New Online Biographical Resource from African American Publications

We're pleased to introduce the *Reference Library of Native North America* and a wonderful, new online biographical resource. This online Web enhancement brings you extended coverage of men and women featured in the *Reference Library of Native North America*, as well as coverage of emerging figures in the Native American community not found in the print publication.

We're pleased to remind you that you have been **automatically authorized** to access the site. Just follow these simple instructions:

• Locate the Web address card in the front matter of Volume I of this publication

• Go to **www.nativepubs.com** and simply access the Registration page

• When registering, be sure to include your invoice/access number

Your students are sure to enjoy these easy-to-read online essays that offer extensive insight into the lives of *hundreds* of fascinating Native American men and women.

Thank you for your interest and enjoy this terrific online biographical resource!

www.nativepubs.com

African American Publications
Phone: 215-321-7742
Fax: 215-321-9568
E-mail: afriampub@aol.com

Reference Library of

NATIVE

NORTH

AMERICA

Reference Library of

NATIVE

NORTH

AMERICA

VOLUME

I

Edited by
Duane Champagne

Distributed exclusively by:

African American Publications
Proteus Enterprises

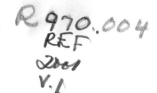

Rebecca Parks, *Editor*
Shelly Dickey, *Managing Editor*
William Harmer, *Contributing Editor*
Laura L. Brandau, *Associate Editor*
Brian J. Koski, *Associate Editor*
Jeffrey Wilson, *Associate Editor*
Mark Springer, *Technical Training Specialist*

Mary Beth Trimper, *Composition and Electronic Prepress Manager*
Evi Seoud, *Assistant Composition and Electronic Prepress Manager*

Kenn Zorn, *Product Design Manager*
Jennifer Wahi, *Art Director*
Barbara Yarrow, *Manager, Imaging and Multimedia Content*
Randy Bassett, *Imaging Supervisor*
Pamela A. Reed, *Imaging Coordinator*
Leitha Etheridge-Sims, Mary K. Grimes, David G. Oblender, *Image Catalogers*

The Reference Library of Native North America/ edited by Duane Champagne
Cover artwork: *The Veteran*, courtesy of Richard Glazer-Danay. *White Hopi Clown Child*, courtesy of
Owen Seumptewa.

Board of Advisors

John Aubrey, *Librarian, The Newberry Library, Chicago, Illinois*
Cheryl Metoyer-Duran, *Librarian, Mashantucket Pequot Research Center and Museum, Mashantucket, Connecticut*
G. Edward Evans, *University Librarian, Loyola Marymount University, Los Angeles*
Hanay Geiogamah, *Professor of Theater, University of California, Los Angeles*
Carole Goldberg-Ambrose, *Professor of Law, University of California, Los Angeles*

Editorial Team at the American Indian Studies Center, University of California, Los Angeles

Editor: Duane Champagne, *Director, American Indian Studies Center, and Professor of Sociology, University of California, Los Angeles*
Assistant Editors: Amy Ware, Alexandra Harris, Tim Petete, Elton Naswood, Jacob Goff, Demelza Champagne, and Garrett Saracho.
Photographic Editor: Roselle Kipp
Bibliographic Editor: Ken Wade
Graphic Artist: James Perkins

Biographers

Angela Aleiss, *American Indian Studies Center, University of California, Los Angeles*
Paola Carini, *English Department, University of California, Los Angeles*
Duane Champagne, *American Indian Studies Center, University of California, Los Angeles*
James Coulon, *Coulon, Ink., San Diego, California*
Troy Johnson, *American Indian Studies Department, California State University, Long Beach*
Richard Keeling, *Ethnomusicology Department, University of California, Los Angeles*
Patrick Macklem, *Faculty of Law, University of Toronto, Toronto, Ontario, Canada*
Tim Petete, *American Indian Studies Center, University of California, Los Angeles*
Amy Kathleen Simmons, *American Indian Studies Center, University of California, Los Angeles*
Amy Ware, *American Indian Studies Center, University of California, Los Angeles*

Contributing Authors

Frances Abele, *School of Public Administration, Carleton University, Ottawa, Ontario, Canada*
Gerald Alfred, *School of Public Administration, The University of Victoria, Victoria, Canada*
Karen Baird-Olson, *Department of Sociology and Anthropology, University of Central Florida, Orlando, Florida*
Russel Lawrence Barsh, *Native Studies, University of Lethbridge, Lethbridge, Alberta, Canada*
Janet Berlo, *Department of Art History, University of Rochester, New York*
Peggy Berryhill, *Native Media Resource Center (NMRC), Bodega Bay, California*
Ted Binnema, *History Department, The University of Northern British Columbia, Prince George, British Columbia, Canada*
Nancy Bonvillain, *Simon's Rock College of Bard, Great Barrington, Massachusetts*
Daniel Boxberger, *Department of Anthropology, Western Washington University, Bellingham, Washington*
Simon Brascoupe, *Department of Sociology and Anthropology, Carleton University, Ottawa, Ontario, Canada*
William Bright, *Department of Linguistics, University of Colorado, Boulder, Colorado*
Tara Browner, *Department of Ethnomusicology, University of California, Los Angeles, California*
Gregory Cajete, *Center for Research and Cultural Exchange, University of New Mexico, Albuquerque, New Mexico*
Edward Castillo, *Native American Studies, Sonoma State University, Rohnert Park, California*
Katherine Beatty Chiste, *Department of Social Sciences, University of Lethbridge, Lethbridge, Alberta, Canada*

Anthony Clark, *Department of Sociology, University of Kansas, Lawrence, Kansas*

Richmond Clow, *Native American Studies, University of Montana, Missoula, Montana*

Heather Coleman, *Faculty of Social Work, University of Calgary, Calgary, Alberta, Canada*

David de Jong, *Prescott High School, Arizona*

Henry Dobyns, *Independent Consultant, Tucson, Arizona*

Leroy Eid, *Department of History, University of Dayton, Dayton, Ohio*

Jo-Anne Fiske, *Anthropology Department, The University of Northern British Columbia, Prince George, British Columbia, Canada*

Donald Fixico, *Department of History, The University of Kansas, Lawrence, Kansas*

Hanay Geiogamah, *Theater Department, University of California, Los Angeles, California*

Douglas George-Kanentiio, *Journalist, Oneida Iroquois Territory, Oneida, New York*

Ian Getty, *Research Director, Stoney Tribe, Nakota Institute, Calgary, Alberta, Canada*

Carole Goldberg-Ambrose, *School of Law, University of California, Los Angeles, California*

Charlotte Heth, *Department of Ethnomusicology, University of California, Los Angeles, California*

Ann Marie Hodes, *Health Services Center, University of Alberta, Edmonton, Alberta, Canada*

Felicia Schanche Hodge, *University of California, San Francisco, and University of Minnesota, Minneapolis*

Cornelius Jaenen, *Department of History, University of Ottawa, Ottawa, Ontario, Canada*

Jennie Joe, *Native American Research and Training Center, University of Arizona, Tucson, Arizona*

Clara Sue Kidwell, *Native American Studies, University of Oklahoma, Norman, Oklahoma*

Rita Ledesma, *Department of Social Welfare, California State University, Los Angeles*

John D. Loftin, *Loftin & Loftin, Hillsborough, North Carolina*

Carol Lujan, *American Indian Studies Program, Arizona State University, Tempe, Arizona*

John A. (Ian) Mackenzie, *Centre for Indian Scholars, Terrace, British Columbia, Canada*

David C. Mass, *Department of Political Science, University of Alaska, Anchorage, Alaska*

Donald McCaskill, *Department of Native Studies, Trent University, Peterborough, Ontario, Canada*

Alan McMillan, *Department of Archaeology, Simon Fraser College, Burnaby, British Columbia, Canada*

Dorothy Lonewolf Miller, *Native American Studies, University of California, Berkeley, California*

C. Patrick Morris, *Department of Native American Studies, Salish Kootenai College, Pablo, Montana*

Ken Morrison, *Religious Studies, Arizona State University, Tempe, Arizona*

Bradford Morse, *Faculty of Law, University of Ottawa, Ottawa, Ontario, Canada*

Joane Nagel, *Department of Sociology, University of Kansas, Lawrence, Kansas*

Elton Naswood, *American Indian Studies Center, University of California, Los Angeles*

David Newhouse, *Department of Native Studies, Trent University, Peterborough, Ontario, Canada*

Brigid O'Donnell, *Department of Ecology and Evolutionary Biology, University of Connecticut*

James H. O'Donnell III, *Department of History, Marietta College, Marietta, Ohio*

Michael O'Donnell, *Director of Distance Education, Salish Kootenai Community College, Pablo, Montana*

Darren Ranco, *Department of Ethnic Studies, University of California, Berkeley*

Audry Jane Roy, *School of Public Administration, The University of Victoria, Victoria, Canada*

Kathryn W. Shanley, *Department of English, Cornell University, Ithaca, New York*

Leanne Simpson, *Department of Native Studies, University of Manitoba, Winnipeg, Manitoba, Canada*

Gerald Slater, *Vice President of Academic Affairs, Salish Kootenai Community College, Pablo, Montana*

Dean Smith, *College of Business Administration, Northern Arizona University, Flagstaff, Arizona*

C. Matthew Snipp, *Department of Sociology, Stanford University, Stanford, California*

Rennard Strickland, *School of Law, University of Oklahoma, Norman, Oklahoma*

Paul Stuart, *School of Social Welfare, University of Alabama, Tuscaloosa, Alabama*

Imre Sutton, *Professor Emeritus, Department of Geography, California State University, Fullerton, California*

Karen Swisher, *College of Education, Arizona State University, Tempe, Arizona*

Steve Talbot, *Department of Sociology and Anthropology, San Joaquin College, Stockton, California*

Wesley Thomas, *Department of Anthropology, Idaho State University, Pocatello, Idaho*

Loretta Todd, *Film Maker, Vancouver, British Columbia, Canada*

Clifford Trafzer, *Department of Ethnic Studies, University of California, Riverside, California*

Ronald Trosper, *Department of Forestry, Northern Arizona University, Flagstaff, Arizona*

Daniel Usner, *History Department, Cornell University, Ithaca, New York*

Joan Vastokas, *Department of Anthropology, Trent University, Peterborough, Ontario, Canada*

Tarajean Yazzie, *School of Education, Harvard University, Cambridge, Massachusetts*

Brother,

    When you first came to this island

    you were as children, in need of food and shelter,

    and we, a great and mighty nation.

    But we took you by the hand

    and we planted you and watered you

    and you grew to be a great oak,

    we a mere sapling in comparison.

    Now we are the children

    (in need of food and shelter).

An opening speech often used by Northeastern Indian leaders at conferences with Europeans during the early colonial period.

Highlights

Persons interested in a comprehensive reference providing information on all aspects of the Native American and Canadian experience can turn to one accurate source: *The Reference Library of Native North America.* The first seventeen chapters are composed of signed essays, annotated directory information, and documentary excerpts; the final chapter presents more than 500 concise biographies of prominent Native North Americans. *The Reference Library of Native North America* covers a broad scope of topics, including:

- History and historical landmarks
- Health
- Law and legislation
- Major culture areas
- Activism
- Environment
- Urbanization and non-reservation populations
- Administration
- Education
- Economy
- Languages
- Demography
- Religion
- Arts
- Literature
- Media
- Women
- Gender Relations

Arrangement Allows for Quick Information Access

The Reference Library of Native North America provides a wealth of information, and its logical format makes it easy to use. The chapters contain subject-specific bibliographies and are enlivened by close to 350 photographs, maps, and charts. Other value-added features include:

- Contents section details each chapter's coverage, including directories and bibliographies
- Alphabetical and geographical lists of tribes
- Multimedia bibliography of sources for further reading and research
- Glossary of Native terms
- Comprehensive keyword index listing tribe and band names (with alternate spellings), personal names, important events, and geographic locations
- Detailed occupational index giving insight into Natives who have excelled in their field of endeavor

Contents

Acknowledgments

The undertaking of the update and revision of this set was a far greater task than originally anticipated, and a great many people contributed to its compilation, writing, editing, and production. I am greatly honored to express thanks to my numerous colleagues who contributed their updated and revised manuscripts, and provided the inspiration for a reference work about contemporary Native North American peoples. The contributors were enthusiastic about updating the *Reference Library;* most thought that over the past seven years many events and changes occurred in Indian Country that required new interpretations and additional material. The set benefits greatly from these many contributors who bring their expertise and understanding into four volumes. We all share the same vision and the understanding of having put forth our best efforts for a worthy cause.

Great credit and thanks are due to people at the Gale Group for their vision and support. Chris Nasso deserves special recognition for developing the idea and groundwork for the set; our readers and the Native peoples are indebted to her for her sympathetic foresight. The Gale editors made workable a long and difficult project. Rebecca Parks deserves special and heartfelt recognition for taking on a difficult and complicated project. With her patience, guidance, and perseverance, the second edition is made possible.

Special mention must also be made of our advisory board. I fondly remember the two days in early summer 1991 when we hammered out the outline and basic entry assignments for the entire set. These sessions are a testament that hard work and engaging company need not be separate events. G. Edward Evans, in particular, provided many insights and a guiding hand, and for this we are grateful. Since the first edition, board member Vee Salabiye passed away, and we miss her insight, knowledge and understanding. She made many comments and contributions that shaped the philosophy and direction of the *Reference Library.*

Many of my friends and associates provided valuable contributions, and I take this opportunity to give them thanks. Roselle Kipp provided greatly needed help in securing photographs and producing digital images; Kenneth Wade worked diligently on the bibliographies, glossaries and some directories; Amy Ware worked cheerfully and tirelessly throughout the entire project in copyediting the manuscript, and we all give thanks for her care, understanding, and concern in creating a quality product. Many students had an opportunity to contribute on parts of the *Reference Library,* and I thank them for their help and effort. In particular I wish to thank Jacob Goff, Demelza Champagne, and Alexandra Harris for their hard work on difficult tasks. Too numerous to thank are the people who helped collect the many illustrations and photographs, but special mention must be made to Ilka Hartmann, Sara Wiles, Carole Lujan, Mary Wentz, Sara Loe, and Mike McClure who all generously made available their artistic and informative photographs and images. Special thanks to Garrett Saracho whose help was indispensable for bringing the entire project to a happy conclusion.

Duane Champagne
March 2001

Preface

The *Reference Library of Native North America* provides historical and contemporary information about the Native peoples of North America. Too often reference books about Native North Americans stop providing information after the 1890s. Consequently, many people cannot find accurate, accessible, and systematic information about contemporary Native culture, art, communities, life, and legal relations. Furthermore, many reference works have given little attention to Canadian Natives, even though Canadian Natives often play a more central role in Canadian constitutional issues and politics than do Native peoples in the United States. In this set, special efforts were made to gather together experts on many aspects of U.S. and Canadian Native life, as well as to include as many U.S. and Canadian Native authors as possible. This effort paid off greatly, since these authors provided many points of view and information that could only come from individuals continually engaged in Native life and issues. In this way, the set represents an overview of the history of Native peoples in North America and provides new and probing perspectives not found in comparable reference works.

At the beginning of the twentieth century, many people believed that Native Americans would disappear and assimilate into Canadian or U.S. society. The experience of the twentieth century, however, has shown that Native communities have survived, and are strongly entrenched in their traditions and institutions. At the beginning of the twenty-first century Native Nations continue to struggle to protect their land, political rights, religions, and cultures. The *Reference Library* informs the reader about the struggle of contemporary Native North Americans and gives considerable insight into their present conditions regarding health, education, economy, politics, art, and other areas. This work is devoted to the student who has had little background or knowledge about Native Americans, and we hope it will inspire, inform, and educate students and the general public about Native peoples. If this set creates greater understanding and appreciation between the peoples of North America and peoples around the world it will have served one of its primary purposes.

Terminology: Is Indian the Right Name?

Throughout the set, a variety of terms are used interchangeably for Native North Americans, such as Indian, American Indian, Native, aborigine, First Nations, First Peoples, and others. The Native peoples of the Americas have the unfortunate distinction of having been given the wrong name, Indians, since the Native people of the Americas were not from the country or civilization of India, the subcontinent in southern Asia. The search for a single name, however, has not been entirely successful. In the United States, Native American has been used but has recently fallen out of favor, and American Indian is now preferred. Nevertheless, American Indian still retains the unfortunate Indian terminology and consequently is not an entirely satisfactory term. Native American also has serious difficulties since anyone born in North or South America may claim to be a "native American."

The Canadians have wrestled with this question of names, and many Native Canadians reject the appellation of Indian. Métis (mixed bloods) and Inuit (often called Eskimos) in Canada will not answer to the name Indian. Similarly, in Alaska the Inuit, Yupik, and Aleut peoples consider themselves distinct from Indian peoples, and do not wish to be called Indian. The Canadians have developed a range of terms such as Native, aboriginal, First Nations, and First Peoples, which in many ways more accurately describes the Native peoples. Throughout the text, we have tried to respect the Canadian preference for avoiding the inclusive term "Indian" for denoting all Native peoples. Many Native people in Canada are called "Indian," and it is appropriate for most Native peoples below the subarctic region, except for the Métis, who consider themselves a distinct ethnic group from Native as well as non-Native Canadians.

The ultimate problem in these terminological difficulties is that Native peoples in North America do not form a single ethnic group but are better understood as thousands of distinct communities and cultures. Many Native peoples have distinct languages, religious beliefs, ceremonies, and sociopolitical organization. Characterizing this diverse array of cultures and peoples with one inclusive name presents serious difficulties from the start, and no one word can characterize such diversity. The inclusive word "Indian" must be seen as something akin to "European," where there is clear recognition of peoples who occupy a contiguous geographic area but have a wide variety of language, culture, and sociopolitical organization. The same applies in Native North America: the term "Indian" or other generic terms can denote only the collection of people who occupied the North American continent, but it says little about the diversity and independence of the cultures.

The best way to characterize Native North Americans is by recognizing their specific tribal or community identities, such as Blackfeet, Cherokee, or Cree. Such identifications more accurately capture the unique and varied tribal and cultural distinctions found among Native North American peoples.

Every effort has been made to keep Native tribal and community identities distinct, but when broader tribal designations were appropriate we allowed the many authors to use their own terms. We do not wish to offend anyone, and we offer our apologies to anyone who is offended, but for ease of presentation and because our many authors used a variety of terms, we have decided not to favor one particular term but rather hoped to see that the various terms were used appropriately in all situations.

The Native North American Peoples

Native North Americans occupied their continent for at least the last ten thousand years, if not for a considerably longer period. Unlike all other groups that live in North America, Natives do not have a recent immigrant experience but rather live in cultures that predate the present institutions and societies of Canada and the United States. Native peoples have legal, cultural, and political claims to priority over Canada and the United States for use of the land, for rights to self-government, and for the practice of their cultures and religions. Over the past five hundred years Native people have experienced considerable change and dislocation, yet most Native communities have survived and will continue as communities into the next centuries. Native North Americans live in thousands of small communities and exhibit considerable differences in culture, language, religion, and social organization. Perhaps the strongest unifying force among these diverse cultures and communities is the general insistence by U.S. and Canadian societies and governments to treat Natives as a homogeneous ethnic group. Nothing could be further from the truth, but since they are treated as homogeneous, there are many situations in which Natives can act collectively to pursue their economic and political goals. Consequently, Natives have operated in mass North American society in increasingly well-organized national organizations and interest groups. These trends will most likely continue and become a major force in contemporary Native affairs.

Scope and Content

The Reference Library of Native North America covers the range of Native history and culture in the United States and Canada, providing a chronology, demographic and distribution descriptions and histories, and discussions of religion and religious change, art, music, theater, film, traditional arts, history, economy, administration, and law and legal issues.

Eighteen chapters were written by over sixty scholarly contributors while students worked to collect information for wide-ranging directories of Native North American communities, major Native cultural events and major writings, films, and videos produced by Native peoples. The range of topics provides an overview and introduction to the history and present-day life of Native North Americans. Each chapter has an ample bibliography for those users interested in further reading or who wish to conduct more specialized studies. Chapter 18 comprises biographical essays on significant Native North Americans, about one-third of whom are historical figures.

An extensive glossary provides definitions of words and concepts that are commonly used in Native affairs and history.

The index provides a quick means to find information on special topics that are discussed throughout the *Reference Library.*

Close to four hundred illustrations—including photographs, line drawings, tables, maps, and figures—complement the text. Every effort was made to use Native photographers and to present views of everyday Native life and scenes.

Suggestions Are Welcome

A work as large as *The Reference Library of Native*

North America may contain oversights and errors, and we appreciate any suggestions for correction of factual material or additions that will make future editions more accurate, sympathetic, and useful. Please send comments to:

Editor
The Reference Library of Native North America
The Gale Group
27500 Drake Rd.
Farmington Hills, MI 48331
Toll Free: (800) 347–4253

Duane Champagne
March 2001

Duane Champagne has been teaching at the University of California, Los Angeles, since 1984. In 1986, he became editor of the *American Indian Culture and Research Journal* and went on to be named professor in 1997.

Dr. Champagne received a doctoral degree in sociology from Harvard University in 1982, and accepted a postdoctoral award from the Rockefeller Foundation in 1982–83. During this time, he completed fieldwork trips to the Tlingit of southeast Alaska and to the Northern Cheyenne in Montana.

Most of Dr. Champagne's writings focus on issues of social, cultural, and political change in American Indian societies as they adapted to European political, cultural, and economic incorporation. He has published in both the sociology and American Indian studies fields, including his two books *American Indian Societies: Strategies and Conditions of Political and Cultural Survival* (1989) and *Social Order and Political Change: Constitutional Governments Among the Cherokee, the Choctaw, the Chickasaw, and the Creek* (1992). He is an active writer and has produced over sixty papers and book publications.

Dr. Champagne is also the director of the UCLA American Indian Studies Center, which carries out research, conducts a master's degree program in American Indian studies, and publishes books for both academic and Indian communities.

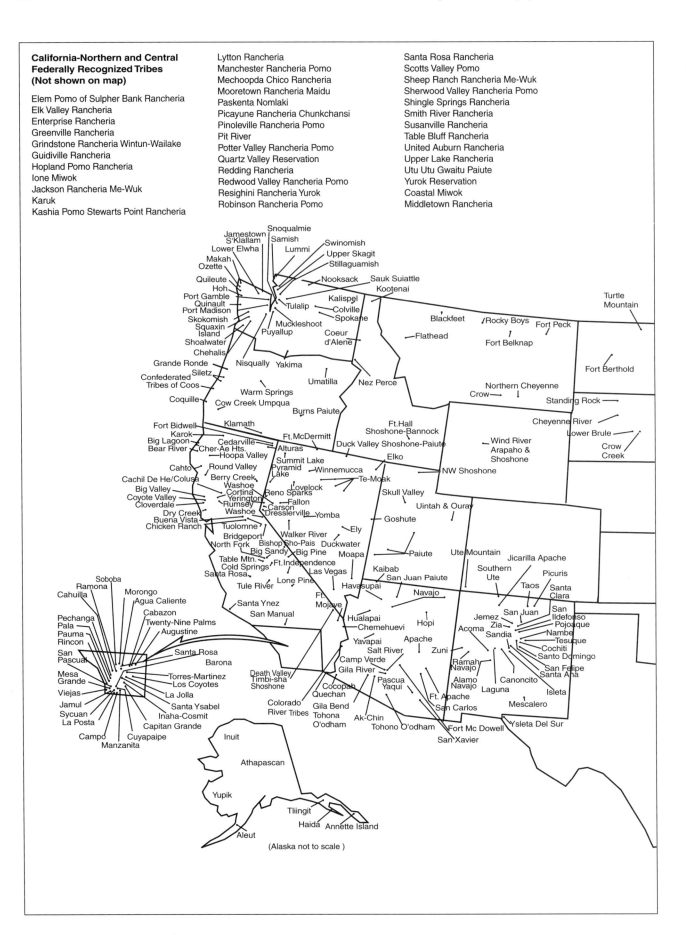

Federally Recognized Native American Tribes

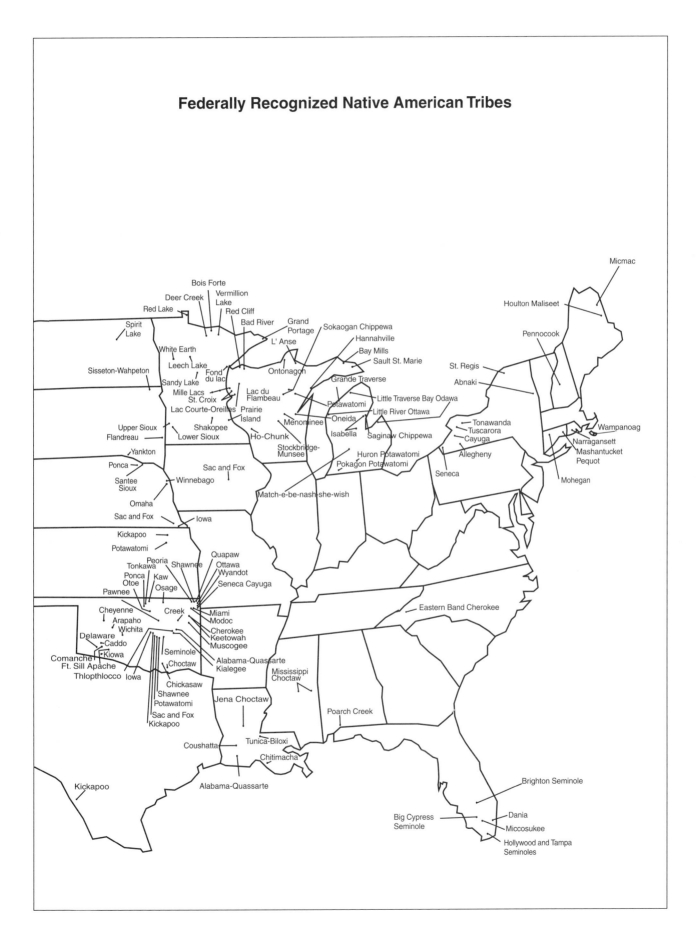

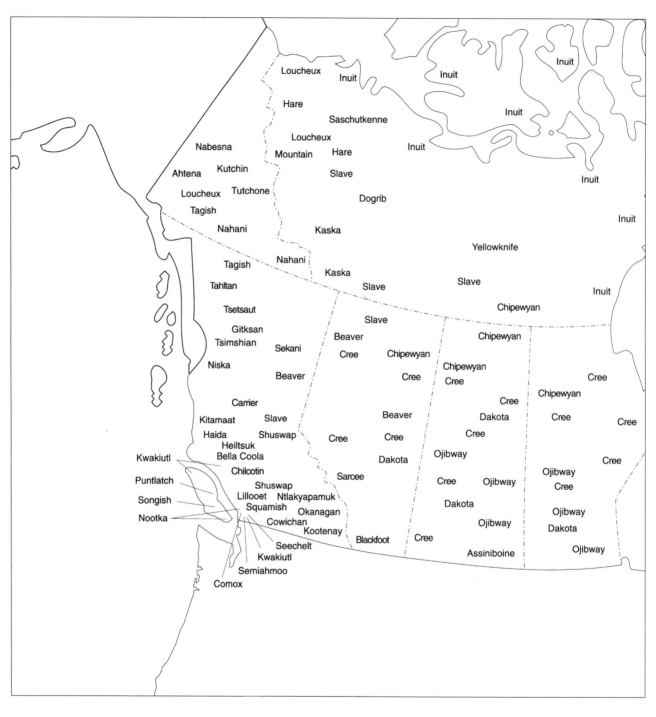

Canadian Native

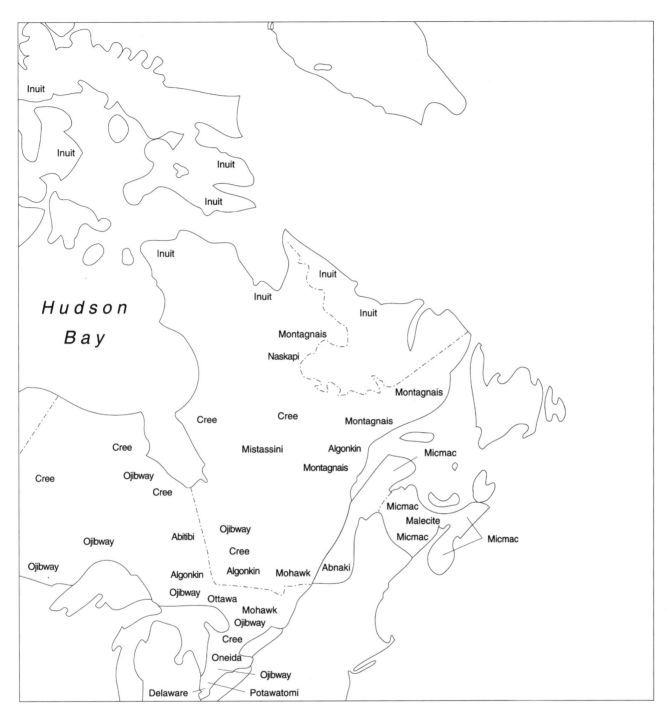

Inuit
Inuit
Inuit
Inuit
Inuit
Inuit
Inuit
Inuit
Inuit

H u d s o n
B a y

Montagnais
Naskapi
Montagnais
Cree
Cree
Montagnais
Cree
Mistassini
Algonkin
Micmac
Cree
Ojibway
Montagnais
Cree
Micmac
Malecite
Cree
Ojibway
Micmac
Micmac
Ojibway
Abitibi
Ojibway
Cree
Ojibway
Algonkin
Algonkin
Mohawk
Abnaki
Ojibway
Ottawa
Mohawk
Ojibway
Cree
Oneida
Ojibway
Delaware
Potawatomi

Culture Groups

Major Native Nations

UNITED STATES

◆ NORTHEAST

Abenaki
Brotherton
Cayuga
Chickahominy
Chippewa (Ojibway)
Fox
Huron
Maliseet
Mattaponi
Menominee
Miami
Mohawk
Mohegan
Montauk
Nanticoke
Narragansett
Nipmuc-Hassanamisco
Oneida
Onondaga
Ottawa
Pamunkey
Passamaquoddy
Paugusset
Penobscot
Pequot
Piscataway
Poosepatuck
Potawatomi
Rappahanock
Sauk
Schaghticoke
Seneca
Shawnee
Shinnecock
Sioux
Stockbridge-Munsee
Tuscarora
Wampanoag

Winnebago

◆ SOUTHEAST

Alabama
Biloxi
Catawba
Cherokee (Eastern)
Chitimacha
Choctaw (Mississippi)
Coharie
Coushatta
Creek
Edisto
Haliwa
Houma
Lumbee
Miccosukee
Santee
Saponi
Seminole
Texas Kickapoo
Tunica
Waccamaw

◆ OKLAHOMA

Apache
Caddo
Cherokee
Cheyenne-Arapaho
Chickasaw
Choctaw
Comanche
Creek
Delaware
Iowa
Kaw
Kickapoo

Kiowa
Miami
Modoc
Osage
Otoe-Missouri
Ottawa
Pawnee
Peoria
Ponca
Potawatomi
Quapaw
Sac and Fox
Seminole
Seneca-Cayuga
Shawnee
Tonkawa
Wichita
Wyandotte

◆ PLAINS

Arikara
Assiniboine
Blackfeet
Cheyenne
Chippewa
Crow
Delaware
Gros Ventre
Hidatsa
Iowa
Kickapoo
Mandan
Omaha
Plains Ojibwa
Potawatomi
Sac and Fox
Sioux
Winnebago
Wyandotte

◆ ROCKY MOUNTAIN AREA

Arapaho
Bannock
Cayuse
Coeur d'Alene
Confederated Tribes of
    Colville
Flathead
Gosiute
Kalispel
Klamath
Kootenai
Nespelem
Nez Percé
Paiute (Northern)
Sanpoil
Shoshoni (Northern)
Spokane
Umatilla
Ute
Walla Walla
Warm Springs
Wasco
Washo
Yakima

◆ SOUTHWEST

Apache
Chemehuevi
Havasupai
Hopi
Hualapai
Maricopa
Mohave
Navajo
Paiute
Pima
Pueblo
Tohono O'Odham (Papago)
Yaqui
Yavapai
Yuma
Zuni

◆ CALIFORNIA

Achumawi
Atsugewi
Cahuilla
Cupeño
Diegueño
Gabrielino
Hupa
Karok
Luiseño
Maidu
Miwok
Mohave
Mono
Ohlone
Paiute
Patwin
Pomo
Serrano
Shasta
Shoshoni (Western)
Tolowa
Washo
Wintu
Wiyot
Yana
Yokuts
Yuki
Yurok

◆ NORTHWEST COAST

Bella Bella
Bella Coola
Chehalis
Chinook
Clallam
Coos
Coquille
Gitksan
Haida
Heiltsuk
Hoh
Kalapuya

Kwakiutl
Lillooet
Lummi
Makah
Molala
Muckleshoot
Nisgha
Nisqually
Nooksack
Nootka
Puyallup
Quileute
Quinault
Rogue River
Sauk-Suiattle
Shasta
Siletz
Siuslaw
Skagit
Skokomish
Snohomish
Squaxin Island
Stillaguamish
Suquamish
Swinomish
Tillamook
Tlingit
Tsimshian
Tulalip
Twana
Umpqua
Wishram

◆ ALASKA

Ahtena
Aleut
Athapascan
Eyak
Haida
Inuit
Tlingit
Tsimshian
Yupik

CANADA

Abenaki
Algonquin
Assiniboine
Beaver
Bella Bella
Bella Coola
Blackfoot
Blood
Carrier
Chilcotin
Chipewyan
Chippewa (Ojibway)
Comox
Cowichan
Cree
Dakota
Dogrib

Gitksan
Gros Ventre
Haida
Haisla
Hare
Heiltsuk
Huron
Inuit
Kootenay
Kutchin
Kwakiutl
Lillooet
Loucheux
Maliseet
Micmac
Mohawk
Montagnais

Nahani
Naskapi
Nisgha
Nootka
Ntlakyapamuk
Okanagon
Potawatomi
Sarsi
Sekani
Shuswap
Slave
Songhees
Squamish
Tagish
Tahltan
Tsimshian

Chronology

◆ CHRONOLOGY OF NATIVE NORTH AMERICAN HISTORY, PRE-CONTACT TO 1500

38,000 B.C.E. Texas. From initial human migration to North America until the end of the Ice Age, big-game hunting is the dominant way of life. Most hunting societies track large Pleistocene game such as woolly mammoths, mastodons, saber-toothed tigers, American lions, camels, bighorn bison, short-faced bears, and other mammals for sustenance. In Lewisville, Texas, the concentration of human and animal remains indicates the presence of early societies in the area. Fingerprints discovered in Pendejo Cave at Fort Bliss, Texas, date back 36,000 years before the present time. Evidence indicates that these societies rely on bone implements and wooden spears. The period from about 50,000 B.C.E. to 25,000 B.C.E. is often referred to as the Pre-Projectile Point Stage.

circa 33,000 to 12,000 B.C.E. Alaska. Over a period of years small bands of hunters steadily make their way across the Bering Sea Land Bridge from Siberia. Anthropologists speculate that these people and their descendants spread throughout North and South America to become the ancestors of all subsequent generations of Native Americans. Some archaeologists believe the first people came across before 18,000 B.C.E. Although questionable, possible bone artifacts found along the Old Crow River in Canada's Yukon Territory were dated at 24,000 to 27,000 B.C.E. Linguistic evidence supports an even earlier appearance, 33,000 B.C.E., of North American peoples.

25,000 B.C.E. North America. New technologies appear among the Paleo-Indian societies of North America. Workable stone—especially flint, chert, and obsidian—is crafted into functional tools such as knives, scrappers, choppers, and, most importantly, spear points. The introduction of stone spear points dramatically alters the subsistence patterns of Paleo-Indians. Different periods of Paleo-Indian history are classified by the types of spear points used and normally bear the name of the site at which a particular stone point has been found, such as Sandia, Clovis, Folsom, and Plano.

25,000 B.C.E. Sandia Mountains, New Mexico. Paleo-Indian societies that develop in the Southwest use the Sandia stone point. From two to four inches long, the Sandia points have rounded bases with a bulge on one side for greater stability. The development of this point, first uncovered in the Sandia Mountains in New Mexico, is limited to the societies of the Southwest. The length and width of the point reveals a reliance on large game for sustenance.

22,000 B.C.E. Northern Pacific Rim. Seafaring ancestors of today's American Indian people may have worked their way along the Northern Pacific Rim in small boats. These people make landfall and gradually migrate to the interior of present-day North and South America.

15,000 B.C.E. North America. The Clovis culture, also referred to as Llano, becomes much more widespread than the Sandia. Although named after the original Clovis site in New Mexico, Clovis stone points are used in every mainland state of the United States. Characterized by its slender point with lengthwise channels on both sides, Clovis points are crafted by pressure flaking, and are used to hunt numerous Pleistocene animals, especially mammoths and mastodons. Widespread use of Clovis stone points disappears around 9200 B.C.E..

11,000 B.C.E. Lindenmeier Site, Colorado. The Paleo-Indians are the first people to come to the Americas. They live a nomadic life based on hunting many types of animals and collecting wild plants. Located just south of the Wyoming border in Colorado, the Lindenmeier site is the first Paleo-Indian campsite studied. It helped verify the antiquity of humans in the Americas.

10,500 B.C.E. Monte Verde, Chile. Wood, bone, and stone tools indicate that people established a sophisticated village site at Monte Verde on the southernmost tip of South America. Evidence suggests that people were at the site as early as 28,000 B.C.E. and that their tools bear no resemblance to those of the vanished Clovis culture. The Monte Verde site is considered one of the oldest verifiable sites in the Americas and casts serious doubt on the Bering migration theory.

10,200 B.C.E. North America. Dogs have always been with people in North America. Dog remains found at the Jones-Miller site in Colorado and other Paleo-Indian sites in the western United States show animals closely related to wolves, but about three-fourths their size.

10,000 B.C.E. North America. Among the first people to come to the Americas are the Clovis hunters and gatherers. They hunt Pleistocene animals, such as mammoths, horses, camels, and bison, and collect a variety of plants. By this date, Clovis people are spread over most of North and South America. Evidence for their distinctive type of tools dies out about 9200 B.C.E.

10,000 B.C.E. Southwest. As big-game animals begin to die off, societal economies in the Southwest become more diversified. People begin to rely on wild plants and nomadic hunting, and use vegetable-grinding tools such as manos, milling stones, and, later, mortars and pestles. Human burial also appear in specific locations, suggesting a belief in an afterlife as well as the growing sedentary nature of many societies in this region. The atlatl becomes a primary tool for hunting. The atlatl is also called a spear-thrower and consists of a slender spear point fitted into a long shaft, secured with plant-fiber twine. A spear launched by an atlatl travels up to 300 feet with great accuracy and is effective against large animals such as deer, elk, horses, and camels.

9200 B.C.E. North America. Following Clovis, a new Paleo-Indian tradition called Folsom emerges across the continent. The Folsom people are hunters and gatherers like their Clovis ancestors, but they make smaller spear points and focus more attention on hunting the now-extinct giant bison called *Bison antiquus*. By the end of the Folsom tradition (8000 B.C.E.), many of the North American Ice Age mammals, such as the giant ground sloth, woolly mammoth, and dire wolf, are extinct.

9000 B.C.E. Arctic. In areas untouched by glaciers, people of the Paleoarctic tradition develop an effective hunting way of life and are the first people in the Americas to find ways of living in the harsh arctic environment. Their tools include scrapers, spear points, and very small, razor-sharp stone tools called microblades. They live in small, highly mobile groups that move over wide territories to take advantage of the best hunting conditions.

9000 B.C.E. Great Basin. Artifacts similar to those found in the San Dieguito complex in California also occur at Danger Cave, west of Salt Lake City, Utah. As defined for California, the San Dieguito complex is a distinctive tradition with a heavy reliance on hunting and no evidence for the use of grinding stones. Some typical San Dieguito artifacts include small, leaf-shaped projectile points and knives, scrapers, and engraving tools. The San Dieguito artifacts may represent a transitional period between the earlier Clovis Paleo-Indians and the later Archaic period cultures in this region.

9000 B.C.E. Great Plains. *Bison antiquus* becomes a major food source. Herds increase greatly following the extinction of predators like lions and short-faced bears, and after the climatic changes foster the expansion of shortgrass prairie.

9000 B.C.E. Blackwater Draw, New Mexico. Early campsites in present-day eastern New Mexico, used by Paleo-Indian groups for more than one thousand years, show that people took advantage of a local environment much wetter than today's. Remains recovered from the site include those of mammoth and other now-extinct species.

8500 B.C.E. Marmes Rockshelter, Washington. At Marmes Rockshelter on the lower Snake River in southeast Washington, some of the best early evidence for human habitation of the Plateau region documents the hunting of a wide variety of animals.

8500 B.C.E. **Agate Basin Site, Wyoming.** Located in extreme eastern Wyoming near the Cheyenne River, the Agate Basin site is one of a growing number of places that reveal the hunting strategies of the Paleo-Indians. In this location bison are driven into an arroyo, or gully, where they are surrounded and killed.

8000 B.C.E. **California.** Seagoing people are living in the Channel Islands off the coast of Southern California.

8000 B.C.E. **California.** Although few artifacts or remains indicate the development of major Paleo-Indian societies in this region, many postglacial societies emerge in southern California during this period. Findings from the Lake Mojave region in the southeast, as well as from the San Dieguito complex near the southern coast, reveal many similarities with the Desert culture of the Great Basin, such as small-game hunting tools.

8000 B.C.E. **Holcombe Site, Western Great Lakes.** At the Holcombe site, just north of Detroit, early Archaic period foraging peoples develop tools such as gravers, scrapers, and various projectile point forms, replacing earlier styles used by Paleo-Indian groups.

8000 B.C.E. **North America.** Across the continent people adapt to a new, more diverse, post-Ice Age environment, marking the end of the Paleo-Indian period in most regions.

8000 B.C.E. **Danger Cave, Utah.** Repeated use by early hunters and gatherers reveals a remarkable record of adaptation to a difficult desert environment.

8000 B.C.E. **Columbia River, Oregon.** From earliest times to the modern day, people have camped along the Columbia River in a stretch of rapids called the Dalles to take advantage of the rich salmon resources. At sites along the great rapids, on the middle portion of the Columbia River, thousands of salmon bones and a wide variety of tools have been discovered.

8000 B.C.E. **Colorado.** At the Olson-Chubbuck site, near the Kansas border in east-central Colorado, hunters stampede almost two hundred bison into an arroyo where they kill and butcher them. Bison kill sites like Olson-Chubbuck are known in several places on the Great Plains.

8000 B.C.E. **Bonfire Shelter, Texas.** At a bison jump site, in Val Verde County, western Texas, Paleo-Indians on at least two separate occasions drive herds of bison over a cliff.

7500 B.C.E. **Southeastern United States.** Near the end of the Paleo-Indian period a tool complex called Dalton is recognized from such places as the Brand site in Arkansas. The Dalton point style is often used as a projectile as well as a knife and is found in association with stone scrapers and woodworking tools.

7300 B.C.E. **Columbia River, Washington.** An unidentified male believed to be Native American and identified as Kennewick Man dies. Kennewick Man's skeletal remains are discovered in 1999 and spark a debate between the Umatilla Indians, who claim that he was one of their ancestors, and anthropologists, who say that the skeletal remains are more like those of the ancient Japanese Ainu than of today's American Indians. Kennewick Man's remains indicate that he led a difficult life and include multiple fractures, a crushed chest, a withered arm, evidence of a skull fracture, and a stone projectile buried in a hip bone.

7000 B.C.E. **Northwest Coast.** As the glaciers retreat, hunting-and-gathering peoples move into the coastal regions from the interior plateau.

6500 B.C.E. **Southeast.** Freshwater mussels and other river resources become a major part of the diet for Archaic-period peoples. Expanding use of these resources probably results from climate change and the beginnings of a lengthy period of river stabilization that increase their availability.

6400 B.C.E. **Hogup Cave, Utah.** People living along the edges of ancient lakes, in the region west of present-day Salt Lake City, collect pickleweed and hunt a variety of water fowl. The remains of nets and traps also indicate the hunting of rabbits and other small game.

6000 B.C.E. **North America.** In many regions, groups adapt to smaller ranges as populations begin to increase. Local cultural differences multiply due to decreased interaction.

6000 B.C.E. **Moorehead Cave, Texas.** At this cave in the Great Bend region of Texas, about 120 miles west of San Antonio, a long history of use associated with the Coahuiltecan cultural tradition verifies a hunting-and-gathering lifestyle that exists until European contact. The people of the Coahuiltecan culture live in small bands that hunt and collect over a vast region of southwest Texas and northern Mexico. They fish in the Pecos River and the Rio Grand and use throwing sticks to hunt rabbits. Because this region is so arid, the Coahuiltecan people never adopt agriculture.

5500 B.C.E. North America. Grinding stones called manos and metates used for processing seeds and other plant products are used in Archaic period sites.

5500 B.C.E. Southern California. Cultures of the Encinitas tradition develop along the California coast from Paleo-Indian ancestors. Grinding stones and remains of abundant shellfish provide evidence for an economy based on marine coastal resources. In the San Diego area, the Encinitas tradition lasts until C.E. 1000.

5000 B.C.E. Arctic and Subarctic. By this time hunting and foraging groups of the Northern Archaic tradition begin exploiting the increasingly ice-free environments. They live in small camps and hunt throughout the tundra and forests. On the northern forest fringes, caribou hunting is a primary occupation. In the dense woodlands slightly farther south, elk, deer, and moose are important.

5000 B.C.E. Aberdeen Lake, Canadian Subarctic. For the next 4,000 years, Northern Archaic tradition hunters camp on Aberdeen Lake, about three hundred miles west of Hudson Bay, to intercept the seasonal migrations of vast caribou herds.

5000 B.C.E. Plateau Region. For the next 2,000 years there is evidence of increased contact and sharing of ideas between peoples of the Plateau and Great Basin.

5000 B.C.E. Southern Great Basin. For the next 3,400 years, Pinto Basin cultures practice a hunting-and-gathering way of life. Some evidence of small circular houses indicates they may have been semisedentary.

5000 B.C.E. Northwestern Great Plains. For the next 2,500 years, a drier climate prevails, causing reduction in prairie grasses and a dwindling of the bison herds. Fewer archaeological sites for this period indicates that human populations also move out of the region.

4500 B.C.E. Northeastern California. People of the Menlo phase (4500–2500 B.C.E.) are the first to build sturdy, semisubterranean earth lodges in this region. From these relatively permanent hamlets they exploit environments ranging from the mountains to the river

valleys. Later in time, the climate becomes drier and the people are forced to move more often to find food. They respond by shifting to lighter, easier-to-build dwellings made of brush.

4000 B.C.E. Ocean Bay, Kodiak Island, Alaska. Kodiak Island, about 215 miles south of present-day Anchorage, is one of the places where Arctic hunters begin adapting their skills to exploit marine resources.

4000 B.C.E. Onion Portage, Alaska. Some of the earliest Northern Archaic artifacts are found at Onion Portage on the Kobuk River in northeast Alaska. They give evidence for increasingly diverse subsistence strategies including a shift to caribou hunting.

4000 B.C.E. Koster Site, Illinois. At least by this date, throughout the Midwest, hunters and gatherers of the Archaic period begin building permanent shelters at base camps. Some of these camps were discovered in southern Illinois, about seventy miles north of St. Louis, at the Koster site.

3000 B.C.E. Umnak Island, Alaska. At Umnak and other islands in the Aleutian chain, people skilled at hunting seals, sea lions, and whales build villages with small oval houses three to five meters in diameter.

3000 B.C.E. Southern California. In some areas along the coast, the Encinitas tradition is replaced by the Campbell tradition, which has a greater orientation toward hunting deer and other game animals. Artifacts of the Campbell tradition include leaf-shaped points and stone mortars and pestles. The Campbell tradition is a precursor to the modern Chumash of the Santa Barbara area.

3000 B.C.E. Southwest. Beginning about this time, favorable conditions for widespread trade and interaction develop, permitting the eventual spread of important domesticated plants from Mexico, especially maize, beans, and squash.

3000 B.C.E. Southwest. Four regional Archaic period traditions of hunting-and-gathering peoples, known collectively as the Picosa culture, take shape. In the west is the little-known San Dieguito-Pinto tradition. The best-known artifact of this tradition is the small Pinto Basin projectile point, but there are a variety of other artifacts, including small grinding slabs and choppers. In the north, the Oshara tradition shows many connections in artifact styles with the western San

Dieguito-Pinto tradition. In the east, the Hueco and Coahuiltecan cultural complexes are known to include many wooden and other perishable objects, such as nets and sandals, recovered from dry caves. In the south, during the Chiricahua and San Pedro phases of the Cochise tradition, people use a wide variety of plant processing and hunting tools.

2600 B.C.E. Southeast. Throughout the region there is an expansion of long-distance trade. It is not clear why trade increases at this time, but there is evidence that expanding populations use trade to maintain good relations with a growing number of neighboring groups. It is also possible that exotic items are becoming important as markers of wealth and status.

2500 B.C.E. Central California. For the next 2000 years people of the Windmiller period (also called the Windmiller pattern) cultures live in permanent villages and practice a wide variety of hunting-and-gathering activities in California's Central Valley. They bury their dead in small mounds. Among the many objects made by Windmiller people are distinctive, large, obsidian (volcanic glass) projectile points, stone smoking pipes, alabaster charmstones, various types of baskets, and grinding stones.

2500 B.C.E. Charles River, Massachusetts. Several large fish traps, called weirs, are positioned at the mouth of the Charles and other rivers as they feed into the Atlantic Ocean. These types of traps are probably used well before 2500 B.C.E. and continue in use into the period of European contact.

2500 B.C.E. Southeast. The earliest pottery north of Mexico is made at sites in Georgia and Florida. The simple styles are constructed using plant fibers as tempering material to strengthen the vessels. This and later pottery represent a major technological advance in the preparation and storage of food and other resources.

2000 B.C.E. Alaska. The Arctic Small Tool tradition develops and spreads east as far as Greenland. These hunters and fishers are the first humans to live in the eastern Arctic, other than Antarctica, the last uninhabited region of the world. The people of the Arctic Small Tool tradition are the ancestors of the modern-day Inuit. They are responsible for developing some of the most remarkable technologies for surviving in the world's harshest environment. They develop special harpoons and techniques for hunting seals, walrus, and whales.

2000 B.C.E. Northwest Coast. Beginning as early as 2000 bc, archaeological remains, designated the Strait of Georgia tradition, point to coastal and interior adaptations that eventually lead to the development of complex societies like the present-day Coast Salish and Bella Bella. Initially, artifact styles are similar to those from Kodiak Island, Alaska, and include a wide variety of harpoons and fishing equipment. By C.E. 400 distinctive Strait of Georgia tradition artifacts include ground slate spear points, barbed points made of bone, and spindle whorls used to make cloth.

2000 B.C.E. Labrador. Ramah Chalcedony, a translucent type of stone easily worked into a variety of tools, becomes an important trade item after the arrival of Inuit peoples. This stone is traded from Labrador to New England.

2000 B.C.E. Midwest. From about this time into the period of European contact, people mine copper in the Lake Superior area. The copper is obtained in relatively pure chunks and is cold hammered into a variety of tools and ornaments. Over time, copper from this region is traded widely across the eastern woodlands.

2000 B.C.E. Eastern United States. By this date, four native plants are being domesticated in this region. Two of these plants, squash and sunflowers, are still commonly used today. The other two, marsh elder and chenopodium, are now thought of as only weeds.

1500 B.C.E. Subarctic. A period of increasing cold causes the southerly retreat of forests. Northern Archaic tradition hunters, who are adapted to forest environments, also move south. For these hunters the migratory caribou herds are a major food source. Not long after the Northern Archaic tradition hunters move south, Inuit (Eskimo) peoples fill the vacuum.

1500 B.C.E. Central California. Flexed burials, some cremation, coiled basketry, wooden mortars, barbed harpoons, and the bow and arrow appear. Village sties become larger and "shell mounds" and other burial sites are built. Evidence of concentrated, economically diversified, and culturally complex societies indicates the growth of unique and dynamic cultures with specialized modes of production and ideological systems.

1500 B.C.E. Subarctic. A period of increasing cold causes the southward retreat of forests. Northern Archaic tradition hunters who are accustomed to forest environments follow the migratory caribou herds. Shortly after the Archaic tradition hunters move south, Inuit (Eskimo) peoples begin living in these northern regions. Many of their communities exist today.

Dogs were domesticated by Native people as far back as 10,000 B.C.E. Paleo-Indians often trained dogs to pull loads during their seasonal migrations. (Photo by Lori Cooper. Courtesy of the UCLA American Indian Studies Center)

1400 B.C.E. Louisiana. By this date, people living along the lower Mississippi River and its tributaries are constructing large mounds and living in planned communities. The best-known example is the Poverty Point site, located fifty-five miles west of Vicksburg, Mississippi, where a massive semicircle of concentric mounds is constructed. Some archaeologists believe Poverty Point is the first chiefdom north of Mexico. There are approximately one hundred lesser sites with cultural connections to Poverty Point.

1000 B.C.E. Southwest. The first evidence of the use of maize in the Southwest is documented at Bat Cave and Jemez Cave in southwest New Mexico, north of Silver City.

1000 B.C.E. Central California. Cultures of the Cosumnes period grow out of the earlier Windmiller culture. Artifactual evidence suggests they rely more on harvesting acorns and fishing than their Windmiller culture ancestors, although hunting continues to be important.

1000 B.C.E. Northeast. Vessels carved from a stone called steatite are a common trade item from New England to the southern Appalachian Mountains.

800 B.C.E. Choris Peninsula, Alaska. The first pottery in Alaska appears in this area of Kotzebue Sound, about 160 miles north of Nome. Styles and methods of manufacture show recent contact with Asia.

700 B.C.E. Foxe Basin and Baffin Island, Canada. In this vast region north of Hudson Bay, Dorset Inuit culture develops, eventually spreading to many parts of the eastern Arctic. Excavations at the Kapuivik site, near Igloolik, reveal the oldest documented occurrence of Dorset culture. Dwellings used by the Dorset people include skin tents, sod houses, and pit houses.

500 B.C.E. Eastern Great Plains. Throughout the eastern border of the Plains for the next 1500 years people of the Plains Woodland tradition build many small mounds.

500 B.C.E. **Southeast.** The older practice of using plant fiber as a tempering agent in pottery is replaced by the use of sand and limestone. At about this time, there is a huge increase in the variety of decorations used on pottery throughout the region. This corresponds with expanding cultural diversity and the shift from a hunting-and-gathering way of life to the establishment of small permanent villages and the cultivation of native plants like sunflower, marsh elder, may grass, and squash. The seeds from the sunflower, marsh elder, and may grass could be collected and ground to produce flour.

500 B.C.E. **Midwest.** In the Ohio River Valley and surrounding regions, an Early Woodland cultural complex, called Adena, develops from late Archaic antecedents. The Adena people build burial mounds and live in small villages of circular semipermanent dwellings.

500 B.C.E. **Southwest.** Beans make their first appearance in the Southwest about this time, becoming more common after 300 C.E. Beans contain vital amino acids, which corn lacks. Beans also return nitrogen to the soil, which corn depletes. Consequently, by growing beans and corn in tandem, Southwestern farmers improve their health and increase the soil's longevity.

400 B.C.E. **Ohio.** People of the Adena Culture build a huge earthwork, today called Serpent Mound. The body of the serpent measures 382 meters long. Today its symbolism is unknown.

350 B.C.E. **Southwest.** Beans and squash, already widely cultivated in Mesoamerica, are introduced and eventually become important food sources.

250 B.C.E. **Eastern United States.** Peoples begin cultivation of locally domesticated plants.

250 B.C.E. **Eastern Great Plains.** A variety of cultures referred to as Plains Woodland develop in this region. They differ markedly from earlier cultures; especially noteworthy is their use of pottery, sedentary villages, and mounds as places for a variety of religious purposes, including burial of the dead.

100 B.C.E. **Midwest.** Centered in Ohio and Illinois, Hopewell societies develop from local roots. The Hopewell people are especially noted for constructing massive, geometric-shaped earthworks. Hopewell societies are also known for participating in trade networks extending from the Great Lakes to the Gulf of Mexico. Some of the items traded include conch shell, shark teeth, mica, lead, copper, and various kinds of stone.

C.E. **1 Eastern Kansas.** For the next 500 years, Hopewellian communities with affinities to the east live in the area of present-day Kansas City. Their semipermanent villages provide evidence for the early cultivation of maize.

C.E. **1 Eastern Woodlands.** In many parts of the present-day eastern United States, small-scale groups develop more complex social hierarchies with leaders whose authority is derived from group consensus.

C.E. **1 Southeast.** Throughout the region small oval mounds are built for the burial of important members of society.

C.E. **1 Southwest.** The roots of the Hohokam cultural tradition emerge in the Sonoran Desert of south-central Arizona and adjacent regions of Chihuahua and Sonora in Mexico. The earlier Hohokam people are hunters and gatherers, but later develop agriculture and build massive irrigation systems to water their fields. The central Hohokam area is in south-central Arizona around the modern city of Phoenix. The Hohokam tradition continues until after European arrival. The ancient Hohokam may be ancestral to the present-day Pima and Tohono O'Odham.

C.E. **100 Southwest.** Maize becomes a significant food crop in the region.

C.E. **100 Louisiana.** Sharing similarities with the Hopewellian peoples farther north, the Marksville culture becomes an important regional variant of the Woodland period. The Marksville people develop an economy based on hunting and cultivation of native plants. They also build mounds for ceremonial purposes, including the burial of important individuals.

C.E. **100 Alaska.** Remains ancestral to modern Inuit peoples are identified in eastern Siberia and western Alaska. By about C.E. 1000 all northern Native Americans from Alaska to Greenland are part of this same cultural heritage, called the Thule or Northern Maritime tradition. Archaeologically, the Thule tradition is recognized for the use of polished slate and elaborately carved bone and ivory tools used for hunting sea mammals.

C.E. **200 Southwest.** Small sedentary villages develop, marking the end of the nomadic hunting-and-gathering lifestyle in many parts of the region.

C.E. **200 New Mexico.** The first evidence for the Mogollon is found in the mountainous areas of southern New Mexico, eastern Arizona, and adjacent portions of Chihuahua and Sonora, Mexico. Like their neighbors to the north and south, the Mogollon people develop first small villages of earth-covered houses and later multistory pueblos and techniques for cultivating crops in a dry environment. Some people of the modern Western Pueblos are believed descended from the Mogollon.

C.E. **200 Southwest.** The Patayan tradition has its origins in southwestern Arizona, but is primarily associated with the Colorado River region. The Patayan tradition occupies a vast area extending from northern Baja California to northwest Arizona. The Patayan people are among the first pottery producers in the Southwest. Several sites excavated south of the Grand Canyon in Arizona give some information on dwellings and subsistence. Their early dwellings are small and made of wood or masonry, usually with an attached ramada or open-air porch. They probably grow corn and squash and hunt a variety of local animals.

C.E. **300 Central Arizona.** Construction of what will become massive irrigation systems begins in the earliest period of the Hohokam cultural tradition.

C.E. **300 Midwest.** Around this date Hopewellian societies give way to cultures of the Late Woodland period. The reason for the decline of Hopewell in the Midwest is not known, but it may be related to the breakup of long-distance trade connections, increased warfare, and climate change.

C.E. **400 Southwest.** Pottery, used for storage and cooking, comes into wide use. Most pottery in the Southwest is made by coiling strips of clay to build up the body of the vessel.

C.E. **400 Southwest.** The Anasazi tradition emerges in the Four Corners region of Arizona, New Mexico, Colorado, and Utah. The Anasazi practice agriculture and through time move from pit-house villages to the construction of large multiroom apartment buildings, some with more than 1,200 rooms. The pueblos in Chaco Canyon in western New Mexico are examples of Anasazi dwellings. The Anasazi produce many distinctive styles of pottery; especially recognizable are the black on white geometric designs. The people of the modern Pueblos of Arizona and New Mexico are descended from the Anasazi.

C.E. **400 North America.** By this date the bow and arrow are in use in several regions and spread rapidly through the continent as a major technological advance for hunting and warfare. Before the bow and arrow, spears and a weapon called the atlatl are used widely. The atlatl, also called a spear thrower, consists of a spear held on top of a long handle. By holding the handle and propelling the spear forward a lever effect is achieved to add throwing force. Although the bow and arrow become very popular, the spear and atlatl still receive some use.

C.E. **450 Lower Mississippi Valley.** The people of the Lower Mississippi Valley build conical burial mounds and some of the first flat-top platform mounds in North America. The flat-top platform mounds are probably used as substructures for temples or residences for important people. Platform mounds become a hallmark of the later Mississippian period.

C.E. **500 Eastern Great Basin.** The Fremont culture develops with a lifeway similar to that of the Puebloan agriculturists to the south. The Fremont culture includes a number of discernibly southwestern characteristics, including cultivation of maize, pottery, pit houses, and later stone architecture. By C.E. 1350, declining rainfall brings an end to widespread agriculture and the Fremont culture.

C.E. **500 Central California.** Hotchkiss period cultures develop out of the earlier Cosumnes period.

Thunderbird. A petroglyph in Jeffers National Park in southern Minnesota. (Photo by Sarah Loe. Courtesy of the UCLA American Indian Studies Center)

An early colonial drawing of an Indian town in the Southwest.

Hotchkiss-period economy is based heavily on acorn gathering, but also fishing, fowling, and hunting.

C.E. 500 Central Arizona. A ball game is played in large oval courts, similar to those found in Mesoamerica at the famous Mayan ceremonial center of Chichén Itzá on the Yucatan Peninsula and the city of Teotihuacan in central Mexico near Mexico City.

C.E. 500 Florida and Georgia. Hopewellian cultures along the Gulf Coast continue to thrive after those of the Midwest disintegrate. One of the largest sites is Kolomoki in southern Georgia, with numerous burial mounds and a large rectangular, flat-top mound. The site may have had a population of about one thousand people.

C.E. 500 Eastern United States. Cultures of the Late Woodland period are widespread. Compared to earlier cultures in the eastern woodlands, Late Woodland peoples build very few mounds and do not often participate in long-distance trade. The Late Woodland groups are organized more simply than their Poverty Point, Adena, or Hopewell ancestors.

C.E. 700 Crenshaw Site, Arkansas. This site, near Texarkana, Texas, is the earliest known ceremonial center linked to the modern Caddo people who once occupied the area of western Arkansas, eastern Louisiana, eastern Texas, and eastern Oklahoma, but were removed to lands in western Oklahoma, where many of them live today. Between C.E. 900 and 1100, at least six mounds were constructed at the Crenshaw site. One of the mounds contained the remains of more than two thousand deer antlers.

C.E. **750 Eastern United States.** The simple cultures of the Late Woodland period begin a process of transformation into the more complex societies of the Mississippian period. In some areas there is a dramatic shift in subsistence and social complexity. At about this time, many groups intensify agriculture based on maize cultivation. This is associated with the growth of elaborate status hierarchies and hereditary leadership.

C.E. **750 Range Site, Southern Illinois.** This site, near eastern St. Louis, provides some of the first tangible evidence for centralized, large-scale storage of food and settlements planned around a plaza. This may represent evidence for the further development of social hierarchies responsible for the distribution of shared resources.

C.E. **800 Toltec Site, Arkansas.** The Toltec site, near Little Rock, Arkansas, consists of ten mounds arranged around a plaza, enclosed by a two-meter-high earth embankment. This is the most complex settlement known in the Southeast at this time. Although named for the Toltec people of Mexico, the site is the outgrowth of local social developments and not the result of a migration of people from Mexico.

C.E. **800 Zebree Site, Arkansas.** At this site about fifty-five miles north of Memphis, Tennessee, some of the first evidence for larger storage pits corresponds to the increased importance of maize throughout the region as an easily stored food resource.

C.E. **850 Great Plains.** Throughout the region, cultures of the Plains Village tradition develop along major and minor river valleys. They practice agriculture in conjunction with bison hunting and wild plant gathering. In the northern and central Plains they build large, well-insulated earth lodges. In the south they construct houses with grass roofs.

C.E. **880 Spiro Site, Oklahoma.** On the uplands near the Arkansas River, twelve miles west of Fort Smith, Arkansas, Caddoans build a series of large, square ceremonial buildings around a plaza. Over the next two hundred years these buildings are periodically destroyed and rebuilt as part of an elaborate ceremonial cycle. By

C.E. 1100, Spiro becomes a major ceremonial center known for its extensive trade connections.

C.E. **900 Southwest.** By this date, agriculture is commonly practiced in most areas. Maize becomes a major crop. Although maize contains less nutritional value than some wild plants, it produces higher and more predictable yields. Southwestern farmers use a variety of irrigation canals, dams, and planting methods to conserve scarce rainfall.

C.E. **900 Alaska.** Thule Inuit (Eskimo) culture begins to spread east, replacing and acculturating existing Dorset groups.

C.E. **900 Eastern United States.** In many areas, cultures referred to as Mississippian take shape. These cultures are organized as chiefdoms, with an economy based on maize cultivation and locally domesticated crops. These societies participate in long-distance trade and a widespread religion termed the Southeastern Ceremonial Complex.

C.E. **900 Kincaid Site, Ohio.** One of the major regional mound centers of the Mississippian period, Kincaid is occupied for five hundred years. The Kincaid site is located at the confluence of the Ohio, Tennessee, and Cumberland rivers, near the town of Paducah, Kentucky. It contains two mound groups, a large village, and a palisade.

C.E. **900–1450 Snaketown, Casa Grande, and the Hohokam Climax.** During the Colonial and Classic periods, consolidation and expansion of many major Hohokam sites occurs. Above-ground adobe structures come into use, irrigation canal systems are greatly expanded, and, in several places, Mesoamerica-style platform mounds and ball courts are constructed. One of the largest Hohokam settlements, Snaketown, serves as an important trading center during this time, linking the Southwest with Mesoamerica groups such as the Toltec. During their Classic phase, the Hohokam build Casa Grande on the Gila River in the Phoenix Basin. The main structure at the Casa Grande site is four stories tall and made with caliche-adobe walls, reflecting pueblo-style architectural influences.

C.E. **950 South Dakota.** People of the Middle Missouri tradition migrate to the Great Plains from Minnesota and Iowa. They bring with them a heritage of farming, and settle along the fertile bottomlands of the Missouri River in present-day South Dakota where maize, squash, and other crops grow in spite of the cold winters and often dry summers. They are recognized as the ancestors of the modern-day Mandan and Hidatsa.

C.E. **985 Greenland.** Thule Inuit encounter the first expedition of Norsemen to reach North America.

C.E. **1000 Owens, Panamint, and Death Valleys, Utah.** By this time, archaeological remains linked with the history of the modern Paiute are identifiable.

C.E. **1000 Central and Southern New Mexico.** Some of the earliest compact villages, later called pueblos by the Spanish, develop around central plazas in the region of the Mogollon cultural tradition.

C.E. **1000 Kansas and Nebraska.** Along the major rivers in this region, cultures grouped as the Central Plains tradition develop a farming lifestyle focused on maize, beans, squash, tobacco, and sunflowers. They live in large, multifamily, earth-covered houses with extended entryways.

C.E. **1000 New York and St. Lawrence River Valley.** During the Owasco period (ad 1000–1300), people build small villages throughout this region and the first clear evidence for cultivation of maize, beans, and squash occurs. By the end of the Owasco period, dwellings consist of multifamily longhouses, some more than two hundred feet long, and villages are surrounded by fortifications, indicating the prevalence of warfare. People of the Owasco period are the ancestors of the Iroquois.

C.E. **1040 Western New Mexico.** Over a period of years, several pueblos with hundreds of rooms are constructed near each other. In Chaco Canyon, construction of the huge pueblos, like Pueblo Bonito and Chetro Ketl, reach their maximum extent between C.E. 1040 and 1150. Chaco Canyon is connected throughout a wide region by a road system stretching many miles across the desert.

C.E. **1060 Chihuahua, Mexico.** At the Casas Grandes site (also called Paquime), 200 miles southwest of El Paso, a large settlement is built with connections probably derived from the west coast of Mexico. It is generally believed that traders from Mexico establish the site to improve trade between the civilizations of Mexico and those of the Southwest. About C.E. 1205 the settlement is destroyed, possibly by a revolt.

C.E. **1100 Casa Grande Site, Arizona.** During the Classic period (ad 1100–1450), the Hohokam build a "big house" on the Gila River in the Phoenix Basin. The building is four stories high and made with caliche-adobe walls. The structure may serve as a chief's house.

C.E. **1100 Eastern United States.** Heavy reliance on starchy foods, especially maize, is linked to the poorer health of Mississippian period populations, especially those living in larger villages.

C.E. **1100 New York Region.** By this date, the archaeological remains linked to the cultural development of the modern Iroquois can be recognized.

C.E. **1100 Northeast.** Beginning about this time many groups construct fortifications around their villages, indicating widespread warfare.

C.E. **1100 Cahokia Region, Southern Illinois.** The Mississippian culture, centered at the Cahokia site near St. Louis, reaches its highest level of complexity. More than one hundred mounds are constructed at Cahokia. The principal mound, Monks Mound, is the largest ancient construction north of Mexico. The town surrounding the mounds hold a population of more than ten thousand people.

C.E. **1100–1300 Mesa Verde Climax.** Inhabited continuously from C.E. 600 to 1300, the Mesa Verde site in southern Colorado reaches its height after 1100. At about this time, the Anasazi residents of Mesa Verde begin to move off the mesas and into sheltered areas in the cliffs below, apparently for defensive reasons. By the time the move is completed, the Fewkes Canyon settlements consist of more than thirty-three cliff dwelling sites, with more than 500 living and storage rooms and sixty kivas. The largest of these, Cliff Palace, contains some 220 rooms and twenty-three kivas, and houses up to 350 people. By about 1300 the entire San Juan drainage, including the Mesa Verde area, is abandoned by the Pueblo peoples, who migrate to the Hopi/Zuni and Rio Grande areas to the south and southeast.

C.E. **1100–1804 Southern California Coast Late Period.** Use of shell money becomes widespread throughout the southern California area, indicating the growing complexity of cultures in this region. The people of this time are the Hokan-speaking Chumash and others, ancestors to the coastal groups that would later meet European explorers and missionaries. Studies of shell beads and other artifacts suggest that

Chumash society may have developed continuously for over 7,000 years in the area now known as the Santa Barbara Channel.

C.E. 1175 Awatovi Site, Arizona. Located seventy-five miles north of Winslow, Arizona, the Hopi call this site "Place of the Bow Clan People." At one point the Pueblo consists of 1,300 ground-floor rooms with a population of more than 1,000. About C.E. 1450, a large two-story Pueblo is built. The Franciscans build a church there in the sixteenth century.

C.E. 1200 Oklahoma. In central Oklahoma the people of the Washita River phase (C.E. 1200–1450) develop villages based on an economy of maize cultivation and the hunting of deer and bison.

C.E. 1220 Texas and Oklahoma Panhandles. Groups move from New Mexico to take advantage of better agricultural conditions resulting from a moister climate.

circa C.E. 1300 Deganawida, Huron Spiritual Leader Flourishes in the Eastern United States. Deganawida is the founder of the Iroquois Confederacy. The confederacy's origin is unknown, but it is generally dated before the landing of Columbus in 1492. In Iroquois history, Deganawida lives in a time when there is little peace among the Iroquois-speaking nations, of which the Huron, Deganawida's tribe (then residing in Ontario) is one. Deganawida has a vision from the Great Spirit that instructs him to give the Great Law of Peace, a set of rules and procedures for working out differences and settling hostilities between nations. Hiawatha becomes the spokesperson for the message of Deganawida and the Great Spirit. Both Deganawida and Hiawatha travel among the Iroquois nations, and convince them to form a confederacy of forty-nine chiefs. Through ceremonies and agreements they settle their disputes and form the Iroquois League. The purpose of the league is to create peace and spread the Great Law of Peace to all nations of the world.

C.E. 1300 Eastern United States. Common beans were present by at least C.E. 1070; however, they do not come into wide usage until C.E. 1300. Although beans are an important nutritional addition to maize-based diets, they are not adopted in all areas.

C.E. 1300–1600 Midwest. Great Temple Mound (or Middle Mississippi) civilization flourishes in the river valleys of Arkansas, Mississippi, Alabama, Tennessee, Missouri, Kentucky, southern Illinois, southern Indiana, and Ohio. These societies are organized into republics dominated by a large city surrounded by smaller cities. Each city consists of a plaza, one or more pyramid-like temple mounds, temples, chief's houses, and other houses.

C.E. 1350 Eastern Great Basin. Hunting-and-gathering peoples associated with the modern southern Paiute, Ute, and Shoshoni replace the earlier Fremont culture.

C.E. 1350 Moundville, Alabama. One of the largest Mississippian-period ceremonial centers is located forty miles south of Tuscaloosa. By this date, the site consists of twenty mounds and an associated village. It is probably the center of a chiefdom that includes a

A circle petroglyph at Jeffers National Park in southern Minnesota. (Photo by Sarah Loe. Courtesy of the UCLA American Indian Studies Center)

Mesa Verde. (Photo by Manny Pedraza)

number of other sites situated along the Black Warrior River and adjacent areas in west-central Alabama.

C.E. **1400 Southern California.** Archaeological remains of the Chumash, a tribe that lived in the vicinity of modern-day Santa Barbara, date through the period of European contact. The Chumash are known archaeologically by the term Canalino.

C.E. **1400 Midwest.** Through a broad section of Missouri and Illinois, including the once densely populated Cahokia region, an "empty quarter" develops, possibly as a result of a poorer climate for agriculture.

C.E. **1450 Nebraska.** Groups related to the Pawnee migrate north to the Missouri River in South Dakota. Their descendants are recognized as the present-day Arikara. Today, the Arikara live in North Dakota and are members of the Three Affiliated Tribes, along with their neighbors, the Mandan and Hidatsa.

C.E. **1492 Caribbean.** The expedition led by Christopher Columbus touches ground on an island in the Bahamas called Guanahani by Natives and San Salvador by Europeans.

C.E. **1500 Caribbean.** Columbus and his successors consolidate Spanish control of the Caribbean and begin a period of exploration and exploitation in North and Central America that has repercussions to the present day.

Troy Johnson
California State University, Long Beach, California

◆ CHRONOLOGY OF NATIVE NORTH AMERICAN HISTORY, 1500 TO 1964

1500 Population Decline. The sixteenth century marks the beginning of a widespread decline in Native population. Over the next four centuries, perhaps as many as sixty million people die primarily of European-imported diseases such as smallpox and scarlet fever.

In the United States, the population decline continues until about 1900, when Indian populations begin to recover.

1502–1503 Early English Contact and Trade.
English fishermen begin making regular trips to the waters off Newfoundland and the East Coast of the United States. Various tribal groups begin occasional trade with European fishermen and whalers. They frequently exchange furs and food for metal goods and cloth. European disease is introduced through microbes contained on and in trade goods.

1511 Priests Decry Spanish Treatment of Native Americans.
Antonio de Montesinos, a Catholic priest, gives a stirring sermon to the Spanish leaders of Hispaniola, condemning them for their treatment of Native Americans. Another priest, Bartolome de las Casas, writes *Destruction of the Indies*, in which he chronicles the Spanish conquistadors' cruelty against Native Americans. These gruesome cruelties include butchering men, women, and children like "sheep in the slaughter house."

1512 Laws of Burgos and the Requerimiento.
De las Casas and others attempt to stop the atrocities and begin a reform movement to alter the Spanish Indian policies. The result is the Laws of Burgos, a series of reforms that outlaws Indian slavery and orders the owners of large tracts of land—taken from the Indians and known as *encomiendas*—to improve the treatment of their Indian laborers. The Spanish conquistadors cannot legally invade, enslave, or exploit Indians without first reading them the Requerimiento, a document outlining the Christian interpretation of creation and the hierarchy of the Catholic Church. Indians are told to surrender their hearts, souls, and bodies to the Church and Spanish Crown or face utter devastation. "We ask and require. . . that you acknowledge the Church," the document reads. If Indians did not obey, the Spanish promised to "make war against you. . . subject you to the yoke and obedience of the Church [and Crown]. . . take you, and your wives, and your children, and. . . make slaves of them. . . take away your goods and. . . do you all the harm and damage we can."

The Requerimiento is intended to offer Native Americans a chance to surrender and submit peacefully to Spanish rule. But as with the Laws of Burgos, the Spanish ignore the substance as well as the spirit of the Requerimiento. The Laws of Burgos fail to end Spanish abuses, for they continue throughout Latin America for four hundred more years.

1513–21 Ponce de Leon.
Juan Ponce de Leon, the governor of Puerto Rico, is given license by the Spanish king to explore and settle Florida, which the Spanish name Bimini, meaning "life source." Though one stated goal of de Leon's mission is to obtain slaves, it is his search for the Fountain of Youth for which he is best known. Ponce de Leon reaches Florida in 1513 and has extensive contact with the peoples of that region. The Saturiwa and Ai nations both greet the expedition with hostility, as do the Calusa, who, in eighty war canoes, drive de Leon's ships away from the coast. Ponce de Leon returns to Bimini in 1521 in an attempt to conquer the Indian Nations. De Leon is shot in the thigh by a Calusa arrow and later dies in Havana from the wound.

Cliff dwellings at Bandelier National Monument near Los Alamos, New Mexico. (Photo by Alexandra Harris)

1520 Hernando Cortes Defeats the Aztec.
The Spanish adventurer, Hernando Cortes, accompanied by

a few hundred Spaniards and a large number of Tlaxcala and other Indian allies, defeat the Aztec at Mexico City. The Spanish thereafter substitute their control over the Indians once subject to Aztec rule. After defeating the Aztec Empire, which controlled most of southern Mexico, Cortes establishes himself as ruler of Mexico.

1520–34 Guayocuya. Within three decades of the establishment of the Spanish colony on Hispaniola, the population of the island drops from estimates of over one million people to only a few thousand. Rebelling against further labor exploitation and the rape of Native women, Guayocuya, a Taino Indian, leads a guerilla war against the Spanish. Guayocuya and his followers refuse to negotiate with the Spanish and after fourteen years of fighting the Spanish submit and Guayocuya and the other refugees are granted land upon which to live in freedom.

1539 Marcos de Niza. As reconnaissance for the impending Coronado expedition, a Franciscan friar named Marcos de Niza explores the region now known as the American Southwest, searching for the fabled Seven Cities of Cíbola. De Niza is accompanied by an escort of Mexican Indians from the Opata region as well as the slave Estevánico, who, as a survivor of the Narv'aez expedition, had traveled through the region several years earlier. Estevánico and the Opata contingent travel some distance ahead of de Niza. Near the six Pueblos of Zuni, de Niza meets fleeing members of the advance party who inform the Franciscan that the Zuni had killed Estevánico and many others. De Niza returns to Mexico falsely claiming that the Zuni Pueblos had wealth greater than the Aztecs or Incas.

1539–43 Hernando de Soto. A Spanish expedition led by Hernando de Soto travels through the present-day southeastern United States. De Soto and his company pillage and fight the Creek, Hitchiti, Chickasaw, Chakchiuma, Choctaw, Tunica, Alabama, and other indigenous nations. The Spanish find little gold and encounter strong resistance from the southeastern Indian nations.

1540–42 Francisco Coronado. Acting on the reports of wealth spread by Friar Marcos de Niza, the Spanish explorer Francisco Coronado travels into present-day Arizona and New Mexico, and perhaps as far east as present-day Oklahoma. The expedition meets with several Pueblo peoples, including the Zuni and Hopi. Hostilities develop because of Spanish atrocities; the Zuni and their Indian allies force the Spanish to retreat in 1542.

1540–1600 Disease Decimates Mississippian Peoples. De Soto and other Spaniards encounter the remnants of the southeastern Mississippian culture, which consists of politically and ceremonially centralized chiefdoms, or small city-states, often managed by priests or sacred chiefs. Diseases transmitted by European explorers, fishermen, and slave raiders decimate Mississippian culture populations. By 1600, most Mississippian ceremonial centers are abandoned and the formerly Mississippian culture groups move up and down the Mississippi Valley and into the present-day southeastern United States, dispersed into decentralized political alliances and confederacies of villages or local kinship groups. By the early 1700s much of the Mississippian culture has disappeared. Some of the remnant Mississippian culture nations are known today as the Creek, Cherokee, Natchez, Chickasaw, Caddo, Pawnee, and Choctaw.

circa 1540–1600 Introduction of Wool. The use of wool is introduced in the Southwest when Indians of that region begin raising sheep brought to North America by the Spanish. At about this time, Pueblo Indians begin weaving on flat looms. The Navajo begin weaving around 1700, learning the skill from their Pueblo neighbors.

1542–1600 Early Displacement. The Iroquoian-speaking nations (Wyandotte, Huron, Five Nations, and others) who live along the St. Lawrence River are invaded and displaced by Algonkian-speaking nations (Montagnais, Ottawa, Algonquin, and others) from the north and west. The Iroquoian-speaking nations retreat south and to the lower Great Lakes area.

1563–65 Huguenots. Protestants known as Huguenots flee Catholic France. They attempt to colonize an area from present-day South Carolina to St. Augustine, in present-day Florida. The colony does not survive because of internal dissension and Spanish attack. The French artist Jacques le Moyne draws some of the earliest known European representations of Native North Americans.

1565–68 Settlement at St. Augustine. The first permanent European settlement in North America is

Town of Secoton in present-day Beaufort County, North Carolina, was engraved by De Bry in the seventeenth century to illustrate the village life of peoples he met. This drawing and those of other settlements visited by early English observers give a visual idea of the lifeways that developed eight hundred years earlier throughout the Southeast and Midwest at the beginning of the Mississippian period. (Courtesy of American Heritage Press)

established at St. Augustine in present-day Florida. Small posts are established up the Atlantic coastline to present-day Georgia; the area is called Guale. Later, Catholic missions, built to Christianize the Natives, will be established throughout Guale.

1578–1579 Sir Francis Drake.　Sir Francis Drake of England explores the California coast and encounters such groups as the Coastal Miwok.

1582–1606 The Spanish Begin Settlement of New Mexico.　Spanish expeditions begin to enter the southern Plains and Pueblo territory by way of the Rio Grande Valley, in eastern New Mexico. In 1598, a Spanish colony is established at San Juan Pueblo, in present-day northern New Mexico. In 1598 and 1599, Indians at Acoma Pueblo revolt against the Spanish, but are put down a year later by a Spanish retaliatory expedition. The Spanish introduce sheep and trade to the Pueblo peoples.

1585–1707 Roanoke Colony.　Sir Walter Raleigh founds the first English colony in the New World on Roanoke Island, present-day North Carolina, but the settlement does not survive. What happens to the English settlers at the Roanoke colony remains a mystery. The Rappahannock people of present-day Virginia come into contact with Spanish and English fishermen, slave raiders, and explorers, although many contacts were probably not recorded.

1598–99 Pueblo Colonization.　Juan de O'nate, governor of New Mexico, leads an expedition through Pueblo territory with the primary mission of subduing the peoples of that region and establishing a Spanish colony. His initial contact with Acoma, a Pueblo situated on a 300-foot mesa, is peaceful, but when Juan de Zaldivar brings reinforcements, diplomacy turns to hostility. Zaldivar is killed. One month later, on 21 January 1599, Vincente de Zaldivar arrives with a force of seventy men to avenge his brother's death. Zaldivar and his men gain access to the village, burn building and slaughter people indiscriminately. By the end of the three-day battle, 800 Acoma are dead. Another 570 are put on trial. Women between the ages of twelve and twenty-five are indentured to twenty years' servitude at the Spanish capital of San Juan. Men are also condemned to servitude, but as an added punishment are publicly mutilated as well. In the plazas of other Pueblos, males over twelve years of age have one foot chopped off. Two Hopi visitors to Acoma are sent home with their right hands severed to show their people what resistance to the Spanish crown will bring.

1606–14 New Mexico Turmoil.　Continual warfare develops between the Spanish and Indians in New Mexico, especially the Navajo, Jeez, and Pueblo refugees. Indians capturing herds of horses are among some of the earliest reports of Native use of these animals in North America.

1607 English Settlement in Virginia.　The British Virginia Company, a monopoly granted by King James I, establishes a settlement at Jamestown (present-day Virginia) on the lands of the Pamunkey Indians, a subgroup of the Powhatan Confederacy. Like those from other European nations, English citizens come to America to exploit its resources and get rich. When the colonizers arrive, they spend much of their time exploring the James River and gathering rocks believed to contain gold. The gold turns out to be pyrite or fool's gold, and the English cast about for another resource.

Wahunsonacock, the leader of the Powhatan Confederacy (referred to simply as Powhatan by the English) warmly receives the colonizers. During the first winter, the Indians save the Englishmen from starvation. George Percy, one of the Jamestown settlers, writes that English rations are reduced to "but a small can of barley, sodden in water, to five men a day." Percy praises God who "put the terror into the sauvages' hearts" so that the "wild and cruel pagans" would not destroy the English. Percy proclaims that God sent "those people which were our mortal enemies, to relieve us with victuals, as bread, corn, fish, and flesh in great plenty." Without the help of Powhatan and his people, they would have all perished.

The English soon repay the Pamunkey by demanding their submission to English rule and the payment of an annual tribute of corn. John Smith, the leader of the Jamestown settlement, advocates an aggressive policy toward the Indians, which causes conflicts between the settlers and the Indians of Chesapeake Bay. At first, Powhatan aids the colonists, but after a few years he becomes disillusioned with the English. He asks, "Why will you destroy us who supply you with food? What can you get by war?" He cannot understand the English animosity toward the Indians and does not comprehend the full extent of European desire for material gain.

1609 Henry Hudson and John Smith.　Henry Hudson, sailing for the Netherlands, opens the lucrative

Proceedings of the Floridians in deliberating on important affairs (1591). Drawing by Le Moyne, from an engraving by T. De Bry, *America,* part 11, plate XXIX. (Courtesy of American Heritage Press)

fur trade with the Lenape, Wappinger, Manhattan, Hackensack, Munsee, and Mohican nations of New Netherlands (present-day New York).

John Smith, of Jamestown colony, is captured by members of the Powhatan Confederacy under suspicion that he participated in a raid on one of their villages. Smith is brought to Powhatan's village. Tradition has it that Pocahontas, Powhatan's young daughter, intercedes and prevents Smith's execution. Captain Smith is released and allowed to return to Jamestown.

1613–14 Marriage of Pocahontas and John Rolfe.
Pocahontas is captured by English settlers and eventually converts to Christianity. In 1614, she marries John Rolfe, the Englishman credited with beginning the European tobacco industry. Pocahontas travels to England, but soon dies of an illness. The marriage further complicates the relationship between Powhatan and the English. Tobacco growing requires new acreage for cultivation every five to seven years; therefore, the colonists seek more land inland in Indian hunting areas

or lands that the Indians have already cleared and used for farming. The extension of the tobacco plantations further aggravates relations between colonists and Indians; Powhatan, however, seeks to keep the peace.

1615 Continued Migration. The confederacy of Algonkian-speaking nations (Ottawa, Potawatomi, Chippewa, and possibly Cree) continue a migration starting near the Atlantic Coast, then through the St. Lawrence River basin, and finally to the Lake Michigan and Lake Superior area. These nations have a tradition of political and ceremonial unity, although they begin to separate into small bands because of the demands of the fur trade economy. Indians trade furs for European manufactured goods such as rifles, metal hatchets and knives, cloth, beads, alcohol, and other items. The Indians quickly recognize the value of the manufactured goods and find that the Europeans are willing to trade for skins and furs, most often deerskins and beaver skins, which are made into leather and hats. Indians begin to hunt for fur-bearing animals more often, for

Pocahontas saving the life of Captain John Smith. From an engraving by T. De Bry, *America,* part XIII, 1634.

longer periods of time, and for the market, instead of for necessity. Consequently, some nations, like the Potawatomi, Ottawa, and Chippewa, migrate into the interior in search of territories that support fur-bearing animals. The fur trade defines the primary economic relation between Europeans and Indians until about 1800.

1615–40s Establishment of Trade Networks. The Wendat (Huron), an Iroquoian-speaking nation of thirty to thirty-five thousand people living near Lake Huron, in alliance with other Iroquoian-speakers—Tobacco, Attiwandaronk (Neutral Nation), and Erie of present-day Ohio—establish a vast trade network in the eastern interior of North America. Goods are exchanged through

trade networks that extend into Mexico, the Gulf of Mexico, and as far west as present-day Minnesota. By the early 1600s these trade networks are distributing manufactured goods, metal knives, guns, tools, cloth, and others items, which are gained in trade with the French in New France (present-day southeastern Canada). By 1635, beaver supplies in the Huron homeland are depleted thanks to European fur demands. The Huron are forced to trade with other nations or hunt on the territories of other Native nations. In the late 1640s the Five Nations (Iroquois of upstate New York), with Dutch supplies of guns, ball, and powder, destroy the Huron and allied nations' trade empire. Under French influence, the Huron and their allies refuse to grant the

Five Nations trade access to the interior from the early 1620s to 1649.

1616–20 Disease. A smallpox epidemic ravages the New England Indians who live along the coastline from present-day Massachusetts to Maine.

1618–31 The First Powhatan War. Powhatan dies in 1618. His brother, Opechancanough, assumes leadership of the tribal confederation. Relations between the colonists and Indians grow more hostile until 1622 when Opechancanough moves against the English, who lose more than one-third of their colony and nearly leave Virginia. The English Crown takes over Jamestown and Virginia, providing aid and protection to the settlers.

Some English feel that the war of 1622 ultimately would be good for the colony. John Smith writes that the conflict "will be good for the Plantation, because we have just cause to destroy them by all meanes possible." Another Englishman writes that the English are "now set at liberty by the treacherous violence of Sauvages." By right of war, the English can now invade Indian lands and thereby "enjoy their cultivated places. . . and possessing the fruits of other labours. Now their cleared grounds in all their villages (which are situated in the fruitfullest places of the land) shall be inhabited by us, whereas heretofore the grubbing of woods was the greatest labour."

The first Virginia War intermittently lasts nearly ten years with many deaths among the Natives and colonists. The territory of the Chickahominy Nation, an ally nation within the Powhatan Confederacy, is ravaged by colonial attacks throughout the 1620s. The Native population in Virginia begins to decline significantly, mostly because of disease, warfare, and most likely migration. In 1608, about thirty thousand Natives live on Chesapeake Bay, but by 1669 only two thousand remain.

1620 Arrival of the Pilgrims. The Pilgrims arrive aboard the Mayflower at Plymouth, Massachusetts. Before landing, they sign a compact calling for self-rule. The Pilgrims barely survive their first winter in Massachusetts, but are helped by several friendly Indians, one of whom was Tisquantum, more commonly known as Squanto. He is captured sometime between 1605 and 1614, when an English ship abducts several Indians and carries them off for sale in Europe. Tisquantum is brought to Malaga Island, Spain, and sold. He makes his way back home by way of England and Newfoundland, only to find that his home village has been wiped out by disease. Tisquantum lives with the Wampanoag and their chief, Massasoit, who enjoys influence over much of present-day Massachusetts and Rhode Island. During his travels, Tisquantum learns some English.

Tisquantum, like other Native Americans, aids the colonists, showing them where to hunt and fish, and how to grow and prepare native crops such as squash, corn, and beans. After the disastrous first winter, the Pilgrims learn quickly from the Indians' lessons. In the fall of 1621 they invite Massasoit to a feast to give thanks; he arrives with ninety people. When the Pilgrims do not have sufficient food, Massasoit asks his people to provide food as well.

1626 Sale of Manhattan Island. Peter Minuit, governor of New Netherlands, the Dutch colony in the New World, trades sixty guilders of goods—legend says worth twenty-four dollars—for Manhattan Island, part of present-day New York City. Minuit buys the land from a band of Shinnecock Indians, but later has to buy it again from the Manhattan band, which claims hunting rights to the island.

Huron dancing ceremony to cure sickness, from Champlain, *Voyages et descouvertures,* Paris, 1620.

1629–33 Establishment of Churches in the Southwest. Spanish missionaries establish Catholic churches at Acoma, Hopi, and Zuni Pueblos.

1630 Arrival of the Puritans. Ten years after the Pilgrims' arrival, the Puritans (a Protestant religious sect) led by John Winthrop, arrive in Massachusetts. The Puritans believe that they are on a mission from God to establish a "City Upon the Hill," a perfect Christian society in which the Puritans form a covenant among themselves and with God to live a holy life. Outsiders are not invited into the covenant unless they agree to subjugate themselves to the rules of the religious community. Most Native Americans do not want to join this covenant and are considered outside of God's law. In fact, Puritan minister Cotton Mather maintains that Indians are the "accursed seed of Canaan" who have been dispatched by Satan "in hopes that the gospel of Jesus Christ would never come here to destroy or disturb his absolute empire over them." Reverend Mather points to the devastating disease that ravages Native populations to prove English superiority. He called the smallpox epidemic of 1633–1635, which kills thousands of Natives, a "remarkable and terrible stroke of God upon the natives." The Puritans argue that God sent the disease to kill Satan's children and to clear the land for his true flock.

1636–37 Pequot Wars. The Puritans attack the Pequot, who are living in present-day Connecticut. In 1634, Indians kill John Stone and eight companions who are hunting for Native slaves. Puritans use Stone's death to claim jurisdiction over the Pequot and to demand their surrender of land, valuable goods, and Stone's killers. The Narragansett, living to the east of the Pequot, are believed to have committed the murders, but the Pequot agree to the Puritan demands. However, they do not abide by the terms of the agreement, and relations with the English grow steadily worse. In 1636, several Narragansett kill an English trader and then flee into Pequot country. When the English demand the return of the Narragansett, the Pequot refuse and a fight ensues. In May 1637, the Massachusetts General Court, the colony's legislature, drafts articles of war, raises an army against the Pequot, and surrounds the Indian village and fort on the Mystic River. Puritans, pilgrims, Mohican, and Narragansett attack and set fire to the Pequot fort, killing as many as seven hundred men, women, and children.

1637–41 Rise of the Ute. Some Spaniards in search of slaves attack the peaceful Ute, who capture Spanish horses, escape, and introduce horses among their people. The Ute then become one of the most powerful people in the Great Basin region.

1638 Early Reservations. The Puritans establish what would now be called a "reservation" for the Quinnipiac Nation living near present-day New Haven, Connecticut. Under the terms of their agreement, the Quinnipiac retain only 1,200 acres of their original land on which they are subject to the jurisdiction of an English magistrate or agent. Under English rule, Quinnipiac people cannot sell or leave their lands or receive "foreign" Indians. They cannot buy guns, powder, or whiskey. They must accept Christianity and reject their traditional spiritual beliefs, which Puritans feel are the teachings of Satan.

1638–84 The Beaver Wars. After failing to gain a reliable trade agreement with the Huron and their trading allies, the Five Nations, with Dutch support and guns and powder, initiate a series of intermittent wars against the Susquehannock, Huron, Neutral Nation, Erie, Wyandotte, Ottawa, and other French trading nations. By 1650, the Huron trade empire is destroyed by the Five Nations. The Ottawa then assume the role of middlemen traders between the interior nations of the Great Lakes area and the French. Thereafter, the Five Nations carry their wars and diplomacy to the Indian nations of the interior, attacking the Chippewa, the Illinois Confederacy, and the Ottawa, and pushing these nations farther into the Great Lakes regions of present-day Michigan and Wisconsin. The Five Nations are generally successful in these wars and are able to supply the Dutch, until 1664, with trade goods. After 1664, the English capture New Netherlands and rename it New York. The English continue the policies of the Dutch traders by supplying the Five Nations with weapons to carry on their trade wars with the interior nations. The French are reluctant to supply their trading partners with guns, and therefore the interior nations are at a disadvantage against the better supplied Five Nations.

1640 Five Nations Exhaust Local Beaver Supplies. The Five Nations (Iroquois) are no longer able to supply their trade requirements by hunting and trapping on their home territory (present-day upstate New York). The Five Nations have come to depend on trade with the Dutch at Fort Orange (present-day Albany, New York) to supply knives, axes, cloth, beads, and guns and powder. After 1640, the Five Nations look to the interior nations to supply them with trade ties or allow them access to beaver territories. During the 1640s, the Five Nations try to negotiate trade and diplomatic agreements with the Huron, Neutral Nation,

Domed wigwam. (Photo by Sarah Loe. Courtesy of the UCLA American Indian Studies Center)

Erie, and Wyandotte, but the French move to prevent permanent trade agreements.

1644–46 The Second Powhatan War.   The Powhatan Confederacy stages a second war against Virginia colony. After the war of 1622, the Indians try to live in peace with the settlers, but the English expand onto Indian lands. Some Indians are held as slaves or servants. By 1641, the English have settled in Maryland and south of the James River and covet the land of the Rappahannock, a major Powhatan ally. By 1642, the English are selecting land sites, even some that include Indian villages. The war of 1644–46 temporarily prevents English territorial expansion.

After two years of warfare, the Indians and colonists negotiate an agreement defining a boundary between the two. The Treaty of 1646 prohibits English land expansion; however, the Indians are left with only a portion of their former lands. The colonists agree to respect Native rights to these territories. Indians become subject to the rule of the colonial Virginia courts and must provide an annual tribute of beaver pelts.

Nevertheless, by 1649 English colonists are already disregarding the treaty and moving farther into Indian territory.

1649 Iroquois Attack Huronia.   The Iroquois Confederacy initiates a concerted attack on Huronia that kills or scatters the entire Huron population. Some survivors are integrated into neighboring groups, including the tribes of the Iroquois Confederacy, others migrate throughout the Great Lakes area where they become known as the Wyandot. In 1652 the Iroquois also destroy the Petun and Neutral.

1650 Cheyenne Migration Begins.   Because of the expanding Iroquois trade empire, the Cheyenne, probably living in present-day southern Ontario or Quebec, are forced to migrate westward. By 1775, they reach the Great Plains of present-day Montana and Dakotas, where they adopt Plains culture with buffalo hunting, an original Sun Dance ceremony, and sacred bundles, given to them by the prophetic figure Sweet Medicine.

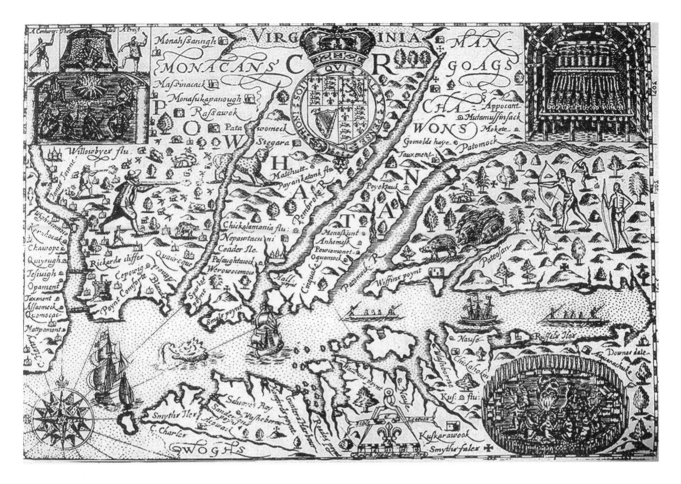

Map of Virginia, 1636, by Ralph Hall.

1660 The Chippewa-Sioux Wars. The Chippewa (Ojibway) living in the upper Great Lakes region start to move west, armed with guns and trade goods. Pushed by colonial and Five Nation expansion, the Chippewa move into Sioux territory in present-day Minnesota. After much fighting with the Chippewa, many Sioux migrate onto the Plains in the 1700s, where they adopt the buffalo-hunting horse culture, for which they are well known in U.S. history. Before this time, the Sioux were a settled horticultural people living in the woodlands east of the Plains area.

1660 Western Apache in the Southwest. Western Apache have control over the area from Sonora and Pima north to the lands of Coninas and to the Hopi area and are said to wage war on all other Indian groups in surrounding areas.

1661 The Chickahominy Are Dispossessed. The Chickahominy Nation, part of the Powhatan Confederacy, move from the Pamunkey River to the Mattaponi River. The Chickahominy sell 2,000 acres of land to an Englishman named Hammond. Phillip Mallory buys 743 acres from the Chickahominy, the beginning of the Mallory family's two-century effort to acquire Chickahominy lands in Virginia.

1661 Spanish Suppression of Pueblo Religions. The Spanish raid the sacred kivas of many Pueblo Indians, destroying hundreds of kachina masks and attempting to suppress Pueblo religions.

1670–1710 Carolina Colony and Early Southern Indian Slave Trade. Charles Town, in present-day South Carolina, is established. Early encounters lead to conflict with local tribal groups such as the Cusabo and Westo. The English attempt to enslave many Indians for plantation work and enlist other nations such as the Creek and Cherokee to raid interior nations like the Choctaw, living in present-day Mississippi and Louisiana, for slaves. During the 1680s and 1690s, the Choctaw are under considerable pressure and lose many

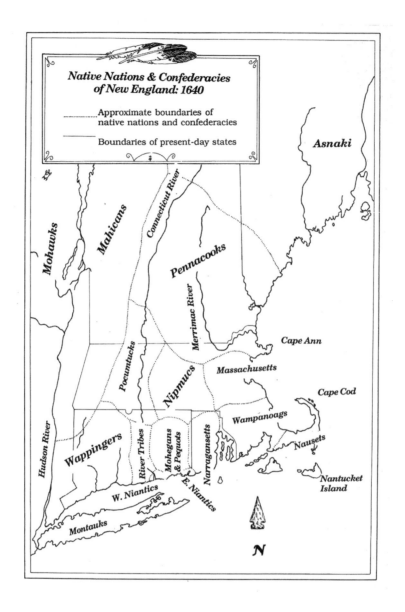

Native nations and confederacies of New England, 1640. (Drawing by John Kahionhes Fadden)

people to slave raids. In 1699, the French establish Louisiana colony, and supply the Choctaw with some weapons, which they use to protect themselves from the English, Creek, and Cherokee slave raids. Some Choctaw regions thereafter are strongly allied to the French in gratitude for their help in preserving the Choctaw Nation. By 1710, the Indian slave trade declines; Indians make poor slaves since they know the local area and escaped often. Thereafter, the fur trade becomes the primary economic relation of the southern Indians to the colonists.

1671–80 Apache Migration. Apaches begin migrating to the Southwest from the southern Plains. They raid Spanish settlements and Indian Pueblos; sheep, horses, and trade goods are stolen. By this time, the Apache are well equipped with guns and horses and are able to elude and challenge Spanish armed forces.

1675–76 King Philip's War. The Puritans proceed to concentrate Indians on reservations and open former Indian lands to Puritan resettlement. By 1671, the Puritans have established fourteen reservations and many Indians have been forced from their homelands. Metacom, the Wampanoag son of Massasoit known to the English as King Philip, protests Puritan policies. He argues that the English set out to destroy Native American cultures and steal Indian lands. In 1671, Puritans arrest Metacom, but release him. He continues to move among the tribes, telling them that the settlers are destroying Indian culture and sovereignty. By 1675, Metacom has a sufficient following to launch a war against the English. Abenaki, Nipmuck, Narragansett, and Wampanoag Indians join forces and attack more than half of the ninety English settlements in New England. The Indians, however, do not stand long against the English. Upon conclusion of hostilities, the English General Court decreases the number of reservations from fourteen to five and places all Indians they can find upon these reserves. The Puritan government has Metacom executed and his wife, son, and hundreds of followers sold into slavery. Many of King Philip's allies, such as the Wampanoag, Nipmuck, and Narragansett, are enslaved or flee to the Mahican, a linguistically related group to the Mohican, in New York, or to the Abenaki Confederation in present-day Maine. The remnant northeastern Indian nations settle down to English rule in small communities, and over the next few centuries establish about fifteen "praying towns" of Christian Indians. These "praying" Indians become socially and economically marginalized in New England society.

1675–77 Bacon's Rebellion. In 1675 and 1676, a third major war erupts between Indians and Virginia settlers. This time Maryland settlers are involved. The Rappahannock flee their villages, and their land is taken by Virginia settlers. The colonists defeat the Susquehannock, who are pressed in the north by expanding Iroquois trade wars. Some Susquehannock move into Virginia territory only to be abused by Virginia traders. The colonists are led by Nathaniel Bacon, who seeks to free Virginia colony from English rule. The English restore order, but not before Bacon's army kills and enslaves many Susquehannock, Occnaneechi, Appomatuck, Manakin, and members of the Powhatan Confederacy. The Indians lose heavily in the war.

In 1677, a treaty of peace is signed between some Indian nations and Virginia colony. This treaty guarantees the signing Indians at least three miles of land in each direction from each of their villages. This leaves the rest of the land open to Virginia settlements and plantations. The Indians of Virginia are forced to acknowledge English law and courts, are subject to Virginian rule, and are left without significant land resources.

1677–1731 Shawnee Migrations and Regroupings. The Shawnee probably occupied present-day northern Kentucky and southern Ohio before European contact. During the late 1600s Chickasaw and Cherokee slave-raiding and fur-trading expeditions force the Shawnee

to retreat from their homeland. Some Shawnee migrate south to Georgia to live on the Savannah River, which is named after them, while others move to present-day western Virginia and Pennsylvania. Others join the Creek Nation, in present-day Alabama, where they establish a permanent village within the Creek Nation. By the 1690s many Shawnee are congregating in present-day eastern Pennsylvania, where they are joined by remnant bands of Delaware, Munsee, and Susquehannock. Sometime before 1680 the Five Nations grant the Delaware, Susquehannock, Shawnee, and other remnant coastal nations the right to occupy territory in present-day eastern Pennsylvania, and many locate near what is now Philadelphia. Most of these nations are now landless, and the Iroquois use the landless Indian nations to create a buffer zone between themselves and the English colonies.

1680 Fur Trade. The Ottawa and Chippewa actively trade with the French. The Iroquois are unsuccessful in persuading or forcing the Algonkian-speaking Indian allies to trade with them or with the English in New York. The Iroquois, however, make greater inroads for hunting and trading south of the Great Lakes area, using both diplomacy and armed forces to attain their commercial ends.

1680–1693 The Pueblo Revolt. Popé, from San Juan Pueblo, leads an armed revolt against the Spanish. The Pueblo Revolt begins at Taos Pueblo in August 1680 and moves steadily southward, driving the Spanish to El Paso del Norte (El Paso, Texas). The Pueblos kill more than four hundred people and recover their homelands. Nine years later, a Spanish army returns. More than six hundred Indians are killed in the initial battle for the reconquest of New Mexico. In 1691, the Spanish military commander Diego de Vargas begins the bloody recovery in earnest, ending four years later. Rather than live under Spanish rule, many Pueblos flee to the small Navajo bands in the north, bringing much knowledge of the Pueblo cultural worldview and economic lifestyle to the Navajo, who until then live mostly by hunting and gathering fruits and nuts.

1682 Pennsylvania Colony and Delaware Treaty. William Penn purchases the present site of Philadelphia, Pennsylvania. The treaty is negotiated with a leading Delaware chief, sometimes called Tammany. An early period of peaceful relations begins between Quakers and the Indians, although relations are not always peaceful with Pennsylvania colony, especially after the 1730s.

Walpi, an ancient Hopi Pueblo village. (Courtesy of Owen Seumptewa)

1683–1690s Shawnee Slave Trade. The Shawnee of the Savannah River dominate trade with South Carolina, getting guns in exchange for furs and slaves. The Shawnee capture their slaves by raiding the Winyah, Appomatuck, Cherokee, and Chatot peoples.

1689–97 King William's War. King William's War initiates a series of colonial conflicts that last until the end of the War of 1812. During this time, there is an undeclared war on the frontier, first between the English and French and their respective Indian allies until 1763, or the end of the French and Indian War. Frontier warfare starts again with the Revolutionary War in 1776 and continues intermittently until 1795. The War of 1812 is the last war before the United States establishes military control over the eastern coastal frontiers. During this period of more than 125 years of intermittent warfare, Indian nations maintain trade relations with one or more European colonies and seek to retain their territory and political independence from colonial domination. Since Indian nations cannot produce metal goods or guns and powder, they depend on trade with European powers to supply these and other more domestic economic requirements. This dependency on trade forces the Indian nations to side with one or the other European power in order to have access to trade and weapons, which becomes increasingly important for defense within the climate of almost constant colonial struggle and warfare. Indian nations often sell themselves as mercenaries to one European power as a means of obtaining goods, other than by trapping furs and trading. In the north, the Algonkian-speaking nations often side with the French, until their defeat in 1760. After 1760, the western Algonkian-speaking nations (Ottawa, Chippewa, Potawatomi, Miami, and others) side with the British against the United States until the end of the War of 1812. Some nations, like the Five Nations and the Creek in the south, try to balance power diplomatically among the European colonies by not taking sides and by threatening an opponent with defection to gain political or trade concessions from the Europeans.

1692 Reconquest of the Pueblos. On August 16, the governor of New Mexico, Diego de Vargas, leaves Guadelupe del Paso to begin preliminary military pacification of the Pueblos. He succeeds through diplomacy in restoring twenty-three Pueblo villages to the Spanish crown. On 13 October 1693, the recolonization of New Mexico begins. Only Santa Ana, Zia, San Felipe, and Pecos Pueblos demonstrate loyalty to the Spanish, while the Tewa, Tano, Picuris, Taos, Jemez, Acoma, and Hopi remain hostile. Considerable force is used to subjugate these groups and whole villages are destroyed and people scattered.

1700 The Missions. Native Americans influenced the Spanish in many areas, particularly with their gifts of foods, natural resources, and architecture. In return, American Indians acquire horses, cattle, sheep, mules, and other livestock. In California and Texas, Indians become skilled cowboys and cowgirls. Some Indians learn the new religion and Christianity spreads widely among the American tribes. Spanish priests, generally of the Jesuit and Franciscan orders, establish missions from the Atlantic to the Pacific. The priests oversee Indian life at the missions where Indians supply the labor to build the beautiful structures so admired today.

The mission system is not a positive experience for most Native Americans. Indians often die from the meager diet and hard work, and sometimes go unattended following injuries or infection. When Indians refuse to work, priests or Christian Indians whip the people, including women and children, into submission. When families flee the missions, presidio soldiers hunt them down and force them to return. Native Americans die in large numbers at the missions from overwork, disease, and unsanitary conditions. Epidemics occur periodically in California under the Spanish occupation, the first recorded one in 1777 at Mission Santa Clara. An epidemic of diphtheria and pneumonia occurs in 1802, ravaging the young from Mission San Carlos to San Luis Obispo. Still another epidemic decimates Native Americans from San Francisco to Santa Barbara with more than 1,600 dead due to measles. Children under the age of ten are almost wiped out in this epidemic. The Native American population declines by as much as 45 percent under the Spanish occupation of California as the direct result of introduced sickness and disease.

circa 1700–60 Early Migration onto the Great Plains. The Shoshone, buffalo hunters of the western plains between the Missouri and the Red Deer rivers, acquire horses for the first time. This gives them an important military advantage over their northern enemies. As a result, the Siksika, Kainai (Blood), Peigan (Blackfeet in Montana, but Blackfoot in Canada), and Atsina retreat toward the Northeast. Horse ownership spreads to most Plains groups by 1760, bringing important changes to Indian societies and to relations among Indian groups. For example, horses make buffalo hunting and transporting goods much easier. Thus, the size of residential bands grows, and horse ownership becomes a symbol of prestige and wealth in formerly egalitarian societies.

1701–55 The Iroquois Adopt Neutrality. The Iroquois shift their policy from alliance with the English to

Iroquois conference, 1753. (Drawing by John Kahionhes Fadden)

neutrality between French (in New France, or present-day Canada) and the English colonies. Late in the 1690s the English begin to occupy Iroquois territory in the Mohawk Valley; this, along with the burden and losses of warfare with the French and their Indian allies, convinces the Iroquois that their English allies were as much a threat as the French. During the 1690s the Iroquois suffered from a series of military setbacks and the new English land threats. In response they developed a new policy of a united front against the Europeans by designating one speaker for the entire confederacy of Five Nations whereby one voice, rather than five chiefs, would speak for their nations.

After a treaty of peace with the French in 1701, the Iroquois Confederacy negotiates commercial agreements with the Ottawa, Chippewa, Illinois Confederacy, and other interior nations. In exchange for allowing the Iroquois to hunt and trade in the interior and Great Lakes area, the interior nations are allowed to travel to Albany, New York, to trade with the English, who had cheaper, better quality goods than the French. This agreement supports Iroquois influence in the region until the 1740s, when Pennsylvania traders follow

the retreating Delaware and Shawnee into the Ohio Valley and beyond. The Iroquois restrict English trade to Albany, but the Pennsylvania traders go directly to the interior villages. Thus, the Iroquois lose their strong trade position, and their power and influence decline. The English continue to support the Iroquois Confederacy as a means to gain trade relations and diplomatic influence over the interior nations.

1702–13 Queen Anne's War. Queen Anne's War, pitting the English against the French and Spanish, starts in Europe, but is also fought in the American colonies. Between 1702 and 1704, the English and Indian allies (Creek and probably Cherokee) attack the Florida mission Indians of Guale (present-day Georgia) and nearly annihilate the entire population of Apalachee Indians, a remnant of which later joins the Creek. The area from the Savannah River (Georgia) to St. Augustine, Florida, is depopulated of Indian people and the Spanish missions are destroyed. Some Yamasee Indians, mission Indians in Guale, migrate to Spanish protection in Florida. The Spanish are unable or unwilling to protect them from English expansion into Florida.

1711–22 Tuscarora War and Migration. The Tuscarora, an Iroquoian-speaking nation living in present-day North Carolina, become involved in war with the English arising from trade disputes. Many Tuscarora become indebted to English traders, who give them credit in the form of goods in the fall of the year and collect the credit in the spring after the hunt. Many Tuscarora cannot pay back the credit, and some traders confiscate the hunters' children and wives to sell as slaves. This manner of collecting the debts leads to war in 1711, and the Tuscarora are defeated by 1713. Many Tuscarora migrate out of eastern North Carolina and travel north, where they find that the Tuscarora and the Iroquois (Five Nations) speak a language similar to their own. The Tuscarora are invited by the Oneida, one of the Five Nations of the Iroquois Confederacy, to live with them and join the confederacy. Between 1715 and 1722, many Tuscarora settle in New York with the Iroquois and are adopted into the confederacy. Nevertheless, the forty-nine chiefs do not wish to create new Tuscarora chiefs, which would violate the sacred constitution of the confederacy, and so the Oneida chiefs speak and represent the Tuscarora, at least until the 1800s, when the confederacy was disrupted. After 1715, the Iroquois Five Nations becomes known as the Six Nations.

1715–17 The Yamasee War and Creek Neutrality. The Yamasee of present-day Georgia, in alliance with the Creek and other smaller coastal nations such as the Hitchiti, Yuchi, and Mikasuki, rise up against the English because of a series of trade abuses and the like. The Yamasee and allies are defeated, and many tribes migrate south into Florida, ultimately forming part of the Seminole Nation, while others join the Creek Confederacy, then occupying what is now central Georgia and Alabama. This defeat convinces the Creek leaders that war against the English is not profitable, and the Creek embark on a policy of neutrality between the English colonies in the Carolinas, the Spanish in Florida and West Florida (now southern Alabama and Mississippi), and the French colony of Louisiana. The Creek balance power among rival European powers and attempt to maximize trade with and diplomatic concessions from the colonists.

1716–27 The Creek and Cherokee War. In the Yamasee War, the Cherokee side with the English against the Creek and their allies. This leads to bloodshed and several failed attempts to reestablish peace. In 1716, a pro-English faction of Cherokee kills a delegation of visiting Creek and Yamasee emissaries, which initiates the war. The Creek and Cherokee carry on a war of raiding parties and revenge attacks against one another.

1720–60 The French Wars on the Chickasaw. The Chickasaw are attracted to an English alliance because they are enticed by the low price and high quality of English trade goods. The English, in turn, seek a Chickasaw alliance because they wish to disrupt the French plan to control the Mississippi Valley by erecting a series of forts and making alliances with the Indian nations along the Mississippi River. In general, the Chickasaw favor the English, although there is a small pro-French faction. Between 1729 and 1752, the French launch four major military expeditions against the Chickasaw villages near the Mississippi in present-day western Kentucky and northwestern Mississippi. The Chickasaw survive all these attacks, although at times they are desperate for supplies and ammunition. In 1739, some Chickasaw migrate to South Carolina for English protection, while others, many of whom are survivors of the Natchez Nation that sought Chickasaw protection from the French in 1729, move to live among the western Creek. The Chickasaw are a major military obstacle to the French plan of enveloping the British colonies and restricting them to the Atlantic seaboard.

1729 Destruction of the Natchez Nation. The Natchez Nation, a Muskogean-speaking society with a centralized sacred chieftain, The Great Sun, and a remnant society of the Mississippian culture, rebels against French attempts to impose taxes and confiscate land in their central village, Natchez. The French at Natchez plantation, in the Louisiana colony, are wiped out. The French and their Choctaw allies counterattack and destroy the Natchez villages. The Great Sun is captured, along with several hundred other captives, and is sold into slavery in the Caribbean Islands. The Natchez descendants still live on the island of St. Helena. Other Natchez escape, some seeking refuge among the Chickasaw, who give them shelter, but this intensifies warring relations between the Natchez and the French and Choctaw.

1739 Arikara Migrate North. About this time, a group of Indians known now as the Arikara (a tribe closely related to the Pawnee) begin to migrate north from the Loup River in present-day Nebraska and travel up the Missouri River to settle eventually in present-day central North Dakota.

1740–1805 Russians Explore the Northwest Coast. The first Russian explorers sail over to Alaska and explore the entire Alaskan coastline and encounter many Pacific Northwest Coast tribal groups, like the Haida, Tlingit, Aleut, and others. In the 1740s and 1750s, following Vitus Bering who in 1741 sighted the North American continent and explored the Bering Sea and

Early colonists often observed Native societies. (Drawing by John Kahionhes Fadden)

Bering Strait, the Russians open trade with Natives for sea otter pelts. Russian fur traders expand their enterprises in the far Northwest and by 1805 reach San Francisco, California. French, Dutch, and Russians establish colonies primarily to exploit the rich resource in fur. They trade guns, powder, lead, pots and pans, knives, fishhooks, beads, and cloth for furs. Indians often alter their traditional lives to obtain furs to trade for these items; in doing so, their cultures change and many become dependent on the European supply of manufactured goods.

In the second half of the eighteenth century, the Russian government sends over many Russian Orthodox priests to convert and protect the Natives. Many of these early Russian Orthodox churches and their Native congregations, sometimes singing mass in archaic Russian, can still be found in several places in Alaska.

1744–48 King George's War. King George's War is initiated in Europe and is fought, in part, by the European colonies in North America. This war pits the French against the English, and each side persuades its Indian allies to fight. It is cheaper and more efficient for colonial governments to hire Indian fighters to engage in war than to import troops from Europe, where they are badly needed. In North America, the war is inconclusive; the Treaty of Aix-la-Chapelle, negotiated in Europe, restores all original boundaries.

1748–51 The Choctaw Civil War. The Choctaw Nation is divided during the 1730s and 1740s between loyalty to the French and cheap trade goods given by the English. One region, the central and northeast villages, favors English trade, while the western and southern villages favor French alliance. Civil war erupts between the regions when Red Shoes, the head warrior of the eastern allied towns, is assassinated for a bounty by a pro-French Indian. Both sides rely on their allies to supply weapons and ammunition, but the British fail to provide enough support and the pro-British eastern villages are defeated. After 1751, Choctaw political relations are organized into three autonomous political regions: the conservative Six Towns district (or *iksa*, a Choctaw term for a matrilineal descent group) in the south favor the French; the western villages, called "people of the long hair," also favor the French; and the northeastern villages, called the "potato people," favor the British. Each district has a chief and a council, and each decides its own internal matters, rarely meeting with the other two districts to discuss national business. The three-district political system lasts among the Choctaw until 1907, when the U.S. government abolishes the government of the Choctaw Nation.

1749–63 French and Indian War. The French and Indian War begins with the French construction of Fort Duquesne (present-day Pittsburgh, Pennsylvania) on land already claimed by Virginia. The European colonies go to war over lands along the Ohio River. Many Iroquois (primarily Mohawk) reluctantly side with the British, while Seneca favor the French for a time. Many Indians align themselves with the French, including the Wyandotte, Shawnee, Chippewa, Ottawa, Miami, Abenaki, and Lenape. At first the war goes well for the French and their Spanish and Indian allies, but in the end the French lose nearly all their claims in the Americas, including Canada and the Illinois-Mississippi River valleys. Indians who fought with the French now find themselves without their allies and without suppliers of arms and trade goods.

1750–1850 The Chickahominy Nation Disperses. The Chickahominy Nation of Virginia breaks into several smaller communities. Some join the Pamunkey, Mattaponi, and other remaining nations living near the Chesapeake Bay area, while others hang onto their lands, living by hunting and fishing. By the 1760s and later, the Chickahominy people are no longer mentioned in the Virginia records.

1754 The Albany Plan. Benjamin Franklin, a prominent citizen and statesman from Pennsylvania, proposes a plan of union for the British colonies. Franklin has several times visited the Iroquois Confederacy (Six Nations) and suggests their model for unifying the colonies. He remarks that it is strange that the Six Nations could form an apparently indissoluble union, while ten or twelve British colonies could not. The plan fails in 1754—for want of interest by more than a few colonists—but is revived later in the U.S. Articles of Confederation (1777–88), the first laws of U.S. government, and the U.S. Constitution (implemented in 1789).

1760–75 The British in Sole Control of Eastern North America. The French defeat by 1760 changes the situation of the eastern Native nations. Since about 1600, there were at least two or more major European powers fighting for control of trade and land. Now only the British remain, and only one nation controls trade relations and supplies of goods, weapons, and ammunition. The British try to regulate the distribution of trade and weapons, which makes the formerly French allied Indians suspicious of British intentions. Furthermore, the British intend to occupy the old French forts, such as Detroit and Chicago, in the Great Lakes area, which was territory the Indians claimed and did not grant British occupation. Ottawa, Wyandotte, Miami, Great Lakes nations, and Shawnee Indians living north of the Ohio River fear British political domination. In the 1760s and early 1770s, the British administration plans to regulate the Indians' trade and activities, but these plans are disrupted by the emergence of the revolutionary war in 1775.

1760–63 The Delaware Prophet. After the French defeat in 1760, and while the British threaten domination, several prophets emerge among the Delaware people. Two major figures teach very different messages. One brings a militant message, involving borrowed Christian concepts of personal salvation in heaven; the other "domestic" Delaware prophet teaches a message also borrowed from Christian ideas of heaven and a central god, but establishes a new religion designed only for the Delaware, not for any other Indian or European nations.

The more militant prophet emphasizes that the Europeans will have to be driven off the continent and the Indians return to the customs of their ancestors before they can be restored to their former prosperous and happy state. This message greatly influences the Ottawa leader Pontiac, who uses it to mobilize warriors from different nations to strike at the English in 1763. The "domestic" Delaware prophet creates a new national religion, reorganizes the Delawares' disrupted kinship system, and creates new and permanent chiefs for the three reorganized kinship-religious divisions of the religiously and politically unified Delaware Nation.

Hendrick, Abraham, and Franklin at the Albany Conference, 1754. (Drawing by John Kahionhes Fadden)

1763 Pontiac's War. Pontiac follows the militant Delaware prophet and, through this religious revitalization movement, forms a confederacy of the Ottawa, Lenape (Delaware), Wyandotte, Seneca, Potawatomi, Kickapoo, Shawnee, and Miami tribes. Pontiac leads the confederacy in a short-lived war, which does not prevent the British from occupying the old French forts of the Ohio and Great Lakes area.

1763 The Proclamation of 1763. The British government's proclamation results in a boundary, the Proclamation Line of 1763, running along the crest of the Appalachian Mountains. Indian country is west of the line from the Appalachian Mountains to the Mississippi River, while colonists can settle lands east of the line. This act recognizes Indian rights to land, but many colonists disregard the act and move across the Appalachians, causing conflict with the Indian nations that regard the colonists as intruders.

1763–74 Pre-Revolutionary Policy. Between 1763 and 1774, most of the nations in the eastern portion of North America reassess their relationship with the

British government and the colonists. Native Americans realize that a rift has developed between the British homeland and the colonists, and many seek positions of neutrality; however, as the British government and the colonists drift closer to war, some of the nations favor alliance with the British. Many Indians believe that in the event of war, the British will win. Many Indians also believe that the colonists, who are interested in acquiring more land, are a greater threat to the Indians than the British government.

1765 Paxton Boys' Massacre. Frustrated by the failure of Pennsylvania's Quaker-dominated assembly to take more aggressive action against the Indians of that state, a group of seventy-five Presbyterians from Paxton in Lancaster County take matters into their own hands. They attack a village of Conestoga Mission Indians (Christianized Susquehannock and others) and violently murder six people, scalping them all. The remaining Conestoga are moved to the Lancaster jail for their own protection. Governor John Penn issues a proclamation denouncing the incident and orders the violence to stop. In spite of his orders the Paxton Boys strike again, breaking into the jail on December 27 and murdering the remaining fourteen Conestoga.

1768 Treaty of Fort Stanwix. Bowing to British insistence, the Six Nations cede land ranging from south of the Ohio River into present-day northern Kentucky. Most of this land comprises the traditional Shawnee homeland, and the Shawnee recognize no right of the Six Nations to sell it to the British. Thereafter, the Shawnee and their ally, the Delaware (both nations then residing in present-day Ohio) organize a pan-Indian confederacy without the leadership of the Six Nations, now seen as puppets of the British. The Six Nations, since about 1700, gain informal leadership of a broad coalition of Indian nations, once boasting that they could muster warriors from fifty nations. Now the influence of the Six Nations declines, and the loose confederacy of western Indian nations are led by the Shawnee, Delaware, and Miami. The Indian confederation tries to keep settlers out of the Old Northwest, the area west of the Ohio River, including the Great Lakes area. This confederacy defends the Old Northwest until the end of the War of 1812.

1769 Missions Established in California. The San Diego Mission, the first in a series of twenty-one religious agrarian settlements to be built approximately a day's journey apart along El Camino Real, the Spanish land route from San Diego to San Francisco, is established. The missions support two Franciscan friars as overseers, a protective military garrison, and hundreds of "Christianized" Indians, who are impressed for mission work and religious conversion. Those who do not obey are subject to a number of punishments, including solitary confinement, lashing, branding, and execution. Mission Indians find life very difficult; the Spanish forbid any practice of traditional cultures and religions, and many Indians die of disease and hardship.

In response to this invasion of their territory, California Indian groups begin to resist almost immediately. The Ipai and Tipai Indians, on whose land the San Diego Mission is built, attack the Spanish camp within a month of its establishment. Six years later on 4 November 1775, under the leadership of two baptized village headmen, a force of 800 Ipai and Tipai destroy the mission there, killing the resident padre. Other acts of rebellion take place, most notably the 1824 revolt at Missions La Purisima and Santa Barbara, when mistreated neophytes capture both missions for a short time. In the end all these revolts are defeated.

1773–74 Lord Dunmore's War. Angry about settlers from Virginia moving onto their lands and sometimes murdering Indians, the Shawnee and their allies

move to protect territories in western Virginia and Pennsylvania. Lord Dunmore, governor of Virginia, musters an army and fights a series of skirmishes with the Indians along the Virginia and Pennsylvania frontier.

1774–75 Formation of the Indian Departments. During the First Continental Congress in 1774, the delegates, worried about Indian loyalties, commit $40,000 to Indian affairs and appoint a Committee on Indian Affairs to negotiate terms of neutrality or support from the Indians. In 1775, the First Continental Congress assumes control over Indian affairs, removing such power from the individual colonies. Northern, southern, and middle departments are created, with commissioners appointed to the head of each. Indian affairs are considered of such importance at this juncture in U.S. history that Benjamin Franklin, Patrick Henry, and James Wilson, all central leaders in the Revolution, are named the first commissioners of the Indian departments. The commissioners are authorized to make treaties and to arrest British agents. They open negotiations with the Six Nations in order to win their neutrality in the impending war, if not their alliance. The commissioners offer trade goods and blacksmith services as a part of a treaty of alliance, but the Six Nations decline the offer.

1775 Cheyenne Receive the Sacred Law. According to their tradition, the Cheyenne are granted their sacred law and covenant with the Creator at this time through the prophet Sweet Medicine. Sweet Medicine receives the law directly from the Creator on a sacred mountain, present-day Bear Butte in South Dakota. Sweet Medicine then gives the Cheyenne instructions to form a council of forty-four chiefs—forty chiefs elected from the ten traditional Cheyenne bands and four chiefs appointed to represent the four sacred directions. The covenant relation obliges the Cheyenne people to uphold the sacred law and ceremonies; in return, the Creator preserves the Cheyenne Nation from physical and cultural destruction.

1777–83 Iroquois Confederacy Is Dispersed. The Revolutionary War permanently disrupts the unity of the Iroquois Confederacy. At the beginning of the war, many Iroquois, especially the Seneca and Onondaga, prefer neutrality and do not wish to join with either warring party. Some Mohawk, led by Joseph Brant, a close family friend to the British agent William Johnson, prefer to fight with the British. The Oneida and Tuscarora, because of local trade and friendship ties with settlers, prefer to side with the United States. This absence of agreement about how to handle the war does not allow the Confederate Council to arrive at a

On 11 June 1776, an Onondaga sachem gave John Hancock an Iroquois name at Independence Hall. (Drawing by John Kahionhes Fadden)

common plan of action (all six nations of the confederacy must agree to all decisions, otherwise each nation acts independently). Since there is no agreement, the individual nations, villages, even families make their own decisions about alliance or neutrality. This causes a deep rift within the confederacy, which is not effectively restored, even after the Revolutionary War. The pro-British Iroquois move to Canada during and after the war and eventually form their own confederacy, and the Iroquois remaining in New York do likewise. Thus, by the early 1800s two independent Iroquois Confederacies emerge.

1777–87 Articles of Confederation. Under the Articles of Confederation—the first U.S. laws of national government—Native Americans are treated as sovereign nations. Under the terms of the Peace of Paris (1783), the United States receives claim to all the land from the Atlantic to the Mississippi River, and from the Great Lakes to the Florida border. Congress has administrative authority over these lands, but most of them belong to Indians. The British long followed the precedent that Native Americans had a "natural right" to the land but that they could relinquish title to the lands through agreements. For the most part, the United States follows this principle, although the country will claim vast areas of land from the Indians by right of conquest. In 1779, the Continental Congress passes a law asserting that only the national government can transfer ownership of Indian lands, and, by the Ordinance of 1787, the United States promises that Native Americans' "land and property shall never be taken from them without their consent; and in their property, rights and liberty, they shall never be invaded or disturbed, unless in just and lawful wars authorized by Congress."

17 September 1778 First U.S.-Indian Treaty Is Signed. At Fort Pitt (now Pittsburgh, Pennsylvania), the Delaware, primarily the Turtle, one of three Delaware divisions, sign a peace treaty with the United States. The treaty offers the Delawares the right to send representatives to Congress and become part of the U.S. nation. This clause, however, is never implemented. The Delaware Treaty is the first of 370 treaties signed with Indian nations between 1778 and 1871, when Congress passes a law forbidding the government to make treaties with Indians.

1783–95 Intermittent Border Wars. After the end of the Revolutionary War in 1783, the political and military situation remains extremely unstable. Between 1783 and 1795 the British continue to occupy the forts of the Old Northwest, at Detroit and Chicago, although by treaty they are to be evacuated. The United States has neither the military strength nor the will to dislodge the British soldiers. The British occupy the forts and supply their Indian allies west of the Ohio River with goods and weapons, hoping that the Indian nations will create a buffer zone between the United States and Canada. The Indian nations (Delaware, Miami, Shawnee, Ottawa, and others) hope to use British support to keep U.S. settlers from streaming across the Ohio River and taking Indian land.

The U.S. government has little money with which to operate, but it claims all Indian land west to the Mississippi River. The new nation makes considerable money by selling western lands in Ohio, Indiana, Kentucky, and Tennessee. In the north, the Wyandotte, Delaware, Shawnee, Miami, Chippewa, Potawatomi, Kickapoo, Ottawa, and some Iroquois warriors join to defy the U.S. invasion of the Old Northwest, bringing war to the settlers in Ohio in their attempt to drive them out. Between 1783 and 1790 perhaps one thousand settlers lose their lives; there are no estimates regarding Indian deaths north of the Ohio River caused by war and disease.

In the 1780s, several unsuccessful treaties are signed between small Indian groups and the U.S. government. The U.S. commissioners negotiate these treaties at Fort Stanwix with the Six Nations (1784); at Fort McIntosh with the Wyandotte, Delaware, Chippewa, and Ottawa (1785); at Fort Finney with the Shawnee (1786); and at Fort Hopewell with the Cherokee, Choctaw, and Chickasaw (1786). The treaties typically contain several articles, including those that cede certain lands to the United States. Not all the Indian leaders of the various nations agree with or sign the treaties. Trouble results when settlers move onto western lands they purchase from land companies. In Ohio, Kentucky, and Tennessee, settlers often find Native Americans still residing on and laying claim to lands that the settlers have bought. Although some settlers and Indians live peacefully beside one another, there is continued conflict over land ownership.

Land disputes result in intermittent skirmishes along the frontier between 1790 and 1794. President George Washington answers the Indian challenge by directing General Josiah Harmer and 1,500 troops to engage the Indians. Kickapoo, Shawnee, and Miami snipers harass the soldiers as they march south of the Maumee River in Ohio. In September 1790 the Indian alliance launches a successful battle that defeats Harmer and provokes Washington into sending Governor Arthur St. Clair and 3,000 troops to the Maumee River, in present-day Indiana, to confront the Indians. Once again Native American forces strike hard, killing and wounding more than 900 soldiers. Still determined to destroy the Indian alliance in the Old Northwest, Washington orders General Anthony Wayne into Ohio. In August 1794, the confederated nations, led by Little Turtle of the Miami Nation, go into battle against Wayne, known to the Indians as Blacksnake, at the Battle of Fallen Timbers, near present-day Fort Wayne, Indiana. Partly because the British fail to come to the Indians' aid at the battle, the Indians are forced to retreat. The Indians' political position further erodes when, in late 1794, the United States and Britain sign Jay's Treaty; the English depart to Canada and withdraw their military support for their Indian allies. This forces the Indians of the Old Northwest to treat with the United States in 1795 at Fort Greenville, in present-day Indiana. The Indian nations recognize the United States as the primary non-Indian power in the area and cede most of Ohio to the United States for $20,000 worth of goods and an annuity of $10,000. The Indian nations of the Old Northwest—the Wyandotte, Shawnee, Delaware, Potawatomi, Miami, Kickapoo, Ottawa, and Chippewa—lose considerable land and power.

In the South, parts of the Cherokee, Creek, Choctaw, and Chickasaw nations side with the Spanish in order to curtail U.S.-settler expansion into their territories. Like the British in the North, the Spanish in Florida and West Florida (present-day Alabama and Mississippi)

On 2 May 1780, Cornplanter addressed Congress in New York City. (Drawing by John Kahionhes Fadden)

provide the southern Indians with trade and weapons. This leads to intermittent warfare between the westward-moving settlers and the Indian nations, who are intent on defending their territory.

Like the British, the Spanish hope to prevent the territorial expansion of the young United States. In 1795, when the Napoleonic Wars begin in Europe, the Spanish turn their attention to Europe and ignore their relatively unprofitable Florida colonies. Thus, the southern Indian nations, in a series of treaties in the middle 1790s, are forced to recognize the United States as the major non-Indian power in the South.

7 August 1786 Federal Indian Reservation. The first federal Indian reservation is established. Congress establishes two departments: the northern, with jurisdiction north of the Ohio River and west of the Hudson River, and the southern, which covers the area south of the Ohio River. A superintendent is appointed to head each department, reporting to the secretary of war. Each of these officials has the power to grant licenses to trade and live among the Indian people.

1787–89 Indians and the U.S. Constitution. In 1787, delegates come to Philadelphia to frame the Constitution. Some Native Americans and scholars argue that the delegates learned much about representative government from the Iroquois, and that the Constitution is patterned after the political ideas of the Iroquois and the political structure of their league. Furthermore, ideas of individual political freedom, free speech, political equality, and political community are recorded in sixteenth- and seventeenth-century encounters with Native societies. Many of these observations are incorporated into the Enlightenment philosophy of the 1700s by such men as Jean-Jacques Rousseau and Voltaire. The Enlightenment philosophy in turn influences contemporary political thought and the organization of democracy in Western nations.

After much debate, the states ratify the Constitution and it becomes the supreme law in the United States. The constitutional delegates want Indian policy to be centralized and determined by Congress. Article 1, Section 8 of the Constitution, often called the Commerce Clause, empowers Congress to make all laws pertaining to the Indian trade and diplomatic relations.

This clause prohibits the original thirteen colonies from negotiating treaties directly with Indian nations and leaves control over Indian land in federal hands, outside individual state's jurisdiction. Through treaty-making, which requires ratification by the Senate with a two-thirds vote and signature by the president, the Indian nations form a legal relationship with the U.S. government. Treaties end wars and cede to the government millions of acres of land.

1787 The Northwest Ordinances. The Northwest Ordinance of 1787 calls for the division of lands north of the Ohio River into territories that can eventually become states. In this way, the Congress establishes the mechanism by which territories and states will be created. In order to open lands for settlement, Congress passes the Ordinance of 1785, which calls for the survey of so-called public land into townships of six miles square divided into thirty-six sections of 640 acres each, costing $640. This method favors land speculators with money to invest. Real estate companies emerge, buying large tracts of land and subdividing them to make purchases more affordable for smaller farmers. Yet, in order for the two ordinances to work, the United States must secure Indian title to the land. The government establishes this through treaties.

1789 Indian Affairs Moved to War Department. Since 1784, Congress has delegated negotiation of treaties to the War Department. In 1786, the secretary of war assumes management of Indian Affairs, and in 1789, with the creation of the new War Department, Indian Affairs are delegated to the first Secretary of War, Henry Knox. Because many Indian nations on the frontier are allied with the British or Spanish and resist U.S. settlement, the War Department is seen as the most appropriate agency to manage Indians relations.

1799 Religious Revitalization and Handsome Lake. Handsome Lake, a Seneca clan leader, becomes so ill that his family and friends gather to pay their respects before he dies. Not long after his apparent death, Handsome Lake recovers and tells everyone that his soul left his body and met three Native angels. They told Handsome Lake to end his drinking, live a good life, and follow the teachings of the Creator who would reveal himself in the months ahead. In the fall of 1799, Handsome Lake has a second vision, in which he meets the Creator and learns lessons that become the hallmark of the revitalized Longhouse religion. By the late 1830s, the religion becomes the Handsome Lake Church. His visions and teachings are known as the Gaiwiio, the good word. He teaches that Native Americans should live in peace with the United States, but that they should spiritually or culturally be Iroquois.

His doctrines stress peace within the family and among all people.

1803 The Louisiana Purchase. The United States buys from France a large portion of land west of the Mississippi River extending in the north to the Pacific Ocean. This land contains large numbers of Indian nations, many of whom have yet to have extended political relations with a European or U.S. government. With the purchase of these western lands, President Thomas Jefferson proposes that many of the Indian nations living east of the Mississippi River be removed west to lands where they would be out of the way of U.S. settlers, and the eastern land would be open to settlement.

1805–1806 Sacajawea Aids Lewis and Clark Expedition. While wintering in present-day North Dakota, explorers William Clark and Meriwether Lewis meet Sacajawea, a Shoshone woman married to French trader Toussaint Charbonneau. Charbonneau is hired as an interpreter and guide. Sacajawea proves invaluable to the men's expedition because she can speak to Indians encountered along the way. Her female presence is seen as a peaceful symbol to them.

1805 The Munsee Prophetess. In the early 1800s U.S. officials in present-day Indiana pressure leaders of the Delaware, Shawnee, and other Old Northwest Indian nations into selling significant tracts of land, resulting in considerable tension and dismay among most members of the Indian nations. Between 1803 and 1805, while the Delaware and Munsee are living in what is now the area between Indianapolis and Munsee, Indiana, several Delaware have visions. But in 1805, a female, now known only as the Munsee Prophetess, has a vision and consequently introduces modifications to the Delaware Big House Religion, the Delaware national religion since the Delaware prophet of the 1760s. The Munsee Prophetess teaches that the Indians must retain their traditions and reject farming, Christianity, trade, and European clothing, otherwise the Delaware Nation will continue to decline politically, economically, and spiritually. When Tenskwatawa, the Shawnee prophet who lives in the Delaware and Munsee villages, emerges in February 1806, the prophetess defers to him.

1806–1809 Tecumseh and Tenskwatawa, the Shawnee Prophet. In February 1806, while living among the Delaware and Munsee, Tenskwatawa reportedly dies. While his family prepares him for burial, he regains consciousness, saying that he had died and visited the Master of Life. Tenskwatawa reports that through him, The Open Door, Native Americans can learn the Way.

Thousands of Indians gravitate toward Tenskwatawa and his teachings, flocking to hear him preach in a village called Prophetstown. So many Native peoples come to the village that resources are depleted, and the prophet is forced to move his town west, settling near the junction of the Tippecanoe and Wabash rivers in eastern Indiana. Through his religious revitalization movement, Tenskwatawa unites many tribes to stand against the United States. Using his brother's spiritual movement, Tecumseh forges a pan-Indian confederacy that is both political and military.

1811 Battle of Tippecanoe.   With a Creek medicine man named Seekaboo, Tecumseh travels to the southern Indian nations, seeking support for his confederacy. Only a portion of the Creek, known as Red Sticks, join the movement. Tecumseh returns to the north to learn that against his instructions, his brother the prophet, entered into battle with U.S. troops. In November 1811, Governor William Henry Harrison, future U.S. president, leads 1,000 soldiers within a few miles of Prophetstown. Tenskwatawa, the prophet, provides ceremonial protection from bullets and encourages his followers to attack the soldier's camp. During the battle the Prophet's followers suffer casualties. Thereafter, most of the Indians abandon the his leadership and religion.

1812–14 The War of 1812.   The War of 1812 devastates the land and populations of the Indians of the Old Northwest. At the Treaty of Ghent, which ends the war, the British agree that all the territory south of the Great Lakes belongs to the United States, and the British agree not to give aid to their ally Indians there. This leaves the Indian nations living east of the Mississippi River entirely within the sphere of the U.S. government's influence. The Indians no longer have the supplies or alliance of a rival European power to balance against the United States. By 1819, the Spanish sell Florida and West Florida to the United States, and U.S. claims to the land east of the Mississippi River are undisputed, except by the Indian nations still living there. After 1817 to 1819, however, the political and diplomatic position of the Indian nations rapidly deteriorates, and they are less able to retain territory and political independence.

1813–14 The Red Stick War.   Angry over U.S. interference and control within the Creek government and influenced by Tecumseh's message of resistance to the United States, Creeks living in present-day Alabama called Red Sticks attack Creek villages allied with the United States. Sometime later the Red Sticks also attack Fort Mims, killing U.S. citizens there and providing an excuse for the United States to enter into the Creek civil war. General Andrew Jackson, with five thousand troops and Indian allies, marches against the Red Sticks at the village of Tohopeka at Horseshoe Bend on the Tallapoosa River. Surrounded and assaulted by cannon fire, the Red Sticks suffer losses of more than eight hundred men, women, and children. The Creek Nation, including the U.S.-allied Creek, is forced to accept the Treaty of Fort Jackson, which cedes 22 million acres of Creek land in Georgia and Alabama to the U.S. government.

1817–18 The First Seminole War.   In Florida, a U.S. attack on Fowltown, home of the Seminole chief Neamathla, officially begins the war on 21 November 1817. Forces led by General Andrew Jackson destroy Seminole villages and farms in northern Florida, leading to the cession of Florida to the United States by Spain. Some Creek Red Sticks join the Seminole in Florida and continue resistance to the United States with the help of English trade companies.

1817–1819 Cherokee Migration.   Because of continuing harassment from U.S. settlers, several thousand Cherokee emigrate beyond the Mississippi River into Arkansas, forming a Cherokee Nation West.

1821 The Cherokee Syllabary.   Sequoyah, a Cherokee living in present-day Arkansas, develops the Cherokee syllabary, a writing code using symbols for syllables rather than for sounds. Many Cherokee quickly learn to read and write in the Cherokee syllabary. Translations of the Bible are made into Cherokee, and Cherokee spiritual leaders and healers record sacred and medicinal knowledge.

1823 *Johnson v. M'Intosh*.   In *Johnson v. M'Intosh*, a case before the U.S. Supreme Court, Justice John Marshall recognizes that Indians have the right to land by their prior use, but rules that Indian tribes cannot sell land to private individuals and must sell only to the federal government. This case curtails Indian control over the use and sale of their own territory.

1827–28 The Cherokee Republic.   The Cherokee watch the drift toward a policy of forced removal and decide upon a unique course of action in their attempt to prevent their own removal. In the early 1820s, the Cherokee establish a capital in New Echota, in present-day Georgia. In 1827, they write a constitution calling for three branches of government, in many ways similar to the U.S. federal constitution. In 1828, the Cherokee ratify the new constitution and elect John Ross, a wealthy Cherokee slaveholder, principal chief. The Cherokee wish to establish their government and right to preserve their homeland in present-day Georgia, Tennessee, and eastern Alabama. In January 1829 the Georgia legislature, wanting to remove the Cherokee from their chartered limits, pass a series of laws that abolish the Cherokee government and appropriate Cherokee territory.

1828–35 The Cherokee Phoenix. *The Cherokee Phoenix*, a weekly newspaper printed in English and Cherokee, is published. The newspaper's first editor is Elias Boudinot, who was educated in Cornwall, Connecticut, after attending primary school among the Moravian missionaries in Tennessee. The newspaper is discontinued when the U.S. government presses the Cherokee Nation to move west. Boudinot joins a minority group in signing the Treaty of New Echota in 1835, which, according to the U.S. government, obligates the Cherokee to move west to present-day Oklahoma.

1830–60 The Removal Era. In 1830, Congress votes in favor of the Indian Removal Act. The removal of Native Americans from their lands becomes an integral element of national Indian policy. During the 1830s and 1840s, the U.S. Army forces thousands of Indian families to leave their belongings and move to lands west of present-day Iowa, Missouri, Kansas, Nebraska, Arkansas, and Oklahoma. The United States forces the Cherokee onto the Trail of Tears, which directly results in the death of four thousand to eight thousand people. One soldier writes: "I fought through the Civil War and have seen men shot to pieces and slaughtered by thousands, but the Cherokee removal was the cruelest work I ever knew."

The Cherokee Nation is not the only Native nation to remove to Indian Territory. Other nations include the Choctaw, Chickasaw, Creek, Seminole, Wyandotte, Ottawa, Peoria, Miami, Potawatomi, Sac, Fox, Delaware, Seneca and many others. The government is ill prepared to handle so many Indians along the trails and in new homes. In 1841, Major Ethan Allan Hitchcock investigates Indian affairs in the West and concludes that the American Indian policy is filled with "bribery, perjury and forgery, short weights, issues of spoiled meat and grain, and every conceivable subterfuge."

1830 Treaty at Dancing Rabbit Creek. The Choctaw sign the Treaty at Dancing Rabbit Creek, ceding more than 10 million acres of land in Alabama and Mississippi. In exchange they are promised peace, friendship, and land in the West. They are not compensated, as promised, for farm buildings, schoolhouses, and livestock that they lose by giving up their homelands.

The move takes nearly three years, and hundreds of Choctaw die during the removal.

1831 Cherokee Nation v. Georgia. Against Georgia's efforts to remove the Cherokee from their homeland, the Cherokee counter with a lawsuit in the Supreme Court. *Cherokee Nation v. Georgia* is based on a clause in the Constitution that allows foreign nations to seek redress in the U.S. Supreme Court for damages caused by U.S. citizens. Chief Justice John Marshall rules that the Cherokee Nation is not a foreign republic, but a domestic dependent nation. Indians are not citizens of the United states but are wards of the government.

1832 Worcester v. Georgia. *Worcester v. Georgia* is brought by the Cherokee Nation with the help of two missionaries, Samuel Worcester and John Butterick. Since the Cherokee are not citizens and the court ruled they are not a foreign nation, the Cherokee must rely on U.S. citizens to make their case against Georgia. The missionaries defy Georgia law by carrying on Cherokee Nation business and refuse to swear allegiance to Georgia, for which they are arrested and sentenced to hard labor. In this case, the Court strikes down the Georgia law arguing that only the federal government has the right to regulate affairs in Indian country, while states cannot extend their laws over Indian governments. The Indian Nations sign treaties recognizing U.S. power, but do not cede rights to self-government or territory. The Cherokee are forced to move between 1835 and 1839. *Worcester v. Georgia* now stands as a major precedent supporting Indian rights to self-government as long as they do not conflict with federal or constitutional law.

1832 The Black Hawk War. Remnant bands of the Sauk and Fox tribes attempt to reclaim land in Wisconsin and Illinois but are quickly repressed by U.S. troops. Black Hawk, a keeper of a major medicine bundle among the Sauk and Fox, is strongly opposed to ceding territory in present-day Illinois.

1835–42 The Second U.S. and Seminole War. U.S. troops battle in the swamps of Florida. The Seminole conduct a guerrilla-style warfare that costs the U.S. government more than $20 million and the lives of 1,500 troops. The Seminole leader Osceola is deceived and captured under a flag of truce and dies in prison in 1838.

1837–53 Kenekuk, the Kickapoo Prophet. After the end of the War of 1812, Kenekuk, a Kickapoo, assumes leadership of a segment of the Kickapoo Nation, then living along the Osage River in Illinois.

Based on Kenekuk's teachings, these Kickapoo form a community of 350 that turns to agriculture and adopts selected Protestant, Catholic, and traditional religious and moral teachings. While strongly resisting removal from their homeland, they are finally forced to migrate to Missouri in 1833 and to present-day Kansas by 1837. There, the prophet converts a group of Potawatomi, who join the prophet's community in 1851. This community survives to the present. Kenekuk dies in Kansas in 1853, but not before promising his faithful that he will rise again after three days.

1837–70 Smallpox Epidemic on the Plains. The once numerous Mandan and Hidatsa, living in present-day central North Dakota, are decimated. Both tribes lose as much as 90 percent of their population, leaving only a few hundred survivors. Other Plains nations are also hit hard, some left with only about 20 percent of their previous numbers. Between 1837 and 1870, at least four smallpox epidemics kill thousands of people among the Plains Indian nations.

1840–60 Indian Territory and the Indian State. During the 1840s and 1850s, U.S. officials adhere to a plan to ultimately move all Indians to Indian Territory, present-day Kansas and Oklahoma. U.S. officials believe that more land can be opened to settlers, and the Indians can be incorporated into the United States by means of their own state, with elected officials representing Indian interests in Congress. In the post–Civil War period, however, this plan is abandoned because many Indian nations do not want to move to Indian Territory, and most do not want to be incorporated under one Indian political government or be included in the U.S. Congress and government.

1846–48 Mexican-American War. Between 1846 and 1848 the United States fights Mexico in a war that ends with the Treaty of Guadelupe Hidalgo. Mexico cedes to the United States any and all claims to California and the Southwest. The U.S. government thus brings American Indian policy to that region of the country and to the Pacific Northwest. As in other parts of the nation, the government considers that Indians have a "natural right" to the land; however, the Indians can also relinquish their lands through treaties. Throughout the West, the United States commissions agents to extinguish Indian title to millions of acres. Nations such as the Navajo, Sioux, Kiowa, and Modoc fight back against the U.S. Army. Others such as the Crow, Caddo, Blackfeet, Hopi, and Nespelem do not. Regardless of the policies followed by the various nations, the ultimate results are the same: the United States asserts its authority through the army and the Indian administration. Lands are taken from the Indians through

treaties or by right of conquest. Western Indians secure for themselves only a minute portion of their former lands and live on lands ruled by Indian agents. Many Indians are relocated to lands controlled by their neighbors. Others are concentrated on reservations with other Indian nations, including former enemies.

1846 Navajo Resistance. At the end of the Mexican-American War, U.S. settlers move into California and New Mexico where the *Diné* (Navajo for "the people") face the U.S. Army. The Navajo are one of the first Indian nations in the American Southwest to deal with the United States. Between 1600 and 1846 the Navajo confront the Nakai, or Spanish, who moved into the Rio Grande Valley of New Mexico onto lands belonging to Pueblo Indians. The Europeans introduce cattle, sheep, and horses to the Natives, and the Navajo take advantage of the innovations by sweeping down on New Mexican villages to steal stock. Comanche, Kiowa, Apache, Ute, and others follow suit, giving rise to an economy based in part on raiding. By 1846, when the United States enters New Mexico, Navajo people already have extensive holdings of cattle, sheep, and horses.

When Colonel Stephen Watts Kearny enters New Mexico in 1846, he promises to end Navajo raids on New Mexican villages and, to this end, he dispatches Colonel Alexander W. Doniphan to Navajo country. Doniphan meets with a group of Navajo Naat'aani (headmen) at Bear Springs near present-day Gallup, New Mexico. He concludes the first treaty with the Navajo, which is ratified by the Senate and signed by the president.

During the 1850s, a number of Navajo leaders sign treaties with the United States intended to end hostilities and establish trade relations between Indian and non-Indian communities of New Mexico. The agreements fail because the Navajo continue to raid New Mexican villages and because New Mexicans enslave Navajo. The conflict centers on livestock and slaves, not land, since most non-Indians consider Navajo land beautiful but unproductive. In 1860, Colonel Edward R. S. Canby, who had fought the Seminole in Florida, leads a campaign against the Navajo. By sending out small raiding parties and striking purposefully at civilian populations, Canby brings the Navajo to the bargaining table. In the spring of 1861 several Navajo leaders, including Manuelito, Barboncito, Armijo, Herrero, and Ganada Mucho, agree to a peace treaty. Canby's campaign probably would have ended the Navajo wars had it not been for the U.S. Civil War.

1848 The California Gold Rush. In 1848, Maidu and other California Indians working for James Marshall, a miller, discover gold on the American River, near Sacramento, California. At first, Native Americans in California work in the gold mines, contributing significantly to their discovery and success. Between 1848 and 1850 California officials estimate that more than one-half of the miners in California were Natives. During the 1850s some California miners abuse and kill many Indian men, women, and children.

1849 The Office of Indian Affairs. The Office of Indian Affairs is transferred from the War Department to the newly created Department of the Interior. The new department is created to manage public land, Indian land, and Indian affairs.

1850–60 Nonratification of California Indian Treaties. In California, numerous treaties are signed by federal officials with the California Indian nations, but non-Indian Californians prevent their ratification in Congress. Many leading Californians believe that Indian lands contained gold. Consequently, most California Indians are not recognized by treaty, and many California Indian communities continue to seek official federal recognition.

1850–80 Genocide of California Indians. Fearing widespread Indian uprisings, non-Indian Californians kill and terrorize California Indians. California militia and self-appointed vigilantes indiscriminately hunt down and kill thousands of peaceful California Indian men, women, and children. Indian women are often kidnapped to be used as prostitutes, concubines, or, along with Indian children, sold into slavery. The Indian population in California declines from about 100,000 in 1850 to 16,000 in 1880.

1850–1907 Religious Renewal in the Northwest.
Many Indian peoples turn to their old spiritual beliefs. Indians of the Northwest Plateau (present-day western Washington) join new religious movements like the Indian Shaker Church, or *Waptashi*, the Feather Religion. Some Indians follow the teachings of Smohalla, the Wanapum prophet, who is said to have died on two occasions and traveled to the Sky World to converse with the Creator. Smohalla was given the sacred dance and ceremony known as the Washat and told to return to his people and remember the ceremonies of thanks for first foods and other gifts of creation. Smohalla leads a fierce resistance to selling land, and provides a new religion that mixes both Christian and traditional northwestern Indian ideas. The new religion helps individual Indians and Indian communities better cope with the rapidly changing political, economic, and social conditions in their lives. His church becomes known

as the Shaker Church and continues to gather congregations among several northwestern Indian nations such as the Nez Percé.

1851–80 The "Final Solution" to the Indian Problem. During these years federal bureaucrats gradually develop plans for "the final solution of the Indian problem." In essence, the plans call for the complete control of tribal affairs by colonial administrators through the Office of Indian Affairs, the complete destruction of the tribal structure, and rapid reduction of the size of the Indian land base. Commissioner Luke Lea sets forth the doctrine in 1851 when he calls for the Indians' "concentration, their domestication and their incorporation." In 1857, Commissioner Denver advocates small reservations that will force the Indians to become farmers and in which the land will be allotted individually. By the 1880s this policy is in full operation.

1853–56 Treaties with Indians. During this period many Indian nations are induced to sell most of their remaining land and accept small parcels of land, commonly called reservations. The Chippewa in the 1850s cede most of their lands in Wisconsin and Minnesota and are relegated to small and scattered reservations. The Indian nations of present-day Washington State cede most of their lands and reluctantly settle on small reservations. Between 1853 and 1856 more than fifty-two treaties are made with Indian groups, and the United States acquires 174 million acres of Indian land. In many cases, the Indian communities are economically destitute and Indians are forced to trade land for goods; in some cases, for example in Washington and Wisconsin, Indians retain the right to hunt and fish on their former lands. These hunting and fishing rights are disputed and ignored by U.S. citizens.

1854 Indian Removal Policy. Indian Commissioner George Manypenny calls for the abandonment of the Indian removal policy, saying: "By alternate persuasion and force, some of these tribes have been removed, step by step, from mountains to valley, and from river to plain until they have been pushed half-way across the continent. They can go no further. On the ground they now occupy, the crisis must be met, and their future determined." By 1854 virtually all Indian tribes, with the exception of small isolated groups, have been removed from their ancestral homelands east of the Mississippi and relocated west of the Mississippi to Indian Territory.

1855–58 The Seminole Form New Government.
The Seminole in Florida again engage U.S. forces. The army cannot defeat the Seminole and allies, who retreat to the southern Florida swamps. Eventually, the

United States reconciles itself to leaving the Seminole in Florida. In previous years, in the 1830s, some Seminole were captured and moved to Indian Territory (present-day Oklahoma), where they were joined with the Creek Nation. Both nations speak Muskogean languages and have a history of kindred relations. By 1855, the Oklahoma Seminole withdraw from the Creek Nation and create their own government, one that very much resembles traditional Creek government, with about a dozen politically independent villages that meet together to form a national council. The government stays in effect until 1907, when the U.S. government dissolves the major Indian governments in Indian Territory.

1855–1907 The Chickasaw Constitutional Government. In 1856, the Chickasaw Nation adopts a constitution, modeled after the U.S. Constitution, with a "governor" as chief executive, a legislature, and a judiciary. In 1834, the Chickasaw sign a removal treaty, but cannot find a new location in the west. In 1838, the Chickasaw agree to join the Choctaw government, then already in Indian Territory (present-day Oklahoma). Between 1840 and 1855, however, most Chickasaw do not wish to live under Choctaw law, feeling they were discriminated against. The Chickasaw appeal to the United States for a return to a independent nationality, and in an 1855 treaty the Chickasaw are granted independence. In 1856, the Chickasaw form a constitutional government, which replaces an older form of government based on clan chiefs and priests. The constitutional government manages Chickasaw affairs until 1907, when the United States abolishes it.

1860–1907 The Choctaw Constitutional Government. In 1860, after twenty-five years of constitutional change and amendment, the Choctaw residing in Indian Territory (present-day eastern Oklahoma) adopt a centralized constitutional government, with a principal chief, three district chiefs (as was the Choctaw political tradition), a national legislature, and a court system. The government remains in power until 1907, when the U.S. government abolishes the Choctaw government and makes Indian Territory into the state of Oklahoma.

1861–68 The Long Walk. Colonel Christopher (Kit) Carson is appointed field commander over an army of volunteers in New Mexico. In weeks, this force captures a group of Mescalero Apache and relocates them to the Bosque Redondo of eastern New Mexico onto a bleak, windswept reservation on the Llano Estacado, or Staked Plains, near the Pecos River. It was the government's plan to gather the Mescalero and Navajo tribes together at Bosque Redondo to civilize and Christianize them. Under orders, Carson pursues Navajo men, women, and children throughout the summer, fall, and winter of 1863 and 1864, causing the deaths of many from hardship, hunger, and exposure. The U.S. government forcefully removes about 8,500 Navajo 350 miles to the Bosque Redondo, a place Navajo call Hweeldi (prison). This forced march is remember bitterly by the Navajo as the Long Walk. There they remain until 1868, when General William Tecumseh Sherman concludes a treaty with the Navajo permitting them to return to a reservation located on a portion of Dinetah.

1862–64 The Minnesota Sioux Uprising. Because of Indian agents' corruption and incompetence in their administration of relations with the Minnesota Sioux, the Sioux almost starve from lack of supplies. Under the leadership of Little Crow, they attack Minnesota settlements. The uprising quickly spreads to other Santee Sioux bands living in the eastern Dakotas. Thirty-eight Sioux are sentenced and hanged for their part in the uprising.

1862–65 Kickapoo Migration to Mexico. Two bands of Kickapoo, about 1,300 people, migrate to Mexico, believing their lands are unfairly treated by the U.S. government and people. Both bands fight battles with Texas troops, who strongly oppose Indians settling or traveling through Texas. Both groups settle in the province of Coahiula, in northern Mexico. Earlier in 1839, a band of Kickapoo had already migrated to Morelos, Mexico, and they were joined by Machemanet, a Kickapoo headman, and six hundred Kickapoo who left Kansas for Mexico, hoping for better treatment at the hands of the Mexican government. By 1865, all Kickapoo, except the band formerly led by the Prophet Kenekuk, leave Kansas because of corrupt handling by U.S. Indian agents and crooked dealings by U.S. citizens. In 1867, about one hundred Kickapoo return from the south and resettle near present-day Leavenworth, Kansas.

1863 The Nez Percé and the Thief Treaty. The Nez Percé Indians of Oregon and Idaho attempt to live in peace with the settlers and remain neutral during the Plateau Indian War of 1855–58. In 1855, the Nez Percé sign a treaty with the United States, securing nearly all their land, but in 1860 non-Indian "traders" discover gold while prospecting on the Nez Percé Reservation in

Idaho. Non-Indians flood onto Indian land. Nez Percé leaders complain to the Indian Service and the government responds in 1863 by writing a new treaty reducing the reservation to one-tenth its original size. When government officials disclose the plan to Nez Percé leaders, almost all the chiefs leave the council, refusing to accept the new treaty. Only Chief Lawyer, upon whose lands the council is held, agrees to its terms. Lawyer and fifty-one Nez Percé sign the document, and it is ratified by the Senate and signed by the president. According to tribal law, Lawyer could speak only for his band and not the tribe as a whole. Chief Joseph and the other Nez Percé leaders refuse to adhere to the Thief Treaty. Chief Joseph objects: "If we ever owned the land we own it still for we never sold it."

1864 The Chivington Massacre.   Colonel John M. Chivington and Governor John Evans of Colorado allow Chief Black Kettle and his peaceful Cheyenne followers to camp near Fort Lyon for the purpose of negotiating at treaty. By night, Chivington deploys his Third Colorado Cavalry around Sand Creek, including 700 men and four howitzers. On November 29, Chivington leads an unprovoked attack on the Indian camp killing up to 164 men, women, and children. The Sand Creek Massacre, as it becomes known, is one of the bloodiest and cruelest events of the Civil War. Although punishment of the parties responsible for the massacre is demanded by the public and by a U.S. congressional committee, no action is taken.

1866 Post–Civil War Indian Reservations.   In 1853, California Superintendent of Indian Affairs Edward Fitzgerald Beale places a number of Indians in the Tejon Valley to become ranchers and farmers. Although this and other reservations meet with only limited success, the system becomes national policy after the Civil War. The Peace Commission meets with many tribes, concluding treaties, and establishing reservations. Some of the tribes, or portions of them, agree to remain on reservations; others do not. In 1867, the commissioners conclude an agreement with some Kiowa and Comanche, creating a reservation in the southwest corner of present-day Oklahoma. At the same time, a portion of Cheyenne and Arapaho country is recognized as a reservation.

1866–74 The Montana Gold Rush.   By the summer of 1866, non-Indians are flooding into Montana to find gold. Many miners take the Bozeman Trail from Fort Laramie, Wyoming, to the new diggings around Virginia City, Montana. The trail, however, runs though the lands of the Oglala and Brule Sioux, who fight to keep the miners out of the region. The army establishes a series of forts along the trail for the miners' protection, but under attack by Sioux and Cheyenne, agrees to abandon them at the Treaty of Fort Laramie in 1868. Under this agreement, some Sioux and Cheyenne leaders agree to move to the reservations in Montana, Wyoming, and the Dakotas. Indians secure for themselves much of the hunting grounds along the Big Horn and Powder rivers (present-day Montana). The treaty does not end U.S. incursion into Indian land, and miners, buffalo hunters, and railroad men continue to trespass on Sioux and Cheyenne country.

In 1874, Colonel George Armstrong Custer leads an expedition to the Paha Sapa, the Sioux word for black hills, of South Dakota where geologists and journalists confirm the presence of gold. A new rush commences, and the Northern Pacific Railroad moves closer to Sioux land.

1867 The United States Purchases Alaska.   The U.S. government purchases Alaska from the Russian government. The purchase does not change the situation of the Aleuts, Eskimos, and Indians living in Alaska. The Russians do not claim Indian lands and the Indians are left undisturbed in possession of their territories.

1867–1907 The Creek Constitutional Government.   In 1867, the Creek Nation, now living in Indian Territory, adopts a constitutional government. The first elections in 1867 are controversial, and a small majority of conservatives demand a return to the traditional Creek government based on central villages and a council composed of village leaders. The United States supports the constitutional government and on various occasions uses marshals and troops to defend it against conservative Creek. Compared to the constitutional governments of the Cherokee, Choctaw, and Chickasaw, the Creek constitutional government is fraught with rebellion and political instability. In 1907, the Creek government is abolished over the protests of the conservative Creek who do not wish to join U.S. society or renounce their treaty and land rights.

1869–71 The First Indian Commissioner of Indian Affairs Is Appointed.   Brigadier General Ely Parker, a Seneca Indian and personal friend of President Ulysses S. Grant, is appointed commissioner of Indian affairs. Parker helps initiate a policy of providing Indians with

Hide-covered tipi, Pipestone National Park. (Photo by Sarah Loe)

food and clothing in exchange for reconciling themselves to life on small, economically marginal reservations of land.

1870–90 The Peyote Road. For centuries Indians in northern Mexico have used the peyote plant in religious ceremonies. Peyote induces a mild hallucinatory state, which brings the user closer to the spirit world. In the late nineteenth century the Peyote religion spreads among the Kiowa, Comanche, Cheyenne, and Arapaho. Tribal members develop their own ceremonies, songs, symbolism, visions, and prayers, incorporating them into the Peyote religion. Peyote is ingested as a sacrament and followers vow to follow the Peyote Road. They promise to be trustworthy, honorable, and community-oriented. Family, children, and cultural survival become a major emphasis of this movement. Elements of Christianity become a part of the worship service, and in 1918 the membership organize themselves into the Native American church.

The Office of Indian Affairs attempts to extinguish the religion but does not succeed. In the twentieth century Indians introduce the church to Native peoples throughout the United States. The Native American Church has survived but continues to face legal attacks during the last decade of the twentieth century.

1870 The First Ghost Dance Movement. Perhaps the best known of the Native American religious revitalization movements is the Ghost Dance. Wodziwob, a Paiute living on the California/Nevada border, is credited with beginning this religion in 1870. Wodziwob was informed by the Creator that non-Ghost Dancers would be swallowed up by a great earthquake. Indians would be spared or resurrected in three days so that they might live much as they had before European contact.

3 March 1871 The End of Treaty Making. Congress passes an act that it will no longer negotiate treaties with Indian nations. All treaties signed between 1778 and 1871 are not invalidated, but are to be upheld by the federal government. After this act, agreements with Indian groups are made by congressional acts and executive orders, which are agreements made by the president or designated official, usually by the secretary of the interior.

1871–90 Extermination of the Buffalo. As early as 1871 U.S. hunters and traders begin a systematic killing of buffalo on the Plains. Hundreds of thousands are killed for their tongue meat and hides. By the late 1880s there are only about one thousand buffalo left; not enough for the subsistence requirements of the Plains Indians. With their economic base destroyed, the Plains Indians are destitute and eventually forced onto small reservations, where they are dependent on the United States for food and supplies, and, consequently, fall under U.S. political and administrative control.

1875–83 The Northern Cheyenne Flee Indian Territory. In 1875, the Northern Cheyenne, then living in present-day Montana and the western Dakotas, reluctantly agrees to migrate to Indian Territory. One band of Northern Cheyenne fight with the Sioux at Little Big Horn against Custer in 1876, but most Northern Cheyenne are induced to migrate to Indian Territory. In 1877, Chief Dull Knife, of the Northern Cheyenne, refuses to remain in Indian Territory and leads an escape of his people to return to their homeland in the northern plains. This dramatic escape captures the imagination of the American people through the press and convinces U.S. officials that it would be extremely difficult to detain unwilling Indian nations in Indian Territory. In 1883, the Northern Cheyenne are granted a reservation in eastern Montana. U.S. Indian policymakers abandon the attempt to relocate Indians nations in Indian Territory and allow them to take reservations within their home territories.

1876–81 Custer and the End of Sioux Resistance.
After gold miners start working in the Black Hills, which is sacred land to the Sioux, several bands of Sioux leave their reservations to protect the Black Hills from sacrilege. Led by Crazy Horse of the Oglala Sioux and Sitting Bull of the Hunkpapa band of Teton Sioux, the Indians gather to face the army, which is protecting the miners. Three columns converge on the Sioux and their Cheyenne and Arapaho allies. One of the columns, led by General Alfred Terry, includes the Seventh Cavalry commanded by Colonel George Armstrong Custer. Terry sent Custer to the southern end of Little Big Horn Valley (present-day eastern Montana) where the colonel and his Crow and Arikara scouts locate a large Indian encampment. On 25 June 1876, Custer divides his force for tactical purposes, and with a command of 225 men advances on the Indian camp. Sioux and Cheyenne meet his advance and kill every man, including Custer, and are only prevented from doing likewise to the other forces because the forces are rescued by General Terry's command. The army pursues the Sioux and in 1877 shoot down Crazy Horse in what the soldiers described as an escape attempt. Sitting Bull and remnants of the Sioux flee to Canada and do not return to the Dakotas until 1881.

1877 The Nez Percé War.   Between 1863 and 1876 the non-treaty Nez Percé continue to reject the Thief Treaty of 1763. After the defeat of Custer at Little Big Horn, the army orders that all nonreservation Nez Percé be placed on reservations. On the way to their assigned reservations, a skirmish breaks out and the Nez Percé and their Palouse allies fight several running battles with the army as they change directions and travel toward Montana. The Nez Percé move into Wyoming, hoping to settle with the Crow and live like buffalo-hunting Plains people. But they are rejected by the Crow and so move farther north heading for Canada. When they are but forty miles from the Canadian border, they are caught and attacked again by the army. After days of fighting, Chief Joseph concludes a conditional surrender whereby the Nez Percé will not be

punished for their resistance but will be allowed to settle on the reservation in Idaho. General Howard and Colonel Nelson A. Miles agree to these conditions, but they are reversed by General William Tecumseh Sherman. Sherman exiles the Nez Percé and Palouse to Fort Leavenworth, Kansas, as prisoners of war, before moving them to the Quapaw Agency in northeastern Indian Territory (present-day Oklahoma) and then to the Ponca Agency.

1877–79 The Nez Percé Exiled and Returned.
Throughout the exile, Joseph presses the government to live up to the terms of the conditional surrender. In 1879, he takes his case to Washington, D.C. More importantly, he gives an interview to the editor of the *North American Review*. The resulting essay clearly reflects his feelings about the injustice of the Nez Percé exile to *Eekish Pah*, the Hot Place, and stirs many people to demand the Nez Percé's return to the northwest. In 1885, the U.S. government agrees to permit the Nez Percé to return. Some Nez Percé relocate to the reservation in Idaho, but Joseph is forced to move to the Colville Reservation in north-central Washington. For years he tries to buy a portion of his homeland, the Wakllowa, the Place of Winding Waters, but settlers living there refuse to sell him any land and he dies on the Colville Reservation in 1904.

1879–90 Civilization and Christianization.   In 1879, the Carlisle Indian School in Pennsylvania is founded in an effort to show that Indians can be educated in the ways of American culture. Other schools are founded in California, Oregon, Oklahoma, New Mexico, and Arizona, as well as on the individual reservations. U.S. reformers take Indian children from their homes and communities in the belief that it would be in the interest of the children to destroy their Native culture. Government teachers force Indian children to learn English and punish them with whippings and food deprivation when they break the rules and use the Native language. Curricula are established for vocational education, since Indians are not considered intelligent enough to learn the professions, but children are taught some academic skills. When the children reach first grade, government agents routinely take them from their families and send them to Indian boarding schools.

1881–84 *A Century of Dishonor* Published.   Helen Hunt Jackson, in *A Century of Dishonor* (1881), writes an indictment of U.S. Indian policy and the treatment of American Indians in U.S. society. Because of her work

Congress forms a special commission to investigate and suggest reforms of Indian affairs. Jackson's research on the special commission provides her with material to write a biographical novel, *Ramona*, about the life of a California Indian woman. The romanticized biography stimulates considerable interest in the United States about the plight and life of Indians.

1887 The General Allotment Act. Congress passes the General Allotment Act, also known as the Dawes Act, dividing reservation land into individual parcels. The Act is intended to safeguard the Indians on the land and, to this end, allotments are to be protected for twenty-five years. The Burke Act (1906) amends the Allotment Act of 1887, extending the original twenty-five year trust period for another twenty-five years. Surplus land is purchased by the U.S. government and then opened to settlement, thus making thousands of acres available. Between 1887 and 1934, when the Allotment Act is repealed, the U.S. government divests Native Americans of about 90 million acres.

1889–90 The Second Ghost Dance Religion and Wounded Knee. Wovoka becomes the second Ghost Dance prophet. He is the son of Tavibo, a Paiute shaman in western Nevada. In 1889, Wovoka reportedly speaks with the Creator, who advises Native Americans to live peacefully with all peoples. The Creator instructs Indians to work hard in this life and pray for an apocalypse that will restore the world to its aboriginal state. If the Indians follow the Ghost Dance path, their dead relatives will rise up, and the game and plants will return.

The Ghost Dance religion spreads to many tribes throughout the West. Some Sioux, devastated by war, reservations, poverty, and disease, turn Wovoka's teachings into a movement advocating violence. Soldiers, settlers, government agents, and missionaries fear for their lives as rumors spread that the Ghost Dance will inspire the Sioux to fight again for their rights and freedom. In 1890, the Office of Indian Affairs outlaws the Ghost Dance, and the U.S. government agents and military strengthens its command on the northern Plains. A group of Sioux Ghost Dancers, led by Big Foot, retreats to a site known as Wounded Knee. They are pursued by the Seventh Cavalry, Custer's old unit. After some misunderstandings about the Ghost Dancers' intentions, the army fires on the Sioux and kills more than three hundred Indian men, women, and children. This incident is known as the Wounded Knee Massacre.

1890–1900 "Vanishing Americans."

At the turn of the twentieth century, most non-Indians believe that the Native peoples are "Vanishing Americans" and will not long survive. The American Indian population declines to a low point of 237,196 in the 1900 U.S. Census. After 1900, however, the Indian population slowly recovers. In 1920, the Census Bureau records 244,437 Native Americans. This number increases to 357,499 in 1950, 1,366,676 in 1980, and 1,959,234 in 1990.

1890–1934 The Assimilationist Policy. After 1890 most Indian nations are located on reservations or are not recognized by the federal government. Reservation Indians come under direct administrative control from U.S. Indian agents. Since most reservation economies cannot support their Indian populations, Indian reservation residents become economically and politically dependent on the Office of Indian Affairs and its field agents. Food, clothing, medicine, education, and ceremonial life come under strict regulations. Traditional tribal governments are inhibited from operating, and ceremonies, like the Plains Sun Dances, are prohibited. Children are sent to boarding schools, where they cannot speak their Native language. Federal policymakers hope to reeducate Indian children and incorporate them into U.S. society, and then abolish the reservations. This policy of assimilation is not successful. Traditional government, traditional ceremonial life, and Indian language and lifestyle persist, despite the efforts to force Indians into U.S. economic and social life.

1900s Struggle and Change in the Twentieth Century. The early years of the twentieth century are difficult times for Native Americans who continue to feel the disastrous effects of the General Allotment Act of 1887. Federal, state, and county officials often work together with the private sector to divest the American Indian of his estate. Railroad, cattle, mining, timber, and oil companies take every opportunity to liquidate Indian title to lands and resources.

Indians living on tribal lands are required to be versatile. Hunting, fishing, gathering, and farming continue and at times government rations are received, but these are not sufficient for survival. For this reason, many Native Americans become wage earners. Indians work as migrant workers, moving from one labor camp to the next during harvests. Indians also work on ranches, performing a variety of menial jobs, while others find employment on the reservations themselves. Sometimes the Office of Indian Affairs hires reservation Indians as police officers and judges. And some

Indians receive an income from leasing their allotments to non-Indian farmers and ranchers.

1902 *Lone Wolf v. Hitchcock*.   In 1902, Lone Wolf, a Kiowa leader, files a lawsuit to prevent the Interior Department from allotting and selling surplus lands guaranteed by the Treaty of Medicine Lodge in 1869. The Supreme Court rules against him in *Lone Wolf v. Hitchcock*, giving Congress the authority to abrogate treaties and dispose of Indian lands. This decision creates the doctrine that Congress has plenary powers in Indian affairs, meaning that there is no higher authority in deciding issues in Indian affairs. *Lone Wolf* affirms the policy that it is within Congress's power to abrogate, or ignore or change, Indian treaties. This decision is a major blow to Indian treaty rights.

16 November 1907 Indian Territory Is Formed into Oklahoma.   The state of Oklahoma is admitted to the Union. Most Indian governments in the former Indian Territory have been abolished, including the constitutional governments of the Cherokee, Choctaw, Chickasaw, Seminole, and Creek nations. Most Indian land is allotted to individuals, sometimes forcibly to conservative Indians who do not recognize U.S. rights to abolish their government or to take their land. In the late 1890s and early 1900s, the Creek Snake Indians under Chitto Harjo and Red Bird Smith among the Nighthawk Keetoowah society, as well as less well known movements among the Seminole, Choctaw, and Chickasaw, resist allotment and dissolution of their national governments and land. Oklahoma citizens urge that the remaining Indian lands be put on the market and that Indian landholdings be taxed. Over the next thirty years, many Indians lose their land allotments owing to debt, legal fraud, and inability to pay taxes. The tribal governments of the former Indian Territory nations are kept up informally, and some are revived starting in the late 1930s. The Choctaw, Cherokee, Chickasaw, Creek, and Seminole regain the right to elect their own governments in the early 1970s, but the governments are now under the jurisdiction of the Bureau of Indian Affairs.

1908 Winter's Doctrine.   The Supreme Court decides that Indians on reservation lands retain the right to sufficient access to water to provide for agriculture. This doctrine is designed to preserve water and is a decision in favor of conservationists, who think Indians would not use as much water as free market users. The doctrine, however, guarantees Indian reservations rights to water for economic and agricultural use. This doctrine becomes very important after the 1960s, when Colorado, Arizona, New Mexico, and California divide scarce water resources. Indian reservations in the area are guaranteed access to water for reservation development, because the western states cannot entirely ignore the Winter's Doctrine.

1911 Ishi, the Last Yahi Indian.   After years of hiding from California settlers, a Yahi Indian known as Ishi allows himself to be captured. He creates a sensation in the newspapers, which refer to him as the "last wild Indian in North America." Ishi survives for five years, living at a museum in San Francisco and providing much ethnographic and linguistic material to the famous anthropologist Alfred Kroeber.

1911 Society of the American Indian Organized.   In April 1911 seven prominent American Indian leaders meet in Columbus, Ohio, and establish a pan-Indian organization known as the Society of American Indians (SAI). A national conference takes place in October 1911. Headquartered in Washington, D.C., SAI lobbies for better educational programs and improved reservation conditions. For about a decade SAI gives Indian people a new dimension of representation, providing a much-needed voice and calling for reforms in federal Indian policy.

1912 Founding of the Alaska Native Brotherhood.   Modeled after religious organizations of the Russian Orthodox and Protestant churches, the Alaska Native Brotherhood is formed in 1912 in Juneau, Alaska, by eleven Tlingits and one Tsimpshian, all strong Presbyterians, who attended the Presbyterian-administered boarding school at Sitka, Alaska, an old Tlingit village. In 1915, an auxiliary organization, the Alaska Native Sisterhood, follows the same path at the Brotherhood. The Brotherhood promotes civil rights issues such as the right to vote, access to public education for Native children, and civil rights in public places such as the right to attend movie theaters. It defends Native workers in the Alaskan canneries, defends the rights of Native fishermen, and fights a major land case for the taking of the Tongass Forest from the Tlingit and Haida tribes of panhandle Alaska. The Brotherhood wins the Tongass Forest case in the 1950s and receives payment of $7.5 million after a long legal struggle starting in 1929. The Brotherhood continues to the present day as an active political force in Alaska Native issues.

1912 Jim Thorpe Wins Olympic Decathlon.   Jim Thorpe, from the Sauk and Fox Nation, wins the decathlon in the 1912 Olympic games held in Norway.

Henry Bond (Choctaw) was the first state tax assessor of Oklahoma, 1907. (Courtesy of James Perkins)

Thorpe's medal is taken away from him, however, because he played semiprofessional baseball; it is formally reinstated in 1978. Thorpe goes on to star in professional football during its early days.

1918 Establishment of the Native American Church. U.S. courts and law officers persecute Indian peyote users. Indians argue that the peyote is used to enhance religious experience, but they are denied the right to worship with peyote because the worshipers do not have a church organization. Consequently, the Native American Church is incorporated into the state of Oklahoma by members of several Oklahoma nations (Kiowa, Comanche, Apache, Cheyenne, Ponca, and Oto). Since the late 1800s the peyote religion has spread quickly across the Plains tribes and reservation communities, where the old forms of religion and culture no longer sustain the Indians under the new conditions of economic poverty and political and cultural suppression.

1923 The Committee of One Hundred. Reformers begin pressing the government to improve Indian living conditions, and in 1923 Secretary of Interior Hubert Work appoints the Committee of One Hundred to survey American Indian policies and to make recommendations. The committee recommends increasing funds for health care, public education, scholarships, claims courts, and a scientific investigation into the effects of peyote usage.

2 June 1924 Indians Are Granted U.S. Citizenship. Because of the services Indian soldiers performed during the World War I and lobbying by the Alaska Native Brotherhood, Congress grants all Indians the rights of U.S. citizenship. The act, however, does not take away rights that Indians have by treaty or by the Constitution. It allows Indians to vote in federal elections, but some states, such as New Mexico, prohibit Indians from voting in state elections.

1928 The Meriam Report. Secretary of Interior Hubert Work also asks the Board of Indian Commissioners to make a study of Indian living conditions, but they provide little help. With a grant from John D. Rockefeller Jr., the Brooking Institute hires Lewis Meriam and nine scholars to investigate the status of Indian economies, health, education, and the federal administration of Indian affairs.

In 1928, Meriam and his committee publish a significant volume, *The Problem of Indian Administration*, commonly known as the Meriam Report. The study describes the conditions of Indian people as "deplorable," particularly because of high infant mortality and deaths at all ages from tuberculosis, pneumonia, and measles. Navajo, Apache, Pima, and other Arizona nations have death rates from tuberculosis seventeen times the national average. The report details the educational failures and poor living conditions found at the boarding schools, and Meriam's committee recommends increased funding for Indian health and education. It also details the incidence of malnutrition, poverty, and marginal land tenure among American Indians. The Meriam Report urges Congress to appropriate money to fulfill its treaty obligations to the tribes in terms of health, education, and subsistence. It urges the president, secretary of the interior, and commissioner of Indian affairs to reform the Office of Indian Affairs.

1934 The Indian Reorganization Act. The Great Depression slows the prospects for Indian reform during President Herbert Hoover's administration. Franklin Roosevelt's administration, however, implements a program of reform. Secretary of Interior Harold Ickes and Commissioner of Indian Affairs John Collier work closely to create an Indian New Deal. The Indian Reorganization Act, or the Wheeler-Howard Act, is passed to fulfill the recommendations of the Meriam Report and to promote the well-being of Native Americans by recognizing the value of their diverse cultures, religions, languages, and economies. Indian tribal governments are allowed to establish their own constitutions, laws, and memberships and are encouraged to form economic business corporations.

1934 The Johnson-O'Malley Act. Congress adopts the Johnson-O'Malley Act, which allows the federal government to contract with states and territories to provide services for the Indians, including health, social welfare, and education. As another part of the Indian New Deal, the commissioner of Indian affairs orders the Indian Service to hire more Indians and to cease interference with Native American spiritual beliefs, ceremonies, and traditions. Indians join the Works Project Administration, the Public Works Administration, and the Civilian Conservation Corps (CCC). While

participating in such programs as the CCC, Indian families are introduced to modern farming, ranching, and forestry techniques and are taught English and basic mathematics. Opinions vary about the effect of the Indian New Deal, but the 1930s would prove to be a watershed in American Indian history and a step toward Native American self-determination.

1941–45 World War II. On 7 December 1941 the United States enters World War II. More than 25,000 Indian men and women join the services, and those who remain home participate in the war effort through work, buying of war bonds, blood drives, and collecting rubber, paper, and metal. A group of Navajo serve as code talkers in the South Pacific, devising a code based on the Navajo language but constructed in such a way that even a Navajo speaker could not decipher it without the key. The Japanese were never able to break the code. The Navajo code talkers most likely saved the lives of thousands of U.S. soldiers. Members of several other tribes serve as code talkers during World War II, employing their Native languages.

1942 *Seminole Nation v. the United States*. In *Seminole Nation v. the United States* the court addresses the issue of payment of trust fund monies and the fiduciary responsibility of the federal government to Indian tribes. In its decision the Supreme Court refers to the federal responsibility toward managing Indian land and assets as a "moral obligation of the highest responsibility and trust." Since then it has been called the "trust responsibility."

1944 The National Congress of American Indians. The Second World War develops a new leadership of Native Americans who are not satisfied with the status quo. In 1944, tribal leaders meet in Denver, Colorado, to form the National Congress of American Indians, a group dedicated to guarding Indian rights and preserving Native culture, reservations, and tribal lands.

1946–49 Reorganization of the Bureau of Indian Affairs. A special congressional commission investigates the Bureau of Indian Affairs (BIA) and recommends reform. For years, the BIA administration has suffered from overcentralization at the Washington, D.C. office. All local agency offices send their requests directly to the capitol, and it often takes months to get responses. The new BIA organization creates twelve

Native Americans, including Choctaw Chief Allen Wright (r.) and Henry J. Bond (far right), lay flowers on the monument to Choctaw Chief Pushmataha in Arlington National Cemetery in Washington, D.C. Pushmataha died in 1824 while visiting on government business. (Courtesy of James Perkins)

area offices among the ninety agency offices on the reservations and the Washington, D.C. office. Much of the day-to-day administrative power of the commissioner of Indian affairs is delegated to the twelve area offices.

1946–78 The Indian Claims Commission. Even as Native Americans began to organize, a conservative movement is growing in the national capitol, calling for a renunciation of New Deal era politics. In 1946, Congress creates the Indian Claims Commission, enabling tribes to sue the federal government for past wrongs. This bill overcomes conservative opposition to become the last piece of Indian New Deal legislation. The claims cases take years to resolve and are a major cost. Although the commission makes several awards to Native Americans, no land is returned and very meager monetary rewards are given to Indian claimants.

1949 The Hoover Commission. In 1949, the Hoover Commission, under former president Herbert Hoover,

recommends that Native Americans be "integrated, economically and politically, as well as culturally." Hoover's report suggests that "when the trust status of Indian lands has ended, thus permitting taxation, and surplus Indian families have established themselves off the reservations, special aid to the state and local governments for Indian programs should end." The commission recommends that the federal government remove itself from regulation of and responsibility for Indian affairs. This program gathers considerable support from congressional leaders. Many reservations contain timber, oil, gas, coal, uranium, water, and other natural resources coveted by non-Indians and major corporations.

1952 Relocation. During the 1950s, the government begins the relocation program, which assists Indian families to move to urban areas. Administrators argue that with housing and employment in urban areas, Indians will find new lives away from their old lands and become integrated into mainstream America. In 1952, the Bureau of Indians Affairs establishes the Voluntary Relocation Program (also known as the Employment Assistance Program), which pays for training, travel, moving, and assistance in finding urban work. The BIA also provides a strong vocational and academic training program for Indians who relocate. By 1960, approximately 35,000 Native Americans have relocated, but one-third of these return home to the reservations.

1953 The Termination Resolution. House Concurrent Resolution 108 is passed. It calls for the end of the special legal relation between Indian governments and the federal government. This legal relation is created by the commerce clause in the Constitution and recognized by a series of court decisions starting in the 1820s and 1830s. The House Resolution sets the tone of Indian Affairs policy by indicating its desire to end the reservation system and to assimilate Indians into U.S. society by terminating Indian treaty rights and legal status as historical nationalities and independent cultural communities.

In the same year, Congress passes Public Law 280, which empowers certain states (California, Wisconsin, Nebraska, Minnesota, Oregon, and, in 1959, Alaska) to assume management over criminal justice on Indian reservations. This law opens the possibility of state jurisdiction over reservation courts. Previously, federal law and courts had upheld the separation of state and Indian government relations because this separation is explicitly written out in the commerce clause of the Constitution.

1954–62 Termination. Congress adopts the policy often termed *termination*, a plan to end tribal sovereignty, health care, and most federal obligations to Indians as specified in past treaties or acts of Congress. Responsive to the national conservative swing in the 1950s, Congress passes a series of laws implementing the termination of Indian reservations. Between 1954 and 1962 more than one hundred bands, communities, and rancherias are terminated or severed from direct relations with the federal government. As a result, the terminated Indian communities lose protections and services formerly provided by the national government. The National Congress of American Indians fights against termination and by the late 1950s the movement has lost its momentum. Termination ends during President John F. Kennedy's administration because of opposition by Indians and state governments, who think the policy will result in higher state service costs to Indians.

James King Overman (Oneida) as a cadet, 1953. During tours in the Korean and Vietnam wars, he earned three Distinguished Flying Crosses, eighteen Air Medals, and the Presidential Unit Citation for Extraordinary Heroism. He retired as a major in 1972. (Courtesy of James Overman)

1959–71 Alaska Native Land Claims. Alaska becomes a state in 1959; the federal government grants the new state the right to select 102 million acres of land. Indian title in Alaska, however, has not been settled, and Alaska Native villages protest state land selections by making claims to land with the Bureau of Land Management. By 1964, Alaska Natives claim more than 300 million acres, and Secretary of the Interior Stewart Udall prohibits the state from selecting land until Indian title is clarified. Alaska Natives mobilize around the land claims issue and other issues like education, health, and jobs. They form local and regional associations of villages. In 1965 and 1966, Alaska Natives create the Alaska Federated Natives (AFN), a statewide organization empowered to pursue land claims and other community interests. The AFN leads Alaska Natives to a Congressional settlement in 1971, called the Alaska Native Claims Settlement Act (ANCSA), which gives control of land, resources, and a portion of the cash settlement to Native people. ANCSA also preserves for the Natives 44 million acres and $962 million for giving up claims to the rest of Alaska.

1961 The Chicago Indian Conference. After mobilizing against the threat of termination in the late 1950s, representatives from ninety tribes meet in Chicago and set out a policy agenda. The new agenda emphasizes greater academic training for Indian children, increased job training, improved housing on reservations, better medical facilities, access to loans for economic development, and increased emphasis on industrial development and employment on the reservations.

1961 The National Indian Youth Council. An activist organization, the National Indian Youth Council, is formed. This organization challenges the approaches of traditional advocate groups such as Christian churches, the National Congress of American Indians, and the Indian Rights Association. The National Indian Youth Council presents a more activist and nationalist orientation to solving Indian problems.

1962 Indian Voting Rights. Indians became U.S. citizens in 1924, but many states refuse to allow Indians to vote in state and local elections (although Congress ensures Indians the right to vote in federal elections). This year, the federal government forces New Mexico to grant its large Indian population the right to vote in state and local elections.

1964 The American Indian Historical Society. Rupert Costo and Jeanette Henry Costo organize the American Indian Historical Society, dedicated to historical research and teaching about Native Americans. The society begins publishing *The Indian Historian*, a journal that presents articles on Indian history primarily from an Indian perspective.

1964–66 Indian Community Action Programs. President Lyndon B. Johnson's Great Society legislation for alleviating poverty is implemented by creation of the Office of Economic Opportunity (OEO). The OEO organizes an Indian Desk for managing antipoverty programs on Indian reservations. The Bureau of Indian Affairs (BIA) insists on administering Indian antipoverty funds, but the OEO, suspicious of paternalistic BIA management of Indian affairs, delivers antipoverty funds

directly to the tribal governments. For the first time, most Indian tribal governments gain direct access to federal funds that are not administered by BIA officials. Community Action Programs (CAP) become the primary funding source and administrative organization for managing Indian antipoverty funds. During the late 1960s and 1970s many tribal governments rapidly expand in personnel, budget, and programs administered. The method of granting funds directly to tribal government control becomes the model for the Self-Determination Policy starting in the early 1970s and for the Self-Determination and Education Assistance Act of 1975.

1964–74 Fishing Rights in Washington State. Treaties dating from the 1850s give many Washington Indian tribes the right to fish at their traditional fishing places and rights to one-half of the fish in the rivers. Over the years, state laws and court decisions increasingly excluded Indians from fishing with traps and certain kinds of fishing nets. Washington Indians become increasingly active in asserting their treaty rights

Billy Mills wins the 10,000-meter event at the 1964 Olympics. (Courtesy of Billy Mills)

to take fish at their traditional fishing camps and with traditional fishing methods. Eventually, the issue is sent before state and federal courts and is partially settled in 1974 by a federal court ruling, often called the Boldt Decision. The decision affirms Indian treaty rights to at least half the fish in many western Washington State rivers.

Troy Johnson
California State University, Long Beach, California

♦ CHRONOLOGY OF NATIVE NORTH AMERICAN HISTORY, 1965 TO 2000

1965 California Indian Land Claims. After many years of hearings, California Indians receive an award of more than $29 million for outstanding land claims. The settlement amounts to only 47¢ an acre for 64 million acres of land taken, nearly two-thirds the state's total area. Since the number of eligible descendants is about 33,000 most California Indians receive less than $900.

7 April 1965 Reexamination of Termination Policy. American Indian National Congress executive director and tribal representatives testify before U.S. Senate subcommission against the termination of the Colville tribe of Washington, D.C. The congressional termination policy began in 1953 with the passage of House Concurrent Resolution 108, whose objective was to solve "the Indian problem" by assimilating Indian people into the American mainstream. This process was to be accomplished by ending the government's relationship with tribes and bands that were considered to have reached a satisfactory level of economic and social achievement. Among the first tribes whose relationship with the federal government were terminated were the Klamath of Oregon and the Menomonee of Wisconsin. Many other smaller groups around the nation were also terminated. By 1965, it becomes increasingly clear that the effect of the termination policy on Indian communities is disastrous.

26 May 1965 Miami Tribe Receives Land Claims Award. The House of Representatives approves a $4.7 million award by the Indian Claims Commission to the Miami Indians of Indiana and Oklahoma for the loss of their lands in the nineteenth century.

15 February 1966 Fish-Ins. Comedian Dick Gregory and his wife are arrested for illegal net fishing, which they engage in with members of the Nisqually tribe in a protest fish-in. The tribe, arguing that they reserve the right to fish according to their own laws in their 1856 treaty with the federal government, protests the application of state game laws that dictate hook-and-line fishing, thereby preventing the tribe from fishing according to their traditional ways.

14–16 April 1966 Tribal Advisory Commission Established. Approximately eighty tribal leaders representing sixty-two tribes attend an "emergency conference" called by the National Congress of American Indians to protest their exclusion from a congressionally sponsored conference. The conference was called by the chairman of the House Commission on Interior and Insular Affairs, Morris Udall, to discuss the reorganization of the Bureau of Indian Affairs. Representative Udall announces the admittance of representatives to the BIA's conference and confirms that the House commission will establish a tribally comprised group to advise him on the BIA's reorganization.

30 April 1966 Bennett Appointed BIA Commissioner. The Senate confirms the appointment of Robert LaFollette Bennett (Oneida) as the BIA commissioner, succeeding Phileo Nash. Bennett is only the second Indian appointed commissioner, following in the footsteps of Ely Parker, a Seneca, appointed by Ulysses S. Grant in 1869.

30 April 1966 Havasupai Reject BIA's Modernization Proposals. The three hundred members of the Havasupai tribe, who live at the base of the Grand Canyon, reject a Bureau of Indian Affairs proposal to modernize their village, Supai. Each year, one to two thousand visitors make the rough eight-mile trek by horseback to the only village on the 518-acre reservation. The council votes against the BIA's goals to link the reservation by roads, chair lifts, and helicopters.

Spring 1966 Rough Rock Demonstration School. The Navajo contract with the BIA to establish the Rough Rock Demonstration School. Impetus for the school's creation comes from the realization that more than one-half of all reservation school students fail to complete their high school education. Studies suggest that the high dropout rate results from the teachers' lack of knowledge about Indian culture and behavior and from discriminatory treatment. The Navajo hope that by running their own school, they will be able to reverse the dropout rate and improve the education of their children.

October 1966 Alaska Federation of Natives. The Alaska Federation of Natives (AFN) meets in Anchorage, Alaska. Originally organized by Emil Notti, president of the Cook Inlet Native Association, the three-hundred-member organization discusses resolutions and strategies for the preservation of their land base. Alaska Natives, who never signed treaties with the U.S. government, are recognized by the government as possessing an aboriginal title to their lands. The exact meaning of aboriginal title, beyond a recognition that Alaska Natives lived on their lands for thousands of years, however, is unclear. The Alaskan Statehood Act of 1958 guarantees the Natives' hunting and fishing rights, and gives the state of Alaska the right to appropriate 102 million acres of land for its own use. As economic development and tourism in Alaska increase, the Natives' subsistence living, based on hunting, fishing, and trapping, becomes increasingly endangered.

November 1966 American Indian Education Conference. The forty-four-year-old Association of American Indian Affairs holds a conference on the dismal record of educating American Indian youth. Attended by thirty-five specialists, including the recently appointed chief of education in the Bureau of Indian Affairs, the group hears grim statistics concerning the lack of educational success achieved by Indian children. Coming under particular attack are the eighty-one boarding schools operated by the Bureau of Indian Affairs for some 30,000 students. In many instances, very young children are forced to attend boarding schools 600 miles from their homes and families because there are no local schools available. Both the boarding school children and the 91,000 other Indian students who attend public, church, or private schools face serious problems of adjustment and discrimination, leading to a 50 percent dropout rate among Indian students.

10 January 1967 President Johnson Addresses Indian Self-Determination. President Lyndon B. Johnson, in his State of the Union message, urges, "We should embark upon a major effort to provide self-help assistance to the forgotten in our midst—the American Indians."

16 January 1967 National Indian Education Advisory Committee Formed. The Bureau of Indian Affairs announces the formation of a National Indian Education Advisory Committee to assist in the improvement of educational services to Indian students.

5 February 1967 Iowa Repeals Discriminatory Law. The Iowa Senate approves the repeal of one of the last examples of discriminatory legislation against Indians: a law that prohibits the sale of liquor to Indians. Congress repealed federal prohibitions against the sale of liquor to Indians in 1954.

20–21 March 1967 Indian Claims Commission Tenure Prolonged. The U.S. Senate and House of Representatives approve a bill to extend the life of the Indian Claims Commission to 1972 and to expand its membership to five. The commission, first established in 1946, still has 347 unadjudicated cases on its dockets.

10 June 1967 Seminole Land Claims Upheld. The U.S. Claims Court upholds a 1964 decision by the Indian Claims Commission finding that the Seminole of Florida and Oklahoma have claims to 32 million acres of Florida lands under the terms of the Seminole Nation's 1823 treaty with the federal government.

6 August 1967 Fiscal Compensation for Sioux Lands. The Indian Claims Commission awards $12.2 million to eight Sioux tribes for the compensation of 29 million acres taken in fraudulent treaties during the 1800s. The illegally taken lands include one-half of Minnesota and parts of Iowa, North and South Dakota, and Wisconsin.

11 September 1967 NAACP Reports on American Indian Genocide. The New York Division of National Association for the Advancement of Colored People (NAACP) announces the preparation of a report detailing the United States' genocide of American Indians. The report is to be submitted to the United Nations.

1968 *Menominee Tribe of Indians v. United States*. In the court case *Menominee Tribe of Indians v. United States*, the U.S. Supreme Court upholds the power of Congress to terminate the Menominee Tribe. The Court gives the 1954 legislation that terminated the Menominee Tribe a narrow interpretation, however. Treaty rights persist unless expressly legislated away, the court observes. Hunting and fishing rights reserved by the Menominee in their 1854 treaty are not mentioned specifically by Congress in 1954 and therefore are not terminated. The Menominee continue to fight for restoration of those tribal rights that were expressly extinguished by Congress in 1954, and finally succeed in obtaining congressional restoration of their legal status in 1973.

6 March 1968 Johnson Sends Message of Self-Determination. Johnson delivers his "Special Message to Congress on the Problem of the American Indian: 'The Forgotten American.'" In announcing his request for a 10 percent increase in federal funding for Indian programs, Johnson outlines three goals in his message: (1) "A standard of living for the Indian equal to that of the country as a whole"; (2) "Freedom of choice: an opportunity to remain in their homelands, if they choose, without surrendering their dignity; and opportunity to move to towns and cities of America, if they choose, equipped with the skills to live in equality and dignity"; and (3) "Full participation in the life of modern America, with a full share of economic opportunity and social justice." The new federal objective, according to Johnson, is "a goal that ends the old debate about 'termination' of Indian programs and stresses self-determination."

The same day, President Johnson signs an executive order establishing the National Council on Indian Opportunity. Chaired by the vice-president and comprised of six Indian leaders and the heads of the departments of interior, agriculture, commerce, labor, health, education, and welfare, and housing and urban affairs and the Office of Economic Opportunity, the council is charged with coordinating efforts to improve programs for Indians.

11 April 1968 American Indian Civil Rights Act Passes. Congress passes the American Indian Civil Rights Act, which guarantees reservation residents many of the same civil rights and liberties in relation to tribal authorities that the U.S. Constitution guarantees all persons in relation to federal and state authorities. The act is introduced by Senator Sam Ervin after seven years of investigations into rights denied to individual Indians by tribal, state, and federal governments.

The act is not fully supported by all tribes, especially the Pueblos, who fear that the act will alter their traditional forms of governments and culture. The act also limits the rights of tribes to levy penalties over crimes committed on their reservations to $1,000 in fines or six months in jail.

Tribal leaders support other provisions of the legislation. Title IV of the act, for example, amends Public Law 280, an act passed by Congress in 1953 that gives states the authority to extend criminal and civil jurisdiction over reservations. The act also allows states to retrocede, or give back, criminal and civil jurisdiction to the tribes. Other parts of the law direct the secretary of the interior to publish updated versions of Charles Kappler's *Indian Affairs: Laws and Treaties*, and Felix Cohen's *Handbook of Federal Indian Law*.

8 May 1968 John Collier Dies. John Collier, U.S. commissioner of Indian affairs from 1935 until 1945, dies in Taos, New Mexico. Collier was responsible for the reaffirmation of tribal authority and the strengthening of tribal governments. He sincerely believed in the values of Indian cultures and that Indian problems were best solved by Indian people. He established the Indian Arts and Crafts Board, and oversaw the passage of the 1934 Indian Reorganization Act (IRA), which stopped the sale of Indian allotments.

18 May 1968 Peace Treaty with Navajo Commemorated. President Lyndon Johnson signs a bill commemorating the centennial of the federal government's peace treaty with the Navajo. The Navajo Nation inhabits a 16-million-acre reservation located in Arizona, New Mexico, and Utah. In terms of population and acreage, the Navajo Nation is larger than twenty-six independent countries in the world.

19 May 1968 Indian Leaders Tour Major Cities. The National Congress of American Indians sponsors a tour by forty-nine Indian leaders from fifteen western tribes. The group, which visits New York City and other cities, is designed to encourage companies to establish businesses on reservations.

27 May 1968 *Puyallup Tribe v. Department of Game*. A unanimous Supreme Court in *Puyallup Tribe v. Department of Game* upholds the right of Washington State to prohibit Indian net fishing for salmon in the interest of conservation. The case is an important departure from previous holdings, because it allows state regulation of some treaty fishing rights. One-hundred-and-fifty Indians march outside the plaza of the Supreme Court building in protest of the Supreme Court's decision in the Puyallup case.

July 1968 AIM Founded. The American Indian Movement (AIM) is founded by Dennis Banks, Clyde

Bellecourt, Eddie Benton-Bonai, George Mitchell, and Mary Wilson in Minneapolis, Minnesota. During a period of general civil unrest and protests by African-Americans and Mexican-Americans, the movement is organized to improve federal, state, and local social services to urban Indian neighborhoods and prevent the harassment of Indians by the local police. AIM members form patrols to monitor police activity and demonstrate against Indian mistreatment.

16 July 1968 Dick Gregory Released from Jail. Comedian Dick Gregory is released from jail in Olympia, Washington, after fasting for six weeks to call attention to the violation of Indian treaty rights.

21 October 1968 Supplemental Appropriations Act. Congress enacts the Supplemental Appropriations Act of 1969, which includes an appropriation for $100,000 to implement the National Council on Indian Opportunity, established by Executive Order 11399 on 6 March 1968. This act is an important piece of President Johnson's efforts to improve Indian socioeconomic conditions. The council is given the following charge: (1) to encourage the complete application of federal programs designed to aid Indians; (2) to encourage interagency cooperation in the implementation of federal programs; (3) to assess the effect of federal programs; and (4) to suggest ways in which government programs can be improved.

24 October 1968 Yavapai Land Settlement. The Yavapai of Arizona and the federal government agree to a $5 million settlement for the loss of over 9 million acres illegally taken from the tribe by the federal government in 1874.

1969 First Native American Studies Program Created. In the spring, the University of California, Berkeley campus chapter of United Native Americans joins the Third World student strike, spurring the creation of a Native American studies program. Leaders of the Indian effort include LaNada Boyer, Patty Silvas, and Jack Forbes. Plans are also being developed for Native American studies centers on other California college campuses. Forbes drafts a proposal for a College of Native American Studies to be created on one of the University of California campuses. The California State Legislature endorses the idea.

21 January 1969 Navajo Community College Opens. The Navajo Community College opens at Many Farms, Arizona. The college is the first tribally established and controlled community college.

5 March 1969 Office of Minority Business Enterprise Established. President Richard Nixon signs an executive order establishing the Office of Minority Business Enterprise. It is the office's function to ensure that a fair proportion of the total government purchases and contracts are awarded to businesses that are owned wholly or in part by minorities and women. Indian tribes, acting in their commercial capacity, are expressly included in the act's provisions. The act's objective is to assist tribes in the economic development of their reservations, where more than one-half of all families live below the poverty level and unemployment on some reservations is as high as 90 percent.

23 March 1969 Life Expectancy Gap Closes. The Indian Health Service reports that the life expectancy for Indians is sixty-four years of age, compared to an average life expectancy of 70.5 years for non-Indians. Despite the gap, the new statistics reveal a major improvement in Indian health care. Twenty years previous, the average life expectancy for an Indian male was only forty-four years.

23 March 1969 Mohawk Trial Begins. The trial of seven Mohawks begins on charges stemming from demonstrations on the International Bridge between the United States and Canada. The bridge is located on the Akwesasne Reservation that straddles Canada and the United States. Demonstrators were protesting the imposition of Canadian custom duties on their goods. The Indians argue that the 1794 Jay Treaty signed between the United States and Great Britain guaranteed tribes' free passage over the border and freedom from import and export taxes on goods traversing the border. Because of the failure of Canada and the United States to recognize the tribes' right to freely export and import goods, Indian families must pay taxes on goods that are only carried from one family member's house to another.

5 May 1969 Momaday Receives Pulitzer Prize. Kiowa author N. Scott Momaday is awarded the Pulitzer Prize for his book *House Made of Dawn*. The book details the life of a young Indian man who leaves the reservation and explores his subsequent difficulties adjusting to the outside world. Momaday is the first American Indian awarded a Pulitzer since the prize's inception in 1917.

18 May 1969 Klamath Tribe Awarded Money for Land Loss. The Klamath tribe of Oregon wins a judgment of $4.1 million from the Indian Claims Commission for the loss of lands resulting from faulty surveys conducted by the government of their reservation in 1871 and 1888.

19 June 1969 NCAI Makes Effort to Bring Business to Reservations. The National Congress of American Indians (NCAI) hosts an exhibition and briefing sessions in New York City in an effort to attract private businesses to reservations. NCAI president Wendall Chino announces that 159 new enterprises have been started on reservations in the previous five years, with a total investment of more than $100 million.

7 August 1969 Bruce Appointed Commissioner of Indian Affairs. President Richard Nixon appoints Louis R. Bruce, a Mohawk-Oglala Sioux and one of the founders of the National Congress of American Indians, the new commissioner of Indian affairs.

23 August 1969 Tribal Representatives Call for New Interior Secretary. Representatives of forty-six North American Indian nations meet at the Onondaga Reservation in New York. Representing traditional peoples, the conference passes a resolution calling for the immediate ousting of Interior Secretary Walter Hickel. They charge that Hickel has not protected Indian resources and is insensitive to the needs of Indian peoples.

September 1969 Corporations Acquire Oil from Alaska Natives. Multinational oil corporations offer hundreds of millions of dollars to acquire oil in Alaska belonging to the Inuit people. They plan the development of an oil pipeline across Inuit and Dene lands. Several Alaska Native villages prevent the construction of an oil pipeline over their land.

7 October 1969 Kennedy Calls for Conference on Indian Problems. U.S. Senator Edward Kennedy calls for a White House conference on Indian problems. Announcing that he will introduce a bill to authorize and finance such a project, Kennedy criticizes the Bureau of Indian Affair's handling of Native American affairs as "unsatisfactory even under the best of circumstances." He calls for the creation of a Select Committee on Human Needs of American Indians, saying, "The BIA is notorious for its resistance to

reform, to innovation, and to discharging its responsibilities in a competent and sensitive fashion."

November 1969 NIEA Organized. The National Indian Education Association (NIEA) is organized in Minneapolis, Minnesota, to improve the quality of Indian education. The organization is established specifically to improve communications on Indian educational issues through national conventions and workshops; to advocate for increased funding and creative programs for the education of Indian children; and to provide technical assistance to educators in the field.

3 November 1969 Final Report on Indian Education Issued. The Senate Subcommittee on Indian Education issues its final report following a two-year investigation. Chaired by Senator Edward Kennedy, who took over following the death of his brother, Robert Kennedy, the committee spends two years reviewing all areas of Indian education. The report concludes that "our national policies for educating American Indians are a failure of major proportions." Their comparative analysis of statistics leaves the committee shocked at "the low quality of virtually every aspect of schooling available to Indian children." The report spells out sixty recommendations to improve Indian education and urges that Indian people be given greater control over the schooling of their children.

20 November 1969 Alcatraz Island Occupied. Indian activists occupy Alcatraz Island in San Francisco Bay and symbolically claim the island for Indian people. The protesters incorporate as Indians of All Tribes, Inc. and offer to purchase the island from the federal government for $24 worth of beads. The occupation of Alcatraz lasts until 11 June 1971. Inspired by the Alcatraz occupation, Indian activists, led by former participants in the protest, occupy over sixty government facilities across the United States, demanding that Indian rights be recognized. During the occupation, President Nixon signs legislation returning the sacred Blue Lake to the Taos people. Nixon formally announces an end to the termination era and the beginning of a government policy of self-determination for Indians.

1970 Indian Demonstrations and Protests. Concerned with Indians' abysmally low economic status in an otherwise healthy and vigorous national economy, Indian youth groups press for change and agitate for a "new look" for the "First Americans." Indian youth set

Members of the Iroquois League protest for their rights to cross the U.S.-Canadian border in accordance with the 1794 Jay Treaty, July 1969. (Courtesy of the Buffalo and Erie County Historical Society)

out to accomplish change through the use of political power and activism. Because of the formal nature of treaty relations with the federal government, activist protests and demonstrations are not considered acceptable by older and sometimes more conservative Indians. Consequently, youth strategies, influenced by the civil rights movements of the 1960s, begin to adopt an overtly proactive stance. Indian groups demonstrate throughout the United States to direct attention to current Indian concerns and inequities.

17 January 1970. A Senate and House of Representatives subcommittee publishes a two-volume report on economic conditions on reservations. Detailed in the report are charges by Bureau of Indian Affairs official William Veeder, a water resources expert, that the government has caused "irreparable damage" to the Indians and to the economic development of Indian reservations. Veeder asserts that the basic problem results from an inherent conflict of interest between the Interior and Justice departments, which are responsible for protecting public lands and streams as well

assuring Indian property rights. Veeder suggests that Congress create an independent governmental agency for the protection of Indian water rights.

8 March 1970 Fonda and Indians Arrested. Actress Jane Fonda and thirteen Indians are arrested following an attempt by a large group of Indians, organized as United Indians of All Tribes, to take over Fort Lawton, Washington, near Seattle. The group demands the base for use as an Indian cultural center. The military uses clubs to beat and forcibly remove the demonstrators. Jane Fonda is taken into custody and given a letter of expulsion banning her from the post.

22–23 March 1970 Protests Lead to Arrests. Nine Indians are arrested near Denver and twenty-three are arrested at the Bureau of Indian Affair's offices in Chicago for sit-in protests against the BIA's employment policies. Similar protests are held in Cleveland, Minneapolis, Sacramento, and Santa Fe.

11 April 1970 Legislation Provides for Tribal Loans. The government enacts legislation to provide for loans to federally recognized tribes or tribal corporations from the Farmers Home Administration for the purpose of acquiring lands or interest to lands within reservation boundaries. The act is an extension of the 1934 Indian Reorganization Act, which sought to prevent the further erosion of the tribal land base and to assist tribes in the consolidation of their lands.

27 April 1970 *Choctaw Nation et al. v. Oklahoma et al.* In the case of the *Choctaw Nation et al. v. Oklahoma et al.*, the Choctaw, Chickasaw, and Cherokee nations of Oklahoma win control of the lower Arkansas River by a vote of four to three. The Supreme Court finds that the government ceded the riverbed and oil and mineral resources beneath the land to the tribes in the 1830 Treaty of Dancing Rabbit Creek and the 1835 Treaty of New Echota.

5 May 1970 Isleta Women Enfranchised. A tribal election at the Isleta Pueblo, located outside Albuquerque, New Mexico, grants women the right to vote.

14 May 1970 Seminole Land Claims Settlement. The Indian Claims Commission awards $12.2 million to the Seminole tribe for the government's illegal taking of lands in Florida. The money is to be distributed among the 1,500 Seminole in Florida and the 3,500 Seminole living in Oklahoma. The Seminole, who fought three successive wars with the federal government resisting forced relocation to Oklahoma, successfully argued to the court that the government had taken title to their lands in Florida under duress.

29 June 1970 Navajo Land Claims Settlement. The Navajo win a decisive court victory to prove title to 40 million acres of western land. The Indians charge that they were inadequately compensated for the lands when put on an 8-million-acre reservation in 1868. The Indian Claims Commission agrees with the Navajo, but the federal government insists that the Navajo could not prove claim to more than 10 million acres. Under court procedures, the Navajo will not receive the land. Instead the precise acreage will be determined and a value affixed to the property; the Navajo are to receive a monetary settlement.

8 July 1970 Nixon Sends Native-Focused Message to Congress. President Richard Nixon delivers a special message to Congress dealing exclusively with American Indians and Alaska Natives, setting forth a legislative program that expresses the idea of self-determination without the threat of termination. "The time has come," Nixon states, "to break decisively with the past and to create the conditions for a new era in which the Indian future is determined by Indian acts and Indian decisions." Nixon proposes that the Termination Act (House Concurrent Resolution 108) be overturned; that tribes secure the means to administer programs now operated by the Bureau of Indian Affairs; that Native peoples gain greater control over Indian education; that Blue Lake be restored to the Taos Pueblo; that greater federal funds be allocated to improve Indian health and the status of urban Indians; that the position of assistant secretary of Indian affairs be created to elevate the status of the BIA within the Department of the Interior; and that an Indian Trust Counsel Authority be established to represent Indians in the protection of their lands and resources.

12 July 1970 Iroquois Meeting. Two hundred members of the Iroquois Confederacy meet in Geneva, New York, to discuss proposals for regaining political power lost to state and federal governments. The Iroquois Confederacy, or Haudenosaunee, established more than five hundred years ago, is comprised of the Onondaga, Mohawk, Seneca, Oneida, Cayuga, and Tuscarora.

15 July 1970 Oglala Sioux Takeover. Members of the Oglala Sioux seize an area on Sheep Mountain, South Dakota, demanding the return of a gunnery range that the military took from the tribe during World War II.

1 August 1970 Puyallup Fish-in. Puyallup Indians set up a camp on the Puyallup River in Washington State and begin fishing to reestablish their tribal fishing rights.

September 1970 Mount Rushmore Takeover. Approximately fifty Indians from different tribes climb to the top of Mount Rushmore and announce their takeover of the historic landmark. The occupiers intend to occupy Mount Rushmore until 123,000 acres of Indian land, unjustly taken for a gunnery range during World War II, is returned.

20 September 1970 Osage Land Settlement. The Justice Department announces a $13.2 million settlement with the Osage Indian Nation of Oklahoma for 28

Indians protesting discrimination in hiring at the Bureau of Indian Affairs office in Denver, Colorado, 1970. (Courtesy of the Denver Public Library, Western History Collection)

million acres of lands purchased by the federal government in Arkansas, Kansas, Missouri, and Oklahoma between 1803 and 1819.

8 November 1970 Occupation of Army Communications Center. Approximately seventy-five Indians seize an abandoned army communications center in Davis, California. The Indians demand that the center be turned over to them for use as an Indian cultural center.

1970 *Mayflower II* Seized. On Thanksgiving, members of the American Indian Movement (AIM) seize the

Mayflower II in Plymouth, Massachusetts. Proclaiming Thanksgiving day a national day of mourning, AIM protests the taking of Indian lands by European colonists. This is one of AIM's first national demonstrations. Previously AIM focused upon providing physical protection against police harassment of Indian people living in Minneapolis, Cleveland, and Washington, D.C.

15 December 1970 Taos Land Bill. President Richard Nixon signs the Taos Land Bill. The legislation returns forty-eight thousand acres of land, including Blue Lake, to the Taos Pueblo. This bill, the first legislation to restore a sizable piece of land to an Indian tribe, acknowledges that the Taos Pueblo Indians practiced their religion at this sacred site for over seven hundred years. The Pueblo lost the lands in 1906 when President Theodore Roosevelt added the area to the Carson National Forest. The Taos Pueblo lobbied sixty years for the return of their sacred lands.

On this date President Nixon also signs legislation authorizing the payment of $1.1 million to the Nez Percé tribe of Idaho and the Confederated Tribe of Colville of Washington State. The funds were awarded to the tribes by the Indian Claims Commission for the illegal loss of tribal lands to the federal government in the nineteenth century.

1971 Tribal Sovereignty Efforts and the Creation of NARF.   The Bureau of Indian Affairs establishes regulations allowing for the direct election of the chiefs of the Five Civilized Tribes. The Five Civilized Tribes—the Cherokee, Creek, Seminole, Choctaw, and Chickasaw—along with more than thirty other tribes, were relocated in the 1800s to Indian Territory, present-day Oklahoma. Despite their promise that the territory would always remain in Indian control, Congress allotted tribal lands in the 1890s and, for the most part, dissolved tribal governments. The BIA was given the authority to appoint a chief for each of the Five Civilized Tribes. Tribes view the return of control over their own electoral system as an important step in government revitalization.

The Native American Rights Fund (NARF) is created with its central office located in Boulder, Colorado, and a branch office in Washington, D.C. NARF was established as a special pilot project of the California Indian Legal Services. Funded by the Ford Foundation, the organization's objectives are to pursue the legal protection of Indian lands, treaty rights, individual rights, and the development of tribal law.

13 January 1971 Report Charges Misuse of Indian Education Funds.   The NAACP Legal Defense and Education Fund and Harvard University's Center for Law and Education release a 162-page report charging state and local officials with a gross misuse of funds appropriated under the Elementary and Secondary Education Act and the 1934 Johnson-O'Malley Act. Funds, the report charges, which are to be used for the benefit and education of Indian children, are frequently used for non-Indian educational purposes. Some 250 examples of alleged impropriety are provided, such as buying expensive equipment for non-Indian schools and reducing non-Indian property taxes. "By every standard," the report emphasizes, "Indians receive the worst education of any children in the community."

14 January 1971 Army Communications Center Given to Indians.   The San Francisco regional office of the Health, Education, and Welfare Department gives custody of a 647-acre army communications center in Davis, California, to local Indians. The Indians who receive the "care, custody, protection and maintenance" of the base occupied the deserted building in November 1970. A spokesman for the group, Jack Forbes, announces plans to establish a college for American Indians and Mexican-Americans on the site. In April 1971 the federal government turns over land title to the trustees of Deganawida-Quetzelquatl University (DQU). The new university takes a hemispheric and indigenous approach to teaching and research.

19–20 February 1971 National Tribal Chairmen's Association Formed.   Tribal leaders from fifty reservations in twelve states meet in Billings, Montana, to discuss the establishment of a national association of tribal council leaders. The decision to establish the National Tribal Chairmen's Association stems from a concern by tribal reservation leaders that national Indian policy is being made in response to the actions of urban Indians and young militant reservation Indians.

25 April 1971 Population Increase.   The U.S. Census Bureau reports that the 1970 Census counted 791,839 Indians, an increase of more than 50 percent from the 1960 Census. The increase in population is primarily due to a declining death rate, high birth rate, and changing Native identities. More people with Native ancestry are willing to identify themselves as Indian.

15 May 1971 Hopi File Suit to Stop Strip-Mining. The Native American Rights Fund files suit in federal court on behalf of sixty-two members of the Hopi tribe to stop strip-mining on one hundred square miles of the Hopi Reservation. The religious leaders contend that Black Mesa is sacred to Hopi religion and culture. The suit is part of a larger effort by other Indians and conservationists to stop the development of a major power grid in the Four Corners area. The Hopi traditionalists' objective is to prevent mining of the coal by the Peabody Company for use in six proposed power plants.

21 May 1971 AIM Occupies Naval Air Station. Members of the American Indian Movement (AIM)

An exuberant occupier of Alcatraz Island flashes the peace sign. (Photo by Ilka Hartmann)

occupy a naval air station in Milwaukee, Wisconsin. The group argues that under the terms of the 1868 treaty between the federal government and the Lakota, all abandoned federal property should revert to Indians.

26 May 1971 OEO Establishes Urban Indian Centers. The director of the Office of Economic Opportunity (OEO) announces the provision of $880,000 in grants to establish a Model Urban Indian Center program. The funds are to be used to establish Indian centers in Los Angeles, Minneapolis, Gallup, and Fairbanks. The program's objective is to provide models for the improvements of services in the forty other existing urban Indian service centers.

According to the 1970 census, 44.5 percent of the Native population lives in urban areas, an increase of almost 15 percent during the previous ten years. Much of the urban migration is facilitated by the Bureau of Indian Affair's relocation program. In an effort to assimilate Indians into the mainstream, tribal members are encouraged to move to the urban areas to find work. Others move on their own, leaving their reservation homes in search of jobs.

6–7 June 1971 Indians Occupy Mount Rushmore. Forty Indians, demanding that the federal government honor its 1868 treaty with the Sioux Nation, which states that all lands west of the Missouri River would belong forever to the Sioux Nation, establish a camp on the top of the Mount Rushmore National Memorial. Police arrest twenty protesters for climbing the monument.

11 June 1971 Alcatraz Occupation Ends. The last fifteen Indians occupying Alcatraz Island are removed by federal marshals, ending the nineteen-month takeover of the island. The activists, approximately one hundred protesters from fifty Indian nations, hoped to turn Alcatraz into a center for Native American studies, an Indian center of ecology, an American Indian museum, and an Indian training school.

14–17 June 1971 Indian Protesters Occupy Army Site. Lakota leader John Trudell and fifty Indians occupy a deserted army missile site near Richmond,

California. One hundred police remove the protesters three days later.

14 June–1 July 1971 Indian Protesters Occupy Missile Site. One hundred Indians occupy an abandoned Nike missile site outside Chicago, protesting the lack of housing for Indians in Chicago.

30 July 1971 Indian Protesters Occupy Missile Site. Seventy-five Indians occupy a former Nike site on the grounds of the Argonne National Laboratories in Hinsdale, Illinois.

14 August 1971 AIM Seizes Abandoned Coast Guard Station. Members of the Milwaukee chapter of the American Indian Movement seize an abandoned Coast Guard station.

26 August–1 September 1971 Report Indicates Low College Enrollment among Indians. The Office of Civil Rights of the Health, Education, and Welfare Department reports that 29,000 American Indians are enrolled in colleges and universities.

16 September 1971 Indian Polytechnic Institute Dedicated. Assistant Secretary of the Interior Harrison Loesch participates in the dedication of the new $13 million Southwestern Indian Polytechnic Institute in Albuquerque, New Mexico. The school will serve seven hundred Indian students from sixty-four tribes. The 164-acre campus will offer training in business management, clerical work, drafting, radio, electronics, commercial food preparation, telecommunications, television, engineering, and optical technology.

5 October 1971 Alaska Natives File Suit against Alaska. The Arctic Slope Native Association files suit against the state of Alaska, claiming the 26,000-acre North Slope of Alaska. The suit claims that the state's selection of this oil-rich area in 1964 violated Native land rights in that the "Eskimo people have occupied, used and exercised dominion" over the area. The region is currently under lease to private oil companies for approximately $1 billion.

9 October 1971 Indian Education Bill Passes. The Senate passes a $390.3 million education bill designed to give greater control to tribes over the education of their children.

13–15 October 1971 First National AIM Convention. The American Indian Movement holds its first national convention. Approximately one hundred delegates representing eighteen chapters attend the conference at Camp Owendigo, Minnesota.

15 December 1971 Navajo Community College Act. The Navajo Community College Act provides $5.5 million for the construction and operation of a new facility for the Navajo Community College.

18 December 1971 Alaska Native Claims Settlement Act. President Richard Nixon signs the Alaska Native Claims Settlement Act (ANSCA) into law. The act extinguishes Alaska Native title to nine-tenths of Alaska in return for 44 million acres and $962.5 million. The House passed the bill on December 14 by a vote of 307 to sixty and the Senate by a voice vote. The legislation provides for the creation of villages and regional corporations under state law for the management of the lands and funds provided by the act.

Although the Alaska Federation of Natives approved the bill by a vote of 511 to fifty-six, the act remains controversial among Alaska Natives who fear that ANCSA will destroy their traditional lifestyle, which is centered on hunting and fishing.

19 February 1972 Chippewa Subsistence Rights Upheld. A federal court order takes effect protecting the Chippewa's right to hunt, fish, trap, and gather wild rice according to tribal laws on their Leech Lake Reservation. The Leech Lake Band of Chippewa Indians won a suit against the state of Minnesota in December 1971, upholding their 1855 treaty with the United States which guaranteed their right to hunt, fish, trap, and gather wild rice on the reservation.

2 March 1972 Stanford Changes Mascot. Bowing to pressures by Indian students on campus, Stanford University in Palo Alto, California, ends a forty-year tradition of using an American Indian symbol for its athletic teams.

4 March 1972 Five Persons Convicted in Murder. Five persons are charged in Gordon, Nebraska, with manslaughter and false imprisonment in the death of R. Yellow Thunder, a forty-one-year-old Oglala Sioux Indian.

7 March 1972 National American Indian Council Formed. Urban Indians hold a conference in Omaha, Nebraska, forming the National American Indian Council. The council is committed to working on behalf of urban Indians nationwide.

23 April 1972 Peaceful AIM Sit-in. Thirty Lakota and Chippewa American Indian Movement members stage a peaceful protest on the Fort Totten Indian Reservation in North Dakota. The sit-in's purpose is to call attention to police brutality on the reservation. According to the protesters, three Indians have died in jail in the last few months.

20 May 1972 Indian Education Act. Congress passes the Indian Education Act of 1972, creating a BIA-level Office of Indian Education as well as a National Advisory Council on Indian Education (NACIE) designed to improve the quality of public education for Indian students through grants and contracts for teachers of Indian students.

President Richard Nixon signs an order restoring 21,000 acres in Gifford Pinchot National Forest to the Yakima Indians of Washington.

June 1972 Lumbee Struggle to Retain Historic Building. Lumbee students at Pembroke State University strive to prevent the destruction of a historic Indian building on the campus. In 1885, the state of North Carolina permitted the Lumbees to operate their own school systems. The state's fifty-year-old constitution recognized the Lumbees as "free people of color,"

Title VII's (Indian Education) program for gifted and talented students provided this electronic video microscope for elementary classes. Patricia C'Hair and Franklin Martel show how the TV monitor can display microscopic views to large groups. (Photo by Mike McClure)

but barred them from attending white schools. Permitting them to operate their own schools proved an important step in Lumbee advancement. The school, started in 1887, became a four-year college in 1935. Old Main, as the building is known, served for many years as the only building on campus. With a current enrollment of 2,500, 92 percent of whom are white, the mostly white campus administration finds itself pitted against the Lumbee who are determined to save the historic building.

24 August 1972 Interior Department Charged with Environmental Failure. The General Accounting Office (GAO) issues a report charging that the Department of Interior has failed to enforce the Environmental Policy Act in its regulation of strip coal-mining on Indian and federal lands.

13 September 1972 Natives Seize BIA Building. Approximately forty Indians seize control of the Bureau of Indian Affairs building in Pawnee, Oklahoma, protesting the use of federal funds and presenting a list of demands to federal and state authorities.

2–8 November 1972 Trail of Broken Treaties. Five hundred Indians arrive in Washington, D.C., with the Trail of Broken Treaties to protest the government's policies toward Indians. The leaders, mostly members of the American Indian Movement, bring with them a twenty-point program, which they plan to present to the administration. Among their demands are that treaty relations be reestablished between the federal government and the Indian nations; that termination policies be repealed, including Public Law 280; that the Indian land base be doubled; that tribes be given criminal jurisdiction over non-Indians on reservations; and that cultural and economic conditions for Indians be improved.

The twenty-point program is quickly forgotten in the wake of a disagreement over housing and food provisions during the march in Washington, D.C. In protest, members of the Trail of Broken Treaties occupy the Bureau of Indian Affairs building in Washington, D.C.

After almost a week of occupation, during which time activists destroy files, furniture, and Indian art, the government agrees to pay for the protesters' return trip home and to consider the demands presented in the twenty-point program. On 9 June 1973 the federal government officially rejects the demands received from the leaders of the Trail of Broken Treaties.

9 November 1972 Paiute Prevail in Case against Interior Department. The Paiute tribe of Nevada wins its suit against the Department of Interior for the

Urban Indian children take care of a baby. (Photo by Ilka Hartmann)

department's management of Pyramid Lake. The court agrees that the Interior Department had violated its trust responsibility by allowing water diversion from the lake, thereby threatening the economic and spiritual existence of the tribe.

14 November 1972 Natives Charge Commission with Inconsistency. The U.S. Commission on Civil Rights hears testimony from American Indian witnesses that the agency directs its attention to the needs of African- and Hispanic-Americans, overlooking the needs of American Indians.

6–8 February 1973 AIM Protest Turns Violent. Two hundred American Indian Movement protesters clash with police in Custer, South Dakota. Thirty-seven Indians are arrested during a melee with police over a judge's decision to grant bail to the white man charged with the stabbing death of Wesley Bad Heart.

12 February 1973 Withhorn Released from Jail. Two hundred-fifty Indians gather in Sturgis, South

Dakota, to witness the setting of bond for Harold Withhorn, whom police have charged with the murder of a non-Indian.

27 February–8 May 1973 Wounded Knee Occupied. Two hundred Indians under AIM leadership occupy Wounded Knee on the Pine Ridge Reservation in South Dakota. American Indian Movement leaders are asked to the reservation by traditionalists to assist them in their struggle against the elected chairman Richard Wilson, whose administration, they charge, is rife with corruption, nepotism, intimidation, and violence.

Federal marshals and Federal Bureau Investigation (FBI) officers immediately surround the hamlet, creating a standoff that draws national and world-wide media attention. The Indian militants, who are well armed, make clear their intention to fight rather than surrender to outside forces. The Indian occupiers are surrounded by 300 federal marshals and FBI agents equipped with guns and armored personnel carriers. The impasse ends after sixty-seven days with a negotiated settlement and the withdrawal of both sides.

March 1973 Clashes between Hopi and Navajo. Clashes occur between Hopi and Navajo over the disposition of the Joint Use Area.

27 March 1973 *Mescalero Apache Tribe v. Jones*. The Supreme Court rules in *Mescalero Apache Tribe v. Jones, Commissioner, Board of Revenue of New Mexico et al.* that Indians are exempt from state taxation on incomes earned within reservation boundaries.

31 March 1973 Cheyenne Order BIA to End Strip-Mining. The Northern Cheyenne Tribal Council of Montana votes to instruct the Bureau of Indian Affairs to cancel strip-mining leases worth millions of dollars negotiated by the BIA on reservation lands. Lawyers for the Cheyenne tribe found thirty-six illegal sections in the leases that the BIA had negotiated on behalf of the tribe.

14 June 1973 BIA Charged with Unfair Trading Practices. The Federal Trade Commission issues a report charging that a number of non-Indian traders, licensed by the Bureau of Indian Affairs, are engaged in unfair trading practices leading to poor economic conditions for the inhabitants of the Navajo Reservation. The report finds that prices charged by the trading posts exceeded off-reservation stores by 16.6 percent and exceeded the national average by 27 percent.

16 July 1973 Census Report Findings. The Census Bureau reports that the median income for Indian families in 1969 was $5,832, compared to a national average of $9,590. Forty percent of Indian families live below the poverty level, compared to 14 percent of all families and 32 percent of Black families. Education statistics indicate the greatest degree of increase since the last census. One-third of all Indians over twenty-five have completed high school, with a median number of 9.8 years of school for all Indians. The number of Indian students in college has doubled since 1960.

13 August 1973 Office of Indian Rights Created. An Office of Indian Rights is created within the Civil Rights Division of the Justice Department. The office is established to investigate and protect individual Indian rights guaranteed under the Indian Civil Rights Act.

17 November 1973 Grand Jury Issues Indictments. The grand jury in Sioux Falls, South Dakota, returns four indictments against Indians arrested following the Wounded Knee standoff.

19 November 1973 *Department of Game of Washington v. Puyallup Tribe et al.* The Supreme Court, in a unanimous decision in *Department of Game of Washington v. Puyallup Tribe et al.*, rules that Washington State had abrogated the Puyallup Indians' treaty rights by prohibiting the tribe from commercial fishing. State law restricted all available fish to sports fishing.

22 November 1973 Arctic-Area Natives Meet. Indigenous peoples of the Arctic area—Eskimos, Lapps, and Indians—meet in Copenhagen, Denmark, to formulate demands for self-government and for control over land and resources. Indigenous peoples from Alaska, Canada, Greenland, Norway, and Sweden attend the four-day meeting.

22 December 1973 Public Law 93–197. President Richard Nixon signs Public Law 93–197 restoring the Menominee Indian tribe of Wisconsin to full federally recognized status.

28 December 1973 Comprehensive Employment and Training Act. Congress enacts the Comprehensive Employment and Training Act of 1973 or CETA, as it is commonly known. Title III of the act, Special Federal Responsibilities, Indian Manpower Programs, is designed to assist unemployed and economically disadvantaged Indians.

21 January 1974 Supreme Court Reversal. The Supreme Court reverses a lower court decision that barred the Oneida Indian Nation from suing the State of New York for rental on 5 million acres of land the tribe claims was taken in illegal state treaties in 1788 and 1795.

7 February 1974 Oglala Sioux Election Runoff. Russell Means, leader of the American Indian Movement, is defeated by incumbent Richard Wilson in a runoff election for chairman of the Oglala Sioux Tribal Council. Means had led in a field of twelve nominees by a small margin in the initial vote on January 22. Means, who lost 1,709 to 1,530, vowed to destroy the "white man's tribal government" and to reestablish "a type of government where all Indians would have a voice." Wilson pledged to continue full cooperation with the federal government. Charges of corruption and illegal vote counting followed the final outcome of the election.

12 February 1974 *United States v. State of Washington*. U.S. District Court Judge Boldt rules in *United States v. State of Washington* that the 1854 and 1855 treaties signed by the tribes of northwestern Washington, in which they reserved "the right of taking fish, at all usual and accustomed grounds and stations... in common with all citizens of the Territory," entitle the tribes to 50 percent of the allowable salmon catch.

16 February 1974 Wounded Knee Trial. Russell Means and Dennis Banks, leaders in the American Indian Movement, are brought to trial for charges stemming from the 1973 occupation of Wounded Knee, South Dakota.

20 February 1974 *Morton v. Ruiz*. The Supreme Court, in *Morton v. Ruiz*, unanimously upholds the right of Indians living off-reservation to receive general welfare payments from the Bureau of Indian Affairs.

12 April 1974 Indian Financing Act. Congress passes the Indian Financing Act, making available $250 million in credits and grants up to $50,000 to facilitate financing the economic development of Indians and Indian organizations.

17 June 1974 Supreme Court Refuses to Review Navajo Case. The Supreme Court declines to review a lower court decision upholding the election of an Arizona county supervisor who is a member of the Navajo nation. Non-Indian voters had challenged his eligibility for office on the grounds that his status as a reservation Indian made him immune from state taxes and the normal legal process.

17 June 1974 *Morton v. Mancari*. The Supreme Court, in *Morton v. Mancari*, upholds the preferential hiring of American Indians within the Bureau of Indian Affairs. The suit, which was brought by non-Indian BIA employees, argued that preferential hiring of Indians violated the equal protection clause of the Constitution. The Court denies the claim, pointing out that the federal government has a special obligation to Indians. Special preferences are given to Indians in BIA employment, the Court said, not because of their membership in a racial group, but because of their membership in quasi-sovereign nations that have entered into a political relationship with the federal government.

28–30 August 1974 Civil Rights Commission Hearings. The New Mexico Advisory Committee of the U.S. Civil Rights Commission holds three days of hearings near Farmington, New Mexico. The hearings are prompted by the beating death of three Navajo men by three white teenagers who had found the men drunk. The teenagers, according to the terms of state juvenile laws, were sentenced to two to three years in a reformatory. Navajo leaders testified to a variety of abuses ranging from commercial cheating to murder suffered by Navajo in off reservation towns located in Colorado, Utah, and New Mexico. Several Navajo leaders request support closing nearby off-reservation taverns.

22 December 1974 Hopi and Navajo Relocation Act. Congress passes the Hopi and Navajo Relocation Act providing for negotiations between the two tribes over their dispute concerning the Joint Use Area. The bill provides for the partition of the 1.8-million-acre Joint Use Area between the Hopi and Navajo and for $16 million to compensate eight hundred Navajo families who will be required to relocate as a result of the partition.

This legislation is the latest attempt by Congress to deal with the long-standing Navajo-Hopi land dispute. The conflict between the Hopi and the Navajo is complex. The Hopi never signed a treaty with the United States. In contrast, the Navajo entered into a treaty with the United States in 1868, following years of hostility and relocations. The treaty established the Navajo Reservation in northwestern New Mexico and northeastern Arizona. Prior to the adoption of this treaty, a number of Navajo families already lived in areas claimed by the Hopi.

In 1882, in response to Hopi complaints about Navajo encroachment, the president issued an executive order establishing the Hopi Reservation. Hopi lands continued to be settled by Navajo and Mormon families.

In an effort to solve the growing conflict between the two tribes, Congress authorized the courts to make a determination as to the competing land claims. In response, the courts created the Joint Use area, composed of 1.8 million acres, while allotting 650,000 acres of the 1882 reservation for the exclusive use of the Hopi.

1 January–4 February 1975 Indians Seize Catholic Novitiate. Forty-five Indians of the Menominee Warrior Society seize a Catholic novitiate in Gresham, Wisconsin. The Warrior Society demands that the Alexian Brothers give the 225-acre complex to the tribe for use as a hospital. The compound, comprised of a twenty-room mansion and another sixty-four room building, is currently unused by the religious order.

2 January 1975 Congress Reviews Tribal-Federal Relations. Congress, pursuant to a joint resolution of both houses, agrees to review the government's historical and special legal relationship with the Indian people. The American Indian Policy Review Commission is chaired by Senator James Abourezk of South Dakota. The task force includes three senators, three representatives, and five tribal representatives.

4 January 1975 Indian Self-Determination and Education Assistance Act. Congress passes the Indian Self-Determination and Education Assistance Act, expanding tribal control over reservation programs and authorizing federal funds to build needed

Wyoming Indian high school students Yvonda Hubbard and Marla Jimerson. (Photo by Mike McClure)

public school facilities on or near Indian reservations. Hailed as the most important piece of legislation passed since the 1934 Indian Reorganization Act, the Self-Determination Act's goal is to contract management of federal programs to tribal governments and other Indian organizations.

8 January 1975 Pine Ridge Election Declared Invalid. A U.S. Commission on Civil Rights report on the tribal chairman's election at Pine Ridge Reservation is termed invalid and recommends a new election. The election race involves Richard Wilson and Russell Means. After reviewing the ballots, the commission reports, "almost one-third of all votes cast appear to have been in some manner improper.... The procedures for ensuring the security of the election were so inadequate that actual fraud or wrongdoing could easily have gone undetected."

13 March 1975 Navajo Plant Closes. The Fairchild Camera and Instrument Corporation announces that it will close its Shiprock, New Mexico, electronic plant on the Navajo Reservation. The plant was occupied by armed members of the American Indian Movement

(AIM) for eight days in protest of the plants layoff of 140 Indian employees. The company, which produces semiconductors and integrated circuits for computers, employed approximately 600 Navajos before the layoffs took effect in February. In assessing the damage of the takeover, which ended March 3, a Fairchild spokesperson stated, "Fairchild has concluded that it couldn't be reasonably assured that future disruptions wouldn't occur."

22 April 1975 Violence Continues on Pine Ridge. A story in the *New York Times* reports that violence on the Pine Ridge Reservation has continued since the end of the Wounded Knee seizure. According to an FBI report, six people have been killed and sixty-seven assaulted since January 1. The violence, according to the story, is the legacy of the 1973 takeover, which divided the reservation into two opposing factions.

16 June 1975 AIM National Convention. The American Indian Movement (AIM) ends its national convention in Farmington, New Mexico, with a statement declaring that the U.S. government, religion, and education are the most potent enemies of Indian people.

26 June 1975 AIM-FBI Shootout. A shootout on the Pine Ridge Reservation in South Dakota between AIM members and the FBI results in the death of two agents. Leonard Peltier is charged and convicted for the murder of the FBI agents and is presently serving two life sentences in prison.

10 July 1975 Alexian Brothers Rescind Offer. The Alexian Brothers Roman Catholic order rescinds its offer to deed to the Menominee tribe of Wisconsin its novitiate in Gresham, Wisconsin, for use as a tribal hospital.

6 August 1975 Voting Rights Act Amendments. President Gerald Ford signs into law the Voting Rights Act Amendments of 1975. The act, which is designed to protect the voting rights of non-English speaking citizens by permitting voting in more than one language, specifically includes the rights of American Indians.

13 August 1975 Report on Farmington, New Mexico, Released. The New Mexico advisory committee to the U.S. Civil Rights Commission issues "The Farmington Report: A Conflict of Cultures." The study concludes that Navajo in San Juan County, New Mexico, which includes Farmington, are subjected to a wide range of injustices and mistreatment. Discrimination, according to the report, is intensified by poverty, severe alcoholism, and substandard health care. The county, the committee points out, has no detoxification or rehabilitation centers, despite the fact that 85 percent of the 21,000 Navajo arrested between 1969 and 1973 were arrested on alcohol-related offenses. The report also takes note of the inadequately staffed and funded Indian Health Service Hospital in Shiprock, and the lack of cooperation and commitment evidenced by local doctors responsible for the care of the Navajo population.

25 November 1975 Four Indians Indicted in South Dakota. A federal grand jury indicts four Indians, Leonard Peltier, Robert Eugene Robideau, Darrelle Dean Butler, and James Theodore Eagle, on charges of the premeditated death of two FBI officers. The officers were killed on July 26 in a gun battle on the Pine Ridge Reservation in South Dakota.

23 December 1975 *Passamaquoddy Tribe v. Morton*. The U.S. Court of Appeals, First Circuit, upholds Judge Edward Gignoux's decision in *Passamaquoddy Tribe v. Morton*. The Passamaquoddy and Penobscot of Maine, two non-federally recognized tribes, argue that the 1790 Trade and Non-Intercourse Act established a trust relationship between them and the federal government. The 1790 act forbade the sale of Indian lands without the approval of the federal government. The colony of Massachusetts (which later divided into the states of Massachusetts and Maine) had purchased land from the Passamaquoddy and Penobscot tribes in treaty. The federal government argued that it was not obligated to represent the tribes in their suit against the state of Maine because the tribes were not federally recognized. Judge Gignoux's decision upholds the principle that the federal government has an obligation to protect the land rights of all tribes, whether recognized or not.

2 March 1976 *Fisher v. District Court*. The Supreme Court rules in *Fisher v. District Court* that the Northern Cheyenne tribe of Montana has exclusive authority over adoption proceedings in which the participants are all tribal members and residents of the reservation.

27 April 1976 *Moe v. Salish and Kootenai Tribes*. The Supreme Court, in *Moe v. Salish and Kootenai Tribes*, rules that the states may not tax either personal property on the reservation or cigarette sales by Indians to Indians on the reservation. The Court, however, rules that tribes must collect cigarette sales tax on the reservation on sales by Indians to non-Indians.

29 May 1976 Indian Crimes Act of 1976. Congress passes the Indian Crimes Act of 1976. The act ensures that all individuals, Indian and non-Indian alike, receive equal treatment when violating crimes on federal lands, including Indian reservations, military installations, and national parks.

8 June 1976 AIM Members Stand Trial. American Indian Movement members Robert Robideau and Darrelle Butler stand trial for the 25 June 1975 murder of two FBI agents on Pine Ridge Reservation.

15 June 1976 *Bryan v. Itasca*. The U.S. Supreme Court rules in *Bryan v. Itasca* that Public Law 280, a statute giving six states criminal and civil jurisdiction over Indian reservations, does not give states the authority to levy state property tax on Indians living within reservation boundaries.

1 September 1976 All Indian Pueblo Cultural Center Opens. The All Indian Pueblo Cultural Center opens in Albuquerque, New Mexico. The $2.3 million Indian Cultural Center is a joint effort of the nineteen Pueblos that lie along the Rio Grande. The center houses a museum, a restaurant, and a gift shop.

16 September 1976 Indian Health Care Improvement Act. Congress passes the Indian Health Care Improvement Act, authorizing seven years of increased appropriations in an effort to improve Indian health care. The bill provides $480 million in funds for recruiting and training Indian health professionals; providing health services, including patient, dental, and alcoholism treatment; constructing and renovating health facilities; and providing services to urban Indians.

8 October 1976 Indian Claims Commission Terminated. President Gerald Ford signs a bill to terminate the Indian Claims Commission on 31 December 1978. Unresolved cases are to be forwarded to the U.S. Court of Claims for final resolution. The bill provides an additional amount, not to exceed $1,650,000 for the dissolution of the Indian Claims Commission on 30 September 1978.

13 October 1976 Mesquakie Land Claims Settlement. The federal government awards $6.6 million to the Mesquakie tribe for lands taken in Iowa, Missouri, Illinois, and Kansas in ten treaties signed between the federal government and the tribe between 1804 and 1867.

31 October 1976 Puyallup Occupy. Approximately sixty members of the Puyallup tribe, including members of the tribal council, occupy the Cascadia Juvenile Diagnostic Center in Tacoma, Washington. After a weeklong occupation, during which time the tribe claimed

Dennis Banks and supporters. (Photo by Ilka Hartmann)

title to the building, the governor of Washington announces an agreement to give six acres of land to the tribe.

13 December 1976 Navajo Radio Network. The Navajo Radio Network broadcasts its first day of news and public interest programming on the reservation in the Navajo language.

13 January 1977 Crow Coal Agreements Rescinded. Secretary of Interior Thomas S. Kleppe rescinds a number of coal leases and lease options on coal reserves on the Crow reservations. The strip-mining agreements, which provided for a royalty payment of 17.5¢ per ton on subtracted coal, came under attack by Crow tribal members. Tribal members filed suits to have leases held by Shell Oil, AMAX Inc., Peabody, and Gulf revoked.

4 April 1977 Catawba Ask Congress to Settle Claims. The Catawba Indians of South Carolina vote 101 to two in a tribal council meeting to ask Congress to settle their claims to 144,000 acres in York and Lancaster counties. The tribe, which is requesting recognition of a reservation within their former lands, argues that their 1763 treaty with Great Britain guarantees their ownership of the land. Barring congressional relief, the tribe agrees to take their suit to court.

5 April 1977 *Rosebud Sioux Tribe v. Kneip*. The Supreme Court, in *Rosebud Sioux Tribe v. Kneip*, rules that the congressional legislation, which opened surplus reservation lands to American settlers in the nineteenth century, diminished the size of the reservation and thereby the tribe's jurisdictional authority over that area.

18 April 1977 Peltier Found Guilty. American Indian Movement member Leonard Peltier, thirty-two, is found guilty of two charges of first-degree murder in the 1975 shooting deaths of two FBI agents on the Pine Ridge Reservation. Two men, previously charged with Peltier, had been acquitted of the charges on 16 July 1976. Peltier is sentenced to two consecutive life terms by a Fargo, North Dakota, court on 2 June 1977.

13 May 1977 Mohawks, State of New York Reach Agreement. A group of Mohawks, who for three years occupy a 612-acre campsite in the Adirondack Mountains, reach an agreement with the state of New York. In return for a grant of two separate sites, the Mohawks agree to vacate within the next five months the site they have renamed Ganienkeh or "Land of the Flint." The larger area of land, consisting of 5,000 acres, is located within the Macomb State Park. A smaller parcel of seven hundred acres lies near the town of Altona, New York. The Mohawks claim the area as part of the land guaranteed to the tribe in an eighteenth century treaty.

18 May 1977 American Indian Policy Review Report Released. Congress releases its multivolume American Indian Policy Review Commission Report. Eleven study groups, comprised of thirty-three members, thirty-one of whom are Indian, worked for two years to produce the report. The commission recommends the formation of a separate Department of Indian Affairs with cabinet status and suggests that stronger self-governing powers be given to tribes, wherein they can levy taxes on their reservations, try reservation offenders in tribal courts, and control Native resources such as waterways, hunting, and fishing. Despite strong support, Indian affairs remain under the authority of the Department of Interior. The commission's final report reveals that more than one hundred tribes are not federally recognized and recommends procedures for their recognition.

2 June 1977 Peltier Sentenced. Leonard Peltier is sentenced by a Fargo, North Dakota, court to two consecutive life terms for the killings of two FBI agents.

13–17 June 1977 First Inuit Conference Convenes. Two hundred indigenous peoples from Alaska, Canada, and Greenland, convene the first Inuit Circumpolar Conference in Barrows, Alaska. The conference is the first attempt to organize the 100,000 Inuits who inhabit the North Pole region. Delegates adopt resolutions concerning the preservation of their cultures and the recognition of self-sufficiency. The delegates also decide on environmental protections and ban all weapons testing and disposal in the Arctic.

17 June 1977 Council Provides List of Grievances to Soviet Union. The *New York Times* reports that the International Indian Treaty Council, which represents ninety-seven tribes, announces its intention to provide the Soviet Union with a list of human rights abuses by the United States against tribes. The list, which includes treaty violations, the destruction of Native cultures and religions, and the interference in

tribal economic and social life, would be provided for Soviet use at the upcoming meetings on the Helsinki Accords in Belgrade, Yugoslavia. The Helsinki Accords, signed by thirty-five nations in 1975, pledge signatory states to respect the self-determination and human rights of all peoples.

24 July 1977 Ute and Comanche End 200-Year Dispute. The Ute and Comanche nations meet to formally end a 200-year-old dispute over hunting rights in jointly claimed territory. More than two thousand members from both tribes attend the traditional ceremony, which includes the exchange of buckskin scrolls, the smoking of a peace pipe, and the shaking of hands.

1 August 1977 Seneca Opens Museum. The Seneca Nation holds an opening ceremony for its new $265,000 museum in Salamanca, New York. The museum, designed and constructed by the tribe from federal grants, houses artifacts from the Seneca Nation and the Iroquois Confederacy, as well as art work.

September 1977 Alaskan Eskimo Whaling Commission Founded. The Alaskan Eskimo Whaling Commission is founded to fight the International Whaling Commission's ban against the hunting of all bowhead whale. Culturally and economically dependent on the hunting of bowhead, the Alaskan Eskimo Whaling Commission commits itself to ensure that all hunts are conducted in a traditional and non-wasteful manner to educate non-Native Alaskans about the cultural importance of whaling and to promote scientific research to ensure the bowhead's continued existence.

13 October 1977 Assistant Secretary of Indian Affairs Appointed. Forrest J. Gerard (Blackfeet) is appointed by President Jimmy Carter as the first assistant secretary of Indian affairs. First proposed by President Richard Nixon, the creation of the position elevates the Bureau of Indian Affairs administration to a level similar to other major agencies within the Interior Department.

2 January 1978 Devils Lake Sioux Land Claims Settlement. The Bureau of Indian Affairs reports that the federal government has reached an out-of-court settlement with the Devils Lake Sioux Indian tribe for the illegal taking of 100,000 acres of land between 1880 and 1890. The tribe will receive $8.5 million for land taken from the Fort Totten Indian Reservation.

11 February–15 July 1978 The Longest Walk. Indian participants begin the Longest Walk at Alcatraz Island, California, in protest of the government's ill

Members of AIM at a San Francisco anti-nuclear rally, c. 1977. (Photo by Ilka Hartmann)

treatment of Indians. The five-month trek begins on Alcatraz Island, the site of the 1969 occupation that lasted nineteen months and gave impetus to many subsequent occupation events. The walk concludes with 30,000 marchers in Washington, D.C. Religious and traditional Indian leaders meet for three hours with Vice President Walter Mondale and Secretary of the Interior Cecil Andrus.

2 March 1978 Narragansett Land Settlement. The Narragansett Indians of Rhode Island receive 1,800 acres in a negotiated settlement with state officials. The tribe filed suit against Rhode Island for the taking of 3,500 acres in violation of the 1790 Trade and Non-Intercourse Act.

6 March 1978 *Oliphant v. Suquamish Indian Tribe.* The Supreme Court rules in *Oliphant v. Suquamish Indian Tribe* that tribal courts do not possess jurisdiction over crimes committed by non-Indians on reservations. The case is brought by two U.S. citizens who were arrested by the Suquamish tribal police for disturbing the peace and resisting arrest

during the tribe's annual Chief Seattle Days. The men argue that tribal governments do not have the inherent authority to exercise criminal jurisdiction over non-Indians. The decision inhibits tribes in the protection of their inherent sovereignty. The ruling also presents tribes with the practical problem of how to protect their lands and citizens from criminal actions by non-Indians. For the most part, state police officers do not have the authority to enforce law and order on Indian reservations.

22 March 1978 *United States v. Wheeler.* The Supreme Court rules unanimously in *United States v. Wheeler* that the United States did not violate a Navajo Indian man's protection against double jeopardy by trying him for rape in a federal court when he had been convicted on a lesser charge arising from the same incident in the Navajo tribal courts. The Court underscores that tribal governments are not creations of the federal government, but are separate sovereigns. As separate sovereigns, they have the authority to make and to adjudicate their own laws within limits established by Congress.

24 March 1978 Mashpee Wampanoag Land Claim Dismissed. The Mashpee Wampanoag land claim in the Cape Cod area of Massachusetts is dismissed by the U.S. District Court in Boston. The tribe, which had initiated its suit three years earlier, suffered a setback on January 6 when a jury ruled that although the Mashpee constituted a tribe in 1834 and 1842, they had lost their tribal status by 1869, when the land passed into non-Indian hands. Because of the tribe's failure to meet the definitions of a tribe after 1869, the court rejected Mashpee claims of more than 11,000 acres.

17 April 1978 Navajo Nation Reaches Agreement with Oil Companies. An agreement between four oil companies and the Navajo Nation is reached, ending a seventeen-day occupation of an Aneth, Utah, oil field. The four companies, Conoco, Phillips, Superior Oil, and Texaco, agree to institute a code of conduct for their oil workers and establish a hiring preference program for Indian employees. The protesters demanded the code of conduct because of the oil workers' use of alcohol on the reservation and their harassment of Navajo women.

19 April 1978 Banks's Extradition Denied. Governor Edmund G. Brown of California refuses an official request from Governor Richard F. Kneip of South Dakota to extradite Dennis Banks to stand trial in South Dakota. Banks, an Ojibway leader in the American Indian Movement, was convicted by a South Dakota court in 1975 of assault with a deadly weapon. The conviction arose out of the ninety-day seizure of Wounded Knee in 1973. Jumping bail, Banks, forty-five, fled to Oregon and then to California, where he has been teaching at a Deganawida-Quetzelquatl University (DQU) near Sacramento. In his letter to the South Dakota governor, Brown referred to "the strong hostility there against the American Indian Movement as well as its leaders." Brown's refusal to extradite Banks to South Dakota was upheld by the California Supreme Court on 20 March 1978.

22 April 1978 Reservation Denies Access to Non-Indians. The Fort Hall Indian Reservation's business council votes to deny access of non-Indians to the reservation for all purposes, including hunting and fishing in the Snake River basin. The action is taken in reaction to the Supreme Court's decision in the *Oliphant* case that tribal governments do not possess criminal jurisdiction over non-Indians.

30 April 1978 Department of Education Established. The Senate passes a bill to establish a new cabinet level agency, the Department of Education. A provision is included to transfer Indian education programs from the Department of the Interior to the newly established Department of Education.

13 May 1978 Reservation Housing Decline. The General Accounting Office reports that substandard housing for reservation families increased from 63,000 in June 1970 to 86,500 in a six-year period. New housing construction on reservations also dropped from 5,000 units to 3,500 units during the same time period.

15 May 1978 *Santa Clara Pueblo v. Martinez*. The Supreme Court rules in *Santa Clara Pueblo v. Martinez* that the Indian Civil Rights Act provides only for review of tribal habeas corpus cases. The case stems from a request by Mrs. Martinez of the Santa Clara Pueblo tribe that the Pueblo's tribal membership law be overturned to allow her children's enrollment. Current tribal law states that the children of enrolled women who marry outside the tribe are ineligible for membership. The ordinance extends membership to the children of men who married outside the tribe. Santa Clara Pueblo reckons descent by patrilineal clan and tribal membership is extended to members of clans, the clan of one's father. Mrs. Martinez charged that the tribal ordinance constituted a denial of equal protection under federal law. The Supreme Court held that Indian tribes have the power to determine membership according to their own rules, and that U.S. law is not applicable.

21 May 1978 Chumash Protests Conclude. Approximately twenty-five Chumash Indians agree to end their three-day protest at the site of an ancient burial ground at Little Cohu Bay, Pt. Conception, California, one of the proposed locations for a $1 billion coast site for the importation of liquefied natural gas. Under the terms of an agreement worked out between the tribe and the utility companies, the tribe will be allowed to have access to the area for religious practices, to protect all ruins and artifacts, and to have six tribal members monitor future excavations.

24 May 1978 AIM Activists Acquitted in Taxi Driver's Death. Two Indian activists, Paul Skyhorse and Richard Mohawk, are found innocent of murder and robbery in the death of a taxi driver. The driver's body had been found on 10 October 1974, near an American Indian Movement campsite north of Los Angeles. In the courts for three-and-a-half years, the case took thirteen months to try and cost $1.25 million to prosecute. Both men, whom supporters argued were framed for their AIM activities, remained in jail during the entire three-and-a-half years.

8 June 1978 Council of Energy Resources Tribes Established. Tribal leaders from twenty-five reservations containing energy resources agree to establish the Council of Energy Resources Tribes. The organization, to be known as CERT, will have its headquarters in Denver, Colorado. Its primary function will be to assist tribes in the development of their energy and mineral resources.

21 June 1978 Aleut Land Claims Settlement. The *Tundra Times* reports the award of $11.2 million by the Indian Claims Commission to the Aleut of Pribilof Islands for mistreatment by the federal government in the sale of seal fur from 1870 to 1946. The award settles a twenty-seven-year struggle by the Aleut to gain recompense from the federal government.

13 August 1978 American Indian Religious Freedom Act. President Jimmy Carter signs the American Indian Religious Freedom Act (AIRFA) in which Congress recognizes its obligation to "protect and preserve for American Indians their inherent right of freedom to believe, express and exercise their traditional religions." The act directs all federal agencies to examine their regulations and practices for any inherent conflict with the practice of Indian religious rights. The drafters of the legislation intend that the act will reverse a long history of governmental actions designed to suppress and destroy tribal religions. Until 1924, for example, the Bureau of Indian Affairs had regulations prohibiting the practice of Indian religion. Violators, if caught, could receive ten days in jail. In more recent times, Indians have been prohibited from entering sacred areas, from gathering and transporting sacred herbs, and from obtaining eagle feathers and meats necessary for ceremonies.

5 September 1978 Federal Acknowledgment Program Established. The Bureau of Indian Affairs publishes regulations for the newly organized Federal Acknowledgment Program. The BIA estimates that more than 250 tribes are unrecognized in thirty-eight states. The regulations create a Federal Acknowledgment Branch, comprised of a historian, an anthropologist, a sociologist, and a genealogist, who will be responsible for deciding if tribal petitions for recognition meet the stated requirements.

To gain recognition, tribes must prove the following: (1) continuous existence as an aboriginal tribe; (2) that they live in a geographically contiguous area; (3) that the group has been under the recognized authority of a governing body from historical times to the present; (4)

that they are currently governed by a constitution or other document; (5) that they have developed membership criteria; (6) that they possess a list of current members; and (7) that the federal government has not previously terminated its relationship with the tribe.

11 September 1978 Andrus Mediates Salmon Dispute. Secretary of Interior Cecil Andrus agrees to mediate a dispute between the Yurok Indians and federal officials over a two-week-old government ban on salmon fishing, imposed in response to a noticeable drop in salmon returning to the Klamath River to spawn. The ban resulted in a violent confrontation between the tribe and game wardens on the Klamath River in northern California, with the tribe arguing that the ban violates their religious rights given the spiritual importance placed upon fishing in Yurok culture. The reduction in the salmon runs is attributed to heavy fishing by all involved in the fishing industry and to the polluting effects of heavy logging in the area.

17 October 1978 Tribally Controlled Community Colleges Act. Congress enacts the Tribally Controlled Community Colleges Act. The legislation provides for grants to tribally controlled colleges, including Alaska Native villages and corporations.

November 1978 Oglala Sioux Television Station Planned. The Oglala Sioux tribe announces plans to construct the first Indian-owned and operated television station. The station will serve 14,000 people on the Pine Ridge Reservation in South Dakota.

1 November 1978 Education Amendment Act. Congress passes the Education Amendment Act of 1978, giving substantial control of education programs to local Indian communities.

8 November 1978 Indian Child Welfare Act. Congress passes the Indian Child Welfare Act (ICWA), establishing a federal policy to promote the stability and security of Indian tribes and families by giving tribal courts jurisdiction over foster care and the adoption of Indian children. Tribal leaders lobbied extensively for passage of the act. Surveys conducted by the Association on American Indian Affairs reported that 25 to 35 percent of all Indian children are raised in non-Indian foster and adoptive homes or institutions. The ICWA established standards for the placement of Indian children in foster homes and provides authority for the secretary of the interior to make grants to Indian tribes and organizations for establishment of Indian child and family service programs.

Indian maiden on the Northern Cheyenne Indian Reservation in Lame Deer, Montana. (Photo by Lori Cooper. Courtesy of the UCLA American Indian Studies Center)

Poster for the Indian Child Welfare Conference at the University of California, Los Angeles. (Courtesy of the UCLA American Indian Studies Center)

29 May 1979 Mohawk Takeover. A nine-hour takeover of the Akwesasne police station ends peacefully. The protest, which stemmed from the arrest of a traditionalist chief over a property dispute, is part of a longstanding issue between Mohawk traditionalists and those tribal members who support the elected form of government. The traditionalists do not recognize the authority of either the state police or the Franklin County Sheriff's Department, despite it being composed of sixteen Indian officers.

13 June 1979 Lakota Nation Refuses Settlement for Black Hills. The U.S. Court of Claims awards the Lakota Nation $122.5 million for the federal government's taking of the Black Hills in South Dakota. The Lakota Nation refuses to accept the award and demands the return of the Black Hills to Lakota jurisdiction. The federal government refuses to return land and holds $122 million, plus accumulating interest, in trust for the Lakota people.

21 July 1979 Silverheels Receives Star on Walk of Fame. Jay Silverheels, who played Tonto in the television series *The Lone Ranger* is the first Indian actor to have a star commemorated in the Hollywood Walk of Fame. Silverheels, a member of the Mohawk tribe and an actor for more than thirty-five years, is the founder of the Indian Actors Workshop.

27 July 1979 Boldt Decision Affirmed. The Supreme Court upholds the Boldt decision, affirming the right of Washington tribes to one-half the salmon catch.

19 August 1979 Narragansett Land Claim Settlement. The 800-member Narragansett Indian tribe of Rhode Island is the first of the eastern tribes to settle its land claim against federal and state governments. Filing suit in 1975 for ownership to 3,500 acres, the tribe will receive 1,800 acres. The tribe will purchase 900 acres with federal funds and receive the other 900 acres

Dennis Banks addresses participants in the 500-mile Indian Marathon from Los Angeles to D-Q University, 1979. (Photo by Ilka Hartmann)

from public state lands. While hailed as a victory by some tribal members, others express dissatisfaction with the agreement, frustrated that the agreement is inadequate for the loss of thousands of acres of land and 300 years of mistreatment.

31 October 1979 Archaeological Resources Protection Act. Congress enacts the Archaeological Resources Protection Act of 1979, which provides protection for all important archeological sites on federal public lands and Indian lands. It further requires that scientists or lay personnel must obtain a special permit before excavation will be allowed. Indians are exempt from obtaining federal permits for excavations on Indian lands.

November 1979 Natives Subjected to Racism Over Fishing Rights. Ottawa and Chippewa are subjected to racist and violent actions as they exercise their right to fish as guaranteed in their treaties with the United States. Indian fishers experience shootings, tire slashings, and the smashing of their boats. Bumper

stickers also begin to appear containing derogatory sayings, such as "Spear an Indian—Save a Fish."

8 December 1979 Oneida File Class-Action Suit. The Oneida Indian Nation files a class-action suit against New York State, local governments, farmers, and cooperatives in an effort to regain control of 3 million acres illegally taken by the state in violation of the 1790 Trade and Intercourse Act.

9 December 1979 Navajo and Hopi Settlement. The Navajo and Hopi tribes agree to a settlement of a one hundred-year-old dispute over control of the Joint Use Area. The dispute between the Navajo and Hopi involves the ownership and use of 1.8 million acres of land. The dispute between the two tribes arises from an 1882 executive order by President Arthur assigning the land to both tribes for their joint use.

9 December 1979 Tribes, States Sign Energy Agreement. Tribal leaders whose reservations contain energy resources and the governors of Alaska, Arizona,

Colorado, Montana, Nebraska, New Mexico, North Dakota, South Dakota, Utah, and Wyoming sign an agreement to ensure that tribal concerns are considered in any national effort to achieve energy independence. Fearing that the more populous eastern portion of the country will enact an energy policy to the detriment of the West, the agreement's objective is to protect western energy resources for the economic benefit of the areas in which they are located. Tribal and state lands in the West contain an estimated 50 percent of the nation's coal, 33 percent of the oil, 22 percent of the natural gas, 92 percent of the uranium, and 100 percent of the most easily developed oil shale.

17 January 1980 Omaha Land Claim Upheld.   The U.S. Court of Appeals upholds the Omaha tribe in their claim to 2,900 acres of land in Iowa. The land, originally on the Nebraska side of the Missouri River, initially belonged to the tribe, as recognized in their 1854 treaty with the federal government.

23 January 1980 Peltier Sentenced to Seven More Years.   Leonard Peltier, the American Indian Movement activist serving two life terms in prison, is sentenced to an additional seven years for escaping from a federal prison. Peltier, considered a political prisoner by many Indian supporters, was convicted of killing two FBI agents on the Pine Ridge Reservation in June 1975. Peltier escaped, with another inmate, from the Federal Correctional Institution in Lompoc, California, in July 1979.

18 February 1980 European Parliament Members Meet with Iroquois.   The Italian representative to the European Parliament, Mario Capanna, holds a meeting with the Grand Council of Six Nation Iroquois Confederation on the Onondaga Reservation. Capanna is one of twenty-two European Parliament members who introduced a resolution in January calling for the Parliament's condemnation of the state sending state troopers into the Mohawk Reservation.

13 March 1980 Case Goes to European Parliament.   Five members of the Iroquois and Lakota tribes take their case to the European Parliament, requesting support for their efforts at the international and national levels to gain recognition for their rights.

April 1980 IHS Issues Report.   The Indian Health Service issues a report stating that the most serious Indian health problems are no longer tuberculosis and gastroenteritis. Accidents, alcoholism, diabetes, mental health, suicides and homicides remain the greatest Indian health threats.

3 April 1980 Congress Restores Relations with Paiute Bands.   Congress passes legislation to restore a federal trust relationship with the 501 members of the Shvwits, Kanosh, Koosharem, and Indian Peaks bands and Cedar City bands of Paiute Indians of Utah. The tribes, whose relationship with Congress was terminated twenty-seven years earlier, will acquire the rights to approximately fifteen thousand acres in southwestern Utah and access to educational, employment training, and health benefits. An estimated 60 percent of the adults are unemployed, and 40 percent of the children do not attend school regularly.

13 April 1980 Court Upholds Washoe Hunting Laws.   The Washoe Nation wins a federal court decision that upholds the tribes right to enforce its own hunting laws on 60,000 acres of off-reservation land in the Pine Nut Mountains of Nevada.

13 April 1980 Harris Selected as Citizen's Party VP.   The Citizen's Party selects environmentalist Barry Commoner as its nominee for president and LaDonna Harris, a Comanche Indian activist from Oklahoma and former wife of Senator Fred Harris, as his vice-presidential running mate.

15 April 1980 Eastern Cherokee Suit Dismissed.   The U.S. Court of Appeals for the Sixth Circuit dismisses a suit brought by members of the Eastern Cherokee who are seeking to prevent the construction of the Tellico Dam in eastern Tennessee. Tribal members argue that the dam, a project of the Tennessee Valley Authority, would flood ancestral lands sacred to the Cherokee and thus violate their right to freely practice their religion as protected under the free exercise clause of the First Amendment. The appeals court, affirming a lower court decision, rules that the plaintiffs are unable to demonstrate that the land in question is indispensable to the practice of the tribe's religion.

20 April 1980 Mohawk, Federal Government Reach Tentative Agreement.   St. Regis Mohawk (in New York State) and the federal government reach a tentative agreement on the disposition of tribally claimed land near the St. Lawrence Seaway. According to the terms of the agreement, the Mohawk of Akwesasne will receive 9,750 acres south of the reservation and $6 million in federal funds.

14 June 1980 Police Sent to Akewsasne.   New York State sends seventy police to Akwesasne, the St. Regis Mohawk Indian Reservation that straddles the Canadian-United States border. For the previous ten months, in an effort to prevent the arrest of several traditional leaders involved in the 1979 takeover of the Akwesasne police station, approximately seventy Mohawk traditionalists maintained a camp on twenty acres along the St. Lawrence.

17 June 1980 Congress Passes Commerce Legislation. Congress passes legislation regulating and protecting Indian tribes in their commercial dealings with federally licensed Indian traders.

22 June 1980 Tekakwitha Beatified. The Vatican beatifies Kateri Tekakwitha, a Mohawk woman who died three hundred years ago at the age of twenty-four. The beatification process is the last step before achieving sainthood in the eyes of the Church. She is the first American Indian beatified by the Catholic Church. She was renamed Kateri at her baptism at the age of twenty (her Mohawk name was Ioragode, or Sunshine).

30 June 1980 *U.S. v. Sioux Nation*. The Supreme Court in *U.S. v. Sioux Nation* upholds the $122 million judgment against the United States by the Court of Claims for the taking of the Black Hills. The Fort Laramie Treaty of 1868 guaranteed the Lakota possession of the Black Hills, or *Paha Sapa*, an area of sacred significance to the tribe. The discovery of gold in 1874, however, brought a flood of prospectors, mining companies, and military units into the area. After enduring years of war and the intentional killing off of the buffalo, the tribe's staple food, the Sioux, or Lakota, signed an agreement in 1876 ceding the Black Hills to the United States.

8 July 1980 Navajo-Hopi Relocation Act. Congress enacts the Navajo-Hopi Relocation Act, which requires the relocation of some Navajo and Hopi families in an effort to settle the joint-use land dispute. The legislation provides for funds to assist in the purchase of additional lands for the Navajo tribe.

18 July 1980 Oglala Sioux File Suit against Federal Government. The Oglala Sioux file a class-action suit against the federal government and the state of South Dakota for $11 billion, seeking $10 billion for the loss of nonrenewable resources from the Black Hills and $1 billion for "hunger, malnutrition, disease and death" incurred by the Sioux resulting from the loss of their traditional lands.

20 July 1980 Martinez Dies. Maria Martinez, ninety-five, dies at San Ildefonso Pueblo, New Mexico. A world renowned potter, Martinez, working with her husband, revived the traditional black pottery of the Pueblos. Her pottery was perfectly crafted and shaped,

even though she worked without the use of a potter's wheel. Her pots appear in collections throughout the world.

18 August 1980 Creek Nation Regains Ownership of Sacred Grounds. The Creek Nation, or Alabama Creek as they are called locally, east of the Mississippi River regains ownership to a thirty-three-acre village site known as Hickory Grounds. The site was the location of one of the most sacred Creek villages before their removal from the Southeast in the 1830s, and was purchased with the proceeds of a $165,000 federal grant. In the 1830s, the village of Hickory Ground was relocated during removal to present-day Oklahoma and the sacred objects and stories were carried to the new location.

4 September 1980 Congress Establishes Reservation for Siletz. Congress establishes a reservation of 3,663 acres for the Confederated Tribes of Siletz Indians of Oregon. Congress terminated its relationship with the confederation of twenty-four tribes and bands in 1956. The Confederated Tribes, with approximately nine hundred members, were restored to federal recognition in 1977.

12 October 1980 Maine Tribes Settle Land Dispute. President Jimmy Carter, using a symbolic feather pen, signs legislation settling the claim of the Passamaquoddy, Penobscot, and Maliseet to two-thirds of Maine. The settlement provides for an $81.5 million settlement to the tribes. The money includes a $27 million trust fund and $54.5 million to purchase 300,000 acres of land. The agreement followed the tribes' claim that the state of Maine inappropriately treated for their homeland, the northern two-thirds of Maine, in violation of the 1790 Trade and Intercourse Act, which granted authority only to the federal government to purchase land from the Indian Nations.

8 November 1980 Helsinki Conference. The U.S. representatives provide the Helsinki Conference, meeting in Madrid, Spain, with a federal study on the United States' compliance with the 1975 Helsinki Accords in its treatment of American Indians. The report concludes that the United States' record is "neither as deplorable as sometimes alleged nor as successful as one might hope."

23 November 1980 Cayuga File Suit against New York. The Cayuga Indian Nation files suit against

New York State for taking former Cayuga lands located in the Finger Lakes region. The Cayuga Nation demands return of 100 square miles, payment of $350 million in damages, and the relocation of 7,000 property owners.

2 December 1980 Russell Tribunal Finds U.S. Guilty of Genocide. The Russell Tribunal, an international human rights body located in the Netherlands, finds the United States, Canada, and several countries in Latin America guilty of cultural and physical genocide and of the unlawful seizure of land in their treatment of their Indian populations. The verdict comes following an eight-day hearing during which the human rights activists heard testimony from fourteen Indian communities. The "judges," many of whom are lawyers, base their decision, which has no legal authority, on the protections afforded to Indian people in the 1975 Helsinki Accords, the International Covenant on Civil and Political Rights, and the Universal Declaration of Human Rights.

22 December 1980 Salmon and Steelhead Conservation Act. Congress passes the Salmon and Steelhead Conservation Act of 1980. The bill, designed in part to meet the guarantees promised by the federal government in treaties signed with the tribes in the mid-1800s, provides for the conservation and enhancement of the salmon and steelhead runs.

3 March 1981 Navajo and Hopi Protest Ski Resort Construction. Navajo and Hopi religious leaders request a federal district court to halt ski resort construction in the San Francisco Peaks mountains. Arguing that the First Amendment protects their right to religious freedom, the tribal leaders' suit states that construction would destroy sacred sites and that the desecration would anger their gods.

18 April 1981 Joint Use Area Divided Equally. A federal court partitions the 1.8 million-acre Joint Use Area equally between the Navajo and Hopi. The division forces the relocation of 3,000 to 6,000 Navajo and one hundred Hopi tribal members. Four days later, Bureau of Indian Affairs officials begin gathering Navajo livestock for removal.

8 May 1981 Tribal Leaders Call for Watt's Resignation. One hundred fifty tribal leaders, attending the National Tribal Government Conference in Washington, D.C., send a letter to President Ronald Reagan demanding the immediate resignation of Secretary of Interior James G. Watt. Citing Watt's unwillingness to consult with tribes as dictated by law, the leaders write: "We find this callous disregard of his lawful function and responsibility as the Federal official with general statutory-delegated authority in Indian matters completely intolerable." Elmer Savilla, spokesperson for the group, called further attention to Reagan's proposal to cut Indian funds by consolidating the financing of ten Bureau of Indian Affairs programs into one block grant, and reducing the allocation of funds by 26 percent. Other administration proposals call for the reduction of adult and child education, housing, employment, assistance, and vocational training programs.

24 May 1981 *Montana v. U.S.*. The Supreme Court rules in *Montana v. U.S.* that the state of Montana has the authority to regulate hunting and fishing on the Bighorn River flowing through the Crow Indian Rreservation. The Court rules that the state assumed title to the riverbed upon its entrance into the Union in 1889. The case is a blow to tribal authority and the tribe's efforts to regulate hunting and fishing within its own boundaries.

11 June 1981 Civil Rights Commission Issues Report. The U.S. Civil Rights Commission issues a major report on the federal government's treatment of American Indians. Commission Chairman Arthur Flemming sums up the government's policy toward American Indians as one of "inaction and missed opportunities." The commission, after a decade of research, proposes several changes in federal policy toward tribes. One of its primary recommendations is that Congress apportion, as in the case of states, federal funds to tribes as block grants. The commission also recommends the establishment of an Office of Indian Rights within the Civil Rights Division of the Justice Department. The report urges the government to act expeditiously and fairly in the resolution of fishing rights disputes and eastern land claims, and impels Congress to pass legislation allowing tribal government the option to assume criminal jurisdiction over all peoples within their reservation boundaries.

10 July 1981 Tribes Win Court Battle Over Fishing Rights. The Bay Mills and Sault Ste. Marie Chippewa and Grand Traverse tribe of Ottawa Indians win a nine-year court battle in the U.S. Court of Appeals for the

Sixth Circuit, recognizing their fishing rights in lakes Michigan, Superior, and Huron. The federal court lets stand a district court decision in which tribes successfully proved that the treaties of 1836 and 1855 guaranteed their right to fish in the Great Lakes. In addition to acknowledging their fishing rights, the courts rule that tribes may continue to use their traditional gill nets, an apparatus banned under state law. The next step is for the tribes to enter into negotiations with the federal government and the state of Michigan for the development of a fishing management plan.

13 August 1981 Omnibus Budget Reconciliation Act. Through the enactment of the Omnibus Budget Reconciliation Act of 1981, Congress allows the Secretary of Health and Human Services to make community block grants to Indian tribes. The legislation also provides for the establishment of Head Start programs on Indian reservations and for improvements in the loan process to small, tribe-owned businesses.

20 August 1981 Montana Orders Crow to Open River to Fishing. The state of Montana orders the Crow tribe to open access to fishing on the Bighorn River. In response, members of the Crow tribe barricade a highway bridge over the river near Hardin, Montana. The tribe, which claims ownership of the river, had closed the river to fishing by non-Indians in 1975. In March, the Supreme Court ruled that the state of Montana owned title to the fifty-mile section of the river under dispute. The blockade of both lanes of Highway 313, consisting of approximately fifteen cars, campers, and pick-ups, was lifted fourteen hours later when federal marshals served notice on the tribe that the blockade was illegal.

14 October 1981 Amnesty International Calls Marshall, Pratt Political Prisoners. Amnesty International, in a 144-page report, charges the U.S. government with retaining Richard Marshall of the American Indian Movement and Elmer Pratt of the Black Panther Movement as political prisoners. The report alleges official misconduct in the investigations and trials of both leaders.

7 January 1982 Nuclear Waste Policy Act. Congress passes the Nuclear Waste Policy Act of 1982. The act calls for the "development of repositories for the disposal of high-level radioactive waste and spent nuclear fuel, to establish a program of research, development, and demonstration regarding the disposal of

high-level radioactive waste and spent nuclear fuel." Section 2 of the act allows the administrator of the Environmental Protection Agency to authorize such repositories to be located within the boundaries of Indian reservations "upon the petition of the appropriate governmental officials of the tribe." Passage of this act draws considerable criticism from several tribes who interpret the act as a federal attempt to desecrate Indian lands.

21 January 1982 Watt Revises Interior's Royalty Policy. In response to a special commission's sharp criticisms of the Interior Department's collection of royalty money, Secretary of Interior James G. Watt announces a revision in the department's policy for obtaining royalties on oil and natural gas on federal lands.

25 January 1982 *Merrion v. Jicarilla Apache Tribe*. The Supreme Court rules in the *Merrion v. Jicarilla Apache Tribe* that Indian tribes have the authority to levy severance taxes on the extraction of minerals from tribal lands, even though the tax falls on nontribal members.

11 June 1982 Tlingit Demand Apology. Tlingit Indians arrive in Washington, D.C., seeking an official apology from the navy for its 1882 shelling of Angoon village in the Admiralty Islands. The navy's actions were undertaken as a means of forcing the Alaskan Indians to return to work for private whalers.

14 August 1982 Reagan Declares Code Talkers Day. President Ronald Reagan declares August 14 as National Navajo Code Talkers Day, commemorating the cadre of Navajo servicemen who sent messages in their tribal language during World War II. The system was never cracked by the Germans or Japanese.

13 October 1982 Thorpe Family Receives Gold Medals. The International Olympic Committee announces that it will restore to Jim Thorpe's family the two gold medals Thorpe won in the 1912 Olympic games for the decathlon and the pentathlon. Thorpe was stripped of his medals for having played minor league baseball for $2 a game. The two medals are returned in a ceremony to Thorpe's daughter Charlotte during the 1984 Olympics in Los Angeles.

2 November 1982 Zah Elected Navajo Chairman. The Navajo Nation elects a new tribal chairman, Peterson

Grace Thorpe, holding a picture of her dad, Jim, on the Oklahoma map, another of him with his baseball team, and one of his gold medals. Prague, Oklahoma, 1997. (Photo by Ilka Hartmann)

Zah, who defeats Peter MacDonald, Navajo chairman for the last twelve years, by a vote of 29,208 to 24,665. Zah, the founder of the reservation's legal aid organization, pledges to stop further exploitation of energy, minerals, timber, and water resources on reservation lands by non-Indians. Zah's platform also includes a proposal that the Navajo and Hopi seek to mediate their dispute over the Joint Use Area without the interference of the federal government.

22 December 1982 Indian Mineral Development Act.   Passage of the Indian Mineral Development Act of 1982 confirms and provides federal support for tribes to enter into commercial ventures for the development of their tribal resources.

30 December 1982 Reagan Recognizes 300 Umpqua.   President Ronald Reagan signs legislation extending federal recognition to approximately three hundred members of the Cow Creek Band of Umpqua tribe in Oregon.

8 January 1983 Congress Allows Texas Kickapoo to Apply for Citizenship.   Congress passes legislation to allow the Texas Kickapoo to apply for U.S.

citizenship and for federal services. The Texas, or Mexican, Kickapoo, as they are called, were part of the larger Kickapoo Nation pushed out of their aboriginal homelands in northern Illinois and southern Wisconsin in the early 1800s. One band sought refuge in Mexico, settling near Nacimiento Kickapoo, eighty miles from the Texas border. Today, the six hundred members of the tribe spend their summers in or near Eagle Pass, Texas, working as migrant laborers. In the winters, they return to their home in Mexico for the tribe's sacred winter ceremonial.

12 January 1983 Federal Oil and Gas Royalty Management Act. Passage of the Federal Oil and Gas Royalty Management Act of 1982 provides for cooperative agreements among the secretary of the interior, Indian tribes, and states for the sharing of oil- and gas-royalty management information.

12 January 1983 Indian Land Consolidation Act. Congress passes the Indian Land Consolidation Act to assist tribes in consolidating fractional land interests in many reservation lands. Tribes whose reservation lands were allotted under the terms of the 1887 General Allotment Act now possess, in some cases, allotments owned by over two hundred individuals. The original allotments of eighty to 160 acres were, by federal regulations, divided equally among allottee heirs. Passage of this act allows for tribes to purchase and consolidate these lands in an effort to make them more economically productive.

14 January 1983 Indian Tribal Tax Status Act. Passage of the Indian Tribal Tax Status Act of 1982 confirms that tribes possess many of the federal tax advantages enjoyed by states. Like states, tribes are acknowledged to have the power to issue tax-exempt bonds to enable tribal governments to fund economic development projects.

19 January 1983 Watt's Televised Comments Incite Indian Country. Secretary of Interior James Watt states during a television interview: "If you want an example of the failures of socialism, don't go to Russia. Come to America, and see the American Indian reservations.... Socialism toward the American Indian," Watt said, "had led to alcoholism, unemployment, venereal disease, and drug addiction." Watt's remarks provoked an outcry across Indian Country demanding his resignation.

24 January 1983 Reagan Issues Policy Statement. President Reagan issues the first Indian policy statement since 1975. Emphasizing that "the Constitution, treaties, laws, and court decisions have consistently recognized a unique political relationship between Indian tribes and the United States," the president states his commitment to deal with Indian tribes on a "government-to-government" basis. The address, which promotes economic development on reservations, states the government's support for industrial development of resources on Indian lands. Tribes and the American society "stand to gain from the prudent development and management of the vast coal, oil, gas, uranium and other resources found on Indian lands." The address is met with skepticism by many Indian leaders who fear an underlying terminationist message.

25 January 1983 *Lac Courte Oreilles Band of Lake Superior Chippewa Indians v. Voigt.* The U.S. Court of Appeals for the Seventh Circuit affirms in *Lac Courte Oreilles Band of Lake Superior Chippewa Indians v. Voigt* that the Chippewa's treaties with the United States in 1837 and 1842 preserved the rights of six Chippewa bands to hunt, fish, and cut timber in lands they ceded to the federal government.

31 January 1983 Reagan's Budget Calls for Cut in Indian Program Funding. President Ronald Reagan sends his first budget to Congress. Proposals include a one-third cut in the total budget for Indian programs.

15 March 1983 Pacific Salmon Treaty Act. Congressional passage of the Pacific Salmon Treaty Act of 1984 clarifies and protects tribal fishing rights as provided in executive orders and Indian treaties as they relate to the United States treaty with Canada over Pacific salmon fishing.

23 March 1983 Onondaga Grants Asylum to Banks. The Onondaga Nation, located south of Syracuse, New York, agrees to grant asylum to American Indian Movement leader Dennis Banks, who is fleeing charges in South Dakota arising from the takeover of Wounded Knee.

30 March 1983 *Arizona v. California.* The Supreme Court rejects in *Arizona v. California* a federally appointed fact finder's report that five Indian reservations—the Cocopah, Ft. Mohave, Ft. Yuma, Colorado River, and the Chemehuevi—are entitled to receive a larger share of water allocation in the lower basin of the Colorado River. The five tribes requested larger water allocations on the basis of an increase in reservation populations.

2 June 1983 Tribal Chairmen Criticize Reagan. The National Indian Tribal Chairman's Association holds a news conference to criticize President Ronald Reagan for his failure to uphold his pledge to free tribes of federal regulations and to provide tribal governments with greater self-determination.

13 June 1983 *New Mexico v. Mescalero Apache Tribe*. The Supreme Court rules in *New Mexico v. Mescalero Apache Tribe* that the state of New Mexico cannot enforce state laws against non-Indians hunting and fishing on tribal lands within reservation boundaries. The imposition of state laws in this instance, the Court stated, would interfere with "Congress' overriding objective of encouraging tribal self-government and economic development."

24 June 1983 *Nevada v. U.S.* The Supreme Court in *Nevada v. U.S.* unanimously upholds a lower court ruling affirming the allocation of water rights to the Pyramid Lake Reservation in western Nevada.

1 July 1983 *Rice v. Rehner*. The Supreme Court rules six to three in *Rice v. Rehner* that states have the authority to enforce liquor laws on reservations. Tribes, according to the opinion written by Justice Sandra Day O'Connor, are required to obtain state licenses before selling liquor on the reservation.

15 July 1983 *Arizona v. San Carlos Apache Tribe*. The Supreme Court rules in *Arizona v. San Carlos Apache Tribe* that state courts have the authority to decide water rights disputes involving Indians. The decision is another blow to tribes in their quest to preserve their water rights. Tribes attempted to prove that water rights disputes must be settled in the federal courts. Tribes feared that the state courts, under pressure to protect the progress and development of major cities and areas throughout the West, would not provide tribes with a fair hearing.

30 July 1983 Seminole Agree to Establish Traditional Judicial System. Fifteen hundred Seminole tribal members, who occupy five reservations in southern Florida, approve a referendum to establish a judicial system reflecting traditional values and principles. Tribal leaders, who are in the process of developing the new judicial system, are giving careful examination to the neighboring system of the Miccousukee tribe, which operates with two judges, one schooled in modern law and the other in traditional law.

13 September 1983 Banks Surrenders. American Indian Movement co-founder Dennis Banks surrenders to state authorities in Rapid City, South Dakota, following nine years as a fugitive. Banks's surrender allows the state to prosecute him for assault and rioting charges stemming from the 1973 Wounded Knee takeover and flight to avoid prosecution. Banks, who states that he feared for his life, explains that he had given himself up for the sake of his family. Banks had spent six years in California, under the protection of Governor Jerry Brown, before fleeing to the Onondaga Reservation in New York when Brown's successor, Governor George Deukmejian, indicated his willingness to extradite Banks to South Dakota. New York governor Mario Cuomo agreed to return Banks to South Dakota but forbade marshals from entering the Onondaga Reservation.

20 October 1983 Mashantucket Pequot Federally Recognized. President Ronald Reagan signs legislation acknowledging the Mashantucket Pequot Indians of Connecticut as a federally recognized tribe with all powers of self-government. The legislation also provides for a $900,000 appropriation to the Pequots for the purchase of land near their reservation. President Reagan vetoed a similar bill on 10 April 1983.

25 March 1984 Cherokees Meet in Tennessee. Members of the Eastern Band of Cherokee and the Cherokee Nation of Oklahoma hold their first joint council meeting in 146 years. An estimated 10,000 tribal members attend the historic meeting held at the Cherokee's sacred ground in Red Clay, Tennessee. The two tribes, which confirmed their permanent split, agree to meet annually in the Council of Cherokees to discuss issues and needs of common concern.

8 June 1984 Senate Select Committee on Indian Affairs Made Permanent. The U.S. Senate agrees to make the Senate Select Committee on Indian Affairs a permanent body. The body, which is responsible for the consideration of Indian affairs and oversight, was established on a temporary basis in 1977.

5 July 1984 Cayuga, New York Reach Agreement. The Cayuga Indian Nation agrees to accept approximately 8,500 acres of land in Cayuga and Seneca counties of New York State in return for relinquishing claims to 64,000 acres.

2 September 1984 Pequote Take Possession of Land. The Mashantucket Pequot Indians from eastern Connecticut take possession of 650 acres of land. Tribal title to the land ends an eight-year struggle by the tribe to regain former reservations lands.

23 September 1984 Santa Fe Publication Apologizes to Santo Domingo. The Santa Fe *New Mexican* apologizes to the Santo Domingo Indian community for the publication of two photos of sacred dances.

Bolinas supports American Indian prisoner Leonard Peltier, San Francisco Federal Building, June 1984. (Photo by Ilka Hartmann)

The community has a posted policy of forbidding the taking of photographs at sacred ceremonies.

8 October 1984 Banks Sentenced. Dennis Banks is sentenced in Custer, South Dakota, to three years in prison for his part in the Custer Courthouse Riot in 1975.

30 November 1984 Reservation Economies Commission Presents Report. The Presidential Commission on Indian Reservation Economies presents its report to President Ronald Reagan. Characterizing the Bureau of Indian Affair's organization and administration as "byzantine," and "incompetent," the report called for the BIA's replacement with an Indian Trust Services Administration. As an illustration of the BIA's top-heavy administration and over-regulation, the report points out that two-thirds of the BIA's budget goes into administration; less than one-third of the federal funds reach the reservation.

Other recommendations in the report include the placement of tribal businesses in individual hands, the subordination of tribal courts to federal courts in interpreting law, the reduction of tribal immunity, and the allowance of tribal taxation only after the vote of all Indian and non-Indian residents on the reservation. The report further recommends that tribal leaders and federal officials tackle the issue of tribal self-determination through private economic development. The report draws a cool reception from many tribes.

9 January 1985 Kickapoo Resettle in Texas. Charitable contributions provide for the purchase of a 125-acre parcel of land on the Rio Grande near Eagle Pass, Texas, for the resettlement of the Kickapoo tribe.

11 January 1985 Tribal Leaders Reject Private-Enterprise Proposal. The National Tribal Council Association, a national group comprised of tribal political leaders, votes eighty-four to eighteen to reject a proposed program for the development of private enterprises on Indian reservations. As explained by Elmer Savilla, the association's executive director, the program's philosophy is in opposition to the "Indian way," which is "to go into business to provide income for tribal members, to provide employment for as many tribal members as you can."

11 February 1985 Federal Government Settles with Wyandotte.   The federal government agrees to pay $5.5 million to Wyandotte Indians in Kansas and Oklahoma for forcing their ancestors to sell their aboriginal lands in 1842 for less than fair market value.

20 February 1985 *Dann et al. v. United States*.   In *Dann et al. v. United States*, the Supreme Court rejects a suit by two Shoshone Indians claiming ownership of 5,100 acres of the tribe's aboriginal homeland. In 1951, the Shoshone tribe sought compensation for the loss of their aboriginal homeland and were awarded $26 million by the Indian Claims Commission. The tribe refused to accept payment of the funds, requesting instead the return of their lands. The courts ruled that once the funds were placed in an interest-bearing account, the tribe's claim to the lands were extinguished.

4 March 1985 *County of Oneida v. Oneida Nation*.   The Supreme Court, in *County of Oneida v. Oneida Nation*, upholds the right of the Oneida Nation of New York State to sue for lands illegally taken in 1795.

5 March 1985 Scientists Find that Natives Developed Calendars.   The *Journal of the Society for American Archeology* reports that scientists, through the analysis of Winnebago calendar sticks, have the first evidence that tribes, through systematic astronomical observations, had developed full-year calendars.

15 March 1985 Pacific Salmon Treaty Act.   After a thirteen-year effort, Congress passes the Pacific Salmon Treaty Act of 1985. The act, which many legislators and biologists hail as the most important key to saving the salmon runs from extinction, was passed following the intervention and support of the northwestern tribes that depend on fishing for cultural and economic survival.

16 April 1985 *Kerr-McGee Corp. v. Navajo Tribe*.   The Supreme Court, in *Kerr-McGee Corp. v. Navajo Tribe*, unanimously upholds the right of the Navajo Nation to tax business on the reservation without first obtaining federal approval. The decision allows for the Navajo to continue taxation of mineral leases on reservation lands.

16 May 1985 Montana Governor, Tribes Reach Water Rights Agreement.   Montana Governor Ted

Schwinden signs an agreement with the Sioux and Assiniboine tribes guaranteeing water allocations between the tribes and their neighbors.

3 June 1985 *Montana v. Blackfeet Tribe*.   The Supreme Court, in *Montana v. Blackfeet Tribe*, upholds a Court of Appeals ruling that Montana could not tax the royalty interests earned by the Blackfeet from leases issued in accordance with the Indian Mineral Leasing Act of 1938. At issue was the legal status of state taxation of oil, gas, and minerals from Indian lands.

2 July 1985 Jicarilla Apache Offer Tax-Exempt Bonds.   The Jicarilla Apache tribe of New Mexico is the first tribe to offer tax-exempt municipal bonds to institutional investors, issuing $30.2 million in revenue bonds.

2 October 1985 Wind River Suicide Rates Skyrocket.   News services report that nine young Arapaho and Shoshone Indians on the Wind River Reservation in Wyoming have hanged themselves in the last two months. The reservation, which has a population of six thousand people and an unemployment rate of 80 percent, reported forty-eight suicide attempts in 1985. The National Center of Health reported that the suicide rate at the Wind River Reservation, 233 suicides per 100,000, is almost twenty times higher than the national average, twelve per 100,000.

22 November 1985 Kickapoo Issued Citizenship Cards.   One hundred forty-three members of the Kickapoo of Texas and Mexico are issued citizenship cards acknowledging their status as a "subgroup" of the Kickapoo tribe of Oklahoma.

22 November 1985 Banks Granted Parole.   American Indian Movement leader Dennis Banks is granted parole from the South Dakota Penitentiary. He served approximately one year of a three-year prison term, which arose from a 1973 disturbance at Custer County Courthouse in South Dakota.

13 December 1985 Swimmer Sworn in as Assistant Secretary of Indian Affairs.   Ross Swimmer, Cherokee and former principal chief of the Cherokee Nation of Oklahoma, is sworn in as assistant secretary of the interior for Indian affairs in Washington, D.C.

14 December 1985 Mankiller Sworn in as Cherokee Principal Chief.   Wilma Mankiller is sworn in as

Activist Rigoberta Menchu (second from the left) with Ilka Hartmann (l.) and Dennis Jennings (r.) in the mid-1980s. Menchu accepted the Nobel Peace Prize for her work on behalf of indigenous peoples. (Photo by Ilka Hartmann)

Principal Chief of the Cherokee Nation of Oklahoma. The nation, the largest Indian tribe in the country after the Navajo, is headed by a fifteen-member council.

14 February 1986 Smithsonian Agrees to Return Skeletal Remains to Tribes. The Smithsonian's Museum of Natural History agrees to return skeletal remains to tribal leaders for reburial when a clear biological or cultural link can be established. Several Indian organizations, while applauding the museum's decision, request that all Indian remains be returned for reburial, as required by Indian spiritual beliefs. Studies estimate that more than one million Indian remains are in the hands of museums and universities.

24 March 1986 White Earth Reservation Lands Settlement Act. Congress signs the White Earth Reservation Lands Settlement Act of 1985, settling "unresolved claims relating to certain allotted Indian lands on the White Earth Reservation, to remove clouds from the titles to certain land," regarding checkerboard non-Chippewa land ownership.

15 May 1986 Lummi Fight IRS Demands. The Lummi Indian tribe of western Washington is fighting a demand from the Internal Revenue Service that Indian fishers pay an income tax on the sale of salmon caught by the tribe in Puget Sound. The tribe argues that their natural resources, as guaranteed to the tribe by treaty, are immune from taxation.

3 June 1986 Supreme Court Denies Catawba Land Settlement. The Catawba lose a major case before the Supreme Court in their quest to reclaim 144,000 acres of aboriginal lands now in private hands. The Court rules that the tribe lost the opportunity to bring a suit due to a statute of limitations.

18 August 1986 Wampanoag Receive Land Claims Settlement. Congress passes legislation to settle the land claims of the Wampanoag Tribal Council of Gay Head, Massachusetts. In exchange for relinquishing further land claims, the state of Massachusetts will pay

$225 million to the tribe for the purchase of tribal trust lands.

27 August 1986 Bands Trust Relations Restored.
Congress restores federal trust relations to the Klamath, Modoc, and the Yahuskin band of Snake Indians of Oregon. The approximately 3,000-member tribe was one of the first terminated by Congress in the 1950s. The Klamaths, Modocs, and Snakes, along with the Menominees of Wisconsin, were the largest tribes to be terminated.

17 October 1986 Institute of American Indian and Alaska Native Culture and Arts Development.
Legislative approval is granted for the establishment of an Institute of American Indian and Alaska Native Culture and Arts Development. The institute, to be administered by a board of trustees, is charged with acknowledging and promoting the contributions of Native arts to American society.

27 October 1986 Indian Alcohol and Substance Abuse Prevention and Treatment Act. Recognizing that alcoholism and alcohol and substance abuse is a severe social and health problem among Indian people, Congress passes the Indian Alcohol and Substance Abuse Prevention and Treatment Act of 1986. When adjusted for age, Indians are four times more likely to die from alcoholism than the general population. Four of the top ten causes of death among Indians are alcohol related. Indians between the ages of fifteen and twenty-four years are twice as likely to die from vehicular accidents, 75 percent of which are alcohol related.

27 October 1986 Indian Civil Rights Act Amended.
Congress revises the Indian Civil Rights Act to allow tribal courts to impose fines of $5,000 and one year in jail for violating tribal criminal offenses.

4 November 1986 MacDonald Elected Navajo Chairman. Peter MacDonald regains his elected position as the tribal chairman of the Navajo Nation. MacDonald, chairman from 1970 to 1982, defeated the incumbent, Peterson Zah.

6 November 1986 Campbell Elected to House.
Ben Nighthorse Campbell, a member of the Northern Cheyenne tribe of Montana, is elected to the U.S. House of Representatives from the third district of Colorado.

Campbell is only the second Indian elected to the U.S. House of Representative in recent times. Ben Reifel, a Sioux from South Dakota, served in the House from 1961 to 1971.

19 November 1986 American Indian Vietnam Plaque Dedicated. The Grandfather Plaque, or American Indian Vietnam Plaque, is dedicated at Arlington National Cemetery in Virginia. The plaque commemorates the service of approximately 43,000 indigenous combatants who served in Vietnam. An estimated one out of every four eligible Indian males served in Vietnam.

1 January 1987 Woman Elected Isleta Governor.
Isleta Pueblo, located near Albuquerque, New Mexico, elects its first woman governor.

25 February 1987 *California v. Cabazon Band of Mission Indians*. In *California v. Cabazon Band of Mission Indians* the U.S. Supreme Court rules that the state of California may not regulate bingo and gaming on the Cabazon and Morongo Indian reservations. The Court rules that Public Law 280 nor the 1970 Organized Crime Control Act carry congressional approval for California state regulation of gaming on Indian land.

23 August 1987 Reagan Cedes Land to Wampanoag. President Ronald Reagan signs a bill ceding to the Wampanoag more than four hundred acres of undeveloped land located on Martha's Vineyard, Massachusetts. The Bureau of Indian Affairs extended federal recognition to the Wampanoag Indians of Gay Head, Massachusetts, on March 8.

18 September 1987 Pope Speaks to Indian Leaders. Pope John Paul II speaks to a group of 1,600 American Indian leaders in Phoenix, Arizona, urging them to forget the past and to focus on the church's current support of Indian rights. An American Indian Catholic attendee responds that the Church still has much to accomplish in the United States.

9 October 1987 Charges Against Seminole Chief Dropped. The U.S. Justice Department drops all charges against Seminole Indian Chief James E. Billie, who killed a rare species of Florida panther, and was arrested for violating the Endangered Species Act. Billie admitted killing the panther in December 1983, but argued that his right to hunt panthers was a religious act that was protected by the Seminole's treaty of

1842 with the United States. Billie's first trial ended in a mistrial on 27 August 1987, when the jury could not agree on how Billie could identify the panther when the hunting occurred at night. Billie's second trial ended in an acquittal October 8.

2 December 1987 Bill Commemorating Cherokee Removal Passed. The U.S. House of Representatives passes a bill commemorating the centennial anniversary of the army's forcible removal of the Cherokees from the southeastern portion of the United States to northeastern Oklahoma.

11 January 1988 Cheyenne Tax BIA Contractors. The Northern Cheyenne tribe in Montana proposes to exercise its inherent right to tax by levying a tax on BIA contractors operating within reservation boundaries.

1 February 1988 Tuscarora Men Hold Newspaper Office, Employees Hostage. Two Tuscarora Indian men seize the newspaper office of the *Robesonian* in Lumberton, North Carolina. They hold seventeen of the newspaper's employees hostage for ten hours, demanding that the paper investigate corruption and discrimination by the police against the African-Americans and Indians of the area. The standoff ends with an agreement by the governor of North Carolina to investigate the charges.

6 February 1988 Reagan Signs Amendments to Alaska Native Claims Settlement Act. President Ronald Reagan signs into law a set of amendments to the 1971 Alaska Native Claims Settlement Act, which extinguished the Natives' title to their lands in exchange for 44 million acres and $962.5 million. The lands and money were distributed among over two hundred village corporations and thirteen regional corporations. According to the 1971 act, individuals would have been free to sell their shares in the corporations, a move that many Alaska Natives feared would result in the loss of Native lands and rights in Alaska. According to the 1988 amendments, corporations may only sell their stock if a majority of the shareholders support the sale.

17 March 1988 Conference on Suicide. The Warm Springs tribe of Oregon hosts a conference on suicide among Indians. The conference follows a rash of suicides on the reservation inhabited by 2,800 members of the Wascoe, Paiute, and Warm Springs tribes. Six young people killed themselves and sixteen others tried in the last two months. Nationwide, young Indian men kill themselves at a rate more than twice the national average.

The conference, which is attended by Indian leaders and families as well as psychologists and social workers, seeks in part to find the answer to the recent epidemics by returning to traditional practices and methods of counseling for young people.

19 April 1988 *Lyng v. Northwest Indian Cemetery Protective Association*. The Supreme Court, in a five-to-three decision, rules in *Lyng v. Northwest Indian Cemetery Protective Association* that the Forest Service is free to build a five-mile logging road through the sacred lands of the Yurok, Karok, and Tolowa tribes of California. Three justices, William T. Brennan Jr., Thurgood Marshall, and Harry Blackmun, dissent, arguing against the majority's "surreal" logic that "governmental action that will virtually destroy a religion is nevertheless deemed not to 'burden' that religion."

28 April 1988 Elementary and Secondary Education Act. As part of the Elementary and Secondary Education Act, H.R. 5, Title V, Congress repeals the termination policy established by House Concurrent Resolution 108, passed in 1953. The act also prohibited the BIA from terminating, consolidating, or transferring BIA-administered schools without the consent of the affected tribes.

2 June 1988 Mohawks Protest Smuggling Charges. Mohawk Indians at Kahnawake', a reserve on the south shore of the St. Lawrence River, block two highways and the Mercier bridge for thirty hours to protest a June 1 police raid in which seventeen Mohawks are charged with smuggling cigarettes from the United States. The Mohawk claim that the Jay Treaty of 1794 gives them the right to bring goods across the border without paying duty.

29 June 1988 U.S. Housing Act Amended to Include Natives. Indians and Alaska Natives are included in the U.S. Housing Act of 1937 with an amendment establishing a separate program under the supervision of the Secretary of Housing and Urban Development.

8 July 1988 *Oklahoma Tax Commission v. Muscogee (Creek) Nation*. In *Oklahoma Tax Commission v. Muscogee (Creek) Nation*, the Supreme

Performance of the Pueblo Indian tale "Arrow to the Sun" at the Wyoming Indian Elementary School. (Photo by Mike McClure)

Court refuses to overturn a lower court ruling that exempted the Creek Nation from paying a state sales tax on their bingo operations. The gaming operation, located in Tulsa, is built on Creek tribal trust lands.

10 August 1988 Reagan Includes Apology to Aleut in Internment Camp Bill. In a White House ceremony, President Ronald Reagan signs into law a reparations bill for Japanese-Americans interned during World War II. Included in the bill are an apology and $12,000 in reparations for the survivors of the several hundred Aleut who were forcibly relocated from their villages on the island of Attu in 1942. Although they were removed for fear of a Japanese attack, the government admitted that the relocation "resulted in widespread illness, disease and death among the residents of the camps."

17 September 1988 Ceremony Commemorates Iroquois Origins. A ceremony is held to commemorate the origin of the Iroquois Confederacy. The confederacy was organized by the Mohawk, Seneca, Oneida, Cayuga, and Onondaga tribes in the mid-1600s. Estimates of the origin of the Iroquois Confederacy vary from 500 to 1,000 years ago.

17 October 1988 Indian Gaming Regulatory Act. It is estimated that by the late 1980s close to one hundred tribes, acting on their inherent sovereignty and freedom from state laws, establish gaming facilities as a means of improving tribal economies and providing employment for tribal members. Pursuant to concerns expressed by non-Indian neighbors, federal officials, and some tribal officials, Congress passes the Indian Gaming Regulatory Act, Public Law 100–497. The legislation provides for the establishment of federal regulations and standards for the conduct of gaming on Indian lands. The act has two basic purposes: to strengthen tribal governments and promote economic self-sufficiency through gaming, and to provide regulation of tribal gaming thereby allaying fears of criminal influences in gaming operations. In order to ensure the effective regulation of gaming operations, the act establishes the National Indian Gaming Commission with the authority to monitor gaming on Indian lands.

12 December 1988 Reagan Meets with Indian Leaders. President Ronald Reagan holds a meeting at the White House with sixteen Indian leaders. Billed as a "meeting among friends," the meeting is an attempt to smooth over the controversy caused by the president's remarks to Russian students in the Soviet Union in May. While speaking at Moscow University, Reagan stated: "Maybe we made a mistake. Maybe we should not have humored them [the Indians] in wanting to stay in that kind of primitive lifestyle. Maybe we should have said: 'No come join us. Be citizens along with the rest of us.'" President Reagan also made reference to the fact that a large number of Indians had become very wealthy due to oil money. Both remarks, which Indians leaders quickly pointed out were incorrect, raised considerable concern in Indian Country as to the level of knowledge possessed by the administration regarding the current state of Indian affairs.

The twenty-minute meeting was viewed as successful by the participants. The vice chairman of the Navajo Nation, Johnny Thompson, stated that "there was a spirit of forgiveness by all of us."

19 January 1989 Seneca, New York Settle Tax Dispute. The Seneca Indians of New York agree to the settlement of a dispute over taxes with outside local governments and with the state of New York. The tribe, standing on its sovereign authority to levy taxes, established stores selling non-taxed goods on the reservation. In response to pressures by outside competitors, the tribe agrees to levy its own tribal tax on goods, thereby making products comparable in price. In return, the state agrees to allow the tribe to keep all tax revenues for tribal programs and to dismiss its suit against the tribe for $10 million in state sales tax for goods sold to non-Indians.

3 March 1989 *Lac Courte Oreilles Band of Lake Superior Chippewa Indians et al. v. State of Wisconsin.* In the case of the *Lac Courte Oreilles Band of Lake Superior Chippewa Indians et al. v. State of Wisconsin*, several Chippewa Indian tribes seek to clarify their rights, based on the treaties of 1837 and 1842, to hunt, fish, and gather on off-reservation lands. Judge Barbara Crabb, presiding over the U.S. District Court for the western district of Wisconsin, rules that the Chippewa are not obligated to negotiate with the state concerning the length of their spearfishing season, the number of lakes to be fished, or the size of the catch. Furthermore, the court rules that the usufructuary rights of the Chippewa Indians, their rights to use the resources of their lands, may only be regulated if it is shown that such regulation is both reasonable and necessary for public health or for the conservation of natural resources. Moreover, it must be shown that such regulation does not discriminate against the Chippewa.

3 April 1989 *Mississippi Choctaw Band v. Holyfield.* In *Mississippi Choctaw Band v. Holyfield*, the Supreme Court upholds the jurisdictional rights of tribal courts under the Indian Child Welfare Act of 1978. The Indian Child Welfare Act addresses issues that resulted from the separation of large numbers of Indian children from their families and their subsequent placement in non-Indian homes. The 1978 act gave sole jurisdiction in custody proceedings to tribal courts. This case involves an attempt by the Mississippi Choctaw band to negate an adoption decree that had been signed by the parents. The Supreme Court of Mississippi originally ruled that the adoption decree was binding in part because the twins were born off-reservation and had never been "domiciled" there and, thus, the decree did not come under the tribal court's jurisdiction. The Supreme Court overturns the lower court's decision and rules that the twins were domiciled on the Mississippi Choctaw Band's reservation and, therefore, that the tribal court has exclusive jurisdiction.

23 April–7 May 1989 Fishing Protests Lead to Arrests. More than one hundred people are arrested in protests against the rights of northern Wisconsin tribes to fish as guaranteed by their treaties of 1837 and 1842. Almost nine hundred individuals assembled to protest the Indian's fishing rights, while more than one hundred people gathered in support of the Indians.

24 June 1989 Stanford Agrees to Repatriate Ohlone Remains. Stanford University agrees to repatriate for reburial the remains of 550 Ohlone Indians to descendant tribes in northern California. Stanford is one of the first universities to agree to a repatriation request by tribal leaders.

28 June 1989 Coquille Tribe of Indians Trust Relationship Act.   The Coquille Tribe of Indians Trust Relationship Act restores Congress' federal relationship with the Coquille Indians of Oregon, which was canceled by the Termination Act of 1954 in an attempt to facilitate the assimilation of the Coquille into American society. In light of the failure of this integration strategy, Congress began to reestablish federal recognition of Indian tribes in the 1970s.

7 July 1989 Brown Sworn in as Assistant Secretary of Indian Affairs.   Eddie Brown, an enrolled member of the Pasqua Yaqui of Arizona, takes the oath of office as Assistant Secretary for Indian Affairs.

21 July 1989 *Brendale v. Confederated Tribes and Bands of the Yakima Indian Council.*   The Supreme Court rules in *Brendale v. Confederated Tribes and Bands of the Yakima Indian Council* that tribal zoning laws do not apply to non-Indian-owned lands within reservation boundaries where that land is surrounded by other non-Indian-owned lands. Non-Indian-owned land surrounded by tribally owned lands is subject to tribal zoning laws.

21 July 1989 State Troopers, FBI Agents Close Casinos, Make Arrests.   Approximately 225 state troopers and FBI agents sweep into the part of the St. Regis Reservation (Akwesasne) located in the United States around Hogansburg, New York, closing down seven suspected casinos and arresting eight people.

22 July 1989 Navajo Nation Riots.   Two individuals are killed and nine injured in a clash in Window Rock, Arizona, between police and the supporters of ousted Navajo Chairman Peter MacDonald. The tribal council had voted on February 17 to place MacDonald on involuntary leave in the wake of bribery accusations.

27 July 1989 New York Police Close Roads to Mohawk Reservation.   New York State police close all roads to the New York portion of the St. Regis Mohawk Reservation. Tribal factions dispute the legality of gambling on the reservation and whether the traditional Mohawk Sovereignty Security Force or the state police properly exercises jurisdiction over the reservation.

4 August 1989 Tohono O'Odham Demand Return of Land.   Tohono O'Odham tribal leaders request Mexican government officials in Mexico City to return thousands of acres of indigenously owned lands to the tribe. The Tohono O'Odham Nation argues that the Gadsden Treaty of 1853 illegally divided its tribal lands by the establishment of the international boundary.

10 August 1989 Mohawk Vote in Favor of Gaming.   State and federally recognized tribal officials report that the St. Regis Mohawk Reservation voted to allow gambling on the United States side within reservation boundaries.

11 August 1989 Working Group on Indian Water Settlements.   Secretary of Interior Manuel Lujan announces the formation of the Working Group on Indian Water Settlements. The group, which will report to the Interior's Water Policy Council, is charged with establishing principles to guide Indian water settlements; assisting in negotiations with tribes; and reporting to the council on the progress of such negotiations.

11 August 1989 Centennial Accord.   Washington Governor Booth Gardner and the state's twenty-six federally recognized tribes sign the Centennial Accord. In the historic agreement, the state recognizes the sovereignty of Washington tribes and agrees to a government-to-government process for solving problems of mutual concern between the two governmental entities.

13 August 1989 New York Returns Wampum Belts to Onondaga.   New York State agrees to return twelve wampum belts to the Onondaga Nation of New York. The wampum belts, woven of shells and beads, signify important historical and cultural events in Onondaga and Iroquois Confederacy history. The New York Senate and Assembly had passed legislation in 1971 requiring the return of five wampum belts to the nation.

21 August 1989 Harvard Museum Returns Sacred Pole.   The Peabody Museum at Harvard University returns the Sacred Pole of the Omaha tribe. The pole, estimated to be three hundred years old, is a symbol of unity to the tribe. The sacred object was placed in the museum's care 101 years ago by Yellow Smoke, the last keeper.

8 October 1989 Inspector General Details BIA Fund Mismanagement.   The inspector general issues a report detailing the Bureau of Indian Affairs' irresponsible management of Indian trust funds. Trust funds totaling $1.8 billion are administered by the BIA under its obligation of trustee for Indian moneys. The report states that some $17 million is missing as a result of sloppy bookkeeping.

17 November 1989 Senate Issues Report on Mismanagement of Indian Lands and Monies. A specially convened Senate panel issues its report following a two-year investigation into the corruption and mismanagement of American Indian lands and money. The report, the first study of its kind in more than a decade, uncovers corruption in the administration of tribal governments and a failure of the federal trust responsibility. Specifically cited as a violation of the trust obligation is Bureau of Indian Affairs management that allowed oil companies to rob tribes of oil proceeds and inadequate monitoring of teachers in BIA boarding schools found guilty of sexually molesting Indian children. The report's major recommendation is that tribes be given greater control over federal funds and programs. In particular, the panel proposes that a new executive agency be given responsibility for providing the more than five hundred Indian tribes and Alaska Native groups with block grants to administer their own programs.

28 November 1989 National Museum of the American Indian Established. Congress approves a bill to establish a National Museum of the American Indian under the administration of the Smithsonian Institution. The museum, which will be devoted to Indian culture and history, will be located in Washington, D.C.

27 February 1990 Tribal Leaders Agree to Defend Treaty Rights. Leaders of several North American tribes enter into an agreement to collectively defend rights granted by their treaties with the government of the United States. In accordance with the agreement, several tribes from both the United States and Canada will assist each other with legal services and lobbying and law-enforcement aid. The tribes also agree to work together in attempting to educate the non-Indian public about federal treaties with Indians.

25 March 1990 Puyallup Settles Land Dispute. The Puyallup tribe of Washington ends a long-standing land dispute with the city of Tacoma and the state. In return for extinguishing its land claims, the tribe agrees to a $162 million package settlement comprised of money, jobs, and education guarantees, and title to a section of the Tacoma waterfront.

17 April 1990 *Oregon v. Smith*. The U.S. Supreme Court rules, six to three, in *Oregon v. Smith* that a state ban against the use of peyote by American Indians did not violate the plaintiffs' First Amendment rights. The decision represents another blow to tribes in their efforts to protect their religious freedoms. The case involved the firing of two Indian drug counselors after testing positive for drug use. As members of the Native American church, the two men had ingested peyote as part of the church's ritual. Formally established in 1918, but based on thousands of years of tradition, the church's beliefs are a mixture of Native traditions and Christianity. Members believe that the taking of peyote allows them to communicate more closely with God.

30 April–3 May 1990 Akwesasne Gambling Dispute. A factional dispute between those in favor of gambling and those opposed on the Akwesasne Reservation results in the killing of two men on the Canadian side of the reservation. Hundreds of New York and Canadian police are sent to seal off the reservation, while negotiators sent by Governor Mario Cuomo attempt to settle the dispute.

22 May 1990 Seneca, Salamanca Reach Agreement. The Seneca Nation, local leaders of Salamanca, New York, and state and federal officials reach an agreement on Seneca land rented by the city of Salamanca. Under the terms of the first lease, negotiated in 1892, the town paid the nation $17,000 annually. Ninety percent of the town of 6,600 lies within the boundaries of the Allegany Reservation. According to the terms of the new lease, the town, which is the only city in the United States built on leased Indian land, will pay the tribe $800,000 a year. In addition, state and federal officials will reimburse the tribe $60 million for the inequities of the previous lease.

29 May 1990 *Duro v. Reina*. The Supreme Court rules in *Duro v. Reina* that tribes do not possess the authority to exercise criminal jurisdiction over nonmember Indians on the reservation. The decision is a major legal and political blow to tribes in their struggle to regain and protect their inherent right of self-determination. The decision also creates a very difficult situation on reservations, where many nonenrolled tribal members have married within the tribe or are working on the reservation. According to the Court's decision, no governmental body currently possesses criminal jurisdiction over these individuals.

2–3 July 1990 Brown Signs Agreements with Tribes. Assistant Secretary of the Interior Eddie

Martin Gutierrez, 12, looks on as Baudelio Gutierrez, 13, shows their grandfather, Thomas Brown, Sr., 78, some of the textbooks during Grandparent's Day activities at Wyoming Indian Middle School. (Photo by Mike McClure)

Brown signs historic agreements with six tribes: the Quinault Indian Nation, Tahola, Washington; Lummi Indian Nation, Bellingham, Washington; Jamestown Klallam Indian tribe, Sequim, Washington; Hoopa Valley Indian tribe, Hoopa, California; Cherokee Nation, Tahlequah, Oklahoma; and Mille Lacs Band of Chippewa Indians, Onamia, Minnesota. The tribes are part of a Self-Governance Pilot Program that will ultimately allow up to twenty tribes the authority to administer and set priorities for federal funds received directly from the government.

August 1990 White House Conference on Indian Education Legislation Passed. Congress passes legislation to convene the White House Conference on Indian Education. The conference is charged with examining the feasibility of establishing an independent Indian Board of Education that will oversee all federal programs directed at Indian education and recommend improvements to current educational programs.

The Bureau of Indian Affairs currently funds 182 schools, attended by 39,000 Indian children. Of these 18,270 are contracted by tribal education committees. Another 400,000 Indian children attend public schools operated by the states.

3 August 1990 Heritage Month Declared. Congress declares November as American Indian Heritage Month.

25 September 1990 Tribally Controlled Vocational Institutional Support Act. Congress enacts the Tribally Controlled Vocational Institutional Support Act of 1990. The legislation provides for grants to operate and improve tribally controlled post-secondary vocational institutions.

28 September 1990 Lujan, Brown Call Tribal Leader Conference. Secretary of Interior Manuel Lujan and Assistant Secretary Eddie Brown call the Indian Tribal Leaders Conference in Albuquerque, New Mexico, to discuss proposals to reorganize the Bureau of Indian Affairs. More than 1,000 Indian tribal leaders attend the first such meeting since 1976.

4 October 1990 Indian Environmental Regulatory Act. Congress passes the Indian Environmental Regulatory Act, which reinforces and clarifies the authority of Interior officials to protect areas of environmental concern in Indian Country.

30 October 1990 Native American Languages Act. Congress enacts the Native American Languages Act which is designed to preserve, protect, and promote the practice and development of Indian languages. The act is important given the government's historic efforts, especially in the nineteenth century, to eradicate Indian languages. It is estimated that more than one-half of all Indian languages are now extinct. Approximately 250 Indian languages remain in existence, although some are spoken by only a few individuals.

31 October 1990 Ponca Restoration Act. Congress passes the Ponca Restoration Act to reestablish all formal ties and services to the Ponca tribe of Nebraska. Federal recognition of the tribe had been taken away in 1962. As with other Indian tribes, the termination policy had negative ramifications for the Ponca both economically and culturally.

6 November 1990 Defense Bill Delays *Duro* Decision. President George Bush signs a defense appropriations bill that includes an amendment to delay enforcement of the *Duro* decision until 30 September 1991. The amendment, according to the bill's authors, filled the vacuum created by "an emergency situation": "Throughout the history of this country, the Congress has never questioned the power of tribal governments to exercise misdemeanor jurisdiction over non-tribal member Indians in the same manner that such courts exercise misdemeanor jurisdiction over tribal members."

16 November 1990 Native American Graves Protection and Repatriation Act. Bowing to intense lobbying efforts by individual tribes and national and local Indian organizations, Congress enacts the Native American Graves Protection and Repatriation Act. The act provides for the protection of American Indian gravesites and the repatriation of Indian remains and cultural artifacts to tribes.

20 November 1990 Zah Elected Navajo Nation President. Peterson Zah is elected President of the Navajo Nation. Zah assumes leadership of the tribe from Peter MacDonald Sr., who was convicted of taking bribes by the Navajo tribal court in October.

28 November 1990 Child Abuse Increase on Reservations. Historically a rare problem, child abuse is being experienced increasingly on tribal reservations. Now, under the terms of the Indian Child Protection and Family Abuse Prevention Act, tribes are required to report abusive situations and to establish tribal programs to treat and prevent future abuse.

28 November 1990 National Indian Forest Resources Management Act. The passage of the National Indian Forest Resources Management Act provides for improved protection and coordination between the Department of Interior and Indian tribes in the management of Indian forest lands.

29 November 1990 Indian Arts and Crafts Act. With the increase in value of tribal art work and jewelry, tribal artists have faced competition from non-Indian, machine-manufactured art works. Now, under the terms of the Indian Arts and Crafts Act of 1990, Congress gives the Indian Arts and Crafts Board, first established by the 1935 Indian Arts and Crafts Act, expanded powers to bring civil and criminal jurisdiction over counterfeit Indian arts and crafts.

December 1990 Lujan Forms BIA Reorganization Task Force. Secretary of Interior Manuel Lujan announces the formation of a forty-three-member advisory task force to recommend reorganization plans for the Bureau of Indian Affairs. The task force is composed of thirty-six Indian tribal leaders and seven Department of Interior and Bureau of Interior representatives.

Although the BIA reports that tribes contracted administration of approximately one-third of all BIA programs, the secretary of the interior urges reorganization so that less funding be used for administering tribal programs. By contracting with the BIA, tribes are free to operate and manage federal programs, some $415 million annually.

29 December 1990 Wounded Knee Centennial. Approximately four hundred people attend the centennial of the Wounded Knee massacre. On October 19, the House of Representatives provided the final approval needed for a resolution expressing "deep regret" over the Seventh Cavalry's massacre on the Pine Ridge Reservation. The Seventh Cavalry rounded up and killed more than three hundred women, men, and children at Wounded Knee, South Dakota, in 1890.

29 January 1991 MacDonald Convicted of Conspiracy. Peter MacDonald Sr., the former Navajo Nation chairman, is convicted by a tribal court on charges of conspiracy, fraud, and ethics violations. The tribal court had previously convicted him and his son of

Indian students march during American Indian Heritage Month. (Photo by Mike McClure)

accepting bribes and violating the tribe's ethics code. At that time, the tribal court suspended MacDonald from tribal office and prohibited him from holding office for four years. In addition, he was sentenced to almost six years in prison and fined $11,000. His son was sentenced to eighteen months in prison and was fined $2,500.

5 March 1991 National Museum of the American Indian Announces Repatriation Policy. The new National Museum of the American Indian, under the auspices of the Smithsonian Institution, announces its policy for the return of Indian artifacts. Tribes may formally request the return of all sacred objects, funerary artifacts, communally owned tribal property, and illegally obtained objects.

4 April 1991 Census Bureau Report. The Census Bureau announces that 1,959,234 American Indians and Alaska Natives live in the United States. Of these numbers, 1,878,285 are American Indian, 57,152 are Eskimo, and 23,797 are Aleut. These figures represent a total increase in population since 1980 of almost 40 percent. The increase is attributed to improved census taking and a greater willingness on the part of individuals to be identified as American Indian. Included in these numbers are 510 federally recognized tribes in the United States and approximately 200 Alaska Native villages and communities.

20 May 1991 Chippewa Tribes Reach Fishing Rights Agreement. Members of the Chippewa tribes of Wisconsin and the state of Wisconsin announce an agreement which ends a seventeen-year dispute over treaty fishing rights in Wisconsin. Based on previous court decisions, the tribes and the state agree to compromise on a number of issues that had divided them for more than a decade. Under the terms of the agreement, tribes will continue to spearfish in Wisconsin lakes, but only according to strictly held conservation limits. The Chippewa also agree not to appeal a ruling that prevents their harvesting timber from off-reservation lands.

24 May 1991 Lujan Approves Pequot Gaming Plans. Secretary of Interior Manuel Lujan approves a request from the Mashantucket Pequot to operate a

Edlore Quiver, Jr., the first Arapaho veteran to return from the Gulf War, is given a hero's welcome at the Riverton Airport in Riverton, Wyoming, by his family and the Arapaho Color Guard. (Photo by Sara Wiles)

gambling casino on tribal lands. Permission is granted under the terms of the 1988 Indian Gaming Regulatory Act, which permits Indian gaming if generally legal under state law. Connecticut state officials seek to block approval. The Pequot casino becomes the only casino on the East Coast besides the operations in Atlantic City, New Jersey.

14 June 1991 Bush Reaffirms Indian Self-Determination. President George Bush issues his policy statement on American Indians in which he reaffirms the government's commitment to the government-to-government relationship between the federal government and the Indian nations.

26 November 1991 National Monument Renamed. Congress passes a bill, after considerable debate, renaming the Custer Battlefield National Monument in eastern Montana as the Little Bighorn Battlefield Monument. At the Little Bighorn site in 1876, Colonel George

Armstrong Custer and more than 250 soldiers of the Seventh Cavalry lost a battle against allied groups of Lakota, Cheyenne, and Shoshone. This well publicized battle is often known as Custer's Last Stand.

December 1991 BIA Publication Reports Responsibilities. According to *American Indians Today*, a publication by the Bureau of Indian Affairs issued in the winter of 1991, the BIA is responsible in its trusteeship capacity for 278 reservations, comprising some 56.2 million acres. (The term *reservation* includes reservations, pueblos, rancherias, communities, and the like.)

The federal government's trusteeship responsibility extends to 510 federally recognized tribes, including about 200 village groups in Alaska. Since the establishment of the Federal Acknowledgment Program in 1978, the BIA has received 126 petitions for federal recognition; it extended recognition to eight Native communities and denied recognition to twelve. The U.S. Congress during this time legislatively recognized twelve previously unrecognized Native communities.

The same publication reports that the Bureau of Indian Affairs currently provides grants for the operation of twenty-two tribally controlled community colleges, enrolling approximately seven thousand students. The BIA further estimates that more than seventy thousand Indian students are attending colleges and universities. More than four hundred Indian students are known to be pursuing graduate or law degrees.

4 December 1991 Indian Self-Determination and Education Assistance Act Amended. Congress passes legislation to amend the Indian Self-Determination and Education Assistance Act. Entitled the Tribal Self-Governance Demonstration Project, the act extends the number of tribes taking part in the tribal self-governance pilot project from twenty to thirty.

1992 Native American Arts Council Hosts Indigenous Leaders Meeting. The Native American Council of New York City hosts a meeting of indigenous leaders for the United Nations opening of the Year of Indigenous Peoples that will begin in 1993. More than 250 delegates attend, including representatives of the aboriginal peoples of Australia, the Saami of Norway, the Mapuche from Chile, and the Nanentz from Russia. Delegates from the Iroquois, Sioux, Navajo, and Cree nations represent the indigenous people of North America.

Columbus Quincentennial. The Columbus Quincentennial focuses the nation's attention on American Indian contributions to the world as well as the injustices of Spain during the period of conquest. A planned voyage of replicas of Columbus's three ships, the *Nina*, *Pinta*, and *Santa Maria*, ends in bankruptcy.

Foxwoods Casino Opens. The same year, Foxwoods Casino, built by the Mashantucket Pequot Tribe opens in Ledyard, Connecticut. It quickly becomes the most profitable casino in the United States.

21 October 1992 PBS Broadcasts Documentary. The Public Broadcasting System (PBS) airs *Surviving Columbus*, a documentary produced in cooperation with KNME television in Albuquerque, New Mexico, and the Institute of American Indian Arts in Santa Fe. The two-hour special represents the Native American response to the Columbus Quincentennial, and traces Pueblo history from European contact to the present. Production includes an all-Indian crew consisting of Edmund Ladd, producer (Zuni); George Burdeau, co-executive producer (Blackfeet); Diane Reyna, director (Taos Pueblo); and Simon Ortiz, writer (Acoma Pueblo.)

November 1992 Campbell Elected to Senate. Ben Nighthorse Campbell, Northern Cheyenne, is elected to the U.S. Senate as a member of the Democratic Party. Campbell is the first Native American to serve in the Senate.

10 December 1992 UN Invites Indigenous Leaders to Headquarters. The secretary general of the United Nations (UN) welcomes more than 200 representatives of indigenous peoples to the New York City, UN headquarters. The representatives gather to mark 1993 as the International Year of Indigenous Peoples. For the first time, indigenous people are invited to address the UN General Assembly. The proceedings begin with a prayer offered by Avrol Looking Horse, keeper of the Lakota sacred pipe.

5 January 1993 Campbell Sworn in as Senator. Representative Ben Nighthorse Campbell becomes Senator Campbell when he and thirty-eight colleagues are sworn in as U.S. senators by Vice President Dan Quayle. Campbell, a Democrat, is the first American Indian to serve in the Senate in more than sixty years. Campbell represented Colorado's third congressional district for three terms before deciding to run for the Senate.

6 February 1993 First Annual Totem Awards. The First Annual Totem Awards are presented to outstanding Native American artists in film, television, theater, and music. The event is organized by First Americans in the Arts, a nonprofit organization dedicated to encouraging the participation of Native Americans in the entertainment industry. The dinner and awards ceremony is held in Beverly Hills, California. Recipients include John Trudell (Santee Sioux), Graham Greene (Oneida), Sheila Tousey (Menominee), Wes Studi (Cherokee), and Hanay Geiogamah (Kiowa).

27 February 1993 AIM Members Remember Wounded Knee II. Members of the American Indian Movement return to Wounded Knee where they waged a seventy-one-day occupation and armed conflict with federal authorities in February 1973. Accompanied by traditional songs and ceremony, several hundred AIM members and their supporters gather around the burial site of the Lakota people killed at Wounded Knee Creek in 1890.

March 1993 Apache Nation Attempts to Halt Telescope Project. The Apache Nation urges the University of Pittsburgh not to involve the school in a $60 million telescope project in Arizona. Raleigh Thompson (San Carlos Apache) informs Chancellor J. Dennis O'Connor that the proposed Columbus Project is being built on land considered sacred to the Apache people. The University of Pittsburgh stated that they had made no commitment to the Mount Graham project and have spent no money on it. "Our involvement in the Project doesn't exist at this time," Vice Chancellor Ben Tuchi says.

April 1993 American Indian Religious Freedom Act Amendments. Over 1,000 Indian people from thirteen states attend hearings at Augsburg College in Minneapolis, Minnesota, to hear testimony concerning proposed amendments to the American Indian Religious Freedom Act (AIRFA). The United States Senate Select Committee conducts field hearings for strengthening AIRFA. Tribal delegates urge greater protection of the Pipestone quarries, Native American airspace, return of the Black Hills to the Lakota Nation, and the repatriation of Native American sacred objects. John Sun Child, a tribal leader, expresses sorrow that laws are required to protect the religion given to the first people. Senator Dan Inouye states that "Eight hundred treaties were entered into by the U.S. government. My predecessors examined and ratified 370. I'm sad to report EVERY treaty was violated."

3 June 1993 First Native American Film Festival. "Wind and Glacier Voices: The Native American Film and Media Celebration" opens at the Lincoln Center for the Performing Arts in New York City. It is the first film festival showcasing works produced solely by the American and Canadian Indian community. The five-day event includes an awards ceremony honoring Native filmmakers and performers, panel discussions on contemporary Indian issues, and daily screenings of independent films. The festival highlights key Indian filmmakers and their works.

17 June 1993 Gabrielino Protest Building on Sacred Land. The American Civil Liberties Union joins Native Americans in opposing California State University, Long Beach's plan to build a mini-mall and parking lot on a location considered sacred by many southern California Indians. Members of the Gabrielino Indians and other California tribes argue that that the university is built on the remains of Puvungna village, a spiritual center that was the birthplace of Chinigchinix, the founder of the Luiseño-Cahuilla religion. Cindi Alvitre, cultural educator of the Gabrielino-Tongva tribal youth council, said the Native Americans oppose the university's proposal for further study. "We want people to understand that we are not just 'malcontented ethnics' crying for public attention," she said. "Puvungna is where our creator. . . had his funeral. Our cry is the same you would hear if someone came to dig Jesus out of his tomb to assess his cultural significance."

June–July 1993 Hanta Virus Takes Indian Lives. During the months of June and July, the Hanta virus, a rodent-borne disease, is responsible for the deaths of sixteen Indian people, primarily Navajo, in the Four Corners region of the southwestern United States. Initially specialists from the Indian Health Service in Albuquerque, New Mexico, stated, "We don't know what causes it." Guided in part by Navajo medicine men, researchers soon traced the contagion to the deer mice, the cotton rat, the white-footed mice, and possibly the rice mice. While the disease is first thought to be concentrated in the southwestern United States, it is now known that it exists in over one-half of U.S. states.

July 1993 Clinton Appoints Deer Secretary of Indian Affairs. Following confirmation hearings, the U.S. Senate confirms Ada Elizabeth Deer (Menominee) as President William Jefferson Clinton's choice for Secretary of Indian Affairs in the U.S. Department of the Interior. She is the first woman, and the sixth Indian, to fill the post.

9–10 July 1993 Ortiz Presented with Lifetime Achievement Award. The Native Writers' Circle of the Americas presents a lifetime achievement award to Simon J. Ortiz at the 1993 international Returning the Gift conference, attended by nearly 400 Native American poets, fiction writers, and playwrights. His published works include *Fightin': New and Collected Stories* and *Woven Stone.*

10 July 1993 Cheyenne Remains Buried. The remains of eighteen Cheyenne people are buried at the Concho, Oklahoma Cemetery after more than 125 years in the collections of the Army Medical Museum and the Smithsonian's National Museum of Natural History. The remains were repatriated under the provisions of the Native American Graves Protection and Repatriation Act of 1990. Five sets of the remains were collected by the U.S. Army following the Sand Creek Massacre of 1864 led by Colonel John Chivington.

7 August 1993 Deer Sworn in as BIA Head. Ada Deer, a Menominee and alumna of the University of Wisconsin-Madison and Columbia University, is sworn in as the new head of the U.S. Bureau of Indian Affairs. During the inauguration ceremony, tribal leaders from across the country praise her and present her with gifts. At a news conference, Deer states that she wants Native American communities to have more autonomy in the use of BIA funding.

28 August 1993 Sac and Fox Declare Nuclear Free Zone. The Sac and Fox Nation becomes the first tribe in Oklahoma to declare a Nuclear Free Zone (NFZ) on their tribal lands. Mary Black Osborn, chairman of the Sac and Fox Nation's health commission and a registered nurse said, "As a nurse, I am probably more aware of the threats to our environment. If the environment is contaminated or polluted, we in the health field are treating symptoms instead of getting at the real problem." The Sac and Fox join several other tribes in North American that have declared their lands to be nuclear free. The Inuit of Alaska appealed to the United Nations to establish a NFZ in the arctic in 1981.

15 October 1993 Senate Approves Study of Uranium Health Effects. The United States Senate authorizes a study on how uranium milling and mining has affected the health of Navajo and others involved in such work over a thirty-year period. The study will focus on the health effects of uranium milling that took place primarily on or near the Navajo reservation from the late 1940s through 1971.

15 October 1993 Cuomo Signs Gaming Compact with Mohawk. New York Governor Mario Cuomo signs a gaming compact with the Mohawk Nation, clearing the way for the state's second legal casino. The Mohawk Casino will offer roulette and blackjack games, but not slot machines. Under the negotiated compact, New York State police will have unlimited access to the casino, as will officials from the state Racing and Wagering Board. No alcohol will be allowed in the facility.

27 October 1993 Catawba Indian Land Claim Settlement Act. President Clinton signs the Catawba Indian Land Claim Settlement Act of 1993, restoring the Catawba Tribe's government-to-government relationship with the United States and ending the 153 years of conflict with the state of South Carolina. The act provides a total of $30 to $40 million in benefits and contributions and a payment of $50 million over five years from federal, state, and local governments and private contributors. These funds will be placed in trust for land acquisition, economic development, education, and social services for the Catawba Tribe.

28 October 1993 Lumbee Receive Federal Recognition. The House of Representatives voted to recognize the Lumbee Tribe of Cheraw Indians of North Carolina, consisting of 40,000 members. After filing for federally recognized status with the Interior Department, Lumbee Indians can adopt a constitution and bylaws. However, the tribe is not entitled to federal services provided by the Bureau of Indian Affairs and the Indian Health Service until Congress appropriates funds for that purpose. Although the state of North Carolina recognized the Lumbee Indians as a tribe

in 1885, the Interior Department opposed numerous congressional bills for granting the Lumbee federal recognition.

November 1993 Milk Creek Battle Memorial Erected. Approximately 1,000 people gathered in Meeker, Colorado, to honor the Ute warriors who died at the Battle of Milk Creek in 1879. This is the nation's first memorial dedicated to Native Americans and erected by Native people. According to Clifford Duncan, an elder of the Uintah-Ouray Ute tribe of Utah, the Ute people have been invisible in U.S. history books. This memorial provides an opportunity for the Ute to voice their own version of the Milk Creek battle.

22–23 November 1993 Spiritual Leaders Meet to Discuss Environmental Issues. American Indian spiritual leaders from the four directions gather at the United Nations to share ancient Native prophecies warning of environmental destruction of the natural world at a historic conference called Cry of the Earth, the Legacy of First Nations. Religious leaders from the Algonquin, Lakota, Hopi, Iroquois, Micmac, Huichol, and Mayan nations deliver powerful messages handed down by oral tradition. Warning that the world is on the brink of self-destruction, Leon Shenandoah, Tadadaho of the Six Nations Iroquois Confederacy states, "Our instructions says that the end of the world will be near when the trees start dying from the tops down—that's what the maples are doing today." The conference was preceded by the Iroquois Confederacy's ceremonial planting of a Tree of Peace in New York's Central Park.

27 November 1993 Black Kettle Descendants Honor Ancestors. Descendants of Cheyenne Chief Black Kettle and approximately 100 tribal members who perished when George Armstrong Custer attacked their sleeping encampment 125 years ago, honored their ancestors with songs and chants during a memorial service. Tribal members in traditional dress sing as replicas of Cheyenne burial gifts are placed on a cottonwood burial scaffold. Most Cheyenne killed were women and children.

30 November 1993 George Posthumously Awarded Medal of Honor. Charles George is posthumously awarded the Congressional Medal of Honor. George was a rifleman in Company C of the 179th Infantry Regiment of the 45th Infantry Division during the Korean War. On 30 November 1952, George threw himself on an enemy hand grenade to save the lives of his comrades. A bronze bust of George is atop the center marker of the Tribal Veterans Monument in Cherokee, North Carolina. The citation that accompanies the Medal of Honor states that "While in the process of

Students at the Arapaho School play the traditional shinny game with willow sticks and leather balls during Heritage Day activities. (Photo by Sara Wiles)

leaving the trenches a hostile enemy soldier hurled a hand grenade into their midst. Private George shouted a warning to one comrade, pushed the other out of danger and with full knowledge of the consequences unhesitatingly threw himself upon the grenade absorbing the full blast of the explosion."

December 1993 Mankiller Releases Autobiography. Wilma Mankiller, Cherokee Nation Principal Chief, tours throughout American cities to promote her autobiography, *Mankiller: A Chief and Her People*, co-authored by Michael Wallis. Mankiller's autobiography recalls her early years as well as some contemporary history of Cherokee.

9 December 1993 Dann Sisters Receive Right Livelihood Award. Carrie and Mary Dann receive the 1993 Right Livelihood Award, known as the alternative Nobel Peace Prize. According to the Right Livelihood Foundation, the Dann sisters are honored for "their courage and perseverance in asserting the rights of indigenous people to their land." Accompanying

this honor is a $200,000 award that the sisters will share with three other women from Israel, Zimbabwe, and India.

17–18 December 1993 AIM Chapters Meet to Restructure. Several American Indian Movement chapters meet in New Mexico to discuss chapter autonomy, the restructuring of AIM, and schedule a tribunal to hear testimony on the alleged disruptive activities of AIM leadership.

1994 Blackgoat Named America's Unsung Woman. Roberta Blackgoat, Navajo, is named America's Unsung Woman by the National Women's History Project for her twenty-year leadership in the environmental and human rights struggle on Black Mesa and the relocation of 12,000 Navajo.

14–24 January 1994 Natives Travel to Rome for Festival. Native American performers and scholars

The Dann sisters, Carrie (l.) and Mary (r.) have fought a decades-long battle for grazing rights. (Photo by Ilka Hartmann)

travel to Rome to participate in the festival "The Feather, The Flute, The Drum," featuring music, dance, and storytelling performances; an art installation; video programs; a panel discussion of history and culture; and demonstrations of herb-use and cooking. The festival begins with a traditional procession and prayer led by Ken Ryan, Assiniboine spiritual leader. Other participants include Litefoot, a Cherokee musician; Kevin Locke, a renowned Lakota flutist and hoop dancer; Sharon Burch, a Navajo musician; and Sara Batges, a Cherokee visual artist.

19 January 1994 Native American Studies Approved at University of Oklahoma.   After months of negotiation and community pressure, the Oklahoma State Board of Regents approves a Native American Studies Program at the University of Oklahoma. As an interdisciplinary program it offers students a wide range of courses, including fine arts, anthropology, and sociology. Students may use the program to work with Native American community organizations or perform library and museum work.

February 1994 Appeals Court Upholds MacDonald Conviction.   A federal appeals court upholds the convictions of former Navajo tribal chairman Peter MacDonald on charges of taking bribes to steer a tribal loan to business associates. MacDonald was chairman of the Navajo Nation in 1971–1983 and 1987–1989. He was convicted in 1992 of racketeering, fraud, and related charges. MacDonald is serving a five-year prison sentence and an additional tribal jail term concurrently with a fourteen-year sentence for a conspiracy conviction in a 1989 riot at tribal headquarters that left two dead and five injured.

1–4 February 1994 Mescalero Apache Sign Nuclear Waste Agreement.   The Mescalero Apache, one of more than fifty tribes approached by the U.S. government, sign a multimillion-dollar nuclear-waste storage planning agreement with the federal government. They are the only tribe to do so and the agreement was reached despite a tribal referendum that defeated the proposed nuclear-storage dump. A second referendum passed by a narrow margin.

7 February 1994 Clinton's Budget Plan Proposes BIA Cuts. The Clinton administration's 1995 budget plan proposes significant cuts in three BIA economic development grant programs. The $2.5 million direct loan program, $4.3 million in technical assistance grants, and $1.4 million for special tribal courts funding are scheduled to be eliminated. According to BIA spokesman Carl Shaw, the direct loan program is a failure because it has experienced a 70 percent default rate. Ada Deer, assistant secretary for Indian affairs, says that the administration's budget proposal continues the transfer of resources from the BIA to tribal government and Indian trust relationship.

11 February 1994 Wisconsin Winnebago Purchases Land. With cash from casino profits, the Wisconsin Winnebago Nation purchases approximately 600 acres of land on the Wisconsin River for $1.2 million. Winnebago elders and others are convinced that the land was once the site of a Winnebago village and contained at least sixty-four sculptured earthen mounds that have spiritual significance in Winnebago culture. The Winnebago plan to locate and mark all sites of the original mounds. With the approval of Winnebago elders, some of the mounds may be restored to their original size and shape. The purchased land will also be used for the construction of a cultural center, a youth camp, prairie restoration, and a buffalo farm.

11 February–3 April 1994 Teters Exhibits Stereotypes. Charlene Teters, Spokane, creates a thought-provoking exhibit, "It was Only an Indian: Native American Stereotypes," that explores how Native Americans have been and continue to be objectified and dehumanized in popular culture. Teters exposes racism toward Native Americans by asking: What does it mean to be the brunt of stereotyping? How would you feel to be examined, probed, and mocked in this manner? Why does this continue to be acceptable? For several years Teters has collected and studied apparently innocuous objects such as Indian head cigarette ashtrays, toilet paper, and potbellied Indian planters, all of which promote stereotyping. Teters works as a placement and alumni director for the Institute of American Indian Arts in Santa Fe, while continuing to actively place racism under public scrutiny.

11 February–15 July 1994 Walk for Justice. AIM co-founders Dennis Banks and Mary Jan Wilson-Medrano lead a Walk for Justice from Alcatraz Island in California to Washington, D.C., bringing public attention to Native issues and collecting signatures requesting executive clemency for Leonard Peltier, who has served eighteen years in prison for allegedly shooting two FBI agents on the Pine Ridge Reservation in South Dakota

in 1975. Other issues brought to public attention by the walk are the James Bay Great Whale Project, where an expanding hydraulic dam threatens fishing and hunting rights of the Cree and Ojibwa tribes; the fishing treaty rights struggle in Wisconsin; continued nuclear testing which is destroying water, land, and health for the Western Shoshone in Nevada; the Dann family's (Shoshone) conflict over land and treaty rights with the Bureau of Land Management; the Big Mountain issue involving involuntary relocation of Navajo from disputed land with the Hopi; and the return of the Black Hills to the Lakota people.

March 1994 NCAI Supports Black Caucus. The National Congress of American Indians (NCAI), a confederation of 162 tribal governments and the nation's oldest and largest Indian organization, agrees to support the Black Caucus of State Legislators, a caucus of 540 African American state legislators from forty-two states in their struggles for African-American rights. In December 1993, the Black Caucus of State Legislators passed a similar resolution to support Native American tribal sovereignty. Both groups agree that since they share similar histories of economic and political oppression in the United States, they need to build coalition networks to fight for basic economic and human rights.

9 March 1994 Indian Students Receive Scholarships, Internships. Greg Powderface, a Gros Ventres graduate student at the Stanford University School of Business, and Wendy Wisdom, a Hopi, Choctaw, and Chickasaw third-year college student majoring in social welfare and Native American Studies, are winners of a scholarship and internship program sponsored by Columbia Pictures and Sony Pictures Entertainment in connection with Columbia Pictures' December 1993 release of *Geronimo: An American Legend*. They, along with several hundred American Indian college student applicants, submitted an essay addressing the question, "How can the media better highlight and honor American Indian culture and heritage?" The program provides summer 1994 internship employment in the Columbia Pictures marketing department and a $2,500 scholarship to each winner.

11 March 1994 Roessel Appointed Deputy Assistant Secretary for Indian Affairs. Faith Roessel, a member of the Navajo Nation and former staff attorney with the Native American Rights Fund (NARF), is appointed deputy assistant secretary for Indian affairs. In her new post, Roessel continues her work of assisting tribal governments in their efforts to protect Indian trust assets.

Tommy White and Baillie wait outside the Wind River Reservation Museum in Wyoming. (Photo by Sara Wiles)

21 March 1994 Mole Lake Chippewa Lose Legal Battle. The Mole Lake Chippewa tribe loses its eight-year legal battle to regain rights to a 144-square-mile area in northeast Wisconsin. The U.S. Supreme Court refuses to consider their claims regarding nineteenth century treaties. The Mole Lake Chippewa state that they never surrendered the disputed land, most of which is now claimed by Exxon Corporation. The tribe sues Exxon in federal court contending that the tribe never surrendered rights received in the 1842 treaty.

21 March 1994 Clinton Meets with Tribal Leaders. President Clinton invites leaders of all 545 federally recognized American Indian and Alaska Native tribes to the White House. President Clinton hosts the tribal leaders at the White House April 29. Attorney General Janet Reno and Interior Secretary Bruce Babbitt travel to Albuquerque, New Mexico, where they meet with tribal leaders on May 5 and 6. Tribal leaders are concerned because President Clinton had made promising statements to Indian people during his bid for the presidency but later said that he wanted to spend less money on Indian health care.

29 April 1994 Clinton Signs Directives. President William Clinton welcomes more than 300 leaders of federally recognized Indian Nations to the White House. Clinton signs two directives before the tribal leaders, one of which was directed to every executive department instructing them to cooperate with tribal governments to accommodate "wherever possible" the need for eagle feathers in the practice of Native religions. The other document directed every executive department and agency of government to remove all barriers that inhibit cooperative relations with tribal governments and to make certain if they take action affecting tribal trust resources they consult with tribal governments before that decision.

10 May 1994 Crazy Horse Malt Liquor Banned. Minnesota Governor Arne Carlson signed into law a bill banning the sale of Crazy Horse malt liquor in the state. This bill makes Minnesota the second state to ban the sale of Crazy Horse beer. A coalition of groups, including members of the American Indian Movement, Honor Our Neighbors Origins and Rights, and the National Coalition on Racism in Sports and the Media,

President Bill Clinton meets with BIA officials. (Photo by Carol Lujan)

spearheaded the passage of the bill. Seth Big Crow Sr., a distant relative of the Sioux leader Crazy Horse, said the "It's monumental to us that there's a group of people out there who believe in doing what is right."

13 June 1994 *Department of Taxation and Finance of New York et al. v. Milhelm Attea & Brothers, Inc. et al.* In *Department of Taxation and Finance of New York et al. v. Milhelm Attea & Brothers, Inc. et al.*, the United States Supreme Court holds that a state tax scheme to collect taxes on cigarettes sold on Indian reservations does not improperly burden Indian trading and does not violate the Indian Trader Statutes.

15 July 1994 Walk for Justice Reaches Washington, D.C. The Walk for Justice that began on Alcatraz Island on 11 February 1994 reaches its destination at the Lincoln Memorial in Washington, D.C. AIM co-founders Dennis Banks and Mary Jan Wilson-Medrano lead the walk. Hundreds of Native American people gather at Ladybird Johnson Park in Arlington, Virginia, to finish the last miles of the five month, 3,800-mile journey that began on Alcatraz Island. The purpose of the Walk for Justice was to bring public attention to Native issues including violation of treaty rights, grave desecration, nuclear waste dumping, and Native prisoner rights.

15 July 1994 FBI Agents Run Ad in *Washington Post.* A group representing 15,000 past and present FBI special agents run an advertisement in *The Washington Post* urging President Clinton to refuse the request for clemency for Leonard Peltier presented by organizers and supporters of The Walk For Justice, which ended in Washington, D.C. FBI Director Louis J. Freeh issues a statement stating that "Peltier's guilt has been firmly established." The advertisement in *The Washington Post* states that "Leonard Peltier is a vicious, violent and cowardly criminal who hides behind legitimate Native American issues."

20 August 1994 White Buffalo Born in Northern Plains. News of the birth of a rare white buffalo is spreading among American Indians, inspiring pilgrimages to the Wisconsin farm where it was born.

The buffalo calf, named Miracle is the first white buffalo born in more than fifty years. The white buffalo is particularly sacred to the Cheyenne, Sioux, and other Indian Nations of the Northern Plains that once relied on the buffalo for sustenance.

5 September 1994 Tlingits Banished for Crime. Andrian Guthrie and Simon Roberts, both Tlingits, are banished to separate uninhabited islands by a Tlingit tribal court for beating and robbing a pizza delivery man. Over the objection of prosecutors in a Washington State courtroom, the Tlingit rendered a decision for banishment. Tribal members made reparation payments to the victims of the crimes and their families, including building them a new home. Four elders accompanied the boys to the island to instruct them in subsistence hunting and fishing skills. A considerable amount of food was provided as well. Guthrie and Roberts were ultimately returned to the state court system for punishment. The boys arranged for others to bring them supplies, and they were seen leaving the islands. The boys disobeyed the tribal council and were returned to the state court, which sentenced them to three-and-a-half to five-and-a-half years in prison.

21 September 1994 Clinton Recognizes Three Michigan Tribal Communities. President Clinton signs legislation awarding federally recognized tribal status to three Michigan Indian communities. The two bills signed by the president recognize the Pokagon Band of the Potawatomi, the Little River Band of Ottawa, and the Little Traverse Bay Band of Ottawa. The legislation excluded all three bands from federal benefits and services. All three bands signed nineteenth-century treaties ceding Michigan land to the federal government.

2 October 1994 Monument to American Indian Civil War Veterans Dedicated. A monument honoring American Indian Civil War veterans is dedicated on the Iowa Reservation near White Cloud, Kansas. The names of forty-nine Indian soldiers serving with the Fourteenth Calvary of the Union Army are inscribed on the monument.

5 October 1994 Tribal Colleges Awarded Land Grant Status. In legislation passed by the House and the Senate, tribal colleges are awarded land grant status. Jack Briggs, president of the Fond du Lack Tribal and Community College, stated that "It's ironic that Indians were the first people of the land, and the last to receive land-grant status." Research conducted in support of land grant status revealed that tribal colleges receive approximately $3,000 per student

through federal sources while the national average is $7,000 per student.

24 October 1994 Tribal Self-Governance Act. President Clinton signs the Tribal Self-Governance Act into law. The act gives permanent self-governance status to the twenty-eight Indian Nations participating in the Self-Governance Demonstration Project. The project was a tribal initiative intended to allow Indian nations greater flexibility and control in meeting the needs of their communities while preserving the trust responsibility of the federal government. The act permits the Department of the Interior to increase the number of tribes participating in self-governance by up to twenty each year.

25 October 1994 National Museum of the American Indian Opens. The National Museum of the American Indian (NMAI) opens an exhibition hall at the Customs House in lower Manhattan in New York City. The George W. Heye Museum, the first of three planned NMAI museum locations, opens to the general public starting on Sunday, October 30.

31 October 1994 American Indian Radio Network Begins Programming. An American Indian radio network linking twenty-five tribal radio stations begins regular programming. AIROS, American Indian Radio on Satellite, will offer a storytelling series as well as interviews with Native Americans, historical specials, and a multi-part series on breaking the cycle of child abuse. Network officials hope to eventually expand into a twenty-four-hour format. The twenty-five stations are located in ten states.

December 1994 Ho Chunk Nation Receives BIA Approval. The Wisconsin Winnebago Tribe has received final approval from the Bureau of Indian Affairs to change its name to Ho Chunk Nation. The name was chosen as part of the tribe's new constitution, which was given final approval by the BIA. The Ho Chunk Nation has 4,900 members, most living in Wisconsin, Illinois, and Minnesota.

1995 Pequot Add Land to Reservation. The U.S. Department of the Interior issues a decision to allow the Mashantucket Pequot to add 247 non-taxable acres to their reservation. Opponents of the decision argued that the Pequot were the "world's richest Indian tribe grossing nearly $1 billion a year." The tribe's highly successful Foxwoods Resorts Casino draws nearly 50,000 visitors a day. The tribe also pays the state of Connecticut millions of dollars a year from slot machine profits for exclusive gaming rights. This year the Pequot are expected to pay $130 million to the state.

Department of Interior officials and Pueblo officials. (Photo by Carol Lujan)

15 January 1995 Global Peace Walk Begins. The United Nations Fiftieth Anniversary Global Peace Walk begins in New York City. As the walkers pass through the Navajo Reservation, Albert Hale, president of the Navajo Nation, states, "World peace is a noble effort that everyone should aim for." Miss Navajo Nation Karen Leupp joins the small group of national and international walkers.

31 January 1995 Mescalero Apache Reject Nuclear Waste Proposal. The Mescalero Apache vote 490 to 362 to reject a planning grant of $10 million to consider hosting a nuclear waste disposal site on their reservation. Proponents argued the proposal ultimately promised about $250 million for schools and capital for diversifying Mescalero Apache businesses. Opponents argue that the site would endanger the environment and the people living on and around the 461,000-acre reservation.

March 1995 Indians Protest Desecration of Sacred Devil's Tower. American Indians petition the federal government to ban climbers on Devil's Tower located in the northeast corner of Wyoming. Indian leaders say that the 860-foot-high monolith is a sacred site where Indian people have traveled to seek religious visions and leave prayer bundles of tobacco and sage. Indians say that climbers are desecrating a sacred site by riveting its face with climbing bolts and urinating on its walls. They also state that increased climbing and tourism interferes with their ability to communicate with the Great Spirit. National park officials have created a task force of climbers, American Indians, and local officials to arrive at a management policy agreeable to all sides. Monument officials hope to have a joint plan implemented by 1996 that would allow a voluntary climbing ban each June when important Indian ceremonies are celebrated.

3 June 1995 St. Regis Elects Smoke Chief. The Mohawk of the St. Regis Reservation in northern New York elect Douglas Smoke as their chief. Smoke opposed gaming on the Akwesasne Reservation. A new written constitution is approved as well and the new chiefs replace a three-chief system. There is an executive branch which includes a chief executive officer and vice chief, a legislative branch consisting of a five-member council, and a judicial branch.

5 June 1995 National Native-Focused Radio Show Begins. "Native America Calling" is the first national call-in radio program devoted to American Indians and hosted by the Public Broadcasting Consortium and the Alaska Public Radio Network. The program informs people about Indian issues and is broadcast out of the University of New Mexico, which helps produce the program. The hour-long show is broadcast Monday through Friday and is distributed via the American Indian Radio on Satellite Network for play on twenty-nine Indian-owned stations in twelve states.

July 1995 Kennedy Visits Menominee Nation. Robert F. Kennedy, Jr., son of the former U.S. attorney general, visits the Menominee Nation to discuss forestry practices with members of the Canadian Nuu-chah-nulth and Menominee Tribal Enterprises delegation. Kennedy recognizes the Menominee Nation for its sustainable forestry practices. The Nuu-chah-nulth is a consortium of fourteen tribes in the Clayoquot Sound area of Canada and is interested in the Menominee program as a model for its own resource preservation program.

Also at this time, the Makah Tribe of Neah Bay, Washington, announces plans to resume their traditional whale harvest. The tribe seeks to harvest up to five whales for ceremonial and subsistence purposes starting in 1996.

22 July 1995 Harjo Receives Lifetime Achievement Award. Joy Harjo, Muscogee (Creek) poet, receives the fourth annual Lifetime Achievement Award from the Native Writer's Circle of the Americas. Harjo receives the award in person at the Oklahoma Memorial Union, University of Oklahoma. Harjo is a professor at the University of New Mexico and is the author of a number of volumes of poetry that have helped to inspire an entire generation of young Native poets.

August 1995 Native American Prep School Opens. The Native American Preparatory School (NAPS) located in the Pecos River Valley, east of Santa Fe, New Mexico, opens as a residential college-preparatory high school. NAPS is dedicated to nurturing the intellectual, ethical, and leadership potential of Indian students.

9 August 1995 International Indigenous Day Honored at UN. International Indigenous Day is honored at the UN. Delphine Red Shirt, Lakota, conducts the World Sacred Pipe Ceremony to honor the first observance of the World's Indigenous People on the grounds of the United Nations Building in New York City.

12 September 1995 One Mind One Voice Prayer Vigil Held. Native Americans hold a One Mind, One Voice, One Prayer Vigil on the Mall near the Washington Monument in Washington, D.C. Indian representatives from tribes from across the nation gather on Capital Hill to protest proposed cuts in federal spending for the BIA, Indian education, and other Indian social programs. Vice President Al Gore states that President Clinton will veto the Department of Interior Bill because of the proposed cuts.

November 1995 Construction Begins on Replacement Fishing Sites. Ground is broken on the first of thirty-one sites intended to be replacements for fishing sites flooded by the Bonneville Dam. The initial 7.8-acre site on the Columbia River's north side will have a campground, drying sheds, water, and sanitation facilities. Treaties between the federal government and Columbia River Nations—Nez Percé, Umatilla, Warm Springs, and Yakama—guaranteed the right to fish at their usual places along the river. Many of these fishing sites were flooded when the massive dams were built.

8 November 1995 Indian Dance Stamps Unveiled. American Indian dance stamp series is announced. Arlin Humeyumptewa, Hopi, a Denver postal clerk, joins with the Denver Postmaster Michael Flores in unveiling the upcoming issue of the American Indian Dance stamp. The stamps, which depict five dance styles are slated to be available for purchase in 1996.

13–15 November 1995 Tribal Leadership Summit. More than 200 tribal and federal natural resource managers, tribal leaders, and representatives from national intertribal natural-resource oriented organizations attend the first Tribal Leadership Summit on Government Relationship and Management of Indian Trust/Natural Resources held in Denver, Colorado. The summit was organized by ten national intertribal natural resource oriented organizations in response to President Clinton's executive order to enhance intergovernmental partnerships. Tribal leaders expressed their views on treaties with the U.S. government and agreed that the government is ignoring treaty obligations. A follow-up meeting is planned in early 1996 to begin addressing the recommendations of the summit.

1996 Native American Free Exercise of Religion Act. Native American Free Exercise of Religion Act is introduced in Congress. The act is designed to negate the Supreme Court ruling that interferes with the free practice of religion by members of the Native American Church and to strengthen religious rights as set out in the earlier American Indian Religious Freedom Act.

January 1996 *In re Bridget R.* The California Second District Court of Appeals in the case *In re Bridget R.*, rules against Richard and Cindy Adams of Long Beach, California, who put their twin daughters Bridget and Lucy up for adoption in November 1993, shortly after they were born. The Adams claim descent from the California Dry Creek Pomo Indian tribe, and claim that the children are approximately one-eighth Pomo. When the children were four months old, the Adams changed their minds and petitioned to have their children returned under provisions of the Indian Child Welfare Act of 1978. Stating that the birth parents appeared to have "no connection, nor ties. . . and apparently no interest at all" in their tribes, the Court of Appeals rules that the Ohio couple who adopted the children could keep the children, thus applying a new interpretation of the ICWA. John Dodd, an attorney for the adoptive parents states that, "essentially, the court approved a new concept of law, what has now become known as the Existing Indian Family doctrine." This interpretation means that the biological parents have to have a meaningful social, cultural, or political relationship with the tribe in order for ICWA to hold any meaning. ICWA contains no such language or provision.

27 March 1996 *Seminole Tribe of Florida v. Florida et al.* In *Seminole Tribe of Florida v. Florida et al.*, the United States Supreme Court finds that states may not be sued by Indian nations even when the states does not negotiate gaming compacts in good faith according to the Indian Gaming Regulatory Act (IGRA). IGRA imposes upon the states an obligation to negotiate in good faith with an Indian tribe toward the formation of a compact and authorizes a tribe to bring suit in federal court against a state for failure to negotiate a compact. The Court holds that IGRA does not supersede a state's right to sovereign immunity, which protects states from lawsuits by their citizens.

5 July 1996 NARF Files Suit against Federal Departments. A class action suit representing 300,000 American Indians is filed in federal court today against the Bureau of Indian Affairs, the United States Treasury, and the Department of the Interior. The suit, filed by the Native American Rights Fund (NARF), alleges that the BIA has mishandled $450 million in revenues from mineral leases on lands held in trust for Indians. This amount is later raised to $2.5 billion. The suit further alleges that no accurate records were kept of the monies collected, and that funds were illegally diverted to other projects.

14 July 1997 Documentary Awarded Golden Apple. Jay Rosenstein's documentary *In Whose Honor?* is named a Golden Apple Award Winner by the National Educational Media Network, the leading organization for educational videos. *In Whose Honor?* highlights Charlene Teters' efforts to eliminate the Chief Illiniwek mascot used by the University of Illinois at Urbana-Champaign.

10 November 1997 Wauneka Dies. Annie Dodge Wauneka, the first woman elected to the Navajo Tribal Council, dies. Wauneka was born in the Navajo Nation near Sawmill, Arizona, and received a bachelor of science degree in public health from the University of Arizona. She was active in the Navajo Tribal Council Health Committee, and hosted a biweekly radio show on KGAK in Gallup. Wauneka also served as a board member of the National Tuberculosis Association and was appointed to the Surgeon General's Advisory Board.

1998 Campbell Introduces Legislation to Identify Sand Creek Massacre Site. Republican Senator Ben Nighthorse Campbell introduces legislation directing the National Park Service to identify the location of the 1864 Sand Creek Massacre. The legislation is signed into law on 6 October 1998.

5 September 1998 Skeletal Remains Found at Oil Refinery. California state officials search for the living descendants of several prehistoric skeletal remains found at the ARCO oil refinery in Carson, California, earlier this month. Workers stumbled across the human skeletal remains while draining water from a sixty-foot by sixty-foot trench. The water caused the sides of the four-foot-deep trench to slough off, exposing the remains. A forensic expert from the Los Angeles County coroner's office determined that the remains were over 1,000 years old and appeared to belong to five humans. A spokesperson from the coroner's office said that the site appeared to be a Native American burial ground.

3 November 1998 Proposition 5 Passes. California voters approve Proposition 5, the Tribal Government Gaming and Economic Self-Sufficiency Act of 1998 by a margin of 62.6 percent to 37.4 percent. Approximately $96 million is spent by both sides, $58 million by California Indian tribes supporting the initiative, and $30 million by Nevada casino interests. The initiative effort for Proposition 5 was organized and conducted

Schoolchildren visit the Assistant Secretary of Interior in Washington, D.C. (Courtesy of Carol Lujan)

by an Indian political coalition named Californians for Indian Self-Reliance, which seeks to obtain a gaming compact with the state of California by means of a state-wide referendum vote, since California state officials will not provide a satisfactory agreement to the California Indian nations.

25 February 1999 Timbisha Shoshone, Federal Agencies Agree to Park Partnership. The Timbisha Shoshone strike an agreement with the federal agencies to serve as partners in the management of a 3.2 million-acre national park. The Timbisha Shoshone have been largely exiled from their traditional homelands in Death Valley since 1933, when Death Valley was added to the National Park System.

June 1999 Sand Creek Massacre Site Identified. Historians and archeologists working with the National Park Service locate the site of the 1864 Sand Creek Massacre. Over 300 artifacts, including shell fragments from artillery used to bombard the Indians, are found. Other artifacts include cooking pot fragments, tin cups, eating utensils, arrowheads, and personal items. A

special resource study that includes future management plans for the site is scheduled for release in October 1999.

6 December 1999 Court Master Blames Treasury Department for Mismanagement of Documents. A special court master blames senior Treasury Department officials for allowing the destruction of 162 boxes of documents that could have helped resolve the claims of thousands of Native Americans who say the government has mismanaged billions of dollars in trust funds it was holding for them in trust. The destruction of these documents is the latest development in a long-running class-action lawsuit against the government filed on behalf of 300,000 Native Americans.

11 December 1999 Class-Action Suit Concludes. U.S. District Judge Royce C. Lamberth calls the government's century-old mismanagement of Indian trust fund money inexcusable. Judge Lamberth pledges to oversee reform of a program that will pay thousands of Native Americans as much as $2.5 billion in royalties. This action caps the largest class-action lawsuit in history against the federal government. Judge Lamberth will require quarterly progress reports from the secretary of the interior and the Bureau of Indian Affairs for as long as five years for trust fund accounting. The trust fund, which affects Native Americans in every state west of the Mississippi River, was established in the 1830s during the administration of Andrew Jackson.

2000 NARF Files Suit against Babbitt, Rubin. The Native American Rights Fund files a class action lawsuit against Bruce Babbitt, secretary of the interior, and Robert Rubin, U.S. treasury secretary, for mismanagement of tribal trust funds. In an audit conducted by the Arthur Andersen accounting firm, the BIA is unable to account for over $2.4 billion in Indian trust fund accounts.

27 January 2000 Clinton Honors Commitment to Native Americans. President Clinton honors America's commitments to Native Americans. In his State of the Union Address, President Clinton states that "I also... [want] to make special efforts to address the areas of our nation with the highest rates of poverty— our Native American reservations and the Mississippi Delta. My budget includes. . . a billion dollars to increase economic opportunity, health care, education and law enforcement for our Native American communities."

8 February 2000 Campbell Calls for Hate-Crime Investigation. Senator Ben Campbell calls on the Department of Justice to launch a hate-crimes investigation into a newspaper advertisement announcing the start of "Indian Hunting Season." The advertisement, which ran in a South Dakota newspaper, is intended to look like a real hunting season announcement. The C.E. declares open season on the Sioux reservations, sets a limit of ten kills per day, and mentions other regulations for where and in what manner Indians may be killed.

11 February 2000 Land Returned to Northern Ute. Utah state, federal, and tribal officials sign an agreement that will return 84,000 acres to the Northern Ute tribe as part of an agreement to clean up tons of uranium waste leaking into the Colorado River. Called the biggest federal return of Indian land in U.S. history, the land was reclaimed by the Ute in 1882 but taken again in 1916 on the eve of the U.S. entry into World War I to create a reserve supply of oil for the U.S. Navy fleet. Under the agreement to return the land, one-half of the estimated $300 million cleanup cost will be absorbed by the federal government. The Ute will pay an estimated $80 million to $100 million toward the cleanup

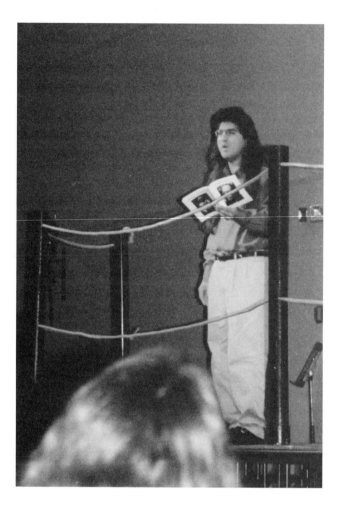

Sherman Alexie (Spokane/Coeur d'Alene) reading poetry. (Photo by Carol Lujan)

and provide added protection to the seventy-five miles of the Green River, which forms the reservation's western boundary.

25 February 2000 Clinton Calls for Passage of Native American Initiative. President Clinton calls for passage of his historic Fiscal Year 2001 Native American Initiative. The president is joined by tribal and congressional leaders, who call for passage of his $9.4 billion Native American fiscal year 2001 budget initiative, an increase in funding of $1.2 billion from the last year, the largest increase ever. President Clinton's initiative recognizes that the entire federal government has a trust responsibility for Native American tribes. The initiative provides funding across many agencies, rather than to the Department of the Interior's BIA and Department of Health and Human Services only. The initiative makes critical investments in education, health care, law enforcement, infrastructure, and economic development in Indian Country.

California Indians campaign for a state constitutional amendment to allow casino gaming on Indian reservations. The referendum was listed as "1A" on the ballot. (Photo by Victor Rocha)

Pechanga Tribal Chair Mark Macarro celebrates victory in Proposition 1A. The California voters strongly supported a state and federal agreement to support Native-owned casino gaming. (Photo by Victor Rocha)

28 February 2000 Appeals Court Rules on Indian Crime.   A federal appeals court rules that an Indian person who commits a crime on another tribe's land and is convicted in tribal court can be prosecuted again, with a longer sentence, in federal court. The Ninth U.S. Circuit Court of Appeals said the multiple prosecutions do not violate the Constitution's ban on double jeopardy, being prosecuted twice for the same crime. The court states that an Indian tribe and the federal government are separate sovereignties and can file separate charges for the same conduct, in the same way that a defendant can be charged in both state and federal court for the same acts.

March 2000 Proposition 1A Passes.   California voters approve Proposition 1A, which provides a state constitutional amendment allowing California Indian tribes to operate slot machines and banked card games, such as black jack. Proposition 1A was introduced as the result of an earlier gaming initiative, Proposition 5, which was approved by California voters in 1998 but struck down by the California Supreme Court in 1999.

May 2000 BIA No Longer Wants Involvement in Recognition.   Kevin Gover, the assistant interior secretary of Indian affairs, announces that the Bureau of Indian Affairs "no longer wants to be the agency that grants federal recognition to American Indian Tribes."

The Senate Committee on Indian Affairs is considering legislation by Senator Ben Nighthorse Campbell that would create a three-person commission appointed by the president to decide which tribes should be federally recognized.

5 June 2000 Complaint Filed Over Alleged Finance Law Violation.   A California group titled California Common Cause files a complaint alleging more than 300 campaign finance law violations by gaming interests, primarily Indian tribes. The report accuses Governor Gray Davis of failing to disclose $169,000 in 1998 contributions, including $113,000 from the Cabazon Band of Mission Indians and $50,000 from the Twentynine Palms Band of Missions Indians, which both operate casinos outside Palm Springs. Governor Davis calls the report "garbage," and states that "This is a typical Common Cause political stunt."

9 June 2000 Makah Whaling Issues Reviewed.   A federal appeals court rejects the environmental assessment that allowed the Makah Indian tribe to hunt gray whales off the coast of Washington, ruling that the government's review was "slanted" in favor of allowing the Makah to hunt. Attorneys for the Makah, a small tribe in northwestern Washington State, sought to revive a long-standing whaling tradition. The federal government conducted an environmental review after it backed the Makah's petition to the International Whaling Commission to engage in subsistence whale hunting. The government concluded that the gray whales' recovery from near extinction in the early part of the century was sufficient to assure the population would not be affected by the Makah's subsistence whale hunting needs.

July 2000 BIA Proposes Changes to Indian Blood Certificate. The Bureau of Indian Affairs publishes a notice in the Federal Register, proposing rules to establish the documentation requirements and standards for filing, processing, and issuing a Certificate of Degree of Indian Blood (CDIB). The proposed rule sets forth the policies and standards that will allow the bureau to issue, amend, or invalidate CDIBs. The Advocates for American Indian Children say that a preliminary analysis of the proposed rules indicate that the bureau will limit access to BIA programs and services by degree of Indian blood.

8 July 2000 Court Sides with Alabama-Coushatta Tribe. A federal court rules that U.S. settlers wrongfully took a 2.8 million-acre tract of Texas forest from the Alabama and Coushatta Indians, possibly entitling the tribe to millions of dollars in reimbursement. On June 19, a three-judge panel of the U.S. Claims Court sided with the 400 members of the Alabama-Coushatta tribe, which began the land rights fight in 1967, and ruled that the tribe has title to land in nine Texas counties, stretching from the Louisiana border to just north of Houston. Congress must ultimately approve any settlement, but tribal leaders hope that the Justice Department will resolve the issue quickly.

13 July 2000 Democrats Criticize Republicans for Anti-Sovereignty Measures. Democratic National Committee National Chair Joe Andrew criticizes the Washington State Republican party for passing a resolution calling for the abolition of tribal governments. "Trying to dissolve tribal sovereignty is an insult to Native Americans across the nation," Andrew says. "I call upon Governor George W. Bush and the Republican National Committees to publicly denounce these unjust and racist actions by the Washington State Republican Party." Tribal leaders call the GOP resolution "outrageous and an affront to their rights under treaties

signed by Congress." Ron Allen, chairman of the Jamestown Klallam Tribe states that "It's absolutely the reverse of what Republican principles stand for—to protect all rights and to uphold the integrity and honor of this nation and of all the commitments it makes."

August 2000 Ishi's Brain Returned. A delegation of Indians from the Pit River tribe of California travel to Washington, D.C. to reclaim the brain of Ishi, presumed to be the last of the Yahi Indians. The preserved brain was found in a Smithsonian Institution warehouse in February 1999. Ishi came to the attention of the American public when he came out of the California mountain country in 1911. Anthropologist Alfred Kroeber took Ishi to the University of California, Berkeley, where he lived and worked at the Phoebe Hearst Museum. Thousands of tourists visited the museum and Ishi became an internationally recognized symbol of the genocide of California Indian people. Ishi died in 1916. His body was cremated against his wishes and his brain was removed and sent to the Smithsonian Institution to join the remains of 18,000 other anonymous Native American people. The Pit River tribal members are descendants of the Yana, the parent tribe of the Yahi. Ishi's brain will be buried in an undisclosed site in the foothills of Mt. Lassen.

3 August 2000 Bush Threatens Tribal Sovereignty. Texas governor George W. Bush states during his acceptance speech of the Republican presidential candidacy that "Now is the time, not to defend outdated treaties but to defend the American people." Taken in light of Bush's 1999 statement when he said Indian affairs were best left to the individual states, Bush's statement is interpreted by many to mean that he will, as president, terminate all Indian treaties and suspend the U.S. Justice Department's role in resolving Indian land claims. Bush's pledge is frightening to Indians because it comes on the heels of a motion by the Washington State Republican Party to supplant Native governments, using force if necessary. Bush also states during a campaign stop in New York State that "Indian Tribes should be subject to state law. My view is that state law reigns supreme when it comes to the Indians, whether it be gambling or any other issue."

7 August 2000 Washington Republicans Apologize. The Washington State Republican Party, scrambling to undo some of the damage resulting from a recent resolution against tribal sovereignty, apologizes and offers a substitute statement that affirms Indian's rights to self-government. The new resolution is adopted by the GOP state executive board at the suggestion of party Chairman Don Benton and is the latest effort at damage control. Indian tribes, human rights groups, Democrats, and newspaper editorials denounced a resolution sponsored by John Fleming, a non-Indian, that called for the federal government to "take whatever steps necessary to terminate all such nonrepublican forms of government on Indian reservations."

8 August 2000 California Gaming Tribes Support Non-Gaming Tribes.   An accountant representing California Indian tribes that operate gaming casinos delivers a check for $34.5 million to California Attorney General Bill Lockyer under an agreement negotiated between California Indian tribes and Governor Gray Davis in 1999. Voters in a March 2000 election ratified the compact. Tribal officials state that part of the $34 million is the first payment by casino operators into a fund to benefit California tribes that have no gaming operations.

15 August 2000 Indian Delegates Gather at Formal Political Caucus.   For the first time in the history of the Democratic Party, American Indian delegates gather at a formal political caucus to plan their political future.

8 September 2000 Cabazon, Firestone Make Deal. The Cabazon Band of Mission Indians of California reaches a deal with the Bridgestone/Firestone tire company to accept almost 5,000 defective Firestone tires a day for the next year from dealers across the Southwest. Bridgestone/Firestone voluntarily recalled 6.5 millions tires in the United States and the number is estimated to grow to 275 million. The tribes will grind the tires into crumbs at a plant near Mecca, east of Palm Springs, California. The crumbs will be turned into asphalt playground surfaces and floor mats.

9 September 2000 Gover Apologizes for BIA Injustices.   Kevin Gover, Pawnee, assistant secretary of the interior, apologizes for the Bureau of Indian Affair's relocations and attempts to wipe out Native languages and cultures. Gover states that he is apologizing on behalf of the BIA, not the federal government as a whole. In his remarks Gover states that the federal Bureau of Indian Affairs apologized for the agency's "legacy of racism and inhumanity" that included massacres, forced relocations of tribes, and attempts to wipe out Indian languages and cultures. Gover said that "never again will we attack your religions, your languages, your rituals or any of your tribal ways.... Never again will we seize your children nor teach them to be ashamed of who they are. Never again."

Assistant Secretary of the Interior Kevin Gover. (Photo by Carol Lujan)

15 September 2000 Resolution 185.   The California Legislature unanimously passes a resolution that points to a genuine concern for American Indian people. The legislature passes Concurrent Resolution 185, written by Assemblyman Jim Battin, a summary of which states that "this measure will reaffirm state recognition of the sovereign status of federally recognized Indian tribes as separate and independent political communities within the United States, encourages all state agencies, when engaging in activities or developing policies affecting Native American tribal rights or trust resources, to do so in a knowledgeable, sensitive manner that is respectful of tribal sovereignty, and, in recognizing their tribal sovereignty, encourages all state agencies to continue to reevaluate and improve the implementation of laws affecting Native American tribal rights"

October 2000 National Tribal Justice Resource Center Established.   The National Tribal Justice Resource Center, a project of the National American Indian Court Judges Association (NAICJA) is established. The Center which is established with start-up

Mary Ann Andreas, chairwoman of the Morongo Band of Mission Indians, presents to the California lieutenant governor 59 handmade arrows, encased in a lucite box, representing the 59 tribal-state compacts signed by California tribes. (Photo by Victor Rocha)

funding from the U.S. Department of Justice's Bureau of Justice Assistance is setting up its offices at the Native American Rights Fund (NARF) at its National Indian Law Library in Boulder, Colorado.

1 October 2000 Babbitt Announces Plans to Repatriate Kennewick Man. Secretary of the Interior Department Bruce Babbitt announces that the department plans to repatriate the Kennewick Man to five claimant Indian tribes in the Pacific Northwest. Babbitt's decision is consistent with the Native American Graves Protection and Repatriation Act, passed in 1990 that allows for repatriation of human remains once a cultural affiliation is determined. Scientists from the Smithsonian Institution fought against the return of the human remains "without the prospect of learning what he [Kennewick Man] has to tell us." Displaying an ongoing insensitivity toward Native American people the scientist said "that there was a wealth of information locked inside those bones."

23 October 2000 Campbell Introduces Bill Honoring Natives. Senator Ben Nighthorse Campbell introduces a bill in Congress to establish a memorial honoring Native Americans killed by the U.S. Army in the 1864 Sand Creek Massacre. The legislation passed by voice vote in the House today and by the Senate earlier. President Clinton has indicated that he will sign the bill. Senator Campbell's ancestors were among the 164 Cheyenne and Arapaho Indians who died on 29 November 1864 when troops under the command of Colonel John Chivington slaughtered Cheyenne and Arapaho women, children, and elderly men. Captain Silas Soule, who rode with Colonel Chivington, later wrote "It was hard to see little children on their knees have their brains beat out by men professing to be civilized."

December 2000 California Tribe Receives Federal Recognition. The Coast Miwok of Northern California receive federal recognition. The 401-member tribe once numbered from 3,000 to 5,000 people, but were

Gila Crossing students. (Photo by Carol Lujan)

decimated by disease, slavery, and murder after European contact. They are one of many California tribes trying to gain federal recognition.

Troy Johnson
California State University
Long Beach, California
Elton Naswood
Tribal Law and Policy Institute

◆ CHRONOLOGY OF CANADIAN NATIVE HISTORY, 1500 TO 2000

Native history has unfolded differently in Canada and the United States. Except for the Native groups living in the St. Lawrence River and Great Lakes area, and along the Pacific Coast, Canadian Native groups were smaller and more decentralized than many U.S. Indian nations. In terms of Native-newcomer relations, Canada today roughly corresponds to the portion of North America where the fur trade dominated the economy for extended periods. Thus Natives in Canada

have a significant history of mutually beneficial economic relations with non-Native newcomers. Furthermore, Canadian Natives did not experience the protracted open conflict with the Canadian government that has marred the experiences of many U.S. Indian nations. In fact, many Native groups in Canada were allied with European powers. By 1867, however, governments in Canada had begun to exert considerable influence over Native life. Even when designed to protect Native interests, outside laws had the effect of undermining Native sovereignty. Between 1880 and 1920 government policy became increasingly coercive. After the 1920s the government became less coercive, but powerful law courts and political interests generally ruled against Canadian Native land claims and Native assertions of self-government. Nevertheless, the latter half of the twentieth century has seen a major revival among Canadian Natives. Arguably the most important turning point was the response of Natives to the Canadian government's White Paper in 1969. The 1970s saw the formation of many Native organizations and direct attempts by Canadian Natives to gain acceptance of Native rights to land and recognition of rights to

Native self-government. Native political influence may have peaked in the 1980s when Native organizations exerted considerable influence in the drafting of Canada's Constitution (1982) which entrenched various aboriginal rights. Since then, the influence of Native organizations has declined as government funding for these organizations dwindled, and as public pressure to include Natives in national discussions waned. However, in 1996, the report of the Royal Commission on Aboriginal People, the largest royal commission in Canadian history, recommended a wholesale change in the way the Canadian government interacts with Native communities. Still, the government has been reluctant to accept many of the recommendations. On the other hand, Native claimants celebrated major victories in the courts and in land claims. Most noteworthy were the Supreme Court's decisions in the *Delgamuukw* case in 1997 and the *Marshall* case in 1999. Also noteworthy was the establishment of the territory of Nunavut in 1999, which had been part of an Inuit land claim submitted in the 1970s, and the implementation of the Nisga'a agreement in 2000, which finally settled a land claim dating to the nineteenth century. Although Canadian Native history has taken some very different turns than U.S. Native history, Natives in both countries face many of the same challenges today. The similarities and differences between the two nations invite comparison.

1503. Various indigenous peoples along the east coast of Canada begin desultory trade with groups of European fishermen and whalers. The Natives trade furs for European manufactures.

1535–36. Villagers from the Iroquois village of Stadacona (Quebec City) trade with French explorer Jacques Cartier, but are annoyed when his party sails upriver to trade at Hochelaga (Montreal). Stadaconans claim the right to control traffic traveling up the St. Lawrence River.

1541–43. Hostility on the part of the villagers at Stadacona prevents the success of a French settlement nearby. The Iroquois resent the newcomers because they make little attempt to establish friendly relations.

1543–88. Instead of establishing permanent settlements, Europeans embark for important Indian coastal trade centers each year. The Montagnais, nomadic hunter-gatherers of the area north of the St. Lawrence River and other Indian traders, greatly improve their returns by trading only when at least two competing ships are on hand.

1576–78. A party of Inuit (aboriginal inhabitants of the Arctic) has a hostile encounter with English mariner Martin Frobisher on Baffin Island in the northeastern Arctic. Frobisher kidnaps one Inuk man, who causes a stir in London.

1588. King Henry III of France grants a fur trade monopoly to nephews of Jacques Cartier. During the following decades monopolies are granted and revoked as monopoly holders fail to force interlopers to honor the monopoly. Indians find increased demand for *castor gras* (greasy beaver), beaver skins that have shed their guard hairs and absorbed perspiration and body oils after being used as clothing for a season or two. Europeans seek *castor gras* to make felt.

1604–1607. French traders establish Port Royal, a year-round trading base on the Bay of Fundy, a large bay separating today's provinces of Nova Scotia and New Brunswick. Micmac chief Membertou concludes an agreement with the French that gives the Micmac access to European weapons in exchange for food and furs. The Micmac are the Native inhabitants of most of Acadia, France's possessions southeast of the St. Lawrence River. Port Royal is abandoned in 1607 because of its poor location.

1608. Samuel de Champlain establishes Quebec City (New France) as the new French trading base. Since 1544 the agricultural, Iroquoian inhabitants have been displaced by nomadic Algonkian-speaking peoples. The Algonkian language family is the largest in Canada. Algonkian languages are spoken by many Indian groups from the Atlantic Ocean to the Rocky Mountains. Iroquoian languages dominate only in the southern Great Lakes-St. Lawrence River region.

1609. A group of Huron led by Chief Ochasteguin and Algonquin led by Chief Iroquet visit Quebec to negotiate a trade alliance. The Huron are Iroquoian, agricultural peoples of the area just east of Lake Huron. The Algonquin are hunter-gatherers of the regions north of the St. Lawrence River. They induce Champlain to join them on a raid against the Iroquois Five Nations Confederacy (Cayuga, Mohawk, Oneida, Onondaga, and Seneca), located southeast of Quebec. The battle initiates almost two centuries of enmity between the Five Nations and the French. Following Indian customs, French and Indians intermarry and Indians accept French emissaries, including missionaries. Some of these emissaries provide valuable information to the French about the area around the Great Lakes.

1610. A lone Cree man trades with an English party led by Henry Hudson on the shores of Hudson Bay. The

In order to cement a trade alliance, Champlain joined a Huron and Algonquin raid on the Iroquois in 1609. This was the first and most successful of several raids that Champlain joined. (Courtesy of the National Library of Canada)

Cree are Algonkian-speaking Indians who today live in areas from Quebec to Alberta.

1615–29. Indian groups accept Roman Catholic Récollet missionaries as emissaries from their French trading partners. They also send some of their children to be educated by the missionaries. In 1615 the Ottawa, Algonkian hunters living east of Lake Huron's Georgian Bay, conduct Champlain as far as Lake Huron.

1615–49. Huron villagers host Champlain at their villages southeast of Lake Huron to conclude a trade and military alliance with the French. As the northernmost agriculturalists in the area, the Huron are central to a web of trade relations between agriculturalists and hunting and gathering societies to the north and west. Thus the Huron are able to distribute European goods widely to other Native groups to the north and west as far away as Hudson Bay and Lake Michigan. (By essentially demanding payment for delivery of goods, Indian intermediaries acquire European goods without having

to trap themselves.) In order to protect their intermediary role, the Huron prevent direct trade between the French and neighboring Indians. Increased wealth allows for increasingly elaborate celebrations of such Huron rituals as the Feast of the Dead, an important Huron burial ceremony held every ten to fifteen years.

1623. The French government grants its first *seigneury* (feudal land grant) in New France. Indians do not acknowledge French sovereignty to any land, just as the French do not recognize aboriginal rights to the land. Thus Indians and the French do not negotiate any land cession treaties (treaties in which one party surrenders its land rights to another).

1635. Jesuits establish residential schools for Indians in New France. The Jesuits arrived in New France in 1632 to begin an intensive missionary effort among the Huron and Algonquin. They replaced the Récollets.

1635–40. Smallpox reduces the Huron population from about twenty thousand to ten thousand.

1639. The Jesuits establish a mission settlement at Sainte-Marie-among-the-Huron (Midland, Ontario).

1641. The French begin selling guns to Huron who profess to be Christian. The Iroquois begin unlimited warfare on the French.

1649–50. In a concerted effort to seize the middle-man role in the French fur trade, the Iroquois crush the Huron. Some Huron are integrated into the Five Nations and other peoples, some relocate to Lorette near Quebec City, and some scatter throughout the Great Lakes region where they become known as Wyandotte. The Ottawa assume the main middleman role. *Coureurs de bois* (traveling French fur traders who spend most of their time among the Indians) also assume an important role in trading with interior Indians. This increases Indian contact and intermarriage with the French.

1666–67. With the two thousand colonists of New France threatened by continual Iroquois attack, French troops attack Iroquois villages. The expedition kills few Indians but destroys Iroquois villages and crops. As a result, the Iroquois and French conclude a truce that lasts ten years.

1667. Iroquois converts move to La Prairie (Caughnawaga) near Montreal. They become allies of the French. Missionaries seek to isolate Indian settlements because they believe Europeans are a corrupting influence on the Indians.

1668. Three hundred Cree trade with men on a British ship at the mouth of the Rupert River along the coast of James Bay, a large bay in Hudson Bay. French fur traders Pierre Esprit Radisson and Médard Chouart des Grosseliers realized the value of the Hudson Bay as a fur-trading base after a foray to the James Bay hinterland earlier in the decade.

1670. Cree and Ojibwa (also referred to as Ojibway and Chippewa), Algonkian hunters centered along the eastern and northern shores of Lake Superior, begin traveling to the Hudson's Bay Company (HBC) posts at mouths of the Rupert, Moose, and Albany rivers on James Bay in present-day northern Quebec and Ontario. The HBC sends no missionaries to the Indians.

1671–73. The French establish forts on the Great Lakes as far northwest as Sault Ste. Marie, at the *sault* (falls) on the St. Marys River, which joins Lakes Superior and Huron, for the purpose of defense, trade, missions, and diplomacy. Competition with the Hudson's Bay Company induces the French to dramatically increase their trade in firearms. Ojibwa ceremonial life

becomes more elaborate as they become important traders around the Sault.

1682–1774. The Hudson's Bay Company establishes York Factory at the mouth of the Nelson and Hayes rivers on the western shores of Hudson Bay in present-day Manitoba. The rivers drain a vast territory as far west as the Rocky Mountains. Cree and Assiniboine become middlemen, trading European goods with Plains Indians as far west and south as the Rocky Mountains and the Missouri River Basin before 1750. Access to European goods, particularly weaponry, increases the wealth and power of Cree and Assiniboine bands. The Assiniboine are Siouan-speaking, a group that inhabited areas south and southeast of Lake Winnipeg (in today's Manitoba) at that time.

1700–1750. The Shoshoni in today's southwestern Alberta become the first Indians residing in present-day Canada to acquire horses. Horses spread to most Plains Indians by 1750, bringing significant changes in social and economic relations, balances of power, and diplomacy.

1701. The Iroquois and French conclude a peace agreement, ending a century of hostilities. Iroquois power and population has been significantly reduced by years of warfare. The Mississauga (Ojibwa) have expanded from the north to occupy most of the former Huron lands north of the Great Lakes.

1713. By the Treaty of Utrecht, France cedes Acadia (renamed Nova Scotia) to England and relinquishes claims to Newfoundland and Hudson Bay. France also recognizes the Iroquois as English subjects. The Micmac (Mi'kmaq) and the Maliseet (Malecite), who occupy lands west of the St. John River (in today's New Brunswick), begin opposing the English, and the Iroquois continue to see themselves as subject to no foreign power.

1713–53. French traders establish fur-trade posts as far west as Lake Winnipeg and the Saskatchewan River. Some of the Ojibwa, originally centered near Sault Ste. Marie, just east of Lake Superior, spread as far west as the prairies.

1717. The Hudson's Bay Company establishes Fort Prince of Wales (Churchill) on the western shores of Hudson Bay (in present-day Manitoba), allowing bands of Chipewyan to establish themselves as middlemen. The Chipewyan are Athapaskan-speaking hunter-gatherers centered in the region of today's northern Manitoba and Saskatchewan and southern Northwest Territories. They guard their role by preventing

Yellowknife and Dogrib, both Athapaskan hunters of the Great Bear Lake and Great Slave Lake area (in today's Northwest Territories) from reaching the post. Secure access to European goods allows them to expand against other Indians and Inuit, leading to acrimonious relations between the Chipewyan and these other Indians. Most Indians in the area that will become northwestern Canada speak an Athapaskan language.

1729. Four hundred Iroquois of Caughnawaga settle at a mission at Lake of Two Mountains (Oka), just west of Montreal.

1752. The Subenacadie band of Micmac sign the Halifax Treaty with the British, easing hostility between the Micmac and the British in Nova Scotia. The British deny that the Indians hold any rights to land in Nova Scotia.

1755. Some Christian Iroquois settle at St. Regis (Akwesasne). Today Akwesasne straddles the Ontario-Quebec-New York State borders near Montreal.

1760. New France falls to the British. The British agree to respect land granted to Indians by the French, but anger Indians by ending the French practice of giving gifts to Indians to cement alliances.

1763–66. Pontiac, a chief of the Ottawa tribe, leads Indian resistance to the British. In 1763 Indian forces capture all British forts west of Niagara Falls except Fort Detroit and Fort Pitt (Pittsburgh). Detroit is besieged for five months.

7 October 1763. The British Royal Proclamation of 1763 recognizes the right of North American Indians to possess all land in British territories outside established colonies (Hudson's Bay Company land is exempt), but claims underlying title for the king. The Crown claims the exclusive right to negotiate land surrender and peace treaties with the Indians and prohibits settlement in areas not covered by land cession treaties. The Indians see the proclamation as a major recognition of their rights. (The proclamation has since been enshrined in Canada's 1982 Constitution.)

1767. Newly surveyed land in Prince Edward Island in the Gulf of St. Lawrence is granted to British proprietors. No land is set aside for indigenous peoples.

1774. The Hudson's Bay Company establishes Cumberland House on the Saskatchewan River as its first inland trading post after learning that Cree and Assiniboine are trading many of their highest quality furs to Canadian traders who have infiltrated the area around Lake Winnipeg (in today's Manitoba).

1774–1800. The Hudson's Bay Company and Canadian traders establish competing fur-trade posts throughout the northern prairies, dramatically reducing the cost of European goods to Plains Indians, who can now trade directly with Euro-Canadians. These Indians are able to displace Indian groups with poor access to trading posts. Former Cree and Assiniboine middlemen assume roles as Home Guard Indians and provisioners at North West Company and HBC posts. Intermarriage between Indians and fur traders produces a sizable mixed-blood population.

1774. Nootka (Nuu-chah-nulth), coastal Indians of Vancouver Island, trade with Spanish explorer Juan Perez. West Coast Indians have already begun trading with Russians. The Indians of the Northwest Coast of North America live in substantial villages and rely heavily on abundant supplies of salmon. Coastal Indians' highly structured, hierarchical societies are unique among Native groups of northern North America.

1775–83. Britain's Indian allies take a prominent role in the American War of Independence. They believe the British best represent their interests.

1779–81. A smallpox epidemic originating in Mexico City spreads as far north as the Chipewyan, devastating Native societies along the way. Smallpox kills up to one-half of the Plains Indians and up to nine-tenths of the Chipewyan.

1779–1821. The North West Company, operating from Montreal, becomes the dominant force in the fur trade and in exploration of the northwest, allowing many northern Indian groups to trade directly with Euro-Canadian traders. This alters interethnic relations in the region. Natives on the prairies supply large amounts of pemmican, a preserved meat usually produced from buffalo and used to feed traders in the north.

1783. By the Treaty of Versailles, the British cede land south of the Great Lakes to the United States, angering their Indian allies who still control the area.

1784. The British negotiate land purchases from Mississauga (Ojibwa) Indians and grant the land to loyalist Indians who had found their land turned over to the United States. Iroquois Captain Joseph Brant (Thyendanega) and more than 1,550 Iroquois are given a tract of land on the Grand River (Six Nations Reserve near Brantford, Ontario), and Captain John Deseronto's

Mohawk are given land near the Bay of Quinte on the north shore of Lake Ontario.

1784. New Brunswick is formed as a separate province as loyalists settle there. Maliseet and Micmac begin to suffer encroachment on their lands.

1785. The Indians of the West Coast begin regular trade with shipborne traders, increasing their returns by trading only when competing ships are at hand. Coastal middlemen trade with Indians well inland. Sea otter pelts and blankets become trade staples, with blankets forming a kind of currency.

1794. The Jay Treaty establishes the border between the United States and British North America beyond the Great Lakes. Britain agrees to withdraw troops and traders from land ceded to the United States in 1783. The British had kept troops posted there to appease

The eighteenth-century engraving, *Indians trading furs,* 1785, demonstrates the importance of the fur trade between Natives and Euro-Canadians. (C. W. Jefferys. Courtesy of the National Archives of Canada)

their Indian allies in the region. Indians are guaranteed unhindered travel across the border.

1812. The Hudson's Bay Company establishes the Red River Colony (Selkirk Settlement) near today's Winnipeg. Chief Peguis's band of Saulteaux (Ojibwa) provides important help to the settlers in their first difficult years.

1812–14. Tecumseh (Shawnee) leads Britain's Indian allies in their important role in the War of 1812. Many Indian groups ally with Britain in the hope that the British will able to create a buffer state for them.

1814. The Treaty of Ghent, ending the War of 1812, ends Indian hopes of a buffer state.

1816. At the Battle of Seven Oaks (Red River), twenty-one Red River settlers and one Métis die in a skirmish. The battle fosters an increased sense of nationhood among the Métis. The Métis, of mixed Indian-European descent, begin to develop a unique society and culture that will be based on trading between their Indian and European kin, small-scale farming, and buffalo hunting.

1818. The British government begins its practice of acquiring Indian land in exchange for annuities rather than lump-sum payments.

1820. John West of the Anglican Church Missionary Society (CMS) arrives to serve the English speaking, non-Catholic population at the Red River Colony. The CMS and the Roman Catholic Oblates of Mary Immaculate become the major missionary groups in the Northwest.

1821. The North West Company and the Hudson's Bay Company merge, retaining the name of the HBC. The HBC reduces employment and opportunities for Indians and mixed-blood inhabitants throughout the northwest. It also reduces trade in alcohol. Many mixed-blood move to the Red River settlement where a large Métis community develops.

1827. With the establishment of Fort Langley on the Fraser River (in the southwestern corner of today's British Columbia), land-based trade in the region begins. The region is the home of Coast Salish, who live in villages and depend heavily on salmon.

1829. Shanawdithit, the last Beothuk, dies. The reclusive Beothuk, the Native inhabitants of Newfoundland, gradually disappeared as a result of disease,

Interior of an Inuit house. (Public domain)

hostilities with Indian and non-Indian enemies, and the unforgiving environment of the island.

1830. Responsibility for Indian affairs in Upper Canada is transferred from military to civilian administrators, reflecting the waning importance of Indians as military allies and a growing emphasis on assimilation of Indians into non-Indian society. The government also adopts a policy of establishing reserves for Indians whenever they sign land surrenders.

1835–40. Smallpox kills up to one-third of some British Columbia coastal Indians.

1836. A plan to relocate Upper Canada's Indians to the Manitoulin Islands (in Lake Huron) is abandoned after humanitarian groups committed to the assimilation of Indians oppose the plan.

1837–38. Smallpox kills up to three-fourths of the Plains Indians. Hudson's Bay Company traders vaccinate the Cree, preventing the spread of the disease to the Cree and their northern neighbors.

1840s. Roman Catholic missionaries (Oblates of Mary Immaculate) arrive in British Columbia.

1841. Methodist missionary James Evans prints a hymnal using the Cree syllabics that he devised. The written Cree language, adapted to Athapaskan and Inuit languages, stimulates the growth of literacy among northern Natives.

1842. The first significant attempt to establish reserves for Indians in Nova Scotia begins.

1844. The New Brunswick government passes legislation restricting Indian reserves to twenty hectares per family.

1844. The Bagot Commission Report on Indian Affairs in the Province of Canada (present-day Ontario and Quebec) recommends an Indian affairs policy with the aim of the complete assimilation of Indians into Canadian society. The Bagot Commission was chosen in 1842 to make recommendations relating to Indian policy.

1850. In a law designed to protect Indian lands in Lower Canada, the government provides the first legal definition of an Indian.

1850. Ojibwa bands sign the Robinson Treaties covering land north of Lake Superior. These treaties, covering twice as much land as all earlier treaties in Upper Canada combined, are the first treaties signed to clear the way for mineral exploration rather than settlement.

1851. Coast Salish Indians of Vancouver Island and James Douglas, governor of the Hudson's Bay Company colony on Vancouver Island, conclude the first of fourteen land cession treaties covering small areas of the island.

1857. The government of the Province of Canada passes the Gradual Civilization Act, which creates a process by which Indians are expected to seek "enfranchisement," the acceptance of citizenship and renunciation of any legal distinction as an Indian. Adult male Indians seeking enfranchisement for themselves and their families will need to demonstrate that they are educated, debt free, capable of managing their own affairs, and of "good moral character." Enfranchised individuals will be granted their share of band funds and ownership of twenty hectares of reserve land and will lose their Indian status. In order to acquaint unenfranchised Indians with the Canadian political system, the act encourages the formation of elected band councils to replace traditional leaders by offering such councils limited powers over reserve affairs.

1858. Thousands of gold seekers come to the lower Fraser River Valley (in present-day British Columbia) and clash with resident Salish Indians.

1860. The Imperial government transfers control of Indian affairs to the Province of Canada.

1862. William Duncan of the Anglican's Church Missionary Society establishes an isolated missionary settlement for Tsimshian Indians at Metlakatla, near Port Simpson, British Columbia. Tsimshian are coastal Indians of the Skeena River Region of British Columbia's north coast. In British Columbia, Anglicans and Roman Catholics focus their efforts in separate regions. As a result, entire Indian communities there become either overwhelmingly Catholic or Protestant.

1862. Indians of the interior of British Columbia clash with thousands of gold seekers rushing to the Caribou region. Smallpox decimates Indians in the interior and coast of British Columbia.

1864. James Douglas retires as governor of Vancouver Island. Joseph Trutch, the new chief commissioner of lands and works in the colony, adopts a policy of refusing to negotiate land surrender agreements with Indians.

1 July 1867. The British North America Act, recognizing Canadian Confederation, grants legislative responsibility for Indian affairs to the new federal government, but gives control of land and natural resources to the provincial governments, thus giving both levels of government an interest in future land-claims negotiations. Land cession treaties have been negotiated only in Ontario, although reserves have been granted in the other provinces.

1868. The Canadian government's first Indian legislation adopts the pre-Confederation Indian policy of the Province of Canada.

1869. The Gradual Enfranchisement Act lays out Canada's Indian policy. Responding to Indian resistance to the establishment of elected band councils, agents are given power to depose traditional leaders for "dishonesty, intemperance and immorality," and to impose elected band councils. This act also stipulates that Indian women and their children will lose their Indian status when they marry non-Indians. It also introduces "location tickets," a means by which provisional individual title to reserve lands can be given to those seeking enfranchisement.

1869–70. Smallpox decimates Natives on the northern plains.

1869–74. After the whiskey trade is repressed in Montana, traders establish posts in the British possessions, bringing serious social problems to the Blackfoot (Blackfeet). The Blackfoot are composed of the Siksika (Blackfoot), Blood, and Peigan (Piegan), Plains Indians who inhabit the southwestern plains of Canada and the northwestern plains of the United States.

1870. Canada acquires Hudson's Bay Company lands from the British government with the provision that it will negotiate land cession treaties with the Indians. Most of the area becomes the North-West Territories, administered by the federal government. As a result of negotiations with a provisional government established by Métis leader Louis Riel, a small area becomes the province of Manitoba. The federal government recognizes Métis land title in the province.

1871. British Columbia (BC) enters the Confederation. It retains control of land and natural resources, but agrees to transfer land to the federal government for use as Indian reserves. The Canadian government is poorly informed about BC Indian policy.

1871. The first of eleven numbered treaties covering former Hudson's Bay Company lands is signed. Treaty 1, covering Manitoba (including the area of the Selkirk treaty of 1817) and areas of the Northwest Territories (today's southern Manitoba), is signed by the Saulteaux (Ojibwa) and Swampy Cree. Treaty 2, covering areas of the Northwest Territories (today's central and southwest Manitoba, and southeast Saskatchewan) is signed by the Ojibwa. Both treaties promise land and farm implements and seed, but make no mention of hunting, fishing, or trapping rights.

1873. The province of Prince Edward Island enters the Confederation having signed no land cession treaties with Indian groups. Responsibility for Indian affairs in the province is handed over to the federal government.

1873. Ten Americans and Canadians kill up to thirty Assiniboine in the Cypress Hills Massacre. The Cypress Hills are in Canada's southwestern prairies. The deaths induce the Canadian government to create a police force for the West.

1873. The Saulteaux sign Treaty 3 covering today's western Ontario and southeastern Manitoba. The treaty promises land and livestock, but also includes hunting, fishing, and trapping rights.

1874. The Plains Cree, Assiniboine, and Saulteaux tribes sign Treaty 4, covering areas of the Northwest Territories (now southern Saskatchewan).

1874. The North-West Mounted Police are sent to the Canadian prairies to stop the whisky trade, prevent such violence as the Cypress Hills Massacre (1873), and prepare the West for peaceful settlement. Not powerful enough to control the Indians by force, the police adopt a conciliatory policy toward the Indians.

1875. The Saulteaux and Swampy Cree sign Treaty 5 covering land in today's northern Manitoba and western Ontario. Treaties 1 and 2 are revised to increase land allotments.

1876. A new Indian Act makes elected band councils voluntary. It also gives such councils wider powers. Location tickets, reintroduced in eastern Canada, are part of a plan to lead Indians to abandon the practice of holding land in common. Location tickets give individuals rights to twenty hectares of reserve land. Indians who farm their allotment over a period of three years

are to be enfranchised and receive absolute title to the land. Only one Indian was enfranchised between 1857 and 1876. The act forbids the sale of alcohol to Indians and bars non-Indians from reserves after nightfall.

1876. Plains Cree, Woodland Cree, and Assiniboine tribes sign Treaty 6, covering areas of the Northwest Territories (today's central Alberta and Saskatchewan). The treaty includes famine relief provisions and a "medicine chest" provision, which later becomes the basis of free health care for all Indians.

1877. The Blackfoot (Blackfeet), Sarcee, and Stoney (Assiniboine) sign Treaty 7, covering areas of the North-West Territories (today's southern Alberta).

1879. Buffalo disappear from the Canadian prairies, forcing Indian bands to follow herds into the United States or face famine. The government rejects a demand by Cree bands led by Piapot, Little Pine, and Big Bear for contiguous reserves in the Cypress Hills. Plains Indian groups gradually settle on reserves in western Canada.

1883. The Canadian government begins establishing residential schools for Indians in the west. Most Indians seek education for their children but resist the assimilative aims of government schools.

1885. Amendments to the Indian Act prohibit Indians from traveling off their reserves without a pass from an Indian Affairs agent, prohibit the reelection of deposed Indian leaders, and prohibit Sun Dances, annual midsummer Plains Indian ceremonies, and potlatches, elaborate ceremonies held among coastal Indians. Agricultural instructors are sent to Indian reserves in western Canada.

1885. At Batoche, North-West Territories (now in Saskatchewan), federal government forces crush a Métis uprising led by Louis Riel. After his execution for treason in November, Riel becomes a powerful symbol for the Métis.

1885. Members of Big Bear's Cree band kill nine people at Frog Lake and members of Cree chief Poundmaker's band raid homesteads near Duck Lake, North-West Territories (now in Saskatchewan). Big Bear, Poundmaker, and forty-two other Indians are jailed.

1889. In the case of *St. Catharine's Milling and Lumber Company v. The Queen* (the Indian Land Title Case), the Privy Council rules that aboriginal land rights were created by the Royal Proclamation of 1763 and can be abolished by unilateral legislative action.

LOUIS RIEL,

CHEF METIS,

Exécuté le 16 Novembre 1885,

MARTYR POLITIQUE !

Coupable d'avoir aimé ses compatriotes opprimés,

Victime du fanatisme orangiste, auquel l'ont sacrifié
des politiciens sans âme et sans cœur.

QUE LES VRAIS PATRIOTES S'EN SOUVIENNENT!!

Louis Riel's execution in 1885 vaulted him to the status of
martyr for the Métis cause. He remains one of the most
controversial figures in Canadian history. (Drawing by
John Vereist. Courtesy of the National Archives of Canada)

1897–99. Thousands of gold seekers disrupt the lives
of Indians in Yukon, in northwestern Canada. Yukon is
created as a separate territory.

1899. The Cree of present-day northern Alberta; the
Beaver, Athapaskan hunters of the Peace River region
of today's northern Alberta; the Sekani, Athapaskan
hunters of the Finlay and Parsnip River region of
northeastern British Columbia; and the Chipewyan of
today's northern Alberta and the North-West Territories south of Great Slave Lake, sign Treaty 8. The
Indians demanded the treaty as the number of non-
Indians in the area increased during the Yukon gold rush.

1905. The Cree and Ojibwa of northern Ontario sign
Treaty 9.

1906. The Chipewyan and Cree of northern Ontario
sign Treaty 10.

1909. The Indian Tribes of the Province of British
Columbia, an alliance of twenty Indian nations, appeals
to the British throne for help in settling their land claims.

1911. About this time, the Canadian Indian population reaches its nadir (under 110,000 persons).

1912. Quebec is granted territory as far north as
Hudson Strait on the condition it will negotiate land
surrender agreements with Natives.

1912–16. A Royal Commission on Indian Affairs in
British Columbia (the McKenna-McBride Commission)
meets to determine the appropriate size for each British Columbia Reserve. Its final report recommends
adding land to some reserves and cutting off land (of
considerably greater value) from others. The recommendations are rejected by the Allied Tribes of British
Columbia.

1914–18. Up to four thousand Indians, approximately
35 percent of those eligible, fight for Canada in
World War I.

1915. Opposition to the conduct of the McKenna-
McBride Commission (1912–16) spurs Reverend Peter
Kelly (Haida) and Andrew Paull (Squamish) to organize
the Allied Tribes of British Columbia. It appeals to the
federal government for help in settling Nishga and
Salish land claims. British Columbia has the longest
history of pan-tribal organization in Canada.

1919–20. Following recommendations of the
McKenna-McBride Commission, the British Columbia
government begins adjusting the size of reserves.

1920. The federal government amends the Indian Act
to allow for compulsory enfranchisement. Only 250
Indians have opted for enfranchisement between 1857
and 1920. Provisions allowing for compulsory enfranchisement are repealed in 1922 but reenacted in 1933.

1921. The Slave, Dogrib, and Hare tribes, all
Athapaskan hunters of western Northwest Territories,
sign Treaty 11, covering land north and west of Great
Slave Lake, Northwest Territories. The Canadian government sought the treaty after oil was discovered at
Norman Wells, along the Mackenzie River in the Northwest Territories.

1923. Several disputed pre-confederation treaties in
southern Ontario are resolved several decades after the
government acknowledged that, because of missing
papers, unclear agreements, or misunderstandings, the
Indians had legitimate claims.

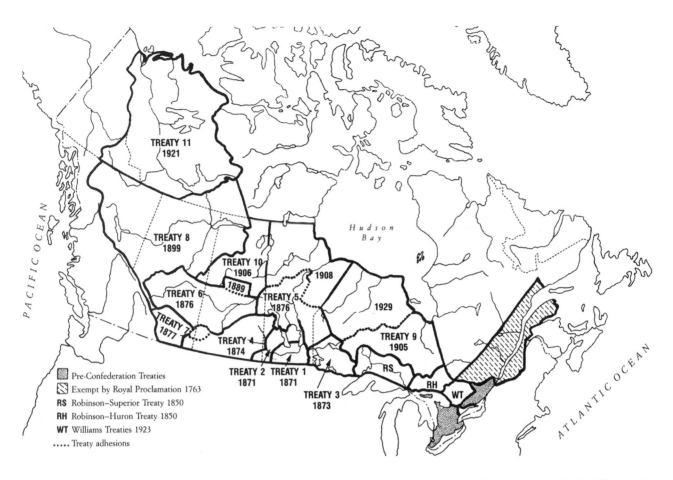

Indian treaty area in Canada. (Map by Brian McMillan from *Native Peoples and Cultures of Canada* by Alan D. McMillan, 1988, published by Douglas & McIntyre. Reprinted by permission)

1927. A joint Parliamentary Committee decides that British Columbia Indians have established no legal claim to land. In place of treaty money, British Columbia Indians will get $100,000 annually. The Allied Tribes of British Columbia collapses soon after the ruling.

1927. An amendment to the Indian Act makes it illegal to raise or donate funds for the prosecution of any Indian land claims. The law remains in force until 1951.

1930–39. The Great Depression brings great hardship to Natives in Canada. Plummeting fur prices affect those who live by trapping, while falling commodities prices affect those employed in resource industries. In parts of Canada, the depression halts a trend of increasing Native participation as wage earners in the Canadian economy.

1931. The Native Brotherhood of British Columbia is formed by Haida Alfred Adams.

1938. Alberta passes the Métis Population Betterment Act, establishing eight Métis settlements in the province.

1939. The Supreme Court of Canada rules that Inuit (Eskimo) are to be legally regarded as Indians. This makes them the responsibility of the federal government.

1939–45. Up to six thousand Indians volunteer for service in World War II. Their status as non-citizens makes them ineligible for conscription or for certain veterans' benefits.

1941. A census shows that the Indian population is growing steadily. Indian populations stopped their decline between 1911 and 1921.

1942. The Pacific Coast Native Fisherman's Association merges with the Native Brotherhood of British Columbia (NBBC), which consists of Protestant British Columbia Indians.

1942–43. Andrew Paull leads the organization of the North American Indian Brotherhood, an attempt to establish a national Indian organization. It becomes dominated by British Columbia Roman Catholics.

1942–43. The Alaska Highway is built from Dawson Creek, British Columbia, to Alaska, bringing dramatic social change and new diseases to Indians in the region.

1946–48. A Joint Senate and House of Commons Committee meets to consider changes to the Indian Act. This committee consults with Indian groups. Its report supports the aim of complete assimilation of Indian peoples but recommends that the Indian Act be revised to eliminate its coercive elements and that a commission be established to settle Indian land claims. Indian organizations reject the aim of assimilation.

1949. British Columbia Indians vote in a provincial election for the first time. Only Nova Scotia Indians already have the franchise. Nishga Frank Calder becomes the first Indian elected to a provincial legislature.

1949. Newfoundland enters the confederation without having negotiated land surrenders with Natives. Under the agreement, Natives in the province are not recognized as status Indians and remain the responsibility of the Newfoundland government.

1951. The federal government passes a new Indian Act, which adopts the main thrust of the Joint Senate and House of Commons Committee report of 1948, significantly reducing the powers of the Indian Affairs Department but retaining the assimilative aim of the Indian Act. The government rejects the establishment of a land claims commission. The new act makes it easier for Indians to be enfranchised and to acquire location tickets. It also makes provisions allowing Indian children to be placed in integrated provincial schools.

1953. Inuit families from Port Harrison, on the eastern shore of Hudson Bay, and Pond Inlet on Baffin Island, in Canada's Arctic, are moved north to new communities at Resolute Bay (Cornwallis Island) and Grise Fiord (Ellesmere Island), both in the high Arctic. Hundreds of Inuit were relocated in government-sponsored relocations beginning in the 1930s.

1955. The construction of the Distant Early Warning (DEW) line (a line of radar stations intended to warn of Soviet attack) in Canada's Arctic increases the presence of non-Natives in northern Canada and increases cross-cultural contact. Increased interest in the resources of the north also increases the non-aboriginal population of the north.

1960. Indians are given the national franchise.

1961. The National Indian Council is formed as the first truly national Indian organization.

1964. The government induces the Ojibwa of Grassy Narrows in northern Ontario to move from their traditional homes to a new mainland reserve where government services can be administered more easily. This phenomenon is common in Canada at the time. The move brings about significant social and economic dislocation.

1966–68. *A Survey of the Contemporary Indians of Canada* (Hawthorn Report) criticizes Canadian Indian policy, noting that Natives are an economically, socially, and politically disadvantaged group. The report, noting that Indians have been treated as "citizens minus," calls for a new Indian policy that would treat them as "citizens plus." Indian leaders endorse the report.

August 1967. *Indians and the Law*, a study commissioned by the Department of Indian Affairs and conducted by the Canadian Corrections Association, issues its report. The report, the first in-depth study of the extent of Natives' problems with the law, criticizes the impact of police and legal services on Indians.

February 1968. The National Indian Council separates into the National Indian Brotherhood (NIB) and the Canadian Métis Society. The NIB will seek to protect benefits status Indians enjoy under treaties and the Indian Act. The Canadian Métis Society will seek to protect the aboriginal rights of Métis and non-status Indians.

25 July 1968. The federal government begins consultations with Indian groups toward establishing a new Indian policy.

March 1969. Quebec Indians become the last Indians in Canada to be given the provincial franchise.

25 June 1969. Jean Chrétien, minister of Indian affairs, releases the federal government's White Paper (policy paper) *Statement of the Government of Canada on Indian Policy, 1969.* The discussion paper rejects the Hawthorn Report's recommendation that Indians be treated as "citizens plus," arguing instead that Indians' special legal status has hindered their social, economic, and political development. Thus the policy paper proposes legislation to end all legal and constitutional distinctions relating to Indians. The Indian Act and the Indian Affairs Department would be abolished in about five years, and reserves, held in trust by the government since before confederation, would pass to Indian ownership. The provinces would assume the same jurisdiction over Indians as they do over other Canadians. During a transition period, Indians would be given aid to alleviate social and economic problems on reserves. The policy paper dismisses aboriginal land claims as too general and vague to be remedied.

June–December 1969. Indians and Indian organizations begin to unite in opposition to the government's White Paper. As early as June 26, Walter Deiter, leader of the National Indian Brotherhood rejects the White Paper, saying that it ignores both the views Indians expressed during the government's consultations and the special status for Indians as guaranteed by treaties. In the following months most aboriginal organizations fight the government's policy.

September 1969. Trent University in Peterborough, Ontario, begins the first Native studies program in Canada.

20 November 1969. In the case of *Regina v. Drybones*, the Supreme Court strikes down sections of the Indian Act that restrict liquor sales to Indians because they contravene sections of the 1960 Bill of Rights guaranteeing all Canadians equality before the law. This, the first ruling on the Bill of Rights, finds that the Bill of Rights prevails over other legislation.

19 December 1969. Lloyd Barber, vice president of the University of Saskatchewan, is appointed land claims commissioner according to guidelines set out in June's White Paper.

1970. The Canadian government begins funding various Indian organizations, thus marking the reversal of its 1927 law repressing Indian political organizations. Funding helps further strengthen organizations established or united by opposition to the White Paper.

4 June 1970. Two hundred Indians from across Canada present *Citizens Plus* (the Red Paper) to Minister of Indian Affairs Jean Chrétien and Prime Minister Pierre Trudeau. The Red Paper was written as the Indian Association of Alberta's response to the government's White Paper. Following some revisions on June 3, Indian organizations from across Canada adopt it as the official Indian response to the White Paper. Taking its title from the Hawthorn Report of 1968, *Citizens Plus* condemns the government's proposal to remove Indians' special status and to transfer responsibility for Indians to the provinces. The Red Paper demands that

the special legal status of Indians be retained and that treaty obligations be kept. It also calls for a reorganization of the federal Indian Affairs Department in order to make it more responsive to the needs and desires of Indian peoples. The Red Paper also calls for the creation of an Indian Claims Commission with the power to settle the claims. Upon receiving the submission, Trudeau implies that the government is willing to withdraw the White Paper.

1 September 1970. A Cree band in northeastern Alberta takes over control of the Blue Quills school from the federal government, thus becoming the first Indian band in Canada to control its own school.

17 March 1971. Jean Chrétien, minister of Indian affairs, formally announces the retraction of the White Paper.

30 June 1971. A House of Commons committee on Indian Affairs recommends that control of education be turned over to Indians rather than to the provinces. Since 1951 an increasing number of Indians are being educated in provincial schools.

17 November 1971. The Union of British Columbia Indian Chiefs releases "A Declaration of Indian Rights— The British Columbia Indian Position Paper," usually known as the Brown Paper. It rejects the White Paper along similar lines as the Red Paper, but puts more emphasis on land claims issues. Since the Red Paper, other Indian groups have also submitted their position papers rejecting the proposed federal policy.

3 May 1972. The Cree and Inuit of northern Quebec file for a permanent injunction to halt construction of the James Bay Hydroelectric Project. This is their first court action to stop the development announced by the Quebec government in April 1971. Phase one of the project would flood about 10,500 square kilometers (4000 square miles) and divert several rivers. The Cree and Inuit of the region, who view the project as a threat to their way of life, were not consulted before the project was announced. Quebec has not negotiated land surrender agreements with the Natives of the region despite a 1912 agreement to do so.

December 1972. The National Indian Brotherhood (NIB) presents "Indian Control of Indian Education," which calls for greater band control of Indian education. The NIB statement calls attention to the fact that Indians do not enjoy parental or local control over education-rights taken for granted by most Canadians.

31 January 1973. The Supreme Court rules in the case of *Calder v. Attorney General* that aboriginal rights to land exist in law, but that the rights of British Columbia Indians and of Nishga claimants specifically have been extinguished by government legislation. On this basis the court rejects the claim of the Nishga of the Nass River Valley in West Central British Columbia but greatly strengthens the case for Indian land claims.

14 February 1973. The Yukon Indian Brotherhood presents the first northern land claim, *Together Today For Our Children Tomorrow*, on behalf of the twelve Indian bands of the Yukon Territory. Prime Minister Trudeau announces that a federal committee will negotiate the claim.

8 August 1973. The Canadian government announces that it will establish an Office of Native Claims, a branch of the Department of Indian Affairs and Northern Development. It will negotiate "comprehensive claims," claims for land not covered by treaty, and "specific claims," claims based on treaties, the Indian Act, or other legislation. The office will deal with only six comprehensive claims at a time. Indian Affairs Minister Jean Chrétien cites the *Calder* ruling as influencing this complete reversal of the White Paper's land claims proposals. Native leaders cautiously approve of the announcement.

27 August 1973. In the case of *Attorney General Canada v. Lavell*, the Supreme Court decides that provisions in the Indian Act that remove Indian status from Indian women who marry non-Indians are an excusable violation of the Bill of Right's equality guarantees. Most treaty Indian organizations welcome the ruling because they fear that the Bill of Rights could be used to strike down the entire Indian Act.

6 September 1973. In *Re Paulette et al. v. Registrar of Titles*, the Supreme Court of the Northwest Territories rules that Northwest Territories Indians have the right to file a caveat (notice of claim) on approximately one-third of the Northwest Territories, because there is significant doubt about whether treaties 8 and 11 are legitimate land cession treaties. The case is appealed to a higher court.

November 1973. The Quebec Superior Court grants the Cree and Inuit of northern Quebec an injunction halting development of the James Bay Hydroelectric Project in northern Quebec on the grounds that Quebec has not kept provisions of the Proclamation of 1763 or its 1912 agreement with the federal government. The Quebec Court of Appeal overturns the injunction a week later, but the Quebec government begins negotiating the Indian and Inuit claims immediately.

July 1974. The federal government establishes the Office of Native Claims to evaluate and negotiate Indian land claims.

28 August 1974. A group of Ojibwa end a five-week occupation of the Anicinibe Park in Kenora (in northwestern Ontario) after reaching a tentative agreement with authorities. The Ojibwa claim the fourteen-acre park occupies land taken from their reserve without their permission in 1959. The confrontation had become an armed siege on August 13.

20 September 1974. Five Indians are arrested for assaulting and obstructing police officers as two hundred Indians, trying to storm the Parliament buildings in Ottawa, battle with police and the military. The protest started September 15 when the Native Caravan began traveling from Vancouver to Ottawa to demand settlement of their land claims and to protest the poor housing conditions and social services on their reserves.

1975. The Union of British Columbia Indian Chiefs and the British Columbia Association of Non-Status Indians collapse (although both organizations are later revived). Both organizations were formed in 1969 to lead opposition to the White Paper. A trend of forming organizations to represent status and non-status Indians of specific tribes lines gains strength. This trend is unique to British Columbia.

April 1975. The federal government creates a Joint Cabinet-National Indian Brotherhood Committee and a Cabinet-Native Council of Canada Committee to improve communication between the government and Native organizations.

24 June 1975. The British Columbia government and the Indians of British Columbia agree to settle the issue of "cut-off" reserve lands. Following the recommendations of the McKenna-McBride Commission the British Columbia government "cut off" (removed) land from twenty-two British Columbia bands in 1919 and 1920, but they did not get the Indians' consent to do so.

19 July 1975. The Indian Brotherhood of the Northwest Territories and the Métis Association of the Northwest Territories issue the Dene Declaration, declaring that the aboriginal peoples of the Northwest Territories form a nation with the right to self-government. Dene means "people" in most Athapaskan dialects.

27 October 1975. Seven Indian bands, including the Lubicon Cree band, submit a caveat on land in northern Alberta. A ruling on a similar caveat filed in the Northwest Territories suggests that such a caveat would be accepted in an Alberta court.

11 November 1975. The East Main Cree, Montagnais, Naskapi (6,500 people), and Inuit (4,200 people) bands of northern Quebec sign the James Bay and Northern Quebec Agreement with the federal and Quebec governments and three Quebec Crown Corporations. In the agreement the Natives surrender their claims to 1,062,000 square kilometers (410,000 square miles) of land for a cash settlement ($225 million over twenty years) and surrender their aboriginal rights in exchange for rights granted them in the agreement. These rights include significant control over their political, economic, and social affairs. The agreement creates three land categories in northern Quebec-Natives will own 14,000 square kilometers (5,408 square miles) and will enjoy exclusive hunting, fishing, and trapping rights on an additional 62,160 square kilometers (24,000 square miles). The general public will have equal access to the rest of the land. The agreement also includes income security for Cree hunters and trappers. Some Natives criticize the deal, claiming it compares poorly with a land claims settlement in Alaska (the Alaska Native Claims Settlement Act) in 1971, which gave the Alaska Natives 44 million acres of land and $962.5 million. Cree Chief Billy Diamond and Inuit Charlie Watt have led the negotiations for the Natives.

27 February 1976. The Inuit Tapirisat of Canada presents its claim to an immense area in Canada's Arctic. The claim, on behalf of all the Inuit of the Northwest Territories, follows a unique federally funded study of Inuit land use and occupancy in the Northwest Territories. It proposes to establish Nunavut ("our land"), as a new territory covering most of Canada north of the treeline. The territory, which would be taken from the Northwest Territories, would be controlled by the Inuit who comprise over 80 percent of the population of that region.

May 1976. The Yukon Indians (status and non-status) reach an agreement-in-principle with the Canadian government to settle their land claim. Under the agreement the Indians would retain title to 52 hectares (128 acres) per person and exclusive hunting, trapping, and fishing rights on an additional 44,000 square kilometers (17,000 square miles). The agreement would have them

surrender subsurface rights to all the land. The membership of the organization rejects the deal because they believe it compares poorly to a settlement in Alaska in 1971.

May 1976. The Saskatchewan Indian Federated College, an independent college integrated with the University of Regina, is organized as the first college under Native control. Intended to encourage Native socioeconomic development and contribute to the general academic community, it will accept aboriginal and non-aboriginal students.

22 June 1976. A team of doctors recommends closing the English/Wabigoon river systems in northern Ontario to all fishing because of mercury pollution. The Ojibwa of Grassy Narrows have been told not to eat fish from the rivers, but they continue to eat them because the rivers remain open to sport fishermen. Experts have found evidence of mercury poisoning among the Indians.

26 October 1976. The Dene of the Northwest Territories present their claim to much of the land in the western Northwest Territories. The claim includes a proposal for an Indian government for the Northwest Territories with powers like that of a province. The Métis Association does not support this claim and instead is asking for separate funds from the federal government in order to fund their own claims research.

20 December 1976. On a technicality, the Supreme Court of Canada rules against the Indians of the Northwest Territories for the right to file a caveat. The ruling does not alter the lower court's finding, which casts doubt on the legality of Treaties 8 and 11 as land cession treaties. On this basis, the federal government has already accepted the Dene claim as a comprehensive claim. The proposed Mackenzie Valley Pipeline would pass through part of the area in question.

1977. The Labrador Inuit Association releases "Our Footprints are Everywhere," a land-use study similar to that done in the Northwest Territories. Later in the year, it presents the claim of the Labrador Inuit to land and sea-ice in northern Labrador.

1977. The Conseil Attikamek/Montagnais, an alliance of Attikamek (Téte-de-Boule) and Montagnais-Naskapi Indians of northern Quebec and Labrador, presents its claim to land in Quebec and Labrador.

March 1977. The Committee for Original People's Entitlement (COPE), established in 1969, presents

Inuvialuit Nunangat, a land claim on behalf of 2,500 Inuit in the western Arctic. COPE was originally part of the Inuit Tapirisat of Canada claim presented in February 1976 but, because of differences of opinion, withdrew in order to present its own claim.

17 March 1977. The Canadian government and the National Indian Brotherhood establish the Canadian Indian Rights Commission to replace the federal government's Indian Claims Commission established in 1969.

15 April 1977. The Mackenzie Valley Pipeline Inquiry (Berger Inquiry) calls for a ten-year moratorium on construction of any pipeline in the Mackenzie Valley to allow time for the Indians and Inuit to settle their land claims with the government and for the residents to prepare for changes the development would bring. Hearings of the inquiry ended in November 1976. The report points out that residents fear the development and that aboriginals have not benefitted from northern developments in the past. The Indian Brotherhood of the Northwest Territories, the Native Council of Canada and the National Indian Brotherhood endorse the report, but the Northwest Territories Métis Association, which supports the principle of the development, expresses disappointment with the report.

May 1977. The Alberta government passes a law that makes it impossible to file a caveat on unpatented Crown land. The law is to be applied retroactively, effectively killing an attempt by several Alberta Indian bands to file such a caveat. The provincial government has been fighting the caveat since October 1975.

29 July 1977. Kenneth Lysyk, the chair of the Alaska Highway Pipeline Inquiry, recommends approval-in-principle of the Alaska Highway Pipeline but recommends that construction be delayed by two years in order that Indian land claims can be settled before construction begins.

3 August 1977. The federal government rejects the proposals for separate Dene and Inuit governments in the Northwest Territories. These proposals are stalling negotiations on northern land claims.

28 September 1977. The Métis and non-status Indians of the Northwest Territories present their claim to land in the Mackenzie Valley in the Northwest Territories to the federal government. This group had been part of the Dene claim of October 1976, but withdrew to present its own claim.

31 October 1977. The James Bay Settlement Acts are passed by the Quebec and Canadian governments.

This gives the James Bay Agreement greater legal force than former Indian treaties.

November 1977. The Naskapi-Montagnais Innu Association of Labrador presents a claim on behalf of the Naskapi and Montagnais tribes in northern Labrador. The claim includes a declaration of sovereignty similar to the 1975 Dene Declaration.

December 1977. The Inuit Tapirisat of Canada presents a revised claim to land in the central and eastern Arctic. The revised claim was made necessary by the withdrawal of the Inuit of the western Arctic from the original ITC claim.

8 December 1977. A special Native commission created by the Native Council of Canada condemns the effects of the Canadian justice system on Natives. It associates the large number of Indians in jails with high unemployment, little education, pervasive poverty, and lack of opportunities among Natives.

12 January 1978. The Naskapi and Inuit of northeastern Quebec sign an agreement parallel to the James Bay and Northern Quebec Agreement of 1975.

30 March 1978. The Indian Brotherhood of the Northwest Territories changes its name to the Dene Nation and opens membership not only to treaty Indians, but also to all Native people, including Métis. The Dene and Métis have claims to the same regions of the Northwest Territories, and differences between the two have complicated negotiations with the federal government since 1976.

13 April 1978. The National Indian Brotherhood (NIB) pulls out of a joint Cabinet-National Indian Brotherhood Committee formed in 1975.

June 1978. The federal government's discussion paper *A Time For Action* calls for Native constitutional issues to be addressed and identified in the upcoming constitutional reform process. Constitutional reform became a prominent issue after Quebec elected a separatist government in 1976.

31 October 1978. The Committee for Original People's Entitlement signs an agreement-in-principle with the Canadian government to settle the Inuvialuit (Inuit of the western Arctic) land claim in the western Arctic.

1979. The Native Council of Canada issues its *Declaration of Métis and Indian Rights*. The document claims Natives have rights to self-determination, to representation in legislatures and in the constitutional reform process, and to recognition of special status in confederation.

January 1979. The Canadian Indian Rights Commission (a joint federal government-National Indian Brotherhood commission) is officially dissolved because of dissatisfaction on the part of the NIB.

5–6 February 1979. Canada's first ministers (prime minister and premiers) meet to discuss constitutional reform. Indian groups are offered observer status at the talks, but boycott the meeting to underscore their demands for direct participation in the talks.

1 July 1979. Three hundred Indian chiefs of the National Indian Brotherhood visit London to press British politicians to block any change to the British North America Act unless Indians are given a greater role in constitutional reform discussions. The Indians are fighting the government's proposed constitutional amendment that would recognize the existence of two founding nations (English and French) in Canada, but would give no special recognition to Aboriginals. Aboriginals demand direct participation in constitutional talks.

1980. The Tungavik Federation of Nunavut, formed by the Inuit Tapirisat of Canada in 1979 to negotiate its claim in the central and eastern Arctic, agrees to set aside demands for the Nunavut Territory in order to get negotiations on its land claim started.

1980. Negotiations resume between the Council of Yukon Indians and the federal and Yukon governments. Negotiations broke off after the Yukon Indians rejected a tentative agreement in May 1976.

1980. In the case of *Hamlet of Baker Lake et al. v. Minister of Indian Affairs and Northern Development*, the federal court rules that the aboriginal inhabitants of the Northwest Territories have hunting, trapping, and fishing rights to the land based on occupancy, not based on the Royal Proclamation of 1763. The court, however, also finds that governments can extinguish aboriginal title unilaterally. The ruling includes criteria by which the court can determine whether a group has proven to have aboriginal rights to land. According to these criteria, members of an organized society have a legitimate claim if they can prove that their ancestors belonged to an organized society that occupied the claimed land to the exclusion of other societies at the time the government asserted its sovereignty over the area. Notwithstanding the ruling, the Indians of Baker Lake lose this case because the court

Indians gather at the home of Grace McCarthy, Human Resources Minister, to protest the British Columbia government's child welfare policies. (Photo by Kate Bird. Courtesy of *Vancouver Sun*–Ken Oakes, October 1980)

finds that aboriginal rights do not allow them to prevent mining in the area.

8–12 September 1980. The first ministers (prime minister and provincial premiers) meet to discuss constitutional reform. Representatives of Native organizations are permitted to attend as observers.

13 October 1980. Seven hundred British Columbia Indians protest the number of Native children placed in non-Native foster homes in the 1960s and 1970s. As a result, the government begins to increase band control of child welfare services, a trend that also begins in other provinces.

7 November 1980. Indian leaders hold a press conference in London to explain why they feel threatened by Canada's constitutional proposals. Prime Minister Trudeau announces that he is willing to include a provision to protect aboriginal rights in the Constitution if such an amendment would be accepted by the premiers.

17 December 1980. National Indian Brotherhood president Del Riley, appearing before a Joint Parliamentary Committee on constitutional reform, protests the lack of Native involvement in the reform process. He says aboriginal peoples want a third level of government that would allow them to control their own land, resources, and people. He also calls for the entrenchment of the Proclamation of 1763 in the new Constitution.

1981. In the case of *R. v. Taylor and Williams*, the Supreme Court of Ontario finds that the terms of a cession treaty (a treaty in which Natives surrender their land rights in exchange for other rights) must be kept even if they do not appear in the treaty document.

30 January 1981. The federal government accepts a constitutional amendment that would entrench the provisions of the Proclamation of 1763. Another amendment would read: "The aboriginal and treaty rights of the aboriginal peoples of Canada are hereby recognized and affirmed." Del Riley, president of the National Indian Brotherhood, endorses the amendments.

2 September 1981. The United Nations Human Rights Commission rules that Canada's Indian Act violates international human rights because it discriminates on the basis of sex. The ruling was made in regard to Sandra Lovelace, a Maliseet, who had lost her Indian status and right to live on her tribal reserve because she married a non-Indian.

2–5 November 1981. Nine of ten provinces accept an amending formula for the Constitution and a Charter of Rights only after amendments guaranteeing aboriginal rights (30 January 1981) are deleted from the package. Several premiers oppose the provisions because they find them too poorly defined. The agreement meets with immediate angry denunciation by Indian leaders across Canada.

26 November 1981. The House of Commons reinstates a reworded version of a constitutional provision agreed upon on 30 January 1981. The new amendment recognized "existing aboriginal and treaty rights." Indian groups demanded the removal of the word "existing" despite assurances that the word would not alter the intended meaning of the section. The House of Commons also adds a provision that guarantees a federal-provincial conference, with Native participation, to define these existing rights.

29 January 1982. The British Court of Appeal rules that Britain no longer has any responsibility for the protection of Indian rights in Canada. Indian groups made the appeal to the British court in an attempt to convince the British government to block patriation (transfer to Canada) of the Constitution.

17 April 1982. Canada's new Constitution and Charter of Rights and Freedoms is proclaimed by the British government despite opposition by Canadian Indian groups. Section 25 of the Charter says that its equality guarantees do not affect aboriginal treaty rights or rights recognized by the Proclamation of 1763. Section 35 of the Constitution recognizes "existing aboriginal and treaty rights of the aboriginal peoples." (Indians, Inuit, and Métis are explicitly identified as aboriginal peoples.) The Constitution also guarantees aboriginal participation at a conference to define what these existing rights are. Indian groups boycott celebrations and denounce the new Constitution.

21 April 1982. David Ahenakew, a Cree from Saskatchewan, is elected to replace Del Riley as the new president of the National Indian Brotherhood. The National Indian Brotherhood announces its reorganization as the Assembly of First Nations (AFN), an association of chiefs rather than an alliance of bands.

July 1982. The federal government announces it will inject $61.4 million to deal with problems with the James Bay Agreement. The announcement follows reviews by the Indian Affairs Department and the Justice Department that found that the federal government is keeping the letter but not the spirit of the 1975 agreement.

22 September 1982. The Parliamentary Sub-Committee on Indian Women and the Indian Act releases its report calling for an end to sexual discrimination in the Indian Act.

March 1983. Alberta, Saskatchewan, and Manitoba associations of the Native Council of Canada withdraw to form the Métis National Council, over differences on the constitutional negotiation process.

15–16 March 1983. At a conference guaranteed by the 1982 Constitution, representatives of aboriginal peoples, the first ministers, and the elected governments of Yukon and Northwest Territories agree to alter Section 25 of the Charter of Rights to recognize all aboriginal rights acquired in past and future land claims settlements. Section 35 of the Constitution will be amended to guarantee gender equality in the enjoyment

Indian chiefs open the first ministers' conference on aboriginal issues, March 1983. This conference, guaranteed by the 1982 constitution, marked the first time that aboriginals were given full participation in constitutional conferences. (Courtesy of CP Pictures Archives)

of treaty rights. Native groups are also guaranteed participation at two more conferences to define the nature and extent of "existing" aboriginal and treaty rights enshrined in Section 35 of the Constitution. This is the first constitutional conference in which Native groups have full participation. Indian leaders endorse the amendments but express frustration at the slow progress being made on central issues.

3 November 1983. The Report of the Special Parliamentary Committee on Indian Self-Government (the Penner Report) unanimously agrees that the aboriginal right to self-government should be entrenched in the

Constitution. The commission also recommends abolishing the Indian Act and the Indian Affairs Department. The report receives unanimous support in the House of Commons.

1984. The Canadian Education Association reports that Indian bands that have taken over control of Indian education have witnessed marked improvement in student achievement. Since 1970 increasing numbers of Indian bands have taken over control of Indian education.

8–9 March 1984. The second first ministers' constitutional conference on aboriginal issues ends with an agreement to amend the Indian Act to guarantee gender equality but without agreement on the major aim of defining aboriginal rights. Six premiers reject a proposed amendment that would recognize the right to aboriginal self-government, complaining that it was too vague.

17 May 1984. Alberta Indians walk out of an Assembly of First Nations (AFN) meeting because of disagreement over the gender equality amendment. The Indian Association of Alberta then withdraws from the AFN for a time.

5 June 1984. The final agreement is reached on the comprehensive claim of the Committee of Original People's Entitlement (COPE) on behalf of the 2,500 Inuvialuit of the Mackenzie Valley. This is the first comprehensive land claims settlement north of the 60th parallel. The agreement calls for the Inuvialuit to surrender their aboriginal rights in return for the rights and benefits provided in the agreement, which include a cash settlement and provisions regarding wildlife, the environment, and economic development. The agreement is unique in that it gives the Inuvialuit outright ownership of 82,880 square kilometers (32,000 square miles) including subsurface rights in 13,000 square kilometers (5,000 square miles). It also allows the Inuvialuit to participate in wildlife management decisions. The federal government also agrees to establish a 13,000 square-kilometer (5,000 square-mile) National Wilderness Area in which the Inuit will enjoy hunting, trapping, and fishing rights. Native leaders criticized the provisions that would have the Inuit give up their aboriginal rights in exchange for the rights specified by the agreement.

12 June 1984. The Micmac of Conne River, Newfoundland, are recognized as an Indian band under the Indian Act. They settled at Conne River in 1870.

21 June 1984. The first amendments to the Canadian Constitution are proclaimed. The two amendments are provisions agreed upon at the first ministers' conference in March 1983.

3 July 1984. The Canadian Government proclaims the Cree-Naskapi (of Quebec) Act according to a provision in the James Bay and Northern Quebec Agreement of 1975. The act gives the Natives of northern Quebec a type of self-government. The Indians no longer fall under the jurisdiction of the Indian Act.

23 October 1984. The Gitksan and Wet'suwet'en (Carrier) Indians of the Skeena and Bulkley River Valleys of northern British Columbia initiate a court action to claim over 57,000 square kilometers of northwestern and north central British Columbia.

November 1984. In the *Guerin* case, the Supreme Court rules that the Canadian government must pay the Musqueam band, in Vancouver, $10 million for violating its legal obligations to the band. The Court rules that aboriginal rights were not created by law.

26 February 1985. Inuit from Grise Fiord, Ellesmere Island, in Canada's high Arctic, meet with Indian Affairs Minister John Crosbie to seek help to move south. The Inuit were relocated from Port Harrison, Quebec, in 1953.

2–3 April 1985. At a constitutional conference on aboriginal issues, four premiers refuse to approve a constitutional amendment that would entrench the Indian right to self-government without a clear definition of such a right. The Assembly of First Nations refuses an amendment that would entrench the principle of self-rule for Aboriginals but would not guarantee a process for defining such powers. The participants agree to meet again in June.

5–6 June 1985. Constitutional talks with first ministers and aboriginal organizations fail to make progress in defining Indian rights to self-government. The federal government announces that it will begin negotiating self-government agreements with individual groups of Indians.

28 June 1985. Passage of Bill C-31 removes sections of the Indian Act that discriminate against women in order to harmonize the Indian Act with the Charter of Rights and Freedoms. Some Indians protest that the federal government has no right to define who is or is not an Indian. Many Indian bands are also concerned about the effect of a sudden influx of new status Indians on reserve life and band funds.

29–31 July 1985. The Prairie Treaty Nations Alliance (PTNA), accounting for approximately one-third of the membership of the Assembly of First Nations, walks out of an Assembly of First Nations convention in Vancouver over disagreements arising out of the AFN's negotiating strategy with the government. The defection follows earlier defections by Alberta and Atlantic organizations. Incumbent AFN leader, David Ahenakew from Saskatchewan, facing questions about the AFN's $3.6 million debt, becomes leader of the PTNA. Dene Georges Erasmus from the Northwest Territories is chosen president of the AFN. Under Erasmus, the Indian Association of Alberta and Atlantic Indians return, and the debt is eliminated.

November 1985. Seventy-two Haida and their supporters are arrested while trying to prevent logging on Lyell Island (Queen Charlotte Islands, British Columbia). The Haida, who have protested logging in the area since 1974, filed a claim in 1983 and set up a blockade on October 30 after the British Columbia government approved logging on the island.

December 1985. Minister of Indian Affairs David Crombie issues *Living Treaties: Lasting Agreements* (the Coolican Report), a revision of the government's comprehensive land claims policy. The new policy notes that little progress has been made in settling land claims. It announces the government's commitment to settling claims through negotiation rather than litigation. The new policy announces that land claims agreements would not necessarily require Natives to surrender their aboriginal rights and would be viewed as flexible over time. The policy also calls for agreements that will allow Native peoples to share in the financial rewards of development in their territories. Native organizations welcome the new policy as a breakthrough.

December 1985. The Ojibwa of the Grassy Narrows Band and nearby Whitedog Reserve in northwestern Ontario accept an offer of $16.7 million from the federal and Ontario governments for compensation for mercury poisoning on both reserves and for land on the Whitedog Reserve flooded by a hydroelectric project in 1958.

9 October 1986. Legislation giving the Sechelt band of Salish Indians in British Columbia self-government is passed. The band has agreed to a form of self-government akin to a municipal government.

December 1986. Indian Affairs Minister Bill McKnight unveils a new comprehensive land claims policy, which announces the government's intention to restrict land claims negotiations to land issues. The government will seek to make one-time settlements with Indians.

26–27 March 1987. The final constitutional conference on aboriginal issues guaranteed by amendments to the Constitution of 1982 ends with no agreement on how to define Indian rights to self-government, and no agreement to meet again. Differences center around the concept of the "inherent" aboriginal right to self-government.

30 April 1987. The prime minister and the premiers unanimously agree on a constitutional reform package, which becomes known as the Meech Lake Accord. The first ministers formulate the new package because

Quebec refused to sign the Constitution of 1982. This reform package makes no reference to aboriginal issues.

28 May 1987. Native leaders hold a press conference to accuse the first ministers of holding a double standard in the Meech Lake Accord. They accuse the governments of being willing to enshrine an undefined recognition of Quebec as a distinct society after rejecting amendments guaranteeing aboriginal rights to self-government because they are undefined. They also protest that they were shut out of these constitutional talks.

1 July 1987. The federal government announces an agreement with the British Columbia government to establish a national park in the South Moresby region of the Queen Charlotte Islands. The Haida have been protesting logging operations in the area.

11 September 1988. The Innu of North West River in Labrador begin protesting low-altitude training at a NATO training base near Goose Bay, which began in 1980 by camping at the end of a runway at the base. The Innu claim that the flights are causing reduction of wildlife populations, particularly of the George River Caribou herd upon which they depend, and is causing distress to the Indians themselves.

22 October 1988. Chief Bernard Ominayak of the Lubicon Lake Cree band reaches a preliminary agreement with Alberta Premier Don Getty on terms to settle the band's long-standing land claim. The agreement would provide the band with a 250 square kilometer (95 square mile) reserve. On October 15, the Lubicon set up a blockade on the road leading to their community after negotiations with the federal government broke down. On October 20, twenty-seven Indians were arrested when the Royal Canadian Mounted Police removed the blockade. The Lubicon gained international attention by organizing a boycott of "The Spirit Sings," an exposition of Native artifacts held during the Calgary Olympics in February 1988. The Lubicon Lake band was missed when the government and northern Alberta Indians signed Treaty 8 in 1899. The band launched a claim in 1933 and was promised a reserve in 1940. However, no reserve was ever given to them. In 1980 an access road was built to their settlement area and about four hundred oil wells were drilled, seriously disrupting the band's traditional self-sufficient dependence on hunting and trapping. Most of the band turned to welfare.

27 February 1989. The Ontario Court of Appeal upholds a 1984 finding that the Teme-Augama Anishnabai (Bear Island People) band of Ojibway had lost title to its land in 1850 even though they had not signed the treaty. The federal government had granted the Indians a reserve at the south end of Lake Temagami, in east-central Ontario, in 1885, but the Ontario government refused to transfer the land in the agreement.

March 1989. The federal government announces a ceiling on funding for Indian students attending post-secondary institutions. Indians protest with sit-ins and hunger strikes in Thunder Bay (western Ontario), claiming that the funding is a treaty right. Special funding for Indians in post-secondary education began in 1968 with the number of Indians in post-secondary institutions increasing dramatically since then.

10 May 1989. Cree of northern Quebec file suit to stop construction of the $7.5 billion Great Whale Project (Phase II of the James Bay Hydroelectric Project) in northern Quebec. Studies by Hydro-Quebec confirmed that mercury levels in reservoirs created by the first phase of the James Bay project increased to up to nine times the federal government's guidelines for safety. The 1975 James Bay and Northern Quebec Agreement made provisions for this second phase, even bigger than the first, but the Quebec government elected to begin construction without the project undergoing the environmental review process established by the agreement.

28 August 1989. The federal government announces that it will settle with a band (the Woodland Cree) composed of Indians it claims have defected from the Lubicon Lake band in northern Alberta. This follows the federal government's rejection of an agreement reached between Chief Bernard Ominayak of the Lubicon Lake band and the Alberta premier in October 1988, and the Lubicon's rejection of the Government's offer of January 1989.

September 1989. The Nisga'a (Nishga) sign a framework agreement with the federal government toward resolving their claim to land in west central British Columbia, but the British Columbia government refuses to recognize the legitimacy of the claim.

26 January 1990. An inquiry in Nova Scotia finds that, because of racism and incompetence in the police force and legal community, Donald Marshall, a Micmac, had been wrongfully convicted of murder in 1972 and spent the next eleven years in prison. The report recommends that the government establish a cabinet committee on race relations and a Native criminal justice system.

7 February 1990. The Nova Scotia government issues an apology to Donald Marshall. The government announces that it will establish a cabinet committee on race relations and establish a Native criminal court as a pilot project.

7 March 1990. The Nova Scotia Court of Appeal rules that provisions in the Constitution Act of 1982 give Micmac Indians the constitutional right to fish for food and give them some immunity from government regulations.

31 March 1990. The Council of Yukon Indians, representing 6,500 Indians, and the federal government and Yukon governments reach an umbrella final agreement to settle their 1973 land claim. This agreement is designed to serve as the blueprint for negotiations between the government and the fourteen First Nations of the Council. It is unique in that it offers the Indians a share of federal royalties from mining and exemption from some forms of taxation, although the status Indians will give up their rights under the Indian Act in exchange for rights specified in the agreement. The Indians will retain title to 41,440 square kilometers (8.6 percent of the land in the Yukon) and will receive $242.7 million over fifteen years.

4 April 1990. The New York State legislature passes a law that will require an environmental assessment of the Great Whale Project before it signs a contract to buy the power from the project. The legislation followed lobbying by the Cree of northern Quebec who oppose the project. The Cree began fighting the project immediately after the government's 1989 announcement that it would begin construction.

9 April 1990. The thirteen thousand Dene and Métis of the Northwest Territories sign a land-claim agreement for the Mackenzie Valley in the western Arctic. The agreement would give the claimants title to 180,000 square kilometers of land. Issues of treaty rights and self-government remain to be negotiated.

23 April 1990. The Teme-Augama Anishnabai Indian band is granted a veto over logging on a tract of land, which they claim as theirs.

24 May 1990. In the case of *R. v. Sioui*, the Supreme Court rules that a 230-year-old treaty signed by the Huron Indians of Quebec supersedes later legislation that contradicts it. The ruling is based upon Section 35 of the Constitution of 1982, which guarantees aboriginal treaty rights.

31 May 1990. The Supreme Court of Canada orders a retrial for Ronald Sparrow, from the Musqueam band

(Vancouver), who had been convicted of violating federal fishing regulations. The Court rules that Section 35 of the Charter supersedes wildlife regulations.

22 June 1990.   Elijah Harper, a Cree-Ojibwa member of the provincial legislature in Manitoba, is able to use procedural rules to prevent the passage of the Meech Lake Accord in the Manitoba legislature. This effectively kills the constitutional reform package that Aboriginals have been opposing since its inception in 1987.

11 July 1990.   A police officer is killed after Quebec police storm a barricade on the Mohawk reserve at Kanesatake (Oka), near Montreal. The Mohawk set up the blockade in March to prevent construction of a golf course on land they claim. After their failed attempt to storm the barricades on July 11, police surround Kanesatake. In sympathy with the Mohawk at Kanesatake, members of the Mohawk Warrior Society at Kahnawake (Caughnawaga), south of Montreal, block access to the Mercier Bridge, a bridge linking the southern suburbs of Montreal with the city. The actions initiate a seventy-eight-day standoff between the police and military and the Mohawk Warriors of Kahnawake and Kanesatake, a conflict that draws worldwide attention.

19 July 1990.   The Dene and Métis reject their comprehensive land claim settlement with the federal government because of concern over the provision that would have them surrender their aboriginal rights.

9 August 1990.   The British Columbia government announces that it is willing to join Indians and the federal government in land claims negotiations based on the legitimacy of aboriginal title. The policy reverses the position held by every British Columbia government since 1864. The promise is made after Indians bands blocked rail lines and roads in the province.

7 September 1990.   The Royal Canadian Mounted Police move in on the Peigan Lonefighters (a revived warrior society) camp, ending a month-long attempt by the Lonefighters to divert the Oldman River around the site of a partially completed dam. The leader of the Lonefighters, Milton Born With a Tooth, is arrested on weapons charges. The Lonefighters oppose the dam because it would flood land they consider sacred and because they fear its environmental effects.

25 September 1990.   Prime Minister Brian Mulroney announces a new government agenda to meet aboriginal grievances. He commits the government to speeding up settlement of all land claims and meeting all its outstanding treaty obligations. For the first time, the government will begin negotiating more than six comprehensive claims at a time. He also announces a commitment to improve housing, sewage treatment, and water facilities on reserves, and to increase aboriginal control over their own affairs.

26 September 1990.   The warriors at Kahnawake and Kanesatake surrender after an eleven-week standoff with police and soldiers. The seventy-eight day armed standoff attracted international attention and made Canadians more aware of the depth of frustration among many Native Canadians. The federal government refused to negotiate with the Indians as long as the standoff continued.

11 October 1990.   The British Columbia government signs an agreement to join the federal government in land claims negotiations with the Nisga'a (Nishga) Tribal Council.

7 November 1990.   The federal government announces that as a result of the rejection by the Dene and Métis of their land claims settlement in July, the government will begin negotiating with individual Indian groups in the western Arctic, saying that such groups had indicated their desire to negotiate separately. Indian leaders accuse the government of adopting a "divide and conquer" strategy.

30 November 1990.   The Naskapi-Montagnais Innu Association signs a framework agreement with the federal and Labrador/Newfoundland governments toward settlement of its land claim in Labrador. The claim was submitted in 1977. Negotiations were slowed by the group's claim to sovereignty, acrimonious relations between the Quebec and Newfoundland governments, and Innu protests of low-level flights at a NATO base at Goose Bay in 1989.

19 December 1990.   The federal and Alberta governments reach an agreement with a band known as the Woodland Cree, formed in 1989 as a breakaway band of the Lubicon Lake band, which has been seeking a settlement since the 1930s.

8 March 1991.   The British Columbia Supreme Court rules in *Delgamuukw v. Attorney-General* that the Gitksan-Wet'suwet'ens of west central British Columbia do not hold aboriginal title to fifty-seven thousand square kilometers they claim, because such title was extinguished by British Columbia before it entered Confederation and because the Proclamation of 1763 does not apply to British Columbia. The Indians announce that they will appeal the decision. The British

Columbia government announces that the decision will not change its policy of negotiating with Indian claimants.

12 June 1991. Ovide Mercredi, a Cree lawyer from Manitoba, is elected as the new president of the Assembly of First Nations.

26 June 1991. Indian Affairs Minister Tom Siddon announces that the government will seek to ameliorate damage done to Indian societies by residential schools. Evidence of physical and sexual abuse at residential schools has been revealed in the past few years.

6 July 1991. The Woodland Cree band, a band created by the federal government in 1989, votes to accept the government's offer to settle its land claim.

13 July 1991. The Gwich'in (Kutchin), Athapaskan Indians of the Mackenzie delta, reach a land claims settlement with the federal government based on the agreement rejected by the Dene and Métis of Northwest Territories in April 1990. The agreement gives the Indians fifteen thousand square kilometers in the Northwest Territories and the Yukon.

12 August 1991. The report of the Manitoba Aboriginal Justice Inquiry finds that aboriginal peoples suffer discrimination in the justice system. It recommends the establishment of a separate aboriginal justice system that would give the aboriginal people the right to enact and enforce laws in their own communities. The inquiry finds that racism played an important part in the deaths of Helen Betty Osborne, a Cree woman murdered by non-Natives in The Pas, in northern Manitoba, and J. J. Harper, a Cree man killed by a Winnipeg police officer.

27 August 1991. The Quebec government announces that construction of the Great Whale Project (Phase II of the James Bay Hydroelectric Project) will be delayed one year. The announcement follows a negotiations between Quebec and New York State. The Quebec government hopes to sell most of the electricity to the northern states of the United States. The Cree of northern Quebec have lobbied New York legislators to refuse to buy the power.

7 December 1991. The Council of Yukon Indians votes to accept their umbrella final agreement on their land claim with the federal government. The agreement establishes guidelines for settlements with the each of Yukon's fourteen First Nations. The Indians will receive title to 41,440 square kilometers (8.6 percent of the Yukon) and $257 million. The agreement includes provisions for self-government for the Indians.

16 December 1991. Indian Affairs Minister Tom Siddon announces that the government has reached a final agreement with the Inuit (Tungavik Federation of Nunavut) of the eastern Arctic. The agreement follows fifteen years of negotiations. The agreement would create a new territory of Nunavut in the eastern Arctic. The new territory would be publicly governed although Inuit presently account for 80 percent of the area's population. The provision resembles part of the Inuit's original claim, but had been rejected earlier by the federal government. The agreement also calls for the Inuit to surrender their aboriginal rights. They would be given cash ($580 million over fourteen years) in exchange for title to most of the land, but would retain 350,000 square kilometers of land (approximately 17.5 percent of the territory).

28 January 1992. Responding to the report of the Manitoba Justice Inquiry, the Manitoba government announces that it will hire more Native judges and improve legal services to Indians in the provinces, but rejects the suggestion that a separate justice system be established in Manitoba.

31 March 1992. The Quebec government blames the Cree of northern Quebec for New York State's decision to cancel a contract to buy power from the Great Whale Project, putting the project in jeopardy. The Cree have lobbied against the project.

April 1992. Representatives of the federal government, nine provincial provinces, two territories, and four aboriginal groups unanimously agree that the Constitution should recognize the inherent aboriginal right to self-government. The exact powers of Indian governments that would form a third level of government has not been negotiated, but aboriginal leaders and governments hail the agreement as the beginning of a new era for Canada's Natives. The Assembly of First Nations announces the creation of a women's committee on constitutional matters to meet criticism that it is ignoring the concerns of Native women. The Native Women's Association of Canada has argued that Native governments must be bound by the Charter of Rights to protect aboriginal women.

22 May 1992. The federal government announces that it will build a healing lodge (federal prison) at Maple Creek, Saskatchewan. It will be designed to allow native women prisoners to be kept near their communities. Up to now all women in federal prisons have been kept in one prison in Kingston, Ontario. While only 3 percent of Canada's population is aboriginal, 15 percent of its female prison population is aboriginal.

20 August 1992. Prime Minister Brian Mulroney, Canada's ten premiers, and the leaders of the Assembly of First Nations, the Native Council of Canada, the Métis National Council and the Inuit Tapirisat of Canada reach unanimous agreement on provisions that would entrench aboriginal self-government in Canada's Constitution (The Charlottetown Accord). All agree that laws passed by aboriginal governments will have to be consistent with laws passed by the federal and provincial governments and with Canadian standards of peace, order and good government. While most Canadians and natives greet the agreement enthusiastically, there are also immediate voices of criticism.

3 September 1992. Prime Minister Brian Mulroney announces that a national referendum will be held on October 26 on the "Charlottetown Accord," a proposed new Constitution for Canada that includes provisions that would grant a form of self-government for Canada's aboriginal peoples.

21 September 1992. Prime Minister Brian Mulroney, British Columbia Premier Mike Harcourt, and British Columbia Indians agree to establish a British Columbia Treaty Commission to facilitate the settlement of land claims in British Columbia.

26 October 1992. In a nation-wide referendum, Canadians reject the Charlottetown Accord. Pollsters suggest that most Canadians did not reject the proposal because of its provisions regarding aboriginal self-government. Nevertheless, status Indians do not appear to have supported the proposal. Sixty-two percent of those on Indian reserves who voted, rejected the Accord. Many natives complained that the self-government provisions were not adequately spelled out. Seventy-five percent of the Inuit voted for the agreement.

20 November 1992. The Federal Court of Appeal rules the federal government of Canada does not have to do an environmental assessment of the Eastmain hydroelectric project because it is authorized by the 1975 James Bay and Northern Quebec Agreement.

13 January 1993. The Sahtu Tribal Council representing 2200 Sahtu (Bearlake) Dene and Métis reach a land claim agreement with the federal government. The agreement will give the Sahtu $75 million dollars over fifteen years. The agreement also grants the Sahtu ownership and subsurface rights to some land and a share of royalties for resources extracted from the region.

19 January 1993. Police seize unlicenced gambling equipment on five reserves in Manitoba. The Indians and the provincial government have disputed the legality of the gambling establishments.

26 January 1993. Television news reports show six Innu children aged twelve to fourteen, at the remote village of Davis Inlet, in Labrador, sniffing gasoline in an apparent suicide attempt. The Innu at Davis Inlet say the level of substance abuse in the village reflects the community's despair. The story captures national and international attention.

9 February 1993. Tom Siddon, Canadian Minister of Indian Affairs announces that the government will pay for the relocation of the Innu village of Davis Inlet to the nearby mainland location at Sango Bay. The Department of Health and Welfare Canada is also paying ($1.7 million) for seventeen Innu children who are being treated for their substance abuse at Poundmaker's Lodge, a Native-run addictions treatment center near Edmonton.

1 June 1993. According to a Canadian census, 783,980 people in Canada identify themselves as Indian (626,000 are status Indians); 212,650 as Métis; and 49,255 Inuit. Sixty-five percent of Canadian natives live west of Ontario.

25 June 1993. The British Columbia Court of Appeal rules in the case of *Delgamuukw v. The Queen* that the 8000 Gitksan-Wet'suwet'en claimants do enjoy some rights to land which they are claiming in west-central British Columbia. The ruling overturns portions of a March 1991 British Columbia Supreme Court ruling which said that any land rights the Gitksan-Wet'suwet'en may have had were extinguished before British Columbia entered the Canadian Confederation. The claimants welcome the decision as a victory. The British Columbia government expresses its commitment to resolve the claim through negotiation.

11 November 1993. New Minister of Indian Affairs Ron Irwin meets with Indian chiefs in an effort to begin negotiations toward an agreement that would establish aboriginal self-government in Canada.

3 February 1994. The recipients of the first Canadian National Aboriginal Achievement Awards are announced. The founder of the award program is John Kim Bell. A special lifetime achievement award was granted to Bill Reid, Haida artist.

22 February 1994. Canadian finance minister Paul Martin announces that Camp Ipperwash, a military training base in southern Ontario, will be returned to the Ojibwa community at the Kettle and Stoney Point reserves. The land was originally taken from the band in 1942 under the War Measures Act. The band struggled ever since to have the land returned. In 1980 the federal government gave the band $2.5 million to compensate for the expropriation, but some members of the band had been occupying the base since last May in efforts to have the land returned.

27 February 1994. The Native Council of Canada is reorganized as the Congress of Aboriginal Peoples during its convention in Ottawa.

16 March 1994. For the sixth straight year, Max Yalden of the Canadian Human Rights Commission points to the discrimination faced by Natives as the most serious human rights problem in Canada.

31 May 1994. The Canadian government introduces legislation to enact its agreement with the Yukon Indians. The agreement is with four First Nations in the Yukon—the Vuntut Gwitchin First Nation, the Champagne and Aishihik First Nation, the Teslin Tlingit Council, and the Nacho Nyak Dunand First Nation. The agreement covers more than 41,000 square kilometers of the Yukon, and will pay the four First Nations $242.6 million over the next fifteen years. The First Nations communities will have control over hunting, fishing, and other land use on their own land. Ten other bands have not yet approved the agreement.

1 September 1994. Phil Fontaine, the grand chief of the Assembly of Manitoba Chiefs announces that his organization has approved a preliminary agreement aimed at dismantling the Department of Indian Affairs in Manitoba and handing over greater powers to Indian communities in Manitoba. Manitoba was chosen for this experiment because leaders like Fontaine are willing to move toward a form of self government without the passage of constitutional amendments or federal legislation.

9 September 1994. Milton Born With a Tooth is sentenced to sixteen months in prison after being convicted of weapons offenses committed during the 1990 standoff at the construction site of the Oldman River Dam in southern Alberta.

5 December 1994. The Ontario government announces that the Rama Ojibwa Reserve in southern Ontario will be the site of Ontario's first Native casino. The decision that the profits from the casino will be shared by the 131 Indian bands in the province sparks protest from nonstatus Native communities and organizations.

6 February 1995. About 150 Innu travel to Voisey's Bay in northern Labrador to protest drilling there. The International Nickel Company discovered a large nickel deposit at Voisey's Bay, near Nain, in 1994, but the Innu do not want the deposit exploited until their claims have been settled.

10 February 1995. The Saskatchewan government reaches a deal with the Saskatchewan Federation of Indian Nations to open four casinos on Indian reserves in the province. The Natives will get 75 percent of the profits of these casinos. Throughout Canada, Native communities have been attempting to assert a right to operate casinos on reserves, much like Indian communities in the United States. Twice, however, the Supreme Court has ruled that provinces have exclusive jurisdiction over gaming. Thus, these communities have found it necessary to work with provincial governments before they could legally establish such gaming operations. The Saskatchewan government shut down a casino operation on the White Bear Reserve in 1993, but chose to negotiate with its First Nations communities rather than fight a protracted battle with them.

20 February 1995. Nova Scotia Indians sign a deal that will see them get one-half of the government's share of profits from a casino planned for Sydney. Manitoba, Ontario, Nova Scotia, and New Brunswick are also working with First Nations communities to share gambling profits.

6 September 1995. Dudley George is shot to death during a protest at Ipperwash Provincial Park, about forty-five kilometers northeast of Sarnia, Ontario. Dissident members of the Kettle and Stoney Point Ojibwa band in southern Ontario took over Camp Ipperwash, an abandoned military base, in July. The 900-hectare parcel of land was taken from the Stoney Point Reserve in 1942 under the authority of the War Measures Act. They were given $50,000 at the time. In 1980 they were given $2.4 million more in compensation. A group of protestors began occupying the base on 5 May 1993, and in February 1994 the government agreed to turn the land over to the band after the military had a chance to clean up the base and dispose of unexploded ammunition. The continued occupation prevented the clean up, however. More recently, the camp has attracted a renegade group that includes Indians from other parts of Ontario and the United States. On July 30, with the protestors becoming more militant, the army abandoned the camp to avoid bloodshed. Then, on September 4, several dozen people including some from the United States, began occupying the adjoining Ipperwash Provincial Park as it was being closed for the season. They claim that the park includes a Native burial site.

17 September 1995.   Rebels who have been occupying land near Gustafsen Lake, near 100 Mile House, British Columbia, since June, surrender after John Stevens, a spiritual leader from Alberta's Stoney Reserve advises them to do so. The owner of the ranch had allowed a group to hold a Sun Dance on his property every year since 1990. The standoff began in June when the owner discovered a group had remained on his property, and refused to abide by an eviction order. The Natives claim that the land is sacred to the Shuswap Indians. The standoff escalated on August 18 when a police officer was shot at. Ovide Mercredi, the leader of the Assembly of First Nations, then attempted to mediate on August 25 and 26, but failed. Mercredi called on the group to surrender, but he accused the police of undermining his mediation efforts, and criticized political leaders for refusing to get involved at all. Tensions rose again on August 27 when two police officers were hit by gunfire. They were uninjured because they were wearing bullet-proof jackets.

26 October 1995.   In a referendum, the Inuit of northern Quebec vote 94 percent to stay in Canada. The vote comes in anticipation of a province-wide referendum sponsored by the Quebec government. The Inuit referendum result is similar to those of a referendum they held in 1980. Indian Affairs Minister Ron Irwin responds to the results by saying that the aboriginal people of Quebec have the right to secede from Quebec in the event of separation, a position that the Quebec government rejects.

30 October 1995.   In a province-wide referendum, the people of Quebec narrowly defeat a proposal to separate from Canada. In that referendum, Quebeckers vote narrowly against separation, but the narrowness of the victory leads some separatist leaders to suggest that ethnic minorities are preventing French Quebeckers from realizing their political aspirations. The referendum and its aftermath lead many to fear reprisals. The 7,500 Inuit and 11,000 Cree of Quebec have been consistent opponents of Quebec separation, as have most of the Indian groups in the province. Approximately 62,000 Indians live in Quebec.

February 1996.   British Columbia abandons land-claim talks with the Gitskan band of northern British Columbia, arguing that the band has been too rigid in its demands. Negotiations began after the British Columbia Court of Appeal ruled in favor of the Gitskan in the *Delgamuukw* case in 1993. Now, however, both sides seem willing to take on the risks and costs involved with an appeal of that decision to the Supreme Court, an appeal that had been suspended as long as the negotiations continued. Some argue that the British

Columbia government has taken a hard line because a provincial election is looming.

26 February 1996.   The Supreme Court rules that Aboriginals do not have an inherent right to govern themselves. The decision will mean that Indian bands will continue to have to negotiate with provincial governments to gain access to gaming profits. Several provinces, including Ontario, have already signed agreements with Indian bands that would see governments share gambling profits with Indian bands, but the ruling that Aboriginals do not have the inherent right to govern themselves will have important implications.

10 March 1996.   The Department of Indian Affairs releases reports that suggest that living conditions for aboriginal Canadians improved noticeably between 1980 and 1995. Still, the numbers study shows that more progress will be necessary before Indians have the same living standards as other Canadians.

28 March 1996.   Quebec Inuit accept an offer from the Canadian government to compensate them for being relocated to the high Arctic in 1953. The government relocated about ninety Quebec Inuit from Inukjuak and Pond Inlet to Resolute Bay and Grise Fiord.

21 August 1996.   The Supreme Court rules that Native people cannot claim an aboriginal right to sell fish unless they can prove that they sold fish historically. Specifically, the court upheld a conviction of Dorothy Van der Peet, a Sto:lo from British Columbia who sold salmon in 1987 without a commercial license.

29 October 1996.   The residents of Davis Inlet vote 97 percent in favor of accepting an agreement reached with the Canadian government in July that would see them relocate to a mainland village at Sango Bay.

21 November 1996.   The Royal Commission on Aboriginal People releases its six-volume, 3,537-page final report. The report includes 440 recommendations. The report calls on the government to commit itself to a comprehensive restructuring of its relationship with aboriginal people. Among its many specific recommendations, it calls on the government to provide new lands and resources for Native communities. It recommends increasing spending by $1.5 billion to $2 billion annually. It also recommends that the government concede Aboriginals the inherent right to self-government. It calls on the government to establish a new independent tribunal to monitor land claims, establish an aboriginal parliament, and apologize for its past mistakes. The commission recommends that the Department of Indian Affairs be replaced by two new departments, one of which would deal with Native governments, while the other would deal with communities not yet prepared for self-government. It urges the government to provide an adequate land and revenue base to all aboriginal communities, including Métis communities. The Royal Commission on Aboriginal Peoples was established during the aftermath of the Oka Crisis in 1990. It has been controversial because of its cost—at $58 million it is the most expensive royal commission in Canadian history—and because the report has been delayed—the commission was originally told to submit its final report in the fall of 1994. The five-volume report is accompanied by thousands of pages of supporting documents and reports. Ron Irwin, the minister of Indian Affairs, responds cautiously to the report, suggesting that it would be too expensive to implement the recommendations.

18 December 1996. The European Union agrees not to ban Canadian fur imports as scheduled in the beginning of January. The move comes after Canada agrees to phase out the leghold trap. The concession is very important for Native people, because more than one-half the trappers in Canada are Native.

14 February 1997. Nine Mi'kmaq bands in Nova Scotia become the first in Canada to take over jurisdiction of their children's education. The federal government hand over $140 million to help them establish their own school boards. The development is seen as a potential precedent for other parts of Canada.

17 April 1997. Natives hold a national day of protest to show their dissatisfaction with the lack of government action in implementing the recommendations of the Royal Commission on Aboriginal Peoples, and to protest proposed changes to the Indian Act. The protests slow traffic in Canada. Indian Affairs Minister Ron Irwin says some of the recommendations of the Royal Commission have already been implemented, but that it would be impossible to implement them all.

May 1997. The Association for the Survivors of the Subenacadie Indian Residential School file a class action lawsuit against the federal government and the Roman Catholic Diocese of Halifax. The claimants say that students at the school suffered as a result of racism and physical, emotional, and sexual abuse. The school, which closed in 1967, educated more than 2,000 students. It was one of seventy-four such schools built by the Canadian government since the 1880s. Former students in schools across the country have begun filing lawsuits to seek compensation for alleged abuse.

20 May 1997. The British Columbia Supreme Court convicts William Jones Ignace (Wolverine) of mischief endangering life for his role in the Gustafsen Lake standoff during the summer of 1995. Several others are convicted of lesser charges.

31 July 1997. Phil Fontaine is elected as the head of the Assembly of First Nations (AFN) at that group's annual meeting. Fontaine proposes to follow a more conciliatory approach than Ovide Mercredi, his predecessor. Fontaine promises to seek partnerships with governments, businesses, community agencies, and special interest groups. The former Minister of Indian Affairs, Ron Irwin, increasingly snubbed Mercredi and the AFN and dealt directly with individual First Nations communities.

8 August 1997. The Pe Sakastew Centre, the first prison built for Native male inmates opens officially at Hobbema, Alberta. The prison will house forty minimum security prisoners. Most of the staff are Aboriginal. Leaders on the Samson Reserve first suggested the idea for the prison six years ago.

7 November 1997. Native leaders in New Brunswick threaten to seek an injunction to stop all logging in New Brunswick unless the provincial government abandons it intention to appeal a recent court decision. On November 4, Justice John Turnbull of the New Brunswick Court of Queen's Bench ruled that the Dummer's Treaty of 1720 gives the aboriginal people of the province the unrestricted right to cut trees on Crown Land. Because of the implications of the decision for New Brunswick (forestry is the largest industry in New Brunswick), and other parts of Canada (especially Nova Scotia and British Columbia), the New Brunswick government has said it will appeal the decision.

11 December 1997. British Columbia Native leader Joe Mathias announces that "Aboriginal title is alive and well and living in the territories of First Nations in British Columbia" after the Supreme Court of Canada makes its landmark ruling in the case of *Delgamuukw v. The Queen*. The decision is one of the most important Supreme Court decisions of the century because it makes the first attempt to define aboriginal title. The court rules aboriginal title is protected by the Constitution, that no province has the power to extinguish that title, that aboriginal lands are communally owned, that Natives have exclusive rights to their lands, and that lands can be used for "modern" purposes as long as those modern uses do not conflict with aboriginal practices. The decision is also important because the court rules that the judge who decided the case in 1991 erred when he did not evaluate the claimants' oral histories correctly. The court rules that oral histories must be given due consideration by the courts. The decision is also of historical interest, because it is rooted in the longest-running land claim in Canada. This decision means that the case must be retried or negotiated. The judges recommend that the dispute be settled through negotiation. In response to this decision the British Columbia and Canadian governments renew their commitment to negotiation.

7 January 1998.   Native leaders give mixed reviews after Indian Affairs Minister Jane Stewart delivers the Canadian government's response to the Royal Commission on Aboriginal Peoples (RCAP) report. Stewart pledges to overhaul the government's relationship with aboriginal people. At the center of the response is an apology on behalf of the Canadian government for past mistreatment of Natives in Canada. Stewart explicitly mentions the residential school experience. She also announces the creation of a $350 million healing fund to help victims deal with the results of abuse suffered at the schools. A seventeen-member management board will administer the healing fund. Several churches involved in the residential schools have already apologized. Over the past year hundreds of lawsuits have been filed in connection with abuse at Native residential schools. Stewart also announces the creation of another $250 million fund to address other problems faced by aboriginal people. It will go to help pay for various programs ranging from improvements to Native housing, employment programs, and policing programs, to the establishment of an aboriginal health institute to help deal with the high rates of AIDS, tuberculosis, and suicide among Natives. Stewart also announces the creation of an independent claims commission to address the backlog of Native claims. These were recommendations of the RCAP.

10 March 1998.   Chiefs at an Assembly of First Nations policy meeting in Edmonton vote seventy-two to twelve to accept Jane Stewart's apology of January 7 and the $350 million healing fund, which will go toward counseling services, healing centers, preservation of Native languages, and job training. The vote is a victory for Phil Fontaine who was urging acceptance of the apology. He described the fund and apology as "the first step into the sunlight after generations of darkness." Many leaders have argued that Stewart's gesture does not go far enough to make up for past abuses. Marilyn Buffalo, the president of the Native Women's Association of Canada, who has been particularly vocal in her criticism of the deal, left the room after the vote. Both Fontaine and Buffalo are former students of residential schools.

22 March 1998.   Tsuu T'ina (Sarcee) woman Connie Jacobs and her son Ty are killed in an exchange of gunfire with police on the Tsuu T'ina Reserve near Calgary. The shooting occurred as authorities were attempting to remove six children from the home.

18 June 1998.   Leaders of the Kettle and Stoney Point First Nation sign an Agreement-in-Principle to return Camp Ipperwash to the Stoney Point Ojibwa. The deal will be worth $26.3 million to the band. The land was expropriated during World War II to establish a military base. In 1980 the government gave the band $2.4 million to compensate for the loss of the land since World War II. Negotiations toward this agreement began in March 1996.

30 November 1998.   Joseph Gosnell, the chief of the Nisga'a people, addresses the British Columbia legislature, an honor normally reserved for visiting heads of state. He is speaking as the legislature considers the historic Nisga'a Agreement. The treaty still requires approval of the Canadian and British Columbia governments, but the treaty is viewed as so significant because it is British Columbia's first comprehensive modern-day treaty. For over a century the British Columbia government refused to negotiate land-surrender agreements with Indians in the province. This deal would give the 6,000 Nisga'a title to 2,019 square kilometers of the lower Nass Valley, limited self-government, extensive fishing and logging rights, and $340 million. The Nisga'a approved the agreement in a referendum earlier this month. It still needs to be ratified by the British Columbia legislature and the House of Commons before it is implemented.

February 1999.   The Samson Cree of central Alberta file a legal claim of $40 billion for control of a 51,800-square-kilometer swath of central Alberta. The claim includes the rich Bonnie Glen and Leduc oilfields. This is the biggest cash claim in Canadian history. The Cree band's lawyer, James O'Reilly, said the band is claiming an 1876 treaty never surrendered Cree control of resource revenue in "traditional lands" around Hobbema, Leduc, and Pigeon Lake.

17 February 1999.   The Supreme Court of Canada rules that the custody of a young Indian boy should go to his non-Native grandparents in Connecticut, rather than his Native grandfather in Vancouver. The case is viewed as significant because the Court rules that the child's biological heritage should play no part in the court's decision regarding the child's best interests, and because it questions the legitimacy of a British Columbia law that encourages the placement of Native children in Native homes. Some Native groups denounce the decision.

1 April 1999. The Inuit in the north celebrate the creation of Nunavut with fireworks. The territory was carved out of the Northwest Territories and covers one-fifth of Canada's land area, from the sixtieth parallel to the northern tip of Ellsemere Island. The territory has a population of 27,000, of whom 85 percent are Inuit. Iqaluit, with a population of 4,500 is its largest community and the area's capital.

10 May 1999. The Labrador Inuit sign an Agreement-in-Principle with the federal and Newfoundland governments to settle their twenty-two-year old claim. The deal is worth $255 million. The deal would give the Inuit 15,800 square kilometers of land, and a settlement area of 72,520 square kilometers. The 5,000 Inuit will also get a central government which will control their education and health and social services. The Inuit will also get a $140 million trust fund and a portion of future mining revenues from their territory, including development of the Voisey Bay nickel deposit.

20 May 1999. In *Corbiere v. Canada (Minister of Indian and Northern Affairs)*, the Supreme Court rules that portions of the Indian Act denying voting privileges to members of reserve communities who are living off reserves contravene the equality provisions of the Canadian Constitution. The ruling has far-reaching implications partly because, since the addition of new band members as a result of Bill C-31, some bands have more non-resident than resident members.

September 1999. Trent University begins the first doctoral program in Native studies in Canada.

The flag of Nunavut. (Public Domain)

1 September 1999. The Aboriginal Peoples Television Network (APTN), Canada's (and the world's) first national aboriginal TV network, broadcasts for the first time. The opening lineup includes singer Susan Aglukark, a comedy duo from Whitehorse called Susie and Sara, and Go For Baroque and the Nikumoon Top Hat Choir singing Cree to Beethoven. The $15-million-a-year project is aimed at giving viewers a taste of the variety of Native life in Canada and around the world.

17 September 1999. In *R. v. Marshall*, the Supreme Court of Canada rules that a 1760 treaty between the Mi'kmaq (Micmac) and the British Crown still gives the Mi'kmaq the right to make a moderate living from commercial fishing. The case involved Donald Marshall Jr., a Cape Breton Mi'kmaq who was arrested in 1993 for catching and selling 210 kilograms of eels out of season and without a license. This is the same man who spent eleven years in prison for a murder he did not commit. In this case, Marshall argued that the Mi'kmaq-British treaty permitted him to catch and sell fish commercially. The Supreme Court agreed, ruling that the treaty allows all Nova Scotia natives covered by the treaty to hunt and fish without a licence at any time of year, although only to fish for their own needs, or to earn a "moderate livelihood." It does not give them the right to establish commercial fishing ventures. Justice Ian Binnie wrote that "The 1760 treaty does affirm the right of the Mi'kmaq people to continue to provide for their own sustenance by taking the products of their hunting, fishing and other gathering activities, and trading for what in 1760 was termed 'necessaries.'"

4 October 1999. The leaders of Quebec's Innu call on the federal government to stop work on a joint Quebec and Newfoundland government hydroelectric project on Churchill Falls. They say they are ready to go to court to stop further development on the $10-billion project unless the governments involved offer a treaty that spells out the Innu's ancestral rights to the land surrounding the proposed dam within sixty days.

26 October 1999. The New Brunswick government seizes a load of lumber harvested from Crown Land by Mi'kmaq loggers and brought to a sawmill at Belledune, near Bathurst. The issue of Native logging in New Brunswick has been simmering for more than two years, but the Supreme Court decision of September 17 has encouraged Mi'kmaq loggers on the Big Cove Reserve to force the issue over aboriginal cutting rights on Crown land. Maritime Natives argue that the decision in the Marshall case gives them a wide-ranging right to log, hunt, and fish.

1 November 1999. A British Columbia court begins hearing evidence concerning how thirty former Nuu-chah-nulth students at the Alberni Indian residential schools should be compensated for physical and sexual abuse. With more than 3,000 claims having been filed for compensation for abuse in Indian residential schools, the decision will be potentially very significant. It is expected that victims across the country will eventually be awarded billions of dollars in compensation. Last June the British Columbia Supreme Court ruled that the United Church and Canadian government share "vicarious liability" for abuse at the school. There were more than eighty residential schools in Canada between 1880 and the 1980s. Approximately 105,000 children attended these schools. Claims are being filed at a rate of approximately fifteen to twenty per week.

16 November 1999. Robert Levi, chief of the Big Cove Reserve on New Brunswick's east coast agrees to a deal that will give his band access to trees on Crown land. Access will be permitted according to the same formula that other bands in the province have already agreed to. Aboriginal loggers will be given 5 percent of the total annual allowable cut. The Mi'kmaq have been in a long struggle with the New Brunswick government over Native logging rights, and the recent Marshall decision has renewed the struggle. The Mi'kmaq insist that the Marshall decision gives them the unrestricted right to harvest trees on Crown land.

17 November 1999. Mi'kmaq (Micmac) leaders in Atlantic Canada are disappointed after the Supreme Court rules that the Canadian government does have the power to regulate the Native fishery in Atlantic Canada. The ruling comes after the Supreme Court refuses to rehear the controversial ruling it handed down in the Marshall case on September 17, but agrees to issue a "clarification" of the decision. Since the decision of September 17 the maritime has witnessed violent confrontations between non-Native fishermen and Mi'kmaq fishermen.

13 December 1999. The Nisga'a treaty overcomes its final political hurdle as the House of Commons votes 217 to forty-eight to pass the treaty into law. It must now pass the Senate, which is expected to happen in February. The bill passed despite the Reform Party's record-setting stalling tactics. The Reform Party conducted a forty-two-hour filibuster in the House of Commons beginning on December 7. The Reform Party opposes the treaty, arguing that because the treaty is based on race it sets a bad precedent for future treaties. It also argues that the treaty does not guarantee that average band members will benefit from the treaty. The party called for a referendum on the treaty in British Columbia.

20 January 2000. The Ontario Superior Court of Justice rules that Métis people have the constitutional right to hunt without a license. The decision will be appealed.

21 March 2000. Dissident members of the Nisga'a file a challenge to the constitutionality of the Nisga'a land claim in British Columbia's Supreme Court. The group from the village of Kincolith argues that the treaty violates sections 25 and 35 of the Constitution Act of 1982 by arguing that the Nisga'a Tribal Council and the government violated the rights of the Nisga'a by claiming that the Tribal Council has authority over the Nisga'a. The plaintiffs argue that the Tribal Council is not a valid aboriginal government.

25 March 2000. Canadian, provincial, and Innu negotiators are nearly ready to sign a framework agreement toward an Agreement-in-Principle to settle the Innu land claim. When completed, the deal may be more extensive than the Nisga'a Agreement that has attracted much attention lately. Despite the optimism, some doubt that an agreement would do much to alleviate the troubled Innu communities in Labrador.

5 April 2000. Indian Affairs Minister Robert Nault tells a parliamentary committee that Indians in Canada are filing court claims against the federal government related to abuse at residential schools at a rate of twenty cases a week. Since 1997 the number of claims has jumped from eighty-four to 3,152. The department expects to spend nearly $1.5 billion in the next three years in order settle all other kinds of Native claims. Meanwhile the department is also grappling with Supreme Court decisions that are undermining the Indian Act. In this context, Nault argues, there is a danger of conflict.

11 April 2000. Two Saskatoon city police officers are charged with unlawful confinement and assault after Darrell Night, an aboriginal man, alleged that the officers drove him to the outskirts of the city in bitterly cold weather last January 28, took his jacket, and told him to find his own way back to the city. The allegations led to the appointment of an RCMP task force in February consisting of fifteen to twenty investigators who took four weeks to look into five suspicious deaths and allegations that the police (both the Saskatoon city police and the RCMP) routinely took Aboriginals to the edge of the city to find their own way back. Night made his allegation shortly after the partially clothed body of

Rodney Naistus, from Onion Lake, was discovered on January 29, and the frozen body of Lawrence Kim Wegner was found on February 3. In March the Federation of Saskatchewan Indian Nations (FSIN) announced that it has also hired investigators to look into the allegations because it does not trust the RCMP to investigate properly. The FSIN has also called for a public inquiry to look into the matter.

13 April 2000. Shortly after the Nisga'a agreement receives Royal Assent, Nisga'a Chief Joseph Gosnell stands on the steps of the Senate chambers and says "The Royal Assent of our treaty signifies the end of the colonial era for the Nisga'a people. It is a great and historic day for all Canadians, and this achievement is a beacon of hope for colonized people in our own country and throughout the world." Surrounded by politicians from the Nisga'a Nation and the Canadian parliament, Gosnell declares that "Today, the Nisga'a people become full-fledged Canadians as we step out from under the Indian Act—forever. Finally, after a struggle of more than 130 years, the government of this country clearly recognizes that the Nisga'a were a self-governing people since well before European contact. We remain self-governing today, and we are proud to say that this inherent right is now clearly recognized and protected in the Constitution of Canada."

13 April 2000. New Brunswick Provincial Court Judge Denis Lordon rules that two eighteenth-century treaties do not give the Mi'kmaq the right to cut trees on commercial land today. In his fifty-page ruling, the judge wrote that "to interpret the right to gather as a right to participate in the wholesale, uncontrolled exploitation of natural resources would alter the terms of the treaty and wholly transform the rights therein conferred." This is the first significant legal test since the Supreme Court's decision in the Marshall case last September. The case is likely to be appealed to the Supreme Court.

13 April 2000. A report by the six-member Indian Claims Commission tabled in Parliament argues that the claims process is not working. It notes that while about 450 claims await evaluation, only five to ten are resolved each year.

17 April 2000. The Manitoba government announces that it will hand over control of child and family services to the First Nations of the province. The announcement comes after the new government of the province established a committee to implement the recommendations of the 1991 Manitoba aboriginal justice inquiry. The committee was established soon after the election of the New Democratic Party last year.

1 May 2000. Hearings begin in the Samson Cree lawsuit against the federal government. The Samson Cree of Hobbema are suing the government for $1.3 billion alleging that the government has misspent and mismanaged the band's oil revenues. Observers predict that if the band is successful, many other bands in Canada could be expected to file their own claims. In February the Samson Cree filed a $40-billion lawsuit in which they argue that they have rights to much of the oil-producing region in Central Alberta.

13 May 2000. Nisga'a Chief Joe Gosnell announces that "we're no longer beggars in our own land," and hundreds of Nisga'a sing "O Canada" as they celebrate the implementation of their agreement with the Canadian government at an elaborate celebration at Gitwinksihlkw, British Columbia, in their homeland in the Nass Valley.

15 May 2000. The British Columbia Supreme Court begins hearing a court challenge of the validity of the Nisga'a Agreement. The British Columbia Liberal Party, which is leading the challenge, argues that the treaty is unconstitutional because it creates a third order of government. They argue that the agreement can stand only if the Constitution is amended—something that, according to British Columbia law, requires a province-wide referendum. If the Liberals win the case, it would very likely end up in the Supreme Court.

16 May 2000. Judge Thomas Goodson releases the result of his fatality inquiry into the death of Connie and Ty Jacobs on the Tsuu T'ina (Sarcee) Reserve on 22 March 1998. The report makes eighteen recommendations, many of which suggest that the tribal police force was understaffed and poorly prepared to deal with the very serious conditions that developed. The report says that the Jacobs may not have died if RCMP officers and paramedics had responded together when the domestic dispute first came to light. Goodson also called for better training for the child and family services workers and First Nations police officers. Band officials and members of the Jacobs' family welcome the recommendations.

31 May 2000. The Sechelt band announces that it is withdrawing from treaty negotiations with the British Columbia government, raising fears that the entire British Columbia Treaty Commission process may be threatened. Last year, the Sechelt became the first band to sign an Agreement-in-Principle after passing through the process. Representatives of the band suggest that recent court decisions suggest that the band should be offered far more than they were offered in the Agreement-in-Principle. More than one hundred First Nation

Nisga'a Chief Joe Gosnell shakes hands with Premier Ujial Dosanjh to finalize the historic treaty. (Photo by Kate Bird. Courtesy of *Vancouver Sun* files)

communities in British Columbia are awaiting land claim settlements with the British Columbia Treaty Commission.

1 June 2000. Officers from the Department of Fisheries and Oceans seize forty-three lobster traps set by Mi'kmaq fishermen in Miramichi Bay, New Brunswick. This action is part of a simmering dispute set off by the Supreme Court's decision in the Marshall case in September. The Mi'kmaq claim the right to fish according to their own rules, while the federal government claims that the Mi'kmaq may fish only if they have federal licenses. Disputes and impasses in various parts of Canada have raised fears that the summer of 2000 will see violent confrontations between Native groups and Canadian authorities.

12 June 2000. The Supreme Court hears arguments from lawyers of the Musqueam band and lawyers of seventy-three leaseholders whose homes are on land owned by the band. The lawyers for the band say that a lower court has set the rents too low, while the leaseholders' lawyers will argue that the rent has been set too high.

12 July 2000. Matthew Coon Come, a Cree from northern Quebec, is elected the new head chief of the Assembly of First Nations, defeating the incumbent Phil Fontaine. Fontaine was accused of being too friendly with the federal government and of ignoring the priorities of most reserve Indians in Canada. During the week leading up to the vote, Coon Come promised to continue employing the openly confrontational approach that made him successful during his struggles with the Quebec government. Coon Come is known as a bold, confident, articulate leader with a sharp sense of practical politics.

23 July 2000. The 2,000 members of the Squamish band in Vancouver vote to accept the federal government's offer to settle their land claim. The federal government offered the band $92.5 million to settle their claim to 600 hectares of land in parcels in and near

Vancouver which was taken from their reserve during the last century. Today, much of the land is prime real estate in Vancouver. The money will go into a trust fund. The Squamish initiated litigation in this case in 1977.

23 July 2000. The Nisga'a of northern British Columbia, and the government of the province, celebrate after Justice Paul Williamson of the Supreme Court of British Columbia rules that the Nisga'a Agreement does not violate the Canadian Constitution. The case was brought to the court by Gordon Campbell, the leader of the British Columbia Liberal Party, who has vowed to appeal the decision.

Theodore Binnema
University of Northern British Columbia

Sites and Landmarks

UNITED STATES

◆ ALABAMA

MOUNDVILLE STATE MONUMENT
P.O. Box 66
Moundville, AL 35474
(205) 371–2572
www.ua.edu/mndvillle.htm

RUSSELL CAVE NATIONAL MONUMENT
3729 County Rd 98
Bridgeport, AL 35740
(256) 495–2672
www.nps.gov/ruca/
Archaic, Woodland, and Mississippian periods.

◆ ALASKA

SITKA NATIONAL HISTORIC PARK
106 Metlakatla P.O. Box 738
Sitka, AK 99835
(907) 747–6281

◆ ARIZONA

AWATOVI RUINS
Keams Canyon, AZ 86034
No phone number available.
(On the National Register of Historical
    Places, 1/30/92)

CANYON DE CHELLY NATIONAL MONUMENT
P.O. Box 588
Chinle, AZ 86503
(520) 674–5500
www.nps.gov/cach

CASA GRANDE RUINS NATIONAL
    MONUMENT
1100 Ruins Dr.
Coolidge, AZ 85228
(520) 723–3172
Hohokam village site, C.E. 500–1450.

CHIRICAHUA NATIONAL MONUMENT
    MUSEUM
H.R.C. 2, Box 6500
Wilcox, AZ 85643
(520) 824–3560

GUEVAVI MISSION RUINS
Nogales, AZ 85621
No phone number available.
(On the National Register of Historical
    Places, 1/30/92)

HUBBELL TRADING POST NATIONAL
    HISTORIC SITE
P.O. Box 150
Ganado, AZ 86505
(520) 755–3475
www.nps.gov/hutr/
Oldest continually operating Indian trading post.

MISSION SAN XAVIER DEL BAC
1950 West San Xavier
Tucson, AZ 85746
(520) 294–2624
Spanish colonial Indian mission.

MONTEZUMA CASTLE MUSEUM
P.O. Box 219
Camp Verde, AZ 86322
(520) 567–3322
www.nps.gov/moca

NAVAJO NATIONAL MONUMENT
HC 71, Box 3
Tonalea, AZ 86044–9704
(520) 672–2366
Site of three cliff villages, of the Kayenta, Anasazi,
and Navajo cultures.

OLD ORAIBI
Hopi Indian Reservation
Oraibi, AZ 86039
No phone number available.
(On the National Register of Historical
Places, 1/30/92)

PUEBLO GRANDE MUSEUM
4619 East Washington St.
Phoenix, AZ 85034
(602) 495–0901
Hohokam site, 300 B.C.E.–C.E.1450

TONTO NATIONAL MONUMENT MUSEUM
HC 02, Box 4602
Roosevelt, AZ 85545
(602) 467–2241
Prehistoric Salado Indian cliff dwellings.

TUMACACORI NATIONAL HISTORICAL PARK
P.O. Box 67
Tumacacori, AZ 85640
(520) 398–2341
www.nps.gov/tuma

TUZIGOOT NATIONAL MONUMENT
P.O. Box 68
Clarkdale, AZ 86324
(520) 634–5564

WALNUT CANYON NATIONAL MONUMENT
Walnut Canyon Rd.
Flagstaff, AZ 86004–9705
(520) 526–3367
www.npsgov/wacca
Sinagua Indian ruins site, C.E. 110–1270

WUPATKI AND SUNSET CRATER NATIONAL
MONUMENT
HC 33, Box 444A
Flagstaff, AZ 86001
(520) 556–7152
Ruins of the Lomaki, Nalakihum Citadel, Wuwoki,
and Wupatki.

◆ **ARKANSAS**

CADDO-HA INDIAN VILLAGE
P.O. Box 669
Murfreesboro, AR 71958
(870) 285–3736
www.caddotc.com
Caddo (mound builders) grounds, site excavation.

TOLTEC MOUNDS ARCHEOLOGICAL
STATE PARK
490 Toltec Mounds Rd.
Scotts, AR 72142
(501) 961–9221

◆ **CALIFORNIA**

DEATH VALLEY NATIONAL PARK
P.O. Box 579
Death Valley, CA 92328
(760) 786–2331
www.npsgov/deva
Exhibits of local basketry; archaeological artifacts.

LA PURISIMA MISSION STATE
HISTORIC PARK
2295 Purisima Rd.
Lompoc, CA 93436
(805) 733–3713
www.parks.ca.gov

LAVA BEDS NATIONAL MONUMENT
P.O. Box 867
Tulelake, CA 96134
(530) 667–2287
Modoc Indian war (1872–73) museum.

◆ **COLORADO**

BENT'S OLD FORT NATIONAL HISTORIC SITE
35110 Highway 194 E.
La Junta, CO 81050
(719) 384–2800
Adobe trading post built in 1833.

GREAT SAND DUNES NATIONAL
MONUMENT
11500 Highway 150
Mosca, CO 81146
(719) 378–2312

HOVENWEEP NATIONAL MONUMENT
McEmo RT.
Cortez, CO 81321
(970) 562–4282
www.nps.gov

MESA VERDE NATIONAL PARK MUSEUM
P.O. Box 38
Mesa Verde, CO 81330
(970) 529–4465
Prehistoric Pueblo dwellings, with museums of
Anasazi remains, c.e. 500–1330

◆ **FLORIDA**

INDIAN TEMPLE MOUND
139 Miracle Strip Pkwy. SE
Fort Walton Beach, FL 32548
(850) 833–9595
www.fwb.org
The largest Mississippian temple mound on the
Gulf Coast.

◆ **GEORGIA**

CHIEF VANN HOUSE
82 HWY 225 NC
Chattsworth, GA 30705
(706) 517–4255

ETOWAH INDIAN MOUNDS STATE
HISTORIC SITE
813 Indian Mounds Rd. S.E.
Cartersville, GA 30120
(770) 387–3747
Seven mounds; excavations.

KOLOMOKI MOUNDS MUSEUM
Rte. 1, Box 114
Blakely, GA 31723
(912) 724–2151
Indian burial mound and village, c. c.e. 1250.

NEW ECHOTA HISTORIC SITE
1211 Chatsworth Hwy. N.E.
Calhoun, GA 30701
(706) 624–1321
www.gastateprkff.org
1825 capital of the Cherokee Nation; a Preservation
Project.

OCMULGEE NATIONAL MONUMENT
1207 Emery Hwy.
Macon, GA 31217
(912) 752–8257
www.npsgov/ocma
Seven mounds, about c.e. 900.

◆ **IDAHO**

NEZ PERCÉ NATIONAL HISTORICAL
PARK MUSEUM
P.O. Box 100
Spalding, ID 83540
(208) 843–2001
www.nps.gov
Early mission site.

◆ **ILLINOIS**

CAHOKIA MOUNDS STATE HISTORIC SITE
INTERPRETIVE CENTER MUSEUM
30 Ramey 3
Collinsville, IL 62234
(618) 346–5160

DICKSON MOUNDS MUSEUM
Rtes. 97 and 78
Lewiston, IL 61542
(309) 547–3721

STARVED ROCK STATE PARK
P.O. Box 509
Utica, IL 61373
(815) 667–4726
dnr.state.il.us
Site of village occupied first by Illinois Indians, then
Ottawa and Potawatomi.

◆ **INDIANA**

ANGEL MOUNDS STATE HISTORIC SITE
8215 Pollack Ave.
Evansville, IN 47715
(812) 853–3956
Mississippian archaeological site; ten mounds, c.e.
1250–1450; reconstructed structures.

CHIEF RICHARDSVILLE HOUSE AND MIAMI
TREATY GROUNDS
Huntington, IN 46750
No phone number available.
(On the National Registry of Historic Places, 1/30/92)

SONOTABAC PREHISTORIC INDIAN MOUND
    AND MUSEUM
P.O. Box 941
2401 Wabash Ave.
Vincennes, IN 47591
(812) 885–4330
Largest ceremonial mound in Indiana.

◆ **IOWA**

CHIEF WAPELLO'S MEMORIAL PARK
Agency, IA 52530
No phone number available.
(On the National Register of Historic Places, 1/30/92)

EFFIGY MOUNDS NATIONAL MONUMENT
151 HWY 76
Harpers Ferry, IA 52146
(319) 873–3491
www.nps.gov/efmo
Burial mounds.

SPIRIT LAKE MASSACRE LOG CABIN
Arnolds Park, IA 51331
No phone number available.
(On the National Register of Historic Places, 1/30/92)

◆ **KANSAS**

CORONADO QUIVIRA MUSEUM
105 W. Lyon
Lyons, KS 67554
(316) 257–3941

FORT LARNED NATIONAL HISTORIC SITE
R.R. 3
Larned, KS 67550
(316) 285–6911
www.nps.gov/fols

KAW-INDIAN MISSION
500 North Mission
Council Groove, KS 66846
(316) 767–5410
www.kshs.org

NATIVE AMERICAN HERITAGE MUSEUM
Highland Mission State Historic Site
1737 Elgin Road
Highland, KS 66035
(785) 442–3304
kshs.org/places/highland.htm

PAWNEE INDIAN VILLAGE MUSEUM
R.R. 1 Box 475
Republic, KS 66964
(785) 361–2255
ww.kshs.org
Best preserved Pawnee earth lodge site on
    the Plains.

PAWNEE ROCK
Pawnee Rock, KS 67567
No phone number available.
(On the National Register of Historic Places, 1/30/92)

SHAWNEE INDIAN MISSION
Mission Road
Fairway, KS 66205
(913) 262–0867

◆ **KENTUCKY**

WICKLIFFE MOUND RESEARCH CENTER
P.O. Box 155
Wickliffe, KY 42087
(270) 335–3681
http:campus.murraystate.edu.htm

◆ **MASSACHUSETTS**

WAMPANOAG INDIAN PROGRAM OF
    PLYMOUTH PLANTATION
P.O. Box 1620
Plymouth, MA 02362
(508) 746–1622
Outdoor living history museum of colonial period.

◆ **MINNESOTA**

GRAND PORTAGE NATIONAL MONUMENT
P.O. Box 668
Grand Marais, MN 55064
(218) 387–2788

LOWER SIOUX AGENCY HISTORY CENTER
Minnesota Historical Society
32469 County Hwy.
Morton, MN 56270
(507) 697–6321, or (888) 727–8386
www.mnhs.org
1835 Indian mission.

PIPESTONE NATIONAL MONUMENT
36 Reservation Ave.
Pipestone, MN 56164–1269
(507) 825–5464
www.nps.gov/pipe
Original Dakota pipestone quarry for
  ceremonial pipes.

◆ MISSISSIPPI

EMERAL MOUND
Natchez Trace Parkway
2680 Natchez Trace Parkway
Tupclo, MS 38804
(662) 680–4025

THE GRAND VILLAGE OF THE NATCHEZ
  INDIANS
400 Jefferson Davis Blvd.
Natchez, MS 39120
(601) 446–6502
mdah.state ms.us
Ceremonial mound center for the Natchez Tribe,
  1250–1730.

WINTERVILLE MOUNDS
2415 Hwy 1 north
Greenville, MS 38701
(662) 334–4684
mdah.state ms.us
Ceremonial center for Prehistoric Tribes, C.E.
  1000–1450.

◆ MONTANA

BIG HOLE NATIONAL BATTLEFIELD
P.O. Box 237
Wisdom, MT 59761
(406) 689–3156
Preserves scene of battle between Nez Percé and
  the Seventh U.S. Infantry, 1877.

CHIEF PLENTY COUPS STATE PARK
  AND MUSEUM
P.O. Box 100
Pryor, MT 59066
(406) 252–1289
Crow Indian Museum.

LITTLE BIGHORN BATTLEFIELD NATIONAL
  MONUMENT
P.O. Box 39
Crow Agency, MT 59022
(406) 638–2621
www.nps.gov/libi
National Cemetery and site where the Battle of the
  Little Bighorn took place on June 25th and
  26th, 1876.

MADISON BUFFALO JUMP STATE
  MONUMENT
Logan, MT 59741
No phone number available.
(On the National Register of Historic Places, 1/30/92)

◆ NEBRASKA

OREGON TRAIL MUSEUM
Scotts Bluff National Monument
P.O. Box 27
Gering, NB 69341–0027
(308) 436–5794

◆ NEVADA

GATECLIFF ROCKSHELTER
Austin, NV 89310
No phone number available.
(On the National Register of Historic Places, 1/30/92)

◆ NEW MEXICO

AZTEC RUINS NATIONAL MONUMENT
P.O. Box 640
Aztec, NM 87410
(505) 334–6174
www.nps.gov/azaru
Pueblo ruins at Chaco Canyon and Mesa Verde.

BANDELIER NATIONAL MONUMENT
HCR 1, Box 1, Suite 15
Los Alamos, NM 87544
(505) 672–3861
www.nps.gov/band
Anasazi ruins, C.E. 1200–1600.

CHACO CULTURE NATIONAL
HISTORICAL PARK
P.O. Box 220
Nageezi, NM 87037
(505) 786–7014
www.nps.gov/chcu/
Thirteen major Anasazi sites; more than 400 smaller
village sites.

CORONADO STATE MONUMENT
P.O. Box 95
Bernalillo, NM 87004
(505) 867–5351
Pueblo ruin, C.E. 1300–1600; reconstructed kiva.

EL MORRO NATIONAL MONUMENT
Rte. 2, Box 43
Ramah, NM 87321
(505) 783–4226
Archaeological site of Inscription Rock;
Pueblo ruins.

PECOS NATIONAL HISTORICAL PARK
P.O. Drawer 418
Pecos, NM 87552
(505) 757–6414
www.nps.gov/peco
Pueblo ruins; Spanish church ruins.

SALINAS PUEBLO MISSION NATIONAL
MONUMENT
P.O. Box 517
Mountainair, NM 87036–0517
(505) 847–2585
Prehistoric pit houses, C.E. 800, ruins, C.E. 1100–1670;
Spanish mission ruins, C.E. 1627–72.

SALMON RUIN
San Juan County Museum Association
975 U.S. Highway 64
Farmington, NM 87401
(505) 632–2013
Anasazi ruin.

◆ NEW YORK

MOHAWK-CAUGHNAWAGA MUSEUM
Rte. 5, Box 55
Fonda, NY 12068
No phone number available.
Located near Tekakwitha Shrine (see next entry).
Excavated Caughnawaga Indian village.

TEKAKWITHA SHRINE
P.O. Box 6298
Fonda, NY 1206
(518) 853–3646
Mohawk Indian castle; residence of Kateri
Tekakwitha.
Religious shrine and historic archaeological site,
1666–93.

◆ NORTH CAROLINA

MUSEUM OF THE CHEROKEE INDIAN
P.O. Box 1599
Cherokee, NC 28719
(828) 497–3481
www.cherokee.museum.org

OCONALUFTEE INDIAN VILLAGE
P.O. Box 398
Cherokee, NC 28719
(828) 497–2315
www.oconaluftee.com
A replica of a 1750 Cherokee village.

TOWN CREEK INDIAN MOUND STATE
HISTORIC SITE
509 Town Mound Rd
Mt. Gilead, NC 27306
(910) 439–6802
www.ah.dcr.state.nc.us/section/hs/town
Reconstructed sixteenth-century Indian ceremonial
center.

◆ NORTH DAKOTA

BIG HIDATSA VILLAGE SITE
Stanton, ND 58571
No phone number available.
(On the National Register of Historic Places, 1/30/92)

◆ OHIO

FORT ANCIENT MUSEUM
Fort Ancient State Memorial
6123 State Route 350
Oregonia, OH 45054
(513) 932–4421
www.ohiohistory.org

HOPEWELL CULTURE NATIONAL
  HISTORICAL PARK
16062 State Route 104
Chillecothe, OH 45601
(740) 774–1125
www.nps.gov/hocu
Twenty-three Hopewell culture burial mounds, 200
B.C.E.–500 C.E.

MOUND BUILDERS STATE MEMORIAL
  AND MUSEUM
99 Cooper Ave.
Newark, OH 43055
(740) 344–1920
www.ohiohistory.org.places.moundbld
The Great Circle Earthworks: Ceremonial grounds of
Hopewell culture, 200 B.C.E.–C.E. 600

PIQUA HISTORICAL MUSEUM
509 North Main
Piqua, OH 45356
(937) 773–2307
Collection of pre-contact tools and weapons from
  the Adena, Hopewell, and Fort Ancient cultures.

SERPENT MOUND MUSEUM
3850 Rte. 73, Box 234
Peebles, OH 45660
(513) 587–2796
(800) 653–6446
Adena culture.

♦ OKLAHOMA

CREEK INDIAN COUNCIL HOUSE MUSEUM
106 W. 6th Street
Council House Square
Okmulgee, OK 74447
(918) 756–2324

SEQUOYAH'S CABIN
Rte. 1, Box 141
Sallisaw, OK 74955
(918) 775–2413
www.ok-history.mus.ok.us
1829 log cabin of Cherokee leader Sequoyah.

♦ PENNSYLVANIA

BUSHY RUN BATTLEFIELD PARK
P.O. Box 468
Harrison City, PA 15636–0468
(724) 527–5584
Site of Chief Pontiac's rebellion, 1763.

♦ SOUTH DAKOTA

BEAR BUTTE STATE PARK
P.O. Box 688
Sturgis, SD 57785
(605) 347–5240
Native American traditional religious site.

INDIAN MUSEUM OF NORTH AMERICA
Crazy Horse Memorial Foundation
Avenue of the Chiefs
Crazy Horse, SD 57730–9506
(605) 673–4681
www.crazyhorse.org
Crazy Horse Memorial project in the Black Hills.

THE HERITAGE CENTER
Red Cloud Indian School
P.O. Box 100
Pine Ridge, SD 57770
(605) 867–5491
www.basec.net/~rchertiage
Art museum near scene of Wounded Knee Massacre.

♦ TENNESSEE

CHUCALISSA INDIAN VILLAGE
1987 Indian Village Dr.
Memphis, TN 38109
(901) 785–3160
Museum and rebuilt Indian village.

PINSON MOUNDS STATE
  ARCHAEOLOGICAL AREA
460 Ozier Rd.
Pinson, TN 38366
(901) 988–5614
Middle Woodland Period ceremonial site; mounds
  and earthworks.

RED CLAY STATE HISTORICAL PARK
1140 Red Clay Park Road S.W.
Cleveland, TN 37311
(423) 478–0339
www.state.tn.us/environment/parks/redclay
Cherokee government seat, 1832–38; Cherokee
  Council site.

◆ TEXAS

CADDOAN MOUNDS STATE HISTORIC SITE
Rte. 2, Box 85C
Alto, TX 75925
(409) 858–3218
Caddoan village and ceremonial center with three
mounds, C.E. 750–1300.

◆ UTAH

ANASAZI STATE HISTORICAL MONUMENT
P.O. Box 1429
Boulder, UT 84716
(435) 335–7308
Excavated Anasazi Indian village, C.E. 1050–1200.

EDGE OF THE CEDARS STATE PARK
AND MUSEUM
600 West, 400 North
Blanding, UT 84511
(435) 678–2238
Anasazi ruins, C.E. 700–1220.

INDIAN CREEK STATE PARK
Monticello, UT 84535
No phone number available.
(On the National Register of Historic Places, 1/30/92)

◆ VIRGINIA

PAMUNKEY CULTURAL CENTER MUSEUM
Rte. 1, Box 787
King William, VA 23086
(804) 843–4792

WOODLAWN HISTORIC AND
ARCHEOLOGICAL DISTRICT
Port Conway, VA
No phone number available.
On the National Register of Historic Places, 1/30/92)

◆ WEST VIRGINIA

MOUND MUSEUM
801 Jefferson Ave.
Moundsville, WV 26041
(304) 845–2773

◆ WISCONSIN

BARRON COUNTY PIPESTONE QUARRIES
Rice Lake, WI 54868
No phone number available.
(On the National Register of Historic Places, 1/30/92)

OLD INDIAN AGENCY HOUSE
Portage, WI 53901
No phone number available.
(On the National Register of Historic Places, 1/30/92)

RICE LAKE MOUNDS
Rice Lake, WI 54868
No phone number available.
(On the National Register of Historic Places, 1/30/92)

WAUKESHA COUNTY HISTORICAL MUSEUM
101 West Main St.
Waukesha, WI 53186
(262) 521–2859
Located on prehistoric burial mound of the Turtle.

CANADA

◆ ALBERTA

WRITING-ON-STONE PROVISIONAL PARK
P.O. Box 297
Milk River, AL T0K 1M0
(403) 647–2364

◆ NEWFOUNDLAND

CASTLE HILL NATIONAL HISTORIC PARK
P.O. Box 10
Jersey Side
Placentia Bay, NF A0B 2G0
(709) 227–2401

◆ ONTARIO

CHAMPLAIN TRAIL MUSEUM
1035 Pembroke St. E.
Pembroke, ON K8A 6Z2
(613) 735–0517
Agricultural artifacts of the 1840s.

LONDON MUSEUM OF ARCHAEOLOGY

1600 Attawandaron Rd.
London, ON N6G 3M6
(519) 473–1360
Archaeological site of a reconstructed 500-year-old
Iroquoian village; prehistory of Ontario.

OLD FORT WILLIAM

Vickers Heights Post Office
Thunder Bay, ON P0T 2Z0
(807) 577–8461
Reconstruction of the nineteenth-century inland
headquarters of the North West Company,
including a living history program reenacting the
fur trade activities of Scottish partners, French-

Canadian voyeurs, and native Ojibwa.

SERPENT MOUNDS PROVINCIAL PARK

R.R. 3
Keene, ON K0L 2G0
(705) 295–6879
Walking path to Indian burial mounds.

SKA-NAH-DOHT INDIAN VILLAGE

Longwoods Rd. Conservation Area, R.R. 1
Mt. Brydges, ON N0L 1W0
(519) 264–2420
A recreated Iroquoian village of about one thousand
years ago. Ska-Nah-Doht means "A village stands
again" (Oneida).

Native American Place Names

UNITED STATES

♦ ALABAMA

Alabama: Name of state and river; meaning "clearers of thickets" (Choctaw)

Autauga: Name of county and creek; meaning "border" (Creek)

Chickasaw: Name of town; derived from tribal name (Chickasaw)

Choctaw: Name of city and county; derived from tribal name (Choctaw)

Conecuh: Name of county, river, and national forest; probably meaning "land of cane" (Creek)

Eufaula: Name of city and wildlife refuge; derived from former village name (Creek)

Mobile: Name of city, county, and river; derived from tribal name, probably meaning "the rowers" (Choctaw)

Natchez: Name of town; derived from tribal name, probably meaning "timber land" (Muskogean)

Sipsey: Name of town and river; meaning "poplar tree" (Chickasaw-Choctaw)

Talladega: Name of city, county, and national forest; derived from village name, meaning "town on the border" (Creek)

Tuscaloosa: Name of city and county; named after chief whose name means "Black warrior" (Choctaw)

Tuscumbia: Name of city; named after chief whose name means "warrior rain maker" (Cherokee)

Tuskegee: Name of town, institute, and national forest; derived from tribal name, meaning "warrior" (probably Creek)

♦ ALASKA

Alaska: Name of state, gulf, and peninsula; meaning "a great country or continent" (Aleut)

Anaktuvuk: Name of river and pass; meaning "dung everywhere" (Inupiat)

Iditarod: Name of river; derived from a former Indian village (Ingalik)

Kenai: Name of lake, mountains, and peninsula; derived from tribal name (Kenai)

Ketchikan: Name of city and lake; meaning "eagle wing river" or "city under the eagle" (probably Tlingit or Haida)

Kodiak: Name of town, island, and national wildlife refuge; meaning "island" (probably Eskimo)

Metlakatla: Name of town; derived from former village name (Tsimshian)

Nunivak: Name of island and national wildlife refuge; probably meaning "big land" (Eskimo)

Sitka: Name of town, national monument, and sound; probably meaning "by the sea" (Tlingit)

Skagway: Name of village and river; probably meaning "home of the north wind" (Tlingit)

Stikine: Name of river and strait; meaning "great river" (Tlingit)

Tanana: Name of village, river, and island; derived from tribal name, meaning "mountain river" (Athapascan)

Unalaska: Name of village, island, bay, and lake; meaning "dwelling together harmoniously" (Aleut)

Yukon: Name of river; meaning "big river" (Yupik Eskimo)

♦ ARIZONA

Ajo: Name of town and mountains; meaning "paint" (Tohono O'Odham, also known as Papago)

Apache: Name of town, county, lake, pass, and peak; derived from tribal name, meaning "enemy" (Yuma or Zuni)

Arizona: Name of state; meaning "small place of the spring" (Tohono O'Odham)

Chinle: Name of town and trading center; meaning "mouth of canyon" (Navajo)

Chiricahua: Name of mountains, peak, and national monument; derived from tribal name, meaning "great mountain" (Apache)

Chuska: Name of mountains; meaning "white spruce" (probably Navajo)

Cochise: Name of county; named after famous chief (Chiricahua Apache)

Coconino: Name of county, plateau, and national forest; derived from tribal name, meaning "pinyon people" (Zuni) or "little water" (Havasupai)

Hopi: Name of Indian reservation; derived from tribal name, meaning "the peaceful ones" (Hopi)

Kaibab: Name of town, plateau, and national forest; meaning "a mountain lying down" (Paiute)

Kayenta: Name of town; meaning "where they fell into a creek" (Navajo)

Maricopa: Name of town and county; derived from tribal name (Pima)

Mohave: Name of county, mountains, and lake; derived from tribal name, meaning "three mountains" (Mohave)

Navajo: Name of Indian reservation and county; derived from tribal name, probably meaning "large area of cultivated lands" (Spanish)

Paria: Name of river and plateau; meaning "elk water" (Paiute)

Pima: Name of town and county; derived from tribal name, meaning "no" (probably Spanish)

Yavapai: Name of county; derived from tribal name, meaning "people of the sun" (Yuman)

Yuma: Name of town, county, and desert; derived from tribal name, probably meaning "sons of the river" (Hokan)

◆ ARKANSAS

Ponca: Name of town; derived from tribal name, meaning "sacred head" (Siouan)

◆ CALIFORNIA

Azusa: Name of town; meaning "skunk hill" (Gabrieleno)

Cahuilla: Name of town and valley; derived from tribal name, probably meaning "master" (Cahuilla)

Chemehuevi: Name of valley; derived from tribal name (Chemehuevi)

Chowchilla: Name of town; derived from tribal name, meaning "to kill" (Yokuts)

Cucamonga: Name of town; meaning "sandy place" (probably Gabrieleno)

Gualala: Name of town; derived from village name, meaning "river mouth" (Kashaya Pomo)

Inyo: Name of mountains, county, and national forest; meaning "dwelling place of a great spirit" (probably Paiute)

Lompoc: Name of town; probably meaning "where the waters break through" (Chumash)

Malibu: Name of city; probably derived from former village name (Chumash)

Marin: Name of county and peninsula; named after a leader (Coast Miwok)

Napa: Name of town and county; meaning "house" or "fish" (probably Patwin)

Ojai: Name of town; meaning "moon" (Chumash)

Otay: Name of town; meaning "brushy" (Diegueo)

Pala: Name of town; probably meaning "water" (Luiseño)

Petaluma: Name of town; derived from village and tribal name, meaning "flat" (Coast Miwok)

Simi: Name of valley; probably meaning "valley of the wind" or "village" (Chumash)

Sonoma: Name of town and county; derived from village name (Coast Miwok)

Tahoe: Name of city, lake, and national forest; meaning "big water" (Washo)

◆ COLORADO

Apishapa: Name of river; meaning "standing water" (Ute)

Kiowa: Name of town and county; derived from tribal name, meaning "principal people" (Shoshonean and Tanoan)

Montezuma: Name of town and county; named after the ruler of Mexico (Aztec)

Uncompahgre: Name of mountains, peak, plateau, river, and national forest; meaning "red water canyon" (Ute)

Yampa: Name of town and river; derived from name of band and name of edible root (Ute)

◆ CONNECTICUT

Connecticut: Name of state and river; meaning "the long river" (Mohican)

Mystic: Name of town; meaning "great tidal river" (Algonkian)

Naugatuck: Name of town and river; meaning "long tree" (Algonkian)

Niantic: Name of town and river; derived from tribal name, meaning "at the point of land on a tidal river" (Algonkian)

Ouray: Name of town, county, and peak; named after chief, probably meaning "the arrow" (probably Algonkian)

Saugatuck: Name of town, river, and reservoir; meaning "tidal outlet" (Paugusett)

Taconic: Name of town and mountain; probably meaning "forest" (Algonkian)

Willimantic: Name of river and reservoir; meaning "good cedar swamp" (Nipmuc)

Yantic: Name of town and river; meaning "tidal limit" (Mohegan)

◆ DELAWARE

Minquadale: Name of town; derived from Iroquoian tribe also known as Susquehanna (Iroquois)

◆ FLORIDA

Alachua: Name of town and county; meaning "grassy, marshy plain" (probably Creek)

Apalachicola: Name of town, river, bay, and national forest; meaning "people on the other side" (Hitchiti)

Chokoloskee: Name of town; meaning "old house" (Seminole)

Chuluota: Name of town; meaning "fox den" (probably Seminole)

Loxahatchee: Name of town and river; meaning "turtle river" (Seminole)

Miami: Name of city; meaning "people of the peninsula" (Ojibway)

Micanopy: Name of town; meaning "head chief" (Seminole)

Miccosukee: Name of town and lake; derived from tribal name (probably Muskogean)

Myakka: Name of town and river; derived from former village name (Timucuan)

Ocala: Name of town and national forest; derived from former village name (Timucuan)

Ochlockonee: Name of river; meaning "yellow water" (Hitchiti)

Okaloosa: Name of county; meaning "black water" (Choctaw)

Okeechobee: Name of town, county, and lake; meaning "big water" (Hitchiti)

Pensacola: Name of town and river; derived from tribal name, meaning "long-haired people" (Choctaw)

Seminole: Name of town, county, and lake; derived from tribal name, meaning "runaway" or "pioneer" (Muskogean)

Steinhatchee: Name of town and river; meaning "manhisriver" (Seminole)

Suwannee: Name of town, county, sound, and river; meaning "echo" (probably Algonkian)

Tallahassee: Name of city and bay; derived from village name, meaning "old town" (Creek)

Tampa: Name of city and bay; derived from village name, meaning "near it" (probably Muskogean)

Wakulla: Name of town, county, river, and springs; meaning "loon" (Seminole)

◆ GEORGIA

Alapaha: Name of town; derived from former village name (Seminole)

Canoochee: Name of town and river; derived from name of an ancient Indian region (Creek)

Catoosa: Name of county; named after chief whose name means "high place" (probably Cherokee)

Chickamauga: Name of town and river; derived from tribal name, meaning "sluggish water" (Cherokee)

Coosa: Name of town; derived from tribal name, meaning "reed" (Creek)

Ellijay: Name of town; derived from former village name (Cherokee)

Hiawassee: Name of town; meaning "meadow" (Cherokee)

Muscogee: Name of county; derived from tribal name (Muskogean)

Ocmulgee: Name of river and national monument; derived from tribal name, meaning "where the water bubbles up" (Hitchiti)

Oconee: Name of town, county, river, and national forest; meaning "water" (Muskogean)

Okefenokee: Name of swamp and national wildlife refuge; meaning "trembling water" (Hitchiti)

Satolah: Name of town and battlefield; meaning "six" (Cherokee)

Savannah: Name of river; meaning "southerner" (Shawnee)

Withlacoochie: Name of river; meaning "little creek" (Creek)

◆ IDAHO

Bannock: Name of county, river, mountain and peak; derived from tribal name, meaning "hair in backward motion" (Shoshonean)

Blackfoot: Name of river and reservoir; derived from tribal name referring to their dyeing their moccasins black (Algonkian)

Kootenai: Name of county, river and national wildlife refuge; derived from tribal name, meaning "water people" (Algonkian)

Lochsa: Name of river; meaning "rough water" (Flathead)

Minidoka: Name of town, county, national wildlife refuge; meaning "broad expanse" (probably Shoshonean)

Nez Percé_: Name of town, county, and national forest; derived from tribal name, meaning "pierced nose" (French version of Indian word)

Pocatello: Name of city; named after Bannock chief, probably meaning "the wayward one" (Shoshonean)

Potlatch: Name of town; meaning "giveaway," a type of public event (Chinook)

Shoshone: Name of town, county, and falls; derived from tribal name (Shoshonean)

Targhee: Name of pass and national forest; probably named after Shoshoni chief (Bannock)

◆ ILLINOIS

Aptakisic: Name of town; named after chief whose name means "halfday" (Potawatomi)

Cahokia: Name of town; derived from tribal name (Cahokia)

Chicago: Name of city and river; meaning "onion place" (Algonkian)

Chillicothe: Name of town; derived from tribal name, meaning "village" (probably Shawnee)

Illinois: Name of state and river; derived from tribal name, meaning "men" (Algonkian)

Iroquois: Name of city, county, and river; derived from tribal name, meaning "real adders" (Algonkian, with French spelling)

Kankakee: Name of town, county, and river; meaning "wolf land" (Mohegan)

Kaskaskia: Name of river; derived from tribal name (Kaskaskia)

Macoupin: Name of county; meaning "potato" (Algonkian)

Ottawa: Name of city; derived from tribal name, meaning "to trade" (Algonkian)

Peoria: Name of town and county; derived from tribal name, meaning "carriers" (Peoria)

Prophetstown: Name of town; named after medicine man, White Cloud (English version of Winnebago word)

Sangamon: Name of county and river; probably meaning "outlet" (Ojibway)

Sauk: Name of town; derived from tribal name, meaning "people of the yellow earth" (Algonkian)

Skokie: Name of town and river; meaning "marsh" (Potawatomi)

Spoon: Name of river; meaning "mussel shell" (Algonkian)

Waukegan: Name of town; meaning "trading post" (Algonkian)

◆ INDIANA

Genesee: Name of city; meaning "beautiful valley" (Algonkian)

Indiana: Name of state and county; derived from the Latinized form of Indian

Kokomo: Name of city; named after chief whose name means "black walnut" (Miami)

Muncie: Name of city; derived from tribal name, meaning "people of the stone country" (Algonkian)

Muscatatuck: Name of river and national wildlife refuge; meaning "clear river" (Delaware)

Wabash: Name of county and river; meaning "white water" (Miami)

◆ IOWA

Black Hawk: Name of city, county, and lake; named after chief of Sauk and Fox tribes

Iowa: Name of state, county, river, and falls; derived from tribal name, meaning "sleepy ones" (Siouan)

Keokuk: Name of town and county; named after Fox chief whose name means "he who moves around alert" (Algonkian)

Lakota: Name of city; derived from tribal name (often called Sioux), meaning "allies" (Siouan)

Maquoketa: Name of town and river; meaning "bear river" (Algonkian)

Muscatine: Name of town, county, and island; derived from tribal name (Muscatine)

Oskaloosa: Name of town; named after one of Osceola's wives whose name means "black water" (Choctaw)

Oto: Name of town; derived from tribal name, meaning "lovers" or "lechers" (Siouan)

Pocahontas: Name of city and county; named after the Indian princess whose name means "radiant" or "playful" (Algonkian)

Poweshiek: Name of county; named after chief whose name means "he who shakes something off" (Fox)

Sac: Name of city and county; derived from tribal name (same as Sauk), meaning "people of the yellow earth" (Algonkian)

Sioux: Name of city, county, and river; derived from Ojibway word, meaning "snakes" or "enemies" (French version of Ojibway word for Dakota)

Wapello: Name of town and county; named after Fox chief whose name means "he, of the morning" (Algonkian)

Wapsipinicon: Name of river; meaning "white potato" (Algonkian)

Winneshiek: Name of county; named after chief (Winnebago)

◆ KANSAS

Comanche: Name of county; derived from tribal name, meaning "always ready to fight" (Shoshonean)

Kansas: Name of state, city, and river; derived from tribal name, meaning "people of the south wind" (Siouan)

Kiowa: Name of county; derived from tribal name, meaning "principal people" (Shoshonean and Tanoan)

Osage: Name of city, county, and river; derived from tribal name, probably meaning "people" (Siouan)

Potawatomi: Name of county; derived from tribal name, meaning "people of the place of fire" (Algonkian)

Satanta: Name of city; named after chief (Kiowa)

Shawnee: Name of city and county; derived from tribal name, meaning "southerner" (Algonkian)

Topeka: Name of city; meaning "good potato place" (Kansa)

Wabaunsee: Name of county; named after Potawatomi chief (Algonkian)

Wichita: Name of city and county; derived from tribal name, meaning "man" (Caddoan)

◆ KENTUCKY

Kentucky: Name of state, lake, and river; meaning "land of tomorrow" (Wyandotte) or "meadow land" (Iroquoian)

Paducah: Name of town; named after chief and derived from tribal name (Chickasaw)

◆ LOUISIANA

Atchafalaya: Name of bay and river; meaning "long river" (Choctaw)

Bogalusa: Name of town; meaning "large stream" (Choctaw)

Caddo: Name of parish and lake; derived from tribal name, meaning "chief" (Caddoan)

Coushatta: Name of town; derived from tribal name, meaning "white canebreak" (Choctaw)

Houma: Name of town; derived from tribal name, meaning "red" (Choctaw)

Kisatchie: Name of town and national forest; meaning "reed river" (Choctaw)

Natchez: Name of city; derived from tribal name, probably meaning "timber land" (Muskogean)

Natchitoches: Name of town and parish; derived from tribal name, meaning "chestnut eaters" (Caddoan)

Tichfaw: Name of town and river; probably meaning "pine rest" (Choctaw)

Tunica: Name of town; derived from tribal name, meaning "the people" (Tunican)

◆ MAINE

Allagash: Name of river; meaning "bark shelter" (Abnaki)

Androscoggin: Name of county, river, and lake; derived from tribal name, meaning "fish spearing" (probably Algonkian)

Aroostook: Name of county and river; meaning "good, beautiful, or clear river" (Algonkian)

Kennebec: Name of county and river; meaning "long lake" (Algonkian)

Kennebunk: Name of town and river; meaning "long cut bank" (Algonkian)

Passadumkeag: Name of town and mountains; meaning "rapids over sandy places" (Abnaki)

Penobscot: Name of county, bay, lake, and river; derived from tribal name, meaning "rocky place" (Algonkian)

Piscataquis: Name of county and river; meaning "at the fork of the river" (Abnaki)

Saco: Name of town and river (Algonkian)

Sagadahoc: Name of county; meaning "mouth of river" (Algonkian)

Sebec: Name of town and lake; meaning "big lake" (Algonkian)

Seboeis: Name of town, lake, and river; meaning "small lake" (Algonkian)

Tulamdie: Name of river; meaning "canoe sandbar" (Algonkian)

◆ MARYLAND

Nanticoke: Name of town and river; derived from tribal name, meaning "tidewater people" (Delaware)

Pocomoke: Name of town and sound; meaning "small field" (Algonkian)

Potomac: Name of city and river; derived from tribal name, meaning "where the goods are brought in" (probably Algonkian)

Wicomico: Name of county and river; derived from tribal name, meaning "pleasant village" (Delaware)

◆ MASSACHUSETTS

Chappaquiddick: Name of island; meaning "seplaceted island" (Wampanoag)

Chicopee: Name of town and river; meaning "swift water" (Algonkian)

Housatonic: Name of town and river; meaning "at the place beyond the mountain" (Mahican)

Massachusetts: Name of state and bay; meaning "great hill" (Algonkian)

Muskegel: Name of channel and island; meaning "grassy place" (Wampanoag)

Nantucket: Name of county, island, and sound; meaning "narrow tidal river at" (Algonkian)

Natick: Name of town; derived from tribal name, meaning "a place of hills" (Algonkian)

Weweantic: Name of river; meaning "crooked river" (Algonkian)

◆ MICHIGAN

Cheboygan: Name of town, county, and river; probably meaning "pipe" (Algonkian)

Chippewa: Name of county and river; derived from tribal name, meaning "voice" and "gathering up" (Ojibway)

Gogebic: Name of county and lake; meaning "high lake" (Ojibway)

Kalamazoo: Name of town and county; meaning "it smokes" (Algonkian)

Mackinaw: Name of town, county, island, and straits; meaning "island of the large turtle" (Ojibway)

Manistee: Name of town, county, river, and national forest; meaning "crooked river" (Ojibway)

Manitou: Name of islands; meaning "spirit" (Algonkian)

Mecosta: Name of county; named after chief whose name means "bear cub" (Potawatomi)

Menominee: Name of town, county, river, and mountains; derived from tribal name, meaning "wild rice people" (Algonkian)

Michigan: Name of state and one of the Great Lakes; meaning "big lake" (Ojibway)

Missaukee: Name of county and lake; after Ottawa chief whose name means "big outlet at" (probably Algonkian)

Munuscong: Name of lake and river; meaning "the place of the reeds" (Algonkian)

Muskegon: Name of town, county, and river; meaning "swampy" (Ojibway)

Ontonagon: Name of town, county, and river; meaning "a place where game was shot by luck" (Ojibway)

Otsego: Name of town, county, and lake; meaning "rock place" (Iroquoian)

Pontiac: Name of city; named after Ottawa chief (probably Algonkian)

Sanilac: Name of county; named after Wyandotte chief (probably Iroquoian)

Shiawassee: Name of county and national wildlife refuge; meaning "straight ahead water" (Algonkian)

Tahquamenon: Name of river and falls; meaning "dark-colored water" (Ojibway)

Tecumseh: Name of town; named after chief whose name means "a panther crouching for its prey" (Shawnee)

Tittabawassee: Name of river; probably meaning "river following the line of the shore" (Algonkian)

Washtenaw: Name of county; meaning "on the river" (Ojibway)

◆ MINNESOTA

Anoka: Name of town and county; meaning "on both sides" (Siouan)

Bemidji: Name of town and lake; named after chief whose name probably means "river crossing lake" (probably Algonkian)

Chanhassen: Name of town and river; meaning "tree with sweet juice" (Siouan)

Chaska: Name of town, lake, and creek; meaning "first-born son" (Siouan)

Chisago: Name of county; meaning "large and beautiful" (Ojibway)

Isanti: Name of town and county; derived from tribal name (probably Siouan)

Kanabec: Name of county; meaning "snake" (Ojibway)

Kandiyohi: Name of county; meaning "buffalo fish come" (Siouan)

Koochiching: Name of county; probably meaning "rainy lake" (Cree)

Mahnomen: Name of town and county; meaning "wild rice" (Ojibway)

Mesabi: Name of mountains; meaning "giant" (Ojibway)

Minneapolis: Name of city; meaning "waterfall" (Siouan) and "city" (Creek)

Minnesota: Name of state, lake, and river; probably meaning "land of many lakes" (Siouan)

Minnetonka: Name of town and lake; meaning "big water" (Siouan)

Wabasha: Name of town and county; a personal name for hereditary chiefs, meaning "red leaf" or "red battle-standard" (Siouan)

Wadena: Name of town and county; meaning "little round hill" (Ojibway)

Waseca: Name of town and county; meaning "fertile" (Siouan)

Watonwan: Name of county and river; meaning "where fish bait can be found" (probably Siouan)

◆ MISSISSIPPI

Biloxi: Name of town, bay, and river; derived from tribal name, meaning "broken pot" (probably Muskogean)

Chickasawhay: Name of river; derived from village name, meaning "potato" (Choctaw)

Escatawpa: Name of town and river; meaning "cane cut there" (Choctaw)

Hatchie: Name of river and natural wildlife refuge; meaning "stream" (Choctaw)

Homochitto: Name of river and national forest; meaning "red chief" (Choctaw)

Issaquena: Name of county; meaning "deer's head" (Choctaw)

Mississippi: Name of state and river; meaning "big river" (Algonkian)

Neshoba: Name of town and county; probably meaning "wolf" (Choctaw)

Noxubee: Name of county and river; meaning "stinking water" (Choctaw)

Oktibbeha: Name of county; meaning "pure water" (Choctaw)

Pascagoula: Name of town and river; derived from tribal name, meaning "bread people" (probably Muskogean)

Pontotoc: Name of town and county; meaning "cattails on the prairie" (Chickasaw)

Tallahatchie: Name of county and river; meaning "town" and "river" (Creek)

Tishomingo: Name of town and county; after chief whose name means "assistant chief" (Chickasaw)

Tombigbee: Name of river and national forest; meaning "coffin makers" (Choctaw)

Tougaloo: Name of city; meaning "fork of a stream" (Cherokee)

Tunica: Name of county; derived from tribal name, meaning "the people" (Tunica)

Yalobusha: Name of county and river; meaning "little tadpole" (Choctaw)

Yazoo: Name of town, county, and river; derived from tribal name, probably meaning "those who are the people" (Tunican)

◆ MISSOURI

Meramec: Name of river; derived from tribal name, meaning "catfish" (Meramec)

Missouri: Name of state and river; derived from tribal name, meaning "muddy water" (probably Siouan)

Neosho: Name of town; meaning "cold, clear water" (Osage)

Pemiscot: Name of county; meaning "place of the long rock" (possibly Fox)

Wyaconda: Name of town and river; meaning "spirit" (Siouan)

◆ MONTANA

Chinook: Name of town; derived from tribal name (Chinookan)

Flathead: Name of county, river, lake, and national forest; derived from tribal name (Flathead)

Kootenai: Name of river and mountains; derived from tribal name, meaning "water people" (Kootenai)

Mackinac: Name of town; meaning "island of the large turtle" (Ojibway)

Missoula: Name of town and county; meaning "feared water" (Flathead)

Tepee: Name of mountains and Indian tent (Siouan)

◆ NEBRASKA

Arapaho: Name of town; derived from tribal name, meaning "he who trades" (Pawnee)

Nebraska: Name of state and national forest; meaning "wide water" (probably Siouan)

Niobrara: Name of river; meaning "spreading water river" (unknown)

Ogallala: Name of city; derived from tribal name, meaning "to scatter one's own" (Siouan)

Omaha: Name of city; derived from tribal name, meaning "those who live upstream beyond others" (probably Siouan)

Pawnee: Name of county; derived from tribal name, meaning "horn," "hunter," or "braid" (Caddoan)

Red Cloud: Name of town; named after chief (Siouan)

Santee: Name of town; derived from tribal name, meaning "knife" (Dakota)

◆ NEVADA

Beowawe: Name of pass to canyon; meaning "an open gate" (Shoshonean)

Hiko: Name of mountain range; meaning "white people" (Southern Paiute)

Pahranagat: Name of valley and mountain range; derived from tribal name, meaning "people of the marshy spring" (Paiute)

Pequop: Name of mountain; derived from tribal name (Algonkian)

Timpahute: Name of mountain range; derived from tribal name, meaning "rock spring people" (Paiute)

Toana: Name of mountain range; meaning "black hill" (Shoshonean)

Toquima: Name of mountain range; derived from tribal name, meaning "black backs" (Shoshonean)

Washoe: Name of town, county, lake, valley, and mountain range; derived from tribal name, meaning "person" (Hokan)

Winnemucca: Name of lake; meaning "bread giver" (Paiute)

◆ NEW HAMPSHIRE

Coos: Name of county; meaning "pine tree" (Pennacook)

Merrimack: Name of town, county, and river; probably meaning "deep place" (Algonkian)

Nashua: Name of town and river; derived from tribal name, meaning "beautiful river with pebbly bottom" (probably Algonkian)

Ossipee: Name of town, lake, river, and mountains; meaning "beyond the water" (Abenaki)

Suncook: Name of town, river, and lakes; meaning "at the rocks" (Algonkian)

Winnisquam: Name of lake; meaning "salmon" (Algonkian)

◆ NEW JERSEY

Hackensack: Name of city and river; derived from tribal name, probably meaning "hook mouth" or "big snake land" (Algonkian)

Hoboken: Name of city; meaning "land of the tobacco pipe" (Delaware)

Hopatcong: Name of city and lake; probably meaning "hill above a body of still water having an outlet" (Algonkian)

Navesink: Name of town and river; meaning "point at" (Algonkian)

Parsippany: Name of town; probably derived from tribal name (probably Algonkian)

Passaic: Name of city, county, and river; probably meaning "valley" or "peace" (Delaware)

Pequannock: Name of city and river; meaning "open field" (Algonkian)

Raritan: Name of city, river, and bay; derived from tribal name, probably meaning "stream overflows" or "forked river" (Algonkian)

Wanaque: Name of city and reservoir; probably meaning "sassafras place" (Algonkian)

Whippany: Name of city and river; probably meaning "arrow stream" (Delaware)

◆ NEW MEXICO

Abiquiu: Name of city and reservoir; probably derived from village name, meaning "chokecherry" (Tewa)

Acomita: Name of city; named after Indian pueblo and people, meaning "whiterock people" (Pueblo)

Aztec: Name of town; derived from tribal name, meaning "place of the heron" or "land of flamingos" (Aztec)

Mescalero: Name of city; derived from a Spanish word for an Apache tribe, referring to their practice of preparing a food called mescal (Spanish)

Mexico: Name of state and gulf; meaning "place of the war god" (Aztec)

Taos: Name of city and county; probably meaning "red willow place" or "at the village" (Tewa)

Tucumcari: Name of city and mountain; meaning "to lie in ambush" (Comanche)

Ute: Name of city and park; derived from tribal name (Uto-Aztecan)

Zuni: Name of city, river, and mountains; derived from village and tribal names (Zuni)

◆ NEW YORK

Adirondacks: Name of town, park, and mountain range; derived from tribal name, meaning "bark eaters" (Iroquoian)

Allegheny: Name of plateau and reservoir; probably from the name for Allegheny and Ohio rivers (Delaware)

Canadaigua: Name of town and lake; meaning "town set off" (Iroquoian)

Cassadaga: Name of town, creek, and lakes; meaning "under the rocks" (Iroquoian)

Cattaraugus: Name of town, county, and creek; meaning "bad smelling shore" (Iroquoian)

Cayuga: Name of town, county, canal, and lake; derived from tribal name, meaning "where they take the boats out" (probably Iroquoian)

Chemung: Name of town, county, and river; meaning "big horn" (Seneca)

Chenango: Name of county and river; meaning "bull thistle" (Onondaga)

Manhasset: Name of town; derived from tribal name (Algonkian)

Manhattan: Name of island and borough; derived from tribal name, probably meaning "island-mountain" (Algonkian)

Mohawk: Name of town and river; derived from a name used by their Algonkian enemies, meaning "man eaters" (Algonkian)

Niagara: Name of town, county, river, and falls; meaning "point of land cut in two" (Iroquoian)

Oneida: Name of town, county, and lake; derived from tribal name, meaning "stone people" (Iroquoian)

Onondaga: Name of county; derived from tribal name, meaning "hill people" (Iroquoian)

Oswego: Name of town, county, river, and lake; probably meaning "the outpouring" or "the place where the valley widens" (Iroquoian)

Poughkeepsie: Name of town; meaning "little rock at water" (Algonkian)

Saratoga: Name of town, county, and lake; meaning "springs from the hillside" (probably Mohawk)

Seneca: Name of county, river, lake, and falls; derived from tribal name, probably meaning "people of the stone" (Mohegan)

Susquehanna: Name of river; derived from tribal name (Iroquoian)

Tuscarora: Name of town; derived from tribal name, meaning "hemp gatherers" (Iroquoian)

◆ NORTH CAROLINA

Alamance: Name of county and creek; meaning "noisy stream" (probably Siouan)

Catawba: Name of town, county, and river; derived from tribal name (probably Siouan)

Cherokee: Name of town, county, and national forest; derived from tribal name, meaning "people of a different speech" (probably Algonkian)

Chowan: Name of county and river; derived from tribal name (probably Algonkian)

Croatoan: Name of city and national forest; probably meaning "talk town" (probably Algonkian)

Currituck: Name of town, county, and sound; derived from tribal name, probably meaning "wild geese" (probably Algonkian)

Nantahala: Name of mountains, gorge, lake, river, and national forest; meaning "place of the middle sun" (Cherokee)

Pasquotank: Name of county; derived from tribal name, probably meaning "divided tidal river" (Weapemeoc)

Perquimans: Name of county and river; derived from tribal name (Weapemeoc)

Tuckaseigee: Name of river; derived from village name, probably meaning "crawling turtle" (Cherokee)

Waccamaw: Name of lake and river; derived from tribal name (probably Siouan)

◆ NORTH DAKOTA

Dakota: Name of states and river; derived from tribal name of people also known as Sioux, meaning "allies" (Siouan)

Mandan: Name of city; derived from tribal name, meaning "those who live along the bank of the river" (Dakota)

Minnewaukan: Name of city; meaning "water of the bad spirit" (Siouan)

Pembina: Name of town, county, and river; meaning "summer berry" (Ojibway)

Wahpeton: Name of town; derived from one of the seven divisions of the Dakotas, meaning "dwellers among the leaves" (Siouan)

◆ OHIO

Cuyahoga: Name of county, river, and falls; meaning "important river" (probably Iroquoian)

Mahoning: Name of county; meaning "salt lick" (Delaware)

Maumee: Name of town and river; derived from tribal name, meaning "people of the peninsula" (Ojibway)

Mississinewa: Name of river; meaning "river of big stones" (Algonkian)

Muskingum: Name of county and river; derived from village name, meaning "at the river" (Algonkian)

Newcomerstown: Name of town; named after chief Netawatwees, whose name means "beaver" (Delaware)

Ohio: Name of state and river; meaning "beautiful" (Iroquoian)

Sandusky: Name of town, county, bay, and river; meaning "source of pure water" (Wyandotte)

Tippecanoe: Name of city; meaning "buffalo fish" (Potawatomi)

Wyandotte: Name of county; derived from tribal name, meaning "islanders" or "peninsula dwellers" (Iroquoian)

◆ OKLAHOMA

Atoka: Name of town and county; named after the Choctaw athlete, Captain Atoka, whose name means "ball ground" (Choctaw)

Broken Arrow: Name of city; derived from a Creek village name (translated from Muskogean)

Cheyenne: Name of city; derived from tribal name, meaning "red talkers" (Algonkian)

Coweta: Name of town; derived from a Creek town name (Muskogean)

Creek: Name of county; derived from tribal name given by the English to the Muskogee tribe (English)

Kiamichi: Name of river; derived from village name (Caddoan)

Muskogee: Name of town and county; derived from tribal name (Muskogean)

Nowata: Name of town and county; meaning "welcome" (Delaware)

Okfuskee: Name of county; meaning "promontory" (Muskogean)

Oklahoma: Name of city, county, and state; meaning "red people" (Muskogean)

Okmulgee: Name of town and county; derived from tribal name, meaning "where water boils up" (Hitchiti)

Oologah: Name of town and reservoir; named after chief whose name means "dark cloud"

Pushmataha: Name of county; named after chief (Choctaw)

Sequoyah: Name of county; named after a Cherokee who devised a written language (Cherokee)

Tonkawa: Name of city; derived from tribal name, meaning "they all stay together" (probably Waco)

Tulsa: Name of city and county; derived from a Creek village name, meaning "old town" (Muskogean)

Wewoka: Name of town and creek; derived from a Creek village name, meaning "water roaring" (Muskogean)

Wichita: Name of mountains; derived from tribal name, meaning "man" (Caddoan)

♦ OREGON

Clackamas: Name of county and river; derived from name of a subtribe (Chinookan)

Clatsop: Name of county; derived from name of a subtribe (Chinookan)

Klamath: Name of county, lake, and river; derived from a tribal name (Chinook)

Metolius: Name of town and river; meaning "light colored fish"

Multnomah: Name of county and falls; derived from tribal name (Multnomah)

Nehalem: Name of river; derived from a tribal name (Chinook)

Oregon: Name of state; probably meaning "place of plenty" or "river of the west" (Shoshonean)

Sacajawea: Name of peak; named after the Shoshoni woman who was part of the Lewis and Clark Expedition, meaning "bird woman" (Shoshonean)

Siskiyou: Name of town, national forest and mountains; meaning "bobtail horse" (probably Cree)

Siuslaw: Name of river and national forest; derived from tribal name, meaning "people of Nehalem" (Chinook)

Tillamook: Name of county, bay, and cape; derived from tribal name (Tillamook)

Umatilla: Name of town, county, river, and dam; derived from tribal name, probably meaning "water rippling over sand" (Umatilla)

Umpqua: Name of town and river; derived from tribal name, meaning "thunder" or "high and low water" (Athapascan)

Wallowa: Name of town, county, lake, river, national forest, and mountains; meaning "triangular stakes," a type of fish trap (Nez Percé_)

♦ PENNSYLVANIA

Aliquippa: Name of borough; named after a Seneca matron (Iroquoian)

Lenape: Name of town; derived from tribal name, meaning "men of our nation" or "real people" (Delaware)

Lycoming: Name of county; meaning "sandy creek" (Delaware)

Monongahela: Name of town and river; meaning "river with the sliding banks" (Delaware)

Pocono: Name of lake, creek, and mountains; probably meaning "valley stream" (Delaware)

Shenango: Name of river and reservoir; derived from village name, meaning "beautiful one" (probably Algonkian)

Susquehanna: Name of county and river; derived from tribal name (Iroquoian)

Tioga: Name of town, county, and river; meaning "at the forks" (Iroquoian)

◆ RHODE ISLAND

Narragansett: Name of city and bay; derived from tribal name, meaning "people of the small point" (Algonkian)

Pascoag: Name of town and reservoir; meaning "forking place" (Algonkian)

Pawtucket: Name of city; meaning "at the falls in the river" (Algonkian)

Wallum: Name of town and lake; meaning "dog" (Nipmuc)

Woonsocket: Name of city; probably meaning "at a steep spot" (Algonkian)

◆ SOUTH CAROLINA

Congaree: Name of river; derived from tribal name (Congaree)

Coosawhatchie: Name of town and river; meaning "stream with cane" (Muskogean)

Edisto: Name of island and river; derived from tribal name (probably Muskogean)

Pacolet: Name of town and river; derived from tribal name (Pacolet)

Wateree: Name of river and lake; derived from a subtribe (Catawba)

◆ SOUTH DAKOTA

Dakota: Name of states; derived from tribal name of people also known as Sioux, meaning "allies" (Siouan)

Wakpala: Name of town; meaning "creek" (Siouan)

Waubay: Name of town and lake; meaning "nesting place for wild fowl" (Siouan)

Wetonka: Name of town; meaning "big" (probably Siouan)

Wewela: Name of town; meaning "small spring" (probably Siouan)

Yankton: Name of town and county; derived from tribal village, meaning "end village" (Siouan)

◆ TENNESSEE

Chattanooga: Name of city; meaning "rock rising to a point" (Creek)

Obion: Name of town, county and river; probably meaning "many forks" (unknown)

Sequatchie: Name of county and river; named after a chief whose name means "hog river" (Cherokee)

Telico: Name of town; derived from village name, probably meaning "place of refuge" (Cherokee)

Tennessee: Name of state and river; derived from village name (Cherokee)

Unicoi: Name of town, county, and pass; meaning "white" (Cherokee)

◆ TEXAS

Anahuac: Name of national wildlife refuge; meaning "plain near the water" (Aztec)

Miami: Name of town; derived from tribal name, meaning "people of the peninsula" (Ojibway)

Nacogdoches: Name of county; derived from tribal name (Caddoan)

Neches: Name of river; derived from tribal name, meaning "snow river" (Hasinai)

Pecos: Name of county and river; meaning "watering place" (Keresan)

Quanah: Name of town; named after chief, meaning "better flowers" (Comanche)

Tehuacana: Name of town; meaning "the three canes" (Wichita)

Waco: Name of lake; derived from tribal name, meaning "heron" (probably Caddoan)

Waxahachie: Name of town; meaning "cow stream" (Tonkawa)

◆ UTAH

Goshute: Name of town; derived from tribal name, meaning "dust people" (probably Shoshonean)

Juab: Name of county; meaning "valley" (Gosiute)

Paiute: Name of county; derived from tribal name, meaning "Ute of the water" (Paiute)

Panguitch: Name of town and lake; derived from tribal name, meaning "fish people" (Paiute)

Parowan: Name of town; derived from tribal name, meaning "marsh people" (Parowan)

Sanpete: Name of county; meaning "homelands" (Ute)

Uinta: Name of river, national forest, and mountains; de—rived from tribal name, meaning "pineland" (Shoshonean)

Utah: Name of state, county, and lake; derived from tribal name, meaning "high up" or "the land of the sun" (Ute)

Wah Wah: Name of mountains; probably meaning "juniper" (Paiute)

♦ VERMONT

Missisquoi: Name of river; meaning "much water fowl" (Algonkian)

Winooski: Name of town and river; meaning "onion land" (Abenaki)

♦ VIRGINIA

Accomac: Name of town and county; derived from tribal name, meaning "the other side" (probably Algonkian)

Alleghany: Name of town and county; named for Allegheny and Ohio Rivers (Delaware)

Appomattox: Name of town, county, and river; derived from tribal name, probably meaning "tobacco plant country" or "curving tidal estuary" (Algonkian)

Chesapeake: Name of city and bay; probably meaning "on the big bay" (Algonkian)

Nansemond: Name of county; derived from tribal name, meaning "whence we were driven off" (Nansemond)

Nottoway: Name of town, county, and river; derived from tribal name, meaning "rattlesnake" (Algonkian)

Powhatan: Name of city and county; named after chief, probably meaning "falls in a current of water" (Algonkian)

Rappahannock: Name of county and river; derived from tribal name, meaning "back-and-forth stream" (Algonkian)

Roanoke: Name of town, county, and river; probably meaning "white-shell place" (Algonkian)

♦ WASHINGTON

Chehalis: Name of city, county, river, and Indian reservation; derived from tribal name, meaning "shining sands" (Salishan)

Clallam: Name of county, river, and bay; derived from tribal name, meaning "big brave nation" (Clallam)

Cowlitz: Name of county and river; derived from tribal name, meaning "capturing the medicine spirit" (Cowlitz)

Duwamish: Name of river; derived from tribal name, meaning "the people living on the river" (Duwamish)

Hoh: Name of river and Indian reservation; derived from tribal name (Hoh)

Kitsap: Name of county and lake; named after chief, meaning "brave" (Kitsap)

Kittitas: Name of town and county; probably derived from tribal name, meaning "shoal people" (Kittitas)

Klickitat: Name of county and river; derived from tribal name, meaning "beyond" (Klickitat)

Lummi: Name of river, island, and Indian reservation; derived from tribal name (Lummi)

Nespelem: Name of town; derived from tribal name, meaning "large, open meadow" (Nespelem)

Okanogan: Name of county, river, and national forest; derived from tribal name, probably meaning "meeting place" (Okanogan)

Puyallup: Name of city and river; derived from tribal name, meaning "generous people" (Puyallup)

Seattle: Name of city; named after chief (Salishan)

Skagit: Name of county, river, and bay; derived from tribal name (Skagit)

Snoqualmie: Name of river, pass, and national forest; derived from tribal name, meaning "moon" (Snoqualmie)

Spokane: Name of city, county, river, and mountain; derived from tribal name, meaning "chief of the sun" (Spokane)

Tulalip: Name of bay and Indian reservation; meaning "bay with a small mouth" (Tulalip)

Walla Walla: Name of city, county, valley, and river; derived from tribal name, meaning "little swift river" (Walla Walla)

Wenatchee: Name of city, lake, national forest, and mountains; derived from tribal name, meaning "river issuing from canyon" (Wenatchee)

Yakima: Name of city, county, and river; derived from tribal name, probably meaning "runaway" (Yakima)

♦ WEST VIRGINIA

Chattaroy: Name of town; derived from tribal name (probably Algonkian)

Kanawha: Name of county and river; derived from tribal name, probably meaning "hurricane" (Kanawha)

Mingo: Name of county; meaning "stealthy" or "treacherous" (Algonkian)

◆ WISCONSIN

Horicon: Name of town and national wildlife refuge; derived from tribal name, probably meaning "silver water" (Horicon)

Kenosha: Name of town and county; meaning "pickerel" (Potawatomi)

Kickapoo: Name of river; derived from tribal name, meaning "he moves about" (Algonkian)

Manitowoc: Name of town and county; meaning "land of the spirit" (Algonkian)

Milwaukee: Name of city, county, river, and bay; probably meaning "good land" (Algonkian)

Monona: Name of town and lake; named after either an Indian divinity or a legendary Indian girl who jumped into the Mississippi River when she thought her lover had been killed (Algonkian)

Namekagon: Name of town, lake, and river; meaning "place for sturgeon" (Ojibway)

Necedah: Name of town and national wildlife refuge; meaning "yellow" (Winnebago)

Oconto: Name of town, county, river, and falls; meaning "pickerel place" (Menominee)

Ojibway: Name of town; derived from tribal name, meaning "puckered up," referring to a style of moccasin (Ojibway)

Ozaukee: Name of county; derived from tribal name, meaning "river mouth people" or "yellow earth" (Ozaukee)

Waukesha: Name of town and county; derived from tribal name (Potawatomi)

Winnebago: Name of town, county, and lake; derived from tribal name, probably meaning "people of the filthy waters" (Algonkian)

Wisconsin: Name of state, river, lake, and rapids; meaning "the gathering of the waters" or "grassy place" (French version of Ojibway word)

◆ WYOMING

Absaroka: Name of mountains; named after a bird, meaning "crow" (Siouan)

Sundance: Name of town and mountain; named after an-nual purification or world renewal ceremony (English)

Washakie: Name of town, county, lake, mountain, creek, and national forest; named after Snake chief (unknown)

Wyoming: Name of state, range, and peak; meaning "large meadows" (Delaware)

CANADA

◆ ALBERTA

Athabaska: Name of river and mountain; meaning "where there are needs" (Cree)

Chipewyan: Name of lakes, river, and Hudson's Bay Company post; derived from tribal name, meaning "pointed skins" (Cree)

Okotoks: Name of town and mountains; meaning "big rock" (Blackfoot)

Ponoka: Name of town; meaning "black elk" (Blackfoot)

Wetaskiwin: Name of city; meaning "hills of peace" (Cree)

◆ BRITISH COLUMBIA

Chilliwack: Name of city; derived from tribal name, meaning "valley of many waters" (Halkomelem)

Coquitlam: Name of river and mountain; derived from tribal name, meaning "stinking of fish slime" (Halkomelem)

Cowichan: Name of village, river, and lake; derived from tribal name, meaning "warm country" (Halkomelem)

Illecillewaet: Name of river, glacier, and mining district; meaning "end of water" (Okanagan)

Kelowna: Name of city; meaning "female grizzly bear" (Okanagan)

Kootenay: Name of river and national park; derived from tribal name, meaning "water people" (Kootenai)

Lillooet: Name of town, district, and river; derived from tribal name, meaning "wild onion" (Lillooet)

Naas: Name of river and bay; meaning "satisfier of the stomach" (Tlingit)

Nanaimo: Name of city, river, and harbor; meaning "strong, strong water" (Halkomelem)

Okanagan: Name of town, valley, and lake; derived from tribal name, meaning "place of water" (Straits Salish)

Skeena: Name of river; meaning "out of the clouds" (Tsimshian)

Stikine: Name of river; meaning "great river" (Tlingit)

◆ MANITOBA

Manitoba: Name of province and lake; meaning "the strait of the spirit" (Cree)

Minnedosa: Name of town and river; meaning "swift water" (Siouan)

Pembina: Name of county, river, and mountains; meaning "summer berry" (Cree)

Tadoule: Name of lake; meaning "floating charcoal" (Chipewyan)

Winnipeg: Name of city, river, and lake; probably meaning "murky water" (Cree)

◆ NEW BRUNSWICK

Great Manan: Name of island; meaning "the island" (Malecite-Passamaquoddy)

Kennebecasis: Name of island, river, and bay; meaning "little, long bay place" (Malecite)

Miramichi: Name of river; meaning "the land of the Micmacs" (Algonkian)

Oromocto: Name of island, village, river, and lake; meaning "good river" (Micmac and Malecite)

Petitcodiac: Name of village and river; meaning "river that bends in a bow fitted to an arrow" (Micmac)

Shippigan: Name of island, village, and harbor; meaning "a small passage through which ducks fly" (Micmac)

◆ NORTHWEST TERRITORIES

Akimiski: Name of island; meaning "the land across" (Cree)

Aklavik: Name of town; meaning "place of the barren land grizzly" (Inuit)

Akpatok: Name of island; meaning "place of birds" (Inuit)

Auyuittuq: Name of national park; meaning "the place where ice does not melt" (Inuit)

Inuvik: Name of locality; meaning "the place of man" (Inuit)

Keewatin: Name of district; meaning "north wind" (Cree)

◆ NOVA SCOTIA

Antigonish: Name of county and harbor; meaning "broken branches" (Micmac)

Arichat: Name of island; meaning "the camping ground" (Micmac)

Chignecto: Name of bay; meaning "foot cloth" (Micmac)

Maccan: Name of settlement; meaning "fishing place" (Micmac)

Missinaibi: Name of lake and river; meaning "pictures on the water" (Micmac)

Pugwash: Name of river and bay; meaning "a bank of sand " or "shallow water" (Micmac)

Scubenacadie: Name of village, river, and lake; meaning "where nuts grow in abundance" (Micmac)

◆ ONTARIO

Abitibi: Name of lake and river; derived from tribal name, meaning "halfway water" (Algonkian)

Brant/Brantford: Name of city and county; named after chief Joseph Brant (Mohawk)

Cataraqui: Name of river; meaning "where river and lake meet" (Iroquoian)

Cayuga: Name of town and county; derived from tribal name, meaning "here they take the boats out" (Iroquoian)

Iroquois: Name of town; derived from tribal name, meaning "real adders" (Algonkian word with French spelling)

Muskota: Name of district, lake, river, and bay; probably named after a chief (Ojibway)

Niagara: Name of township, river, and falls; probably meaning "thunderer of waters" or "resounding with great noise" (Iroquoian)

Oneida: Name of township; derived from tribal name, meaning "people of the upright stone" (Iroquoian)

Ottawa: Name of city and river; derived from tribal name, probably meaning "to trade" (Algonkian)

Petawawa: Name of township, village, and river; meaning "where one hears the noise of water far away" (probably Algonkian)

Saugeen: Name of township and river; meaning "river mouth" (Huron)

Tecumseh: Name of township; named after chief whose name means "a panther crouching for its prey" (Shawnee)

Toronto: Name of city; probably meaning "fallen trees in the water" or "a place of meeting" (Huron)

◆ QUEBEC

Arthabaska: Name of county and cantons; meaning "a place obstructed by reeds and grass" (Cree)

Chibougamau: Name of settlement, river, and lake; meaning "the water is stopped" (Algonkian)

Chicoutimi: Name of city, county, and river; meaning "end of the deep water" (Montagnais)

Matane: Name of town, county, river, and lakes; meaning "beaver ponds" (Micmac)

Pontiac: Name of county; named after Ottawa chief (probably Algonkian)

Quebec: Name of city, county, and province; meaning "where the river narrows" (Algonkian)

Shawinigan: Name of lake, river, and falls; meaning "a portage shaped like a beech-nut" (probably Cree)

Temiscouata: Name of county and lake; meaning "deep lake" (Cree)

Ungava: Name of bay; meaning "an unknown, faraway land" (Inuit)

◆ SASKATCHEWAN

Assiniboine: Name of river; derived from a word for a Sioux tribe, meaning "he who cooks with stones" (Ojibway)

Saskatchewan: Name of province and river; meaning "swift-flowing river" (Cree)

Saskatoon: Name of city; named for edible red berry (Cree)

Wakaw: Name of lake; meaning "crooked lake" (Cree)

◆ YUKON TERRITORY

Dezadeash: Name of lake; meaning "a native fishing method" (Athapascan)

Itsi: Name of lake and mountains; meaning "wind" (Athapascan)

Klondike: Name of village and river; meaning "river full of fish"

Teslin: Name of town, lake, and river; meaning "long waters" (Athapascan)

Ulu: Name of mountain; named for a knife with a crescent-shaped blade and a handle of bone or wood (Inuit)

Yukon: Name of river and mountain; meaning "great river" (probably Athapascan)

Tribal Collections

UNITED STATES

◆ ALASKA

AKUTAN ALEUT MUSEUM
P.O. Box 89
Akutan, AK 99553

CHICKALOON NUKDIN ITNU TRIBAL
    MUSEUM
Chickaloon Village, Box 1105
Chickaloon, AK 99674
(907) 745–0707

UNIVERSITY OF ALASKA MUSEUM
907 Youkon Dr.
Fairbanks, AK 99775
(907) 474–7505
www.uaf.edu/museum

NANA MUSEUM OF THE ARTIC
P.O. Box 49
Kotzebue, AK 99752
(907) 442–3441

◆ ARIZONA

AK-CHIN HIM DAK ECO MUSEUM
Ak-Chin Indian Community
47685 N. Eco Museum Rd.
Maricopa, AZ 85239
(520) 568–9480

COLORADO RIVER INDIAN TRIBES MUSEUM
Rte. 1, Box 23B
Parker, AZ 85344
(520) 669–1335
Mohave, Chemehuevi, Navajo, and Hopi.

COCOPAH TRIBAL MUSEUM
County 15 & Aveune G
Somerton, AZ 85350
(520) 627–1992

DINE MUSEUM
Navajo Community College
Box 35
Tsaile, AZ 86556
(520) 724–6653

NAVAJO NATION TRIBAL MUSEUM
P.O. Box 1840, Hwy. 264
Window Rock, AZ 86515
(520) 871–7941

◆ CALIFORNIA

HOOPA TRIBAL MUSEUM
P.O. Box 1348
Hoopa, CA 95546
(530) 625–4110
Hupa, Yurok, and Karuk.

MALKI MUSEUM
Morongo Reservation
P.O. Box 578
11–795 Fields Rd.
Banning, CA 92220
(909) 849–7289
www.the-pass.com/Malki/fallg.html
Cahuilla, Serrano, Luiseño, and other California
    Tribal Groups.

◆ COLORADO

SOUTHERN UTE INDIAN MUSEUM
1482 Hwy. 172 N.
Ignacio, CO 81137
(970) 563–9583

UTE INDIAN MUSEUM
17253 Chiopeta Rd.
Montrose, CO 81401
(970) 249–3098

◆ CONNECTICUT

TANTAQUIDGEON INDIAN MUSEUM
Rte. 32, Norwich-New London Rd.
Uncasville, CT 06382
(860) 848–9145
Built and maintained by descendants of uncas, chief of the Mohegans.

◆ DELAWARE

NANTICOKE INDIAN MUSEUM
Rte. 4, Box 107A
Millsboro, DE 19966
(302) 945–7022

◆ FLORIDA

AH-TAH-THI-KI MUSEUM
HC 21, Box 21A
Clewiston, FL 33440
(863) 902–1113
www.seminoletribe.com/museum

COO-TAUN CHOBE MUSEUM
Bobby's Seminole Indian Village and Gift Shop
5221 North Orient Rd.
Tampa, FL 33610
(813) 620–3077

SEMINOLE OKALEE INDIAN VILLAGE AND MUSEUM
5845 South State Rd. 7
Fort Lauderdale, FL 33314
(954) 792–1213

◆ IDAHO

SHOSHONE-BANNOCK TRIBAL MUSEUM
P.O. Box 793
I-15, Exit 80
Fort Hall, ID 83203
(208) 237–9791

◆ KANSAS

MID-AMERICA ALL INDIAN CENTER MUSEUM
650 North Seneca
Wichita, KS 67203
(316) 262–5221

◆ MAINE

MAINE TRIBAL UNITY MUSEUM
Unity College
HC 78 Box 1
Quaker Hill Rd.
Unity, ME 04988
(207) 948–3131

PENOBSCOT NATION MUSEUM
5 Down Street
Indian Island, ME 04468
(207) 827–4153

◆ MICHIGAN

MUSEUM OF OJBIWA CULTURE
500 N. State St.
St. Ignaces, MI 49781
(906) 643–9161
www.stignace.com

◆ MINNESOTA

MILLE LACS INDIAN MUSEUM
43408 Oodena Dr.
Onamia, MN 56359
(320) 532–4181

◆ MISSISSIPPI

THE CHOCTAW MUSEUM OF THE SOUTHERN INDIAN
Mississippi Band of Choctaw Indians
P.O. Box 6010
Philadelphia, MS 39350
(601) 656–5251

◆ MONTANA

CHEYENNE INDIAN MUSEUM
Ashland, MT
(406) 784–2744

FLATHEAD INDIAN MUSEUM
Flathead Indian Reservation
P.O. Box 460 I
1 Museum Ln.
St. Ignatius, MT 59865
(406) 745–2951

FORT PECK TRIBAL MUSEUM
Assiniboine Sioux Tribes
Fort Peck Indian Reservation
P.O. Box 1027
Poplar, MT 59255
(406) 768–5155 ext. 328

◆ NEW MEXICO

PICURIS PUEBLO MUSEUM
P.O. Box 127
Penasco, NM 87553
(505) 587–2957

SAN ILDEFONSO PUEBLO MUSEUM
Rte. 5, Box 315-A
Santa Fe, NM 87501
(505) 455–2424

◆ NEW YORK

AKWESASNE MUSEUM
Rte. 37
Hogansburg, NY 13655
(518) 358–2461

IROQUOIS INDIAN MUSEUM
P.O. Box 7 Cavers Rd
Howes Cave, NY 12092
(518) 296–8949
www.iroquoismuseum.org

SENECA-IROQUOIS NATIONAL MUSEUM
Allegany Indian Reservation
794814 Broad St.
Salamanca, NY 14779
(716) 945–1738

◆ NORTH CAROLINA

MUSEUM OF THE CHEROKEE INDIAN
P.O. Box 1599
Drama Rd. Hwy. 44
Cherokee, NC 28719
(828) 497–3481
www.cherokeemuseum.org

◆ NORTH DAKOTA

THREE AFFILIATED TRIBES MUSEUM
P.O. Box 147
New Town, ND 58763
(701) 627–4477

◆ OKLAHOMA

CHEROKEE NATIONAL MUSEUM (TSALAGI)
Cherokee Heritage Center
P.O. Box 515
Tahlequah, OK 74465
(918) 456–6007

CHICKASAW COUNCIL HOUSE MUSEUM
200 N. Fisher P.O. Box 717
Tishomingo, OK 73460
(580) 371–3351

CHOCTAW NATION MUSEUM
Hc 64 Box 3270
Tuskahoma, OK 74574–9758
(918) 569–4465

CREEK COUNCIL HOUSE MUSEUM
Town Square
Okmulgee, OK 74447
(918) 756–2324

DELAWARE TRIBAL MUSEUM
c/o Delaware Executive Board
P.O. Box 825
Anadarko, OK 73005
(405) 247–2448

OSAGE TRIBAL MUSEUM
Osage Agency Reserve
P.O. Box 779
819 Grand View Ave.
Pawhuska, OK 74056
(918) 287–4622

POTAWATOMI INDIAN NATION ARCHIVES
AND MUSEUM
1901 South Gordon Cooper Dr.
Shawnee, OK 74801
(405) 275–3121

SEMINOLE NATION MUSEUM
524 South Wewoka, Box 1532
Wewoka, OK 74884
(405) 257–5580

TONKAWA TRIBAL MUSEUM
P.O. Box 70
Tonkawa, OK 74653
(580) 628–2561

♦ OREGON

MUSEUM AT WARM SPRINGS
P.O. Box 753
Warm Springs, OR 97761–0753
(541) 553–3331

♦ RHODE ISLAND

TOMAQUAG INDIAN MEMORIAL MUSEUM
Box 386 Summit Rd.
Exeter, RI 02822
(401) 539–7213

♦ SOUTH DAKOTA

BUECHEL MEMORIAL LAKOTA MUSEUM
350 S. Oak St.
P.O. Box 499
St. Francis, SD 575572
(605) 747–5509

♦ TENNESSEE

SEQUOYAH BIRTHPLACE MUSEUM
576 Hwy 360 P.O. Box 69
Vonore, TN 37885
(423) 884–6246
www.sequoyahmuseum.org

♦ TEXAS

ALABAMA-COUSHATTA INDIAN MUSEUM
Rte. 3, Box 640, Hwy. 190
Livingston, TX 77351
(409) 563–4391

♦ UTAH

UTE TRIBAL MUSEUM
P.O. Box 190, Hwy. 40
Fort Duchesne, UT 84026
(801) 722–4992

♦ VIRGINIA

MATTAPONI INDIAN MUSEUM AND
TRADING POST
Mattaponi Indian Reservation
Rte. 2, Box 255
West Point, VA 23181
(804) 769–2194

MONACAN INDIAN ANCESTRAL MUSEUM
2009 Kenmore Rd.
Amherst, VA 24521
(804) 946–5391

♦ WASHINGTON

COLVILLE CONFEDERATED TRIBES
MUSEUM
P.O. Box 233
Coulee Dam, WA 99116
(509) 634–4711

PUYALLUP TRIBE MUSEUM
2215 East 22nd St.
Tacoma, WA 98404
(206) 597–6200

SUQUAMISH MUSEUM
15838 Sandy Hook N.E.
P.O. Box 498
Suquamish, WA 98392
(206) 598–3311

♦ WISCONSIN

ONEIDA NATION MUSEUM
Oneida Nation Cultural Center
P.O. Box 365
Oneida, WI 54155
(414) 869–2768

STOCKBRIDGE-MUNSEE HISTORICAL
LIBRARY AND MUSEUM
Rte. 1, Box 300
Bowler, WI 54416
(715) 793–4270

WINNEBAGO INDIAN MUSEUM
3889 North River Rd.
P.O. Box 441
Wisconsin Dells, WI 53965
(608) 254–2268

♦ WYOMING

ARAPAHO CULTURAL MUSEUM
P.O. Box 8066
Ethete, WY 82520
(307) 332–2660

CANADA

♦ ALBERTA

TSUT'INA K'OSA (SARCEE)
3700 Anderson Rd. S.W.
Box 67
Calgary, AB T2W 3T0
(403) 238–2677

♦ ONTARIO

CHIEFSWOOD MUSEUM
Hwy 54 Chiefswood Rd.
P.O. Box 640
Ohsweken, ON N0A 1M0
(519) 752–5005

NORTH AMERICAN TRAVELING
COLLEGE MUSEUM
Rt 3
Cornwall Island, ON K6H 5R7
(613) 932–9452

WOODLANDS MUSEUM
184 Mowhawk St.
Brantford,ON N3S 2X2
(519) 759–2650

♦ BRITISH COLUMBIA

KSAN HISTORICAL VILLAGE AND MUSEUM
P.O. Box 326
Hazelton, BC V0J 1Y0
(250) 842–5544

SECWEPEMC MUSEUM AND NATIVE
HERITAGE PARK
Kamloops Indian Reserve
345 Yellowhead Hwy.
Kamloops, BC V6H 1H1
(250) 828–9801
www.ohwy.com/bc/s/secwepem.htm

♦ QUEBEC

MUSEE DE ABENAKIS
108 Waban-Aki
Odanak, QB J0G 1H0
(450) 568–2600

MUSEE AMERINDIAN DE MASHTEWIATSH
1787 Amishk St
Mashteuiatsch, QB G0W 2H0
(418) 275–4842

Major Museums

United States

◆ ALABAMA

BIRMINGHAM MUSEUM OF ART
2000 Eighth Ave. N.
Birmingham, AL 35203–2278
(205) 254–2566
www.artsBMA.org
North, Central, and South American Indian art.

◆ ALASKA

ALASKA STATE MUSEUM
395 Whittier St.
Juneau, AK 99801–1718
(907) 465–2901
www.museums.state.ak.us/asmhome.html
Alaskan Native Gallery (companion museum to
Sheldon Jackson Museum).

ANCHORAGE MUSEUM OF HISTORY
AND ART
121 West Seventh Ave.
Anchorage, AK 99501
(907) 343–4326
www.ci.anchorage.ak.us/Services/Departments/
Culture/Museum/index.html
Alaskan tribes, Plains; Cook Inlet Region, Inc.,
Community Collection (CIRI).

SHELDON JACKSON MUSEUM
104 College Dr.
Sitka, AK 99835–7657
(907) 747–8981
www.museums.state.ak.us/sjhome.html
Alaskan Native Gallery (companion museum to
Alaska State Museum).

◆ ARIZONA

THE AMERIND FOUNDATION MUSEUM
2100 N. Amerind Road
P.O. Box 400
Dragoon, AZ 85609
(520) 586–3666
www.amerind.org
North America; emphasis on regional prehistoric.

THE HEARD MUSEUM
22 East Monte Vista Rd.
Phoenix, AZ 85004
(602) 252–8840
www.heard.org
Southwestern Native American Artists Resource
Collection contains documentation of individual
artists' achievements.

◆ ARKANSAS

ARKANSAS STATE UNIVERSITY MUSEUM
P.O. Box 490
State University, AR 72467
(870) 972–2074
www.astate.edu/docs/admin/museum/index.html
Northeast Arkansas regional emphasis.

◆ CALIFORNIA

PHOEBE A. HEARST MUSEUM OF
ANTHROPOLOGY
103 Kroeber Hall
University of California
Berkeley, CA 94720–3712
(510) 642–3682
www.qal.berkeley.edu/~hearst/
North America, especially California.

SAN DIEGO MUSEUM OF MAN
1350 El Prado
San Diego, CA 92101
(619) 239–2001
www.museumofman.org
Native cultures of the western Americas, especially
    California and the Southwest.

SOUTHWEST MUSEUM
234 Museum Dr.
Los Angeles, CA 90065
(323) 221–2164
www.southwestmuseum.org
Native people of the Americas, especially California
    and Southwest.

◆ COLORADO

DENVER MUSEUM OF NATURE AND
    SCIENCE
2001 Colorado Blvd.
Denver, CO 80205
(303) 322–7009 (800) 925–2250
www.dmnh.org
Emphasis on regional, including the original Folsom
    point (found at Folsom site, New Mexico,
    between the ribs of an extinct buffalo).

UNIVERSITY OF COLORADO MUSEUM
Henderson Bldg., Campus Box 218
Boulder, CO 80309–0218
(303) 492–6892
www.Colorado.EDU/CUMUSEUM/index.html
North American prehistory, especially the Plains and
    Southwest.

◆ CONNECTICUT

THE INSTITUTE FOR AMERICAN INDIAN
    STUDIES
P.O. Box 1260
Off Route 199, 38 Curtis Rd.
Washington, CT 06793–0260
(860) 868–0518
Primarily Northeast Woodlands, including Indian
    Village.

PEABODY MUSEUM OF NATURAL HISTORY
Yale University
170 Whitney Ave.
New Haven, CT 06511–8902
(203) 432–5050
www.peabody.yale.edu
Extensive archaeological collection, especially
    regional.

◆ DELAWARE

DELAWARE STATE MUSEUMS
102 S. State Street
Dover, DE 19901
(302) 739–5316
www.destatemuseums.org
Regional emphasis.

◆ DISTRICT OF COLUMBIA

NATIONAL MUSEUM OF THE
    AMERICAN INDIAN
National Mall
Washington, D.C.
Executive Offices:
470 L'Enfant Plaza S.W.
Suite 7103
Washington, D.C. 20560–0934
(202) 357–3164
www.si.edu/nmai
Currently under construction with completion
    scheduled for 2002.

NATIONAL MUSEUM OF NATURAL HISTORY
Department of Anthropology
10th Street and Constitution Avenue N. W.
NHB 112, Smithsonian Institution
Washington, D.C. 20560–0112
(202) 357–2363
www.nmnh.si.edu/departments/anthro.html/
Indians of the Americas (over two million objects);
    Human Studies Film Archives; American Indian
    Program internships and fellowships; National
    Anthropological Archives; Arctic Studies Center;
    Handbook of North American Indians.

◆ FLORIDA

LOWE ART MUSEUM
University of Miami
1301 Stanford Dr.
Coral Gables, FL 33124–6310
(305) 284–3535
www.lowemuseum.org

The Americas, especially the Alfred I. Barton
Collection of Southwest Indian art.

◆ GEORGIA

COLUMBUS MUSEUM
1251 Wynnton Rd.
Columbus, GA 31906
(706) 649–0713
www.columbusmuseum.com
Artifacts from Paleo through Mississippian cultures,
especially Yuchi.

◆ IDAHO

IDAHO STATE HISTORICAL MUSEUM
610 North Julia Davis Dr.
Boise, ID 83702
(208) 334–2120
www.state.id.us/ishs/index.htm
Northwest Coast, Alaskan, and Plains, especially
Upper Great Basin.

◆ ILLINOIS

FIELD MUSEUM OF NATURAL HISTORY
1400 S. Lake Shore Dr.
Chicago, IL 60605–2496
(312) 922–9410
www.fmnh.org
North and South America, diverse and extensive;
Pawnee earth lodge.

ILLINOIS STATE MUSEUM
Corner of Spring and Edwards Streets
Springfield, IL 62706–5000
(217) 782–7387
www.museum.state.il.us
Paleo into historic. Archaeological site branch:
Dickson Mounds Museum, Lewistown, IL 61542;
phone: (309)547–3721.

◆ INDIANA

EITELJORG MUSEUM OF AMERICAN INDIAN
AND WESTERN ART
500 West Washington St.
Indianapolis, IN 46204
(317) 636–9378
www.eiteljorg.org
Primarily North American, especially Northeast
Woodlands, Great Plains, Southwest.

WILLIAM HAMMOND MATHERS MUSEUM
Indiana University
601 East Eighth St.
Bloomington, IN 47408
(812) 855–6873
www.indiana.edu/~mathers
North America, especially Plains and Alaskan
Eskimo; Wanamaker Collection of American
Indian Photographs.

◆ IOWA

STATE HISTORICAL SOCIETY OF IOWA
State of Iowa Historical Building
600 East Locust St.
Des Moines, IA 50319
(515) 281–5111
www.iowahistory.org/museum/index.html
Emphasis on Western Great Lakes and Plains.

◆ KANSAS

MUSEUM OF ANTHROPOLOGY
Spooner Hall
University of Kansas
Lawrence, KS 66045
(785) 864–4245
www.ukans.edu/~kuma/
North America, especially regional, Southwest, and
Northwest Coast.

◆ KENTUCKY

THE SPEED ART MUSEUM
2035 South Third St.
Louisville, KY 40208
(502) 634–2700
www.speedmuseum.org
Primarily Plains.

WILLIAM S. WEBB MUSEUM OF
ANTHROPOLOGY
Department of Anthropology
211 Lafferty Hall
University of Kentucky
Lexington, KY 40506–0024
(859) 257–8208
www.uky.edu/AS/Anthropology/Museum/
museum.htm

◆ LOUISIANA

MUSEUM OF NATURAL SCIENCE
119 Foster Hall
Louisiana State University
Baton Rouge, LA 70803
(225) 388–2855
www.museum.lsu.edu
North America; regional emphasis.

◆ MAINE

THE ABBE MUSEUM
Sieur de Monts Spring in Acadia National Park
P.O. Box 286
Bar Harbor, ME 04609
(207) 288–3519
www.acadia.net/abbemuseum
Primarily Maine and Maritime Provinces (Canada),
    prehistoric and historic.

THE PEARY-MACMILLAN ARCTIC MUSEUM
    AND ARCTIC STUDIES CENTER
Hubbard Hall
Bowdoin College
Brunswick, ME 04011
(207) 725–3416
www.bowdoin.edu/dept/arctic/
Labrador, Baffin, and Greenland Inuit and Indian.

◆ MARYLAND

NATIONAL MUSEUM OF THE AMERICAN
    INDIAN CULTURAL RESOURCES CENTER
4220 Silver Hill Road
Suitland, MD 20746
301–238-6624
Curatorial offices, conservation facilities and
    repository for the NMAI collections.

◆ MASSACHUSETTS

PEABODY MUSEUM OF ARCHAEOLOGY AND
    ETHNOLOGY
Harvard University
11 Divinity Ave.
Cambridge, MA 02138
(617) 496–1027
www.peabody.harvard.edu
North America, especially dynamics of interactions
    between Indians and whites over past 500 years.

◆ MICHIGAN

CRANBROOK INSTITUTE OF SCIENCE
39221 Woodward
Bloomfield Hills, MI 48303–0801
(877) 462–7262
www.cranbrook.edu/institute
North America, especially Woodlands and Plains.

UNIVERSITY OF MICHIGAN MUSEUM OF
    ANTHROPOLOGY
Natural Science Museum Building
1109 Geddes Ave.
Ann Arbor, MI 48109–1079
(734) 764–0485
www.umma.lsa.umich.edu/museum.html
North America.

◆ MINNESOTA

MINNESOTA HISTORICAL SOCIETY MUSEUM
345 Kellogg Blvd. West
St. Paul, MN 55102–1906
(651) 296–6126
www.mnhs.org/places/historycenter/index.html
Minnesota emphasis, especially Dakota (Sioux) and
    Ojibwa (Chippewa).

◆ MISSOURI

KANSAS CITY MUSEUM
3218 Gladstone Blvd.
Kansas City, MO 64123–1199
(816) 483–8300
www.kcmuseum.com
Southern and Central Plains, Eastern Woodlands,
    Southwest, Northwest Coast; extensive.

MUSEUM OF ANTHROPOLOGY
University of Missouri
104 Swallow Hall
University of Missouri
Columbia, MO
(573) 882–3573
www.missouri.edu/~anthmjo/
Missouri and regional emphasis.

ST. LOUIS SCIENCE CENTER
5050 Oakland Ave.
St. Louis, MO 63110
(314) 289–4400
www.slsc.org
Emphasis on midwestern cultures, especially
    Mississippian.

◆ MONTANA

MUSEUM OF THE PLAINS INDIAN
Junction of U. S. Highways 2 and 89 West
Box 410
Browning, MT 59417
(406) 338–2230
www.doi.gov/iacb/museum/museum_plains.html
Northern Plains. Administered by the Indian Arts
and Crafts Board.

◆ NEBRASKA

MUSEUM OF THE FUR TRADE
6321 Highway 20
Chadron, NE 69337
(308) 432–3843
www.furtrade.org
North American Indian cultures; influence of fur
trade on cultures.

MUSEUM OF NEBRASKA HISTORY
131 Centennial Mall North
Lincoln, NE 68501–2554
P.O. Box 82554
(402) 471–4754
www.nebraskahistory.org/sites/mnh/index.htm
Emphasis on Nebraska and Central Plains.

◆ NEVADA

NEVADA HISTORICAL SOCIETY MUSEUM
1650 North Virginia St.
Reno, NV 89503
(775) 688–1190
lahontan.clan.lib.nv.us/polpac/html_client/default.asp
(via State Library, Division of Museums and
History)
Emphasis on Washo, Northern Paiute, Southern
Paiute, Western Shoshone.

NEVADA STATE MUSEUM
600 N. Carson Street
Carson City, NV 89701
(775) 687–4811
lahontan.clan.lib.nv.us/polpac/html_client/default.asp
(via State Library, Division of Museums and
History web site).
Emphasis on Nevada.

◆ NEW HAMPSHIRE

HOOD MUSEUM OF ART
Dartmouth College
Wheelock Street
Hanover, NH 03755
(603) 646–2808
www.dartmouth.edu/acad-support/hood/Menu.html
North, Central, and South America, especially
Southwestern and New England.

◆ NEW JERSEY

MORRIS MUSEUM OF ARTS AND SCIENCES
6 Normandy Heights Rd.
Morristown, NJ 07961
(973) 538–0454
www.morrismuseum.org
Woodlands, Northwest Coast, Southwest, Plains.

NEW JERSEY STATE MUSEUM
205 West State St.
P.O. Box 530
Trenton, NJ 08625–0530
(609) 292–6464
www.state.nj.us/state/museum/musidx.html
Emphasis on New Jersey and the surrounding
region.

◆ NEW MEXICO

INSTITUTE OF AMERICAN INDIAN ARTS MUSEUM
108 Cathedral Place
Santa Fe, NM 87501
(505) 983–1777
www.iaiancad.org/museum/
Paintings, graphics, sculpture, ceramics, textiles,
costumes, jewelry, and ethnographic material,
primarily by Native American students.

MAXWELL MUSEUM OF ANTHROPOLOGY
University of New Mexico
Albuquerque, NM 87131–1201
(505) 277–4404
www.unm.edu/~maxwell/
Archaeology and ethnography, especially Southwest.

MUSEUM OF INDIAN ARTS AND CULTURE
Laboratory of Anthropology
Museum Plaza, Camino Lejo
P.O. Box 2087
Santa Fe, NM 87504–2087
(505) 476–1250
www.miaclab.org/
Primarily Southwest; emphasis on Pueblo,
    Navajo, Apache.

WHEELWRIGHT MUSEUM OF THE
    AMERICAN INDIAN
704 Camino Lejo
P.O. Box 5153
Santa Fe, NM 87502
(505) 982–4636
www.wheelwright.org/
North America, especially Southwest; emphasis
    on Navajo.

♦ **NEW YORK**

AMERICAN MUSEUM OF NATURAL HISTORY
79th St. and Central Park West
New York, NY 10024–5192
(212) 769–5100
www.amnh.org
Extensive and diverse.

GEORGE GUSTAV HEYE CENTER
National Museum of the American Indian
Alexander Hamilton U.S. Custom House
One Bowling Green
New York, N.Y. 10004
(212) 514–3700
www.si.edu/nmai/abmus/index.htm
Public exhibition spaces, photography collection,
    film and video center, and resource center.

♦ **NORTH CAROLINA**

INDIAN MUSEUM OF THE CAROLINAS
607 Turnpike Rd.
Laurinburg, NC 28352
(910) 276–5880
Southeast, primarily North and South Carolina.

MUSEUM OF THE NATIVE AMERICAN
    RESOURCE CENTER
University of North Carolina, Pembroke
Old Main Bldg.
Pembroke, NC 28372
(910) 521–6282
www.uncp.edu/nativemuseum/
North and South America, especially Eastern
    Woodlands.

SCHIELE MUSEUM OF NATURAL HISTORY
    AND PLANETARIUM
1500 East Garrison Blvd.
Gastonia, NC 28056
(704) 866–6908
www.schielemuseum.org
Extensive collection from twelve cultural areas,
    especially Southeast and North Carolina.

♦ **NORTH DAKOTA**

BUFFALO TRAILS MUSEUM
Main Street
P.O. Box 22
Epping, ND 58843
(701) 859–4361
Upper Missouri area.

STATE HISTORICAL SOCIETY OF
    NORTH DAKOTA
North Dakota Heritage Center
612 East Boulevard Ave.
Bismarck, ND 58505
(701) 328–2666
www.state.nd.us/hist
Primarily northern Great Plains.

♦ **OHIO**

CLEVELAND MUSEUM OF NATURAL
    HISTORY
1 Wade Oval Dr., University Circle
Cleveland, OH 44106–1767
(216) 231–4600
www.cmnh.org
North America, especially Ohio.

OHIO HISTORICAL CENTER
1982 Velma Ave.
Columbus, OH 43211
(614) 297–2300
www.ohiohistory.org
Emphasis on regional prehistory.

◆ OKLAHOMA

GILCREASE MUSEUM

1400 Gilcrease Museum Rd.
Tulsa, OK 74127–2100
(918) 596–2700
www.gilcrease.org/
North America, prehistory to present; extensive.
    World's largest collection of art of
    American West.

PHILBROOK MUSEUM OF ART

2727 South Rockford Road
Tulsa, OK 74114
(918) 749–7941
www.philbrook.org
North America, notable basketry and pottery
    collections.

SAM NOBLE OKLAHOMA MUSEUM OF NATURAL HISTORY

University of Oklahoma
2401 Chatauqua
Norman, OK 73072
(405) 325–4712
www.snomnh.ou.edu/
North America, especially Southern Plains,
    Southwest, Northwest Coast, Spiro Mounds.

SOUTHERN PLAINS INDIAN MUSEUM

715 East Central Boulevard
Anadarko, OK 73005
(405) 247–6221
www.doi.gov/iacb/museum/museum_s_plains.html
Tribes of western Oklahoma: Kiowa, Comanche,
    Kiowa–Apache, Southern Cheyenne, Southern
    Arapaho, Wichita, Caddo, Delaware, Fort Sill
    Apache. Administered by the Indian Arts and
    Crafts Board.

◆ OREGON

MUSEUM OF NATURAL HISTORY

University of Oregon
1680 East 15th Ave.
Eugene, OR 97403–1224
(541) 346–3024
natural-history.uoregon.edu/
North America, especially Northwest Coast and
    Pacific Rim.

PORTLAND ART MUSEUM

1219 SW Park Ave.
Portland, OR 97205
(503) 226–2811
www.pam.org
North and Middle America, especially
    Northwest Coast.

◆ PENNSYLVANIA

THE CARNEGIE MUSEUM OF NATURAL HISTORY

4400 Forbes Ave.
Pittsburgh, PA 15213–4080
(412) 622–3131
www.clpgh.org/cmnh/
North and South America, especially Upper Ohio
    Valley.

◆ RHODE ISLAND

THE HAFFENREFFER MUSEUM OF ANTHROPOLOGY

Brown University
300 Tower Street
Bristol, RI 02809
(401) 253–8388
www.brown.edu/Facilities/Haffenreffer/
The Americas, especially Arctic and Red Paint
    (Maine).

◆ SOUTH CAROLINA

CHESTER COUNTY HISTORICAL SOCIETY MUSEUM

107 McAiley Street
P.O. Box 811
Chester, SC 29706
(803) 385–2330
Regional; over 30,000 Catawba Indian artifacts.

◆ SOUTH DAKOTA

SIOUX INDIAN MUSEUM

222 New York Street
P.O. Box 1504
Rapid City, SD 57709
(605) 394–2381
www.doi.gov/iacb/museum/museum_sioux.html
North America, especially Sioux. Administered by
    the Indian Arts and Crafts Board.

THE W. H. OVER STATE MUSEUM
1110 Ratingen Street
Vermillion, SD 57069
(605) 677–5228
www.usd.edu/whover
Emphasis on South Dakota Sioux.

◆ TENNESSEE

FRANK H. MCCLUNG MUSEUM
University of Tennessee, Knoxville
1327 Circle Park Dr.
Knoxville, TN 37996–3200
(865) 974–2144
mcclungmuseum.utk.edu
Regional emphasis.

THE TENNESSEE STATE MUSEUM
505 Deaderick St.
Nashville, TN 37243–1120
(615) 741–2692
Regional emphasis; prehistoric Mississippian.

◆ TEXAS

PANHANDLE-PLAINS HISTORICAL MUSEUM
2401 Fourth Ave.
WTAMU Box 60967
Canyon, TX 79016
(806) 656–2244
www.wtamu.edu/museum/
Emphasis on Comanche, Kiowa.

TEXAS MEMORIAL MUSEUM
University of Texas, Austin
2400 Trinity
Austin,, TX 78705
(512) 471–1604
www.utexas.edu/depts/tmm
Emphasis on Texas, Southwest, Latin America.

WITTE MUSEUM
3801 Broadway
San Antonio, TX 78209
(210) 357–1900
www.wittemuseum.org
North America, emphasis on Texas and Southwest.

◆ UTAH

MUSEUM OF PEOPLES AND CULTURES
Brigham Young University, Allen Hall
700 North 100 East
Provo, UT 84602
(801) 378–6112
fhss.byu.edu/mpc/
North America, emphasis on Maya, Anasazi,
    Fremont, Mogollon, Casas Grandes.

UTAH MUSEUM OF NATURAL HISTORY
University of Utah
1309 E. President's Circle
Salt Lake City, UT 84112–0050
(801) 581–6927
www.umnh.utah.edu/
Regional, Great Basin, Southwest.

◆ VERMONT

ROBERT HULL FLEMING MUSEUM
University of Vermont
61 Colchester Ave.
Burlington, VT 05405
(802) 656–2090
www.uvm.edu/~fleming/
North America.

◆ VIRGINIA

JAMESTOWN SETTLEMENT
P.O. Box 1607
Williamsburg, VA 23187
(888) 593–4682
www.historyisfun.org
Virginia Indian artifacts; reconstruction of
    Powhatan's lodge.

◆ WASHINGTON

BURKE MUSEUM OF NATURAL HISTORY
    AND CULTURE
Box 353010
University of Washington
Seattle, WA 98195–3010
(206) 543–7907
www.washington.edu/burkemuseum/
Emphasis on Northwest Coast.

CHENEY COWLES MUSEUM
Eastern Washington State Historical Society
2316 West First Ave.
Spokane, WA 99204
(509) 456–3931
www.cheneycowles.org
Americas; emphasis on Plateau tribes.

◆ WISCONSIN

LOGAN MUSEUM OF ANTHROPOLOGY
Beloit College
700 College St.
Beloit, WI 53511
(608) 363–2677
www.beloit.edu/~museum/logan/index.html
Regional emphasis; North and South America.

MILWAUKEE PUBLIC MUSEUM
800 West Wells St.
Milwaukee, WI 53233
(414) 278–2700
www.mpm.edu/
North America, especially Midwest archaeology.

◆ WYOMING

PLAINS INDIAN MUSEUM
Buffalo Bill Historical Center
720 Sheridan Ave.
Cody, WY 82414
(307) 587–4771
www.bbhc.org
Primarily Northern Plains; recreation of 1890
　Sioux camp.

WYOMING STATE MUSEUM
Barrett Bldg.
2301 Central
Cheyenne, WY 82002
(307) 777–7022
spacr.state.wy.us/cr/wsm/index.htm
Primarily Northern Plains.

CANADA

◆ ALBERTA

GLENBOW MUSEUM
130 9th Ave. S.E.
Calgary, AB T2G 0P3
(403) 268–4100
www.glenbow.org/museum.htm

Primary focus Northern Plains; also Northwest
　Coast, Arctic and Subarctic.

PROVINCIAL MUSEUM OF ALBERTA
12845 102nd Ave.
Edmonton, AB T5N OM6
(780) 453–9100
www.pma.edmonton.ab.ca/
Emphasis on Alberta, Northern Plains, Inuit.

◆ BRITISH COLUMBIA

MUSEUM OF ANTHROPOLOGY
University of British Columbia
6393 N.W. Marine Drive
Vancouver, BC V6T 1Z2
(604) 822–3825
www.moa.ubc.ca/menu.html

MUSEUM OF NORTHERN BRITISH COLUMBIA
P.O. Box 669
Prince Rupert, BC V8J 3S1
(250) 624–3207
Northwest Coast, especially Tsimshian, Haida,
　Tlingit.

ROYAL BRITISH COLUMBIA MUSEUM
P.O. Box 9815 Stn. Prov. Govt.
675 Belleville St.
Victoria, BC V8W 9W2
(250) 387–3701
rbcm1.rbcm.gov.bc.ca/
Regional archaeology; totem pole exhibit in
　Thunderbird Park.

◆ MANITOBA

MANITOBA MUSEUM OF MAN AND NATURE
190 Rupert Ave.
Winnipeg, MB R3B ON2
(204) 956–2830
www.manitobamuseum.mb.ca
Regional; relationship between humans and
　environment.

◆ NEWFOUNDLAND

NEWFOUNDLAND MUSEUM
285 Duckworth St.
St. Johns, NF A1C 1G9
(709) 729–2329
www.nfmuseum.com/
Regional, especially Beothuk and Naskapi.

◆ NORTHWEST TERRITORIES

DENE CULTURAL INSTITUTE
P.O. Box 207
Yellowknife, NT X1A 2N2
(403) 873–6617

NORTHERN LIFE MUSEUM AND NATIONAL
    EXHIBITION CENTRE
110 King Street
P.O. Box 420
Fort Smith, NT X0E 0P0
(867) 872–2859
Regional, especially Athapascan and Inuit.

◆ NOVA SCOTIA

MUSEUM OF NATURAL HISTORY
Nova Scotia Museum
1747 Summer St.
Halifax, NS B3H 3A6
(902) 424–7353
museum.gov.ns.ca/
Regional Paleo-Indian through Woodland cultures,
    especially Micmac.

◆ ONTARIO

THE NORTH AMERICAN INDIAN TRAVELING
    COLLEGE
THE LIVING MUSEUM AND WOODLANDS INDIAN
    VILLAGE
R.R. 3, Cornwall Island
Cornwall, ON K6H 5R7
(613) 932–9452
Eastern Woodlands cultural and educational center;
    traditional structures, and crafts.

ROYAL ONTARIO MUSEUM
100 Queen's Park
Toronto, ON M5S 2C6
(416) 586–5549
www.rom.on.ca/
North America, especially Canada, Arctic, regional.

◆ PRINCE EDWARD ISLAND

PRINCE EDWARD ISLAND MUSEUM AND
    HERITAGE FOUNDATION
2 Kent St.
Charlottetown, PEI C1A 1M6
(902) 368–6600

◆ QUEBEC

CANADIAN MUSEUM OF CIVILIZATION
100 Laurier St.
Box 3100, Station B
Hull, PQ J8X 4H2
(819) 776–7000
www.civilization.ca/
Extensive First Nations' collections.

◆ SASKATCHEWAN

ROYAL SASKATCHEWAN MUSEUM
2445 Albert Street
Wascana Park
Regina, SK S4P 3V7
(306) 787–2810
www.gov.sk.ca/rsm/
Regional, especially Cree, Assiniboine, Saulteaux,
    Dakota, Dene.

◆ YUKON TERRITORY

MACBRIDE MUSEUM
1st Avenue and Wood Street
P.O. Box 4037
Whitehorse, YT Y1A 3S9
(867) 667–2709
Regional, especially Athapascan, Tlingit, Inuvialuit.

Archives and Special Collections

United States

◆ ALABAMA

ALABAMA DEPARTMENT OF ARCHIVES AND
  HISTORY
624 Washington Ave.
Montgomery, AL 36130–0100
(334) 242–4363
www.archives.state.al.usa

◆ ARIZONA

ARIZONA HISTORICAL SOCIETY
  RESEARCH LIBRARY
949 East Second St.
Tucson, AZ 85719
(520) 628–5774
Maps of Indian reservations; manuscripts of
  teachers, doctors, and agents on their
  observations of various reservations.

CAPITOL MUSEUM
1700 West Washington St.
Phoenix, AZ 85007–2896
(602) 542–4675
www.lib.az.us/museum/index.html

HEARD MUSEUM LIBRARY AND MUSEUM
NATIVE AMERICAN ARCHIVES
2301 N. Central Ave.
Phoenix, Az 85004–1323
(602) 251–0267
www.heard.org

MUSEUM OF NORTHERN ARIZONA
301 N. Fort Valley Rd.
Flagstaff, AZ 86001
(520) 774–5211
www.musnaz.org
Natural history and Native American museum;
  one of the largest collections in the country,

containing more than two million Native
American artifacts.

PUEBLO GRANDE MUSEUM AND
  ARCHEOLOGICAL PARK
4619 East Washington St.
Phoenix, AZ 85034
(602) 495–0901
www.pueblogrande.com

◆ ARKANSAS

ARKANSAS STATE UNIVERSITY MUSEUM
Arkansas State University
P.O. Box 490
State University, AR 72467
Quapaw, Osage, and Cherokee mound builders.

◆ CALIFORNIA

AMERICAN INDIAN RESOURCE CENTER
Los Angeles Public Library
6518 Miles Ave.
Huntington Park, CA 90255
(323) 583–1461

AMERICAN INDIAN STUDIES CENTER
  LIBRARY
University of California
3220 Campbell Hall
Los Angeles, CA 90024–1548
(310) 206–7510
www.sscnetucla.edu/indian/

BANCROFT LIBRARY AND THE HEARST
  MUSEUM OF ANTHROPLOGY LIBRARY
University of California
103 Kroeber Hall
Berkeley, CA 94720
(510) 642–3781
www.library.berkly.edu
California Indians.

HUNTINGTON LIBRARY
1151 Oxford Rd.
San Marino, CA 91108
(626) 405–2141

RANCHO LOS CERRITOS HISTORIC SITE
4600 Virginia Rd.
Long Beach, CA 90807
(565) 570–1755
www.ci.long-beach.ca.us/parks/ranchlc.htm
California and Western history.

◆ COLORADO

CENTER FOR THE STUDY OF NATIVE
    LANGUAGES OF THE PLAINS AND
    SOUTHWEST
University of Colorado
Department of Linguistics CB 295
Boulder, CO 80309
(303) 492–2728

COLORADO HISTORICAL SOCIETY
Stephen H. Hart Library
1300 Broadway
Denver, CO 80203
(303) 866–2305

MUSEUM OF WESTERN STUDIES COLORADO
    ARCHIVES
248 S. 4th Street
Grand Junction, C0 81501
(303) 242–0971

NATIONAL INDIAN LAW LIBRARY
Native American Rights Fund
1522 Broadway
Boulder, CO 80302
(303) 447–8760
Collections exclusively on federal Indian law.

◆ CONNECTICUT

THE INSTITUTE FOR AMERICAN INDIAN
    STUDIES AND RESEARCH
38 Curtis Rd. Box 1260
Washington Green, CT 06793
(203) 868–0518

MASHANTUCKET PEQUOT RESEARCH
    LIBRARY
ARCHIVES AND SPECIAL COLLECTIONS
CHILDREN'S RESEARCH LIBRARY
110 Pequot Trail, P.O. Box 3180
Mashantucket, CT 06339
(800) 411–9671

◆ DISTRICT OF COLUMBIA

THE LIBRARY OF CONGRESS
101 Independence Ave. S. E.
Washington, DC 20540
(202) 707–5522
www.loc.gov
Records of tribal council minutes; manuscripts on
    the relations of tribes with the United States;
    prints and photographs.

NATIONAL ANTHROPOLOGICAL ARCHIVES
Natural History Museum
Smithsonian Institution
10 Street Constitution Ave.
Washington, DC 20560–0152
(202) 357–1976
www.nmhs.si.edu/naa

NATIONAL ARCHIVES AND RECORDS
    ADMINISTRATION
8th & Pennsylvania Ave. NW
Washington, DC 20408
(202) 501–5395
www.nara.gov

UNITED STATES DEPARTMENT OF THE
    INTERIOR LIBRARY
Mail Stop 1151
Washington, DC 20240
(202) 208–5815
library.doi.gov/ill.html
Manuscripts of treaties between the federal
    government and Indians; Indian Claims
    Commission annual reports.

◆ FLORIDA

BILLY OSCEOLA MEMORIAL LIBRARY
Route 6, Box 668
Okeeochoee, FL 34974
(941) 763–4236

HISTORIC MUSEUM OF SOUTHERN FLORIDA
101 W. Flagella St.
Miami, FL 33130
(305) 375–1492

JOHN C. PACE LIBRARY
Special Collection Division
University Of West Florida
11000 University Parkway
Pensacola, FL 32514
(850) 474–2758

WILLIE FRANK MEMORIAL LIBRARY
HC 61 Box 46 A
Clewiston, FL 33440
(941) 983–6724

◆ GEORGIA

HARGRETT RARE BOOKS AND
    MANUSCRIPT LIBRARY
University of Georgia
Athens, GA 30602
(706) 542–7123
www.libs.uga.edu/hargrett/speccoll.htlm
Rare manuscripts and photographs of the Cherokee
    and Creek; holdings of the Cherokee Phoenix
    (probably the first American Indian newspaper).

◆ ILLINOIS

MADISON COUNTY HISTORICAL MUSEUM
715 North Main St.
Edwardsville, IL 62025
(618) 656–7562
John R. Sutter Collection: regional and
    Southwest items.

◆ INDIANA

LILLY LIBRARY
Indiana University
Bloomington, IN 47405
(812) 855–2452
www.indiana.edu/~liblilly/text/lillyhome.html
Collection of folk tales of North American Western
    Indian groups; record of interviews of Indian
    survivors from Custer's Last Stand.

◆ MAINE

THE PEARY MACMILLAN ARCTIC MUSEUM
Bowdoin College
9500 College Station
Brunswick, ME 04011
(207) 725–3416
www.bowdoin.edu/dept./Arctic

ROBERT ABBE MUSEUM
P.O. Box 286
Bar Harbor, ME 04609
(207) 288–3519
www.abbemuseum.org

◆ MASSACHUSETTS

CHAPIN LIBRARY OF RARE BOOKS
Williams College
Williamston, MA 012267
(413) 597–2462
www.ohwy.com/ma/c/chaplirb.htm

FRUIT LANDS MUSEUM
102 Prospect Hill Rd.
Harvard, MA 01451
(978) 457–3924

TOSSER LIBRARY
Harvard University
21 Divinity Ave.
Cambridge, MA 02138
(617) 495–2248

◆ MICHIGAN

FORT ST. JOSEPH MUSEUM
508 East Main St.
Niles, MI 49120
(616) 683–4702
Plym/Quimby Collection of Sioux Indian artifacts,
    1881–83, including drawings by Sitting Bull and
    Rain-in-the-Face.

WILLIAM CLEMENTS LIBRARY
HATCHER GRADUATE LIBRARY
University of Michigan
Ann Arbor, MI
(313) 764–2347
www. clements.umich.edu/clempage.html

◆ MINNESOTA

MINNESOTA HISTORICAL SOCIETY LIBRARY
Research Center
345 Kellogg Blvd. W.
St. Paul, MN 55102–1906
(651) 296–2143
www.mnhs.org
Print, sound, and visual collections of Plains Indians,
especially the Ojibwa and Dakota.

◆ NEBRASKA

LIBRARY AND STATE ARCHIVES
Nebraska Historical Society
1500 R Street
Lincoln, NE 68501
(402) 471–3270
Central Plains Indians.

◆ NEW JERSEY

FIRESTONE LIBRARY
PRINCETON COLLECTIONS OF WESTERN
    AMERICANA
Princeton University
1 Washington
Princeton, NJ 08544
(609) 258–3222

◆ NEW MEXICO

INDIAN PUEBLO CULTURAL CENTER
2401 12th St. N.W.
Albuquerque, NM 87102
(505) 843–7270
Archival collection on the Southwest; owned and
    operated by nineteen pueblos of New Mexico.

LABORATORY OF ANTHROPOLOGY LIBRARY
Museum of Indian Arts & Culture
P.O. Box 2087
Santa Fe, NM 87504
(505) 476–1263
www.myaclab.org

SAN JUAN COUNTY ARCHAEOLOGICAL
    RESEARCH CENTER AND LIBRARY AT
    SALMON RUIN
P.O. Box 125
Broomfield, NM 87413
(505) 632–2013
Anasazi artifacts; oral history collection,
    especially Navajo.

SCHOOL OF AMERICAN RESEARCH
Indian Arts Research Center
P.O. Box 2188
Santa Fe, NM 87501
(505) 954–7204
www.sarweb.org
Southwestern American Indian art.

ZUNI CULTURAL RESOURCE ENTERPRISE
P.O. Box 1149
Zuni, NM 87327
(505) 782–4814
Archaeological site records, maps, air photos of Zuni
    Reservation; unpublished manuscripts on Zuni.

◆ NEW YORK

HUNTINGTON FREE LIBRARY
9 Westchester Sq.
Bronx, NY 10461
(718) 829–7770
Outstanding archival collections on American Indian
    languages and newspapers; field notes of
    prominent archaeologists.

NEW YORK PUBLIC LIBRARY
Humanities and Social Sciences Library
General Research Department
Fifth Ave. and 42nd St.
New York, NY 10018
(212) 930–0827

◆ NORTH CAROLINA

HUNTER LIBRARY
Special Collections Department
Western Carolina University
Cullowhee, NC 28723
(828) 227–7307
Collections on the Cherokee.

NORTH CAROLINA STATE ARCHIVES
Department of Cultural Research
109 East Jones St.
Raleigh, NC 27601–2807
(919) 733–3952
www.ah.dcr.state.nc.us
North Carolina Indian records.

◆ OHIO

THE HISTORY LIBRARY OF THE WESTERN
    RESERVE HISTORICAL SOCIETY
10825 East Blvd.
Cleveland, OH 44106
(216) 721–5722

OHIO HISTORICAL SOCIETY ARCHIVES AND
    LIBRARY DIVISION
1982 Velma Ave.
Columbus, OH 43211
(614) 297–2352
www.ohiohistory.org
Ohio Indians.

◆ OKLAHOMA

ARCHIVES AND MANUSCRIPTS DIVISION,
    OKLAHOMA HISTORICAL SOCIETY
2100 North Lincoln Blvd.
Oklahoma City, OK 73105
(405) 522–5209
www.ok-history.mus
Five Civilized Tribes in Oklahoma.

MUSEUM OF THE GREAT PLAINS
601 NW Farris Ave.
Lawton, OK 73502
(580) 581–3460
www.museumofthegreatplains.org
Photograph collections of the Great Plains.

WESTERN HISTORY COLLECTIONS
University of Oklahoma Libraries
630 Parrington Oval, Room 452
Norman, OK 73091
(405) 325–3641
One of the largest collections on North American
    Indians, especially on Southern Plains Indians.

◆ PENNSYLVANIA

AMERICAN PHILOSOPHICAL SOCIETY
    LIBRARY
105 South Fifth St.
Philadelphia, PA 19106–3386
(215) 440–3423
www.amphil/soc.org
Field notes of prominent anthropologists who
    worked closely with Indians.

READING PUBLIC MUSEUM AND ART
    GALLERY
500 Museum Rd.
Reading, PA 19611
(215) 371–5850
www.readingpublicmuseum.org
Special collection of southeastern Pennsylvania
    lithic objects; Speck Collection of Delaware
    material; mound pottery.

VAN PELT LIBRARY AND UNIVERSITY
    MUSEUM LIBRARY
University of Pennsylvania
3420 Walnut Street
Philadelphia, PA 19104
(215) 898–7091
www.library.upenn.edu

◆ RHODE ISLAND

JOHN CARTER BROWN LIBRARY
Brown University
P.O. Box 1894
Providence, RI 02912
(401) 863–2725
www.jcbl.org
Rare manuscripts; Americana collections from
    1492 to 1830.

◆ SOUTH DAKOTA

CENTER FOR WESTERN STUDIES
Augustana College
P.O. Box 727
Sioux Falls, SD 57197
(605) 336–4007
Native American Historical Research and
    Archival Agency.

I.D. WEEKS LIBRARY
University of South Dakota
414 East Clark St.
Vermillion, SD 57069
(605) 677–5371
www.usdedu/edulibrary/idweeks.htm
Upper Great Plains Sioux Indians.

MUSEUM OF SOUTH DAKOTA
Historical Society
900 Governors Dr.
Pierre, SD 57501
(605) 773–3458
www.state.sd.us/deca/
    culturalarchivesmanuscripts.collections
Special Plains Indian collection.

SIOUXLAND HERITAGE MUSEUM
200 West Sixth St.
Sioux Falls, SD 57102
(605) 367–4210
Pettigrew-Drady Indian Collection, primarily Dakota
    artifacts, 1870–1920; Photograph Collection,
    1870–1900.

◆ TEXAS

CROCKETT COUNTY MUSEUM
404 11th Street
Ozona, TX 76943
(915) 392–2837
Frank Mills Indian Collection.

SOUTHERN METHODIST UNIVERSITY
FIKES HALL OF SPECIAL COLLECTIONS
De Golyer Library
P.O. Box 750396, SMU Station
Dallas, TX 75275
(214) 692–2253
History and archaeology of the American West.

◆ UTAH

FAMILY HISTORY LIBRARY
35 North West Temple
Salt Lake City, UT 84150
(801) 240–4750
Genealogical information on American Indians.

◆ WASHINGTON

ALLEN LIBRARY
Manuscripts Special Collections and Archives
    Department
University of Washington
Box 352900
Seattle, WA 98195
(206) 543–1929
www.washington.edu/admin/ada/allenlib.htm
Pacific Northwest region.

◆ WEST VIRGINIA

WEST VIRGINIA STATE MUSEUM
Department of Culture and History
1900 Kanawha Blvd. E.
Charleston, WV 25305–0300
(304) 558–0220
Migration records of Indian groups.

◆ WISCONSIN

FAIRLAWN HISTORICAL MUSEUM
Harvard View Pkwy.
Superior, WI 54880
(715) 394–5712
David F. Barry Collection of Sioux Indian Portraits;
    Catlin Lithographs of Indians of the Plains.

THE RAHR PUBLIC MUSEUM
610 North Eighth St.
Manitowoc, WI 54220
(414) 683–4501
Manitowoc County Indian Artifacts Collection.

◆ WYOMING

AMERICAN HERITAGE CENTER
University of Wyoming
P.O. Box 3924
Laramie, WY 82071
(307) 766–4114
www.uwadmnweb.uwyo.edu/ahc/

CANADA

◆ ALBERTA

PROVINCIAL MUSEUM OF ALBERTA
Archeological & Ethnological Research Division
12845–102 Ave.
Edmonton AB T5N 0M6
(780) 453–9147
www.gov.ab.ca/mcd/mhs/pma/pma.htm

◆ BRITISH COLUMBIA

KAMLOOPS MUSEUM AND ARCHIVES
207 Seymour St.
Kamloops BC V2C 2E7
(250) 828–3576
www.museumsassn.bc.ca/museums/kma.html

MUSEUM OF ANTHROPOLOGY AND LIBRARY
University of British Columbia
6353 N. W. Marian Dr.
Vancouver BC V6T 1W5
(250) 228–5087

♦ MANITOBA

DEPARTMENT OF CULTURAL AFFAIRS AND
    HISTORICAL RESOURCES PROVINCIAL
    ARCHIVES
200 Vaughn St.
Winnipeg, MB R3C 0V8

ESKIMO MUSEUM LIBRARY
242 La Verendrye St.
Churchill, MB R0B 0E0
(204) 675–2541

♦ NEWFOUNDLAND

MEMORIAL UNIVERSITY OF NEW
    FOUNDLAND
Centre For New Foundland Studies
Queen Elizabeth II Library
St. John's, NF A1B 3Y1
(709) 737–7476

♦ NORTHWEST TERRITORY

DENE MUSEUM AND ARCHIVES
c/o General Delivery
Fort Good Hope, NT X0E 0H0

♦ NOVA SCOTIA

SCHOOL OF SOCIAL WORK LIBRARY
Maritime School of Social Work
Dalhousie University
6420 Coburg RD
Halifax, NS B3H 3J5

♦ ONTARIO

MUSEUM OF INDIAN ARCHEOLOGY
University of Western Ontario
Lawson Jury Bdg
London, ON N6G 3M6
(519) 473–1360

NORTHERN DEVELOPMENTAL LIBRARY
Department of Indian Affairs
Ottawa, ON KIA OH4
(819) 997–0811

ROYAL ONTARIO MUSEUM
100 Queens Park
Toronto, ON M5S 2C6
(416) 586–5724
www.rom.on.ca/

♦ SASKATCHEWAN

NATIVE LAW LIBRARY
NATIVE LAW CENTRE
University Of Saskatchewan
101 Diefenbaker Centre
Saskatoon, SK S7N 5B8
(306) 966–6189
www.usask.ca/nativelaw/index.html

♦ QUEBEC

CANADIAN MUSEUM OF CIVILIZATION
P.O. Box 3100, Station "B"
Hull, PQ J8X 4H2
(819) 776 8430
www.civilization.ca/

Historical Societies and Scholarly Organizations

United States

◆ ARIZONA

ARIZONA HISTORICAL SOCIETY
Central Arizona Division
1300 N. College Ave.
Tempe, AZ 85281
(480) 929–0292
www.tempe.gov/ahs/

SOCIETY FOR HISTORICAL ARCHAEOLOGY
P.O. Box 30446
Tucson, AZ 85751
(520) 886–8006
sha.org/

◆ ARKANSAS

ARKANSAS HISTORY COMMISSION
One Capitol Mall
Little Rock, AR 72201
(501) 682–6900
www.state.ar.us/ahc/

ORDER OF THE INDIAN WARS
P.O. Box 7401
Little Rock, AR 72217
(501) 225–3996
lbha.org/oiw.html

◆ CALIFORNIA

CALIFORNIA HISTORICAL SOCIETY
2099 Pacific Ave.
San Francisco, CA 94109
(415) 567–1848
www.calhist.org/index.html

SOCIETY FOR THE STUDY OF THE
    INDIGENOUS LANGUAGES OF THE
    AMERICAS
P.O. Box 555
Arcata, CA 95518
www.ssila.org

◆ CONNECTICUT

CONNECTICUT HISTORICAL SOCIETY
1 Elizabeth St.
Hartford, CT 06105
(203) 236–5621
www.chs.org

◆ DISTRICT OF COLUMBIA

AMERICAN HISTORICAL ASSOCIATION
400 A St. SE
Washington, DC 20003–3889
(202) 544–2422
www.theaha.org/

NATIONAL GEOGRAPHIC SOCIETY
1145 17th Street N.W.
Washington, D.C. 20036–4688
(800) 647–5463
www.nationalgeographic.org/

SOCIETY FOR AMERICAN ARCHAEOLOGY
900 Second Street NE #12
Washington, D.C. 20002–3557
(202) 789–8200
www.saa.org

◆ IDAHO

IDAHO STATE HISTORICAL SOCIETY
450 North 4th Street
Boise, ID 83702
(208) 334–5335
www.state.id.us/ishs/index.html

◆ ILLINOIS

AMERICAN INDIAN LIBRARY
   ASSOCIATION (AILA)
American Library Association
Office of Library Outreach Services (OLOS)
50 East Huron St.
Chicago, IL 60611
(800) 545–2433 Ext. 4294
www.nativeculture.com/lisamitten/aila.html

AMERICAN SOCIETY FOR ETHNOHISTORY
For information about the Society contact:
Anne McMullen, Secretary-Treasurer
National Museum of the American Indian
Cultural Resources Center
4220 Silver Hill Street
Suitland, Maryland 20746
(301) 238–6624
www.ethnohistory.org/index.html

◆ INDIANA

SOCIETY FOR ETHNOMUSICOLOGY
Indiana University
Morrison Hall 005
Bloomington, IN 47405–2501
(812) 855–6672
www.ethnomusicology.org/

◆ KANSAS

KANSAS STATE HISTORICAL SOCIETY
6425 SW Sixth Avenue
Topeka, KS 66615–1099
(785) 272–8681
www.kshs.org/

◆ MASSACHUSETTS

AMERICAN ANTIQUARIAN SOCIETY
185 Salisbury St.
Worcester, MA 01609
(508) 755–5221
www.americanantiquarian.org/

ARCHAEOLOGICAL INSTITUTE OF AMERICA
Boston University
656 Beacon Street, 4th floor
Boston, MA 02215–2006
(617) 353–9361
www.archaeological.org/

◆ MICHIGAN

MICHIGAN HISTORICAL CENTER
717 West Allegan
Lansing, MI 48918–1800
(517) 373–3559
www.sos.state.mi.us/history/museum/explore/
   explore2.html

◆ MINNESOTA

MINNESOTA HISTORICAL SOCIETY
345 Kellogg Blvd. West
St. Paul, MN 55102–1906
(651) 296–6126
www.mnhs.org/places/historycenter/index.html

◆ MISSOURI

MISSOURI HISTORICAL SOCIETY
225 S. Skinker
P.O. Box 11940
St. Louis, MO 63112–0040
(314) 746–4500
www.mohistory.org/

◆ MONTANA

MONTANA HISTORICAL SOCIETY
225 North Roberts
Helena, MT 59620
(406) 444–2694
www.his.state.mt.us/

◆ NEBRASKA

NEBRASKA STATE HISTORICAL SOCIETY
P.O. Box 82554
1500 R Street
Lincoln, NE 68501
(402) 471–4746
www.nebraskahistory.org/index.html

◆ NEVADA

NEVADA HISTORICAL SOCIETY
1650 North Virginia St.
Reno, NV 89503
(775) 688–1190
lahontan.clan.lib.nv.us/polpac/html_client/default.asp
    (via State Library, Division of Museums and
    History)

◆ NEW MEXICO

THE ARCHAEOLOGICAL CONSERVANCY
5301 Central Avenue NE, Suite 1218
Albuquerque, NM 87108–1517
(505) 266–1540
www.americanarchaeology.com/aaabout.html

WESTERN HISTORY ASSOCIATION
University of New Mexico
1080 Mesa Vista Hall
Albuquerque, NM 87131–1181
(505) 277–5234
www.unm.edu/~wha/

◆ NORTH CAROLINA

CHEROKEE HISTORICAL ASSOCIATION
P.O. Box 398
Cherokee, NC 28719
(828) 497–2315
(828) 497–2111 [off season]
www.oconalufteevillage.com

◆ NORTH DAKOTA

STATE HISTORICAL SOCIETY OF
    NORTH DAKOTA
612 East Blvd. Avenue
Bismarck, ND 58505–0830
(701) 328–2666
www.state.nd.us/hist/index.html

◆ OKLAHOMA

CHEROKEE NATIONAL HISTORICAL SOCIETY
P.O. Box 515
Tahlequah, OK 74465
(918) 456–6007
www.powersource.com/heritage/

CHICKASAW HISTORICAL SOCIETY
P.O. Box 1548
Ada, OK 74820
(580) 332–8685
www.chickasaw.net/heritage/journal/

OKLAHOMA HISTORICAL SOCIETY
2100 North Lincoln Blvd.
Wiley Post Historical Blvd.
Oklahoma City, OK 73105–4997
(405) 521–2491
www.ok-history.mus.ok.us/#

◆ OREGON

OREGON HISTORICAL SOCIETY
1200 SW Park Avenue
Portland, OR 97205–2483
(503) 222–1741
www.ohs.org/

◆ RHODE ISLAND

RHODE ISLAND HISTORICAL SOCIETY
110 Benevolent St.
Providence, RI 02906
(401) 331–8575
www.rihs.org/

◆ SOUTH CAROLINA

SOUTH CAROLINA HISTORICAL SOCIETY
100 Meeting Street
Charleston, S.C. 29401
(843) 723–3225
www.schistory.org/

◆ SOUTH DAKOTA

SOUTH DAKOTA STATE HISTORICAL
  SOCIETY
Cultural Heritage Center
900 Governor's Drive
Pierre, SD 57501–2217
(605) 773–3458
www.state.sd.us/deca/cultural/sdshs.htm

◆ VERMONT

VERMONT HISTORICAL SOCIETY
109 State St.
Montpelier, VT 05609–0901
(802) 828–2291
www.state.vt.us/vhs/

◆ VIRGINIA

AMERICAN ANTHROPOLOGICAL
  ASSOCIATION
AMERICAN ETHNOLOGICAL SOCIETY
4350 North Fairfax Drive, Suite 640
Arlington, VA 22203–1620
(703) 528–1902
www.aaanet.org/

VIRGINIA HISTORICAL SOCIETY
428 North Blvd.
Richmond, VA 23220
(804) 358–4901
www.vahistorical.org/

◆ WASHINGTON

WASHINGTON STATE HISTORICAL SOCIETY
Research Center
315 North Stadium Way
Tacoma, WA 98403

(253) 798–5914
www.wshs.org/

◆ WISCONSIN

STATE HISTORICAL SOCIETY OF WISCONSIN
816 State St.
Madison, WI 53706
(608) 264–6400
www.shsw.wisc.edu/

CANADA

CANADIAN ANTHROPOLOGICAL SOCIETY
Wilfrid Laurier University Press
75 University Avenue
Waterloo, ON N2L 3C5
socserv2.socsci.mcmaster.ca/~casca/

CANADIAN ARCHAEOLOGICAL ASSOCIATION
Executive Assistant
Department of Anthropology and Archaeology
University of Saskatchewan
55 Campus Drive
Saskatoon, Saskatchewan S7N 5B1
(306) 966–4188
www.canadianarchaeology.com

CANADIAN HISTORICAL ASSOCIATION
395 Wellington St.
Ottawa, ON K1A 0N3
(613) 233–7885
www.yorku.ca/research/cha

CANADA'S NATIONAL HISTORICAL SOCIETY
478—167 Lombard Ave
Winnipeg MB R3B OT6
(204) 988–9300
www.historysociety.ca/

Cultural Centers

UNITED STATES

◆ ALASKA

ALASKA NATIVE HERITAGE CENTER
8800 Heritage Center Dr.
Anchorage, AK 99506
(907) 330–8000
www.alaskanative.net

ALASKAN INDIAN ARTS, INC.
P.O. Box 271
23 Fort Sewards Dr.
Haines, AK 99827
(907) 766–2160
Tlingit and Chilkat.

INUPIAT HERITAGE CENTER
P.O. Box 749
Barrow, AK 99723
(907) 852–4594

SOUTHEAST ALASKA INDIAN CULTURAL
    CENTER, INC.
106 Metlakatla St.
Sitka, AK 99835
(907) 747–8061

◆ ARIZONA

APACHE CULTURAL CENTER AND MUSEUM
P.O. Box 507
Fort Apache, AZ 85926
(520) 338–1392

FORT MCDOWELL MOHAVE-APACHE
    CULTURAL CENTER
P.O. Box 7779
Fountain Hills, AZ 85269
(480) 733–8113

HOPI CULTURAL CENTER MUSEUM
P.O. Box 7
Second Mesa, AZ 86043
(520) 734–2401
www.psv.com/hopi.html

SAN CARLOS APACHE CULTURAL CENTER
P.O. Box 760
Peridot, AZ 85542
(520) 475–2894
www.carizona.com/super/attractions/san_carlos.html

◆ CALIFORNIA

AGUA CALIENTE CULTURAL CENTER
219 S. Palm Canyon Dr.
Palm Springs, CA 92262
(760) 323–0151
www.prinet.com/accmuseum

CUPA CULTURAL CENTER
PALA INDIAN RESERVATION MUSEUM
P.O. Box 445
Pala, CA 92059
(760) 742–1590
hometown.aol.com/lmir635563/

◆ COLORADO

SOUTHERN UTE INDIAN CULTURAL CENTER
3066 Country Rd. 311
Ignacio, Colorado 81137–9130
(970) 563–9583

◆ FLORIDA

MICCOUSUKEE TRIBE CULTURAL CENTER
P.O. Box 440021
Miami, FL 33144
(305) 894–2375

◆ LOUISIANA

TUNICA-BILOXI REGIONAL INDIAN CENTER
    AND MUSEUM
P.O. Box 1589
Marksville, LA 71351
(318) 253–8174
www.tunica.org

◆ MICHIGAN

CULTURAL HERITAGE CENTER
Bay Mills Community College
Brimly, MI 49715
(906) 248–5852

◆ MINNESOTA

LITTLE FEATHER INTERPRETIVE CENTER
317 4th St., NE
P.O. Box 334
Pipestone, MN 56164
(507) 825–3579
www.littlefeathercenter.com

MINNEAPOLIS AMERICAN INDIAN CENTER
1530 E. Franklin Ave.
Minneapolis, MN 55404
(612) 879–1755

UPPER MIDWEST INDIAN CULTURAL
    CENTER
PIPESTONE INDIAN SHRINE ASSOCIATION
P.O. Box 727
Pipestone, MN 56164
(507) 825–5463

◆ MONTANA

THE PEOPLE'S CENTER MUSEUM
P.O. Box 278
Pablo, MT 59855
(406) 675–0160
www.peoplescenter.org/museum.htm
Salish, Kootenai and Pend d'Orielle Tribal Nations.

◆ NEW JERSEY

POWHATAN RENAPE NATION
    CULTURAL CENTER
P.O. Box 225
Rancocas, NJ 08073
(609) 261–4747
www.powhatan.org/museum.html

◆ NEW MEXICO

ACOMA TOURIST AND VISITOR CENTER
P.O. Box 309
Pueblo of Acoma
Acomita, NM 87034
(800) 747–0181
www.acomazuni.com/acoma.cfm

A-SHIWI AWAN MUSEUM AND
    HERITAGE CENTER
122 Hwy. 53
Zuni, NM 87034
(505) 782–4403
www.nmculture.org/cgi-bin/showInst.pl?InstID=AISH

INDIAN PUEBLO CULTURAL CENTER
2401 12th St. NW
Albuquerque, NM
(505) 242–4943
www.indianpueblo.org

MESCALERO CULTURAL CENTER
P.O. Box 176
Mescalero, NM 88340
(505) 671–4494

WATATOWA VISITOR CENTER
7413 Hwy. 4 Box 100
Jemez Pueblo, NM
(505) 834–7235
www.jemezpueblo.org

◆ NEW YORK

AKWESASNE MUSEUM
AKWESASNE CULTURAL CENTER
RR1 Box 14C
Hogansburg, NY 13055
(518) 358–2240
library.usask.ca/native/directory/english/
    akwesasne.html

◆ NORTH CAROLINA

THE MUSEUM OF THE NATIVE AMERICAN
    RESOURCE CENTER
P.O. Box 1510 UNCP
Pembroke, NC 28372
(910) 521–6282
www.uncp.edu/nativemuseum

◆ NORTH DAKOTA

TURTLE MOUNTAIN CHIPPEWA
  HERITAGE CENTER
P.O. Box 257
Belcourt, ND 58316
(701) 477–6140
chippewa.utma.com/index2.html

◆ OKLAHOMA

CADDO CULTURAL CENTER
P.O. Box 487
Binger, OK 73009
(405) 656–2344

CHEYENNE CULTURAL CENTER
2250 NE Route 66
Clinton, OK 73601
(580) 323–6224

CHICKASAW CULTURAL CENTER
520 Arlington Rd.
P.O. Box 1548
Ada, OK 74820–1548
(580) 332–1990
www.chickasaw.net/museum/index.htm

WITCHITA TRIBAL CULTURAL CENTER
P.O. Box 726
Anadarko, OK 73005
(405) 247–2425

◆ SOUTH CAROLINA

CATAWBA CULTURAL CENTER
611 E. Main St.
Rock Hill, SC 29730
(803) 328–2427
www.ccppcrafts.com

◆ SOUTH DAKOTA

H.V. JOHNSTON AMERICAN INDIAN
  CULTURAL CENTER
Cheyenne River Reservation
P.O. Box 857
Eagle Butte, SD 57625
(605) 964–2542

◆ TEXAS

TIGUA PUEBLO CULTURAL CENTER
305 Yaya Ln.
El Paso, TX 79907
(915) 859–5287

◆ VERMONT

ABENAKI CULTURAL CENTER
HCR1 Box 110
Morrisville, VT 05661
(802) 868–2559

◆ WASHINGTON

MAKAH CULTURAL RESEARCH CENTER
Bayview Ave., Highway 112
P.O. Box 160
Neah Bay, WA 98357
(360) 645–2711
www.makah.com/museum.htm

STEILACOOM TRIBAL CULTURAL CENTER
1515 LaFayette St.
P.O. Box 88419
Steilacoom, WA 98388
(253) 584–6308
www.ohwy.com/wa/t/tribaccm.htm

WANAPUM DAM INTERPRETIVE CENTER
P.O. Box 878
Ephraita, WA 98823
(509) 932–3571 ext 2571

◆ WISCONSIN

LAC DU FLAMBEAU CHIPPEWA
  CULTURAL CENTER
P.O. Box 804
Lac du Flambeau, WI 54538
(715) 588–3333

◆ WYOMING

EASTERN SHOSHONE TRIBAL
  CULTURAL CENTER
P.O. Box 1008
Fort Washakie, WY 82514
(307) 332–9106

CANADA

◆ ALBERTA

ANDERSON NATIVE HERITAGE AND
　CULTURAL CENTRE
13140 St. Albert Tr.
Edmonton, AB T5L 4R8
(401) 455–2200

NINASTAKO CULTURAL CENTRE
P.O. Box 1299
Standoff, AB T0K 0K0
(403) 737–3774

OLDMAN RIVER CULTURAL CENTER
P.O. Box 70
Brocket, AB P0K 0H0
(403) 965–3939

◆ BRITISH COLUMBIA

HEILTSUK CULTURAL EDUCATION CENTRE
Box 880
Waglisla, BC V0T 1Z0
(250) 957–2626

SHESHAHT CULTURAL CENTRE
5211 Wilkinson Rd.
Port Alberni, BC V9Y 7B2
(604) 723–5421

U'MISTA CULTURAL CENTRE
P.O. Box 253
Alert Bay, BC V0N 1A0
(604) 974–5403

◆ MANITOBA

BROKENHEAD OJIBWA NATION HISTORICAL
　VILLAGE
General Delivery
Scanterbury, MB R0E 1W0
(204) 766–2483

MANITOBA INDIAN CULTURAL
　EDUCATION CENTER
119 Sutherland Ave.
Winnipeg, MB R2W 3C9
(204) 942–0228

NORWAY HOUSE CREE NATION CULTURAL
　EDUCATION CENTER
Norway House, MB R0B 1B0
(204) 359–6296
www.schoolnet.ca/autochtone/norway/index-e.html

◆ ONTARIO

LAKE OF THE WOODS OJIBWA
　CULTURAL CENTER
P.O. Box 159
Kenora, ON P9N 3X3
(807) 548–5744
www.schoolnet.ca/aboriginal/kenora/index-e.html

OJIBWA AND CREE CULTURAL CENTRE
210 Spruce St. S., Suite 306
Timmins, ON P4N 2M5
(705) 267–7911
www.schoolnet.ca/aboriginal/occc/index-e.html

◆ QUEBEC

KANESATAKEHRO:NON TSI
　NIHATWEIENNO:TEN CULTURAL CENTRE
664 Ste. Philomene
Kansehsatake, PQ J0N 1E0
(514) 479–1783
www.schoolnet.ca/aboriginal/kanesata/index-e.html

KANIEN'KEHAKA RAOTITIOHKWA
　CULTURAL CENTER
P.O. Box 969
Kahnawake, PQ J0L 1B0
(450) 638–0880
library.usask.ca/native/directory/english/
　kanienkehaka.html

◆ SASKATCHEWAN

SASKATCHEWAN INDIAN CULTURAL
　CENTRE
120 33rd St. E.
Saskatoon, SK S7K 0S2
(360) 244–1146
www.schoolnet.ca/aboriginal/sicc-cat/

References

Before AD 1500

Cordell, Linda S. *Prehistory of the Southwest*. Orlando,
　Fla.: Academic Press, 1984.

Deetz, James. *Invitation to Archaeology.* Garden City, N.Y.: Published for the American Museum of Natural History by the Natural History Press, 1967.

Jelks, Edward B. and Juliet C. Jelks, eds. *Historical Dictionary of North American Archaeology.* New York: Greenwood Press, 1988.

Jennings, Jesse D., ed. *Ancient Native Americans.* San Francisco: W. H. Freeman, 1978.

Milanich, Jerald T. and Charles H. Fairbanks. *Florida Archaeology.* New York: Academic Press, 1980.

Moratto, Michael J. *California Archaeology.* Orlando, Fla.: Academic Press, 1984.

Morse, Dan F. and Phyliss A. Morse. *Archaeology of the Central Mississippi Valley.* New York: Academic Press, 1983.

Ritchie, William A. *The Archaeology of New York State.* Rev. edition. Garden City, NY: Published for the American Museum of Natural History by the Natural History Press, 1969.

Smith, Bruce D., ed. *Mississippian Settlement Patterns.* New York: Academic Press, 1978.

Snow, Dean R. *The Archaeology of New England.* New York: Academic Press, 1980.

Taylor, R. E. and Clement W. Meighan, eds. *Chronologies in New World Archaeology.* New York: Academic Press, 1978.

Wedel, Waldo R. *Prehistoric Man on the Great Plains.* Norman: University of Oklahoma Press, 1961.

U.S. Indians, 1500–1965

Aberle, David. *The Peyote Religion among the Navaho.* Chicago: Aldine, 1966.

Baird, W. David. *Peter Pitchlynn: Chief of the Choctaws.* Norman: University of Oklahoma Press, 1972.

Bannon, John F. *The Mission Frontier in Sonora, 1620–1687.* Edited by James A. Reynolds. New York: U.S. Catholic Historical Society, 1955.

Berthrong, Donald J. *The Southern Cheyennes.* Norman: University of Oklahoma Press, 1963.

Casas, Bartolome de las. *A Short Account of the Destruction of the Indies.* New York: Penguin, 1992.

Cohen, Felix S. *Handbook of Federal Indian Law.* Albuquerque: University of New Mexico Press, 1971.

Corkran, David H. *The Cherokee Frontier: Conflict and Survival, 1740–62.* Norman: University of Oklahoma Press, 1962.

Debo, Angie. *A History of the Indians of the United States.* Norman: University of Oklahoma Press, 1971.

———. *And Still the Waters Run.* Princeton: Princeton University Press, 1940.

Edmunds, R. David. *The Shawnee Prophet.* Lincoln: University of Nebraska Press, 1983.

———. *Tecumseh and the Quest for Indian Leadership.* Boston: Little, Brown, 1984.

Foreman, Grant. *Indian Removal: The Emigration of the Five Civilized Tribes of Indians.* Norman: University of Oklahoma Press, 1932.

———. *Last Trek of the Indians.* Chicago: University of Chicago Press, 1946.

Gibson, Arrell M. *The American Indian: Prehistory to the Present.* Lexington, Mass.: D.C. Heath, 1980.

———, ed. *America's Exiles: Indian Colonization in Oklahoma.* Oklahoma City: Oklahoma Historical Society, 1976.

Grinde, Donald A. and Bruce E. Johansen. *Exemplar of Liberty: Native America and the Evolution of Democracy.* Los Angeles: American Indian Studies Center, UCLA, 1991.

Hagan, William T. *Indian Police and Judges: Experiments in Acculturation and Control.* Lincoln: University of Nebraska Press, 1980.

Heizer, Robert A., ed. *The Destruction of California Indians.* Santa Barbara, Calif.: Peregrine Smith, 1974.

Hertzberg, Hazel. *The Search for an American Indian Identity: Modern Pan-Indian Movements.* Syracuse, N.Y.: Syracuse University Press, 1971.

Hoig, Stan. *The Sand Creek Massacre.* Norman: University of Oklahoma Press, 1961.

The Indian Historian. San Francisco: American Indian Historical Society, 1967–1979.

Jackson, Helen Hunt. *A Century of Dishonor.* New York: Harper & Brothers, 1881.

Jahoda, Gloria. *The Trail of Tears.* New York: Holt, Rinehart and Winston, 1975.

Jane, Cecil, trans. *Select Documents Illustrating the Four Voyages of Columbus.* Vol. 1. London: Hakluyt Society, 1930.

Josephy, Alvin M., Jr. *The Indian Heritage of America.* New York: Knopf, 1968.

———. *Now That the Buffalo's Gone: A Study of Today's American Indians.* New York: Knopf, 1982.

La Barre, Weston. *The Ghost Dance: Origins of Religion.* Garden City, N.Y.: Doubleday, 1970.

Miner, Craig H. *The Corporation and the Indian: Tribal Sovereignty and Industrial Civilization in Indian Territory.* Columbia: University of Missouri Press, 1976.

Otis, Delos S. *The Dawes Act and the Allotment of Indian Lands.* Norman: University of Oklahoma Press, 1973.

Philp, Kenneth R. *John Collier's Crusade for Indian Reform, 1920–1954.* Tucson: University of Arizona Press, 1977.

Ruby, Robert H. and John A. Brown. *Indians of the Pacific Northwest: A History.* Norman: University of Oklahoma Press, 1981.

Satz, Ronald N. *American Indian Policy in the Jacksonian Era.* Lincoln: University of Nebraska Press, 1975.

Szasz, Margaret C. *Education and the American Indian: The Road to Self-Determination, 1928–1973*. Albuquerque: University of New Mexico Press, 1974.

Thompson, Gerald. *The Army and the Navajo: The Bosque Redondo Reservation Experiment, 1863–1868*. Tucson: University of Arizona Press, 1976.

Trafzer, Clifford E. *The Kit Carson Campaign: The Last Great Navajo War*. Norman: University of Oklahoma Press, 1982.

Trafzer, Clifford E. and Richard D. Scheuerman. *Renegade Tribe: The Palouse Indians and the Invasion of the Pacific Northwest*. Pullman: Washington State University Press, 1986.

Trennert, Robert A., Jr. *Alternative to Extinction: Federal Indian Policy and the Beginnings of the Reservation System, 1846–51*. Philadelphia: Temple University Press, 1975.

Tyler, S. Lyman. *A History of Indian Policy*. Washington, D.C.: U.S. Department of the Interior, Bureau of Indian Affairs, 1973.

Unrau, William E. *The Kansa Indians: A History of the Wind People*. Norman: University of Oklahoma Press, 1971.

Utley, Robert M. *Frontier Regulars: The United States Army and the Indian, 1866–1891*. New York: Macmillan, 1974.

Vaughan, Alden T. *New England Frontier: Puritans and Indians, 1620–1675*. Boston: Little, Brown, 1965.

Washburn, Wilcomb E., comp. *The American Indian and the United States: A Documentary History*. New York: Random House, 1973.

U.S. Indians, 1965–2000

American Antiquity. Washington, D.C., 1935–present.

American Friends Service Committee. *Uncommon Controversy: Fishing Rights of the Muckleshoot, Puyallup and Nisqually Indians*. Seattle: University of Washington Press, 1970.

American Indians Today: Answers to Your Questions. Washington, D.C.: U.S. Department of the Interior, Bureau of Indian Affairs, 1991.

Cahn, Edgar, ed. *Our Brother's Keeper: The Indian in White America*. Washington, D.C.: New Community Press, 1969.

Castile, George P. and Robert L. Bee. *State and Reservation: New Perspectives in Federal Indian Policy*. Tucson: University of Arizona Press, 1992.

Cohen, Felix S. *Felix S. Cohen's Handbook of Federal Indian Law*. Charlottesville, Va.: Michie: Bobbs-Merrill, 1982.

Deloria, Vine, Jr. *Behind the Trail of Broken Treaties: An Indian Declaration of Independence*. New York: Delacorte Press, 1974.

———. *Custer Died for Your Sins: An Indian Manifesto*. New York: Macmillan, 1969.

———. *We Talk, You Listen: New Tribes, New Turf*. New York: Macmillan, 1970.

Dorris, Michael. *The Broken Cord*. New York: Harper & Row, 1989.

Fixico, Donald L. *The Urban Indian Experience in America*. Albuquerque: University of New Mexico Press, 2000.

———. *Urban Indians*. New York: Chelsea House, 1991.

Gibson, Arrell M. *The American Indian: Prehistory to Present*. Lexington, Mass.: D.C. Heath, 1980.

Indian Country Today. Rapid City, S.Dak. 1992–2000.

Iverson, Peter. *We Are Still Here: American Indians in the Twentieth Century*. Wheeling, Ill.: Harlan Davidson, 1998.

Johnson, Troy R. *The Occupation of Alcatraz Island: Indian Self-determination and the Rise of Indian Activism*. Urbana: University of Illinois Press, 1996.

Josephy, Alvin Jr. *Now That the Buffalo's Gone: A Study of Today's American Indians*. Norman: University of Oklahoma Press, 1984.

Josephy, Alvin Jr., Joane Nagel, and Troy Johnson, eds. *Red Power: The American Indians' Fight for Freedom*. Rev. ed. Lincoln: University of Nebraska Press, 1999.

Kappler, Charles J., comp. and ed. *Indian Affairs: Laws and Treaties*. Washington, D.C.: GPO, 1903–1941.

Messerschmidt, Jim. *The Trial of Leonard Peltier*. Boston: South End Press, 1983.

Momaday, N. Scott. *House Made of Dawn*. New York: Harper & Row, 1968.

News From Indian Country. Hayward, Wis. 1990–2000.

O'Brien, Sharon. *American Indian Tribal Governments*. Norman: University of Oklahoma Press, 1989.

Prucha, Francis P. *American Indian Policy*. Norman: University of Oklahoma Press, 1986.

———. *The Great Father: The United States Government and the American Indians*. 2 vols. Lincoln: University of Nebraska Press, 1984.

Smith, Paul Chaat, and Robert Allen Warrior. *Like a Hurricane: The Indian Movement from Alcatraz to Wounded Knee*. New York: New Press, 1996.

Steiner, Stan. *The New Indians*. New York: Harper & Row, 1968.

Tundra Times. Anchorage, Alaska, 1962–1982.

Troy Johnson
Elton Naswood

Canadian Natives, 1500–2000

Abel, Kerry. *Drum Songs: Glimpses of Dene History*. Montreal: McGill-Queen's University Press, 1993.

Allen, Robert S. *His Majesty's Indian Allies: British Indian Policy in the Defence of Canada, 1774–1815*. Toronto: Dundurn Press, 1992.

Calloway, Colin G. *Crown and Calumet: British-Indian Relations, 1783–1815*. Norman: University of Oklahoma Press, 1987.

Carter, Sarah. *Lost Harvests: Prairie Indian Reserve Farmers and Government Policy*. Montreal: McGill-Queen's University Press, 1990.

Coates, Kenneth. *Best Left as Indians: Native-White Relations in the Yukon Territory, 1840–1950*. Montreal: McGill-Queen's University Press, 1991.

Coates, Ken S. & Robin Fisher, eds. *Out of the Background: Readings on Canadian Native History*. 2d ed. Toronto: Copp Clark, 1996.

Gibson, James R. *Otter Skins, Boston Ships, and China Goods: The Maritime Fur Trade of the Northwest Coast, 1785–1811*. Montreal: McGill-Queen's University Press; Seattle: University of Washington Press, 1992.

Jenness, Diamond. *The Indians of Canada*. 7th edition. Toronto: University of Toronto Press, 1977.

Miller, James Rodger. *Shingwauk's Vision: A History of Native Residential Schools*. Toronto: University of Toronto Press, 1996.

———. *Skyscrapers Hide the Heavens: A History of Indian-White Relations in Canada*. 3d ed. Toronto: University of Toronto Press, 2000.

———. *Sweet Promises: A Reader on Indian-White Relations in Canada*. Toronto: University of Toronto Press, 1991.

Nichols, Roger L. *Indians in the United States and Canada : A Comparative History*. Lincoln: University of Nebraska Press, 1998.

Ray, Arthur J. *I Have Lived Here Since the World Began: An Illustrated History of Canada's Native People*. Toronto: Lester Pub., 1996.

Titley, E. Brian. *A Narrow Vision: Duncan Campbell Scott and the Administration of Indian Affairs in Canada*. Vancouver: University of British Columbia Press, 1986.

Trigger, Bruce G. *Natives and Newcomers : Canada's "Heroic Age" Reconsidered*. Kingston: McGill-Queen's University Press, 1985.

Ted Binnema

Demography

- ◆ Native Demography Before 1700
- ◆ Geographic and Demographic Change During the Eighteenth Century
- ◆ Indian Geographic Distribution, Habitat, and Demography During the Nineteenth Century
- ◆ Indian Land Tenure in the Twentieth Century
- ◆ Canadian Native Distribution, Habitat, and Demography

◆ NATIVE DEMOGRAPHY BEFORE 1700

Indian groups moved from place to place in search of adequate food sources, for protection, or to escape changing climatic conditions, such as long droughts in the region. Many Indian peoples tell stories of migrations, which sometimes send people on religious quests. For example, one Creek story claims that the people migrated east for many years in search of the home of the sun. Upon reaching the Atlantic Ocean, however, they gave up the quest and decided to settle. While there were some migrations prior to 1500, Indian migrations and population changes began to increase rapidly after the arrival of European colonists. The territorial expansion of the European colonies pushed many coastal Indian nations into the interior, where they were incorporated into other Indian nations or where they resettled, far from their original homelands. New trade relations with the Europeans, especially the fur trade, induced many Indian nations to seek new hunting territories, which often expanded into the other nations' lands. Perhaps the greatest change to Indian populations came with the introduction of several European diseases, such as smallpox and scarlet fever, previously unknown to Indians. These diseases caused many deaths among the Indians, and were possibly responsible for 60 million deaths in North and South America by 1900, when the U.S. Indian population declined to a low point of about 250,000. These events are often referred to as a demographic catastrophe. Native American demography is especially interesting because of the rapid decline and dispersion of the population after colonial contact.

Paleo-Indians

Archeologists, students of ancient cultures, believe that the first human beings entered the Americas by way of a land bridge that connected Siberia and Alaska toward the end of the last glacial period, approximately 15,000 to 25,000 years ago. At this time, huge continental glaciers contained so much frozen water that sea level had fallen below the bottom of what is now the Bering Strait. After crossing, the first Americans spread rapidly beyond present-day Alaska, and by the end of glacial times, about 12,000 years ago, had settled throughout North and South America.

It is important to note that some Native Americans do not believe that their ancestors walked across the Bering Strait. Most Indian cultures have oral traditions recounting the origins of people on earth. Many of these stories are analogous to the stories of Adam and Eve in the Bible. Other Indians have traditions of eastward migrations. For example, the Lenape, or Delaware Indians, who are considered by many Indian nations to be the grandfather of the Algonkian-speaking nations, have a long epic tradition of migration from the northwest to the Atlantic coast in present-day New England. Other nations, such as the Cherokee, Choctaw, Chickasaw, and Creek, have similar migration stories in which their entire nation was led by the instructions of a sacred pole, which each day pointed in the direction of that day's journey, and finally indicated the end of the march and new homeland by remaining upright. The migration traditions are not inconsistent with archeologists' Bering Strait theory, and considering the age of many creation stories, it is possible that these ancient traditions have roots that predate a migration over the Bering Strait.

For a few thousands years after the glacial period, many large game animals, including woolly mammoths and large bison, roamed North America. These animals died out about 10,000 years ago, probably because of changing climatic conditions caused by the retreat of the glaciers north. Early Paleo-Indian cultures revolved around hunting these animals. Paleo-Indians were large game-hunting Indian peoples whose cultures predate the adoption of horticulture and the bow and arrow. Because of large game animals' extinction, Native Americans hunted smaller game, fished, and foraged for wild plant foods for the next seven or eight thousand years. Sometime around 1500 B.C.E. Indian groups began to plant crops such as corn, squash, and beans. Particularly in the present-day eastern and southwestern United States, Indian groups became increasingly dependent on horticulture, or farming with hand tools.

Native Americans slowly increased in numbers for several millennia. People acquired and transmitted specialized knowledge to their descendants about the natural resources in different regions and eventually regional culture areas formed. These cultural areas are now known as the Northeast, Southeast, Plains, Southwest, Great Basin, California, Plateau, Pacific Northwest, Subarctic, and Arctic (see the culture area sections of chapter 3).

By C.E. 1500, between seven and fifteen million people inhabited the present-day United States. Many people resided in the Southeast and Mississippi Valley where they dry-farmed or irrigated their crops. In the dry-farming Southeast, large towns grew on the natural levees flood waters formed along the edges of the major rivers. Levees rose high enough to keep settlements safe from most floods and to support a large assortment of plants that attracted game animals, making hunting easy and efficient near the towns. Townspeople depended significantly on fish caught from backwater lakes left by stream channel shifts. This cultural pattern is usually called *Mississippian*.

In the Southwest sometime after C.E. 1200, the Hohokam, ancestors of the present-day Piman-speaking tribes, began constructing multi-story, earthen-walled buildings. The Hohokam gardened using irrigation methods, and stored their crops within the earthen buildings. Ancestors of the present-day Pueblos began building similar multi-stories as early as C.E. 900. The Spanish word *pueblo* applies to these compact, multi-storied fortress towns. Pueblo peoples sharing a common culture, despite linguistic differences, occupied hundreds of *pueblos* by C.E. 1500.

The peoples of California, the Pacific Northwest, the Great Basin, and the Subarctic and Arctic by 1500 had not adopted horticulture and continued surviving as hunters and gatherers as they had for thousands of years.

Sixteenth Century

Few records dating from 1500 to 1620 describe life in what is now the United States. Yet the available documents consistently attest that European diseases rapidly spread throughout the Native American groups. By the time of his second voyage in 1493, Christopher Columbus' crews and colonists had transmitted diseases to the Native Americans. The "Columbian Exchange" of microbes and viruses turned into a demographic catastrophe for the Indians.

The Southeast. In the early 1500s, the Indians of the Southeast met the Spanish. One disease of unknown type reached present-day Florida by 1514, and in 1528 Spanish castaways transmitted an undiagnosed ailment to their Galveston Island hosts on the modern Texas coast. Although it killed half the area's Natives, we do not know how far the disease spread. From 1539 to 1543, Fernando de Soto's Spanish army marauded through the Southeast, slaughtering warriors, kidnapping women, and transmitting diseases to the Natives. De Soto found several Indian villages that were already unoccupied owing to diseases that preceded his arrival. Natives probably contracted these diseases from unrecorded Spanish explorations or trading expeditions, and Native travelers and traders most likely transmitted the diseases from one village to another.

In 1559, a Spanish colonizing expedition carried epidemic influenza from Veracruz, Mexico, to Florida's Pensacola Bay. Colonists traveled inland seeking supplies from some of the populous towns de Soto had visited. The colonists stayed hungry because the populous and prosperous southeastern Indian nations that de Soto's marauders had seen dispersed into small village groups between 1543 and 1559. Malaria and stomach disorders probably caused most of the mortality, although the plague might have spread from the Spanish occupation of Mexico. In the Southeast, disease caused a significant loss of life as well as the reorganization of Native political and social structures. Many of the southeastern Indians were part of centralized Mississippian culture groups with hierarchical bodies of priests and chiefs. After the population declined, these Mississippian cultures collapsed and the Indians regrouped as egalitarian coalitions of villages. It was these egalitarian Indian nations that the colonists encountered in the 1700s. Known today as the Cherokee, Catawba, Creek, and Choctaw, these groups survived by constantly incorporating remnant peoples.

The Northeast. In 1535, Jacques Cartier, a French explorer, and his crews transmitted a lethal disease to the Iroquois who were living along the Saint Lawrence River. Before the century's end, the Iroquois would abandon their homeland because Algonkian-speaking

Drawing depicting the storing of crops by Southwest Natives in the public granary. Twice a year the crops are gathered, carried home in canoes, stored in low and roomy granaries built of stone and earth, and thickly roofed with palm branches and soft earth. (Drawing by John White and Jacques Le Moyne and engraved by Theodore de Bry)

nations—the Chippewa, Ottawa, and others—invaded the Saint Lawrence area. Some Iroquois probably migrated to join the Mohawk in present-day upstate New York. By the end of the 1500s, Chippewa, Ottawa, Potawatomi, and other Algonkian-speaking tribes were beginning to migrate from eastern Canada toward the Great Lakes. Iroquois and Algonkian communities dispersed and were forced to migrate inland because of rampant disease and new colonial occupation.

Southward, in the middle Atlantic area of present-day Virginia, Europeans reported outbreaks of smallpox in 1564 among Indian peoples ranging from the Timucuan in Florida to the Chesapeake Bay people, such as the Powhatan, Pamunkey, and Mattaponi. The virus apparently spread north up the Susquehanna River through present-day Pennsylvania, carried by Native traders and travelers. As a consequence, the Susquehannock lost so many people to disease that the entire nation was reduced to a single village by 1580.

English colonists carried lethal disease to Roanoke Island Natives in 1585. Viral diseases evidently killed one-quarter of North Carolina's Indian population during that same year. In 1586, English explorer Francis Drake attacked the Spanish at Saint Augustine, Florida, and transmitted disease to the Timucuan, a major tribe of the region.

The Southwest.   Because colonists often could not diagnose diseases that struck Natives, it is difficult to estimate how far the diseases spread. As the Native population declined, survivors abandoned some settlements and amalgamated in others. The sequence of abandonment of Hopi pueblos on the Little Colorado River in present-day Arizona provides clues to epidemic disease among all Pueblo peoples. About 1500, the Hopi, a western Pueblo nation, inhabited about ten, riverine pueblos. When Spaniards arrived in 1540, seven were still inhabited, indicating that disease perhaps had spread from New Spain, or present-day Mexico.

In 1583, when the Spaniards next encountered the Hopi, only five riverine pueblos were occupied. This attrition indicates that one or more of the four major epidemics that afflicted Mexico during the interval had spread among the Pueblo, resulting in abandonment and amalgamation. Hopi inhabited four pueblos in 1598 and epidemics of smallpox or measles probably reached them sometime between 1592 and 1593. This epidemic caused significant mortality and abandonment of one pueblo. After the 1613 to 1620 plague epidemic, the Hopi abandoned the remaining pueblos on the Little Colorado River. The survivors migrated to join five Hopi pueblos at Black Mesa, sixty miles to the north, also in present-day Arizona. Thus, between 1519 and 1650, the ten formerly populous Hopi pueblos were decimated and abandoned.

Historic attrition among other Pueblo language groups shows that depopulation was typical among all Pueblos. By 1630 Franciscan missionaries had consolidated 6,000 Piro from fourteen pueblos in three missions and one village, a 71 percent reduction in the number of Piro Pueblo settlements. Southern-Tiwa speakers inhabited sixteen Rio Grande Valley pueblos in 1540; by 1641 only three Tiwa pueblos were left, an 81 percent reduction in settlements. Other Pueblo peoples, such as the Jemez and Towa speakers in the Rio Grande Valley, suffered similar declines in population.

Thanks to European records of the 1500s, we know more about the demography of the East and Southwest Indian groups than we do about the demography of the Native peoples of the Subarctic, Northeast Coast, California, Plateau, or Great Basin areas during this time. While we know virtually nothing about these groups during the 1500s, there is more information about these peoples from the following century.

Seventeenth Century

As European colonies proliferated so did records of migrations and epidemics. In contrast to the 1500s, which were marked by severe demographic change due to disease, the 1600s were characterized more by the intensification of trade relations and the expansion of colonial empires. Indian nations came under great pressure to adapt to European trade and political pressures, and many Indian nations were forced to migrate into the interior for relief from colonial expansion, while some remained in their homelands and attempted to accommodate the new laws and political domination of the European colonists. Despite increased pressure to migrate and adapt, disease and death continued as a persistent feature of Indian life during the 1600s.

The Northeast. When English colonists came to what became Jamestown in present-day Virginia, they encountered the Powhatan, a confederacy of twenty-seven tribes on the James, York, and Potomac rivers, with a total population exceeding 10,000. Sixteen other Algonkian-speaking groups, numbering about 15,000

people, also lived in the same coastal area. In 1607 the English colonists invaded the Powhatan territory, causing some deaths among the Powhatan and their neighboring allies. Between 1613 and 1617 the Powhatan and allies suffered a plague epidemic that originated with Florida's Indian population. In an apparent response to the loss of life and continued colonial aggression, the Powhatan rose up against the colonists in 1622. The war lasted intermittently for about ten years, causing many deaths on both sides. The surviving Powhatan rose up against the colonists again in 1644 and 1646 but were defeated and forced to cede their lands between the York and Blackwater rivers. By the late 1600s, most of the Indians in the area were dispossessed and made subject to Virginia law.

In 1614, Dutch merchants on the Hudson River in present-day New York established a trading post in Mahican territory near present-day Albany, New York. The fur trade—the exchange of beaver, deer, and other skins for European manufactured goods (especially metal goods such as guns, hoes, and hatchets)—became the most significant exchange between the early colonists and Indian nations. Indians quickly realized the value of European goods over their own stone tools, and soon found the Europeans willing to trade for furs, which were sold as beaver hats, leather goods, and coats in Europe. After a few years, the Indians began to prefer trade goods and discontinued production of many traditional arts and crafts. Soon, many Indian nations were not willing or able to meet their own material or economic needs, and came to depend on the trade of furs to fill basic economic and manufacturing needs. Thereafter, the Indians were dependent on the Europeans to supply many basic needs; they could no longer live without trade with the colonists.

For three years, from 1614 to 1617, Algonkian-speaking Mahican collected tribute from the Mohawk, the easternmost nation of the Five Nations Iroquois Confederacy, for crossing their territory to trade with the Dutch. In 1624 the Dutch built Fort Orange, now Albany, and a Mahican village moved nearby. From 1624 to 1648, the Mohawk waged war on the Mahican and ousted them from the area around the new European outpost.

Death rates ran high among Natives on New England's frontier. For example, between 1613 and 1617, plague killed half of Florida's Native population. The plague spread northward along the Atlantic coast, weakening the Powhatan. It killed so many Massachusetts Indians that the Puritans who settled in the area during the 1630s believed that God had cleared the lands of infidel Natives, preparing it for Puritan arrival and settlement. In 1634 the Nipmuck lost 450 of 1,000

Taos Pueblo. (Photo by Manny Pedraza)

inhabitants of one town. Colonists compounded the impact of scarlet fever with the Pequot War in 1637, which started when the Pequot allowed Dutch traders to establish a post east of the Connecticut River at present-day East Hartford. The English raised an army, including Narragansett and Mohegan allies, and burned down a major Pequot village, killing at least 300 men, women, and children. Two hundred survivors were sold into slavery.

Because the Natives depended on trade, they began fighting over areas of access to European trading posts and to areas that were endowed with fur-bearing animals that could be traded to Europeans. In 1643 the Mahican conquered three Algonkian-speaking tribes and several hundred others fled to Manhattan and Pavoia where the Dutch massacred them, ensuring Mahican dominance. This conflict cost about 1,000 Native lives.

Because of a scarlet fever epidemic in 1638, 600 Wenro, an Iroquoian-speaking nation living along the lower Great Lakes, abandoned their territory and moved in with the Huron, another Iroquoian-speaking group living nearby. Other Wenro found refuge among other Iroquoian-speaking nations.

Epidemics might have motivated the Mascouten, Kickapoo, Fox, Sauk, and Potawatomi to leave Michigan's lower peninsula in about 1641 to migrate to Winnebago territory at Green Bay. The once powerful Winnebago lost 1,500 men to an epidemic and lost another 500 men to war with the Fox, which greatly weakened the Winnebago's ability to prevent other Indian nations from moving into their territory.

By the 1640s, the Iroquois, or the Five Nations, had already over-exploited their fur-bearing territories and were looking westward to gain access to other trade or hunting areas. Most tribes in the Great Lakes region sided with the French, who wished to prevent Iroquois expansion into the interior, since the Iroquois were Dutch and English trading allies. In the late 1640s, unable to secure trade agreements with the interior nations (the Huron, the Erie, the Petun, the Neutral Nation, and others), the Iroquois initiated military action to secure access to fur-bearing territories. Dutch traders supported the Five Nations by supplying them with guns and powder, giving the Five Nations an advantage over the French-allied Indians, since the French were reluctant to trade weapons with the Indians. Between 1649 and 1700, the Iroquois waged a series of conflicts with interior nations such as the Illinois Confederacy, the Ottawa, the Huron, and others. These wars, called the Beaver Wars, represent a period of almost constant warfare in the northeast region among the Five Nations, the French, and their Indian trade allies.

During the winter of 1649 and 1650, an Iroquois army marched west and dispersed the Petun people, and a Seneca and Mohawk army, composed of two of the Five Nations of the Iroquois Confederacy, then attacked the Neutral Nation traders and its refugees, dispersing them. The campaign demonstrated that the Seneca and Mohawk were extremely dependent on European goods. In 1652 the Iroquois defeated the Susquehannock people, taking from 500 to 600 prisoners, reducing the Susquehannock's population to between 2,000 and 3,000. In 1653, the Iroquois waged war on the Erie people and dispersed them. Between 1649 and 1670, most of the Iroquoian-speaking nations of the lower Great Lakes, such as the Huron, the Petun, the Erie, and the Neutral Nation, were either destroyed, dispersed, or adopted by the Five Nations' military expansion.

At the time of the Iroquois expansion, New England's colonists openly waged a genocidal war of territorial conquest against Native peoples in 1675. The Wampanoag of Massachusetts bore the brunt of the assault. The colonists virtually exterminated the Wampanoag in a war the colonists called King Philip's War after a Wampanoag leader. By this time the Massachusetts Indians had been so reduced by disease that the colonists ignored them. Although the Narragansett people of Connecticut and Rhode Island did not participate early in King Philip's War, a colonial army invaded their territory and broke their power. The Narragansett either found refuge with the Niantic people or left New England altogether. The New England Indians were thereafter subject to English law and many lived on the outskirts of English settlements, eking out a marginal existence. About fifteen New England Indian villages adopted Christianity; they became known as Praying Towns and, to a certain extent, lived in the tradition of New England town government and Puritan religion.

By the late 1600s, the Indian nations of Virginia and Maryland were also subject to colonial law and were to a large extent dispossessed of their original coastal lands. Disease and war caused their populations to decline significantly, and the colonists already outnumbered them in the colonial territories. By 1700, the colonial governments largely ignored most Indians in the middle Atlantic colonies; the Indian communities persisted, however, and remained targets of land speculators, who often succeeded in purchasing the remnants of their land.

Not every Indian nation was dispossessed of its homeland by the colonists. During most of the 1600s, the Shawnee lived in northern Kentucky, southern Ohio, and western Virginia. By the late 1690s, however, the Chickasaw and Cherokee constantly raided the tribe for slaves, whom they sold to English colonists. The Shawnee abandoned their homeland in the 1690s. Some moved to present-day Georgia, others migrating to join the Creek Nation, while still others joined the Delaware in eastern Pennsylvania. There, on land granted by the Five Nations, and under obligation to pay tribute to the Iroquois Empire, the Shawnee joined in alliance with the Delaware, who themselves had retreated from the coastal areas of New York and New Jersey in search of fur-bearing territories and refuge from colonial expansion. Both the Shawnee and Delaware nations were buffeted throughout their history by colonial expansion, and were subjected to trade dependency, requiring them to work as hunters for European traders. Both nations were eventually forced to migrate into Ohio, Indiana, and by the early 1800s to Kansas or Indian Territory, present-day Oklahoma. Many nations of the Northeast were also forced to migrate further west, but the Delaware and Shawnee illustrate the fate of a people ultimately forced to migrate halfway across the North American continent to find refuge from colonial expansion.

The Susquehannock, who during the late 1600s lived in southern present-day Pennsylvania, virtually disappeared because of disease and colonial expansion. Although they held their native Susquehanna River against Iroquois assaults until 1675, mortality from epidemic influenza that spread among the Iroquois and New England's Native peoples in 1675 during King Philip's War might have been the decisive factor in the Susquehannock's decline and subjugation. Suffering calamitous losses during the Iroquois wars against the French beginning in 1677, many of the remaining Susquehannock joined the Shawnee and Delaware who were living near present-day Philadelphia between 1677 and 1700.

Further west, in the Great Lakes area, many of the Algonkian speakers and other nations were also affected by the Beaver Wars and colonial expansion. The Potawatomi who lived between Lake Michigan and Green Bay, Wisconsin, were by 1670, expanding south along the western shore of the lake, into Winnebago territory. The Winnebago entered the fur trade in 1665, abandoning their former warlike actions against the western migrating Indian nations. Indeed, Winnebago married Ojibwa, Potawatomi, Sauk, and Fox, all of whom were invaders into Winnebago territory.

New fur trade opportunities and rivalries among Indian nations motivated a shift in inter-group alliances and residence. For example, in 1667 traders reached the Menominee living northwest of Green Bay. After the Menominee entered the fur trade, they quickly abandoned their villages and scattered in small bands. In 1666 the Mascouten, Kickapoo, and Miami shared with some Peoria a large trading village upstream from Green Bay. The fur trade had become so economically important to Native Americans that several tribes that had never lived near each other before came together to live in one trading village.

The nations of the Illinois Confederacy—including the Kaskaskia, the Cahokia, the Peoria, and others—were also displaced as a result of the Beaver Wars and new trade opportunities. According to French reports, the Illinois Confederacy numbered about 100,000 people in the mid-1600s, inhabiting sixty villages in present-day Iowa, Illinois, and Wisconsin. Chequamegon Bay on Lake Superior became a trading center for Illinois trappers, and the Illinois began migrating further north from their original territories. In 1682 French traders built a post at Starved Rock in northern Illinois and attracted nearly 18,000 Illinois, Miami, and Shawnee. At about the same time, the nations of the Illinois Confederacy came under attack by the Iroquois interested in Illinois fur-trading lands. For example, the Espenimkia tribe of the Illinois Confederacy was virtually destroyed by an Iroquois attack. The Iroquois, in search of access to beaver producing areas, continued to invade and attack the Illinois Confederacy villages until the end of the 1600s. By 1700 there remained only about 6,500 members of the Illinois Confederacy.

Further west, in present-day Minnesota, the Chippewa, who were migrating from the east (in part, because of the Iroquois military expansion for fur-bearing territories), invaded Dakota (Sioux) lands. The Sioux and the Chippewa would fight over this land for the next century. In the end, the Chippewa forced many Sioux to migrate onto the Plains, where they adapted to the horse riding and buffalo hunting lifestyle for which they are now well known. The Chippewa ultimately moved into the Minnesota region, where they continued to hunt, trade, and harvest wild rice.

The Southeast.   Unlike the Northeast, where permanent settlements began in the 1620s, the Southeast did not have permanent European settlements until after 1670. Spanish Florida, established at Saint Augustine in 1565, was the exception. The Spanish built a series of Catholic missions for the Indians throughout Florida and present-day Georgia. These missions soon failed because diseases killed the Indians, and English attacks destroyed the remaining missionary efforts in the 1690s. In spite of this initial Spanish settlement, scholars know less about southeastern Indian demography than about the Northeast for most of the 1600s.

In the mid-1660s, yellow fever and smallpox decimated Florida Natives. Measles killed more than 10,000 Florida Natives in 1658, and a smallpox epidemic between 1665 and 1667 affected Natives from Florida to Virginia, with unknown death tolls. As their numbers declined, Native peoples amalgamated despite traditional animosities and linguistic differences. For example, some Algonkian-speaking Weanock joined the Iroquoian-speaking Nottaway in the Virginia Piedmont region before 1700. The once powerful Natchez gave refuge to remnants of other nations that were abandoning their homelands near the coast of the Gulf of Mexico. By 1700 migrating Tunican tribes joined the Natchez villages on the Mississippi River in present-day west Mississippi.

After the 1670 settlement of Charles Town in South Carolina, many tribes, such as the Creek and Cherokee, started to trade with the English. During this period, the English were interested in acquiring slaves for their plantations; they traded guns and other manufactured goods to Indians who accompanied them on slave raids in the interior Indian nations. For example, the Shawnee in the 1680s and 1690s suffered severe losses as a result of English, Chickasaw, and Cherokee slave raids. In particular, the Choctaw, a populous nation that once lived in present-day Mississippi and Louisiana, were decimated during this period by such slave raids. Some traditional districts of the Choctaw Nation were so depleted by slave raids that it is now virtually impossible to reconstruct their original social and political organization. The beleaguered Choctaw found an ally in the French, who established the Louisiana Colony in 1699. The French supplied the Choctaw with guns, which they used to withstand the continuing English-supported slave raids.

Between 1670 and 1710, trade relations between the Indians and the English were dominated by the capture and sale of Indian slaves. Indians, however, did not make very good slaves. Enslaving people in their homeland was difficult because they knew the land and the people much better than their English captors. For this reason, the Indian slaves found it relatively easy to escape and hide. After 1700, the English began to transport Indian slaves to the Caribbean, where escape

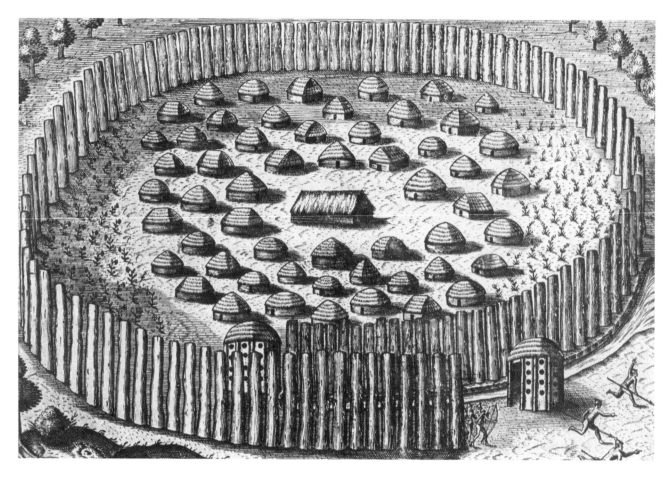

Construction of Fortified Towns among the Floridians. Drawing by Le Moyne, engraving from Theodore de Bry, *America*, part II, 1591, plate XXX. (Courtesy of American Heritage Press)

was more difficult. Thereafter, the English imported slaves from Africa to work the plantations.

The Plains. During the 1600s, the people living on the Plains began to be greatly affected by the northward migration of the horse, which the Spanish had brought to the Southeast and Mexico during the mid-1500s. The horse's ability to travel far and fast eventually transformed the grassy Plains from a nearly vacant zone into an overpopulated area. Nearly constant intergroup strife and horse rustling characterized life on the Plains. As was true of the Northeastern tribes, the Plains peoples soon became dependent on trade goods. Plains tribes traded horses, mules, and tanned hides for firearms, axes, knives, and other tools. French and English demand for horses and mules drove the posthorse Plains economy. Because Plains Natives did not breed horses and mules, they rustled them from each other and from Spanish settlements.

By the late 1600s many formerly horticultural nations began migrating to the Plains area from places farther east. During the 1500s, many of the nations living in the Mississippi Valley had been part of the Mississippi Culture, which built elaborate mounds and ceremonial centers. Some, such as the Caddoan and Siouan nations, had large populations in small towns; they were decimated by the epidemics of the 1500s, however, and by the early 1600s, only small local groups without strong central organization remained. These small tribal groups began feeling the pressure of the expanding eastern trade networks and wars, and encountered the western-moving Indian nations that were forced westward by the colonists and the expansive Iroquois, or Five Nations.

Before 1600, most nations in the Plains area survived through horticultural means. By the late 1600s, the adoption of horses made it possible to raid corn-fields and put pressure on nations that preferred to grow corn and to remain in settled villages. As the horse raids became increasingly effective, more and more of the Indian peoples living on or near the Plains were forced to acquire horses for self-defense and retaliatory raids. This situation led to an intensification of economic raids and revenge attacks among the different nations; peoples with horses had clear advantages in these early skirmishes.

Nevertheless, many nations, such as the Hidatsa, Mandan, and Cheyenne, were reluctant to give up horticulture. While the Cheyenne gradually began to specialize in buffalo hunting and raiding, the Hidatsa and Mandan tried to maintain their villages and horticultural economy. Such tribes' efforts reflected the old Indian traditions more than did the new culture associated with raiding, buffalo hunting, the Sun Dance (an annual world renewal ceremony), warrior societies, and annual tribal hunts, all of which are considered representative of high Plains culture as it developed over the next two centuries. This Plains culture has become the most recognized image of American Indians, even though it does not have a long history and does not represent a long-standing tradition among any Indian nation.

Many Mississippi Valley Indian nations moved westward in the late 1600s. Native migrations from the Great Lakes forced several Siouan-speaking nations, including the Iowa and Chiwere, into the Minnesota and Iowa region. By the 1680s, some of the first Sioux, or Teton Dakota, moved onto the Plains, while most other Sioux remained and fought with the invading Chippewa. The Osage, Caddoan speakers living in present-day western Missouri, continued to grow corn, squash and pumpkins, but turned to replenishing their horses by raiding other Caddoan-speaking nations in present-day Oklahoma. The Hidatsa and Mandan, also Caddoan speakers from old Mississippian mound-building cultures, migrated up the Missouri River, where they began trading horticultural products for European goods by the late 1600s. The Crow, led by a religious leader who claimed he had visions of a new sacred land, left the Hidatsa to wander northward on the Plains. The religious leader took the Crow people on a pilgrimage into the Canadian plains and finally settled in the 1700s in the western and northern Plains, in what is approximately present-day Montana.

Many of the Indian nations that migrated to the southern Plains were Athapascan—Apache and Navajo—hunters and gatherers who had very different traditions from the horticultural peoples moving onto the Plains in the north. The southern Athapascan migrated south from northeastern Canada or Alaska during the thirteenth or fourteenth centuries, and remained big-game hunters and wild-food collectors. They fitted pack-dogs to travois, or small sleds, and carried trade goods between the Pueblo villages on the Rio Grande and the Caddoan horticulturists along the Mississippi Valley.

Southern Athapascan acquired horses from the Spanish, who arrived in 1598. Beginning soon after 1600, Apache, with the aid of horses and Spanish-style lances, dominated the southern Plains. The Apache prospered, grew in number, and divided into several different bands. Jicarilla and Faraon Apache lived on the Canadian River in northeastern New Mexico and the Texas Panhandle. Carlana Apache lived on the Purgatoire River tributary of the Arkansas River in modern-day Colorado, and Cuartelejo Apache inhabited the upper Arkansas River Valley. Paloma Apache resided along the upper Republican River in present-day Nebraska and Lipan Apache migrated over much of what is now Texas. Although they rustled Pueblo and Spanish livestock, Apache peoples traded slaves for stock and other commodities at Taos and Pecos Pueblo, where periodic trading took place.

A few southern Athapascan acquired not only horses, but also sheep, which they learned to pasture and breed. By 1630 the Spanish recognized these Athapascan as "Navajo." With the increase in the standard of living associated with the permanent supply of domesticated mutton, the Navajo population began to increase steadily. The Navajo are now the largest U.S. Indian nation, with nearly 200,000 people.

The Southwest. Although the Apache lived primarily on the southern Plains, by the second half of the 1600s they also traded with and raided Pueblo and Spanish settlements in the Southwest. In 1670 a disease killed many Apache horses. The Apache subsequently migrated into New Mexico, where they depended on hunting and fighting for their survival. By 1672 they began to rustle what they could not purchase. Almost overnight, traditional horse traders became horse raiders. When their traditional Apache trading partners turned into rustlers, residents of five Pueblos—Tajique, Chilili, Quarai, Abó, and Pueblo de los Jumanos—migrated to Pueblo villages along the Rio Grande.

In 1680 most Pueblo peoples used weapons to force Spanish colonists from Indian lands. The Spaniards, along with loyal Pueblos, retreated down the Rio Grande to present-day El Paso, Texas, where their descendants still live.

The collapse of the eastern Pueblo frontier, coupled with the Spanish retreat, removed a military barrier that in effect allowed the Apache to remain on the southern Plains. By 1698 an Apache vanguard migrated westward to the mountains on the present-day Arizona-New Mexico border and would later evolve into eight bands. Meanwhile, Spaniards re-colonized Pueblo territory in 1694, and in 1696, a smallpox epidemic triggered an abortive revolt. Tewa Pueblo people who refused to live under Spanish rule fled west to Hopi First Mesa. As a minority group, the Tewa Pueblo learned the Hopi language and served as interpreters and traders, and assisted in Hopi defense.

The Jemez people defended a mesa-top town until 1695, when they submitted to the Spanish by returning to their fields. In the 1696 growing season, the Jemez joined other Pueblo and rebelled against the Spaniards in the wake of a smallpox epidemic. After slaying resident Spaniards in Jemez pueblo, the Jemez retreated to their mesa-top fortification. After repelling a Spanish attack, they dispersed. Having established close relations with the Navajo between 1680 and 1694, many of the Jemez fled to them. Inasmuch as the Navajo reckon descent through the mother, the children of Jemez women created a new Navajo clan. The refugee Jemez people had great influence on Navajo ceremony, religion, crafts, and horticulture.

Conclusion

Disease and military expansion greatly changed Indian demography and social and political order even before they had direct and sustained contact with Europeans.

During the 1600s the best, although fragmented, evidence of Native Americans is found among the nations of the Plains, Northeast, Southeast, and Southwest. We know very little about the demography of Indian peoples before 1700 in the Great Basin, California, the Pacific Northwest, the Plateau, the Subarctic, and the Arctic regions. In the East, by the late 1600s, very few Native Americans escaped the military turmoil of European expansion. European diseases continued to infect Native Americans and diminished their numbers. By 1700, two centuries of European diseases reduced Native American populations in the Northeast, Southeast, and Southwest to less than one-tenth of what their numbers had been in 1500. Many groups simply disappeared. Those who endured by amalgamating the survivors of villages, towns, and former tribes became much more egalitarian than the populous, socially stratified societies that thrived prior to 1500. The Mississippi Culture, with its full-time artists and priests, had mostly perished from disease and military turmoil. Between 1500 and 1700 so many Native Americans died that they lost a considerable amount of knowledge about their traditional cultures and political

Three Ojibwa grave houses on the Bad River Reservation in Odanah, northern Wisconsin. (Photo by Sarah Loe)

systems; most of what is known about Indian societies is based on documents and knowledge of the post-1700 societies. Because these societies were greatly changed during the period between 1500 and 1700, they only partially reflect the age-old traditions of thousands of years of culture that existed before European arrival.

Henry Dobyns

◆ GEOGRAPHIC AND DEMOGRAPHIC CHANGE DURING THE EIGHTEENTH CENTURY

The eighteenth century brought a wide variety of geographic and demographic changes to the many Native American societies across North America. Numerous diverse cultures had experienced close contact with European colonies since the sixteenth century.

Others were just entering into direct relationships with colonial societies, while many more remained distant from the expansion of European empires. The contest over Indian trade and territory among Spain, France, and England affected all Native American societies in some way before the end of the eighteenth century.

At the beginning of the 1700s the French implemented a strategic plan of encircling the English colonies on the Atlantic coast by creating a chain of Indian alliances and forts along the Mississippi River. In the late 1690s, the French created Louisiana Colony and struggled with the English until the end of the French and Indian War in 1760. The period between the 1690s and the end of the eighteenth century was marked by constant warfare in eastern North America with such campaigns as Queen Anne's War, King William's War, the French and Indian War, and the American War of Independence, as well as considerable intermittent border warfare during times of undeclared war. Warfare and trade relations greatly affected the location and political relations of the Native nations, which managed their affairs and interests within the context of increasingly powerful and competitive colonial governments.

Many changes in the location of Indian peoples were made on their own initiatives and for their own objectives. As the colonies grew more powerful, some Indians acted to protect their economic and trade interests by establishing neutrality and bargaining relations with the rival European colonists, as was the case with the Iroquois and Creek. Other Indian nations sought close trade and political relations with specific European colonies, as did the Cherokee who often sought trade and diplomatic ties with Carolina Colony, or the Ottawa who had long-standing trade ties with the French in New France. In order to develop greater capacities for managing trade and diplomatic relations with the colonists, some nations, such as the Creek and Iroquois, created confederacies and sought to strengthen political and trade relations among themselves. Sporadically throughout the 1700s, the Iroquois stated that they commanded the men of fifty nations, although this was a bluff intended to impress English and French diplomats and military officers. Nevertheless, the confederacy of western Indian nations that the Iroquois led was passed onto other nations, especially after the 1750s, when Iroquois power was declining and the British government openly supported the Iroquois in order to gain trade and indirect diplomatic control over the western Indian nations.

During the 1750s the Delaware and Shawnee increasingly took the initiative in forming a confederacy of Indian nations that fought to prevent westward colonial expansion. During the early 1760s, the Delaware Prophet emerged, preaching that God commanded the Indian nations to unite and drive the Europeans from the continent; only then would prosperity and happiness be restored to the Indian peoples. Pontiac, the Ottawa leader, used the teachings of the Delaware Prophet to muster attacks on the British forts in the Great Lakes area in 1763. Although Pontiac was not able to drive the British out of Indian land, he temporarily convened a military confederacy of western Indian nations. During the 1780s and early 1790s Little Turtle, a Miami war chief, led the western nations. The Indian confederacy resisted U.S. attempts to settle the Ohio and Great Lakes area. After Little Turtle's death, the Shawnee leader Tecumseh and his brother, the Shawnee Prophet, revived the confederacy of Indian nations from 1806 to 1813. After the War of 1812, the Indian confederacy of Ohio and Great Lakes Indians disbanded.

While the eighteenth century did not see major demographic movements among Indian nations, political and economic change greatly affected their economies and political relations. By the beginning of the century, most eastern Indian nations were engaged in trading furs for European manufactured goods, especially guns, powder, metal goods, and textiles. Most tribes became quickly dependent on trade in order to secure newly desired and needed goods, and hence trade became a new way of life. In the Southeast, Indian slaves were sought, but were found difficult to contain; thus, they were exported to the Caribbean Islands, while Black slaves from Africa were imported to the continent to work on tobacco and other plantations. Since interior Indians became victims of slave raids by coastal Indians and their English allies, guns and ammunition soon became necessary, and the eastern nations found that they had to develop trade and diplomatic relations with one or more European colonies to secure a steady supply of guns, powder, ball, and other trade goods.

Epidemics and wars had traumatically reduced Native American groups along the Atlantic seaboard by 1700, but through coalescence and adaptation many refugees from different tribes reorganized themselves into new communities. In the early eighteenth century, Wampanoag and Pequot in southern New England, Chickahominy and Nanticoke in the Chesapeake Bay region, and Catawba and Apalachee in the South managed to maintain a degree of political autonomy while securing stable social and economic relations with neighboring settlements and towns. However, in the Southeast, slave-raiding starting in the 1680s decimated many nations, such as the Shawnee in present-day Kentucky and the Choctaw in present-day Mississippi and Louisiana. The Shawnee Nation was dispersed. Some joined the Delaware near present-day Philadelphia, others joined the Creek Nation in present-day Alabama, and a third group settled for awhile in Georgia, but decided to rejoin the Shawnee in Pennsylvania. The raids on the Choctaw were so severe that the several major groups within their social order were permanently disrupted and Choctaw social and political relations gravitated toward secular, local, and regional organization. Choctaw society was so disrupted by slave raids that it might be impossible for historians to reconstruct the traditional relations of clans, villages, and government.

The Yamasee War of 1715 and the Natchez War of 1729 were the last major struggles of resistance waged by coastal tribes in the eastern woodlands. The Yamasee War started because many Indians incurred debts to English traders, and the traders employed harsh methods, such as taking and enslaving children, in order to satisfy the debts. The powerful Creek Confederacy sought to aid the coastal Yamasee in the war, but when the war ended badly, the Creek turned to a new strategy of balancing diplomatic and trade relations among the English colonies on the east coast, the Spanish in Florida, and the French in Louisiana Colony. The Natchez War (1729) started because the French wished to impose taxes on the Natchez fur trade. The Natchez were one of the few remaining Mississippian culture societies still intact in the early 1700s, and their leader was the sacred priest-leader called the Great Sun. The French, with their Choctaw allies, quickly destroyed the Natchez Nation and captured the Great Sun, who was deported into slavery to the Caribbean Islands with several thousand other Natchez. Some Natchez fled to live with the Chickasaw in present-day northern Louisiana and western Tennessee; others went to live among the Creek in present-day Alabama. The Natchez and Chickasaw thereafter fought a constant war, with several major campaigns waged against the French and Choctaw from 1729 to 1760, when the French were defeated by the English in the French and Indian War.

These wars and slave raids, together with English raids against mission Indians in Spanish Florida in the early 1700s, caused the death of thousands of Indian people and the exportation of thousands more, as slaves, to the West Indies. Some refugees from these southeastern conflicts migrated into the territory of larger Indian nations such as the Creek and Chickasaw. After fighting several battles with North Carolina militia in the early 1710s, the Tuscarora fled North Carolina

and joined their Iroquoian brethren in New York, becoming the sixth nation of the Iroquois Confederacy.

In the mid-Atlantic region, discontent over settlers' encroachment and traders' abuses drove Delaware, Shawnee, Nanticoke, and smaller groups up the Susquehanna River during the 1720s and 1730s. Eventually, most of these Indian migrants resettled in the Ohio River Valley. The Great Lakes and Ohio River region already had become a dynamic world of pan-tribal migration and mixture. Under the influence of French trade, Wyandot, Miami, Potawatomi, Ottawa, and tribes farther west interacted across a vast and fluid network of villages and posts. Intermarriage with French traders created a Métis population, which grew in close association with Indian villagers. When the Seven Years' War erupted between Great Britain and France in 1754, Native American nations in the Great Lakes area entered a long and difficult period of military resistance against the English and, after 1783, against U.S. expansion, which lasted until the end of the War of 1812.

Most interior tribes of the Eastern woodlands experienced a measure of peace and stability during the first half of the eighteenth century. The Iroquois Nations in the Northeast and the Cherokee Nation in the Southeast developed strong trade ties to English colonies, but did not relinquish their avenues to French diplomacy and commerce. During the 1600s, the Iroquois allied themselves to the Dutch and English against the French, but by 1700 the expanding English colonies alerted the Iroquois, who thereafter embarked on policy-neutral diplomatic and trade relations with the French and English colonies. The populous and tribally diverse Creek Confederacy maintained an effective position of neutrality among British, Spanish, and French colonies along its borders. In the lower Mississippi Valley, the powerful Choctaw were highly regarded trade partners and military allies of French Louisiana. The Chickasaw allied themselves with the British and were consequently in continuous conflict with the French and their Indian allies. Even during times of stability and peace, all these large Native American groups suffered population decline from contagious diseases introduced by European settlers and traders. Their involvement in the Seven Years' War and in the American Revolution during the second half of the eighteenth century took an especially heavy toll on the Iroquois and Cherokee peoples.

Geographic and demographic changes occurred in various forms among Native Americans in the eighteenth-century Southwest. By 1696 the Spanish had completed their re-conquest of New Mexico, following

A bent framing for a wigwam at Itasca State Park in northern Minnesota. (Photo by Sarah Loe. Courtesy of the UCLA American Indian Studies Center)

the Pueblo Revolt of 1680. Pueblo communities worked out a stable social and economic relationship with Hispanic settlements. They accepted missionaries into their towns on the condition that they not meddle with traditional beliefs and rituals. The Hopi maintained the greatest degree of independence among Pueblo peoples, destroying the mission town of Awatowi in 1700. Depopulation slowed over the eighteenth century, but diseases continued to plague the Native American populations of the Southwest. The Pueblo and Hispano developed closer ties to the Navajo, Ute, and Apache occupying territory around New Mexico in scattered, mobile bands. The Navajo incorporated sheep-herding into their already diversified livelihood, setting themselves on a course of geographic and demographic expansion. The migration of Comanche onto the southern Plains during the eighteenth century circumscribed colonial expansion in the northern Rio Grande Valley until peace was established in 1786.

The migration of Native American groups to the Great Plains was perhaps the most significant demographic and geographic movement of the eighteenth

century. From the eastern woodlands around Lake Superior, Cheyenne and Lakota Sioux migrated across the Missouri River to the northern Plains. The Sioux and Cheyenne were woodland people who farmed corn, collected wild plants, and hunted, but they soon took up the Sun Dance, buffalo hunting, horse riding, and migratory lifeways characteristic of the Plains culture. From the Rocky Mountains came the Kiowa and Comanche, who eventually populated the southern Plains. These emigrants combined uses of the gun and horse to develop a vibrant culture and economy based on buffalo hunting. Meanwhile, the townspeople who had occupied the lower Missouri River and its tributaries for centuries—Pawnee, Oto, and Mandan, among others—suffered a steady decline in population. The Hidatsa, Arikara, and Crow migrated up the Missouri River and eventually settled near present-day Bismarck, North Dakota. These sedentary horticultural peoples depended heavily on corn production and lived in houses that looked like earthen mounds. They represented the primary form of social and economic life found on the Plains before the introduction of the horse. The migrant Lakota began to raid the corn fields of the sedentary nations, putting considerable economic pressure on them. By the end of the century, the sedentary Indian nations were facing intensive trade pressures from Europeans along with competitive territorial pressures from Cheyenne and Sioux newcomers.

Throughout most of the eighteenth century, other trans-Mississippi Native Americans experienced little or no direct contact with Europeans. Trade goods from the Hudson's Bay Company's expansive Subarctic and northern Plains network began to reach Rocky Mountain and Great Basin societies. Through raiding and trading, these same people also acquired horses. Ute in the southern Rockies and Nez Percé in the Columbia Basin, for example, attained greater mobility in procuring food, fighting enemies, and trading with allies. Contagious diseases introduced by Europeans from different directions undoubtedly affected most Native Americans in the western interior, but migration and intertribal relations were still determined principally by their own design.

During the second half of the eighteenth century, external forces began to reach the Far West from the Pacific Coast. In 1769 Spain established its first mission among California Native Americans at San Diego. Poor living conditions and diseases rapidly took their toll on mission Indians along the California coast, from the Diegueo northward to the Miwok. Expeditions to replace them intimidated interior tribes like the Yokut and Wintun. Throughout the remainder of the eighteenth century, Spanish Franciscan missionaries established missions at locations farther north in California. Thousands of Indians were brought into the missions and induced to become Christians. They worked as laborers to support and build the California missions, and many died from overwork and disease, while many others no longer practiced their traditional cultures.

Russian explorers began sailing along the Alaska coast by 1741 and reported good prospects for trade in seal and sea otter skins. During the 1700s these skins were in high demand in China, where they were used to make clothing. By the 1760s Russian traders and Russian Orthodox priests were extending political and cultural control over the Aleutian Islands and along the southern coastal regions of Alaska. Russian forts and trading establishments extended as far south as present-day northern California. In particular, the Aleut suffered greatly from Russian colonization, and many were forced to hunt and secure furs. Aleutian culture significantly disintegrated under the force of Russian political and cultural domination. Nevertheless, the

Tlingit, living on the Alaska Panhandle, kept their political and cultural independence from the Russians, although the Russian-American Company located its center of operations at New Archangel, present-day Sitka, Alaska, which is near a long-standing Tlingit village. The Tlingit quickly joined in the fur trade with the Russians and added the newfound wealth to their traditional potlatches, where significant quantities of food, tools, art, sacred objects, and symbolic goods were exchanged in ceremonies designed to honor clan ancestors.

In the Pacific Northwest, British and American merchants began commerce with coastal Native Americans for sea otter pelts and other furs. By the 1790s the Chinook, Nootka, and Tlingit were trading regularly with ships from New England and Europe. The Russian-American Company's trade settlements along the Gulf of Alaska drew large quantities of seal and sea otter skins from Native American hunters. The vibrant life of this commercial frontier produced a growing number of people of mixed Native American and Russian descent. Many Alaska Natives converted to the Russian Orthodox religion, as missionaries and churches usually accompanied the establishment of major trade posts.

Meanwhile, in the Eastern Woodlands, Native American societies were facing the aftermath of the American Revolution. The Treaty of Paris (1783) rearranged the geopolitical map of North America more profoundly than any previous agreement made in Europe during the colonial period. The creation along the Atlantic seaboard of a new nation by rebellious English colonies set in motion forces that Native Americans had not experienced before. As the United States asserted power over much of eastern North America, and as European governments wound down their imperial contest over the continent, Indian nations lost their former allies and found themselves face-to-face with an ambitious new republic. Military resistance by Ohio Valley and Great Lakes tribes climaxed in costly defeat by 1794. Many of the Indian nations of the Ohio and Great Lakes area, already immigrants from eastern territories, tried to prevent U.S. expansion across the Ohio River, which the Indians considered a border between themselves and the United States. Several battles were fought in the Indiana and Ohio areas. Nevertheless, the signing of Jay's Treaty by the United States and England in late 1794 changed the diplomatic situation dramatically, and the Indian nations were forced to recognize the United States as the major power in the region. The British agreed not to support the Indian nations, who wished to prevent U.S. occupation of the forts and towns in the Ohio and Great Lakes region.

In the Southeast, the Creek Confederacy, especially the towns in present-day Alabama, allied itself to the Spanish colony in Florida and hoped to resist U.S. territorial expansion. A segment of the Cherokee Nation called the Chickamauga also waged a war of resistance against encroaching settlements and began to migrate west of the Mississippi River during the 1790s. As long as the Chickamauga and Creek had military support from the Spanish, they had access to military supplies that enabled them to resist U.S. efforts to occupy their territory. In 1795, however, the Spanish government turned its attention to the wars in Europe and decided to limit investment in Florida Colony. Like their northern Indian neighbors, the southern Indian nations were forced to sign treaties after 1795 that recognized the United States as the predominant power in the region.

Migration was selected by several Native American societies as a means of preserving their autonomy against U.S. aggression. Following the Revolutionary War, many Iroquois people decided to take permanent refuge in British Canada. Many had joined the British cause during the Revolutionary War and after the war the British offered their Iroquois allies a relatively small tract of land in southern Ontario, which constitutes the present-day Iroquois reserve. Other Iroquois who fought with the colonists during the war stayed on to live in New York within their traditional homeland. Nevertheless, because of increasing impoverishment and U.S. land pressures, by 1796, the Iroquois land base was reduced to a handful of small tracts of land. The once influential Iroquois Nation had to reconcile itself to life under the powerful shadow of the United States.

The movement of many Creek Indians into Florida during the late eighteenth century resulted in the formation of a new tribal group called the Seminole. As early as the 1750s, many Creek and Hitchiti Indians migrated into Florida and ceased to communicate with the Creek Nation. The Seminole, discontented with English colonial relations, formed a loose confederacy and created a new nation. Sizable groups of Shawnee, Delaware, Peoria, and Piankashaw sought social and economic security by migrating across the Mississippi River into Missouri and Arkansas country, on lands offered them by Spanish Louisiana. Southeastern Indian emigrants, especially Choctaw, Tunica, Biloxi, Apalachee, and Coushatta, began settling parts of Louisiana and east Texas in the 1790s.

Encroachment on Native Americans' territory and disruption of their livelihood escalated significantly in eastern North America by the end of the eighteenth century. Epidemic disease continued to besiege Indian societies at varying rates, and demographic and geographic change became increasingly determined by the expansionist policies of the United States. By 1800 the U.S. government began a policy of assimilating Indians into Christianity and farming culture. It was reasoned that if Indians turned to farming they would no longer need large areas of land to carry on their hunting and fur-trading practices. As farmers, Indians would be more willing to sell land to the United States and also enter into citizenship. Missionaries were hired to teach school, religion, farming, and homemaking to the Indians. Some of these first missions were to the Seneca reservations in western New York.

With the Louisiana Purchase of 1803, however, Native Americans across western North America began to face unprecedented challenges and threats. Early in the nineteenth century, the prospect of U.S. expansion across the continent changed early policies of quick assimilation and later focused on removal and reservations. Strategies of adaptation and resistance tested over the eighteenth century, especially migration and consolidation, would serve many of the Native American groups effectively in future struggles for cultural and political survival.

Daniel H. Usner Jr.
Cornell University

♦ INDIAN GEOGRAPHIC DISTRIBUTION, HABITAT, AND DEMOGRAPHY DURING THE NINETEENTH CENTURY

Indian America after 1800

Indian America after 1800 was soon to become a place of constantly relocated displaced-persons camps under military surveillance, located primarily for the benefit of non-Indians. Most of the U.S.-Indian treaties negotiated between 1817 and 1849 dealt with tribal removals to the so-called vacant lands in the West. In 1800, most surviving tribes of the Northeast woodlands were already on their way to reservations west of the Mississippi River or to the extreme northern and western regions of the Great Lakes. Removing a large percentage of the estimated 100,000 Indians east of the Mississippi River did not take place all at once, but proceeded in an evolutionary manner that reflected the historical vagaries of the advancing European-American settlement frontier. The Delaware (or Lenni Lenape)

Indians, who led a seasonal hunting, fishing, and gathering life, met William Penn on the Atlantic Coast in the 1680s. In 1800, however, the tribe was tentatively living in Indiana. Some Delaware were already living in Missouri, from which they were moved successively to Arkansas, Texas, Kansas, and finally Oklahoma. Tribes regularly splintered during this period. In the 1840s some Kickapoo moved to Texas, some to Missouri, and some to Kansas. Very few Northeast groups, such as the remnants of the Five (Six) Nation Iroquois of upstate New York and the Chippewa (Ojibwa) of the lower Great Lakes, remained in part of their original tribal homelands. By 1812 Indian title had been lost in much of Ohio, Indiana, and Illinois. By 1840, Michigan, Wisconsin, Iowa, and Minnesota were largely left open to non-Indian exploitation. An 1842 congressional report listed 82,118 Indians on the frontier who had been "removed west by Government."

Most Indians wound up in John C. Calhoun's creation, the so-called Indian Territory, which originally included Nebraska and Kansas. When reduced in size to present-day Oklahoma, it came to possess the greatest number of Indians of any state. After the period of forced dislocations, Indian Territory had nine times as many tribes as before. Indians moving there encountered a variety of land forms that supported different lifestyles. In the east were the Ozark mountains and plateaus; in the southeast were level plains similar to those of Louisiana, Mississippi, and Alabama; and in the rest of the territory were the gradually rising plains from the Central Lowlands west to the Great Plains and the High Plains of the western half of the Oklahoma Panhandle.

The first tribes to be exiled to Oklahoma were the five nations of the Southeast: the Cherokee, Creek, Chickasaw, Choctaw, and Seminole. Their removal has become the symbol of American attitudes toward Indians in general. While the numerous southern coastal tribes had mostly disappeared by 1800, the large and adaptive tribes of the southern piedmont and mountainous areas approached the new century with some confidence. Nevertheless, an 1802 agreement between the new federal government and the state of Georgia would be used by an aggressive frontier culture as the club to force out these five "civilized" tribes by the late 1830s.

At the turn of the nineteenth century in Texas, California, and the Gila and Rio Grande River areas of Arizona and New Mexico, the Spanish continued to interact with quite disparate Indian societies in 1800. The ancient inhabitants of the Southwest had evolved characteristic cities and farm communities, or pueblos. On the outskirts of these stable communities lived the Navajo and the even more nomadic Apache and Comanche peoples. In Texas, the nomadic Plains Indians met the wandering gatherers of the deserts of southern Texas. Relying particularly on Pueblo Indian allies, Spanish officials tried to restrain the nomadic groups. The marauding nomadic tribes had, for their part, found the Spanish and their Indian allies to be unending sources of revenue. The Pueblo Indians paid lip service to Spanish rule and religion, and then did what they pleased.

This was certainly not the case in 1800 for the Indians of California whose lives had long centered on the dependable supply of acorns gathered from groves of oak trees. Starting in 1769, the Spanish were systematically assaulting the peaceful and sedentary California Native peoples along the coast through the founding of church missions and military presidios as far north as the San Francisco area. Friars and soldiers combined to impose a penitentiary-like existence on many California Indians. Some interior tribes moved east to avoid both the mission-induced epidemics and the near-slavery of mission life. In 1800 there were indications that their newly acquired equestrian skills and newly found love of horse meat would energize the interior tribes of California to resist further white aggression. However, the northern California gold strike of 1848 doomed the California Indians within a decade.

North of California, the fishing life of the Indians of the Pacific Northwest (Oregon and Washington) was hardly touched by any European menace in 1800. In 1805 the Lewis and Clark expedition would end Northwest Indian isolation, and by the 1850s survivors of epidemics and wars would already be relegated by the Americans to military supervision on small reservations.

The Lewis and Clark expedition also initiated U.S. claims to the Plains. For several decades before Americans could appear in force, however, Indian life on the Plains would be greatly enriched by European artifacts. With horses acquired from the Spanish borderlands in the Southwest and guns gained from Europeans and Americans through the fur trade, Plains Indians would revel for a full generation as lords of the lands between the Mississippi River and the Rockies. Many Indians, including the Flathead, Kutenai, or Nez Percé, living in the Plateau area between the Rocky Mountains and the California Mountains also participated in this Plains lifestyle. It must be stressed that most of the tribes enjoying this lifestyle were originally immigrants, and some, such as the Dakota and Cheyenne, had fled misery caused ultimately by the westward movement of the Americans. The early nineteenth century for these fugitive groups was simply a period of rest before they would again be uprooted. By the 1870s they would be subjected to American rule, often on reservations quite far from their Plains homelands.

A number of Indians had met very few Europeans by 1800. These were the ill-defined groups, such as the Paiute, who lived in the quite inhospitable Great Basin region. That harsh and stingy environment had long forced them to live the simplest of any Indian tribe as they moved constantly in search of food. Additionally, their lot had worsened by 1800 because Plains, Plateau, and Southwest marauding Indians all raided the Great Basin looking for captives to trade for Spanish and American goods. Nevertheless, in 1800 nobody desired their land, and they would not be elbowed aside by covetous Americans for another half a century.

In summary, Indian America circa 1800 witnessed flourishing Native American lifestyles in the Southeast, the Plains, the Northwest, and the Plateau areas. In the Southwest and the western part of the Northeast, Indian lifestyles were under attack but still so strong that Spanish and American leaders feared their power. In California, however, Indian lifestyles were under heavy assault, and very few Indians could be found east of Ohio.

Population

The most important reason for the success of the continuing assault on Native America, most scholars agree, was the terrible number of deaths resulting from the introduction of European diseases. In 1837, the Mandan, who were agriculturists of the Missouri River, were dramatically reduced by smallpox from 1,600 to 31. The Blackfeet, Comanche, and Kiowa tribes of the Great Plains also suffered similar disastrous epidemics. Seventy-four percent of 220 Hopi who refused Western medicine in an 1898 smallpox epidemic died. Such high mortality rates have been verified by comparison with various epidemics striking the Amazon Indians in the twentieth century. This disease fueled depopulation, constituting the most important part of the seizure of Indian lands in what has been called the European and American conquest of Native America.

Scholars traditionally estimated that north of the Rio Grande the aboriginal Indian population never exceeded more than one million people. Today some important scholars argue that the population was many times larger than one million. Even so, by 1800 the "widowed"

Indian population seemed close to the older traditional figures. A conservative estimate by the Office of Indian Affairs (1943) projected an 1800 Indian population of around 600,000. Jedediah Morse, who was sent by the federal government on a fact-finding tour of Indian tribes, carefully collected information for his *Report on Indian Affairs* (1822) and estimated the Indian population to be slightly over 471,000, not counting California. The vast dislocation of Indians in the East and Plains, the extraordinary decline of California Indians, and the demoralization among all Indians forcibly relocated, initiated a sharp decline in the Indian population in the nineteenth century.

Many of the northeastern tribes moved west of the Mississippi, and Kansas, as part of the northern half of Indian Territory, was a temporary home for many displaced Eastern Indians. Although the western two-thirds of Kansas belongs to the Great Plains, the many hills and valleys of the eastern third was familiar to these exiles. Some of the most prominent of the nearly thirty tribes to settle there were the Wyandot and Shawnee from Ohio, Miami (with the Wea and Piankashaw) from Indiana, Kaskaskia and Peoria from Illinois, Ottawa and Potawatomi from Michigan, Kickapoo, Sauk, and Fox from Wisconsin, and some Cherokee from Tennessee. In the early 1850s both pro- and anti-slavery factions agreed that these Indians must be pushed out of Kansas and Nebraska. In punishing the Five Civilized Tribes for joining the Confederacy in the American Civil War, the United States acquired land in Oklahoma to relocate Kansas tribes. Some of these Indians (Shawnee, Wyandot, and Ottawa) were fortunate in 1867 in finally being placed in the extreme northeast part of Oklahoma where a scenic beauty combines with fertile soil. On the other hand, the numerous members of the Osage, Kansa, and Ottawa tribes were nearly halved as a result of difficulties suffered under this second Trail of Tears.

California Indian population declined from an estimated 300,000 to approximately 20,000—a decline of 90 percent—between 1770 when the Spanish missions started and 1900. Although the Catholic priests in charge of the California missions were often of good intent, living conditions in the missions caused lethal diseases to flourish. By the end of Mexican occupation (1846–1847), the Native California population was down to around 150,000. The Gold Rush decade quickly added to the death toll in a brutal (even genocidal) fashion as the number of Indians quickly dropped to 50,000.

By 1850 the nation's entire Indian population, according to the U.S. Census, dropped to around 400,000.

By 1900, the U.S. Census estimated a further drop in the Indian population to only 237,000 Indians, not counting those in Alaska. In short, there was a marked decline in the Indian population in the nineteenth century, and the end of the century marked the Indian population's nadir.

Land Hunger and Racism

Just as disease and relocation accounted for the decline in Indian population, land hunger and racism were the major reasons for mistreatment of Indians. Americans and European immigrants wanted the land that Indians had lived on for millennia. Called the Westward Movement by historians and rationalized by participants as Manifest Destiny, the central thrust of nineteenth-century America was the acquisition of as much land as possible, by any means possible. The federal government revealed an array of techniques for acquiring Indian land: secretly paying and gifting leaders; feting Indian delegates; bringing Indian leaders to Washington, D.C.; establishing stores with liberal credit guaranteeing that Indians would become deeply in debt; dealing with minority chiefs; buying land from groups that did not actually control it; deliberately withholding annuity payments to force negotiations or compliance; allowing non-Indians to squat illegally on Indian land and to harass Indian farmers and cattlemen; permitting whites to acquire individually owned Indian land (allotments) by any method; and—behind every other technique—the use of naked power. In short, Indians may have delayed the inevitable, as Kenekuk did for the Indiana Kickapoo, but in the end they were forced off their land.

Frontier ruffians and entrepreneurs fueled the Jacksonian Indian removal policy. Few tribes were left unaffected by such a harsh policy. Even tribes such as the Wyandot (Huron), which included many white people through marriage, was noted for its long and sincere acceptance of Christianity, and individual land-allotments, and its inclusion of many American citizens, still suffered inequality, impoverishment, and settler depredations in Kansas. Some tribes driven out of Kansas by such mistreatment, such as the Kickapoo, Wea, and Piankashaw, had already undergone similar processes elsewhere.

By 1816, the defeats of Tecumseh, the Shawnee leader, and the Red Stick faction of the Creek Nation in the War of 1812 guaranteed that there would be no permanent Indian barrier to American expansion. American frontier pressures splintered tribes into conflicting factions. Some segments voluntarily moved west. Some entire Indian groups would be forced to move because of battle-hardened Indian enemies who were better equipped militarily. For example, the Chippewa (Ojibwa) continued successfully to push north, west, and south against Indian enemies in the first half of the nineteenth century. More generally, however, tribes were simply trying to get out of the way of lawless American frontiersmen.

Any national or individual guilt over how Indians lost their lands was partially assuaged by the fallacious arguments that Indians had wasteful ideas of land ownership and no concepts of personal property. It was almost universally accepted that Indians must stop roaming over vast territories and settle down on a reasonable number of acres that could be farmed. In fact many Indians did farm and, indeed, Indian farming before allotment was growing at a substantial rate. Such farming generally was carried out on individual plots with tribal recognition of each family's plot of ground. Americans assumed, nevertheless, that Indians had to substitute an individualistic concept of property for their ancient communal concept of ownership. In fact, many Indians, particularly with the passage of time, did possess concepts of personal property. The Yakima and Flathead Indians of the Plateau, for example, had a workable system of individual property in place before the arrival of the forced allotment period.

In any case, the argument that Indians could not understand the European concept of private property was a red herring. Mexico in the 1830s believed in private property in the European sense, but that did not keep America from coveting its Texas and California lands. President James Polk almost took all of Mexico. National and individual land hunger explains in great part the despoliation of Indian lands.

Racism joined with avarice to guarantee that Indians would not be able, in general, to live the lives of frontier farmers. What Chief Justice Taney in the *Dred Scott* decision declared of Blacks was true in practice for Indians: they possessed "no rights which the white man was bound to respect."

The history of many of the Sauk and Fox Indians in Kansas (originally part of the Indian Territory) is typical of Indians pushed out of an area even though they were making efforts to live like typical westerners (see maps of Indian Territory in Oklahoma section of Chapter 3). After the Indians accepted personal allotments of land, speculators defrauded hapless Indians of their property, and many of the successful Indians were coerced into selling and moving to an Indian Territory reservation.

The key legal consideration that forced most Indians to leave Kansas (as well as other states) were the difficulties involved in becoming state citizens. For example, tribal leaders could suddenly face state laws levying huge fines for anyone functioning as the leader of the tribe. President Andrew Jackson, who served as president from 1828 to 1836, knew what he was doing in 1829 when he gave Indians only two options: move west or become subject to the selective and discriminatory enforcement of state laws. Observers knew that Indians believed that no state would place them on an equal footing with U.S. citizens. Georgia, for example, forbade the Cherokee from mining their own gold, and many states refused to allow Indians to testify against non-Indians. As late as 1908, Oklahoma passed a law declaring that all adult Indians were incompetent to legally manage their farms. The federal government, for its part, refused to give treaty-guaranteed protection against exploitation and cheating. Indeed, President Jackson had earlier negotiated several questionable Indian treaties, and his refusal to enforce an 1832 ruling by the U.S. Supreme Court (*Worcester v. Georgia*) ensured Georgian domination over the Cherokee.

Inevitably, the American commissioner would appear to make an offer for land that could not be refused. By every method possible, tribes would be forced to cede—or appear to cede—their lands. Chief Spotted Tail of the Sioux is supposed to have tongue-in-cheeked the quip, "Why does not the Great Father put his red children on wheels, so he can move them as he will?" Indians were not just pushed off one parcel of land; they were forced to relocate on different assigned lands. These reserved lands in time would then be either totally eliminated or taken away piecemeal by new treaties (or by negotiation after 1871), unjust state laws, or individual acts of barbarism. Shortly after the end of the nineteenth century, most of the remaining lands were lost through a process called allotment, in which Indians were forced to live on small parcels of privately owned land. By 1900, most tribes had lost their communal lands, and most Indian people would soon lose the allotted land given them.

By the turn of the twentieth century, the continuing decline of the total Indian population and the continuous loss of most of the valuable Indian lands reinforced the idea that the Indian was disappearing. No one realized that the low point of Indian population figures had been reached and that Indians would multiply dramatically in the twentieth century. Certainly, no such renaissance was possible in land ownership—the Indian land heritage was forever gone, and oftentimes the old lifestyle tied to that land was only a memory

among tribal elders. Of the nearly three billion acres of pre-Columbian Indian America, Indians owned only 48 million acres, a great deal of it located on unproductive land, in 1934.

Representative Case Studies

The Abenaki (Penobscot and Passamaquoddy) of New England are an example of New England tribe members who barely maintained themselves on small parcels of their old land. In 1786 they refused to sign a treaty with Massachusetts, but in 1794 they ceded the state more than one million acres. By 1820, the Abenaki owned only a few thousand acres. By 1850, they were confined to two separate villages. Some were even forced out of villages in Vermont by whites and fled to relatives in Canada. It would be 130 years before the federal government paid them $81.5 million for land taken illegally.

The Miami-speaking Indians are an Eastern tribe, most of whose members were forcibly relocated in the West, although a significant number were allowed to stay on allotted land in Indiana. The Piankashaw, a small Miami-speaking tribe, had begun selling their Indian lands as early as 1804 and had been moved as prisoners of war in 1814 to Missouri. In 1832, the Piankashaw had to cede their lands in Missouri and go to Kansas. The tribe then was moved again to the Indian Territory. Another closely related Miami-speaking group, the Wea, ceded their lands in Indiana in 1820 and 1824. The Wea then moved to Missouri and like the Piankashaw were forced to emigrate to Kansas. Large groups of the Miami left Indiana at various times beginning in the early 1830s. After several treaties failed to convince the remaining Miami to emigrate (infuriating President Jackson), their head chief suddenly announced in 1838 that the last part of the tribe was ready to move. The rapid influx of hostile squatters into Miami areas seems to have been the final motivator. Another chief skillfully procrastinated until rather good terms had been negotiated for the removal of the tribe and for the sale of tribal lands. Families and relatives of the principal chiefs, and most of the mixed-bloods, were exempted from the movement west by the terms of the treaty. Although only the presence of the army insured the movement to Kansas of the less-influential Miami, the 1846 exodus was more humane in general than many such forced migrations. The reluctant Miami were also convinced by the fact that government annuities would now be paid only to Indians in the new western lands. A few years later they were forced to move again, this time to the Oklahoma Indian Territory.

The fate of the Catawbas, a Siouan-speaking tribe of the coastal Carolinas, illustrates how some minuscule Indian groups survived in the southern coastal region. Although in 1763 the British Crown had given them 144,000 fertile acres, by 1800 disease had so decimated the tribe that they could offer no resistance to white encroachment. After South Carolina purchased the 144,000 acres in 1840, a number of Catawbas moved to the Indian Territory. So many Catawbas would not leave the state, or returned after being unpleasantly rejected from North Carolina, that South Carolina started a 630-acre reservation in 1841. That miniature Catawba state lasted until 1962, when a billion-dollar court claim filed by the Catawbas kept the issue of the treatment of Indians in the Jacksonian Era alive.

The 1830s Trail of Tears that involved the Five Tribes of the Southeast is a rather well known example of the personal and communal tragedies that accompanied the many forced deportations of Indians during most of the nineteenth century. By the end of the 1830s, the Southeast had lost 60 to 90 percent of the estimated 150,000 Indians counted at the start of the decade. The history of the Southeastern Indians represents the most thoroughgoing application of the Jacksonian removal policy.

The Cherokee, whose unhappy relocation from Alabama, Georgia, and Tennessee to the West seems to have been the worst migratory experience in American history, saw the first group leave to present-day Arkansas after an 1808 treaty. Another Cherokee land cession and emigration took place between 1817 and 1819. The state of Georgia increasingly insisted that the federal government live up to the Compact of 1802 in which Georgia gave up the territory that became Alabama and Mississippi in return for the federal government's help in extinguishing Indian title to land within the state. At the same time, Andrew Jackson emphasized the "Indian must move west" policy, which had been enunciated in 1824 by President Monroe and accepted by his successor, John Quincy Adams, as the only solution to the Indian situation. Indeed, as early as 1804, at Thomas Jefferson's request, Congress gave the president the power to exchange lands west of the Mississippi River for ceded Indian lands east of the river.

Faced with this long history of antagonism, a small group of Cherokee signed the Treaty of New Echota in 1835, exchanging all Southeast Cherokee lands for land in southeast Oklahoma. Although 15,000 Cherokee signed a petition denouncing the treaty, the U.S. government proceeded to force the Cherokee out. In the summer of 1838, the U.S. Army rounded up and imprisoned in stockades individual Cherokee after burning their homes and crops. In the suddenness of the attack, parents and their children often became separated. Water and food were at a premium in the stockades. Leaving late in the fall, some detachments were delayed as much as six months on the 800-mile journey west. In traveling to their new homes in the winter of 1838–1839, between one-fourth and one-third of the 13,000 reluctant émigrés died. Meeting the survivors in Indian Territory were the "Old Settlers," or the 1808 Cherokee group, recently ejected by whites from their Arkansas homes.

Only about one thousand Cherokee in western North Carolina—most of whom descended from Cherokee who had accepted American citizenship and 640 acres of land in the 1819 treaty—were not forced west by General Winfield Scott. Along with some who escaped detection and some who returned over the years, this 1819 group became the present Eastern Cherokee of the Great Smoky Mountains.

All the other Southeast tribes suffered similar fates. The Choctaw Nation of southern Mississippi and Alabama was the first to go west, leaving over three years (1831–1834) in parties of 500 to 1,000. Hundreds died from exposure to winter blizzards, cholera epidemics, and lack of necessary supplies. The death rate in the new environment continued to be high for some years.

Two Southeast tribes fought back. In the Creek War of 1836, General Winfield Scott had to capture and shackle the Indian leaders. On the way to Oklahoma, the sinking of a steamboat cost 300 Creek lives. The usual diseases, hunger, and exposure also claimed a large number. Over 20 percent of the 15,000 Creek died within a short period as a result of exposure and the unhealthy conditions in the new homeland. Seminole in Florida fought the Second Seminole War (1835–1842) to protest migration. In the end, however, 90 to 95 percent of the Seminole were removed.

Historians consider the forced migration of the Chickasaw of northern Mississippi and Alabama as the least lethal among the Southeast tribes. The Chickasaw made the best financial arrangements concerning the sale of their ancient lands. Even so, they suffered the usual deprivations and epidemics on the journey. For several years, the Chickasaw lived in tents in immigrant camps. They found that hostile Plains tribes (Kiowa and Comanche) and marauding Shawnee and Kickapoo Indians had made the assigned area nearly uninhabitable for a decade.

Unlike the Five Tribes, the California Indians were often of marked pacifist tendencies. Miwok and Yokut carried on an effective hit-and-run guerrilla war in the 1830s against the Mexicans, but this military expertise was atypical. California Indians were pushed aside early. In addition, Indians in California lacked any legal control of land, for neither Spain nor Mexico acknowledged Indian land ownership. The secularization of the Catholic missions in 1834 benefited the Indians not a whit. When in 1851 and 1852 the Indians' negotiation with the federal government led to treaties promising 7 million acres of reservation lands, the Californians responded so violently that Congress rejected the treaties. Nevertheless, the lands ceded in those rejected treaties were considered valid cessions. One militarily adept tribe, the Hupa, did indeed gain land in their homeland. However, the participants in the 1870s Modoc War in northern California found themselves exiled to Oklahoma. The Yokayo Pomo found a new secure home only because they paid for it out of their own funds. When reservations began to appear in the 1880s in California, the Mission Indians found that their reservations in southern California were practically worthless because of an inadequate water supply. The Ohlone of the San Francisco Bay Area illustrate the severity of Indian decline in California. From a populous group possessing some thirty to forty permanent villages in the years before the Spanish arrival in 1768, the Ohlone could be found only as parts of small multi-Indian nation ghetto-like villages by the 1860s. By 1900 all communal Ohlone life had ceased (for more detail, see the California section of Chapter 3).

Almost all Great Plains Indians had a history different from such people as the Ohlone, who from time immemorial lived in just one fixed locale. In the late seventeenth century the Cheyenne, for example, were a farming people in the northeast and north-central parts of Minnesota. By the 1750s, they had moved (under Sioux pressure) both south to the Minnesota River area and west to the Sheyenne River of North Dakota. By 1780 they were buffalo hunters in South Dakota. At the beginning of the 1800s, they were on the Cheyenne River at the southwestern corner of South Dakota. Under constant pressure from Indian enemies they moved even farther west to the upper branches of the Platte River. There in the Rocky Mountains they became completely involved in the nomadic horse culture. By 1851, the Southern Cheyenne lived on the Arkansas River in southern Colorado and the Northern Cheyenne lived at the headwaters of the Platte and Yellowstone rivers. After the Medicine Lodge Council of 1867, the United States assigned them a reservation in western Oklahoma. A well-publicized desertion in 1878 of some 300 Northern Cheyenne under Dull Knife

and their continuing escape from some thirteen thousand pursuing U.S. troops caused an embarrassed U.S. government to allow the Northern Cheyenne to settle in Montana, while the Southern Cheyenne stayed in Oklahoma (see also the Plains section of Chapter 3).

Like the Plains Indians, the dramatically reduced number of Plateau Indians of western Oregon and Washington, Idaho, and Montana struggled in several wars to save their lands. By the 1850s, however, they began to be placed on reduced portions of their former lands. The Americans, by then, succeeded in building a wall between Indians in the eastern parts of Oregon and Washington and whites in the fertile valleys near the coast. The Cayuse Indians, one prominent Plateau tribe, had first brought on the wrath of the Americans in 1847 by killing a missionary (Marcus Whitman), his wife, and twelve others. A vigilante army wreaked havoc on the Cayuse. A year after the 1855 Walla Walla Treaty council, a general war broke out between most of the Plateau Indians and the United States. In essence, the Indians wanted their lands back, but the Cayuse were unable to keep their Walla Walla Valley and had to move to the Umatilla Reservation. Disease and drink continued to undermine the tribe. When settlers noticed the beautiful grazing land on the Umatilla Reservation, the reservation was reduced in 1886 by about one-fourth.

While relatively few readers may know about the Cayuse and their troubles, many among the reading public know about the 1864 Long Walk of the Navajo, the culmination of a long period of hostility between Navajo and U.S. society. Previously the Navajo had come into constant conflict with Spanish and then Mexican slave catchers. The Americans continued the hostile Hispanic approach when they arrived in the late 1840s. In 1858, the Bonneville Treaty drastically reduced the size of the area that the Navajo considered theirs. In 1860 one thousand Navajo unsuccessfully attacked Fort Defiance, located in the heart of their country. In 1862 General Carleton arrived with a column of troops from California, bringing with him the Californian Indian extermination policy. Carleton ordered Kit Carson and the New Mexico Volunteers to move against the Navajo, and in early 1864 Carleton's scorched earth policy led to the surrender of the Navajo bastion of Canyon de Chelly. The Navajo were walked under duress 800 miles to a forty-square-mile reserve at Fort Sumner (Bosque Redondo), New Mexico. Ten percent of 2,500 Navajo died in a March 1864 convoy to Fort Sumner. Whites enslaved stragglers and captured their livestock. Absolutely no mercy was shown the trekking Navajo.

Plains social dance, 1893. (Photo by J.A. Anderson. Courtesy of South Dakota State Historical Society)

Some 9,000 Navajo (and 500 Mescalero Apache) herders and hunters were to be made into farmers. At Fort Sumner crops failed because of lack of water, alkaline soil, and hordes of grasshoppers. Available wood was five to eighteen miles away; the local Comanche Indians were hostile; and inadequate government financial support led to starvation and suffering. Conditions were so bad that the Santa Fe, New Mexico newspaper publicized the fort's more inhumane shortcomings. For such reasons, the government in 1868 allowed the Navajo to return to a portion (10 percent) of the hills and mesa of their old homeland. Ten years later, more land was added to the reservation, the first of many additions made to a tribe whose population began to rise dramatically. While the Navajo were quite pleased with these additions, the neighboring Hopi reservation saw with chagrin that they had become completely surrounded by the Navajo and their herds.

Besides the Navajo Apache, most of the other Apache of the Southwest were militarily inclined Indians. Their homeland, Apacheria, was the last Indian area to lay down its arms. Because the Apachean-speaking tribes

of the Southwest were not a centralized group, their history is accordingly complex. The Mescalero Apache of southeastern New Mexico, Texas, and the Chihuahua and Coahuila areas of Mexico were placed first on two tiny reservations in Texas. When vigilante Texans vigorously objected, the Apache were moved to safety in Oklahoma. In 1862, some five hundred Mescalero complied with an order to join the Navajo on the Pecos River wasteland at Bosque Redondo. Most soon deserted. A decade later, they were moved to reservations in south central New Mexico near Fort Stanton. For a time, the Jicarilla Apache also lived there. In 1922, Congress finally did for the Mescalero Reservation what Spain never did: it confirmed the Indians' title to their land.

Through administrative indecision, the Jicarilla Apache of northeastern New Mexico were, in 1873, the only New Mexico tribe not living on a reservation. Only in 1887 did the Jicarilla finally get a reservation that annoyed neither Washington, D.C., local New Mexican whites, nor the Jicarilla. Of course, it was still a most wrenching move, since it was a bit west of the historic

Jicarilla home and most of the valuable lands were already owned by non-Indian farmers and ranchers.

The various groups comprising the Western Apache began to receive reservations in 1871 and 1872, although keeping them on the reservations to the east of Phoenix was a constant problem. Discovery of gold in their territory in 1863 began the troubles between the Americans and the Tonto Apache. However, the more northerly White Mountain and Cibecue Apache remained, rather uneasily, at peace.

Particularly hard to keep on any reservation were the Chiricahua Apache of southern New Mexico and Arizona, who lived just west of the Mescalero. The Chiricahua first had run into problems when tough silver and gold miners flooded their country in 1852. For a while, the Chiricahua had a reservation in the extreme southeastern corner of Arizona abutting the international line. Then the American government tried to move them into the quite different environment of the San Carlos Reservation on the Gila River in Arizona, where the Western Apaches were living. Discovery of coal brought intrusive miners, and whites seized water rights on the Gila River. Such difficulties led to more than two decades of war (1860–1886) against the Americans under leaders such as Mangas Coloradas, Cochise, and Geronimo. After a final sixteen-month flight (1885–1886), they were captured and treated as prisoners of war. They were punished by being sent to Florida, then to Alabama, and finally to Oklahoma. Later, in 1913, most surviving Chiricahua chose to go to the Mescalero Reservation rather than become allottees in Oklahoma.

The history of the Yuman (or Quechan) tribe also represents the treatment accorded a hostile military group of the Southwest. In 1884, a reservation (Fort Yuma) of 45,000 acres of land on the California side of the Colorado River was established. As usual, the tract included only a small portion of the territory the tribe had previously controlled, and contained a good portion of land unfit for farming. The reservation was allotted, or divided into individual portions, in 1893. The usual governmental mismanagement, Indian hostility to agricultural pursuits, and white cupidity led to many Indians not receiving the ten-acre allotment, at least not in the valuable irrigable area.

By the 1870s, there were no more places to exile Indians when whites wanted their lands. Some principle for concentrating Indians on smaller areas was needed to augment the reservation policy. As seen in the Yuman case, an old technique could be used to separate the Indians from most of their good land.

Many of the sixty treaties concluded between 1853 and 1857 called for the allotment of tribal lands. In 1887, after eight years of congressional debate, President Grover Cleveland signed the Dawes General Allotment Act into law. The president was given the authority to subdivide communal Indian land into private ownership of individual plots, a practice sometimes referred to in legal language as "fee simple ownership." The traditional plot of a homesteader (160 acres) was given to the head of a family and smaller plots were awarded to others. Acreage was doubled on reservations suited only for grazing. A group could be punished as were the recalcitrant Kickapoo in Indian Territory, who were only assigned eighty acres each. The land so awarded could not be sold for twenty-five years. In general, only some northern Plains and Southwest Indians escaped allotment.

Allotment was supposed to guarantee the assimilation of Indians into the American mainstream. Instead, it led to permanent underclass status as Indian real estate began to shrivel in three ways during the allotment era. Outside pressures and internal weaknesses combined to encourage tribes to lease out communal tribal lands. For example, in the early 1880s seven cattlemen had leases on the Cheyenne and Arapaho Reservation in Oklahoma ranging in size from 140,000 to 570,000 acres. More ominously, unallocated reservation lands were declared surplus and put up for sale to non-Indians. In addition, laws had been passed allowing many Indians to sell their land earlier than the original twenty-five year no-sale period. In 1891 alone, one-seventh (17.4 million acres) of all remaining Indian lands were lost. In 1881, 155 million acres were Indian owned; in 1900, this number dropped to about 78 million. Land ownership figures, however, are misleadingly high. When it was noticed that a large percentage of Indian land was held by women, orphans, children, and incapacitated males, a law was passed in 1891 allowing these groups to lease their allotted land. Thus, quite quickly reservations often had the majority of their acres leased to non-Indians. In the decades after the 1887 allotment law, Indians lost at least two-thirds of all their landholdings. Ninety percent of the acres originally allotted in Oklahoma are no longer owned by Oklahoma Indians.

Originally, intense opposition from the Five Tribes in Indian Territory left them exceptions to the Dawes Act. Nevertheless, between 1897 and 1902 the Dawes Commission forced them to accept allotment, and today Oklahoma has no reservations. Congress began to open up the Indian Territory (Oklahoma) to non-Indian settlers early. In fact, a number of trespassers were already "booming" the rich lands while waiting for the federal government to legalize their squatter actions. In 1889, President Benjamin Harrison opened up nearly two million acres of land in the "Oklahoma District" in central Oklahoma. On 22 April 1889, the army supervised people recklessly seeking homesteads in an area known for its fertility and which in time produced great petroleum wealth. One hundred thousand non-Indians participated in the 5.7-million-acre Cherokee (plus Pawnee and Tonkawa "surplus" land) Outlet Run on 16 September 1893. The model for these nearly instantaneous transfers of land from Indian to individual non-Indian settler was the earlier opening of the rich Iowa farm lands on 1 May 1843 (with a second run in 1845) of what had once been the domain of the Sauk and Fox. Similar Oklahoma "runs" opened up 868,000 acres of Iowa, Sauk and Fox, and Potawatomi-Shawnee lands on 22 September 1891; the 3.5-million-acre Cheyenne-Arapaho areas on 19 April 1892; and the 85,000-acre Kickapoo land in Oklahoma on 23 May 1895. In 1901, the 3.2 million acres of the Kiowa-Comanche and the Wichita-Caddo reservations were opened, and 170,000 persons registered for a drawing of 13,000 quarter-sections.

The imperative to force Indian cession of lands—which lay behind the allotment principle—also led Congress in 1889 to break up the Great Sioux Reservation of North and South Dakota into six smaller reservations: Pine Ridge, Rosebud, Cheyenne River, Standing Rock, Lower Brule, and Crow Creek. In 1851, at Fort Laramie, the Dakota Sioux signed a treaty defining the boundaries of their domain. In 1868, a new Fort Laramie treaty reduced the reservation to give U.S. miners access to Montana's gold. After Custer's defeat in 1876, the Sioux were punished by having the western part of their land, which includes the Black Hills, sliced off the reservation. In 1889, another eleven million acres were lost.

Another large group of Indians who had to accept the same allotment treatment in 1889 was the Chippewa of Minnesota. Through the years, the Chippewa of the Lake Superior region were forced to cede huge areas, including a large section of west central Wisconsin and east central Minnesota in 1837, most of northern Wisconsin in 1842, and the northeastern portion of Minnesota in 1854. Civil War era treaties limited the Chippewa of Minnesota to a number of large reservations where the land was to be allotted. In 1889, six Chippewa reservations had to cede land to the government, which in turn sold the land to non-Indians with the proceeds held in trust for the tribe. The individual Chippewa were given the choice of either accepting allotments on the original reservation or relocating to the White Earth Reservation and taking allotments there.

A similar rapid disappearance of land can be seen in the history of the Comanche, another Plains tribe. The Treaty of the Little Arkansas (1865) allowed these non-Apache Plains nomads to retain 30 million acres. Then, just two years later, in the Medicine Lodge Treaty, the United States bowed to Texan objections by cutting Comanche land back to 3 million acres. By 1901, other cessions had reduced the Comanche tribal estate to 1 percent of the 1865 area.

One Plains tribe landed on its feet, despite land cessions, frequent forced relocations, and allotment. Challenged by both eastern immigrant and Plains tribes, the once-powerful Osage had little ability to resist American pressure. In a series of treaties in 1808, 1818, 1825, and 1870, the Osage watched the ground disappear from under them. In 1872 they had to leave Kansas for Oklahoma, a removal so traumatic that nearly 50 percent of the tribe died between 1877 and 1884. Then it was discovered that the bluestem grass covering their new acres provided excellent grazing, and that the ground below contained oil. Just as important, Osage intransigence allowed them to reserve all mineral rights for the tribe as a whole, and this communal factor protected a great deal of the wealth flowing in. In forty years, the Osage received about $300 million in royalties. Finally, they were able to acquire individually 658 acres of land because they won the right to allot all their lands to the tribe. There was no Sooner-type or open run land grab.

It should be noted, also, that one large group of Indians neither was moved nor suffered a large amount of land loss. Possessing a relatively secure niche in Spanish New Mexican colonial society, the Pueblo Indians were divided into the Eastern Pueblo along the Rio Grande in New Mexico, and the Western Pueblo in western New Mexico and northeastern Arizona. A liberal interpretation by the Spanish governor of an 1812 Spanish constitution allowed the Pueblo by the late 1820s full citizenship and legal equality. In addition, the Pueblo Indian population not only stabilized, but also was steadily increasing. On the other hand, during the short-lived period of Mexican rule, the Pueblos received a great deal less protection from rapacious neighbors than they had been able to wring from Spanish officialdom. The later violent history of Indians in Mexico centered on the Mexican policy (particularly after 1857) of breaking up corporate Indian land holdings and placing land tenure on a completely individual basis. Fortunately for the Pueblo Indians in the

Omaha dance. (Courtesy of the South Dakota State Historical Society)

territory newly acquired by the Americans after the Treaty of Guadalupe Hidalgo in 1848, Congress confirmed thirty-five Spanish grants to the Pueblo, totaling 700,000 acres. This enlightened Indian land-ownership policy compares radically to the governmental philosophy in California and Texas after the Mexicans were ejected. Greedy settlers, of course, began to move in on much of the choice irrigable land. Since the Pueblos are not a single entity, their autonomous villages often lacked the funds and leadership to oppose interlopers on their lands. Only in 1924 did Congress assure the Pueblo the right to their prime agricultural land.

For the general history of American Indians, the Osage and Pueblo success stories represent exceptions to the rule. More generally, American Indians were clobbered during the nineteenth century by having most of their communally owned and individually allotted lands taken away, their people reduced by some 40 percent, and their frequent relocations anytime their homelands looked attractive to non-Indians. Understandably, even among the over 50 percent of Indians who were American citizens by 1900, there remained an abhorrence of the American way of life. Even without a land base, the Native American was not Americanized.

Leroy Eid
University of Dayton (Ohio)

Cheyenne Indians hunting buffalo near the newly laid tracks of the Union Pacific railroad and telegraph lines. (Courtesy of the Utah Historical Society)

◆ INDIAN LAND TENURE IN THE TWENTIETH CENTURY

By the beginning of the twentieth century, few tribes and Indian communities continued to hold land tenure as they did at the time of contact and well into the early national period. Most Indian groups and societies once had occupied and claimed territory in common as hunting bands, farming communities, and as larger political entities. The environment was revered and respected, and their utilization of natural resources depended upon need. Land was never treated as a commodity and, although examples of individual holdings existed, the practices of private property exhibited by Western culture were alien to most Indians. Land cessions by treaty and dispossession by other means, including armed force, reduced Indian occupation to reservations, representing fragments of indigenous geography and territoriality. Thus, a new order supplanted the traditional and evolving land institutions, reflected in the policies of the government as administered by the Office (later the Bureau) of Indian Affairs (BIA).

Subsequently, three major federal policies affected the way Indians lived. In the first three decades, Indians were still mostly isolated on reservations. Owing to laws enacted in the nineteenth century and still in force into the 1920s, Indians continued to lose considerable land through the process of allotment, which divided up the tribal estate. During this period, the government was too often more preoccupied with the management of Indian realty than with the sound planning and development of reservation-based economies. Simply keeping maps up to date and maintaining a cadastral office consumed much of their efforts. Yet the Bureau of Indian Affairs, the designated trustee, provided some aid and participated in construction—irrigation systems, for example—to abet subsistent land use.

A later policy, especially after World War II, saw the migration of Indians to urban areas stemming from a federally funded relocation program. In part, this program sought to alleviate economic and environmental conditions on many reservations by reducing the resident number living on the land. Ultimately, more than

75 percent of the Indian population ended up living in either urban settings or in rural areas adjacent to many reservations. The latest major policy came in 1975 with the enactment of the Indian Self-Determination and Education Assistance Act that gave the tribes increased autonomy over the management of their trust lands. This 'government-to-government' policy, which has continued into the twenty-first century, has liberated many tribes from the constraints of federal supervision and given Indians renewed options to pursue different environmental and economic goals. Yet the land tenure structure in place has not basically changed in more than one hundred years.

The Geography of Reservations

Most Indian reservations and other trust lands for Native Americans (Indians, Aleuts, and Eskimos) are found in the Great Plains and in the West, including Alaska. A smaller number of reservations exist in the eastern United States. The larger land units are occupied by the Lakota, Oglala, and other Sioux tribes in the Dakota states, and by the Navajo, whose reservation in the Southwest is equivalent in area to West Virginia. But in upstate New York remnant lands of the Iroquois exist as trust holdings; and other reservations can be found in the Lake States and in the South. The majority of southern tribes were forcibly relocated in the Trail of Tears during the 1830s and ended up in what is today Oklahoma. In that state the majority of trust lands comprise non-contiguous, scattered parcels in a number of counties; only the Osage hold a single, identifiable reservation.

Reservations, to be sure, represent but a fraction of original tribal territory. For example, the Zuni Reservation in New Mexico comprises nearly 500,000 acres of an original 15,000,000. A few tribes—the Menominee (WI), the Quinault (WA), and the White Mountain Apache (AZ)—hold significant forest reserves. Many reservations contain arable lands but lack sufficient water to develop them and/or capital in order to compete in the marketplace. Fragmentation of individual holdings reduces the economic utilization of much cultivable acreage. Another group of reservations—including the Osage, the Uintah and Ouray, and the Navajo—contain important oil and mineral reserves. The most ubiquitous resource cutting across Indian Country is grazing land, some of which sustains favorable range condition for year-round or seasonal grazing. The vast majority of the acreage, however, is marginal and subject to erosion and loss of browsable vegetation.

As we move into a new century, what has become quite valued is location, specifically selective trust lands that lie within reach of major metropolitan areas. Examples of such sites include those occupied by the Agua Caliente Indians at Palm Springs (CA), located within one hundred miles of Los Angeles, and the Mashantucket Pequot, who occupy a reservation near Ledyard (CT), located within a two- to three-hour drive from New York, Boston, and other urban centers. Such locations have encouraged many tribes to establish casinos which will draw upon this vast urban population. But location alone does not govern the option to open a casino: trust status of the land is primal.

Land Allotment

Prior to 1900 U.S. policymakers had already come to believe that the reservation system would pacify Indians and thereby stabilize land relations with settlers. As early as 1887 the government implemented policies to assimilate Indians into U.S. society. Part of the assimilation plan involved a major readjustment of Indian land tenure by allotting reservation lands. This land policy not only led to the breakup of tribal lands but also ultimately caused the fragmentation of holdings within reservations. Proponents of land allotment held that the ideal policy was to separate individual Indians from their tribe. They asserted that if Indians were granted private land, or an allotment, which is analogous to a homestead, they would soon become productive yeoman farmers. Thus Congress passed the General Allotment Act of 1887 (known also as the Dawes Act), which authorized the BIA to survey reservation lands in order to lay out individual farms. Under the act, farmer/teachers were assigned to work with Indians during an apprenticeship period. After twenty-five years, Indians would receive a fee title or a deed to their allotments; once obtained, this deed "liberated" an Indian from his trustee. So long as Indian land remained in trust, no property taxes could be assessed. This tax-free status has provided considerable security for individual Indians, although other aspects of allotment have continued to diminish this trust security.

Many Indians, whom BIA officials judged as "competent," received fee title well before the twenty-five-year period. Many of these Indians tended to sell their lands or just abandon them; others leased their allotments, moved to cities, or worked on non-Indian lands within or outside of reservation borders. Still others were forced to live with more prudent relatives or to live on surviving tribal holdings that had not been allotted to individuals. Congress, in amending the Allotment Act in 1906, required that if Indians did not exploit their lands in a manner acceptable to policy, the government could lease their lands. In the early twentieth century, at least 25 percent of allotted lands were so leased; today, that percentage is much greater.

Once the government surveyed and distributed allotted lands among living tribal members—even over their protests—it opened the remaining Indian lands to settlement by non-Indian homesteaders. One of many shortcomings of this policy was that the unborn would not receive an allotment at a later date. Besides locating non-Indians side by side on the land with Indians, opening the reservations encouraged the establishment of towns such as Toppenish on the Yakama Indian Reservation (WA), which contains far more non-Indian than Indian residents. Other towns include Parker on the Colorado River Indian Reservation (AZ), Browning on the Blackfoot Indian Reservation (MT), and, uniquely, Palm Springs, which occupies a checkerboard with the Agua Caliente Indian Reservation (CA). Nearly a half-century later, by 1934, Indians had lost ownership of about 90 million acres through allotment. Moreover, since many Indian allottees left no wills that designated their heirs, this land became subject to state inheritance laws as authorized in various allotment statutes. Thousands of allotments thus became encumbered by multiple joint heirship. Over time, the joint undivided shares have resulted in plots of land much too small to farm profitably and thousands of acres continue to stand idle and unmanaged.

The New Deal and the Indian Reorganization Act

Land allotment disrupted tribal culture and fragmented reservation lands and resources. In *Red Man's Land/White Man's Law*, the late historian Wilcomb E. Washburn noted that Indians had been "forced to limit their life and their vision to an incomprehensible individual plot of 160 or so acres in a checkerboard of neighbors, hostile and friendly, rich and poor, white and red" (p. 75). In the 1920s, even conservative officials sought to modify what had become a destructive process. In 1934, as part of the New Deal administration, Congress stopped the process of land allotment by creating the Indian Reorganization Act (IRA). The IRA restored some surplus lands to tribal ownership, added some new lands, and authorized tribal restoration of allotted lands by purchase, provided it was fiscally possible. The IRA also encouraged tribal self-government and economic enterprises. New Deal planners contended that what many religious groups and national leaders had believed—that holding land in private property would lead to the acculturation and assimilation of Indians—simply was an untenable idea. In reality, speculative interests in Indian cropland, range, minerals, and timber successfully urged Congress to sustain and even step up the pace of granting title to Indians, because it too often meant the sale or lease of Indian land. Ultimately, many Indians were

dispossessed of their land and became dependent on government social services. Such destruction of tribal institutions could not be entirely reversed and tribal opposition to New Deal measures did not help the cause.

All reform efforts have their proponents and opponents, and New Deal measures for the tribes were no exception. For example, many tribal governments did not support the IRA; of 258 tribal communities at the time only seventy-seven accepted the measure. Many tribes voted against the IRA out of fear that treaties would be annulled. Despite the intent of the IRA, tribal governments did not gain appreciable authority over the expenditure of their funds or over signing leases, for the BIA continued to overrule tribal council decisions. In effect, the IRA allowed some tribal governments to form new constitutions but in the end did not grant them any new or considerable powers. In fact, a criticism then still persisted until into the 1980s: tribal government was nearly autonomous on paper, but in reality, much less in charge than the tribes expected. Public officials and academic scholars alike agreed that the onerous allotment practice had to be reversed but that the government needed to move more slowly and be sensitive to tribal concerns, among them the establishment of conservation programs. A number of such programs enlisted cooperation from other agencies, including the Forest Service and the Soil Conservation Service.

Termination of Trust Status

Despite the efforts of Commissioner of Indian Affairs John Collier (1933–1945) to make the Indian Reorganization Act work, Congress in the post-World War II era elected to discontinue the trusteeship of Indian tribes. By House Resolution 108 (1953), Indians became subject to the same laws, privileges, and responsibilities of all U.S. citizens. This resolution aimed to end Indian wardship. Under this policy of termination, the U.S. government intended to sever all special legal ties and social service relations with Indian communities. In 1954, Congress terminated the Klamath Indians of southern Oregon; four Paiute bands, and the Uintah and Ouray of Utah; and the Alabama and Coushatta of Texas. Other terminations followed over the next few years, including the Menominee of Wisconsin and numerous rancherias (very small reservations) in central and northern California.

Most tribes affected by this policy could not survive outside the legal protections of trusteeship. The Menominee, terminated despite their appeals and fears of additional taxes, were obliged to sell valuable lakefront property to non-Indians. The former Menominee Reservation became a county under Wisconsin law. The

Menominee struggled to sustain their lumber operations, the tribe's major source of income, but many tribal members became impoverished. Because of their economic plight, the Menominee sought to be reinstated as an Indian nation; they appealed to Congress for restoration of their federal recognition. By the mid-1970s, the Menominee became the first Indian nation to regain federal recognition after termination. Several terminated Indian groups, including the Siletz of Oregon and more than a half-dozen California rancherias, later regained trust status.

Land Restoration and Claims

At various times, Congress has enacted legislation returning some former "surplus" lands or adding acreage to reservations. Congress has restored some lands subsequent to land claims litigation as with the Havasupai, a recognized tribe, and has restored land subsequent to acknowledging an unrecognized tribe such as the Timbisha. Recognized tribes gain several benefits from services and federal funding, whereas unrecognized Indian communities neither receive these benefits nor hold trust lands. In the case of the Havasupai, whose ancestral home was reduced to a small parcel within the Grand Canyon, the tribe regained land that had become part of national forests and parks; similarly, a small portion of land within Death Valley National Park has been restored to the Timbisha.

During the last quarter of the century, other tribes continued to litigate claims to gain access and exclusive use of sites of Native cultural heritage, notably burial grounds and sacred places. The Yakama in Washington and the Taos and Zuni Pueblos in New Mexico succeeded in regaining limited sacred acreage. When restoration has not transpired, some tribes have turned to the provisions of the American Indian Religious Freedom Act (AIRFA) and the Native American Graves and Repatriation Act (NAGPRA) in order to secure access to land for the exclusive purpose of religious worship. Navajo and Hopi sued the U.S. Forest Service to stop the development of a ski resort located on the slopes of the San Francisco Peaks north of Flagstaff (AZ), arguing that the mountains, as part of a sacred place, should in part be restored to them. The tribes, however, did not convince the court that they made exclusive use of the sacred places. Unfortunately, tribes that have evoked the AIRFA or NAGPRA have not always found these laws supportive of their cause. In 1990 the Havasupai filed suit against the Forest Service, alleging that the agency failed to uphold requirements of an environmental impact statement (EIS) as they sought to determine if the Canyon Uranium Mine located within the Kaibab National Forest (AZ) should be

established at a site declared to be sacred but lying outside lands restored to the tribe. The mine location lay near Red Butte, which is believed to be the locus of an "earth navel" through which ancestors climbed to the present world. The record shows that the Forest Service went to great lengths to determine if environmental constraints and religious concerns should prohibit mining operations and found none. Ultimately, the mineral market declined and the mine became inoperative.

Unlike the Havasupai, the Hopi Indians have chosen to enter a partnership with the Kaibab National Forest as a means to have a voice in the preservation of sacred shrines on ancestral lands, some of which were adjudicated by the Indian Claims Commission. The Hopi have established a Cultural Preservation Office that interacts with a tribal liaison officer of the forest.

In recent years, issues and litigation over the preservation of Indian cultural, historic, or sacred places on federal lands have also invoked the First Amendment, especially the Free Exercise Clause. In 1999 Devil's Tower, known as Bear Lodge and perceived as a sacred site by various Sioux tribes, the Crow, and other Indians, was the subject of litigation. The National Park Service (NPS), which administers the tower as a national monument, attempted some accommodation by denying permits for commercially guided climbs during June and asked the public to voluntarily refrain from climbing at that time. June is the month when Indians revere the tower. But the tower is also generally acknowledged to be a popular rock-climbing natural feature. While the court found the voluntary closure permissible, the ban against commercial use was declared unconstitutional. At issue is the comparative rights of (Native) religion versus rock climbing. For the claimant Indians, exclusive access was to be protected by the American Indian Religious Freedom Act (AIRFA), but the court did not contend that the establishment clause denied them a separate religious right. Instead, the court sustained the argument that rock-climbers had an equal right to exercise their outdoor activity. This is but one of several cases in which the Free Exercise Clause, rather than the Establishment Clause, has been the point of law defeating tribes that invoked the AIRFA.

Tribal hopes fell dramatically when land claims litigation did not result in land restoration. In 1946 Congress created the Indian Claims Commission (ICC) so that one tribunal would hear all land claims from Indian tribes. Congress empowered the ICC to establish ground rules and procedures for the research and adjudication of hundreds of tribal claims over wrongful taking of land. It is possible that Congress intended to

Indian Land Claims: Adjudicated Areas

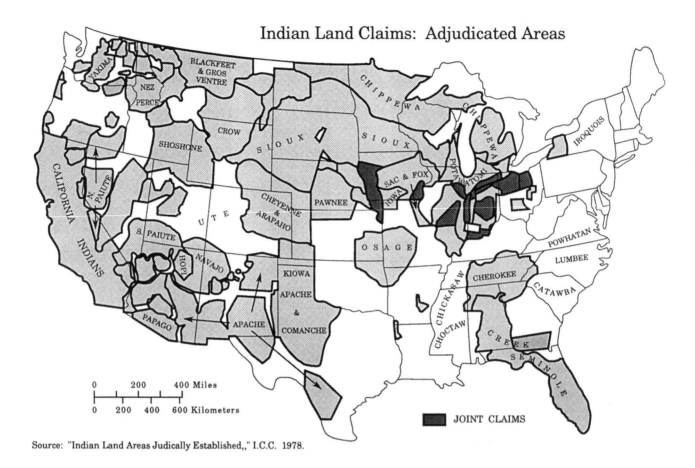

Source: "Indian Land Areas Judically Established,," I.C.C. 1978.

This map is based on "Indian Land Areas Judicially Established," as published in the *Final Report,* Indian Claims Commission, 1978, and published by permission of the University of New Mexico Press. (Courtesy of Imre Sutton)

retire outstanding claims that clouded title to properties long held by non-Indians. Moreover, the claims process coincided in time with federal sentiments toward selective termination of trust responsibilities. Many tribes expected the ICC to award land, the title to which had passed out of Indian hands primarily in the nineteenth century. Unfortunately, the ICC chose early on to interpret its authority as limited to awarding money, not land. Many tribes, even those accepting money, have been disappointed or angered by this day in court, for the acceptance of a monetary award signaled the final quieting of all aboriginal claims to the territory litigated.

The claims process focused on the geographic extent of aboriginal territory—that is, recognized title lands or those ceded by treaties and original title lands based on historic and ethnographic reconstruction relying, in part, on Indian informants—as the basis for ascertaining the amount of money that tribes would net for their loss of land. Researchers for the plaintiff tribes and for the defendant U.S. government examined the historic documentary record and explored the

ethnographic past. While the tribes hoped for the largest geographic adjudication, the defendant government sought a much reduced acreage figure. The process based monetary awards on the market value of an acre at the time of taking, which was usually much less than $1.

Many Indians openly rejected the judicial process, condemning it as a means to exhaust Indian land claims. The noted legal scholar, Vine Deloria, Jr. (Standing Rock Sioux), observed that many Indians who accepted monetary awards suffered an irrevocable loss of land. Accepting the adjudication was an emotionally painful decision that few Indians made willingly. It meant that the tribes acquiesced in the decisions of the ICC and the courts and readily acknowledged the termination of their aboriginal land rights. This reasoning, in part, explains why the Oglala and Teton Sioux continue to reject an award of more than $100 million for the loss of the Black Hills in South Dakota. As recently as February 2000, the Western Shoshone continued to argue among themselves over the acceptance or rejection of an award of $116 million. It is anticipated that in the near future a resolution may be at hand to distribute this money for the loss of nearly 24 million acres in the heart of the Great Basin. While many tribal members willingly intend to accept the money, others will stand with those few tribes still holding out for land restoration. Although involving much less acreage in northern California forests, the Pit River Indians still refuse their award despite the fact that the bulk of the California Indians accepted a meager monetary award following the adjudication of their claims in the 1960s.

Even though the retirement in 1978 of the ICC presumably signaled the finality of claims litigation, the Federal Claims Court has continued to hear both unresolved cases and new ones. In 1991 the Zuni Indians won a $25 million award for the loss of 15 million acres. Other tribal claims have been resolved by a combination of litigation, negotiation, and congressional involvement. For example, the Catawba of South Carolina argued a claims case before several courts, but ultimately Congress passed a settlement act in 1993 that conveyed a sizable monetary grant which has led to the quieting of ancient titles but makes possible the purchase of land and development of tribal resources. Settlement acts result when Congress steps in to terminate long drawn-out litigation. Other recent acts include the Saddleback Mountain Settlement Act of 1995, which finally resolved a controversy between the city of Scottsdale (AZ) and the Salt River Pima-Maricopa Indians over lands abutting the northern boundary of their reservation. This act provides for joint purchase of land and the preservation of about half of it in a natural state for a public park and recreation grounds. Congress also funded other eastern tribes to help them purchase lands. The Penobscot and Passamaquoddy of Maine, for instance, will ultimately acquire about 300,000 acres of forest lands.

In a different way, some land restoration did take place in the later 1990s. A small group of Western Shoshone—the Timbisha—whose home territory always embraced parts of Death Valley (CA), pursued the restoration of some aboriginal acreage which today lies within Death Valley National Park. The Timbisha, acknowledged as a tribe by the BIA in 1982, and the NPS reached an agreement in 1999 that allows the Timbisha to own and develop 300 acres at Furnace Creek, enjoy exclusive use of an adjacent 1,000 acres, and share in the management of a 300,000 acre expanse of parkland to be known as the Timbisha preservation area. Another 6,000 acres lying outside the park, currently administered by the Bureau of Land Management, will be turned over to the tribe.

Even though few efforts to regain land have been successful, a group of Abenaki of New England holds some expectation of restoration of acreage and/or a financial settlement for a claim against Vermont. The Abenaki claim that their land title was extinguished by Vermont without consent of Congress, yet the Vermont Supreme Court ruled that the "increasing weight of history" supported a view that the longer time passed without federal protection of tribal lands, the assumption would be that the federal government intended to extinguish Indian title. Vermont contends that Abenaki title was extinguished when the Republic of Vermont severed from New York. Had the court acknowledged the Abenaki claim, then Congress would likely pass a settlement act, but perhaps one encumbered by Mohawk claims to lands within Vermont.

Trust Lands and Economic Options

Today government programs seek to encourage individual and family farming or ranching and small business enterprises, in addition to tribally operated agriculture, ranching, lumbering, and tourism. Many Indians hope that the economic development of their reservations will sustain tribal lifeways, improve Indian income, and minimize interaction and confrontation with non-Indians. With the assistance of the BIA and other field agencies, the Apache, Arapaho, Blackfeet, Navajo, and other Indian nations have developed grazing programs. Many Indians—among them, the Arapaho and Shoshone of Wind River, and the Zuni—manage housing projects for resident families. Generally, such housing occupies tribal lands and if Indians purchase the homes, they hold only land occupancy rights. Several tribes have entered into short- and long-term contracts for lease developments of timber, minerals, and other resources; they have also established various forms of manufacturing in conjunction with the private sector. The White Mountain Apache in Arizona borrowed and repaid funds to develop a lumber industry to harvest pine and Douglas fir on the reservation and have employed more than three hundred Indians. The Blackfeet in Montana have established a pen-and-pencil factory, which employs mostly Indians. Crow Indians in Montana have entered into leases for the exploitation of coal and oil. Many reservations—such as the Yakama, the Acoma Pueblo, and Gila Bend—have established visitor centers, museums, and craft stores, while others, such as the Fort Hall Indian Reservation (ID), operate tribally run gas stations and other commercial ventures.

Because only a small percentage of Indians benefit from economic developments on reservations, many resident families receive welfare support and live at or below the poverty level. Indians are usually reported at the bottom of national income statistics and high unemployment characterizes most reservations. Among

Pit River land claims protests. (Photo by Ilka Hartmann)

the poorest of reservations is Pine Ridge in South Dakota, where, it is estimated, there is nearly 75 percent unemployment. Tribal enterprises such as resort developments—including the one found at Warm Springs Indian Reservation (OR)—as well as lumber operations—such as the business at Menominee, Warm Springs, and White Mountain Apache—have successfully employed a number of Indians on a regular basis. However, Indian enterprises are not immune to general market downturns, and there are inadequate numbers of enterprises on reservations. By and large, enterprises run by tribal governments as corporate entities fare better than those operated by individuals or families on allotments. However, not all tribes choose to invite non-Indian industry or business onto the reservation.

Heirship, as one unfortunate legacy of land allotment, continues to thwart economic growth of countless acres of allotted lands. The severity of the heirship problem is most critical among Sioux tribes in the northern Great Plains, but it persists on many reservations in the West. Some tribes have sought to consolidate encumbered allotments by invoking the Indian

Land Consolidation Act (1983), but this has led to litigation brought by heirs and relatives of deceased allottees, who contend that the escheat provision—whereby a tribe can unilaterally take back allotted lands—is unconstitutional. The act did intend to enable tribes to acquire marginal lands held in undivided interests. But in recent litigation the courts argued that tribal acquisitions under the act constituted a "taking," requiring just compensation; ultimately, the U.S. Supreme Court declared the act unconstitutional.

Certainly, individual Indians and families are entitled to equal protection under the law, yet tribal acquisition of allotments seems an appropriate option—laudable in terms of the better environmental management of reservation resources. Heirship problems so limit land use because too many heirs cannot agree on utilization or cannot be found in order to render appropriate land use decisions. The tribes are deemed the legitimate first claimants of such encumbered acreage. Congress even attempted to revise the act, yet the Supreme Court continued to rule against its constitutionality. Of course, tribes can continue to purchase inherited parcels, making them part of tribal holdings.

Tribal efforts at land consolidation, of course, predicate a more holistic planning concept, which countless tribes invoke.

When land does not directly support tribal members, many of them have turned to employment in administrative and supervisory roles in tribal government. They may work in the administration directly, as elected or appointed officials, or as staff personnel in tribal planning, housing, health services, or more recently in various environmental programs such as archaeology and water management. Some Indians, of course, work for the BIA, and today one finds qualified Indians employed in other field agencies. An increasing number of young Indians have successfully completed high school, and some have attended, if not completed, college. In general, better educated Indians are more likely to work off the reservation and many tribes may be desperate to hold onto their own by creating suitable positions. But few reservation communities have a sufficient number of college-educated Indians who might assume positions demanding professional skills. In response to this fact, the University of Oklahoma established a graduate program in American Indian Natural Resource Management, which is, to date, the nation's sole academic program aimed at educating professional Indians to manage or co-manage tribal resources. There are a number of Native American college programs, but few of them focus attention on indigenous planning and resource management. One exception is the Menominee of Wisconsin, who in 1997 began to develop, implement, and maintain a reservation and county-wide multipurpose land information system and subsequently has developed an advanced computer lab utilizing digitized maps that will enhance local capabilities and also provide on-reservation training. These efforts are part of a larger program of the tribal Sustainable Development Institute.

Reservation economies, in order to succeed, have followed the general trend toward increased mechanization and specialization, and both preclude the need for a large work force but do necessitate the employment of skilled and professional Indians. No better example of this need is the implementation of Geographic Information Systems (GIS), which provide cartographic and other technical data to help assess reservation resource bases and coordinate environmental planning. Until recently, the BIA's branch of natural resources assisted tribes in this endeavor. Tribal leaders and planners are realistic in recognizing that reservation resources are far too limited in order to support all resident members. Aside from some limited high quality farm or ranch lands and notable timber and mineral resources, most reservations offer few long-term economic options. Many Indians, however, do not willingly choose to be farmers and do not care to engage in rural economic enterprises. Some Indians have done reasonably well in ranching, despite the overgrazed status of much of the tribal range.

Another factor that is gradually being selectively overcome is the absence of investment capital and business experience and entrepreneurship. Tenure structure of many reservations encourages non-Indian enterprises, which outweigh Indian enterprises unless the tribe is well-capitalized and takes on the economic venture itself. Consequently, leasing offers a way out for many Indians. In fact, in recent decades 60 percent of irrigated lands and 75 percent of dry-farmed acreage have been leased. While approximately fourteen reservations receive the bulk of the lease income from timber sales, most of the saw-timber cut on reservations in the Pacific Northwest is milled outside the area by non-Indian companies. In 1975 some twenty-two tribes formed the Council of Energy Resource Tribes (CERT), which has since expanded to forty-nine tribes. The CERT members collectively hold about 60 percent of all Indian lands and represent about half of all reservation Indians. CERT has emphasized the prudent development of tribal energy resources and improved tribal managerial skills, and it advises tribes about leasing in order to avoid contracts that return too little. The Blackfeet, Navajo, Osage, and Uintah and Ouray earn substantial income from natural resource sales. The Northern Arapaho and Eastern Shoshone, who share the Wind River Indian Reservation (WY), earn modest incomes from the sale of oil, normally about $75 a month. In spring 2000 they demonstrated that fluctuations in oil prices related to the downturn in production of the OPEC nations led to minor increases in monthly income. For Indians at Wind River, there are potential royalties from 200 oil leases on a reservation that has little else to support its membership; fluctuations in the market can be both a blessing and a curse.

The BIA's administrative control over reservation resources continues to confound many tribes. While individuals and families freely engage in agriculture, ranching, and some forms of commerce, the BIA still supervises leasing for oil and other minerals. This and other inconsistencies in administrative practice rankle the tribes and contribute to skepticism over the purpose of government programs.

Residence, Mobility, and Relocation

Membership in a tribe is a basic determinant of the right to reside on a reservation. Non-Indian spouses of members and their children usually enjoy most privileges akin to membership. They would sustain an ownership interest in allotted lands, but without the tribal member they may not retain tenure rights to tribal resources or land. At one time the BIA passed on all tribal rules regarding residence as well as membership. Today many tribes determine their own rules and may deny residence on the grounds that someone is less Indian due to intermarriage with a non-Indian. Countless Indians moved away in past generations and today their descendants may not be perceived as sufficiently Indian in culture and association. More critically, however, is a very different demographic fact: on many reservations, non-Indians have come to outnumber Indians living on the reservation. The presence of a large non-Indian population, sometimes the majority, makes it increasingly difficult for Indians to manage their own government and to control their economic institutions. Largely a result of the allotment process that led to the opening of reservations to non-Indians, the Native population on many reservations averages less than 50 percent. On reservations in Arizona, the Dakotas, and New Mexico, Indians generally represent more than 90 percent of the populations, whereas in California, in some Great Lakes states, and in Washington, Indians represent less than 30 percent of the reservation populations. Policy makers once envisioned that the mix of Indian and non-Indian neighbors on reservation lands would hasten the assimilation of the tribes. Nevertheless, recent history demonstrates that simply mixing populations does not dissolve Indian identity and community but does create an unfortunate arena for conflict and litigation.

Motivated by the expectation that Indians would find gainful employment in cities, the BIA also sought an alternative means to enable Indians to assimilate more readily. In the 1950s, the BIA instituted the Voluntary Relocation Program that sought to encourage Indians, especially younger ones, to leave reservations in order to live and work in larger urban centers such as Chicago, Dallas, Denver, Los Angeles, Oklahoma City, and Seattle. Reservation Indians understood that relocation would not normally diminish their tenure rights. Despite financial and social assistance, many Indians have had considerable difficulty securing employment and adjusting to urban life, and often seek out other Indians in a perceived hostile environment. Unfortunately, the longer some Indians remain away from their tribal homeland, their potential return may be hindered by political changes on the reservation, and individuals may suffer from a state of mind known as anomie in which Indians become alienated by being too imbued by non-Indian culture that they can not be readily accepted by tribal members. Simply stated, they no longer fit in.

Although the urbanization of Indians began well before the second World War, only 25 percent of all Indians were urbanized by 1960. According to the 1990 Census, 62 percent of all Indians lived in towns and cities. More than 20,000 Indians live in each of several metropolitan areas such as Los Angeles, Oklahoma City, Phoenix, and Tulsa, and at least 10,000 resided in some dozen smaller urban centers. Unfortunately, the living circumstances of urban Indians mirror those of most reservation Indians: urbanizing Indians too often exchange rural poverty for urban poverty—inadequate housing, unemployment, and discrimination in the city. An unaccountable number of urban Indians remain enrolled tribal members who still retain legal and cultural ties to a tribe. As such, they may occasionally benefit from per capita monetary distributions, such as have occurred with land claims awards and, most recently, owing to gaming income. Even though they live in urban areas, many tribally affiliated Indians continue to own or hold undivided interest in trust land; they may frequently return to reservations to visit relatives, to attend powwows and council meetings, to hunt and fish or generally recreate, and possibly to vote in elections. Non-residence on a reservation has not generally precluded the right to vote in tribal elections. Membership and tenure rights in tribal assets often outweigh on-reservation residence as for those Western Cherokee and Chickasaw who live in California and other states. For example, in election years, candidates from these tribes have campaigned in California. It is to be expected that some Indians would choose to be buried on tribal land. Conversely, reservation residents also frequent nearby towns and cities. They, too, may be visiting relatives, but usually they hold permanent or temporary jobs to which they commute. They also take advantage of nearby local commercial and public services. Many reservation Indian students attend schools in nearby non-Indian communities, while some non-Indian students living on or adjacent to reservations attend reservation schools and colleges. Since tribal Indians more often sustain a legal tie to the tribe and the land, reservation residence is non-obligatory. However, it is also safe to say that many generations of urbanized Indians no longer know of their birthright.

Self-Determination

As the core concept of a redirected Indian policy, self-determination ideally recognizes tribal sovereignty. Tribal governments, for example, when they face no federal prohibitions, are autonomous within the borders of reservations. Sovereignty applies to the tribe, its membership, and the reservation but not to individual Indians living or even working away from the reservation. The policy of self-determination intends to shift more responsibility to the tribes, but this has not always been translated into a working reality. For example, although empowered by the Clean Water Act, few tribes have yet to assume regulatory authority over water quality standards on reservations. When Congress passed the Indian Self-Determination and Education Assistance Act in 1975, it granted tribes greater negotiating authority to "plan, conduct and administer programs" independent of the BIA but still dependent on federal funding. As early as 1980, 370 tribal communities contracted for millions of dollars of federal services, most often coming from Housing and Urban Development (HUD) and Health and Human Services (HHS). Many tribes now assume fuller responsibility for the management of their funds and for reservation programs such as housing and water development. Provisions of this act have both strengthened tribal government and encouraged tribes to take on functions of taxation, planning, and the regulation of reservation activities. While some tribes have embraced the goals of self-determination, others continue to fear that a show of too much independence or an assertion of inherent sovereignty might lead to the reinstatement of the dreaded termination policies of the 1950s. One example of this independence occurs whenever tribes attempt to tax non-Indian landholdings and enterprises.

Several tribal activities demonstrate how effective self-determination can be when Indians assume responsibilities for their own affairs. The Zuni provide a good example of what is possible under the policy: they wrested control of federal programs such as housing, decentralized authority to the community level, replaced many officials with tribal officers and staff, and even required other BIA personnel to move into the Indian community to foster closer interaction. The tribe, not Washington, D.C., supervises BIA staff. On an even grander scale, the Navajo expanded their functions, and even established a Washington office. Education is crucial to self-determination; many tribes assumed supervision of reservation schools and, following the Navajo lead, established community colleges. Health programs and tribally-run health centers increased. Many tribes quickly learned how to manipulate the federal system in order to achieve their goals and to gain the services they required.

Since the advent of the self-determination policy, several other agencies have assumed or have been assigned aspects of the trust responsibility by the tribes. Among the most notable is the Administration for Native Americans (ANA). This agency has worked closely with CERT, and has provided grant funds for priority projects encouraging economic growth and tribal governance. Since its establishment in 1974, ANA has directly aided such tribal enterprises as the 110-unit Best Western Hotel on the Tulalip Indian Reservation in

Washington. On the Yakama Indian Reservation, ANA helped fund a major wildlife resource management program that enhanced a public hunting program. This tribe markets its own hunting licenses and anticipates a multi-million-dollar revenue in the coming decades. When the ANA came up for renewal in 1991, Gregg Bourland, chair of the Cheyenne River Sioux (SD), expressed his tribe's support in these words: "[The ANA] has consistently increased the ability of many tribes to further their struggle for self-sufficiency... without imposing unnecessary and restrictive policies." Michael Pablo, chair of the Confederated Salish and Kootenai (MT), also spoke in laudatory terms: "The ANA is more than just a model of an effective government agency.... [I]t is also a key player in the renaissance of Indian Self-Determination." Such statements by Indians demonstrate that many tribes have increasingly relied upon support and assistance of a number of agencies exclusive of or in addition to the BIA.

In a different way, self-determination has encouraged tribes to seek out assistance or partnerships with other federal and state agencies. In the past, the U.S. Forest Service assisted in the management of tribal forests and the Soil Conservation Service (now the Natural Resources Conservation Service) established field projects in soil and water conservation. On reservations today, the Bureau of Reclamation assists some tribes with water development projects; and the National Park Service has guided Indian communities in the management of tribal parks. In fact, the NPS has been a supporter of the creation of a Wounded Knee National Tribal Park, which would include areas within both the Pine Ridge and Cheyenne River Indian reservations (SD). The park would be managed by Indians with the assistance of the NPS. Unfortunately, to date Congress has not established this park. The Army Corps of Engineers and the Environmental Protection Agency have also become more supportive of tribal goals. Pursuant to a Secretarial Order in 1997, the Departments of Commerce (National Marine Fisheries Service) and the Interior (Fish and Wildlife Service) have sat down with tribes over the designation of critical habitats that include tribal lands. Despite the wording of the Endangered Species Act (ESA), the government has withdrawn the designation of critical habitats on such reservations as the Nez Percé, Yakama, Umpqua/ Siuslaw, Hoopa Valley, and others because of tribal protests that say the ESA unfairly encumbers economic development on reservations.

Off reservation, tribes have been encouraged to interact especially with public land agencies. For example, in the late 1990s the Forest Service, perhaps hoping to create a better image of an agency sensitive to tribal concerns, established the position of tribal liaison to be filled by a person who works with tribes toward the protection of Indian cultural heritage on former tribal lands. As such the Hopi, Havasupai, Yavapai, and other Indian communities have been working in partnership with the agency on the Kaibab National Forest in Arizona. In a similar way, a tribal liaison officer has been interacting with Indians who lay claim to territory that includes the Midewin Tallgrass Prairie, administered by the Forest Service, in Illinois.

In the 1990s, in response to a presidential memorandum on government-to-government relations, the Army Corps of Engineers began to conduct workshops and data-collecting to "assess the scope, extent and quality of Corps-tribal interactions." Long known to be insensitive to the tribes, the corps came to recognize that "a conflict exists between the Corps' multistage execution of its water resource missions and its obligations, as a Federal agency, to honor the commitments made to Federally Recognized Tribes. . . . " To the tribes, corps assistance in the protection of traditional cultural properties relative to provisions of NAGPRA was and continues to be central to their concerns.

It should be emphasized that, in the past, many agencies besides the BIA were often found to be involved in conflicts-of-interest with the tribes. Besides the aforementioned conflicts with agencies that protect wildlife, the Bureau of Reclamation comes to mind because its construction of dams have led to the inundation of tribal lands as in the Missouri River Valley and elsewhere in western watersheds. The Army Corps, of course, also has been identified with negative environmental impacts on tribal lands, not only on the Missouri River, but also on the Allegheny River, a tributary of the Ohio River in Pennsylvania and New York, where Allegheny Seneca have been displaced.

As changing policy follows the mandate for self-determination, tribes perforce remain furtive, not knowing just when new laws and court decisions will undermine the gains made under this policy. To be sure, tribes embrace the greater autonomy but do not want to see the erosion of funding and other benefits. Critics of the policy of self-determination note that the BIA and other agencies still make basic decisions, and the policy, as Philip Deloria (Standing Rock Sioux), a law professor at the University of New Mexico, noted, is a "tactical shift in the fundamental commitment of society to bring Indians into the mainstream, not a movement toward true recognition of permanent rights to exist." Moreover, historian Paul Francis Prucha suggests that Indians' drive for self-determination and sovereignty is contradicted by the "seeds of dependency." More than one critic contends that tribes cannot

have political self-determination without economic self-determination, yet most tribes continue to depend upon federal funds. The American Indian Policy Review Commission, also established in 1975, strongly endorsed tribal sovereignty and self-determination, yet demonstrated that almost all the demands of tribes included the request for federal funds. Policy makers and their critics often seem ambivalent about the role of self-determination: at one extreme it maintains dependence, while at the other extreme it implies independence, which is seen as one step closer to termination of the trust relationship.

Trust Land as the Locus of Indian Gaming

Because Indian gaming is predicated on the unique land tenure structure that sustains Indian Country, it is germane to consider some of its long-term implications. Since tribes are sovereign and generally immune from state laws, gaming may flourish on trust lands; this is a political, not proprietal, role of the reservation. However, the Indian Gaming Regulation Act of 1988 invites state participation by requiring tribes to uphold state gaming laws. In order to establish a casino, the tribe must enter into a compact or agreement with the state. If estimates are correct, more than one hundred tribes have established casinos on trust lands since the passage of the act.

The development of tribal gaming has not arrived on the scene without controversy. Many states have sought ways to prevent Indian gaming, many have not negotiated in good faith, and others, having once signed agreements, no longer are so supportive of tribal casinos. Casino income has been lucrative; it has filled a critical void in on-reservation employment and funding, and it has become a major political force in some states. Because gambling nets well into the millions of dollars yearly, California gaming bands (equivalent to tribes but smaller in number) invested heavily in an election campaign that saw an initiative placed on the ballot in early 2000 that has led to a major change in the state constitution's provisos governing gambling. Encouraged by this gain, some Indians want to buy land in better locations, hoping to gain trust status for it in order to establish a casino. California casinos have generated so much revenue that gaming bands and tribes that are members of the California Indian Gaming Alliance are distributing funds to non-gaming Indian communities and absorbing nearly all funding that otherwise has come from the federal government. At the other end of the continent, Foxwoods Casino near Ledyard (CT), run by the Mashantucket Pequot, is perhaps the most well known. Indian casinos are found in nearly every state in which there are Indian reservations.

Indian Country and Tribal Sovereignty

An Indian reservation is property and a political unit. It comprises real estate held by tribes, by their members as tenants-in-common, and by allottees or their heirs. Probably half of all reservations include non-Indian-owned former allotted lands, which constitute a part of reservations even though non-Indians are not part of the on-reservation body politic. Because of the existence of tribal governments, reservations are also political places. It is better to characterize reservations as one political entity in tripartite Indian Country: federal, tribal, and state (or its civil divisions such as cities and counties). While in legal usage, the term *Indian Country* normally applies only to trust lands, in its political/geographical reality, Indian Country also embraces civil divisions such as towns, cities, and counties. All non-Indian land lying within Indian Country predicates the existence of multiple governing units, which form the bases for continued conflicts. Although state laws rarely apply to trust lands or tribal governments, since the 1970s states and local governments have been asserting jurisdiction over environmental and other matters and tribes have resisted this intrusion through litigation. In this regard, for example, the EPA has come to their aid.

Historically, Congress established federal law-and-order jurisdiction on reservations while retaining exclusive authority to enforce the law. At various times, Congress has granted some measure of authority to the states. In 1952, for example, limited criminal and civil authority was transferred to several states: Iowa, Kansas, New York, and North Dakota. The following year, Congress, in Public Law 280, expanded this law-and-order authority onto reservations in California, Nebraska, Minnesota, Oregon, and Wisconsin, and offered other states the option to adopt similar laws. This jurisdiction, which excluded the authority to tax or encumber Indian lands, was misinterpreted and became the vehicle for state intervention into tribal affairs. Congress amended this policy in the Indian Civil Rights Act (1964) so that states could not assume law-and-order jurisdiction without tribal consent, and tribes could seek retrocession of any existing state law-and-order authority. This new legislation did not necessarily curtail state intervention or clear up the confusion over state and tribal jurisdictions.

Tribal assertions of sovereignty or autonomy resurfaced as early as the termination era. By 1968, the American Indian Movement (AIM) was organized and spread across the nation, drawing its membership from both reservation and urban Indians. Litigation and a new spirit of militancy overshadowed the efforts of older Indian advocacy organizations dominated by non-Indian supporters (the Indian Rights Association and the Association on American Indian Affairs). The takeover of Alcatraz Island in northern California in 1969 and the caravan of protesters who marched on Washington, D.C. in the fall of 1972 in the so-called Trail of Broken Treaties contributed to Indian agitation. The confrontation in 1973 between tribal members and local law enforcement and the FBI at Wounded Knee on the Pine Ridge Reservation in South Dakota demonstrated that Indians were increasingly demanding greater autonomy within Indian Country. Resolution of the controversial Native land claims in Alaska finally came about through the passage of the Native Alaska Land Settlement Act in 1971. Indians in the 1970s and since have been demanding that the government fully honor all treaties. Federal funding created the Legal Services Corporation and the Native American Rights Fund (NARF) which, together with other organizations, help to defend Indians and to mount successful lawsuits against non-Indians as well as public agencies (see Chapter 7 on Activism).

Conversely, toward the end of the last century, federal courts were becoming less supportive of tribal sovereignty even as the executive branch championed self-determination. For example, in a case argued by the Devils Lake Sioux, the U.S. Supreme Court decided in favor of a dichotomous jurisdiction on the Fort Totten Indian Reservation (ND). This decision has undermined tribal efforts to establish holistic environmental management. The plaintiff tribe contended that the Court must look at demographics in evaluating the Indian character of the reservation. Despite earlier declines in numbers up to the 1930s, and a commensurate increase in non-Indian numbers, today it is the reverse. However, the Court based its decision on the fact that non-Indian land ownership, concentrated in larger farms on the peripheries of the reservation, had diminished Indian character so that some state jurisdiction applied. As the Court put it, "tribal sovereignty is present where its exercise affects mainly tribal members and not present where its impact falls mainly on nontribal members."

In similar litigation, the Yakama lost holistic jurisdiction over land use where non-Indians formed the majority of owner/operators of lands within reservation borders. On the Yakama Indian Reservation, open and closed areas were designated, the former being mostly non-Indian and thus not subject to tribal authority, the latter constituting an exclusively Indian area. In the late 1990s, the Confederated Salish and Kootenai on the Flathead Indian Reservation (MT) failed to sustain tribal authority despite the provisos in the Clean Water Act that empower tribes to assume regulatory jurisdiction over non-Indians on reservations in terms of setting water standards. The EPA asserted that tribal authority had to fall within the scope of inherent sovereign powers. Such litigation causes tribes much anxiety, for case law points to a direction the courts seem to be taking to diminish tribal authority over non-Indians within reservation borders despite the congressional intent of self-determination.

Retrospect and Prospect

Logically enough, trust lands have been the locus of experimentation in Indian affairs for the past century. The treatment of tribes as nations and later as self-governing entities, and the treatment of Indians as wards and then later as citizens, reflects efforts to modify the trust relationship. Ambivalently, policy makers have urged tribes to take control of reservation economic affairs and to assert tribal property rights. Some critics feel that the BIA lacks accountability in terms of abetting Indian economic growth and that tribes need grassroots entrepreneurial capital and employers. Moreover, today the tribes are equally concerned with protecting, preserving, and managing their environments according to their traditional beliefs. Lawmakers, administrators, and scholars alike recognize the need for multiple approaches in Indian affairs. Not all tribes are equally ready to go independent. Yet some Indians, such as the Navajo, White Mountain Apache, and Warm Springs are moving toward levels of autonomy that provide them with greater opportunities to pursue their own goals. One failing of policy has been the slow pace of acknowledging dozens of unrecognized Indian communities. They neither hold land in trust, nor benefit from services and funding unless they are among the recognized tribes that are the corpus of trust responsibility.

While more tribal Indians will likely move to cities or otherwise separate themselves from the land, there is some indication that a number of Indians have chosen to return to reservations where they may find employment in the casinos or otherwise receive tribal income. Despite the urbanizing trend, Indian residence on the land will continue to reflect a desire to sustain a way of life and ethnic identity, as well as a territorial link to the past, all of which helps to sustain tribal culture and society.

Imre Sutton
California State University, Fullerton

◆ CANADIAN NATIVE DISTRIBUTION, HABITAT, AND DEMOGRAPHY

Aboriginal Peoples in Canada

Canada's constitution (Canada Act, 1982) specifies three categories of "aboriginal peoples": Indians, Inuit, and Métis. The term *Indian* is a historical misnomer. Although it is still required in various legal contexts (such as those referring to the Indian Act), the preferred term today is *First Nations*, with its implication of many separate and formerly sovereign entities. In total, aboriginal people today are estimated to form approximately 2.7 percent of Canada's population.

Indians (First Nations) form by far the largest and most diverse of these categories. Upon contact with Europeans, Indian people occupied all but the northernmost reaches of Canada. Great differences in language, culture, and history separate Canadian First Nations, impeding common political action. In all, 610 Indian bands exist as independent legal and administrative units. Land claims and similar issues tend to be negotiated at the local level, often involving tribal councils of neighboring and related bands. At the national level, the Assembly of First Nations acts as the political voice for Canadian Indians. As of 31 May 2000, a total of 666,335 people were legally recognized by the Canadian government as Indians.

The Inuit, once known as the Eskimo (a term that has now almost totally disappeared in Canada), are the aboriginal occupants of the Arctic. They are a distinct people who are culturally and biologically separate from other aboriginal Canadians. They form a much more homogeneous population in Canada than Indian groups, speaking dialects of a single language (Inuktitut) from the Mackenzie River delta in the west near the Alaska border to Labrador in the east on the Atlantic Ocean. They fall under several political jurisdictions, but are united in a national political body, the Inuit Tapirisat of Canada. Unlike Indians, individual Inuit are not registered by the federal government, so population figures are less exact, but estimates state that there are approximately 45,000 Inuit in Canada.

The Métis, unlike the previous two groups, emerged in Canada only in the historic period. They are a product of the unions between male fur traders, most commonly of French-Canadian origin, and Native women, particularly Cree. The resultant population of mixed ancestry forged a common identity on the Canadian Plains during the nineteenth century. Aspirations for a Métis Nation in the Canadian West ended with their suppression by military forces in Saskatchewan in 1885. After this time they were expected to blend in with the dominant population, and the federal government took no administrative responsibility for them. Only in recent years have the Métis reemerged into public consciousness. Despite being recognized as one of the aboriginal peoples of Canada when the constitution was enacted in 1982, it is still not clear how Métis should be defined today or how many people should be considered under this category.

Aboriginal peoples in Canada can be divided into eleven language families, with approximately fifty different languages. Algonkian is by far the largest and most widespread of the language families. Cree and Ojibwa, the two largest Algonkian languages, are spoken by Native people from Alberta to northern Quebec. The other large language family is Athapascan, with many closely related languages, spread across the northwestern portion of the country. Siouan, spoken by several groups on the Plains, and Iroquoian, around the eastern Great Lakes, are other major language families. Inuktitut, the language of the Canadian Inuit, belongs to the Eskimoan family. Six more families, some consisting of a single language, are restricted to the western portion of the country, in British Columbia.

The great majority of the aboriginal languages of Canada, however, are endangered. Colonial policies of suppressing indigenous languages, particularly through the residential school system, resulted in great language loss. In the Aboriginal Peoples Survey of 1991 only 36 percent of Native adults responded that they could carry on a conversation in an aboriginal language. Only three aboriginal languages—Cree, Ojibwa, and Inuktitut—are spoken over large areas today and are considered to have excellent chances of survival. Many aboriginal communities are making determined efforts to halt or reverse the gradual erosion of their languages. Language and cultural programs have been established in many schools, and a substantial percentage of aboriginal children now receive some form of Native language instruction.

The Algonkians of Eastern Canada

Members of the far-flung Algonkian family occupy a vast area of eastern and central Canada. They include the Ojibwa and their relatives around the western Great Lakes, the Cree of northern Ontario and Quebec, the Innu (formerly known as the Naskapi and Montagnais) of Labrador and adjacent Quebec, and the Mi'kmaq and Maliseet of the Maritime Provinces of the east coast. All have traditional territories in the woodlands and northern forests. The Algonkians of the Plains will be covered in a later section.

The first aboriginal Canadians to come into continuous contact with Europeans were the Beothuk, the occupants of the island of Newfoundland. Their early extinction has left us too little evidence even to be certain that their language belongs to the Algonkian family. These were the original "Red Indians," a term that referred to their fondness for painting the body with red ochre and grease that was later commonly but erroneously applied to other North American First Nations. They were primarily a coastal people, collecting shellfish and hunting both land and sea mammals. Bark-covered canoes allowed them to travel out into the stormy north Atlantic to harpoon seals and collect bird eggs from offshore islands. During the late autumn and winter the Beothuk moved into the interior forests where they constructed long wooden barriers to channel the caribou herds to where the hunters waited with spears or bows and arrows. Enough meat had to be taken and preserved from these hunts to last through the severe winters.

The historic extinction of the Beothuk is one of the tragic chapters in Canada's history. Increasing European settlement along the coastline forced the Beothuk into the interior of the island. Introduced diseases and hostile encounters with the newcomers greatly reduced their population. By the early nineteenth century, they were reduced to a small group, plagued by tuberculosis and malnutrition, living near the center of the island. When Shanawdithit, a Beothuk captive who was the last known survivor, sucumbed to tuberculois in 1829, the Beothuk passed into extinction.

The Mi'kmaq (formerly written Micmac) occupied the east coast of the Canadian mainland, including all three Maritime Provinces (Nova Scotia, New Brunswick, and Prince Edward Island) and Atlantic Quebec. During the early historic period, the search for new sources of furs also led them to settle in southern Newfoundland. The closely related Maliseet were more inland, along the St. John River valley in western New Brunswick.

Like the Beothuk, the Mi'kmaq moved with the seasons between coast and interior. Fish played a major role in their diet, along with shellfish, other seafoods such as lobster, sea birds and their eggs, and seals. Land mammals such as beaver and moose were hunted inland. They carried out this seasonal round with the use of bark-covered canoes along the coast and with snowshoes, sleds, and toboggans (the latter taking its English name directly from the Mi'kmaq) for the deep snow of the interior.

The numerous groups collectively known today as Ojibwa (or Ojibway, or, particularly in the United States, Chippewa) were originally centered on the western Great Lakes area. During the fur trade they expanded rapidly, east as far as Saskatchewan, north into northern Ontario, and south into southern Ontario and such

American states as Michigan and Wisconsin. No collective identity was held across this vast area; they consisted of numerous small independent bands speaking a continuum of mutually intelligible dialects. Numerous separate groups, known in the historic records as Saulteaux, Ottawa, Nipissing, Mississauga, and others, are considered to be Ojibwa, based on a common language and shared traditions.

Ojibwa subsistence was based on an annual round of hunting, fishing, and plant collecting. Sizable populations congregated seasonally at particularly good fishing locales, such as the rapids at Sault Sainte Marie on Lake Superior. The shallow lakes of the area provided wild rice, which was an important part of the diet for many Ojibwa. Maple sugar was prepared from the sweet sap of the maple tree and used as a seasoning for a wide range of foods. Some of the southern groups, in contact with the Iroquoian-speaking Huron, practiced marginal agriculture or traded fish and furs for agricultural produce.

To the north were the Cree, who occupied the northern forests from Alberta to Quebec, along with the Innu (Naskapi and Montagnais) of Labrador and northeastern Quebec. As their environment provided fewer wild plant resources and good fishing locations, the northern groups relied more heavily on hunting. Moose, caribou, bear, and beaver were the major game species. This was a precarious lifestyle, particularly in winter when few resources were available, and winter starvation was an ever-present threat.

Numerous shared features characterize the Algonkian people of the woodlands. Social organization usually took the form of small, highly mobile bands, although southern groups were able to gather seasonally in larger numbers. Societies were essentially egalitarian, although status distinctions developed among some of the larger groups. To meet the needs of a mobile population, housing had to be simple and portable. Birchbark provided the ideal cover, although moose or caribou hide was used in the north. These could be rolled up and carried between camps, then quickly stretched over a framework of poles to form the dome-shaped structure known throughout eastern North America by the Algonkian term *wigwam*. Birchbark also provided lightweight cover for the canoes that were so important to summer travel throughout the region. Snowshoes were essential in winter.

A fundamental part of Algonkian religious belief was respect for the animals they hunted. The hunter's skill alone was not enough; the animal had to offer itself to the hunter. Only through proper ceremonial acts could humans wrest from nature what they needed to survive. Feasts were held after the kill of larger game to celebrate and honor the animal. Particular care had to be taken with the bones, so that the animals would not be offended and avoid the hunters on future occasions. Animal skulls were hung from trees, and special platforms were built to keep the bones out of reach of the camp's dogs. Divination rituals were also practiced to determine the location of the animals or to predict the outcome of the hunt. All the Algonkian groups had shamans, who used their ties to the supernatural world to cure diseases or to foretell the future. A widespread ritual was the shaking tent, where the violent movements of a small shelter announced the arrival of spirit visitors to assist the shaman in such endeavors.

European arrival and the subsequent fur trade caused major changes in Algonkian life. Trade relations may have begun even prior to the earliest recorded contact. When Jacques Cartier first encountered the Mi'kmaq off the east coast in 1534, they were waving furs and hailing the ship, signaling their desire to trade. Iron knives and hatchets, copper kettles, blankets, and other European goods soon replaced many objects of aboriginal manufacture. A French writer in the 1630s noted that the Indians of the St. Lawrence River, the major trade artery of the early historic period, had already forsaken their traditional garb for European clothing, and copper kettles had completely replaced traditional vessels of bark. Establishment of trading posts throughout Algonkian territory further tied Native groups to the fur trade and led many to relocate their villages around the posts. Alcohol was widely used in trade, with devastating effects on many Natives. Diseases also arrived with the traders, causing great loss of Native life. The search for new trapping lands for beaver and other fur-bearers led many Cree and Ojibwa groups to spread north and west; their far-flung distribution today is largely a result of the new opportunities offered by the historic fur trade.

Today the Algonkians are scattered in small reserves across a large part of the country. Hunting, fishing, and trapping are still important activities for many groups, particularly in the north. Environmental degradation, however, poses major problems. Massive hydroelectric projects in northern Quebec and in northern Manitoba have flooded large areas and threaten the Cree way of life. In northwestern Ontario, industrial wastes have resulted in mercury pollution of the waterways, making fish, the mainstay of the Ojibwa economy, unsafe to eat. In Labrador, the Innu maintain that low-level military training flights over their hunting grounds have scattered the caribou and destroyed traditional hunting activities.

Although many Algonkian groups signed historic treaties, no such land surrenders took place in Quebec and Labrador. The Cree and Naskapi of northern Quebec signed the first land claims agreements in modern

Canadian history in the 1970s. Other groups are still pressing for resolution of their claims.

The Iroquoians of the Eastern Great Lakes

The Iroquoians were part of a large linguistic stock centered on the area around the eastern Great Lakes. At contact, the Canadian Iroquoians consisted of the Huron, Petun, and Neutral in southern Ontario, and the lesser-known St. Lawrence Iroquoians, primarily in southern Quebec. Most in Canada today, however, are Iroquois proper or Six Nations, whose arrival in Canada from upper New York State stems from the tumultuous events of the historic period.

An agricultural economy distinguished the Iroquoian groups from all other aboriginal Canadians. They grew corn, beans, and squash, supplementing this agricultural diet by fishing and hunting. The everyday meal was a thick corn soup, to which pieces of fish, meat, or squash might be added for variety. Tobacco was also grown in their fields; in fact, the Jesuits referred to the Petun as "the Tobacco Nation."

Villages were large collections of longhouses, some containing several thousand individuals. The bark-covered longhouses sheltered multiple families, and could easily be extended in length if populations grew. Raised benches or sleeping platforms ran the length of each side, leaving a central corridor for the cooking fires. Fish and corn, as well as personal belongings, hung from the roof of the house or were kept in covered pits. Many villages were surrounded with palisades of poles twisted into the ground, often in several rows. Exhaustion of nearby soils and firewood supplies meant that villages had to be moved every ten to fifteen years.

The first to be encountered by Europeans were the Iroquoians of the St. Lawrence River. Jacques Cartier sailed up the St. Lawrence in 1535 and wintered near the village of Stadacona (where modern Quebec City now stands). Cartier provides few details on the appearance of Stadacona but has left a fuller account of his brief visit to Hochelaga, a larger village upriver at the location of modern Montreal. Typical of Iroquoian villages, it was situated well back from the river for defensive reasons, requiring a walk through extensive fields of corn. Cartier describes about fifty bark-covered longhouses surrounded by a triple row of palisades, with ladders leading to platforms where defenders could stand during an attack.

The St. Lawrence Iroquoians were also the first casualties in a series of extinctions that were to overtake the northeastern groups early in the historic period. After Cartier's departure, no further historic records exist until the arrival of Samuel de Champlain on the St. Lawrence in 1603. By this time the Stadaconans and Hochelagans had vanished, leaving only Algonkian and Mohawk war parties locked in bitter conflict over control of this vital trade waterway.

The Ontario Iroquoians, consisting of the Huron, Petun, and Neutral, survived into the mid-seventeenth century. The closely related Huron and Petun had coalesced by the early historic period around Georgian Bay, at the eastern end of Lake Huron. The Huron had particularly close ties with the French, who were drawn into this area by a combination of colonial policy, a lucrative fur trade, and missionary zeal. The most important source of information on traditional Huron culture is the voluminous writings of the Jesuits, chronicling their missionizing activities among the Huron from 1634 to 1650. The Neutral were to the south, concentrated around the western end of Lake Ontario. Their rejection of the Jesuits' proselytizing efforts means that details of their traditional culture are less well known.

All three groups were confederacies of separate tribes, linked in a common council. Village affairs were conducted by local councils, one concerned with feasts, ceremonies, and other peaceful pursuits, and another dedicated to matters of war. Councils attempted to reach a consensus, and all present were able to express their views.

Warfare shaped much of Iroquoian life. Prior to the disruptions of the early historic period, it seems to have been primarily motivated by a desire to avenge previous deaths and acquire personal prestige. Later the Iroquoians became embroiled in bitter warfare over access to furs and fur trade routes. Captives and trophies of enemies killed were taken back to their villages. Some captives were tortured and killed, while others were adopted and incorporated into the society. The latter was an important historic method of replacing individuals lost in warfare.

Infectious diseases brought by Europeans greatly weakened the Ontario Iroquoian groups, but it was warfare that destroyed them as distinct political entities. Between 1648 and 1651 the Huron, Petun, and Neutral were overwhelmed by the military force of the League of the Iroquois, particularly the Seneca and Mohawk. Many perished at the hands of the Iroquois, others were driven out of their homelands to form refugee populations and eventually lose their distinct identity, and still others were taken captive and incorporated into Iroquois groups. When the Jesuits abandoned their base among the Huron and fled to Quebec City in 1650, they took with them several hundred Huron survivors. Known as the Huron of Lorette, or more recently as the Nation Huronne Wendat, this

French-speaking community of several thousand people in present-day Quebec is the only recognized vestige of Huron culture in Canada.

The great majority of Iroquoian people in Canada today are Iroquois proper, members of the famed League of the Iroquois, whose homeland was in New York State. From west to east these were the Seneca, Cayuga, Onondaga, Oneida, and Mohawk. Early in the eighteenth century, an additional Iroquoian group, the Tuscarora, joined the league. The term Six Nations is commonly applied to the league members after this time.

The first of the League Iroquois to move into Canada came as a result of the missionizing efforts of the Jesuits. Large numbers of converts to Catholicism, primarily Mohawk, settled along the St. Lawrence River during the late seventeenth century. Eventually these settlements became the modern Mohawk communities of Kahnawake and Kanesatake, near Montreal, and Akwesasne, straddling the international border with portions in Ontario, Quebec, and New York.

The largest wave of Iroquois arrived in Canada after the American Revolution. The Mohawk had been staunch British loyalists, and most of the Iroquois fought on the British side during the war. After the war, they were granted lands in Canada for their loyalty. One group of Mohawk moved to the Bay of Quinte on northern Lake Ontario. A larger group, under the famed Mohawk war leader Joseph Brant, settled along the Grand River in southern Ontario near modern Brantford. The several thousand individuals who arrived with Brant included members of all six Iroquois nations, plus a considerable number of Delaware (an Algonkian-speaking people) and others who had lost their homelands and sought refuge in the league. Each established separate tribal villages along the Grand River. Today this land grant, although greatly reduced in size, is home to the largest Native community in Canada, the Six Nations of the Grand River. Over 20,000 people, in thirteen separate "registry groups" (stemming from the original settlements), are members of this First Nation.

A final arrival came with several hundred Oneida in the 1840s. Loss of their traditional lands and a desire to reunite with other members of the league led to their movement into southern Ontario. Today they are a large community known as the Oneida Nation of the Thames.

The Canadian Iroquois now outnumber those who remain in their American homeland. Three of the four largest First Nations in Canada are Iroquois. The Mohawk predominate, and it is the Mohawk language that has the best chance of survival. Mohawk insistence on controlling their own educational programs, particularly at Kahnawake, helps safeguard the language.

The Iroquois are in a unique situation in Canada. They consider themselves to be a sovereign people, entering Canada as loyal allies. They have rejected the policies of the Canadian government, which treats them as dependents. For many traditionalists, the only valid government structures are the hereditary councils within the League of the Iroquois. This position has led to numerous clashes with the Canadian and U.S. governments.

This tension erupted in violence during the summer of 1990. The flashpoint was at Kanesatake, the Mohawk community at Oka, just west of Montreal. Expansion of a municipal golf course onto lands the Mohawk considered theirs led to resistance. When armed provincial police stormed the Mohawk barricades, the Mohawk responded with armed force. Mohawk from other communities rushed to join the defenders at the Oka barricades, and the people of Kahnawake forcefully closed the bridge that runs through their reserve, cutting off one of the major traffic arteries into Montreal. The Canadian government sent the army into what became a seventy-eight-day military standoff. Although the situation was eventually defused, the underlying issues have not been resolved. It did, however, focus the attention of the Canadian government and people on Native grievances across the country.

First Nations of the Plains

The environment of the Canadian Plains is the flat, semi-arid grasslands extending across the southern portions of Alberta, Saskatchewan, and Manitoba. Vast herds of bison once roamed across this open land, providing the economic basis for all Plains Natives. Not only did the Plains hunters rely on the bison for meat but also for the hides, which provided shelter and clothing. The stereotyped image of Indians in the public imagination is the Plains bison hunter and warrior, on horseback and clad in buckskin and feathers.

Despite the common image of the warrior on horseback, horses were not always part of Plains culture. Throughout the millennia prior to European contact, Plains people traveled and hunted on foot, using dogs to help carry their goods. Horses arrived with the Spanish and were in common use among the southern Plains tribes by the mid-seventeenth century. It was a century later, however, before they were a significant feature in the lives of the Canadian Plains groups. Once horses were available in considerable numbers they transformed Plains societies, fostering greater mobility, increased trade and warfare, larger social groupings, and more elaborate material culture.

Speakers of Algonkian languages dominated the northern Plains. In the west were the members of the

Assiniboine Indian running a buffalo. Painting by Paul Kane from his travels in the 1840s. (Courtesy of Royal Ontario Museum)

powerful Blackfoot Confederacy, composed of the Siksika (formerly known as Blackfoot), Blood, and Peigan Nations. Their bitter foes throughout much of the historic period were the Plains Cree and Plains Ojibwa, recent arrivals from the woodlands to the east, along with their Assiniboine allies, who were members of the Siouan language family. Finally, a small Athapascan-speaking group, the Sarcee, arrived on the Plains from the north early in the historic period and became part of the Blackfoot Confederacy.

All Plains groups based their lives on the vast herds of bison. With the arrival of the horse, hunters could ride along with the stampeding herd, selecting the animal with care and dispatching it with the bow and arrow. Techniques that had been used for millennia continued throughout the historic period. Communal hunting methods, where large numbers of bison could be taken, include jumps, where bison were driven over a cliff edge, and pounds, where they were driven into a corral or natural trap. Both required considerable preparation, including construction of long drive lines to funnel the animals to the desired location. The cliffs at Head-Smashed-In in southern Alberta, perhaps the most

famous of such sites, were used repeatedly for nearly 6,000 years, most recently by the historic Blackfoot.

Essential to the nomadic lifestyle were the tipi and travois. A cover of sewn bison hides was supported on a framework of poles to form the conical tipi. Flaps at the top helped control smoke from the central fire. An inside liner protected the occupants from drafts. Sleeping robes laid around the walls served as couches during the day. When the camp was set to move, the tipi could be taken down quickly and the cover packed with other possessions on a travois, a framework of poles that was dragged behind the horse.

Warfare was a pervasive part of the culture and provided the major route to prestige for young men. Military excursions ranged from a few individuals setting out to steal horses to large parties of allied groups engaged in full-scale war against traditional enemies. Warrior societies kept order in camp and on the hunt and provided a common bond linking the various bands into larger political organizations.

Religion permeated everyday life. Supernatural power could reside in any unusual object or feature of the landscape. Young people sought supernatural assistance by fasting and praying in secluded locations, hoping for a vision. Medicine bundles, the most important ritual possessions, contained sacred objects, often those indicated through supernatural encounters. Opening the bundle required elaborate ceremonies, as did its transfer to a new owner, each object being reverently displayed while prayers and songs invoked its spiritual power. Important religious events, such as the Sun Dance, brought together large numbers of people to participate in the ceremonies. These tradional religious beliefs have survived the period of historic suppression; ceremonies such as the Sun Dance are again being held and medicine bundles are being repatriated from museums for ritual use.

Introduced diseases and destruction of the bison herds struck at the heart of Plains cultures. Smallpox epidemics swept the Plains at intervals during the eighteenth and nineteenth centuries, taking great tolls on Native life. Wanton slaughter of the bison and opening of the prairies for European agricultural settlement meant disappearance of the herds by the early 1880s.

The Natives of the Plains, with their populations reduced and the bison largely gone, were in no position to resist government offers of assistance in exchange for signing treaties. Between 1871 and 1877, the Canadian Plains tribes ceded by treaty all claims to their lands. The treaties allocated reserves and provided small payments of money and farm equipment. Instructors were sent to the reserves to supervise the transition to farming, which was frequently a failure. Widespread hunger and disease, along with suppression of traditional customs and beliefs, characterized this period.

Refugees from American battles also moved into Canada during this time. The Dakota (also known as the Sioux) arrived in two waves. The first were eastern (Santee) Dakota from Minnesota, fleeing their homeland after a disastrous uprising and defeat in 1862. Initially settling near Fort Garry in southern Manitoba, many followed the declining bison herds west and north. The second arrival involved the western (Teton) Dakota and their famed chief Sitting Bull, seeking sanctuary after their annihilation of George Custer's troops at the Battle of the Little Big Horn. Thousands of Dakota, including Sitting Bull, arrived in Saskatchewan during 1876 and 1877. By this time, however, the bison were nearly gone and the other Plains Natives were being confined to reserves. The Teton were denied land and rations, eventually forcing most to leave. Today the Dakota in Canada are primarily Santee, although one Teton community remains. All were eventually assigned reserves and are administered as Canadian Indians, although without treaty.

Despite miserable living conditions, outbreaks of violence were few. The only exception occurred in 1885 with the Métis resistence under Louis Riel in Saskatchewan (see Riel's biography in "Prominent Native North Americans"). Several groups of Plains Cree and Assiniboine, under chiefs Big Bear and Poundmaker (see their biographies in "Prominent Native North Americans"), took up arms in sympathy, but the members of the Blackfoot Confederacy refused to be drawn into the conflict. The rebellion was short-lived and failed to win any consideration of Native grievances.

Today many reserve communities, particularly in Manitoba and Saskatchewan, lack any real economic base. Movement to the cities is a common response, with Regina and Winnipeg having among the highest percentages of Native residents in the country. In Alberta, oil and gas revenues for some bands and ranching for others have offered higher levels of economic security.

The Plateau

The high, generally arid Plateau lies between the Rocky Mountains on the east and the Coast Mountains on the west. The environment varies from sagebrush near-desert in the rainshadow of the Coast Mountains to heavily forested mountain slopes on the edge of the Rockies. Only the northern half of the Plateau is in Canada, in southern British Columbia.

Three Native language families can be found in this area. The largest is the interior branch of the Salish family, containing four languages: Lillooet, Thompson, Okanagan, and Shuswap. The Kutenai, in the mountainous southeast of British Columbia, are a linguistic isolate. The Plateau Athapascans consist of the now-extinct Nicola in the central Canadian Plateau and the Chilcotin and several groups of southern Carrier in the north.

The Interior Salish, along with neighboring Athapascans, practiced a way of life based on hunting, fishing, and gathering plant foods, moving with the seasons as resources became available. Salmon played the major role in the economies of most groups, and much of the late summer and fall was spent intercepting the spawning runs. Canyons provided particularly good fishing locations, where masses of fish teemed in the eddies and could be easily scooped out of the water in large dip-nets or could be harpooned or taken in traps. Large numbers of people congregated around such locations, resulting in very high population densities in favored parts of the Plateau, such as the territory of the Thompson and Upper Lillooet. Large quantities of salmon were cut into thin strips and dried in the warm canyon breezes, providing an assured supply of food for the long winter months and a valued trading commodity to groups lacking adequate supplies of this vital resource.

The dominant type of winter dwelling in the Plateau was the semi-subterranean pit house. A log superstructure over a circular pit was covered with bark and earth, providing effective insulation against the cold. Winter villages consisted of a small cluster of pit houses, each sheltering several families. Each of these villages was politically autonomous. A few groups did not use the pit house, instead banking earth and snow against their mat-covered lodges. In the warmer months people dispersed to their fishing, hunting, root-digging, or berry-picking camps, living in simple structures of bark or mats over a framework of poles.

The Kutenai (spelled Ktunaxa by the tribal council), on the mountainous eastern edge of the Plateau, differed considerably from other Plateau groups. They are a distinct people, speaking a unique language. Many of their culture traits resemble those of the Plains, where they were first encountered by European explorers. The Upper Kutenai, higher into the Rockies and closest to the Plains, had the strongest Plains cast to their culture. They hunted big game such as elk, deer, and mountain goats and sheep, and crossed the mountains several times a year to hunt bison on the Plains. Such excursions brought them into conflict with the Blackfoot, requiring the full military organization of Plains warriors. The Lower Kutenai, further down the Kootenay River and along Kootenay Lake, relied on more typical Plateau resources such as deer, ducks, and fish. The Plains-style, bison-hide-covered tipi was the year-round dwelling among the Upper Kutenai, while the Lower Kutenai resided in mat-covered tipis, with elongated mat-covered lodges as winter dwellings. Both groups wore the typical tanned hide clothing of the Plains and Plateau.

Initial contacts with Europeans came with Alexander Mackenzie's travel through Shuswap and Chilcotin lands to the Pacific in 1793 and with Simon Fraser's epic journey down the Fraser River in 1808. Fraser noticed copper kettles and other European goods traded in from the coast among the Plateau Salish. Extensive disruption of Native cultures, however, did not occur until 1858, with the gold rush in the Fraser Canyon. The sudden influx of thousands of gold-seekers resulted in Natives being displaced from their traditional lands. Smallpox and other diseases greatly diminished their numbers. During the 1870s and 1880s, they were assigned small, scattered reserves. The Plateau groups, however, never ceded their land through treaties. Today land claims are among the most contentious issues, along with such other grievances as legal restrictions on Native fisheries.

The Northwest Coast

Rainforest blankets the rugged Pacific coastline of British Columbia. The mountainous terrain, with its myriad islands, bays, and inlets, provided a bountiful environment for cultures adapted to a maritime way of life. Large dugout cedar canoes once traversed these waterways, providing the only means of transportation along the coast. Villages of cedar-plank houses were nestled in locations sheltered from the winter storms. Coastal culture extended far up the major rivers—the Nass, the Skeena, and the Fraser—so that even groups lacking direct access to salt water shared the coastal lifestyle.

This is by far the most linguistically diverse area of aboriginal Canada. Sixteen mutually unintelligible languages, clustered into five separate language families, are spoken. In the north are the Haida of the Queen Charlotte Islands and the Tsimshian on the mainland, along with the Tlingit, who occupied southeastern Alaska and extended a short distance into Canada. Haida and Tlingit are linguistic isolates, but Tsimshian has three languages—Coast Tsimshian, Nisga'a (Nass River), and Gitksan (Skeena River). To the south are members of the large Wakashan family, divided into northern and southern branches. The northern Wakashans, from north to south, are the Haisla, Heiltsuk, and Kwakwaka'wakw or Kwagiulth (historically known as the "Southern Kwakiutl"). The southern Wakashans, on the west coast of Vancouver Island, are the Nuu-chah-nulth and the closely related Ditidaht (both formerly but erroneously referred to as the "Nootka"). The large Salish family includes the Nuxalk (formerly called the Bella Coola) on the central coast, and the Comox, Sechelt, Squamish, Halkomelem, and Straits languages on the southern coast. Four of these five language families occur only on the Northwest Coast, and all five are unique in Canada to British Columbia.

Everywhere along the coast people relied on the bounty of the sea, beach, and rivers. Salmon was the fundamental resource for almost all groups. Huge quantities were taken by hook and line, nets, traps, and harpoons, with much being dried and stored for winter use. Halibut, cod, and other fish were also important. Herring were valued for the spawn, and eulachon, a small greasy smelt, was rendered down for its oil, providing a sauce to enliven the taste of dried foods. Seals and sea lions were hunted by all groups, although only the Nuu-chah-nulth went out onto the open sea to harpoon whales. Digging clams, prying mussels off the rocks, and collecting other such beach foods were important tasks, as was collecting various plant foods such as berries, shoots, and roots. Effective exploitation of various resources frequently required shifting residence in a seasonal pattern of movement. Important resource locations, such as salmon streams or productive berry patches, were jealously guarded private property. The abundance and security of the food supply supported the densest aboriginal populations in Canada.

The western red cedar provided the basis for the technology of all Northwest Coast groups. The wood's long, straight grain allowed large planks to be split from a cedar log, using wedges of antler or hardwood tapped with a stone hammer. Most of the material culture items, from houses to canoes to storage and cooking boxes, were made of cedar. Architectural styles varied from north to south, but all shared a basic pattern. Massive cedar posts supported huge roof beams and a series of rafters, forming a framework covered with split-cedar planks. These were large structures, meant to shelter a number of related families. Inside support posts could be carved with crest animals, and at the front of the house might stand a number of carved cedar monuments, the famous totem poles of the Northwest Coast. These were primarily heraldic in function, as important chiefs commissioned artists to depict family-owned crest images. Regional art styles differed considerably, and not all groups carved free-standing poles, but all had some tradition of monumental artwork in wood.

While woodworking was a male task, responsibility for weaving fell to the women, who used the bark and roots of the cedar to craft beautiful basketry, matting, and clothing. Most everyday clothing on the coast was woven from strips of cedar bark, pounded until soft and supple. Wide-brimmed woven hats protected both sexes from the sun and rain. Men wrapped cedar-bark blankets around their bodies, often fastening them with a pin at the front. Women wore skirts of shredded cedar bark and blankets or capes. In colder weather fur robes were added. For special occasions, chiefs were wrapped in beautifully woven blankets of mountain goat wool. Most people went barefoot year-round; only the upriver and most northerly groups used footgear. The hide moccasins and tailored hide clothing worn across the rest of aboriginal Canada were poorly suited to the wet conditions of the Northwest Coast.

The primary social unit all along the coast was a group of kin who shared a name and a tradition of descent from a common ancestor. Among the northern groups, membership in this kin group was matrilineal (traced through the mother). Elsewhere on the coast, membership could be claimed through either the male or female lines. These kin groups held ownership to all important resource locations, as well as such intangibles as names, ritual dances, and rights to depict certain crest figures such as ravens or killer whales.

Northwest Coast people placed great emphasis on inherited rank and privileges. Chiefs and nobles held high-ranking names and controlled access to group-owned territories and rights. Management of the group's resources allowed chiefs to accumulate wealth, which could be publicly distributed at feasts and potlatches to enhance their status. High-ranking individuals sought marriage partners of equivalent rank in other social groups, providing an opportunity for political alliance and the transfer of wealth, including names and ceremonial prerogatives. Commoners, who lacked important inherited rights, were essential to provide the labor necessary to accumulate food and wealth. Slaves, obtained through purchase or warfare, performed the most menial tasks.

The major ceremony was the potlatch, which played an essential role in the ranking system. Any change in status required a chief and his kin to invite others to witness their claim. A high-status marriage, birth of an heir, the assumption of an inherited name, or the raising of a totem pole were examples of such occasions. An essential feature of the potlatch was the distribution of large quantities of gifts to all present. Performances of masked dancers also enlivened such events. As much theater as dance, the performances reenacted ancestral encounters with supernatural beings, when important rights were transferred to the human world. Some of the finest examples of Northwest Coast art are the masks, rattles, and other items used in these performances.

Contact with Europeans did not occur until the 1770s. Fleeting contact with several Spanish expeditions preceded the arrival of Captain James Cook among the Nuu-chah-nulth in 1778. These early expeditions set the stage for the period of intensive trade that followed. Vessels from several nations descended on the coast beginning in the mid-1780s in a quest for valuable furs, particularly those of the sea otter. In return the coastal people received metal tools and other European goods, which sparked new heights in potlatching and artistic production. Introduced diseases also arrived with the traders' ships. Destruction of the sea otter stocks brought this period to a close early in the nineteenth century.

The land-based fur trade period soon followed. Hudson's Bay Company trading posts were established at key locations along the coast. Many Native groups resettled around the posts, requiring extensive changes in their economic and social systems. Readily available European goods, such as the Hudson's Bay Company blanket, replaced many items of aboriginal manufacture. Firearms from the traders made inter-tribal warfare more deadly, and alcohol brought social problems and demoralization to many groups. The more settled conditions around the posts also fostered the spread of epidemic diseases, taking great tolls of Native life.

The arrival of settlers led to the establishment of colonial governments, first on Vancouver Island and later on mainland British Columbia. Fourteen colonial treaties were signed with individual Native groups on Vancouver Island between 1850 and 1854, allocating small reserves and payments of money. Reserves were based on traditional use of the land, resulting in each group receiving a number of small scattered locations corresponding to seasonal villages and fishing stations. After British Columbia entered the Canadian confederation in 1871, responsibility for Indian administration shifted to the federal government. The process of establishing numerous small reserves based on traditional use of the land continued, although no further treaties were signed. Native customs were attacked by government agents and missionaries, leading in 1884 to the outlawing of the potlatch through a provision in the Indian Act.

Land claims have continued to be the paramount political concern for the First Nations of British Columbia. The Nisga'a of the north coast were the first to form a tribal council to pursue their claims. Their legal suit against the Canadian government (the Calder case) reached a historic, although inconclusive, decision in the Supreme Court in 1973. Although the judgement was a technical defeat for the Nisga'a, it demonstrated the strength of their legal case and forced the federal government to reconsider its position. The resulting negotiations were prolonged, but an agreement among the Nisga'a, Canada, and British Columbia was finally reached in 1998. This agreement, after ratification by all three parties and the Senate, came into legal effect in 2000. It provides the Nisga'a with lands, financial compensation, and a wide range of self-governing powers. Other bands and tribal councils are now engaged in similar negotiations.

A cultural revival has occurred in recent decades. Northwest Coast art has been recognized as one of the world's great art forms, and a number of artists have achieved national and international acclaim. Dances and ceremonies are continuing or being reestablished in many Native communities. Local councils are taking control of their own educational programs, ensuring that their languages and histories are being taught to their children.

The Athapascans of the Western Subarctic

Members of the large Athapascan language family occupy much of northwestern North America, from the west side of Hudson Bay to interior Alaska. More than twenty Athapascan languages, including those in Alaska, have been defined for the Subarctic. All are closely related and tend to grade into one another through a series of intermediate dialects. Athapascan languages in the Canadian Subarctic, in rough order of number of speakers today, are: Chipewyan, Carrier, Slavey, Gwich'in, Tutchone, Tahltan, Dogrib, Hare, Beaver, Kaska, Sekani, Han, and Tagish. The latter two hang on the brink of extinction. Many Athapascans, particularly those in the north, refer to themselves collectively as the Dene.

Northern boreal forest covers the land, which is crossed by numerous rivers and dotted with lakes. The region is physiographically diverse, with three broad divisions. In the east is the rocky country of the Canadian Shield. In the center are the Mackenzie Lowlands, sloping gradually to the Mackenzie River Delta. In the west are the mountains and valleys of the Cordillera, extending from the Yukon to central British Columbia.

Caribou and moose were the among the most important game animals for the Athapascan hunters. Bison herds were also available to some of the more southerly groups, and in the Cordillera mountain goats and sheep were hunted. Smaller mammals, especially the snowshoe hare, played an important role in the diet. Great numbers of migratory waterfowl could be taken for brief periods each year, and the lakes and rivers provided whitefish, lake trout, grayling, and other fish. Groups on the western edge of the Subarctic, where rivers flow to the Pacific, had access to bountiful runs of salmon.

Athapascan societies were small and highly mobile, following game across a large area. Snowshoes and sleds or toboggans were essential to winter transportation, while in summer people traveled along the lakes and rivers in bark-covered canoes. Housing differed by region, but most groups used simple hide-covered conical or domed structures. Group size and economy varied with available resources, but throughout the Subarctic population density was low. Groups lacked formal chiefs, but individuals could take leadership roles for specific tasks, such as hunting, trade, or war. The social organization was flexible, and cultures differed with the environment. The Chipewyan and the Tahltan provide good examples of differing local adaptations.

The Chipewyan, the most numerous and widespread of the Subarctic Athapascans, were an "edge-of-the-forest" people, wintering in the northern forest and following the caribou herds far out onto the tundra or barrenlands during the summer. Caribou were taken along their migration routes, often by driving the herds into large circular brush enclosures where they could be more easily killed. The meat was dried for winter use; the hides were made into clothing and lodge covers, and cut into strips for snares, nets, and snowshoe lacings; the antlers and bones were important raw materials for tools, and the sinew was essential for sewing clothing. Fishing also provided a major part of the diet.

In the mountains of the Cordillera to the west are the Tahltan of northwestern British Columbia. The Stikine River provided the salmon runs that formed the basis of their economy, although they also hunted caribou, mountain goats, and other game. Contact with the Tlingit downriver resulted in the adoption of many Northwest Coast traits, such as potlatching and matrilineal clans. Their location allowed the Tahltan to become intermediaries in trade between the Tlingit on the coast and the Athapascans further inland.

The historic fur trade brought major changes to the Western Subarctic. Posts were established on western Hudson Bay as early as 1682, although initially the trade was dominated by the Cree. Access to firearms and other goods gave the Cree an advantage in warfare, causing losses in lives and land among the Chipewyan. To bring the Chipewyan into direct trade, the Hudson's Bay Company constructed Fort Churchill in 1717, after negotiating a peace with the Cree. The Chipewyan did not embrace the fur-trade lifestyle as fully as the Cree had done, but some groups moved further south to get better access to fur-bearing animals, abandoning their northern caribou hunts.

Following the epic travels of Alexander Mackenzie to the mouth of the Mackenzie River in 1789 and to the Pacific in 1793, the North West Company established fur trade posts throughout Athapascan territory, forcing the Hudson's Bay Company to move inland and do likewise. This period of competition ended with the merger of the two companies in 1821. Many Athapascan groups settled around the trading posts, focusing their economies on trapping animals for furs and trading for European goods. Metal tools and European clothing replaced aboriginal counterparts, and firearms and ammunition became essential trade items.

Discovery of gold brought massive cultural disruptions to the Cordilleran Athapascans. The Caribou gold rush, which reached its height in 1862, brought large numbers of gold-seekers into Carrier territory. The 1898 Klondike gold rush profoundly affected the Yukon Athapascans, nearly destroying the Han whose lands were at the center.

Increased non-Indian settlement in the northwest led the Canadian government to negotiate treaties with the Athapascans. Much of the Western Subarctic is covered under large federal treaties, signed between 1899 and 1921. In other areas, modern political efforts have focused on land claims. Recent agreements have been reached with the Athapascans of the Yukon and Mackenzie Delta areas.

Athapascan communities in northern Canada today rely on some combination of trapping, government assistance, and wage labor. Continued encroachment of resource industries and non-Native settlement threatens local trapping and subsistence hunting. Native political organizations, such as the Dene Nation in the Northwest Territories, are fighting for recognition of Native land claims and right to self-determination.

The Inuit

The Inuit are the aboriginal occupants of the Arctic, the lands lying north of the tree line. The Arctic is physiographically varied, ranging from the rugged mountains and fjords of the eastern islands, to the rocky rolling terrain of the interior barrenlands, to the flat plain of the Mackenzie Delta. Winters are long and extremely cold, with a midwinter period in the northern regions where sunlight is entirely absent. Summers are short and moderate in temperature, with long daylight hours.

Inuktitut, the Inuit language, was spoken across the entire Canadian Arctic. Population density across this vast area was low. Social groups were generally small, although certain seasonal tasks, such as winter sealing among the Central Inuit and whaling among the Mackenzie Delta Inuit, brought together larger numbers. Leadership was informal, with the opinion of the most experienced and respected elder carrying greatest weight.

All groups relied on some combination of hunting land and sea mammals, along with fishing. Caribou were by far the most important of the land mammals, while seals were the vital sea mammals, although walrus and whales were taken by some groups. Caribou were also essential for their hides, taken in fall when they were in best condition and used to make warm winter clothing. Sealskin boots were also essential for wetter conditions. Women's clothing was often more elaborate than men's, with extra space at the back of the coat to carry babies against the mother's skin. Regional differences in clothing style and decoration were evident.

The successful food quest also required strict observation of taboos. One of the most widespread was the belief that products of land and sea must not be mixed. As a result, seal and caribou meat could never be cooked together, and all sewing of caribou skins for winter clothing had to be completed before the people moved to their sealing camps on the sea ice. Shamans held supernatural power, which enabled them to cure the sick, prophesy the future, and locate the game animals.

In the west were the Inuit of the Mackenzie Delta region, who were closely related to Inuit groups in northern Alaska. Whaling was an important part of their economy. The large bowhead whale was hunted on the Beaufort Sea from umiaks (large, hide-covered open boats), and the small beluga whales were hunted in the shallows of the delta from kayaks. This economy allowed the densest concentration of Inuit people in Canada, living in large villages of semi-subterranean driftwood log houses along the delta. Infectious diseases nearly wiped out these people by the end of the nineteenth century, and the population has been replaced in subsequent years by more recent arrivals from Alaska. These people consider themselves distinct from other Canadian Inuit today, referring to themselves as the Inuvialuit.

In the central Arctic are the Copper, Netsilik, Iglulik, and Baffinland Inuit. In the winter most groups moved far out onto the sea ice, hunting seals through their breathing holes in the ice. During this time they lived in dome-shaped snow houses, or igloos, which were lit and heated by blubber lamps made of soapstone. In summer and fall people lived inland, fishing and hunting caribou while living in sealskin tents. The closely related Caribou Inuit occupied the interior barrenlands west of Hudson Bay. Theirs was a specialized way of life, relying almost totally on hunting caribou. Such reliance on a single resource is perilous, and periods of starvation did occur.

In the east were the various Inuit groups of northern Quebec and Labrador. They relied heavily on hunting sea mammals, including walrus and several species of seals and whales. These were harpooned from kayaks or umiaks in summer and from the ice edge in winter. Caribou and fish were also important.

Initial contact between Inuit and Europeans goes back to the Norse settlement of Greenland in the tenth century. The Inuit of the eastern Canadian Arctic were also in at least fleeting contact with the Norse. Shortly after 1500, European fishermen and whalers arrived in the waters off the Labrador coast and undoubtedly encountered Natives. The voyages of Martin Frobisher, beginning in 1576, began a new period of European exploration in the Arctic.

Moravian missionaries were active among the Inuit of Labrador by the 1770s. For the rest of the Canadian Arctic, however, sustained contact did not begin until the whalers arrived in the late nineteenth century. European whalers began to winter over in northern Hudson Bay, while American whalers established a base on the northern Yukon coast. European goods became commonplace, while diseases drastically reduced Inuit populations. The Sadlermiut of Southampton Island in Hudson Bay went extinct, and the Inuit of the Mackenzie Delta were reduced to a small remnant population.

After the collapse of the whaling industry around 1910, European presence was limited to a relatively small number of trading posts, police posts, and mission stations. This lasted until World War II brought large numbers of military personnel into the Arctic. Following the war, the Canadian government took a much more active role in Inuit administration. Schools and medical stations were built, and housing programs were established. The Inuit were encouraged to move out of their hunting camps and relocate in settlements.

The Inuit Tapirisat of Canada is the national political organization formed to promote Inuit culture and identity and to provide a common front on political and economic issues. Four regional branches represent the people of the western Arctic (the Inuvialuit), the central Arctic (Nunavut), northern Quebec (Nunavik), and Labrador. Canadian Inuit also participate in the Inuit Circumpolar Conference, an international organization bringing together Inuit from Greenland, Canada, Alaska, and Russia to strengthen pan-Inuit communication and cultural activities, as well as to provide international cooperation in protecting the Arctic environment.

Land claims have been a major part of modern Inuit political struggles. Settlements were finalized with the Inuit of northern Quebec in 1975 and the Inuvialuit of the western Arctic in 1984. The largest and most complex settlement, however, was the 1993 agreement with the Tungavik Federation of Nunavut, representing most Inuit in what was then the Northwest Territories. In addition to establishing Inuit lands and financial compensation, a major feature of this agreement involved a commitment to partition the Northwest Territories, creating a new self-governing homeland for the Inuit in the eastern portion. This new Canadian territory, known as Nunavut, which translates to "Our Land" in Inuktitut, came into being in 1999. It is the largest jurisdiction in Canada, covering one-fifth of the country's land mass. It is governed by an elected legislative assembly responsible for all residents. However, the Inuit majority (approximately 85 percent of the population) ensures that this will be a primarily Inuit government. Inuktitut, along with English and French, is an official language of the new territory and the primary language of administration.

The Métis

The Métis, whose name derives from an old French word meaning "mixed," emerged during the historic fur trade as the product of unions between the European male traders and Native women. Racial mixture by itself, however, does not determine a person's social or political identity. The numerous offspring from casual encounters during the early years of contact on Canada's east coast were simply raised as Indians, without a separate social group developing. The term *Métis* is best applied to those who, during the nineteenth century, forged a common identity on the eastern Plains and their descendants.

As the fur trade moved westward from the St. Lawrence River, many French-speaking men followed, establishing stable unions with Cree and Ojibwa women. Kinship ties from such unions provided alliances that facilitated trade. Native wives served as interpreters and performed such skilled tasks as making snowshoes, drying meat, and dressing furs. Male children frequently also became traders, and a distinct group of mixed heritage individuals began to emerge.

To the north, the English and Scottish employees of the Hudson's Bay Company established unions with the surrounding Cree, despite company restrictions on racial mixture. In the early years of contact, such traders usually returned to Britain at the end of their service, leaving their "country-born" offspring at the forts. Only a few high-ranking officers sent their mixed-race sons to be educated in England.

By the mid-eighteenth century, a large mixed-blood population had settled around the Great Lakes. Substantial communities of log cabins emerged at such strategic locations as Sault Sainte Marie. Intermarriages contributed to a common identity, merging the separate elements of their heritage. Depleted fur stocks and increased settlement from the east, however, led many to move westward to the Plains, where the distinctive Métis culture finally emerged.

The Métis heartland was at the confluence of the Red and Assiniboine rivers (modern Winnipeg, Manitoba). There they established themselves as buffalo hunters and provisioners for the North West Company, serving as an essential link in the long trade chain from Montreal to the northwestern posts. Geographic and social isolation, as well as a shared lifestyle, promoted a group identity, although differences still remained between the predominant French-speaking Métis, who were Catholics, and the Protestants of partial English

and Scottish descent. Years of bitter confrontation between the two great fur trade companies helped forge the concept of a Métis Nation in the Canadian West.

The Métis lifestyle was threatened when the Hudson's Bay Company granted lands along the Red River for an agricultural colony in 1811. The North West Company, along whose main trade route the new colony lay, fueled the sparks of emerging Métis nationalism. The Métis organized under Cuthbert Grant, and the subsequent clash in 1816, known as the Battle of Seven Oaks, left the colony's governor and twenty settlers dead and forcefully established Métis rights in the area. After merger of the two fur trade companies in 1821 the Métis community at Red River grew rapidly and flourished in virtual isolation for nearly half a century.

The communal bison hunt was crucial to the Métis economy and central to their self-identity. Large parties set out on the hunt in their two-wheeled Red River carts pulled by horses or oxen. Once the herds were located, the bison were killed from horseback. The meat was cut into strips, dried, pounded into coarse powder, mixed with melted fat, and sewn into hide bags. This pemmican was a vital part of the fur trade economy, meant as provisions to the trading posts of the distant northwest. By the 1850s, however, the bison herds were disappearing, forcing the hunters to move further and further afield. Many began to winter out on the Plains, shortly followed by more permanent Métis settlements.

A serious threat to the Métis of the Red River area came with the transfer of Hudson's Bay Company lands to the Canadian government in 1869. Government surveyors began laying out lots without regard to local residents' holdings. Métis resistance was led by Louis Riel. They seized Fort Garry, the center of the Red River settlement, and established a provisional government. Their demands led to the Manitoba Act of 1870, by which Manitoba became a province of Canada. Despite provision for Métis land grants in the act, the new settlers and troops usurped most Métis lands, and their open hostility led the majority of the Manitoba Métis to move west, establishing new communities in Saskatchewan. Despite his election to the Canadian Parliament, Louis Riel was forced into exile and was never able to take his seat.

The Métis communities in Saskatchewan soon faced encroachment from the east. Government failure to deal with Métis claims to the land led to the Northwest Rebellion of 1885. Led again by Louis Riel, along with Gabriel Dumont as military commander, the Métis declared a provisional government at their capital of Batoche. Several groups of Cree and Assiniboine to the west joined in the uprising. The Canadian military eventually overran the Métis at Batoche, and Riel was

Métis hunting buffalo. Painting by Paul Kane from his travels in the 1840s. (Courtesy of Royal Ontario Museum)

hanged at the Saskatchewan capital of Regina for his role in the rebellion.

The defeat at Batoche brought the end of aspirations for a Métis Nation. Some Métis drifted south to Montana, while others moved north into the boreal forest, reaching as far as the Mackenzie River, where they could live by hunting and trapping. Those who remained found themselves largely excluded from the new economic order. As the Métis were expected to disappear, they were ignored by the Canadian government. Sir John A. Macdonald, the prime minister, denied their existence as a people, stating, "If they are Indians, they go with the tribe; if they are half-breeds they are whites." Excluded from reserves and federal programs for Indians, many Métis existed in poverty.

In the 1930s, several prominent Métis leaders emerged, and the Métis Association of Alberta was formed. Political pressure on the Alberta government led to the passage of the Métis Betterment Act in 1938, which set aside lands for Métis settlements. The eight settlements that remain in Alberta, which are home to about 6,000 people, are the only major communal Métis

lands in Canada today. In 1990, the province of Alberta transferred title to these lands to the Métis and allowed for limited self-government.

After nearly a century as Canada's forgotten people, the Métis are experiencing a cultural and political awakening. Part of the stimulus came from the 1982 constitutional recognition of the Métis as one of the "aboriginal peoples of Canada," although it is still uncertain what benefits have been obtained and who is entitled to share in them. The Native Council of Canada (now the Congress of Aboriginal Peoples), the national organization for aboriginal peoples not recognized by government, drew little distinction between Métis and non-status Indians. In 1983 the Métis of the Plains withdrew to form the Métis National Council, which has pressed for recognition of their distinct aboriginal identity and rights, including entitlement to a land base. Population estimates vary widely, but even a narrow definition of Métis would include over 100,000 people. The Métis today are primarily in the provinces of Manitoba, Saskatchewan, and Alberta, but substantial numbers are also in western Ontario, northeastern

British Columbia, and the Mackenzie Valley region of the Northwest Territories.

Early Indian Administration

At confederation, the British North America Act, now known as the Constitution Act of 1867, assigned the federal government responsibility for "Indians and Lands reserved for Indians." This has meant that Indians are treated differently than all other Canadians, who receive most services, such as education, health, and welfare, from the provincial governments. In order to administer its charges, the federal government passed the first Indian Act in 1876. This again isolated Indian people, putting them under different legislation than other Canadians. The act provided government control over all aspects of Indian life, and served as a vehicle of assimilation by legally suppressing such Native ceremonies as the Sun Dance on the Plains and the potlatch on the Pacific coast. Although the act was extensively rewritten in 1951 and prohibitions on Native traditions were dropped, the act remains essentially a nineteenth-century colonial document.

Indian status comes from being registered on a list held by the federal government, which had the power to decide who was an Indian. Decisions were only partially based on race. Enfranchisement, the voluntary or involuntary loss of Indian status, was a peculiar provision of the Indian Act from its inception until 1985. It reflects the initial belief that Indian status was a transitional measure, providing protection only until a certain level of acculturation had occurred. The most infamous example is the provision that took away Indian status from all Indian women who married non-Indian men. As dependent children also lost status, a large population of non-status Indians emerged. The sexist nature of this provision is clear from the fact that Indian males did not lose status when they married non-Indians; instead, their wives became Indians under the Indian Act, regardless of their racial origins. In 1985 an amendment to the Indian Act (Bill C-31) removed the section on enfranchisement. Status now can neither be gained nor lost. People who had been enfranchised, plus their first generation descendants, can now reclaim status, a process that has swelled the number of legally recognized Indians.

Indian reserves were set aside for the "use and benefit" of specific Indian bands, the administrative units recognized by the federal government. The earliest reserves appear to have been established in New France by the Catholic church. Later, reserves were determined through treaties in many areas; in others, such as Quebec and most of British Columbia, reserves were allocated without treaties. The process remains incomplete, as few reserves have been established in the Yukon and Northwest Territories. Title to reserve land is held by the Crown, making the reserves pockets of federal jurisdiction within the provinces. Under the terms of the Indian Act, a band cannot sell or otherwise dispose of reserve lands without surrendering them to the Crown. As reserves are set apart physically and legally, they have served to isolate Indian communities and, at the same time, have helped maintain distinct ethnic identities. Many bands are now moving toward self-government, and federal control of reserve lands is increasingly being challenged.

Responsibility for education of Indian children was initially taken by Catholic religious orders in New France. Later, Protestant churches also became active in Indian education. By the nineteenth century, government policy involved the establishment of church-run residential schools. Such facilities supported government goals of acculturation by removing Indian children from their families, prohibiting their languages, and promoting a Christian Euro-Canadian lifestyle. The federal government continued to use the residential schools to meet their responsibilities for Indian education into the mid-twentieth century.

The Inuit are also considered a federal responsibility, although they are not subject to the provisions of the Indian Act and do not have reserves. Non-status Indians and Métis are not administered by the federal government. They fall under the jurisdiction of the provinces, as do all other Canadians, and receive no benefits or government recognition of Native status.

Historic Treaties with Canada's First Nations

The earliest treaties between the British government and Indians were the "peace and friendship" treaties on the east coast, signed in the late seventeenth and eighteenth centuries. The British sought to forge alliances with First Nations to gain their assistance in wars with the French. These early treaties did not include purchase or surrender of the land. After the defeat of the French and with increased European settlement, the focus of the treaties shifted to land surrenders. Between about 1780 and 1850, small land conveyance treaties were negotiated with the Indians of what was to become southern Ontario. These treaties varied greatly but often involved only small, one-time payments for land.

In 1850, treaties with the Indians of the upper Great Lakes were negotiated by Commissioner W. B. Robinson. Known as the Robinson-Superior and Robinson-Huron treaties, they involved the surrender of large areas of land in exchange for reserves, lump-sum cash payments, annual payments to each member of the band, and promises of hunting and fishing rights over unoccupied Crown lands. These provided a model for later federal treaties.

The final pre-confederation treaties were negotiated on the Pacific coast between 1850 and 1854. Fourteen small treaties were signed on Vancouver Island, at that time a separate crown colony. In return for surrendering their land, the Indians were confirmed in possession of their village sites, assured that they would be "at liberty to hunt over the unoccupied lands, and to carry on fisheries as formerly," and given small payments.

After confederation, Canada sought to extinguish Native claims in the west, in order to open the land for settlement. The federal "numbered treaties" began in 1871 with Treaty Number 1, affecting the Ojibwa and Cree of southern Manitoba. By the time Treaty Number 7 was signed with the Indians of southern Alberta only six years later, the lands from western Lake Superior to the Rocky Mountains had been covered. Except for a northward addition to Treaty Number 6, treaty-making came to a halt for twenty-two years, until gold and oil discoveries in the north brought about new negotiations. Between Treaty Number 8 in 1899 and Treaty Number 11 in 1921, Native title was extinguished across much of northern Canada, from northern Ontario to the Mackenzie River in the Northwest Territories. Finally, the Williams treaties of 1923, which extinguished Native title to the last unsurrendered lands in southern Ontario, brought treaty-making in Canada to a halt (see the map of Canadian treaties in the Canadian Chronology section of chapter 1).

Only minor differences exist in the terms of the federal treaties. Indians agreed to "cede, release, surrender, and yield up" their rights to the land in exchange for reserves, small cash payments, ammunition, uniforms and medals for the chiefs, small annual payments to each band member, and promises of continued hunting and fishing rights. Lasting benefits have been few. Gifts such as flags and medals were meant to enhance the illusion that these were pacts of friendship, when they were primarily deeds of sale. Not all reserve lands or other benefits promised under treaty were allocated, leading to a number of modern specific claims. Hunting and fishing rights have been eroded by subsequent legislation. The 1982 constitution guarantees protection of existing treaty rights but cannot restore rights lost prior to that time.

Land Claims and Modern Treaty-Making

Two types of land claims are recognized in government negotiations. Comprehensive claims are those based on aboriginal title, while specific claims are based on breach of lawful obligation. Specific claims frequently involve unfulfilled treaty promises. These include reserve lands which were never allocated or resources, such as cattle, which were never provided. Other specific claims allege mismanagement of Indian lands or assets. Numerous claims of this type have been made in recent years, and a considerable number have been settled.

Comprehensive claims apply to areas where aboriginal title has never been extinguished through treaty or other legal process. Aboriginal title derives from Native ownership of the land prior to European colonization. An important part of the legal argument stems from the Royal Proclamation of 1763. This decree by King George III states that any lands not ceded to the crown are reserved for Indians. Thus, it has been argued, treaties are legally mandatory to extinguish Native title, and any land not ceded by treaty is still Native land. The colonial and dominion practice of signing treaties with Indians clearly indicates some recognition of aboriginal rights to the land. Recent court cases have also clearly specified that aboriginal rights, including claims to the land, are still in effect unless explicitly extinguished through legal means, such as a treaty.

In the 1970s, federal government policy changed to allow recognition of Native land claims. In part this was a response to the legal claim of the Nisga'a of northern British Columbia and the failure of the Supreme Court of Canada to come to a conclusive decision in 1973. The Office of Native Claims was established in Ottawa in 1974 to receive proposals for negotiation and the Nisga'a were the first to present their claim.

Modern treaty-making has occurred primarily in Canada's north, where no historic treaties were signed. The first such settlement, the James Bay Agreement, was reached with the Cree and Inuit of northern Quebec in 1975. This was in response to provincial plans for massive hydroelectric development in the area. In 1978 the agreement was extended to include the Naskapi of northeastern Quebec. Then in 1984 the Inuvialuit of the western Arctic reached an agreement. Also in the Northwest Territories, agreements were signed with the Gwich'in of the lower Mackenzie River (1992) and Sahtu-Dene and Métis of Great Bear Lake (1993). All these settlements extinguished Native claim to the land in exchange for monetary compensation, ownership of some traditional lands, hunting and trapping rights, and control of social programs such as education and health. A tentative agreement with the Dene of the Mackenzie Valley, however, floundered over government insistence on extinguishment of aboriginal rights.

In the Yukon a 1993 agreement was signed with the Council for Yukon Indians, representing fourteen separate First Nations. Under the terms of the Umbrella Final Agreement, Yukon First Nations agree to "cede, release and surrender" their aboriginal claims in exchange for title to certain lands and financial compensation. Separate agreements with individual First Nations, only half of which have been completed as yet, are required to deal with specific issues. The Umbrella Agreement also allows each Yukon First Nation to negotiate separate self-government agreements, removing them from the jurisdiction of the Indian Act and providing them with authority over a wide range of local issues.

The largest of these northern agreements was the 1993 settlement with the Tungavik Federation of Nunavut, representing the Inuit of what was then the eastern portion of the Northwest Territories. The Inuit agreed to "cede, release and surrender" all aboriginal claims to the land in exchange for title to about 350,000 square kilometers, about 10 percent of which includes mineral rights. They retain their right to hunt, fish, and trap throughout their former territories and will have joint control with the federal government over land-use planning and wildlife management. The settlement also provides about $1.15 billion in financial compensation and resource royalty sharing. Integral to the agreement were parallel negotions that culminated in the 1999 splitting of the Northwest Territories to create Nunavut, a new political jurisdiction in which the Inuit majority ensures control of the legislative assembly.

Native groups in other non-treaty areas of Canada, such as Labrador and most of British Columbia, are also pursuing comprehensive claims. In British Columbia this is taking place at the level of individual bands or regional tribal councils. The only completed agreement is with the Nisga'a Tribal Council of the north coast. This 1998 agreement removes the Nisga'a from the jurisdiction of the Indian Act and allows them to establish their own government with authority over a wide range of local issues. Almost 2,000 square kilometers became Nisga'a lands, not Indian reserves, and a substantial financial settlement compensates for traditional lands which were not included. Similar combinations of financial compensation, lands, and self-government powers feature in negotiations currently underway with fifty-one different bands or tribal councils through the British Columbia Treaty Commission process.

Land claims represent one of the major areas of unfinished business between Canadian Natives and government. They are seen by many as a validation of their aboriginal rights and as a mechanism by which economic independence can be achieved. As many aboriginal groups are moving toward their goal of self-government, land claims are seen as vital to ensure an economic base.

Modern First Nations Populations

First Nations and Inuit populations in Canada are young and rapidly growing (as the Métis are an undefined group, no demographic profile is available). The number of registered First Nations people has more than doubled in the past twenty years. This stems from both a natural rate of growth that is substantially higher than the Canadian average and from changes in the Indian Act (Bill C-31) that allowed additional enrollments. Almost half (48 percent) of the population is under twenty-five years of age, compared to about 34 percent in the Canadian population as a whole. Only 5 percent of the registered Indian population is over sixty-five, compared to about 12 percent in the general population. Ontario has the largest First Nations population, at about 23 percent of the total, followed by British Columbia, Manitoba, and Saskatchewan. Although absolute numbers are lower in the Yukon and Northwest Territories, First Nations people make up the largest percentage of the total population in those jurisdictions.

The registered Indian population is divided into 610 bands, now generally known as First Nations. Almost one-third of this total is in British Columbia, where bands tend to be small. The average band size in Canada is slightly over one thousand people, while in British Coumbia it is only half that number. The small and scattered nature of First Nations populations impedes effective economic development. In many areas, neighboring and related First Nations have formed tribal councils to provide greater political voice and more effective economic programs.

There are about 2,500 reserves in Canada. Most (about two-thirds) are in British Columbia, where the average size is very small. The majority of Canadian reserves are in rural or remote areas. Almost 20 percent of the on-reserve population is characterized as living in remote or "special assess" (no year-round road access) locations. The small, scattered, and isolated nature of most reserves hinders the provision of adequate facilities and any economic self-sufficiency.

Problems of poverty plague many modern reserve communities. Inadequate housing, which is often overcrowded and lacking running water, is a common feature of reserve life, particularly for those in remote locations. Poor economic conditions also affect Native health; despite considerable progress in recent decades, Native life expectancy is still about six years less than the national average.

A major concern for many band councils today is to initiate developments that will provide employment on their reserves. Native businesses, many aided by federal funding, have sprung up on reserves across Canada. Some fortunate bands hold valuable real estate near modern urban centers or have natural resources such as oil and gas on their land. For bands with small isolated reserves and few resources, opportunities for economic development are minimal, and conditions of poverty are widespread.

The search for employment and better economic conditions has led many Native people to relocate to the cities. About 42 percent of registered Canadian Indians now normally reside off-reserve, a figure nearly double that of two decades ago. The figures are highest for Ontario, Saskatchewan, and British Columbia, where nearly one-half of registered Indians do not live on reserves. A considerable proportion of this off-reserve population resides in urban centers. Métis and non-status Indians also swell the numbers of urban Natives. Substantial inner city Native populations now characterize such Canadian centers as Winnipeg, Manitoba, and Edmonton, Alberta. Reserve populations, however, also continue to increase.

Canadian First Nations are increasingly taking control of administering their own lands and finances. A government committee on Indian self-government released its findings in 1983, dismissing the Indian Act and the present system of administration as unacceptable for the future. The committee report supported the right of Indian people to self-government and recommended that this be explicitly stated and entrenched in the Constitution of Canada. First Nations governments would then be recognized as a distinct order of government within Canada. However, constitutional conferences with federal, provincial, and First Nations leaders collapsed in failure, largely due to provincial concerns over the undefined terms and costs of aboriginal self-government. The attempt to recognize self-government in the constitution has been abandoned, at least temporarily. Many First Nations are now looking to land claims agreements to achieve control of their own affairs.

Education plays a key role in Native plans for the future, both for the preservation of Native cultures and languages and in providing modern skills needed for self-government. Most Canadian First Nations now administer all or part of their educational programs. Three aboriginal groups, the Nisga'a of British Columbia and the Cree and Inuit of northern Quebec, operate

Larry Pierre of the Okanagan on the occasion of the First Nations constitutional conference, 1980, demanding native participation in constitutional tasks. (Courtesy of CP Pictures Archives)

their own school boards. At the post-secondary level, federal funding for Indian and Inuit students to attend colleges and universities is resulting in the appearance of many young, articulate, educated Native leaders.

The First Nations of Canada have rejected the assimilationist policies of the Canadian government since confederation. Despite government assumptions, evident in some of the provisions of the Indian Act, First Nations were not doomed to disappear as distinct cultures. Today, populations of Indian, Inuit, and Métis peoples are rapidly growing and determined steps are being taken to preserve their languages and cultures. Aboriginal self-governments are emerging as an opportunity to take control over their own lives and ensure the survival of their cultures.

Alan D. McMillan
Simon Fraser University

References

Native Demography Before 1700

Borah, Woodrow W. and Sherburne F. Cook. *The Aboriginal Population of Central Mexico on the Eve of the Spanish Conquest.* Ibero-Americana, 45. Berkeley: University of California Press, 1963.

Cook, Noble D. *Born to Die: Disease and New World Conquest, 1492–1650.* New York: Cambridge University Press, 1998.

Cook, Noble D. and W. George Lovell, eds. *Secret Judgments of God: Old World Disease in Colonial Spanish America.* Norman: University of Oklahoma Press, 1991.

Cook, Sherburne F. and Woodrow Borah. *Essays in Population History: Mexico and the Caribbean.* Berkeley: University of California Press, 1971 (vol. 1); 1974 (vol. 2).

———. *Essays in Population History: Mexico and California*, vol. 3. Berkeley: University of California Press, 1979.

———. *The Indian Population of Central Mexico, 1531–1610.* Ibero-Americana, 44. Berkeley: University of California Press, 1960.

Crosby, Jr., Alfred W. *The Columbian Exchange: Biological and Cultural Consequences of 1492.* Westport, Conn.: Greenwood Publishing Company, 1972.

———. *Ecological Imperialism: The Biological Expansion of Europe, 900–1900.* Cambridge: Cambridge University Press, 1986.

Daniels, John D. "The Indian Population of North America in 1492." *William and Mary Quarterly* 49:2 (April 1992): 298–320.

Denevan, William M., ed. *The Native Population of the Americas in 1492.* 2d ed. Madison: University of Wisconsin Press, 1992.

Dobyns, Henry F. "Estimating Aboriginal American Population: An Appraisal of Techniques with a New Hemispheric Estimate." *Current Anthropology* 7, no. 4 (1966): 395–416.

———. *Native American Historical Demography: A Critical Bibliography.* Bloomington: Indiana University Press in cooperation with the Newberry Library Center for the History of the American Indian, 1976.

———. *Their Number Become Thinned: Native American Population Dynamics in Eastern North America.* Knoxville: University of Tennessee Press in cooperation with the Newberry Library Center for the History of the American Indian, 1983.

Stearn, E. Wagner and Allen E. Stearn. *The Effect of Smallpox on the Destiny of the Amerindian.* Boston: B. Humphries, 1945.

Stiffarm, Lenore A. and Phil Lane, Jr. "The Demography of Native North America: A Question of American Indian Survival." In *The State of Native America: Genocide, Colonization, and Resistance*, edited by M. Annette Jaimes, 23–53. Boston: South End Press, 1992.

Thornton, Russell. *American Indian Holocaust and Survival: A Population History Since 1492.* Norman: University of Oklahoma Press, 1987.

Verano, John and Douglas H. Ubelaker, eds. *Disease and Demography in the Americas.* Washington: Smithsonian Institution Press, 1992.

Henry Dobyns

Geographic and Demographic Change During the Eighteenth Century

Anderson, Gary C. *Kinsmen of Another Kind: Dakota-White Relations in the Upper Mississippi Valley, 1650–1862.* Lincoln: University of Nebraska Press, 1984.

Cook, Sherburne F. *The Conflict Between the California Indian and White Civilization.* Berkeley: University of California Press, 1976.

Edmunds, R. David. *The Potawatomis: Keepers of the Fire.* Norman: University of Oklahoma Press, 1978.

Gutierrez, Ramn A. *When Jesus Came, the Corn Mothers Went Away: Marriage, Sexuality, and Power in New Mexico, 1500–1846.* Stanford, Calif.: Stanford University Press, 1991.

Jackson, Robert H. *Indian Population Decline: the Missions of Northwestern New Spain, 1687–1840.* Albuquerque: University of New Mexico Press, 1994.

Jennings, Francis. *Empire of Fortune: Crowns, Colonies, and Tribes in the Seven Years War in America.* New York: Norton, 1988.

McConnell, Michael N. *A Country Between: The Upper Ohio Valley and Its Peoples, 1724–1774.* Lincoln: University of Nebraska Press, 1992.

Merrell, James H. *The Indians' New World: Catawbas and Their Neighbors from European Contact through the Era of Removal.* Chapel Hill: University of North Carolina Press in cooperation with the Institute of Early American History and Culture, 1989.

Ray, Arthur J. *Indians in the Fur Trade: Their Role as Trappers, Hunters, and Middlemen in the Lands Southwest of Hudson Bay, 1660–1870.* Toronto: University of Toronto Press, 1974.

Richter, Daniel K. *The Ordeal of the Longhouse: The Peoples of the Iroquois League in the Era of European Colonization.* Chapel Hill: University of North Carolina Press in cooperation with the Institute of Early American History and Culture, 1992.

Salisbury, Neal. "Native People and European Settlers in Eastern North America, 1600–1783." In *The Cambridge History of the Native Peoples of the Americas.* Vol. 1: *North America,* edited by Bruce G. Trigger and Wilcomb E. Washburn, pt. 1, 399–460. Cambridge: Cambridge University Press, 1996.

Usner, Jr., Daniel H. *Indians, Settlers, and Slaves in a Frontier Exchange Economy: The Lower Mississippi Valley before 1783.* Chapel Hill: University of North Carolina Press in cooperation with the Institute of Early American History and Culture, 1992.

White, Richard. *The Middle Ground: Indians, Empires, and Republics in the Great Lakes Region, 1650–1815.* New York: Cambridge University Press, 1991.

Dan Usner

Indian Geographic Distribution, Habitat, and Demography During the Nineteenth Century

Bee, Robert L. *The Yuma.* New York: Chelsea House, 1989.

Boyd, Robert T. *The Coming Spirit of Pestilence: Introduced Infectious Diseases and Population Decline Among Northwest Coast Indians, 1774–1874.* Seattle: University of Washington Press, 1999.

Calloway, Colin G. *The Abenaki.* New York: Chelsea House, 1989.

Calloway, Colin G., ed. *Our Hearts Fell to the Ground: Plains Indian Views of How the West Was Lost.* Boston: Bedford Books of St. Martin's Press, 1996.

Carlson, Leonard A. *Indians, Bureaucrats, and Land: The Dawes Act and the Decline of Indian Farming.* Westport, Conn.: Greenwood Press, 1981.

Dobyns, Henry F. *The Pima-Maricopa.* New York: Chelsea House, 1989.

Fisher, Robin. "The Northwest From the Beginning of Trade with Europeans to the 1880s." In *The Cambridge History of the Native Peoples of the Americas.* Vol. 1: *North America,* edited by Bruce G. Trigger and Wilcomb E. Washburn, pt. 2, 117–182. Cambridge: Cambridge University Press, 1996.

Fowler, Loretta. "The Great Plains From the Arrival of the Horse to 1885." In *The Cambridge History of the Native Peoples of the Americas.* Vol. 1: *North America,* edited by Bruce G. Trigger and Wilcomb E. Washburn, pt. 2, 1–56. Cambridge: Cambridge University Press, 1996.

Gibson, Arrell M. *The American Indian: Prehistory to Present.* Lexington, Mass.: D. C. Heath, 1980.

Green, Michael D. "The Expansion of European Colonization to the Mississippi Valley, 1780–1880." In *The Cambridge History of the Native Peoples of the Americas.* Vol. 1: *North America,* edited by Bruce G.

Trigger and Wilcomb E. Washburn, pt. 1, 461–538. Cambridge: Cambridge University Press, 1996.

Lamar, Howard R. and Sam Truett. "The Greater Southwest and California From the Beginning of European Settlement to the 1880's." In *The Cambridge History of the Native Peoples of the Americas.* Vol. 1: *North America,* edited by Bruce G. Trigger and Wilcomb E. Washburn, pt. 2, 57–116. Cambridge: Cambridge University Press, 1996.

Maxwell, James A., ed. *America's Fascinating Indian Heritage.* Pleasantville, N.Y.: Reader's Digest Association, 1978.

Merrell, James H. *The Catawbas.* New York: Chelsea House, 1989.

Olson, James S. and Raymond Wilson. *Native Americans in the Twentieth Century.* Provo, Utah: Brigham Young University Press, 1984.

Prucha, Francis Paul. *Atlas of American Indian Affairs.* Lincoln: University of Nebraska Press, 1990.

Simmons, William S. *The Narragansett.* New York: Chelsea House, 1989.

Spicer, Edward H. *The American Indians.* Cambridge, Mass.: Belnap Press of Harvard University Press, 1980.

Tanner, Helen H., ed. *Atlas of Great Lakes Indian History.* Norman: University of Oklahoma Press in cooperation with the Newberry Library, 1987.

Trigger, Bruce, ed. *Northeast.* Vol. 15 of *Handbook of North American Indians,* edited by William C. Sturtevant. Washington, D.C.: Smithsonian Institution, 1978.

Washburn, Wilcomb, ed. *History of Indian-White Relations.* Vol. 4 of *Handbook of North American Indians,* edited by William C. Sturtevant. Washington, D.C.: Smithsonian Institution, 1988.

Wright, Muriel H. *A Guide to the Indian Tribes of Oklahoma.* Norman: University of Oklahoma Press, 1986.

Leroy Eid

Indian Land Tenure in the Twentieth Century

Burt, Larry W. *Tribalism in Crisis: Federal Indian Policy, 1953–1961.* Albuquerque: University of New Mexico Press, 1982.

Carlson, Leonard A. *Indians, Bureaucrats, and Land: The Dawes Act and the Decline of Indian Farming.* Westport, Conn.: Greenwood Press, 1981

Castile, George P. and Robert L. Bee. *State and Reservation: New Perspectives on Federal Indian Policy.* Tucson: University of Arizona Press, 1992.

Champagne, Duane. *American Indian Societies: Strategies and Conditions of Political and Cultural Survival.* Cultural Survival Report 32. Cambridge, Mass.: Cultural Survival, 1989.

Cohen, Fay G. *Treaties on Trial: The Continuing Controversy over Northwest Indian Fishing Rights.* Seattle: University of Washington Press, 1986.

Deloria, Vine, Jr., ed. *American Indian Policy in the Twentieth Century.* Norman: University of Oklahoma Press, 1985.

Deloria, Vine, Jr. *Behind the Trail of Broken Treaties: An Indian Declaration of Independence.* New York: Delacorte, 1974.

Deloria, Vine, Jr., and Clifford Lytle. *American Indians, American Justice.* Austin: University of Texas Press, 1983.

Deloria, Vine, Jr., and David E. Wilkins. *Tribes, Treaties, & Constitutional Tribulations.* Austin: University of Texas Press, 1999.

Getches, David H., Charles F. Wilkinson, and Robert A. Williams, Jr. *Case and Materials on Federal Indian Law*, 4th Ed. St. Paul: West Pub., 1998.

McCool, Daniel. *Command of the Waters: Iron Triangles, Federal Water Development, and Indian Water.* Berkeley: University of California Press, 1987.

McDonnell, Janet A. *The Dispossession of the American Indian, 1887–1934.*, Bloomington: Indiana University Press, 1991.

Momaday, N. Scott. *House Made of Dawn.* New York: Harper & Row, 1968.

Philp, Kenneth R., ed. *Indian Self-Rule: First Hand Accounts of Indian-White Relations From Roosevelt to Reagan.* Salt Lake City: Howe Bros., 1986.

Prucha, Francis P. *American Indian Treaties: The History of a Political Anomaly.* Berkeley and Los Angeles: University of California Press, 1994.

———. *Atlas of American Indian Affairs.* Lincoln: University of Nebraska Press, 1990.

———. *The Indians in American Society: From the Revolutionary War to the Present.* Berkeley: University of California Press, 1985.

Shipek, Florence C. *Pushed Into the Rocks: Southern California Indian Land Tenure, 1769–1986.* Lincoln: University of Nebraska Press, 1988.

Snipp, C. Matthew. *American Indians: The First of This Land.* New York: Russell Sage Foundation, 1989.

Sutton, Imre. *Indian Land Tenure: Bibliographical Essays and a Guide to the Literature.* New York: Clearwater, 1975.

———., ed. *Irredeemable America: The Indians' Estate and Land Claims.* Albuquerque: University of New Mexico Press, 1985.

Vecsey, Christopher and William A. Starna, eds. *Iroquois Land Claims.* Syracuse, N.Y.: Syracuse University Press, 1988.

Vogel, Virgil J. *This Country Was Ours: A Documentary History of the American Indian.* New York: Harper & Row, 1972.

Washburn, Wilcomb E., ed. *History of Indian-White Relations.* Vol. 4 of *Handbook of North American Indians.* Washington, DC: Smithsonian Institution, 1988.

Washburn, Wilcomb E. *Red Man's Land/White Man's Law: A Study of the Past and Present Status of the American Indian.* New York: Scribner, 1971.

Wilkinson, Charles F. *American Indians, Time and the Law: Native Societies in a Modern Constitutional Democracy.* New Haven: Yale University Press, 1987.

Imre Sutton

Canadian Native Distribution, Habitat, and Demography

Damas, David, ed. *Arctic.* Vol. 5 of *Handbook of North American Indians*, edited by William C. Sturtevant. Washington D.C.: Smithsonian Institution, 1984.

Dickason, Olive P. *Canada's First Nations: A History of Founding Peoples from Earliest Times.* 2nd ed. Toronto: Oxford University Press, 1997.

Fisher, Robin and Kenneth Coates, eds. *Out of the Background: Readings On Canadian Native History.* 2nd ed. Toronto: Copp Clarke, 1996.

Frideres, James S. *Aboriginal Peoples in Canada: Contemporary Conflicts.* 5th ed. Scarborough, Ont.: Prentice-Hall Canada, 1998.

Hedican, Edward J. *Applied Anthropology in Canada: Understanding Aboriginal Issues.* Toronto: University of Toronto Press, 1995.

Helm, June, ed. *Subarctic.* Vol. 6 of *Handbook of North American Indians*, edited by William C. Sturtevant. Washington, D.C.: Smithsonian Institution, 1981.

Long, David A. and Olive P. Dickason, eds. *Visions of the Heart: Canadian Aboriginal Issues.* Toronto: Harcourt Brace Canada, 1996.

McMillan, Alan D. *Native Peoples and Cultures of Canada: An Anthropological Overview.* 2nd ed. Vancouver: Douglas & McIntyre, 1995.

Miller, J.R. *Skyscrapers Hide the Heavens: A History of Indian-White Relations in Canada.* 3rd ed. Toronto: University of Toronto Press, 2000.

Morrison, R. Bruce and C. Roderick Wilson, eds. *Native Peoples: The Canadian Experience.* 2nd ed. Toronto: McClelland and Stewart, 1995.

Ponting, J. Rick., ed. *Arduous Journey: Canadian Indians and Decolonization.* Toronto: McClelland and Stewart, 1986.

Ponting, J. Rick. *First Nations in Canada: Perspectives on Opportunity, Empowerment, and Self-Determination.* Toronto: McGraw-Hill Ryerson, 1997.

Richardson, Boyce, ed. *Drum Beat: Anger and Renewal in Indian Country.* Toronto: Summerhill Press, 1989.

Suttles, Wayne, ed. *Northwest Coast*. Vol. 7 of *Handbook of North American Indians*, edited by William C. Sturtevant. Washington, D.C.: Smithsonian Institution, 1990.

Trigger, Bruce G. *Natives and Newcomers: Canada's "Heroic Age" Reconsidered*. Kingston, Ont.: McGill-Queen's University Press, 1985.

———, ed. *Northeast*. Vol. 15 of *Handbook of North American Indians*, edited by William C. Sturtevant. Washington, D.C.: Smithsonian Institution, 1978.

Alan McMillan

Glossary

A

aboriginal   The first people or native people of an area. The Native Americans are the aboriginal people of North America. Under the Canadian Constitution Act of 1982, an aboriginal person is defined as being an Indian, Inuit, or Métis. Aboriginal is often used interchangeably with the terms *native* and *indigenous*.

aboriginal rights   Rights enjoyed by a people by virtue of the fact that their ancestors inhabited an area from time immemorial before the first Europeans came. These rights include ownership of land and resources, cultural rights, and political self-determination. There are widely divergent views on the validity of these rights. On one end of the spectrum, some deny the existence of aboriginal rights; on the other end, some claim that aboriginal rights give natives the inherent right to govern themselves and their lands.

aboriginal title   The earliest discussion of aboriginal title in Canada came in a nineteenth-century lawsuit involving Indian lands in Ontario. At that point, aboriginal (then "Indian") title was understood to be of a usufructuary nature, that is, to give Indians a temporary right to use their lands for subsistence purposes. Indian title was not understood to equal "fee simple" ownership. A century later, however, the doctrine of aboriginal title has been expanded to include in practical terms much broader rights. *See* fee-simple ownership *and* usufructuary.

abrogation   The termination of an international agreement or treaty, for example, when Congress enacts a law completely abolishing a treaty and breaking all the U.S. promises to an Indian nation.

acculturation   The transference of culture from one group to another, usually from a more dominant group to a less dominant one, which thereby loses its previous culture.

age grades   A series of social and ceremonial associations based on age. Members enter the first grade at the appropriate age and then proceed through the set.

agriculturalists   Indian peoples who depended to a significant extent on crops which they planted themselves.

Alaska Native Claims Settlement Act (ANCSA)   A 1971 congressional act that extinguished Alaska Natives' claims to land. In compensation, the Alaska Natives retained 44 million acres and received $962.5 million.

Algonkians   A group of Indian peoples who speak an Algonkian language. This is the largest language group in Canada. It includes many peoples with very different cultures, from the Atlantic coast to the western prairies.

alienate   Transfer of an ownership interest, for example, when tribal land is sold to nontribal members.

alkaloid   Any of a number of colorless, crystalline, bitter organic substances, such as caffeine, morphine, quinine, and strychnine, having alkaline properties and containing nitrogen. Alkaloids are found in plants and, sometimes, in animals and can have a strong toxic effect on the human or animal system.

allotment   The policy, peaking in the 1880s and 1890s, of subdividing Indian reservations into individual, privately owned ("patented" or "fee patent") parcels of land. The division of communally held lands on many Indian reservations into individually owned parcels, thereby nearly eliminating communal ownership of land and resources, which was a defining element of tribal life. The allotment policy was ended in 1934, but it left a legacy of "checkerboard" land ownership on reservations, where often, the tribe, non-Indians, and Indian allottees own small and scattered segments of land. *See* General Allotment Act of 1887.

Amargosa complex   A series of artifacts linked to the ancient hunting and gathering peoples of the Mohave Desert in the southwest, dated from 1600 B.C.E. to C.E. 1000.

American Indian Movement (AIM)   An Indian activist organization originating in Minneapolis, Minnesota, in the 1960s. AIM was originally organized to protect urban Indians from police harassment and to assist Indian children in obtaining culturally sensitive education. In the 1970s, AIM expanded its activities to include more traditional issues, such as assertion of treaty rights, tribal sovereignty, and international recognition of Indian nations.

Anasazi   An early pueblo culture that flourished between C.E. 900 and 1200. The present-day Hopi Indians are believed to be descendants of the Anasazi, which in Hopi means *ancient ones*.

annuities   In the United States, annuities are annual payments for land in accordance with Indian treaties. Instead of paying for Indian land in one large sum, the U.S. government usually spread the expense by paying smaller sums over a number of years. In Canada, annuities were small annual payments made to bands, which surrendered lands to the Crown, or English monarch, who formally claimed public land in Canada.

archaeology   The study of past cultures through an analysis of their physical remains, such as tools or pottery. From such remains, archaeologists piece together an idea of what ancient cultures may have been like.

Archaic period   The time between eight thousand and two thousand years ago defined in most areas by cultures dependent on hunting and gathering.

Articles of Confederation   The original agreement among the thirteen original U.S. colonies to form a new, independent country. The articles were adopted on November 15, 1777, ratified by the thirteen colonies in 1781, and remained in force until 1789, when the present constitution was ratified.

artifacts   Any products of human cultural activity, such as tools, weapons, or artworks, found in archaeological contexts.

Assembly of First Nations (AFN)   The successor organization to the National Indian Brotherhood (NIB) as the national political body representing first nations of Canada at the national political level, such as at the First Ministers' Conferences, where the Canadian prime minister and provincial leaders met to discuss provisions of a new Canadian constitution. The chiefs of each Indian first nation represent their bands at the national assemblies of chiefs, which constitutes the AFN.

assimilation   The idea that one group of people, usually a minority, are becoming like another and are being absorbed by a majority society. For example, for many years it was believed that U.S. Indians were assimilating into the dominant culture, but that idea no longer holds much credence.

associated funerary objects   Objects believed to have been placed with individual human remains at the time of death or later as a part of the death rite or ceremony of a culture and which, along with the human remains, are currently in the possession or control of a federal agency or museum. Items exclusively made for burial purposes or to contain human remains are also considered associated funerary objects.

Athapaskan   A group of Indian peoples who speak an Athapaskan language. These languages dominate in northwestern Canada south of the tree line.

B

band   (1) A small, loosely organized social group composed of several families. (2) In Canada, originally a social and economic unit of nomadic hunting peoples, but, since confederation, a community of Indians registered under the Indian Act. Registered Indians are called "status Indians." Each band has its own governing band council, usually consisting of one or more chiefs and several councillors. Today, many bands prefer to be known as First Nations. *See* status Indians.

band council   In Canada, the local form of native government consisting of a chief and councillors, who are elected for two- or three-year terms to carry on band business. Community members choose the chief and councillors by election, or sometimes through traditional custom. The actual duties and responsibilities of band councils are specified in the Indian Act. *See* Indian Act.

band council resolution   The method by which Canadian band councils pass motions or record decisions. Band council resolutions are statements outlining a decision of the band council. The minister of Indian and Northern Affairs Canada, or senior officials of that department, must approve band council resolutions whenever they involve band lands or monies.

Berengia   During the last glacial age, before fifteen thousand years ago, a land mass between Asia and Alaska in the Bering Sea that served as a land bridge for the first migrations to the continents of the western hemisphere.

bicultural/bilingual education   An education system that combines the languages, values, and beliefs of two cultures in its curriculum to give students the skills to live and function in both cultures.

bilateral kinship   A system of descent and inheritance that recognizes relationship to both a person's mother's and father's kin.

Bill C-31   The pre-legislation name of the 1985 *Act to Amend the Indian Act* of the Canadian Parliament that restored legal status to aboriginal women and their children who had lost status through marriage to non-Indians. The bill corrected a section of the Indian Act that revoked status for women married to non-Indians while permitting Indian men to confer Indian status upon non-Indian wives. While aboriginal women's groups welcomed this change, many Indian communities opposed the bill as an intrusion into their jurisdiction over band membership. Bill C-31 enabled people affected by the discriminatory provisions of the old *Indian Act* to apply to have their Indian status restored. Since 1985, over 100,000 individuals have successfully regained their status.

bill of rights   A statement of fundamental rights guaranteed to members of a nation. The U.S. Bill of Rights consists of the first ten amendments to the Constitution and were adopted in the late 1780s. Canada adopted its first bill of rights in 1960. The fundamental purpose of the Canadian Bill of Rights was to ensure equality of rights, and, as a consequence, Canada's native people were allowed to vote in Canadian federal elections.

boarding school   A school run by the government or a religious or private organization, in which the children live. Boarding schools designed to educate native children took them away from the influence of their family and culture.

"booming"   Forceful nineteenth-century advocacy of the desirability of seizing most of the remaining land of Native Americans.

Bosque Redondo   The Navajo reservation in present-day eastern New Mexico where for four years (1864–1868), the Navajo were forced to live after being rounded up and concentrated together.

branch   In linguistics, a subdivision of a language grouping (either a phylum or a family of languages).

Branch of Acknowledgement and Research (B.A.R.)   Established in 1978 by an act of Congress, a Bureau of Indian Affairs department, and at that time called the Federal Acknowledgement Project (F.A.P.), that established procedures to extend federal recognition to previously unrecognized Indian tribes and communities. About 150 Indian communities have applied to the U.S. government for certification as Indian tribes. *See* federal recognition.

British North America Act (1867)   The legislation passed by the British Parliament in 1867 that created the country of Canada. The British North America Act was renamed the Constitution Act, 1867. The act outlines in section 91 the areas of federal (Canadian national government) jurisdiction, and sub-section 24 of section 91 gives the Canadian Parliament exclusive powers to pass legislation concerning "Indians, and lands reserved for the Indians."

Bureau of Indian Affairs (BIA)   A federal agency charged with the trust responsibility for tribal land, education, and water rights.

C

Cadastral   Mapping property boundaries and other details of realty, as well as of territory, hence reservations, and keeping such records in a cadastre (map office).

California Missions   The twenty-one individual Catholic missions founded between 1769 and 1823, containing a church, a dormitory for Native Americans, and successful farm and cattle operations based on forced Indian labor.

camas   A plant (Camassia quamash), the bulbs of which were an important source of food for the native people of the Northwest Coast and the Columbia Plateau. The bulbs were gathered in the late summer and baked to prepare for eating or storage.

Campbell tradition   Archaeological remains of a group of California cultures dated from 3000 B.C.E. to C.E. 1500 and later. The remains are believed to be ancestral to the present-day Chumash from the Santa Barbara area.

Canada Originally this designation referred only to part of France's possessions in Canada (roughly corresponding to today's southern Quebec). After 1791 it came to refer to the two Canadas, Lower Canada (southern Quebec) and Upper Canada (southern Ontario). With confederation by the British North American Act in 1867, it came to refer to all the provinces and territories collectively.

Canadian Aboriginal Economic Development Strategy (CAEDS) Launched in 1989, a program that seeks to promote economic development among native people. The program coordinates funding services of several federal agencies to focus on aboriginal economic development problems. Participating federal agencies include the Indian and Northern Affairs Canada (INAC), the Department of Employment and Immigration Canada (EIC), and the Department of Industry, Science and Technology. The program emphasizes long-term planning and is geared toward business ventures and entrepreneurship.

Canadian Charter of Rights and Freedoms This section of the Canadian Constitution Act, 1982, combines protection of individual rights, such as freedom of conscience and religion, with group rights involving issues such as language. Judicial decisions involving the charter are having a profound impact on Canadian society. In the 1982 Constitution, aboriginal and treaty rights were not included in the charter itself but in a separate part of the text. A provision of the Canadian charter that differentiates it from the U.S. Bill of Rights allows governments to "opt out" of charter requirements through legislative fiat.

Canadian test of basic skills A test of a student's reading, writing, and mathematical skills commonly used in Canada.

castor gras A French term meaning *greasy beaver*, which referred to beaver pelts that had been used as clothing long enough for the long guard hairs to fall out and for the shorter barbed hairs to absorb body oils and perspiration. Especially during the early fur trade, Europeans sought castor gras because of its value for making felt.

cautery The act of cauterizing, which is to burn with a hot iron or needle, or with a caustic substance, so as to destroy dead or unwanted tissue in order to prevent the spread of infection.

caveat Meaning "caution." A legal action by which a person or party claims ownership of, or interest in, land registered in the name of another party.

cession Giving up of Indian land, often in exchange for a reservation or grant of land set aside for the Indians' permanent and exclusive use and occupancy.

Charlottetown Accord (1992) An attempt at constitutional reform in Canada, named after the Prince Edward Island city where it was reached. It would have entrenched the inherent right to aboriginal self-government in the Constitution, as well as decentralizing many aspects of Canadian government. In the process of drafting this accord, national aboriginal leaders were included as quasi-equal participants for the first time. However, in a national referendum in October 1992, both aboriginal and other Canadians rejected the Charlottetown Accord, and aboriginal political aspirations were again forced to seek out non-constitutional forums.

chiki A Seminole word for their open-sided, thatched-roof shelter, which evolved in Florida from the Creek cabin of their ancestors.

cimarrone A Spanish term for wild or untamed. Cimarrone was applied to the Lower Creek Indians who migrated into Florida in the latter part of the eighteenth century and later became the Seminole Indians.

circle sentencing A way of dealing with community members who have broken the law, that is most frequently practiced in Canada and several communities in Minnesota. Based on traditional practices, the process emphasizes peacemaking, consensus decision making, and taking the interests of the offender, the victim(s), and the community as a whole into account as the offender accepts responsibility for the crime. The participants sit in a circle, speaking in turn as a "talking piece" comes to them, and express themselves concerning the matter at hand and their support for all concerned. Each participant must agree on the outcomes that emerge from the discussion. These outcomes are the sentence.

"citizens plus" In Canada, the concept that Indians are a distinct class of persons with special rights by virtue of their aboriginal title and treaty rights, which non-Indian citizens do not enjoy.

civil law The body of law developed from Roman law that is codified into a single comprehensive body of laws, as opposed to developed from case law or custom. Civil law is the legal system used in most non-English speaking jurisdictions. It is also used in the state of Louisiana and the province of Quebec in Canada. The term "civil law" is also used within the common law system to refer to all non-criminal laws.

civil service reform   Late nineteenth-century movement in the United States to reform government service. The policy separated politics from government office holding, which meant in the Indian Service that elected officials were prevented from directly appointing political friends to well-paying positions. Appointment to and retention of government administrative positions became based on competence and the possession of formal qualifications of individual applicants and job holders.

"civilization" or forced acculturation   A major U.S. Indian policy from 1887 to 1934 that included pacification of Indians, their conversion to Christianity, and their adoption of a "civilized" occupation such as farming. *See* acculturation *and* assimilation.

clan   The basic social and political organization of many, but not all, Indian societies, which consists of a number of related house groups and families. In some cases, persons claim to be related and share a common symbol or totem, often an animal, such as the bear or the turtle.

Clovis points   Ancient spearheads made in a style of polished, tapered, and cylindrical shape, which first appeared among North American peoples about 10,000 B.C.E. These peoples practiced a hunting and gathering way of life that depended on many now-extinct species such as woolly mammoth and dire wolf.

Cochise culture   The name that refers to groups of hunters and gatherers who lived in present-day southeastern Arizona and southwestern New Mexico from about 13,000 to 500 B.C.E. This cultural period is named in honor of the Apache leader, Cochise, who in the late 1800s resisted U.S. troops in the same area.

common law   The body of law that is based on principles developed by judges in case law as opposed to statute. First developed in England, this system of law forms the legal foundation in English speaking jurisdictions including the United States (except Louisiana) and Canada (except Quebec). The term "common law" is also used to refer to the legal principles created within the royal courts of England in contrast to those principles coming from the courts of equity.

Community Health Representatives (CHR) Program   A Medical Services Branch (MSB) program to train Indian and Inuit people at the community level in elementary public health, so that they can provide a link between their community and the health facility in that community.

Compact of 1802   Agreement between the state of Georgia and the U.S. federal government in which the latter retained rights to negotiate land treaties with Indians in present-day Mississippi, Georgia, and Alabama, while Georgia was restricted to its present-day boundaries and given assurance that the federal government would peaceably remove any Indian nations from within Georgia's chartered limits.

comprehensive claim   According to the Canadian government's land-claims policy, an aboriginal claim, based on aboriginal rights, to land not covered by treaty.

concentration   A major U.S. government Indian policy of the mid-nineteenth century involving concentration of Indian tribes on reservations west of the Mississippi River. *See* Removal Act.

Concordat   In Roman Catholic Church law ("canon law" or sacred law), a treaty made by the Vatican (or "Holy See" or the Pope).

confederacy   An alliance of friendship among several tribes or bands in which they agree to regulate some of their activities under common rules and obligations. This could mean the obligation to give military aid if attacked or the right to seek redress for personal or group injuries suffered from other alliance members before the body of the confederacy. The latter was the case within the Iroquois Confederacy of upstate New York.

consensus   Universal agreement. Indian political or social decisionmaking usually required that all interested groups agree to a proposition before it was binding. Majority rule was not sufficient for a decision, but rather all groups (bands, clans, lineages, villages, or triblets) had to agree, otherwise each group acted the way it thought proper or best.

conservatives   Members of an Indian nation who followed traditional ways of living, often claiming the native American way as preferred. Conservatives often represent a cultural and political segment of an Indian nation and usually live differently. They have political and cultural goals of preserving Indian culture and identity that other members of the nation might be willing to give up.

constituencies Groups of individuals, where each group forms a district for purposes of representation.

constitution The written form of a country's governing structure, which establishes the basic functions and division of powers between different levels of government, such as federal and provincial governments in Canada, or federal, state, and city governments in the United States. In the United States, the Constitution was adopted in 1789, but since then several amendments or changes have modified the original document. The Canadian constitution is set forth in the Constitution Act 1867, 1930, and 1982. *See* British North America Act.

Contract Health Service (CHS) The purchase of health care by the Indian Health Service (IHS) through contractual arrangements with hospitals, private physicians, and clinic groups, and dentists and providers of ancillary health services to supplement and complement other health care resources available to American Indians and Alaska Natives.

Council on Energy Resource Tribes (CERT) An organization formed by U.S. Indian tribes who have substantial marketable natural resources on their reservation lands. CERT provides its member tribes with expertise for marketing and managing their resources.

Crown The formal head of state, symbolized by the king or queen of England. In Canada, the Crown is divided between the federal government, "the Crown in right of Canada," and the provincial governments, as "the Crown in right of (name of province)."

crown lands Land under the sovereign ownership or protection of the Canadian federal government or the provincial governments. The treaties recognized the Indians' right to hunt and fish on "unoccupied Crown lands," which has been greatly diminished by privatization of land, designation of national parks or wilderness parks, or reservation by legislation (i.e., "occupied") by any purpose.

cultural patrimony Refers to any object having ongoing historical, traditional, or cultural importance central to the Native American group or culture itself, rather than property owned by an individual Native American. It therefore cannot be alienated, appropriated, or conveyed by any individual regardless of whether the individual is a member of the tribe. Any such object is considered inalienable, not for sale, by such Native American group at the time the object was separated from the group.

culture The nonbiological and socially transmitted system of concepts, institutions, behavior, and materials by which a society adapts to its effective natural and human environment.

culture area A device anthropologists have used to discuss large numbers of people in a contiguous geographical area. Generally, it is assumed that the various peoples in a culture area are similar in lifeways.

D

Dawes Act *See* General Allotment Act of 1887.

demography The statistical study of populations, including migration, birth, death, health, and marriage data.

dependence (1) In nineteenth-century international law and federal Indian law, the relationship between a weak country and a strong country that agrees to protect it. In 1831, the Supreme Court labeled Indian tribes as "domestic nations," because the United States had agreed, by treaty, to protect them from others. (2) The situation by which Indians came to depend on trade of animal furs for European manufactured goods, especially metal goods like hoes, guns, and hatchets. Indians stopped producing their own stone tools and came to depend on trade to supply some necessary economic goods.

diminutive In linguistics, a grammatical construction conveying a meaning of smallness.

discouraged workers Unemployed workers who have abandoned their search for a new job.

diuretic An agent that increases the amount of urine.

domestic dependent nation The expression was used by U.S. Supreme Court Justice John Marshall in the case *Cherokee Nation v. Georgia* in 1831, which denied the Cherokee Nation, and all Indian nations, status as independent foreign nations. Instead, Justice Marshall described the relation of the Indian governments to the United States as more akin to "domestic dependent nations."

Dorset culture An Inuit (Eskimo) cultural tradition dated from 1000 B.C.E. to C.E. 1000. They were adapted to the harsh environments of the Canadian Arctic, relying heavily on fishing and hunting sea mammals.

E

Economic Opportunity Act of 1964   A congressional act that provided funding to local Community Action Programs (C.A.P.) and authorized Indian tribes to designate themselves as C.A.P. agencies for the purposes of the act.

economy   The sphere of society in which individuals and the community organize to satisfy subsistence needs with production of food, clothing, shelter, and, in some societies, personal wealth.

edema   An abnormal accumulation of fluid in cells, tissues, or cavities of the body, resulting in swelling.

egalitarianism   The view that people are equal, especially politically or socially.

EIR or EIS   The first is an Environmental Impact Report and the second is an Environmental Impact Statement. The former is usually employed by states and local governments while the latter by the federal government.

Encinitas tradition   Archaeological remains of a group of cultures derived from Paleo-Indian ancestors. The Encinitas people depended heavily on fishing and collecting shellfish along the California coast. The Encinitas tradition dates from 5500 to 3000 B.C.E.

encomienda   A practice by which the Spanish king rewarded public service with grants of land and rights to demand work from the local population. Encomiendas were granted in the Southwest and throughout Latin and South America. Local Indians were forced to work for the landlords, who in turn tried to convert the Indians to Christianity.

encroach   The illegal and sometimes forcible entry of an individual or group on the land or property of another. For example, during much of the 1800s, Indian nations often complained that U.S. settlers established farms on Indian lands without permission and in violation of treaties with the U.S. government.

enema   A liquid injected into the colon through the anus, as a purgative or for medicinal purposes.

enfranchisement   In Canada's Indian Act, a process by which an aboriginal Canadian gives up legal status as an Indian and assumes all the rights of a citizen of Canada. Until 1960, this was the only procedure for a Canadian Indian to gain the right to vote or to purchase alcohol. Few native people chose enfranchisement because they would lose their treaty rights, they would have to accept their share of band trust funds, and they would surrender all rights to reserve lands or participation in band elections or community affairs.

Equal Protection Clause   Part of the Fourteenth Amendment to the U.S. Constitution, adopted in the wake of the Civil War, which requires the equal treatment of all citizens—except "Indians not taxed" (tribal Indians).

ergative   In linguistics, a grammatical construction in which the subjects of some verb forms are treated similarly to the objects of other verb forms.

ethnography   A descriptive account of a particular culture. Ethnographies generally discuss the economic, political, social, and religious life of a people.

ethnopoetics   The study of traditional oral literature, concerned with how linguistic features are used for artistic effect.

etiology   The causes of a specific disease.

evidential   In linguistics, a construction indicating the source of validity of the information in a sentence.

exclusive   In linguistics, referring to a first-person plural pronoun, which excludes the person spoken to, "I and someone else, but not you."

extended family   A family unit consisting of three or more generations.

extinguished   The act of giving up claims to land in exchange for compensation such as money, parcels of land, and goods and services.

extradition   The process by which a person who has escaped from the country where he or she is accused of a crime is demanded by and then returned forcibly to that country to stand trial. Extradition is usually governed by treaties between the countries concerned. There is no general principle in international law that requires governments to return fugitives.

F

family   In linguistics, a group of languages clearly descended from a single "parent" language.

Federal Acknowledgment Project (F.A.P.) *See* Branch of Acknowledgment and Research. *See also* federal recognition.

federal agency Any department, agency, or instrumentality of the United States.

federal lands Any land, other than tribal lands, that are controlled or owned by the United States.

federal recognition Acknowledgment by the U.S. government of government-to-government relationships with certain Indian tribes. Federal recognition can be obtained by satisfying the criteria of the Federal Acknowledgment Process administered through the U.S. Department of the Interior, by federal statute enacted by Congress, or by court decree. *See* Federal Acknowledgement Process *and* federally recognized tribes.

federally recognized tribes Those Indian tribes with which the U.S. government maintains official relations, as established by treaty, executive order, or act of Congress.

Federation of Saskatchewan Indian Nations (FSIN) An association organized along with the Indian Association of Alberta in the 1940s, which has a mandate and objective to serve the political interest of the native bands with federal treaties within the province of Saskatchewan. *See* Indian Association of Alberta.

fee-simple ownership A form of individual ownership of property, usually land, where the owner has the sole right to sell the land to any buyers, and no other parties have significant claims to the land.

fiduciary A relationship founded in trust and responsibility for looking after the best interests of a group, organization, or committee.

Fifth Amendment Part of the Bill of Rights of the U.S. Constitution, which forbids any taking of "private property" without "due process of law" and compensation. Indian treaties and reservation lands are now recognized as being "property" within the meaning of this provision.

First Ministers' Conference (FMC) A recently developed Canadian political tradition, the FMC is a gathering of Canada's "first ministers"—the ten provincial premiers and the national prime minister. In the 1990s, leaders of the Canadian territories have been included on occasion along with aboriginal leaders. At first, FMCs were oriented toward specific issues and problems; however, increasingly the FMC is supplanting traditional parliamentary politics as the primary decision-making forum in Canada.

first nations A term that came into common usage in the 1970s to replace the word "Indian" which many people found offensive. The term distinguishes and gives recognition to Canada's Indian nations as the original peoples on the North American continent. Although the term First Nation is widely used, no legal definition of it exists. Among its uses, the term "First Nations peoples" refers to the Indian people in Canada, both status and non-status Indians and treaty Indians.

Five Civilized Tribes A name given to the Cherokee, Choctaw, Chickasaw, Creek, and Seminole tribes during the second half of the 1900s because they adopted democratic constitutional governments and schools.

Folsom points Ancient flaked and grooved pieces of flint that were used as spearheads by paleo-Indians, or Stone Age Indians, before 10,000 B.C.E.

foraging economy An economic system based on obtaining foods from naturally occurring sources, hunting, fishing, and gathering plants.

Formative period A term used to describe the period of early settlement of Indians into villages. In the Southwest, the settlement of villages, with some dependence on farming, occurred between C.E. 200 and 900.

freedmen Former slaves who were freed after the Civil War and by the Thirteenth Amendment to the U.S. Constitution. The Cherokee, Choctaw, Chickasaw, Creek, and Seminole all held slaves and, after the Civil War, in one way or another included their freedmen into their national institutions.

fricative In linguistics, a consonant produced by letting the air pass through the mouth with audible noise, as contrasted with a stop, when the air is abruptly held in the mouth.

G

General Allotment Act of 1887 A law that applied the principle of allotting in severalty tribal reservation lands to individual resident tribesmen. Generally, a tract of 160 acres for a head of household, 80 acres for single people, and 40 acres per child was received in trust status for a period of twenty-five years; thereafter, the allottee owned the land in fee simple. The General

Allotment Act was designed to divide Indian reservations into small, privately owned plots and release the surplus lands to U.S. settlers. Under the General Allotment Act, between 1887 and 1934, over 90 million acres of Indian land were sold to U.S. citizens. This law is often referred to as the Dawes Act, named for the law's principle author, U.S. Senator Henry Dawes of Massachusetts.

General Revenue Sharing Program (1972–1986) A federal program to share federal tax revenues with state and local governments in the United States, including states, counties, cities, towns, and Indian tribes and Alaska Native villages, "which perform substantial governmental functions."

genetic relationship In linguistics, the relationship between "sister" languages descended from a single parent language.

Ghost Dance Part of a largely religious movement in the 1870s and into the late 1880s and early 1890s. The movement hoped to restore the buffalo herds to the Plains and restore the old Indian Plains life. It was believed that many of the people lost in epidemics and warfare would be returned to life if certain ritual and religious precautions were observed. *See* the biography of Wovoka and information on the Great Basin and Plains in the 1870s to 1890s.

glottal stop In linguistics, a consonant produced by closing and opening the vocal cords, interrupting the flow of air.

glottalization In linguistics, a closure and re-opening of the vocal cords simultaneously with the production of a sound in the mouth.

government-to-government relationship The official relation between the U.S. federal government and the tribal governments of Indian tribes, which is defined by the mention of Indian tribes in the U.S. Constitution and through legal rulings. In this relation, the U.S. government recognizes inherent rights of Indian tribes to self-government and to the ownership of land.

Great Basin Elevated region covering a great deal of several western U.S. states (Nevada, eastern California, western Colorado, Utah, eastern Oregon, and western Wyoming), which contains no drainage for water outside the region. Consequently, water must drain toward the center, hence the name Great Basin.

Great Society Name given to domestic policy during the administration of President Lyndon B. Johnson (1963–1969), especially anti-poverty and social welfare measures.

H

habeas corpus Literally, from Latin "you have the body." A claim presented to a court stating that a person is being held in custody or jail in violation of law. In Indian country, normally this writ of habeas corpus is available only to criminal defendants who have been convicted in tribal courts and who claim that their convictions were obtained without adherence to the Indian Civil Rights Act (for example, evidence was improperly seized or the criminal statute used as the basis for conviction violated rights of free speech).

Haudenosaunee The name of the people often called the Iroquois or Five Nations, or Six Nations after 1717. Literally, it means "The People of the Long House," referring to the extended multifamily houses in which the Iroquois lived.

Health and Welfare Canada The department of the Canadian federal government responsible for the health of all Canadians. It is divided into several branches; the Medical Services Branch serves the health needs of Inuit and Indians.

health status A measurement of the state of health of a given population, usually reported in numbers per 1,000 population and utilizing such indicators as morbidity, mortality, and infant death rates.

heathens Anyone of another religion with different fundamental views of religion. Indians were considered heathens by the early Catholic Spanish explorers and by the Puritans in New England. Indians considered Europeans also to have little understanding of religion or culture. For example, the Choctaw regarded early English traders as untutored and nonspiritual beings because they did not understand Choctaw religious views and did not practice correct religious rituals and social etiquette.

hierarchical Structured by class or rank.

Home Guard Indians In Canada, bands of Indians who lived near fur trade posts and had a relatively more intense trading relationship with traders than most Indian bands. Home Guard bands and traders exchanged various goods and services, and also tended to develop kinship ties.

homestead With reference to the federal lands (public domain), a homestead is a parcel of land—usually 80 to 160 acres—acquired by an adult who had to develop a portion of the land and build a minimal home on the site. The Homestead Act of 1862 was the initial law that made homesteading possible on public lands.

hunters Indians who depended on hunting, fishing, or gathering, as opposed to farming, for their food. Most aboriginal groups in Canada were hunting peoples.

I

IHS Service Population Those American Indians, Eskimos, and Aleuts (as identified by the census) who reside in the geographic areas in which the Indian Health Service (IHS) has responsibilities. These areas are the thirty-two reservation states (including California), and the geographic areas are defined as on or near reservations or within a contract health service delivery area (CHSDA).

Immersion schools Canadian schools where the language used is different from the students' first language. For example, Indian children who spoke their native language were often sent to schools where only English was spoken. This was a method of getting them to speak English and learn Canadian culture.

in situ "In place." A term applied to archaeological remains found in their original, undisturbed location or position.

inalienable In linguistics, referring to a noun for which a possessor must always be specified, especially kin terms and body parts.

inclusive In linguistics, referring to a first-person plural pronoun that includes the person spoken to, "I and you."

incorporation In linguistics, refers to the object of a noun being part of a verb form.

Indian (1) In Canada, according to the Indian Act first passed in 1876 and revised in 1985, a term that describes all the Aboriginal people in Canada who are not Inuit or Métis. Indian peoples are one of three groups of people recognized as Aboriginal in the *Constitution Act*, 1982. The act specifies that Aboriginal people in Canada consist of Indians, Inuit and Métis people. In addition, there are three legal definitions that apply to Indians in Canada: status Indians, non-status Indians and treaty Indians. (2) In the United States, any individual who self-identifies as an American Indian or Alaska Native and who is determined by his tribe to be a fully enrolled tribal member.

Indian Act In Canada, the overriding legislation that sets forth the policies of the federal government towards native people. This legislation passed by the Canadian government defines the legal status of Indians. First passed by the Canadian Parliament in 1876, the act was revised in 1951 and subsequently amended in 1985. Essentially, the Indian Act had four major objectives. First, it defined status Indians. Second, it established the reserve system. Third, it created legal entities known as bands with governments to administer reserve communities. And fourth, it created a national administrative structure, now known as Indian and Northern Affairs Canada, to administer the act. Under the Indian Act, the head of this administrative structure holds ministerial and trust responsibility for "status Indians" recognized by the Canadian federal government. The minister's responsibilities include managing certain monies belonging to First Nations and Indian lands, and approving or disallowing First Nations by-laws. *See* band, band council, British North America Act, *and* status Indians.

Indian agents In Canada, government agents appointed to Indian regions to increase contact between the Crown and Indian nations. Their presence marked the replacement of traditional Indian governments by elected governments, largely controlled by these agents.

Indian and Northern Affairs Canada (INAC) The Canadian government department (formerly known as the Department of Indian Affairs and Northern Development) that administers the *Indian Act* and delivers authorized federal funds and programs, often through provincial governments, to those Aboriginal people who qualify to receive them.

Indian Association of Alberta (IAA). Officially incorporated in 1944, IAA serves as an organization representing the political interests of the treaty Indians of the province of Alberta. The IAA promotes unity and spiritual strength of Indian nations in the protection of their lands, rights, and cultures. The organization receives its mandates from the chiefs, councillors, and members of the Alberta first nations, the member native bands of Alberta.

Indian country Land where Indian government and custom rule. In more recent times, Indian country refers to Indian reservations where Indian tribal governments are regulated by federal law and the Bureau of Indian Affairs.

Indian Delegation Act of 1946 (Public Law 687)
A congressional act that authorized substantial delegations of formal authority from the secretary of the interior to the commissioner of Indian affairs and from the commissioner to his subordinates, the twelve area directors who work on a day-to-day basis with local BIA agency offices and tribal governments on Indian reservations.

Indian Education Act (1972)   A congressional act that provided education financial assistance to communities with Indian students in their schools.

Indian Health Care Improvement Act (Public Law 94–437)   Through a program of increased funding levels in the Indian Health Service budget, the act was intended to improve the health status of American Indians and Alaska Natives up to a level equal to the general U.S. population. Funding was directed to urban populations and funds were used to expand health services, and build and renovate medical and sanitation facilities. It also established programs designed to increase the number of Indian health professionals and to improve care access for Indian people living in urban areas.

Indian Health Service (IHS)   The seventh agency within the U.S. Public Health Service, this federal agency's mission is to upgrade the health status of American Indians to the highest level possible. The IHS is composed of eleven regional administrative units called area offices. Within these units, the IHS operates 45 hospitals, 65 health centers, 6 school health centers, and 201 other treatment programs. In 1987, the state of California was designated an area office, the latest addition to the IHS. There are no IHS facilities in California, only Indian-operated and -managed clinics.

Indian New Deal   Legislation enacted in the early 1930s during the Roosevelt administration promoting tribal government and economic recovery programs for reservations.

Indian Removal   The United States government policy, beginning in the 1820s and lasting through the 1850s, of moving all Indian tribes west of the Mississippi River, to make room for U.S. settlement of the lands in the east. By 1860, this policy resulted in the removal of most eastern Indian nations to locations in present-day Kansas and Oklahoma.

Indian Reorganization Act of 1934 (IRA)   A congressional act providing reservation communities the opportunity to re-organize their tribal governments and adopt a new tribal constitution and tribal charter, and organize tribal business corporations. It also provided a revolving loan fund and other support services to participating tribes.

Indian Self-Determination and Education Assistance Act of 1975 (Public Law 93–638)   This act enabled tribes to contract, at their own option, to provide any service currently being provided by either the Bureau of Indian Affairs or the Indian Health Service. If the tribes change their policies about contracting government services, they have the right to return the administration of a contracted service to the relevant federal agency. The Self-Determination Act was designed to give Indian tribes and organizations more direct control over federal programs that operated within reservation communities.

Indian status   In Canada, an individual's legal status as an Indian, as defined by the *Indian Act*.

Indian Territory   The area west of the Mississippi River, primarily present-day Kansas and Oklahoma, to which the United States once planned to move all of the eastern Indians. Indian Territory was the home of nearly one-third of all U.S. Indians in 1880. Parts of Indian Territory were opened to U.S. settlers, over Indian objections, in 1889. By 1907, the last remnants of Indian Territory were admitted to the Union as the state of Oklahoma, as non-Indians had become an overwhelming majority of the population.

Indian tribe   Any tribe, band, nation, or other organized group or community of Indians recognized as being eligible for special programs and services provided by the United States because of its status. *See* federally recognized tribes.

indigenous   Native to the area.

industry   A term used in a classification system of economic activity in which firms that produce similar goods or services are grouped together into distinct categories.

infant death rate   A ratio of infant deaths within the first year of life to the total live births in a particular time period, usually five or ten years.

injunction   A court order prohibiting a person or legal entity from carrying out a given action, or ordering a person or organization to carry out a specific task. For example, in 1832, the U.S. Supreme Court in the case *Worcester v. Georgia* ruled that the Georgia government had no legal right to abolish the Cherokee government, which had its capital in territory claimed by Georgia. The Court, however, did not issue an injunction to the state of Georgia to prohibit it from extending its laws over the Cherokee nation.

inpatient   A patient admitted to a bed in a hospital to have treatment and stay overnight at least one night.

intransitive   In linguistics, characterizing verbs that have subjects but not direct objects, opposite of transitive.

Inuit   Formerly known as Eskimos, Inuit are members of one of several peoples who traditionally inhabited areas north of the treeline in northern Alaska, northern Canada, and Greenland. They all speak dialects of the same language. In Canada, Inuit have the same legal status as Indians. The word Inuit means *people* in the Inuit language– Inuktitut. The singular of Inuit is Inuk. Forming a majority in the new Canadian territory of Nunavut, they are in effect self-governing since the turn of the twenty-first century.

Inuk   The singular of Inuit.

Iroquoian   Indian peoples who speak an Iroquoian language, such as the Huron, Mohawk, and Onondaga.

Iroquoian League   The Iroquois Confederacy, an alliance of government and cultural and legal unity, which was formed before European colonization by the Mohawk, Cayuga, Onondaga, Oneida, and Seneca nations of present-day upstate New York. Also called the Five Nations and, after being joined by the Tuscarora in the early 1700s, the Six Nations.

isolate (language isolate)   A language without close historical relationships to other languages.

J

Jim Crow Legislation   After 1890, laws passed by many southern states designed to segregate the U.S. population by race. Many native people were automatically classified as black.

Johnson-O'Malley Act of 1934   Permitted the Indian Office to contract with the states to provide education, health, and welfare services to Indians on reservations within their borders. For example, the act allowed Indian children to attend public schools at the expense of the Indian Office.

jurisdiction   The empowerment of a governing body to oversee regulations and laws within an assigned area. The extent of legal power of a government, legislature, or of a court over its people and territory. Jurisdiction is defined in terms of persons, subject matter, and geography. For example, Alabama courts have jurisdiction in cases involving people, property, or activities only in the state of Alabama.

K

Kachina   A deity or group of benevolent spirit beings among the Pueblo.

kiva   Among the Pueblo cultures, an underground ceremonial chamber formed in the shape of a circle. A cycle of often-secret annual rituals takes place in the kivas. Leaders gather in the kivas to discuss religious and other important issues concerning the pueblo community.

L

labiovelar   In linguistics, characterizing consonants produced with the rear part of the tongue, with simultaneous rounding of the lips.

labor force participation   An individual who is working or looking for work is considered to be participating in the labor force. Anyone who does not have a job and is not looking for work is not in the labor force.

land cession treaty   A treaty in which a group of people surrender certain rights to land in exchange for other rights, usually hunting rights or an annual payment.

land claim, comprehensive   In the 1970s, the Canadian government agreed to negotiate comprehensive land claims with aboriginal groups whose ancestors had not ceded their land rights by signing a land surrender treaty. Claims negotiations involve a lengthy process, which, when successful, leads to cash settlements, land title, and devolution of authority. When settled, comprehensive claims agreements acquire the constitutional status of treaties.

land claim, specific   Specific land claims are made against the Canadian state where it is argued that treaty commitments have not been met. The meaning of treaty rights themselves has expanded considerably over the years, allowing ever more specific claims to be made on treaty grounds. But usually specific land claims refer to as-yet unallocated lands.

land tenure　Land tenure has to do with how land is held—by communities, tribes, nations, individuals—and how it functions in terms of utilization, devisement, etc. In Indian affairs, land tenure is basically dichotomous; tribal and individual (allotment), but reservations may include non-Indian allotments, federal public lands, and even state lands.

language area　A geographical region in which languages of different families have become similar due to borrowing.

law　A measure or set of rules passed by a governing body to regulate the actions of the people in the interest of the majority of the nation.

legend　A folktale that deals with the experiences of individuals or happenings of a distant past.

libertarian　A person who places great value on individual consent and personal freedom.

life expectancy　The average number of years remaining to a person at a particular age, based on a given set of age-specific death rates, generally the mortality (death rate) conditions existing in the period mentioned.

line　A unit in the structure of a literary composition, defined in terms of its parallelism of structure with an adjacent line.

lineage　A group of people who can trace actual descent from a common ancestor.

lingua franca (trade language)　A mixed language used for communication between people of different native languages.

linguistics　The study of language. Usually the sounds, structure, and meaning of a language are analyzed and compared with other languages.

litigation　The use of courts or a legal process to achieve an end or contest an issue. For example, when in the early 1830s, the state of Georgia extended its laws over the Cherokee nation, the Cherokee appealed to the U.S. Supreme Court to resolve their differences with the Georgians.

location ticket　In Canada, the right granted by the government to an Indian to use part of reserve land as if it were private property. Location tickets were part of the Canadian government's attempts to encourage Indians to accept private property rather than hold land in common.

Long Walk　The 300-mile forced walk in 1864 from the Navajo's home in the west to an assigned reservation, Bosque Redondo, near Fort Sumner, 180 miles southeast of Santa Fe, New Mexico. During the 1970s and early 1980s, several long walks by Indians traveling across the country were organized to protest treaty and Native issues. Often the long walks started at Alcatraz Island, or on the West coast, and ended in Washington, D.C. In 1972, one such long walk ended in the pillaging of the BIA offices in Washington D.C. Sacred runs continue to be organized.

longhouse　In the Northwest Coast, a longhouse is a dwelling in which several nuclear families share the structure. Usually, the families are related to one another. The Iroquois or Six Nations of upstate New York also had a similar tradition of living in longhouses with related extended families.

loyalists　An expression used during the Revolutionary War (1775–83) for persons who chose the side of the British and attempted to help the British cause.

M

Magna Carta　An agreement of fundamental rights, also known as the Great Charter of England, signed in 1215 C.E. by King John and his English noblemen. Many of our modern ideas on government and democracy have developed from this fundamental constitutional document, empowering freedom and justice. *See* Proclamation of 1763.

maize　Also known as corn, an important crop plant, initially domesticated in Mexico over six thousand years ago.

Manifest Destiny　During the 1900s, a broadly held belief among the U.S. population that it was inevitable that the U.S. nation would expand across the North American continent from the Atlantic to the Pacific Ocean. Belief in Manifest Destiny served as a rationalization for the seizure of Indian land, and, in 1846, to justify war with Mexico, which led to the annexation of Texas, New Mexico, Arizona, and California.

materialism　The belief that economic well-being or wealth are of central human concern, while spiritual or cultural understandings or comforts are of secondary concern or relatively meaningless.

Matrilineal descent　A kinship system in which relationships are traced through women. Children belong to their mother's kin group. Inheritance of names, wealth, or other property transfer through the mother's family and/or clan.

matrilocal residence   A pattern of residence where a married couple lives with or near the wife's family.

Medical Services Branch (MSB)   The branch of the Department of National Health and Welfare of the Canadian federal government responsible for Indian and Inuit health.

Medicine Chest Clause   A clause in Treaty No. 6 (1876) between the Canadian government and the Indian tribes in Northern Alberta on which is based the claim that Indian people in Canada have a perpetual right to free health care provided by the Canadian federal government.

mega-fauna   The large animals, such as woolly mammoth, ground sloth, and saber-toothed tiger, which died off about 8,000 B.C.E. after the last glacier receded far north.

Meriam Report of 1928   An exhaustive investigation of Indian administration and a major criticism of Indian policies and administration since passage of the General Allotment Act of 1887. The report had a major influence on Indian affairs during the administrations of Presidents Herbert Hoover (1929–1933) and Franklin D. Roosevelt (1933–1945). It helped formulate the policies of the Indian New Deal, which originated with passage of the Indian Reorganization Act of 1934, and allowed Indians greater self-government and the right to retain cultural ceremonies and events. Produced by the Brookings Institution's Institute for Government Research, the actual title of the report is *The Problem of Indian Administration*.

mescaline   A white, crystalline alkaloid, psychedelic drug obtained from the cactus *Lophophora williamsi* (peyote).

metate   A stone with a slightly hollow center that is used for grinding corn.

Métis   French for "mixed-blood." This term has been used in several different ways. Usually it refers to mixed-blood people in western Canada who are conscious of belonging to a distinct community. The Canadian Constitution recognizes Métis as aboriginal peoples. The term is also used to refer to any person of mixed Indian-European descent, and more specifically to a descendant of a native parent, usually Cree or Ojibway, and a non-native parent, usually French, but also some English, who settled in the Red River area of

what is now the province of Manitoba during the days of the fur trade, which lasted from the 1700s to the late 1800s.

Mississippian period   The period between C.E. 900 and 1500 when in the eastern United States there arose complex chiefdom societies and maize-farming communities. The Mississippian tradition is associated with the building of flat-topped earthen mounds, which were religious and political centers. Many of the Mississippian towns, sometimes holding as many as thirty thousand people, were fortified with palisades. One of the largest Mississippian societies was located at Cahokia, near present-day St. Louis, Missouri.

moiety   A French expression which means divided into two halves. For anthropologists, the term refers to a society divided into two major clusters of clans. For example, among the Tlingit, there are Eagle and Raven moieties, which divide the society into two groups of about twenty-five clans. Among the Tlingit, moiety relations govern marriage rules, since Raven moiety members must marry an Eagle and vice-versa.

morphology   In linguistics, the formation of words by combinations of stems, prefixes, and suffixes, as contrasted with syntax.

mortality   The proportion of deaths to population.

moxa   A soft, downy material, burned on the skin as a cauterizing agent or counter-irritant.

Muskogean   A family of related languages spoken by many Indian nations of the southeast including the Choctaw, Chickasaw, Creek, Seminole, and Natchez.

myth   A narrative tale concerned with the Creator, spirits, and the nature and meaning of the universe and humans.

N

Nation   A community of people who share the right to political self-rule, and/or who share a common identity, and who usually share a similar culture, the same language, the same economy, and a mutually recognized territory.

National Indian Brotherhood (NIB)   Founded in 1968, a Canadian national Indian political organization. The NIB now serves as the legal executive office for the Assembly of First Nations. *See* Assembly of First Nations.

Native American   Of or relating to a tribe, people, or culture indigenous to the United States.

need   An estimate of the amount of medical care required to provide adequate services to a population in terms of the amount of disease present or preventable, often contrasted to demand.

New Deal   Name given to domestic policy during the administration of President Franklin D. Roosevelt (1933–1945).

New Frontier   Name given to domestic policy during the administration of President John F. Kennedy (1961–1963).

non-IHS-service population   Those Indians who do not reside in the geographic areas in which Indian Health Service has responsibility.

non-recognized tribe   Indian communities that do not have official government-to-government relations with the U.S. government because they did not sign a treaty with the United States, lost their recognized status by termination, or have no executive orders or agreements that require the U.S. government to provide services or to protect their land and resources in a trust relationship.

non-status Indians   People in Canada who consider themselves to be Indians but whom the Canadian government does not recognize as Indians under the Indian Act because they have failed to establish or have lost or abandoned their Indian status rights.

non-treaty Indians   Canadian Indian people whose relationship with the government is not affected by any treaties. Non-treaty Indians can be either status or non-status Indians.

Northwest Passage   As late as the 1790s, Europeans believed there was a short ocean passage in the northern latitudes connecting the Atlantic and Pacific Oceans. Many of the earliest European explorations in northern North America were prompted by this myth.

Northwest Territories (NWT)   Today this term refers to the western central portion of Canadian territory (capital city, Yellowknife) north of the 60th parallel. The territory of Nunavut was formed in 1999 from the province of Northwest Territories as constituted at that time. Originally (1870), the Northwest Territories referred to most of Canada west of Ontario except

British Columbia, including present-day Alberta and Saskatchewan and most of Manitoba.

numeral classifier   In linguistics, a grammatical element used in counting, indicating the form or shape of the objects counted.

Nunavut   As of 1 April 1999, a new territory (previously part of the Northwest Territories), which covers the majority of Canada north of the tree line. Inuit are the majority of the region's population. The establishment of Nunavut was part an aboriginal land claim.

O

occupation   A term used in a classification system of economic activity in which jobs that require similar activities are grouped together into distinct categories.

Oklahoma "Runs"   Spectacular one-day chances to legally acquire former Indian land in present-day Oklahoma. Most of the "runs" occurred in the 1890s.

"On or near"   The federal regulation that Contract Health Service can be provided only to American Indians residing on a reservation or in a county that borders a reservation.

Oolichan (Eulachon)   A small fish (Thaleichthys pacificus) captured in freshwater streams by the Northwest Coast people. Oolichan were especially important as a source of oil.

oral history   A historical research method that investigates the past by speaking to people rather than relying on the written word.

outpatient   A patient who receives diagnosis or treatment in a clinic or dispensary connected with a hospital but is not admitted as a bed patient. (Sometimes used as a synonym for ambulatory.)

P

Paleo-Arctic tradition   A term used to describe the tools left behind by the first Native Americans, who lived in the arctic regions of Alaska and Canada. The Paleo-arctic tradition began between 9000 and 8000 B.C.E. and continued as late as 5000 B.C.E.

paleo-Indians   The ancestors of contemporary Native Americans and the first people to come to North America over fourteen thousand years ago.

Paleo-Plateau tradition   A term used to describe the various Archaic period cultures of the Columbia-Fraser Plateau of Washington state and British Columbia. The Paleo-Plateau tradition lasted from 8,000 to 3,000 B.C.E.

Papal Bull   A decree made by a Catholic Pope. Bulls used to have the force of law within the Roman Catholic Church, but today are considered to be statements of policy only.

patriarchy   A social system in which men have exclusive control over power and wealth in the society.

patrilineal descent   A kinship system in which relationships are traced through men. Children belong to their father's kin group.

patrilocal residence   A pattern of residence where a married couple lives with or near the husband's family.

patronage   Providing jobs in exchange for political services. For example, before 1890 most jobs with the U.S. Indian administration were jobs gained through patronage relations with congressmen and other high government officials.

Penner Report   A report prepared in 1983 by a special committee of the House of Commons on Indian self-government in Canada. The report is named after committee chairman, Keith Penner, a member of Parliament for the Liberal party.

per capita   A Latin term meaning by or for each person, equally to each individual. It is one way used for distributing funds to every adult member of a tribe.

peyote   A bitter stimulant obtained from the button-like structures of the mescal cactus plant, which some Indian groups use as part of their religious practices. The peyote buttons are taken during ceremonies of the Native American Church, which was officially established in 1918, but began on the Plains as early as the 1860s.

phoneme   In linguistics, one of the set of contrasting sound units in a language.

phylum   Plural phyla. In linguistics, a group of language families hypothesized to be descended from a single parent language.

pictograph   A simplified pictorial representation of an historical occurrence.

Piedmont   A region in the southeast United States marked by rolling hills and open valleys located between the relatively flat coastal plain and the more rugged Appalachian Mountains.

Pinto Basin tradition   A term describing a series of archaeological hunting and gathering cultures from the Great Basin, dating over the period of 5000 to 1500 B.C.E.

plenary power   The exclusive authority of Congress (as opposed to the states of the Union) to make laws concerning Indian tribes. This special power can be traced to Article I, Section 8 (the "Indian Commerce Clause") of the Constitution. Plenary means full or complete.

policy   A statement that outlines the means and philosophy by which a group or government will try to fulfill one or more of its major goals or interests.

polyandry   A marriage involving one woman and two or more men.

polygamy   Having more than one spouse at the same time.

polygyny   A marriage involving one man and two or more women.

polysynthetic language   In linguistics, a type of language marked by long word forms with complex morphologies, which may often function as complete sentences.

potlatch   A feast in recognition of important life events, e.g., birth, death, marriage. The giving of a potlatch conferred value, prestige, and honor to all those involved. During a potlatch, or "giveaway," the hosts gave food, clothes, songs, and culturally significant gifts, such as copper engraved valuables, to the guests. The potlatch ceremony was practiced by tribes in the Pacific Northwest. "Giveaways" are similar events held in other regions of North America.

poultice   A hot, soft, moist mass, as of flour, herbs, mustard, etc., sometimes spread on cloth, applied to a sore or inflamed part of the body.

preemption   The power of the federal government to override state law in fields such as Indian affairs. This power comes from Article VI, Section 2 of the U.S. Constitution (the "Supremacy Clause"), which says federal laws and treaties are "the supreme Law of the Land."

presidio   Spanish military post in the American Southwest.

Privy Council (Judicial Committee of the Privy Council)   In the British Empire, the Privy Council in London was the final court of appeal from the colonial governors and courts. It was a committee of Peers (titled noblemen) chosen by the Crown (the reigning King or Queen). Until 1949, the Privy Council, in London, England, was the highest court of appeal in Canada and was therefore somewhat analogous to the U.S. Supreme Court.

Proclamation of 1763   The document signed by King George III issued as a declaration of policy by the British government to address the unauthorized settlement of Indian land. The Proclamation was never fully implemented, in part due to the outbreak of the American Revolution. The commitments contained within were, however, often renewed to obtain alliances with most Indian nations in fighting against the rebels. In areas that later became part of the United States, the policy reserved the land west of the Appalachian Mountains for Indian use, and restricted English settlements to land east of the divide, or central ridge, of the Appalachians. In Canada, the Proclamation provides the basis of English recognition of Indian rights to use and live on their territory, but only at the pleasure of the British Crown, which by this act claimed ownership of all Indian lands. It remains part of the Canadian Constitution.

proto-language   The prehistoric parent language from which several historical languages are descended.

Public Law 280 (1953) 67 Stat. 588   A congressional act that transferred criminal and civil jurisdiction in Indian country from the federal government to the states of California, Minnesota, Nebraska, Oregon, and Wisconsin (and after 1959 to Alaska). Other states were given the option to assume jurisdiction by legislation. In 1968, P.L. 280 was amended to require tribal consent to the transfer of jurisdiction.

pueblo   A Spanish word for the multi-storied stone or adobe Indian villages of the American Southwest. Also a name used for the Indians who inhabited such communal buildings.

R

radiocarbon dating   A technique that measures the natural radioactive content of organic materials, such as charcoal, in order to measure the approximate age of the materials or objects found in archaeological sites.

rancheria   A Spanish word applied to the numerous, small Indian reservations of California.

range condition   The annual health of browsable vegetation that supports domesticated animals—e.g., cattle, sheep, etc. The determination of a range condition will decide how many head will be permitted to graze given areas in a given year or season.

ratification   The confirmation of a treaty by the national legislature—in the United States, by the Senate. In most countries, a treaty must be ratified before it becomes law.

recognized   *See* federally recognized, state recognized, *and* nonrecognized tribes.

recognized & original title   Recognized title lands refer to those ceded by treaties or statutes and original title lands are those that have had to be reconstructed on the basis of ethnographic and historic research, including information provided by Indian informants.

red power   A term applied to an Indian social movement and a series of protest activities during the 1960s and 1970s.

reduplication   In linguistics, repetition of part of a stem, often used to indicate plurality or habitual action.

referenda   Referring measures passed upon or proposed by the legislature to the voters for approval or rejection. In some states a referenda can be placed on the ballot by petition of registered voters.

registered Indians   *See* status Indians.

relocation   In 1951, the federal government established the Direct Employment Assistance program to encourage reservation Indians to move to urban areas such as Los Angeles, Chicago, Minneapolis, and Denver. This and subsequent programs came to be known as "relocation" programs.

Removal Act   A congressional act passed in 1830 which authorized and funded the peaceful exchange of lands and removal of Indians to Indian Territory, west of the Mississippi River.

repatriation   Through court cases and legislative lobbying, tribes have demanded the return of museum-

and university-held skeletal remains of Indians and funerary objects for reburial or other appropriate disposition.

reservation/rancheria   Lands set aside by U.S. government authority for use and occupation by a group of Indians.

reservation state   An area within which the Indian Health Service has responsibilities for providing health care to American Indians or Alaska Natives.

reserve   In Canada, land set aside for specific Indian bands. "Indian reserve lands" as defined by the Indian Act. Essentially the same meaning as the U.S. term "reservation." In Canada, legal title is held in trust by the federal Crown in the right of Canada and may not be leased or sold until "surrendered" to the Crown by a referendum by band members.

reserved-rights doctrine   A legal theory that Indian communities and governments maintain all rights to self-government, exercise of cultural rights, religious freedom, land, water, and other resources, unless Congress expressly takes those rights away.

residential schools   Schools administered by the Canadian government and religious organizations that housed and educated many Indian and Inuit children in the 19th and 20th centuries. The use of such schools was intended to achieve the goal of complete assimilation of Indians into Canadian society by way of isolating children from their families and communities. Many instances of physical and sexual abuse took place at such schools and the Canadian government as well as the churches involved are facing lawsuits as a result.

residual resource   The final or remaining course of action for patients seeking medical care from a provider.

restitution   Transfer of property or payment of money to prevent an unjust loss from the acts of another.

retrocession   A bureaucratic procedure of the Bureau of Indian Affairs that allows Indian communities within Public Law 280 states (California, Alaska, Wisconsin, Oregon, Nebraska, and Minnesota) to petition the federal government to bar state government regulation of courts and law enforcement on the reservation.

revitalization   A social movement carried out by a group, usually in response to major changes in its society, such as pressures to assimilate. Revitalization

attempts to create new culture with beliefs, values, and attitudes that blend some aspects of the old culture with the new living conditions.

Robinson Superior Treaty of 1850   On 7 September 1850, at Sault Ste. Marie, Ontario, the Honorable William B. Robinson of Toronto, Ontario, acting on behalf of the British Crown, met with three chiefs and five principal men representing Michipicoten, Fort William, and Gull River bands of Ojibwa Indians to sign a document referred to as the Robinson Superior Treaty, the first modern Indian treaty in Canada.

According to the treaty, the Ojibwa people surrendered considerable land, and were paid two thousand pounds in English money and allotted three reserves. A similar agreement, referred to as the Robinson Huron Treaty of 1850, removed Indian land claims from the north shore of Lake Huron.

Rose Spring phase   A term given by archaeologists to a time period (1500 B.C.E. to C.E. 500) when hunter and gatherer cultures occupied the region of the Owens Valley of present-day eastern California.

Royal Commission on Aboriginal Peoples   This Commission was appointed in 1991 by the federal government of Prime Minister Brian Mulroney "to examine the economic, social and cultural situation of the Aboriginal Peoples of Canada." Seven commissioners visited 96 communities, held 178 days of hearings, heard briefs from 2,067 people and accumulated more than 76,000 pages of testimony. The five-volume report constitutes the most in-depth analysis ever undertaken on Aboriginal people in Canada. Highly controversial due to its recommendations and its cost, the current government has yet to implement any of its proposals.

royal prerogative   The rights and privileges of a sovereign over subjects independent of both statutes and the courts.

rural Indian   An Indian residing in a non-urban area, generally on or near a reservation.

S

sacred objects   Specific ceremonial objects needed by Native American religious leaders for the practice of traditional Native American religions.

San Dieguito tradition   A distinctive artifact tradition known from present-day California and Nevada and dating to about 8000 to 6000 B.C.E. The tools of the

San Dieguito people show a heavy reliance on hunting, but with some evidence of gathering of wild plants.

scrip   A document given to Métis people during the late nineteenth century in order to extinguish aboriginal title. Scrip could be exchanged for money or land.

secular   A word referring to the mundane or ordinary and nonreligious aspects or times of everyday life.

sedentary   A term that refers to permanent settlement, where the people usually engage in farming for a livelihood and, for the most part, have abandoned hunting or nomadic herding as the mainstay of their economy.

self-determination   Indians exercising their right to govern and make decisions affecting their own lives and affairs on their own land. In international law, the right of every "people" to choose its own form of government and control its own future. Since the 1970s, Congress has used this word to describe programs designed to give Indian tribes greater control over the schools, health facilities, and social services on reservations. *See* Indian Self-Determination and Education Assistance Act.

seminars   Roman Catholic schools that teach religion and other subjects.

settlement acts   The term refers to laws enacted by Congress that finally end conflict and litigation over designated tribal land claims. Many of these acts carry the term within their title—e.g., The Saddleback Mountain Settlement Act of 1995.

severance tax   A tax assessed by a government on mining or petroleum companies when they remove minerals or natural resources from the ground.

Shaker Religion   A religious movement that began with the prophet John Slocum, whose death and re-birth in the 1880s started a movement among the native people of Puget Sound. The movement combined many elements of traditional Coast Salish religion with Christianity. It soon spread through the northwest United States.

shaman/shamanism   An individual versed in supernatural matters who performed in rituals and was expected to cure the sick, envision the future, and help with hunting and other economic activities. Often, a shaman is a healer who uses spiritual encounters or contacts to enact a cure on the patient. Many shamans deal with ailments that are spiritual rather than physical.

Siouan   A large language family that includes Siouan-related languages such as Lakota, Nakota, Dakota, and Crow.

site   In archaeology, a location of past cultural activity of defined space with more or less continuous archaeological evidence.

smallpox   A highly contagious disease which left survivors with badly scarred skin. Native Americans often died by the thousands because their ancestors had not developed resistance to the infection, which was introduced to North America by Europeans.

smoke shop   An Indian-owned store on a reservation that sells cigarettes at a relatively cheap price because state sales tax need not be included.

Snyder Act of 1921   Provided permanent funding authorization for "the general support and civilization of the Indians." To carry out these objectives, the act authorized the Indian Office to provide educational, health, and welfare services to Indian people, to irrigate and make other improvements on Indian lands, and to employ personnel to support these objectives. The Snyder Act signaled a change toward a permanent Indian-federal government relationship.

socialize   A process by which an individual learns to adjust to the group by acquiring social behaviors of which the group approves.

Sooner   Frontiersmen who illegally squatted on Indian land before the U.S. government had extinguished Indian land claims and title.

sovereignty   Deriving from *sovereign*, which means a ruler or king. In international law, being completely independent and not subject to any other ruler or government. The inherent right of a nation to exercise complete and absolute governance over its people and its affairs. In U.S. federal Indian law, sovereignty means having a distinct, but not completely independent government.

specific claim   According to Canadian government land claims policy since 1973, an aboriginal claim based on rights set out in treaties, Indian acts, or other legislation.

Spirit Dance   In the Northwest Coast, a song and dance performed by an individual who has had a guardian spirit encounter. The Spirit Dances are held in the winter months.

squatter   A person who occupies land without having title to it.

state-recognized tribes   Those Indian communities whose governments and land are officially recognized by their surrounding state government, but are not usually recognized by the federal government as an Indian reservation.

status Indians   In Canada, if a person meets the definitional requirements of the Indian Act, they are entitled to be registered on the Indian Register (or Band Membership List) kept by Indian and Northern Affairs Canada in Ottawa. The guidelines for determining status are complex. The criteria is legal rather than based on racial characteristics or blood quantum. All treaty Indians are status Indians, but not all status Indians are treaty Indians. In 1985, Parliament passed an amendment to the Indian Act that allows each native band to adopt its own rules for determining band membership. Many of the new band codes for determining Indian status vary among themselves and with the old rules of the Indian Act.

statute   A law enacted by the highest legislature in the nation or state.

statutory   Refers to those provisions enacted by law by a legislative body.

stop   In linguistics, a consonant produced by shutting off the flow of air momentarily.

Strait of Georgia tradition   An archaeological cultural tradition from the western coastal area of Canada believed to be ancestral to the Coast Salish and other present-day Native American groups of the area. The Strait of Georgia tradition dated from 3,000 to 200 B.C.E.

subsistence   A term that describes a small and localized economy oriented to the production of goods and services primarily for household use, and bound by rules of kinship, sharing, and reciprocity.

sui generis   So unique that it constitutes a class of its own. A term that is used to explain the status of aboriginal title in Canada. It is unique and is therefore inalienable to anyone but the Crown.

Sun Dance   An annual world renewal and purification ceremony performed with some variation among many of the northern Plains Indian nations such as the Cheyenne and the Sioux. One striking aspect of the ceremony was the personal sacrifice that some men made by self-torture in order to gain a vision that might provide spiritual insight and knowledge beneficial to the community.

sweat lodge   A sacred Indian ceremony involving construction of a lodge made of willow saplings bent to form a dome and covered with animal skins, blankets or canvas tarp. A hole is dug in the middle of the lodge in which hot rocks are placed and water poured over them, often by a medicine man, in a ceremonial way often accompanied by praying and singing. The ceremony can have many purposes including spiritual cleansing and healing.

sweetgrass ceremony   A ceremony in which braided sweetgrass is burned and participants "smudge" themselves with the smoke, similar to incense in other religions.

syllabary   A type of writing system in which the basic unit represents a sequence of consonant plus vowel, constituting a syllable. In comparison, alphabets have either a consonant, a letter, or a vowel (in English—a, e, i, o, u), which compose the basic unit of the writing system, as in English or Latin. The famous Cherokee writing system invented by Sequoia is a syllabary and not an alphabet.

syncretic movements   A religious belief system that combines symbols and beliefs from two or more religions. In native North America, there are many native religions that combine elements of traditional religion with Christianity. Some such Indian religious movements are the Delaware Prophet movement of the early 1760s, the Handsome Lake movement beginning in 1799, the Ghost Dances of the 1870s and early 1890s, the ongoing Shaker movement of the Pacific Northwest, and the Native American Church or Peyote cult.

syntax   In linguistics, the combination of words into sentences, as contrasted with morphology, the formation of words by combinations of stems, prefixes, and suffixes.

T

termination   The policy of Congress in the 1950s and 1960s to withdraw federal trust status from Indian bands, communities and tribes. Those tribes that were "terminated" by an act of Congress no longer functioned as governments that made their own laws, but instead were placed under state laws.

theocracy A government or society led by religious leaders.

Thule tradition The archaeological culture, dated from C.E. 100 to 1500 and later, defined as the direct ancestral culture of the present-day Inuit throughout the Arctic. The Thule people were hunters skilled at exploiting sea mammals.

trade language (lingua franca) A mixed language used for communication between people of different native languages.

traditional ecological knowledge The knowledge of Indigenous Peoples including worldviews, values, processes and factual information.

Trail of Tears In the 1830s, a series of forced emigrations by groups of Cherokee, Creek, Seminole, and perhaps some Choctaw, from the Southeast to Indian Territory, present-day Oklahoma, caused by the removal policy.

transitive In linguistics, a characterizing verb that has both subject and direct object, opposite of intransitive.

treaties Agreements negotiated between two parties, which set out the benefits both sides will receive as a result of one side giving up their title to a territory of land. In Canada, commonly referred to as Modern Treaties or Numbered Treaties. After Canada gained its own constitution under confederation in 1867, the new federal government of Canada signed a series of modern treaties numbered 1 through 11 between 1871 and 1921. Also included as "modern " treaties are the Robinson-Superior and Robinson-Huron treaties of 1850 with the Ojibway of Ontario occupying the north shores of Lake Huron and Lake Superior. The government negotiator, the Honorable William B. Robinson of Toronto is recognized for establishing the "treaty method" of obtaining Indian "title surrenders" to land in return for "treaty rights." The Chippewa and Missassauga Agreements of 1923 were the last formally negotiated Indian treaties in Canada. *See* treaty.

treaty (1) In Canada, an agreement between Indian peoples and the Canadian government. Some maintain that these treaties are comparable to treaties between independent nations, while others claim they are merely contracts between the government and some of its subjects. Between 1871 and 1923, the Canadian government made twelve numbered treaties with native bands. Since 1923, the Canadian government has stopped using this term in its agreements with aboriginal peoples. (2) A formal agreement between two or more sovereign nations on issues of war, peace, trade, and other relations. Before 1871, the U.S. government ratified about 270 treaties with Indian nations. After 1871, the U.S. government stopped making treaties with Indians. *See* treaties.

treaty Indian In Canada, descendants of Indians entitled to benefits under the treaties signed by the Crown and specific Indian bands between 1725 and 1921. Those who "took treaty" and surrendered their land rights for specific benefits.

tribal corporation An enterprise owned and operated by a tribe under articles of incorporation, thereby protecting tribal assets not held by the corporation from lawsuits. While providing economic opportunities for tribal members, tribal corporations often employ many non-members as well.

tribal groups A term, especially in British Columbia, for various language and culture groups that reject centralized bureaucracies, whether attached to government or native organizations.

tribal sovereignty The powers of self-government held by Indian communities.

tribe A group of natives sharing a common ancestry, language, culture, and name.

tripartite A term meaning divide into or composed of three parts or parties. A reference to the three distinct governments within Indian Country: federal, tribal, and state.

trust Property that is protected from being taxed or sold by the federal government for a period of time and is held in benefit of a trustee. In U.S. Indian affairs, the government holds trust of Indian lands and resources.

trust responsibility The responsibility of the federal government to protect Indian lives and property; to compensate Indians for any loss due to government mismanagement; and, generally, to act in the best interests of Indians. Originally called "guardianship" and sometimes described by lawyers as a "fiduciary duty."

trust status A legal relationship of an Indian person or tribe with the United States, within which the U.S. government has final and broad authority over the actions of individual Indians or over tribal governments.

U

unemployment rate A statistic published by the federal Bureau of Labor Statistics. It is the percent of the labor force without employment. Unemployed persons who have given up their search for work are not counted in this statistic because they are not considered part of the labor force.

unilaterally "On its own," often referring to U.S. government policy when it abandoned a treaty promise without agreement or compensation to an Indian nation.

unilineal descent A system of kinship relations and inheritance where descent is traced through only women (matrilineal) or men (patrilineal).

urban Indian An Indian residing in urban metropolitan areas or cities.

usufructuary (1) In Canada, the inherent right to use and enjoy the natural products of lands (e.g., game, fish, plants, fruits) of which the underlying title belongs to another, usually the Crown. (2) A way of using land, common among Indian farmers and hunters, where land belongs to an individual, clan, or village as long as that group has a history of continual usage of the land, hunting area, or fishing site. Usufruct rights are recognized by others and are lost whenever a group discontinues use.

uvular In linguistics, a feature of a consonant sound made with the back of the tongue and the rear of the soft palate or uvula.

V

values The generally agreed upon goals, purposes, and issues of importance in a community.

variety In linguistics, a local language variant, referring either to languages of the same family or to dialects of the same language.

velar In linguistics, characterizing consonants produced with the rear part of the tongue. *See* labiovelar.

vision quest A sacred Indian ceremony that involves an individual, often a teenage boy, going to a secluded place to fast (go without food or water) for a period of time (usually a few days) to learn about the spiritual side of himself and possibly have a vision of his spiritual helper, a spirit being who will give him guidance and strength.

voiced In linguistics, a sound pronounced with vibration of the vocal cords.

voiceless In linguistics, a sound pronounced without vibration of the vocal cords.

vowel harmony In linguistics, a process in which vowels change to resemble vowels in nearby grammatical environments.

W

wampum Small, cylindrical, blue and white beads cut from the shell of the quahog, a large Atlantic coast clam. Long strings of wampum were used as trade exchange, while broad, woven "belts" of wampum were used to record treaties among the tribes and, later, with Europeans.

Wapato A plant (Sagittaria latifolia) that grows in shallow lakes and marshy areas. The root was an important source of food for many groups in the Northwest Coast.

wardship According to some legal theories, the relationship between the U.S. government and Indians, where the government has trust responsibility over the affairs and resources of the Indians.

weir A fishing device that operates by blocking off a portion of a stream with a fence-like structure. Migrating fish are then forced to find openings in the weir where the people then capture them.

Westward movement Name given the displacement of Native American peoples by the movement of Americans from the eastern shoreline in the seventeenth century to the West Coast in the nineteenth century.

Woodland period A major time period usually dating from 500 B.C.E. to C.E. 900. During this period, Native American cultures developed complex ceremonial centers that included construction of large mounds. The Woodland period cultures were the first to practice farming in northeastern North America.

world view The unconscious philosophical outlook held by the members of a society.

General Bibliography

♦ General Studies ♦ Anthropology ♦ Architecture ♦ Art ♦ Atlases
♦ Autobiography ♦ Demography ♦ History ♦ Image/Stereotype ♦ Land
♦ Legal Status/Law ♦ Literature and Poetry ♦ Oral Tradition ♦ Policy ♦ Prehistory
♦ Religion ♦ Sociology ♦ Urbanization ♦ Women ♦ Canada

♦ GENERAL STUDIES

Armstrong, Virginia Irving. *I Have Spoken: American History Through the Voices of the Indians*. Athens, Ohio: Swallow Press, 1971.

Bierhorst, John. *The Mythology of North America*. New York: Morrow, 1985.

Boas, Franz. *Race, Language and Culture*. New York: Macmillan, 1940.

Bowden, Henry Warner. *American Indians and Christian Missions: Studies in Cultural Conflict*. Chicago: University of Chicago Press, 1981.

Boxberger, Daniel L., ed. *Native North Americans: An Ethnohistorical Approach*. Dubuque, Iowa: Kendall/Hunt, 1990.

Champagne, Duane. *American Indian Societies: Some Strategies and Conditions of Political and Cultural Survival*. Cambridge, Mass.: Cultural Survival, 1989.

Davis, Mary B., ed. *Native America in the Twentieth Century: An Encyclopedia*. New York: Garland Pub., 1994.

Edmunds, R. David. *American Indian Leaders: Studies in Diversity*. Lincoln: University of Nebraska Press, 1980.

Feest, Christian F. *Indians and Europe: An Interdisciplinary Collection of Essays*. Lincoln: University of Nebraska Press, 1999.

Hamilton, Charles. *Cry of the Thunderbird: The American Indian's Own Story*. Norman: University of Oklahoma Press, 1972.

Hoxie, Frederick E., ed. *Encyclopedia of North American Indians*. Boston: Houghton Mifflin Company, 1996.

Hoxie, Frederick E., and Harvey Markowitz. *Native Americans: An Annotated Bibliography*. Pasadena, Calif.: Salem Press, 1991.

Leitch, Barbara A. *A Concise Dictionary of Indian Tribes of North America*. Algonac, Mich.: Reference Publications, 1979.

Malinowski, Sharon, ed. *The Gale Encyclopedia of Native American Tribes*. Detroit: Gale, 1998.

Mihesuah, Devon A., ed. *Natives and Academics: Researching and Writing about American Indians*. Lincoln: University of Nebraska Press, 1998.

Moerman, Daniel E. *Native American Ethnobotany*. Portland, Oreg.: Timber Press, 1998.

Swisher, Karen Gayton, and AnCita Benally. *Native North American Firsts*. Detroit: Gale, 1998.

Thornton, Russell, ed. *Studying Native America: Problems and Prospects*. Madison, Wis.: University of Wisconsin Press, 1998.

Weeks, Philip. *The American Indian Experience: A Profile, 1524 to the Present*. Arlington Heights, Ill.: Forum Press, 1988.

White, Phillip M. *American Indian Studies: A Bibliographic Guide.* Englewood, Colo.: Libraries Unlimited, 1995.

◆ ANTHROPOLOGY

Bean, Lowell John. *Mukat's People: The Cahuilla Indians of Southern California.* Berkeley and Los Angeles: University of California Press, 1972.

Biolsi, Thomas. *Organizing the Lakota: The Political Economy of the New Deal on the Pine Ridge and Rosebud Reservations.* Tucson: University of Arizona Press, 1992.

Biolsi, Thomas, and Larry J. Zimmerman. *Indians and Anthropologists: Vine Deloria, Jr., and the Critique of Anthropology.* Tucson: University of Arizona Press, 1997.

Deloria, Vine, Jr. *Red Earth, White Lies: Native Americans and the Myth of Scientific Fact.* New York: Scribner, 1995.

———. *We Talk, You Listen: New Tribes, New Turf.* New York: Macmillan, 1970.

Eggan, Fred. *Social Anthropology of North American Tribes.* 2nd enlarged ed. Chicago: University of Chicago Press, 1970.

Ewers, John Canfield. *Plains Indian History and Culture: Essays on Continuity and Change.* Norman: University of Oklahoma Press, 1997.

Fowler, Loretta. *Shared Symbols, Contested Meanings: Gros Ventre Culture and History, 1778–1984.* Ithaca: Cornell University Press, 1987.

Lowie, Robert. *Indians of the Plains.* 1954. Reprint. Lincoln: University of Nebraska Press, 1982.

Miller, Jay. *Tsimshian Culture: A Light Through the Ages.* Lincoln: University of Nebraska Press, 1997.

Nabokov, Peter, ed. *Native American Testimony: A Chronicle of Indian-White Relations From Prophecy to the Present, 1492-2000.* Rev. ed. New York: Penguin, 1999.

Ortiz, Alfonso. *The Tewa World: Space, Time, Being, and Becoming in a Pueblo Society.* Chicago: University of Chicago Press, 1969.

Parker, Arthur C. *Parker on the Iroquois.* Edited by William N. Fenton. Syracuse, N.Y.: Syracuse University Press, 1968.

Sando, Joe S. *Nee Hemish, a History of Jemez Pueblo.* Albuquerque: University of New Mexico Press, 1982.

———. *Pueblo Nations: Eight Centuries of Pueblo Indian History.* Santa Fe, N.Mex.: Clear Light, 1992.

Stands In Timber, John. *Cheyenne Memories.* 1967. Reprints. Lincoln: University of Nebraska Press, 1972; New Haven, Conn.: Yale University Press, 1998.

Sturtevant, Willam C., ed. *Handbook of North American Indians.* 11 vols. to date. Washington, D.C.: Smithsonian Institution, 1978–.

Swanton, John R. *The Indian Tribes of North America.* 1952. Reprint. Washington, D.C.: Smithsonian Institution Press, 1968.

———. *The Indians of the Southeastern United States.* 1946. Reprint. Grosse Pointe, Mich.: Scholarly Press, 1969.

Swindler, Nina, et al., eds. *Native Americans and Archaeologists: Stepping Stones to Common Ground.* Walnut Creek: AltaMira Press, 1997.

Watkins, Joe. *Indigenous Archaeology: American Indian Values and Scientific Practice.* Walnut Creek, Calif.: AltaMira Press, 2001.

◆ ARCHITECTURE

Krinsky, Carol H. *Contemporary Native American Architecture: Cultural Regeneration and Creativity.* New York: Oxford University Press, 1997.

Morgan, William N. *Precolumbian Architecture in Eastern North America.* Gainesville, Fla.: University Press of Florida, 1999.

Nabokov, Peter, and Robert Easton. *Native American Architecture.* New York: Oxford University Press, 1989.

◆ ART

Berlo, Janet C., ed. *The Early Years of Native American Art History: The Politics of Scholarship and Collecting.* Seattle: University of Washington Press; Vancouver: UBC Press, 1992.

————. *Plains Indian Drawings, 1865–1935: Pages From a Visual History.* New York: Harry N. Abrams in association with the American Federation of Arts and the Drawing Center, 1996.

Berlo, Janet C. and Ruth B. Phillips. *Native North American Art.* Oxford and New York: Oxford University Press, 1998.

Brody, J. J. *Anasazi and Pueblo Painting.* Albuquerque: University of New Mexico Press, 1991.

————. *Indian Painters & White Patrons.* Albuquerque: University of New Mexico Press, 1971.

Dockstader, Frederick J. *Indian Art in America: The Arts and Crafts of the North American Indian.* Greenwich, Conn.: New York Graphic Society, 1966.

Feder, Norman. *Two Hundred Years of North American Indian Art.* New York: Praeger, 1972.

Feest, Christian F. *Native Arts of North America.* London: Thames and Hudson; New York: Oxford University Press, 1980.

Grant, Campbell. *Rock Art of the American Indian.* New York: Crowell, 1967.

Heth, Charlotte, ed. *Native American Dance: Ceremonies and Social Traditions.* Washington, D.C.: Smithsonian, 1992.

Lester, Patrick D. *The Biographical Directory of Native American Painters.* Tulsa, Okla.: SIR Publications; distributed by University of Oklahoma Press, 1995.

Mathews, Zena Pearlstone, and Aldona Jonaitis. *Native North American Art History: Selected Readings.* Palo Alto, Calif.: Peek Publications, 1982.

Matuz, Roger, ed. *St. James Guide to Native North American Artists.* Detroit: St. James Press, 1998.

National Museum of the American Indian. *The Changing Presentation of the American Indian: Museums and Native Cultures.* Washington, D.C.: National Museum of the American Indian; Seattle: University of Washington Press, 2000.

Penney, David W. *Art of the American Indian Frontier: The Chandler-Pohrt Collection.* Detroit: Detroit Institute of Arts; Seattle: University of Washington Press, 1992.

Porter, Frank W., III. *The Art of Native American Basketry: A Living Legacy.* New York: Greenwood Press, 1990.

Rushing, W. Jackson, III, ed. *Native American Art in the Twentieth Century.* London and New York: Routledge, 1999.

Wade, Edwin L., ed. *The Arts of the North American Indian: Native Traditions in Evolution.* New York: Hudson Hills Press; Tulsa: Philbrook Art Center, 1986.

Wyckoff, Lydia J. *Visions and Voices: Native American Painting From the Philbrook Museum of Art.* Tulsa: Philbrook Museum of Art; Albuquerque, N.Mex.: Distributed by the University of New Mexico Press, 1996.

◆ ATLASES

Coe, Michael D., Dean Snow, and Elizabeth Benson. *Atlas of Ancient America.* New York: Facts on File, 1986.

Ferguson, Thomas J. *A Zuni Atlas.* Norman: University of Oklahoma Press, 1985.

Goodman, James M. *The Navajo Atlas: Environments, Resources, People, and History of the Dine Bikeyah.* Norman: University of Oklahoma Press, 1982.

Prucha, Francis P. *Atlas of American Indian Affairs.* Lincoln: University of Nebraska Press, 1990.

Sturtevant, William C. *Early Indian Tribes, Culture Areas, and Linguistic Stocks.* Reston, Va.: Dept. of Interior, U.S. Geological Survey, 1991.

Tanner, Helen Hornbeck, et al., eds. *Atlas of Great Lakes Indian History.* Norman: Published for the Newberry Library by the University of Oklahoma Press, 1987.

Waldman, Carl. *Atlas of the North American Indian.* Rev. ed. New York: Facts On File, 2000.

◆ AUTOBIOGRAPHY

Allen, Elsie C. *Pomo Basketmaking: A Supreme Art for the Weaver.* Rev. ed. Happy Camp, Calif.: Naturegraph, 1972.

Bennett, Kay. *Kaibah: Recollection of a Navajo Girlhood.* Los Angeles: Westernlore Press, 1964.

Bettelyoun, Susan Bordeaux. *With My Own Eyes: A Lakota Woman Tells Her People's History.* Lincoln: University of Nebraska Press, 1998.

Blackman, Margaret B. *During My Time: Florence Edenshaw Davidson, A Haida Woman.* Seattle: University of Washington Press, 1982.

———. *Sadie Brower Neakok, An Inupiaq Woman.* Seattle: University of Washington Press, 1989.

Blaine, Martha Royce. *Some Things Are Not Forgotten: A Pawnee Family Remembers.* Lincoln: University of Nebraska Press, 1997.

Blowsnake, Sam. *Crashing Thunder: The Autobiography of an American Indian.* 1926. Reprint. Lincoln: University of Nebraska Press, 1983.

Brave Bird, Mary. *Lakota Woman.* New York: Grove Weidenfeld, 1990.

Brumble, H. David. *American Indian Autobiography.* Berkeley and Los Angeles: University of California Press, 1988.

———. *An Annotated Bibliography of American Indian and Eskimo Autobiographies.* Lincoln: University of Nebraska Press, 1981.

Campbell, Maria. *Halfbreed.* 1973. Reprint. Lincoln: University of Nebraska Press, 1982.

Cruikshank, Julie. *Life Lived Like a Story: Life Stories of Three Yukon Native Elders.* Lincoln: University of Nebraska Press, 1990.

Cuero, Delfina. *The Autobiography of Delfina Cuero, a Diegueno Indian.* 1968. Reprints. Banning, Calif: Malki Museum Press, 1970; Menlo Park, Calif.: Ballena Press, 1991.

Dauenhauer, Nora. *Life Woven with Song.* Tucson: University of Arizona Press, 2000.

Eastman, Charles Alexander. *From the Deep Woods to Civilization.* 1916. Reprint. Lincoln: University of Nebraska Press, 1977.

———. *Indian Boyhood.* 1902. Reprint. New York: Dover, 1971.

Fools Crow. *Fools Crow.* Lincoln: University of Nebraska Press, 1990.

Giago, Tim A. *The Aboriginal Sin: Reflections on the Holy Rosary Indian Mission School.* San Francisco: Indian Historian Press, 1978.

Greene, Alma. *Forbidden Voice: Reflections of a Mohawk Indian.* 1971. Reprint. Toronto: Green Dragon Press, 1997.

Hale, Janet Campbell. *Bloodlines: Odyssey of a Native Daughter.* New York: Random House, 1993.

Harris, LaDonna. *LaDonna Harris: A Comanche Life.* Lincoln: University of Nebraska Press, 2000.

Hopkins, Sarah Winnemucca. *Life Among the Piutes: Their Wrongs and Claims.* 1882. Reprint. Reno: University of Nevada Press, 1994.

Horne, Esther Burnett. *Essie's Story: The Life and Legacy of a Shoshone Teacher.* Lincoln: University of Nebraska Press, 1998.

Johnson, Broderick H. *Stories of Traditional Navajo Life and Culture.* Tsaile, Navajo Nation, Ariz.: Navajo Community College Press, 1977.

Kakianak, Nathan. *Eskimo Boyhood: An Autobiography in Psychosocial Perspective.* Lexington: University Press of Kentucky, 1974.

Krupat, Arnold. *For Those Who Come After: A Study of Native American Autobiography.* Berkeley and Los Angeles: University of California Press, 1985.

La Flesche, Francis. *The Middle Five: Indian Schoolboys of the Omaha Tribe.* Madison: University of Wisconsin Press, 1963.

Lame Deer, John (Fire). *Lame Deer, Seeker of Visions.* New York: Simon and Schuster, 1972.

Left Handed. *Left Handed, Son of Old Man Hat: A Navajo Autobiography.* 1938. Reprint. Lincoln: University of Nebraska Press, 1996.

Little Coyote, Bertha. *Leaving Everything Behind: The Songs and Memories of a Cheyenne Woman.* Norman: University of Oklahoma Press, 1997.

Lurie, Nancy Oestreich, ed. *Mountain Wolf Woman, Sister of Crashing Thunder: The Autobiography of a Winnebago Indian.* Ann Arbor: University of Michigan Press, 1966.

Mankiller, Wilma, and Michael Wallis. *Mankiller: A Chief of Her People.* New York: St. Martin's Griffin, 2000.

Mitchell, Frank. *Navajo Blessingway Singer: The Autobiography of Frank Mitchell: 1881–1967.* Tucson: University of Arizona Press, 1978.

Modesto, Ruby, and Guy Mount. *Not for Innocent Ears: Spiritual Traditions of a Desert Cahuilla Medicine Woman.* Angelus Oaks, Calif.: Sweetlight Books, 1980.

Mohatt, Gerald V., and Joseph Eagle Elk. *The Price of a Gift: A Lakota Healer's Story.* Lincoln: University of Nebraska Press, 2000.

Mourning Dove. *Mourning Dove: A Salishan Autobiography.* Lincoln: University of Nebraska Press, 1990.

Scott, Lalla. *Karnee: A Paiute Narrative.* Reno: University of Nevada Press, 1966.

Snell, Alma Hogan. *Grandmother's Grandchild: My Crow Indian Life.* Lincoln: University of Nebraska Press, 2000.

Two Leggings. *Two Leggings: The Making of a Crow Warrior.* 1967. Reprint. Lincoln: University of Nebraska Press, 1982.

Underhill, Ruth Murray. *Papago Woman.* New York: Holt, Rinehart and Winston, 1979.

Waheenee. *Waheenee: An Indian Girl's Story, Told by Herself to Gilbert L. Wilson.* Lincoln: University of Nebraska Press, 1981.

Yava, Albert. *Big Falling Snow: A Tewa-Hopi Indian's Life and Times and the History and Traditions of His People.* New York: Crown Publishers, 1978.

Yellowtail, Thomas. *Yellowtail, Crow Medicine Man and Sun Dance Chief: An Autobiography.* Norman: University of Oklahoma Press, 1991.

Zitkala-Sa. *American Indian Stories.* 1921. Reprint. Lincoln: University of Nebraska Press, 1985.

◆ DEMOGRAPHY

Cook, Sherburne F. *The Conflict Between the California Indian and White Civilization.* Berkeley and Los Angeles: University of California Press, 1976.

Crosby, Alfred W., Jr. *The Columbian Exchange: Biological and Cultural Consequences of 1492.* Westport, Conn.: Greenwood Publishing Company, 1972.

Dobyns, Henry F. *Their Number Become Thinned: Native American Population Dynamics in Eastern North America.* Knoxville: University of Tennessee Press in cooperation with the Newberry Library Center for the History of the American Indian, 1983.

Duffy, John. *Epidemics in Colonial America.* Baton Rouge, Louisiana State University Press, 1953.

Reddy, Marlita A., ed. *Statistical Record of Native North Americans.* 2nd ed. Detroit: Gale Research, 1995.

Shoemaker, Nancy. *American Indian Population Recovery in the Twentieth Century.* Albuquerque: University of New Mexico Press, 1999.

Snipp, C. Matthew. *American Indians: The First of This Land.* New York: Russell Sage Foundation, 1989.

Stearn, Esther W. *The Effect of Smallpox on the Destiny of the Amerindian.* Boston: Bruce Humphries, Inc., 1945.

Stuart, Paul. *Nations Within a Nation: Historical Statistics of American Indians.* New York: Greenwood Press, 1987.

Thornton, Russell. *American Indian Holocaust and Survival: A Population History Since 1492.* Norman: University of Oklahoma Press, 1987.

Verano, John, and Douglas H. Ubelaker, eds. *Disease and Demography in the Americas.* Washington: Smithsonian Institution Press, 1992.

◆ HISTORY

Calloway, Colin G. *First Peoples: A Documentary Survey of American Indian History.* Boston: Bedford/St. Martin's, 1999.

———., ed. *New Directions in American Indian History.* Norman: University of Oklahoma Press, 1988.

———. *Our Hearts Fell to the Ground: Plains Indian Views of How the West Was Lost.* Boston: Bedford Books of St. Martin's Press, 1996.

Costo, Rupert, and Jeannette Henry Costo. *The Missions of California: A Legacy of Genocide*. San Francisco: Indian Historian Press, American Indian Historical Society, 1987.

Debo, Angie. *A History of the Indians of the United States*. Norman: University of Oklahoma Press, 1970.

Gibson, Arrell M. *The American Indian: Prehistory to the Present*. Lexington, Mass.: D.C. Heath, 1980.

Hoxie, Frederick E., and Peter Iverson. *Indians in American History: An Introduction*. 2nd ed. Wheeling, Ill.: Harlan Davidson, 1998.

Hurt, R. Douglas. *Indian Agriculture in America: Prehistory to the Present*. Lawrence, Kan.: University Press of Kansas, 1987.

Hurtado, Albert L., and Peter Iverson. *Major Problems in American Indian History: Documents and Essays*. Lexington, Mass.: D.C. Heath, 1994.

Josephy, Alvin M., ed. *America in 1492: The World of the Indian Peoples Before the Arrival of Columbus*. New York: Knopf, 1992.

Kehoe, Alice. *North American Indians: A Comparative Account*. 2nd ed. Englewood, N.J.: Prentice Hall, 1992.

Leacock, Eleanore Burke, and Nancy O. Lurie, eds. *North American Indians in Historical Perspective*. Prospect Heights, Ill.: Waveland Press, 1988.

McNickle, D'Arcy. *Native American Tribalism: Indian Survivals and Renewals*. New York: Oxford University Press, 1973.

———. *They Came Here First: The Epic of the American Indian*. Rev. ed. New York: Harper & Row, 1975.

Olson, James S., and Raymond Wilson. *Native Americans in the Twentieth Century*. Provo, Utah: Brigham Young University Press, 1984.

Prucha, Francis Paul. *American Indian Treaties: The History of a Political Anomaly*. Berkeley and Los Angeles: University of California Press, 1994.

Spicer, Edward H. *Cycles of Conquest: The Impact of Spain, Mexico, and the United States on the Indians of the Southwest, 1533–1960*. Tucson: University of Arizona Press, 1962.

Trigger, Bruce G., and Wilcomb E. Washburn, eds. *North America*. Vol. 1 of *The Cambridge History of the Native Peoples of the Americas*. New York: Cambridge University Press, 1996.

Waldman, Carl. *Biographical Dictionary of American Indian History to 1900*. Rev. ed. New York: Facts on File, 2001.

◆ IMAGE/STEREOTYPE

Bataille, Gretchen, and Charles L.P. Silet, eds. *The Pretend Indians: Images of Native Americans in the Movies*. Ames: Iowa State University Press, 1980.

Berkhofer, Robert F. *The White Man's Indian: Images of the American Indian from Columbus to the Present*. New York: Knopf, 1978.

Bird, S. Elizabeth. *Dressing in Feathers: The Construction of the Indian in American Popular Culture*. Boulder, Colo.: Westview Press, 1996.

Boehme, Sarah E., et al. *Powerful Images: Portrayals of Native America*. Seattle: Museums West in association with the University of Washington Press, 1998.

Deloria, Philip J. *Playing Indian*. New Haven: Yale University Press, 1998.

Dippie, Brian W. *The Vanishing American: White Attitudes and U.S. Indian Policy*. Lawrence, Kan.: University Press of Kansas, 1991.

Hauptman, Laurence M. *Tribes & Tribulations: Misconceptions About American Indians and Their Histories*. Albuquerque: University of New Mexico Press, 1995.

Hirschfelder, Arlene B., Paulette Fairbanks Molin, and Yvonne Wakim. *American Indian Stereotypes in the World of Children: A Reader and Bibliography*. 2nd ed. Lanham, Md.: Scarecrow Press, 1999.

King, C. Richard, and Charles Fruehling Springwood, eds. *Team Spirits: The Native American Mascots Controversy*. Lincoln: University of Nebraska Press, 2001.

Mihesuah, Devon A. *American Indians: Stereotypes & Realities*. Atlanta, Ga., 1996.

Moses, Lester G. *Wild West Shows and the Images of American Indians, 1883–1933*. Albuquerque: University of New Mexico Press, 1996.

National Museum of the American Indian. *The Changing Presentation of the American Indian: Museums and Native Cultures*. Washington, D.C.: National Museum of the American Indian; Seattle: University of Washington Press, 2000.

Rollins, Peter C., and John E. O'Connor, eds. *Hollywood's Indian: The Portrayal of the Native American in Film*. Lexington: University Press of Kentucky, 1998.

Slapin, Beverly, and Doris Seale, eds. *Through Indian Eyes: The Native Experience in Books for Children*. Los Angeles: American Indian Studies Center, University of California, Los Angeles, 1998.

Spindel, Carol. *Dancing at Halftime: Sports and the Controversy Over American Indian Mascots*. New York: New York University Press, 2000.

Stedman, Raymond W. *Shadows of the Indian: Stereotypes in American Culture*. Norman: University of Oklahoma Press, 1982.

◆ LAND

Berger, Thomas R. *Village Journey: The Report of the Alaska Native Review Commission*. Rev. ed. New York: Hill and Wang, 1995.

Clow, Richmond L. and Imre Sutton, eds. *Conservation and the Trustee: Environmental Essays on the Management of Native American Resources*. Boulder: University Press of Colorado, 2001.

Confederation of American Indians, comp. *Indian Reservations: A State and Federal Handbook*. Jefferson, N.C.: McFarland, 1986.

Fixico, Donald L. *The Invasion of Indian Country in the Twentieth Century: American Capitalism and Tribal Natural Resources*. Niwot, Colo.: University Press of Colorado, 1998.

Frantz, Klaus. *Indian Reservations in the United States: Territory, Sovereignty, and Socioeconomic Changes*, Geography Research Paper 242. Chicago: University of Chicago Press, 1999.

Hart, E. Richard. *Zuni and the Courts: A Struggle for Sovereign Land Rights*. Lawrence, Kan.: University Press of Kansas, 1995.

Johansen, Bruce E. *Shapers of the Great Debate on Native Americans—Land, Spirit, and Power: A Biographical Dictionary*. Westport, Conn.: Greenwood Press, 2000.

Kickingbird, Kirke, and Karen Ducheneaux. *One Hundred Million Acres*. New York: Macmillan, 1973.

LaDuke, Winona. *All Our Relations: Native Struggles for Land and Life*. Cambridge, Mass.: South End Press, 1999.

Sutton, Imre, ed. *Irredeemable America: The Indians' Estate and Land Claims*. Albuquerque: University of New Mexico Press, 1985.

Tiller, Veronica E. Velarde, ed. *Tiller's Guide to Indian Country: Economic Profiles of American Indian Reservations*. Albuquerque, N.Mex.: BowArrow Publishing Co., 1996.

Vecsey, Christopher, and William A. Starna. *Iroquois Land Claims*. Syracuse, N.Y.: Syracuse University Press, 1988.

White, Richard. *The Roots of Dependency: Subsistence, Environment, and Social Change Among the Choctaws, Pawnees, and Navajos*. Lincoln: University of Nebraska Press, 1983.

◆ LEGAL STATUS/LAW

Burton, Lloyd. *American Indian Water Rights and the Limits of Law*. Lawrence, Kan.: University Press of Kansas, 1991.

Canby, William C., Jr. *Indian Law in a Nutshell*. 3rd ed. St. Paul: West Pub. Co., 1998.

Clark, Blue. *Lone Wolf v. Hitchcock: Treaty Rights and Indian Law at the End of the Nineteenth Century*. Lincoln: University of Nebraska Press, 1994.

Cohen, Felix S. *Felix S. Cohen's Handbook of Federal Indian Law*. 2d ed. Charlottesville, Va.: Michie/Bobbs-Merrill, 1982.

Deloria, Vine. *Tribes, Treaties, and Constitutional Tribulations*. Austin: University of Texas Press, 1999.

Deloria, Vine, and Clifford M. Lytle. *American Indians, American Justice*. Austin: University of Texas Press, 1983.

Deloria, Vine, and Raymond J. DeMaille, comps. *Documents of American Indian Diplomacy: Treaties, Agreements, and Conventions, 1775–1979.* Norman: University of Oklahoma Press, 1999.

Falkowski, James E. *Indian Law/Race Law: A Five-Hundred Year History.* New York: Praeger, 1992.

Getches, David H. *Cases and Materials on Federal Indian Law.* 4th ed. St. Paul, Minn.: West Group, 1998.

Kappler, Charles J., comp. and ed. *Indian Affairs. Law and Treaties.* 7 vols. 1904–1971. Reprint. New York: AMS Press, 1972.

Norgren, Jill. *The Cherokee Cases: The Confrontation of Law and Politics.* New York: McGraw-Hill, 1996.

O'Brien, Sharon. *American Indian Tribal Governments.* Norman: University of Oklahoma Press, 1989.

Pevar, Stephen L. *The Rights of Indians and Tribes: The Basic ACLU Guide to Indian and Tribal Rights.* 2nd ed. Carbondale, Ill.: Southern Illinois University Press, 1992.

Shattuck, Petra T., and Jill Norgren. *Partial Justice: Federal Indian Law in a Liberal Constitutional System.* New York: Berg, 1991.

Wilkinson, Charles F. *American Indians, Time, and the Law: Native Societies in a Modern Constitutional Democracy.* New Haven: Yale University Press, 1987.

◆ LITERATURE AND POETRY

Alexie, Sherman. *The Business of Fancydancing: Stories and Poems.* Brooklyn, N.Y.: Hanging Loose Press, 1992.

————. *Indian Killer.* New York: Atlantic Monthly Press, 1996.

————. *The Lone Ranger and Tonto Fistfight in Heaven.* New York: Atlantic Monthly Press, 1993.

————. *Old Shirts & New Skins.* Los Angeles: American Indian Studies Center, University of California, Los Angeles, 1993.

————. *One Stick Song.* Brooklyn: Hanging Loose Press, 2000.

Allen, Paula Gunn. *The Sacred Hoop: Recovering the Feminine in American Indian Traditions.* Boston: Beacon Press, 1986.

————, ed. *Song of the Turtle: American Indian Literature, 1974–1994.* New York: Ballantine Books, 1996.

————, ed. *Spider Woman's Granddaughters: Traditional Tales and Contemporary Writing by Native American Women.* Boston: Beacon Press, 1989.

————, ed. *Studies in American Indian Literature: Critical Essays and Course Designs.* New York: Modern Language Association of America, 1983.

————, ed. *Voice of the Turtle: American Indian Literature, 1900–1970.* New York: Ballantine Books, 1994.

————. *The Woman Who Owned the Shadows.* San Francisco: Spinsters Ink, 1983.

Brant, Beth. *Food & Spirits: Stories.* Ithaca, N.Y.: Firebrand Books, 1991.

————. *Mohawk Trail.* Ithaca, N.Y.: Firebrand Books, 1985.

Bruchac, Joseph. *Survival This Way: Interviews with American Indian Poets.* Tucson: University of Arizona Press, 1987.

Bush, Barney. *Inherit the Blood: Poetry and Fiction.* New York: Thunder's Mouth Press, 1985.

————. *My Horse and a Jukebox.* Los Angeles: American Indian Studies Center, University of California, Los Angeles, 1979.

Conley, Robert J. *Mountain Windsong: A Novel of the Trail of Tears.* Norman: University of Oklahoma Press, 1992.

————. *The Way of the Priests.* New York: Doubleday, 1992.

————. *The Witch of Goingsnake and Other Stories.* Norman: University of Oklahoma Press, 1988.

Cook-Lynn, Elizabeth. *Aurelia: A Crow Creek Trilogy.* Niwot, Colo.: University Press of Colorado, 1999.

————. *I Remember the Fallen Trees: New and Selected Poems.* Cheney, Wash.: Eastern Washington University Press, 1998.

Cronyn, George W., ed. *The Path on the Rainbow: An Anthology of Songs and Chants from the Indians of North America*. 1918. Reprint, *American Indian Poetry: An Anthology of Songs and Chants*. New York: Fawcett Columbine, 1991.

D'Aponte, Mimi. *Seventh Generation: An Anthology of Native American Plays*. New York: Theatre Communications Group, 1999.

Dorris, Michael. *A Yellow Raft in Blue Water*. New York: H. Holt, 1987.

Erdrich, Louise. *Beet Queen*. New York: Holt, 1986.

———. *The Bingo Palace*. New York: HarperCollins, 1994.

———. *Love Medicine*. New York: Holt, Rinehart, and Winston, 1984; Bantam, 1985; new and expanded version, New York: H. Holt, 1993; HarperPerennial, 1993.

———. *Tracks*. New York: Henry Holt, 1988.

Geiogamah, Hanay, and Jaye T. Darby, eds. *American Indian Theater in Performance: A Reader*. Los Angeles: UCLA American Indian Studies Center, 2000.

———. *Stories of Our Way: An Anthology of American Indian Plays*. Los Angeles: UCLA American Indian Studies Center, 1999.

Glancy, Diane. *Firesticks: A Collection of Stories*. Norman: University of Oklahoma Press, 1993.

———. *Iron Woman: Poems*. Minneapolis, Minn.: New Rivers Press, 1990.

———. *The Voice That Was in Travel: Stories*. Norman: University of Oklahoma Press, 1999.

Hale, Janet Campbell. *The Jailing of Cecelia Capture*. New York: Random House, 1985.

———. *Women on the Run*. Moscow, Idaho: University of Idaho Press, 1999.

Harjo, Joy. *A Map to the Next World: Poetry and Tales*. New York: W.W. Norton & Co., 2000.

———. *In Mad Love and War*. Middletown, Conn.: Wesleyan University Press, 1990.

———. *She Had Some Horses*. New York: Thunder's Mouth Press, 1983.

Harjo, Joy, and Gloria Bird, eds. *Reinventing the Enemy's Language: Contemporary Native Women's Writings of North America*. New York: W. W. Norton & Company, 1997.

Hogan, Linda. *The Book of Medicines: Poems*. Minneapolis: Coffee House Press, 1993.

———. *Mean Spirit*. New York: Atheneum, 1990.

Kabotie, Michael. *Migration Tears: Poems About Transitions*. Los Angeles: American Indian Studies Center, University of California, Los Angeles, 1987.

Lesley, Craig, ed. *Talking Leaves: Contemporary Native American Short Stories*. New York: Laurel, 1991.

Lincoln, Kenneth. *Native American Renaissance*. Berkeley and Los Angeles: University of California Press, 1983.

Mathews, John Joseph. *Sundown*. 1934. Reprint. Norman: University of Oklahoma Press, 1988.

———. *Talking to the Moon*. 1945. Reprint. Norman: University of Oklahoma Press, 1981.

McNickle, D'Arcy. *The Surrounded*. 1936. Reprint. Albuquerque: University of New Mexico Press, 1978.

Momaday, N. Scott. *The Ancient Child: A Novel*. New York: Doubleday, 1989.

———. *House Made of Dawn*. New York: Harper & Row, 1968.

———. *The Way to Rainy Mountain*. Albuquerque: University of New Mexico Press, 1969.

Mourning Dove. *Cogewea, the Half-Blood: A Depiction of the Great Montana Cattle Range*. 1927. Reprint. Lincoln: University of Nebraska Press, 1981.

Niatum, Duane, ed. *Harper's Anthology of 20th Century Native American Poetry*. San Francisco: Harper & Row, 1988.

Ortiz, Simon J. *A Good Journey*. Berkeley, Calif.: Turtle Island, 1977.

———. *From Sand Creek*. Reprint. 1984. Tucson: University of Arizona Press, 1999.

———. *Men on the Moon: Collected Short Stories.* Tucson: University of Arizona Press, 1999.

———. *Woven Stone.* Tucson: University of Arizona Press, 1992.

———, ed. *Speaking for the Generations: Native Writers on Writing.* Tucson: University of Arizona Press, 1998.

Owens, Louis. *Bone Game: A Novel.* Norman: University of Oklahoma Press, 1994.

———. *Other Destinies: Understanding the American Indian Novel.* Norman: University of Oklahoma Press, 1992.

Rainwater, Catherine. *Dreams of Fiery Stars: The Transformations of Native American Fiction.* Philadelphia: University of Pennsylvania Press, 1999.

Rose, Wendy. *Bone Dance: New and Selected Poems, 1965–1993.* Tucson: University of Arizona Press, 1994.

Sarris, Greg. *Grand Avenue.* New York: Penguin, 1995.

———. *Keeping Slug Woman Alive: A Holistic Approach to American Indian Texts.* Berkeley and Los Angeles: University of California Press, 1993.

Silko, Leslie M. *Almanac of the Dead.* New York: Simon & Schuster, 1991.

———. *Ceremony.* New York: Viking, 1977.

———. *Gardens in the Dunes: A Novel.* New York: Simon & Schuster, 1999.

———. *Storyteller.* New York: Seaver Books, 1981.

Spatz, Ronald, ed. *Alaska Native Writers, Storytellers & Orators.* Anchorage: University of Alaska, 1999.

TallMountain, Mary. *The Light on the Tent Wall: A Bridging.* Los Angeles: American Indian Studies Center, University of California, Los Angeles, 1990.

Tapahonso, Luci. *Saanii Dahataal, The Women Are Singing: Poems and Stories.* Tucson: University of Arizona Press, 1993.

Tedlock, Dennis. *The Spoken Word and the Work of Interpretation.* Philadelphia: University of Pennsylvania Press, 1983.

Treuer, David. *Little.* Saint Paul, Minn.: Graywolf Press, 1995.

Vizenor, Gerald R. *The Heirs of Columbus.* Middletown, Conn.: Wesleyan University Press, 1991.

———. *Shadow Distance: A Gerald Vizenor Reader.* Hanover, N.H.: Wesleyan University Press, 1994.

———. *Wordarrows: Indians and Whites in the New Fur Trade.* Minneapolis: University of Minnesota Press, 1978.

Walters, Anna Lee. *Ghost Singer: A Novel.* Flagstaff, Ariz.: Northland Publishing, 1988.

———. *The Sun is Not Merciful: Short Stories.* Ithaca, N.Y.: Firebrand Books, 1985.

Welch, James. *The Death of Jim Loney.* 1979.

———. *Fools Crow.* New York: Viking, 1986.

———. *The Indian Lawyer.* New York: W.W. Norton, 1990.

———. *Riding the Earthboy 40.* New York: World Pub. Co., 1971.

———. *Winter in the Blood.* New York: Harper & Row, 1974.

Witalec, Janet, ed. *Native North American Literature: Biographical and Critical Information on Native Writers and Orators From the United States and Canada From Historical Times to the Present.* New York: Gale Research, 1994.

Young Bear, Ray A. *Black Eagle Child: The Facepaint Narratives.* Iowa City, Iowa: University of Iowa Press, 1992.

◆ ORAL TRADITION

Bullchild, Percy. *The Sun Came Down.* San Francisco: Harper & Row, 1985.

Clements, William M., and Frances M. Malpezzi. *Native American Folklore, 1879–1979: An Annotated Bibliography.* Athens, Ohio: Swallow Press, 1984.

Erdoes, Richard, and Alfonso Ortiz, eds. *American Indian Myths and Legends.* New York: Pantheon Books, 1984.

———. *American Indian Trickster Tales*. New York: Viking, 1998.

Garter Snake. *The Seven Visions of Bull Lodge*. Ann Arbor, Mich.: Bear Claw Press, 1980.

Margolin, Malcom, ed. *The Way We Lived: California Indian Reminiscences, Stories, and Songs*. Berkeley: Heyday Books, 1981.

Norman, Howard A., trans. *The Wishing Bone Cycle: Narrative Poems From the Swampy Cree Indians*. Expanded ed. Santa Barbara, Ca.: Ross-Erikson, 1982.

Quam, Alvina, tr. *The Zunis: Self-Portrayals, By the Zuni People*. Albuquerque: University of New Mexico Press, 1972.

Swann, Brian, ed. *Coming to Light: Contemporary Translations of Native Literatures of North America*. New York: Random House, 1994.

———. *Smoothing the Ground: Essays on Native American Oral Literature*. Berkeley and Los Angeles: University of California Press, 1983.

◆ POLICY

Castile, George P. *To Show Heart: Native American Self-Determination and Federal Indian Policy, 1960–1975*. Tucson: University of Arizona Press, 1998.

Castile, George P., and Robert L. Bee. *State and Reservation: New Perspectives on Federal Indian Policy*. Tucson: University of Arizona Press, 1992.

Deloria, Vine, Jr. *Behind the Trail of Broken Treaties: An Indian Declaration of Independence*. New York: Dell, 1974.

Deloria, Vine, Jr., ed. *American Indian Policy in the Twentieth Century*. Norman: University of Oklahoma Press, 1985.

Dippie, Brian W. *The Vanishing American: White Attitudes and U.S. Indian Policy*. Middletown, Conn.: Wesleyan University Press, 1982.

Fixico, Donald L. *The Invasion of Indian Country in the Twentieth Century: American Capitalism and Tribal Natural Resources*. Niwot, Colo.: University Press of Colorado, 1998.

———. *Termination and Relocation: Federal Indian Policy, 1945–1960*. Albuquerque: University of New Mexico Press, 1986.

Green, Donald E., and Thomas V. Tonnesen, eds. *American Indians: Social Justice and Public Policy*. Milwaukee: Institute on Race and Ethnicity, University of Wisconsin System, 1991.

Horsman, Reginald. *Expansion and American Indian Policy, 1783–1812*. East Lansing: Michigan State University Press, 1967.

Joe, Jennie R., ed. *American Indian Policy and Cultural Values: Conflict and Accommodation*. Los Angeles: American Indian Studies Center, University of California, Los Angeles, 1986.

Josephy, Alvin M., Jr., Joane Nagel, and Troy Johnson, eds. *Red Power: The American Indian's Fight for Freedom*. 2nd ed. Lincoln: University of Nebraska Press, 1999.

Legters, Lyman H., and Fremont J. Lyden, eds. *American Indian Policy: Self-Governance and Economic Development*. Westport, Conn.: Greenwood Press, 1994.

McNickle, D'Arcy. *Native American Tribalism: Indian Survivals and Renewals*. New York: Oxford University Press, 1973.

Mihesuah, Devon A. *Repatriation Reader: Who Owns American Indian Remains?* Lincoln: University of Nebraska Press, 2000.

Philp, Kenneth R. *John Collier's Crusade for Indian Reform, 1920–1954*. Tucson: University of Arizona Press, 1977.

———. *Termination Revisited: American Indians on the Trail to Self-Determination, 1933–1953*. Lincoln: University of Nebraska Press, 1999.

Prucha, Francis P. *The Great Father: The United States Government and the American Indians*. 2 vols. Lincoln: University of Nebraska Press, 1984.

Prucha, Francis Paul, ed. *Documents of United States Indian Policy*. 3rd ed. Lincoln: University of Nebraska Press, 2000.

Satz, Ronald N. *American Indian Policy in the Jacksonian Era*. Lincoln: University of Nebraska Press, 1975.

Sheehan, Bernard W. *Seeds of Extinction: Jeffersonian Philanthropy and the American Indian*. Chapel Hill: University of North Carolina Press, 1973.

Snipp, C. Matthew. *Public Policy Impacts on American Indian Economic Development*. Albuquerque: Institute for Native American Development, University of New Mexico, 1988.

Trennert, Robert A. *Alternative to Extinction: Federal Indian Policy and the Beginnings of the Reservation System, 1846–51*. Philadelphia: Temple University Press, 1975.

Washburn, Wilcomb E. *Red Man's Land/White Man's Law: The Past and Present Status of the American Indian*. 2nd ed. Norman: University of Oklahoma Press, 1995.

◆ PREHISTORY

Aveni, Anthony F., ed. *Native American Astronomy*. Austin: University of Texas Press, 1977.

Dixon, E. James. *Bones, Boats, & Bison: Archaeology and the First Colonization of Western North America*. Albuquerque: University of New Mexico Press, 1999.

Fagan, Brian M. *Ancient North America: The Archaeology of a Continent*. Rev. and expanded ed. New York, N.Y.: Thames and Hudson, 1995.

Fowler, Melvin L. *The Cahokia Atlas: A Historical Atlas of Cahokia Archaeology*. Rev. ed. Urbana, Ill.: Illinois Transportation Archeological Research Program, University of Illinois, 1997.

Gibbon, Guy. *Archaeology of Prehistoric Native America: An Encyclopedia*. New York: Garland, 1998.

Jennings, Jesse D. *Prehistory of North America*. 3rd ed. Mountain View, Calif.: Mayfield Pub., 1989.

Jennings, Jesse D., ed. *Ancient Native Americans*. San Francisco: W.H. Freeman, 1983.

Shaffer, Lynda. *Native Americans Before 1492: the Moundbuilding Centers of the Eastern Woodlands*. Armonk, N.Y.: M.E. Sharpe, 1992.

Snow, Dean R. *The Archaeology of North America*. New York: Viking Press, 1976.

———. *The Archaeology of North America*. New York: Chelsea House Publishers, 1989.

◆ RELIGION

Beck, Peggy V., and Anna L. Walters. *The Sacred: Ways of Knowledge, Sources of Life*. Flagstaff: Northland, 1990.

Black Elk. *Black Elk Speaks: Being the Life Story of a Holy Man of the Oglala Sioux*. 21st-century ed. Lincoln: University of Nebraska Press, 2000.

Bonvillain, Nancy. *Native American Religion*. New York: Chelsea House Publishers, 1996.

Coffer, William E. *Spirits of the Sacred Mountains: Creation Stories of the American Indian*. New York: Van Nostrand Reinhold, 1978.

Deloria, Vine, Jr. *For This Land: Writings on Religion in America*. New York: Routledge, 1999.

———. *God is Red: A Native View of Religion*. 2nd ed. Golden, Colo.: North American Press, 1992.

Gill, Sam D. *Native American Religions: An Introduction*. Belmont, Calif.: Wadsworth Publishing, 1982.

———. *Native American Religious Action: A Performance Approach to Religion*. Columbia: University of South Carolina Press, 1987.

Hall, Robert L. *An Archaeology of the Soul: North American Indian Belief and Ritual*. Urbana: University of Illinois Press, 1997.

Harrod, Howard L. *Becoming and Remaining a People: Native American Religions on the Northern Plains*. Tucson: University of Arizona Press, 1995.

———. *Renewing the World: Plains Indian Religion and Morality*. Tucson: University of Arizona Press, 1987.

Hittman, Michael. *Wovoka and the Ghost Dance*. Expanded ed. Lincoln: University of Nebraska Press, 1997.

Hultkrantz, Ake. *Native Religions of North America: The Power of Visions and Fertility*. San Francisco: Harper & Row, 1987.

Loftin, John D. *Religion and Hopi Life in the Twentieth Century*. Bloomington, Ind.: Indiana University Press, 1991.

McLoughlin, William G. *The Cherokee Ghost Dance: Essays on the Southeastern Indians, 1789–1861.* Macon, Ga.: Mercer, 1984.

Mooney, James. *The Ghost-Dance Religion and the Sioux Outbreak of 1890.* Lincoln: University of Nebraska Press, 1991.

Powers, William K. *Oglala Religion.* Lincoln: University of Nebraska Press, 1977.

Stewart, Omer C. *Peyote Religion: A History.* Norman: University of Oklahoma Press, 1987.

Sullivan, Lawrence E., ed. *Native Religions and Cultures of North America.* New York: Continuum, 2000.

Treat, James, ed. *Native and Christian: Indigenous Voices on Religious Identity in the United States and Canada.* New York: Routledge, 1996.

Vecsey, Christopher. *Handbook of American Indian Religious Freedom.* New York: Crossroad, 1991.

Zolbrod, Paul G., trans. *Dine Bahane: The Navajo Creation Story.* Albuquerque: University of New Mexico Press, 1984.

◆ SOCIOLOGY

Champagne, Duane. *American Indian Societies: Some Strategies and Conditions of Political and Cultural Survival.* Cambridge, Mass.: Cultural Survival, 1989.

———. *Social Order and Political Change: Constitutional Governments Among the Cherokee, the Choctaw, the Chickasaw, and the Creek.* Stanford, Calif.: Stanford University Press, 1992.

Faiman-Silva, Sandra L. *Choctaws at the Crossroads: The Political Economy of Class and Culture in the Oklahoma Timber Region.* Lincoln: University of Nebraska Press, 1997.

Fixico, Donald L. *The Urban Indian Experience in America.* Albuquerque: University of New Mexico Press, 2000.

Guillemin, Jeanne. *Urban Renegades: The Cultural Strategy of American Indians.* New York: Columbia University Press, 1975.

Kurkiala, Mikael. *Building the Nation Back Up: The Politics of Identity on the Pine Ridge Indian Reservation.* Uppsala: Uppsala University, Department of Cultural Anthropology, 1997.

Ross, Luana. *Inventing the Savage: The Social Construction of Native American Criminality.* Austin: University of Texas Press, 1998.

Sorkin, Alan L. *The Urban American Indian.* Lexington, Mass.: Lexington Books, 1978.

Thornton, Russell. *We Shall Live Again: the 1870 and 1890 Ghost Dance Movements as Demographic Revitalization.* New York: Cambridge University Press, 1986.

Weibel-Orlando, Joan. *Indian Country, L.A.: Maintaining Ethnic Community in Complex Society.* Rev. ed. Urbana: University of Illinois Press, 1999.

White, Richard. *The Roots of Dependency: Subsistence, Environment, and Social Change Among the Choctaws, Pawnees, and Navajos.* Lincoln: University of Nebraska Press, 1983.

◆ URBANIZATION

Danziger, Edmund J. *Survival and Regeneration: Detroit's American Indian Community.* Detroit: Wayne State University Press, 1991.

Fixico, Donald L. *The Urban Indian Experience in America.* Albuquerque: University of New Mexico Press, 2000.

Guillemin, Jeanne. *Urban Renegades: The Cultural Strategy of American Indians.* New York: Columbia University Press, 1975.

Lobo, Susan, and Kurt Peters. *American Indians and the Urban Experience.* Walnut Creek, Calif.: Altamira Press, 2000.

Neils, Elaine M. *Reservation to City: Indian Migration and Federal Relocation.* Chicago: Dept. of Geography, University of Chicago, 1971.

Sorkin, Alan L. *The Urban American Indian.* Lexington, Mass.: Lexington Books, 1978.

Stanbury, W. T. *Success and Failure: Indians in Urban Society.* Vancouver: University of British Columbia Press, 1975.

Waddell, Jack O. and O. Michael Watson, eds. *The American Indian in Urban Society.* 1971. Reprint. Lanham, Md.: University Press of America, 1984.

Weibel-Orlando, Joan. *Indian Country, L.A.: Maintaining Ethnic Community in Complex Society.* Rev. ed. Urbana: University of Illinois Press, 1999.

♦ WOMEN

Albers, Patricia, and Beatrice Medicine. *The Hidden Half: Studies of Plains Indian Women.* Washington, D.C.: University Press of America, 1983.

Allen, Paula Gunn. *The Sacred Hoop: Recovering the Feminine in American Indian Traditions.* Boston: Beacon Press, 1986.

Alvord, Lori Arviso, M.D. *The Scalpel and the Silver Bear.* New York: Bantam-Doubleday Books, 1993.

Bataille, Gretchen M., ed. *Native American Women: A Biographical Dictionary.* New York: Garland, 1993.

Bataille, Gretchen M., and Kathleen Mullen Sands. *American Indian Women, Telling Their Lives.* Lincoln: University of Nebraska Press, 1984.

Benedek, Emily. *Beyond the Four Corners of the World: A Navajo Woman's Journey.* Norman: University of Oklahoma Press, 1998.

Boyer, Ruth McDonald, with Narcissus Duffy Gayton. *Apache Mothers and Daughters: Four Generations of a Family.* Norman: University of Oklahoma Press, 1992.

Green, Rayna. *Native American Women: A Contextual Bibliography.* Bloomington: Indiana University Press, 1984.

Green, Rayna, ed. *That's What She Said: Contemporary Poetry and Fiction by Native American Women.* Bloomington: Indiana University Press, 1984.

Harjo, Joy, and Gloria Bird, eds. *Reinventing the Enemy's Language: Contemporary Native Women's Writings of North America.* New York: W. W. Norton & Company, 1997.

Klein, Laura F., and Lillian A. Ackerman, eds. *Women and Power in Native North America.* Norman: University of Oklahoma Press, 1995.

Landes, Ruth. *The Ojibwa Woman.* 1938. Reprint. Lincoln: University of Nebraska Press, 1997.

Perdue, Theda. *Cherokee Women: Gender and Culture Change, 1700–1835.* Lincoln: University of Nebraska Press, 1998.

Peters, Virginia. *Women of the Earth Lodges: Tribal Life on the Plains.* Norman, Okla.: University of Oklahoma Press, 2000.

Powers, Marla. *Oglala Women: Myth, Ritual, and Reality.* Chicago: University of Chicago Press, 1986.

Schweitzer, Marjorie M., ed. *American Indian Grandmothers: Traditions and Transitions.* Albuquerque: University of New Mexico Press, 1999.

Shoemaker, Nancy, ed. *Negotiators of Change: Historical Perspectives on Native American Women.* New York: Routledge, 1995.

Sonneborn, Liz. *A to Z of Native American Women.* New York, New York: Facts on File, 1998.

Spittal, W. G., ed. *Iroquois Women: An Anthology.* Ohsweken, Ont.: Iroqrafts, 1990.

♦ CANADA

Adams, Howard. *Prison of Grass: Canada From a Native Point of View.* Rev. ed. Saskatoon, Sask.: Fifth House, 1989.

Asch, Michael. *Home and Native Land: Aboriginal Rights and the Canadian Constitution.* Toronto and New York: Methuen, 1984; Vancouver: UBC Press, 1993.

Barron, F. Laurie, and James B. Waldram. *1885 and After: Native Society in Transition.* Regina, Sask.: Canadian Plains Research Center, University of Regina, 1986.

Boldt, Menno, and J. Anthony Long, eds., in association with Leroy Little Bear. *The Quest for Justice: Aboriginal Peoples and Aboriginal Rights.* Toronto: University of Toronto Press, 1985.

Brown, Jennifer S.H. *Strangers in Blood: Fur Trade Company Families in Indian Country.* Vancouver: University of British Columbia Press, 1980.

Cairns, Alan C. *Citizens Plus: Aboriginal Peoples and the Canadian State.* Vancouver: UBC Press, 2000.

Canada. Royal Commission on Aboriginal Peoples. *Report of the Royal Commission on Aboriginal Peoples.* 5 vols. Ottawa, 1996.

Carter, Sarah. *Lost Harvests: Prairie Indian Reserve Farmers and Government Policy.* Montreal: McGill-Queen's University Press, 1990.

Castellano, Marlene Brant, Lynne Davis, and Louise Lahache. *Aboriginal Education: Fulfilling the Promise.* Vancouver: UBC Press, 2000.

Clark, Bruce A. *Native Liberty, Crown Sovereignty: The Existing Aboriginal Right of Self-Government in Canada.* Montreal: McGill-Queen's University Press, 1990.

Coates, Ken S., and Robin Fisher, eds. *Out of the Background: Readings on Canadian Native History.* Toronto: Copp Clark, 1996.

Dewdney, Selwyn H. *They Shared to Survive: The Native Peoples of Canada.* Toronto: Macmillian of Canada, 1975.

Dickason, Olive P. *Canada's First Nations: A History of Founding Peoples From Earliest Times.* Norman: University of Oklahoma Press, 1992.

————. *The Myth of the Savage and the Beginnings of French Colonialism in the Americas.* Edmonton, Alta.: University of Alberta Press, 1984.

Frideres, James S., with Lilianne Ernestine Krosenbrink-Gelissen. *Aboriginal Peoples in Canada: Contemporary Conflicts* 5th ed. Scarborough, Ont.: Prentice Hall Allyn and Bacon Canada, 1998.

Getty, Ian A. L., and Antoine S. Lussier, eds. *As Long as the Sun Shines and Water Flows: A Reader in Canadian Native Studies.* Vancouver: University of British Columbia Press, 1983.

Grant, John W. *Moon of Wintertime: Missionaries and the Indians of Canada in Encounter Since 1534.* Toronto: University of Toronto Press, 1984.

Innis, Harold A. *The Fur Trade in Canada: An Introduction to Canadian Economic History.* Rev. ed. Toronto: University of Toronto Press, 1956.

Isaac, Thomas. *Aboriginal Law: Cases, Materials and Commentary.* Saskatoon, Sask.: Purich Pub., 1999.

Jenness, Diamond. *Indians of Canada.* 7th ed. Toronto: University of Toronto Press, 1977.

King, Thomas, ed. *All My Relations: An Anthology of Contemporary Canadian Native Fiction.* Norman: University of Oklahoma Press, 1992.

Krotz, Larry. *Indian Country: Inside Another Canada.* Toronto: McClelland and Stewart, 1990.

Little Bear, Leroy, Menno Boldt, and J. Anthony Long, eds. *Pathways to Self-Determination: Canadian Indians and the Canadian State.* Toronto: University of Toronto Press, 1984.

Long, J. Anthony, Menno Boldt, eds., in association with Leroy Little Bear. *Governments in Conflict? Provinces and Indian Nations in Canada.* Toronto: University of Toronto Press, 1988.

Lowes, Warren. *Indian Giver: A Legacy of North American Native Peoples.* Penticton, B.C.: Theytus Books, 1986.

Manuel, George, and Michael Posluns. *The Fourth World: An Indian Reality.* Toronto: Collier-McMillan Canada; New York: Free Press, 1974.

McMillan, Alan D. *Native Peoples and Cultures of Canada: An Anthropological Overview.* 2nd ed. Vancouver: Douglas & McIntyre, 1995.

Miller, Christine, and Patricia Chuckryk, eds. *Women of the First Nations: Power, Wisdom, and Strength.* Winnipeg, Man.: University of Manitoba Press, 1996.

Miller, David R., et al. *The First Ones: Readings in Indian/Native Studies.* Craven, Sask.: Saskatchewan Indian Federated College Press, 1992.

Miller, James Rodger. *Shingwauk's Vision: A History of Native Residential Schools.* Toronto: University of Toronto Press, 1996.

————. *Skyscrapers Hide the Heavens: A History of Indian-White Relations in Canada.* Toronto: University of Toronto Press, 1989.

————., ed. *Sweet Promises: A Reader on Indian-White Relations in Canada.* Toronto: University of Toronto Press, 1991.

Morrison, R. Bruce, and C. Roderick Wilson, eds. *Native Peoples: The Canadian Experience.* 2d ed. Toronto: McClelland and Stewart, 1995.

Morrisseau, Norval. *Legends of My People: The Great Ojibway*. New York: McGraw-Hill Ryerson Press, 1965.

Pelletier, Wilfred, and Ted Pool. *No Foreign Land: The Biography of a Northern American Indian*. New York: Pantheon Books, 1974.

Perreault, Jeanne, and Sylvia Vance, eds.*Writing the Circle: Native Women of Western Canada: An Anthology*. Norman: University of Oklahoma Press, 1993.

Peterson, Jacqueline, and Jennifer S. H. Brown, eds. *The New Peoples: Being and Becoming Métis in North America*. Lincoln: University of Nebraska Press, 1985.

Price, John A. *Indians of Canada: Cultural Dynamics*. Scarborough, Ont.: Prentice-Hall of Canada, 1979.

Ponting, J. Rick, and Roger Gibbins. *Out of Irrelevance: A Socio-Political Introduction to Indian Affairs in Canada*. Toronto: Butterworths, 1980.

Purich, Donald. *Our Land: Native Rights in Canada*. Toronto: Lorimer, 1986.

Ray, Arthur J. *I Have Lived Here Since The World Began: An Illustrated History of Canada's Native People*. Toronto: Lester Publishing and Key Porter Books, 1996.

———. *Indians in the Fur Trade: Their Role as Hunters, Trappers and Middlemen of the Lands Southwest of Hudson Bay, 1660–1870*. Toronto: University of Toronto Press, 1974.

Redbird, Duke. *We Are Métis: A Métis View of the Development of a Native Canadian People*. Willowdale, Ont.: Ontario Métis & Non Status Indian Association, 1980.

Russell, Daniel. *A People's Dream: Aboriginal Self-Government*. Vancouver: University of British Columbia Press, 2000.

Smith, Donald B. *Sacred Feathers: The Reverend Peter Jones (Kahkewaquonaby) & the Mississauga Indians*. Lincoln: University of Nebraska Press, 1987.

Tennant, Paul. *Aboriginal Peoples and Politics: The Indian Land Question in British Columbia, 1849–1989*. Vancouver: University of British Columbia Press, 1990.

Trigger, Bruce G. *Natives and Newcomers: Canada's "Heroic Age" Reconsidered*. Kingston: McGill-Queen's University Press, 1985.

Waldram, James B., Ann D. Herring, and T. Kue Young. *Aboriginal Health in Canada: Historical, Cultural, and Epidemiological Perspectives*. Toronto: University of Toronto Press, 1995.

Warry, Wayne. *Unfinished Dreams: Community Healing and the Reality of Aboriginal Self-Government*. Toronto: University of Toronto Press, 1998.

Weaver, Sally M. *Making Canadian Indian Policy: The Hidden Agenda 1968–70*. Toronto: University of Toronto Press, 1981.

Occupation Index

Subject Index

Personal names, place names, events, organizations, and various subject areas or keywords contained in *The Reference Library of Native North America* are listed in this index with corresponding page numbers indicating text references. Page numbers appearing in boldface indicate a major biographical profile. Page numbers appearing in italics refer to photographs, illustrations, and maps found throughout the *Reference Library*.

C

F

G

M

N

Q

R